2018

Toward a 21st-Century School Library Media Program

Edited by

Esther Rosenfeld
David V. Loertscher

The Scarecrow Press, Inc.
Lanham, Maryland • Toronto • Plymouth, UK
and
Hi Willow Research and Publishing
2007

SCARECROW PRESS, INC.

Published in the United States of America
by Scarecrow Press, Inc.
A wholly owned subsidiary of
The Rowman & Littlefield Publishing Group, Inc.
4501 Forbes Boulevard, Suite 200, Lanham, Maryland 20706
www.scarecrowpress.com

Estover Road
Plymouth PL6 7PY
United Kingdom

British Library Cataloguing in Publication Information Available

Library of Congress Cataloging-in-Publication Data

Toward a 21st-century school library media program / edited by Esther Rosenfeld, David V. Loertscher.
    p. cm.
 Includes bibliographical references and index.
 ISBN-13: 978-0-8108-6031-5 (pbk. : alk. paper)
 ISBN-10: 0-8108-6031-7 (pbk. : alk. paper)
 1. School libraries. 2. Instructional materials centers. 3. Teacher-librarians. I. Rosenfeld, Esther. II. Loertscher, David V., 1940– III.
Title: Toward a twenty-first century school library media program.

Z675.S3T645 2007
027.8—dc22   2007032428

The paper used in this publication meets the minimum requirements of
American National Standard for Information Sciences—Permanence of
Paper for Printed Library Materials, ANSI/NISO Z39.48-1992.
Manufactured in the United States of America.

Contents

Part IV: Learning Leadership: 21st-Century Skills

Part V: Learning Leadership: Literacy and Reading

Part VI: Learning Leadership: Partnerships

Part VII: Learning Leadership: Issues and Management

Introduction

Esther Rosenfeld and David Loertscher

We are all aware that today's kindergarten to grade 12 students, often referred to as "Millennials" or "Net Geners," come from a profoundly different world than did previous generations of students. Today's students are heavily influenced by information technology and have never known life without computers, the Internet, video games, cell phones, high-speed networks, instant messaging, social networking sites, iPods, YouTube, and Google. In this first decade of the 21st century, schools are responding in various ways to the twin challenges of this new generation of learners and the rapidly changing information environment. As part of the conversation about how schools need to change in order to teach 21st-century skills to 21st-century learners, specific questions need to be asked about the role of school libraries:

- What is the place of the school library in a 21st-century school?
- How should the school library be responding to the needs of today's students?
- What type of program should exist in the 21st-century school library?
- How can the school library program become the center of teaching and learning?

This book's purpose is to provide some answers to these questions and to help you as teacher-librarians move your school library's program forward so that it serves the needs of 21st-century students. The articles (previously published in *Teacher Librarian* with a few added from *VOYA*) in this book all promote the following philosophy of school libraries and the leadership roles of teacher-librarians:

- The school library exists to provide a learning program and resources to improve student learning and student achievement.
- The school library focuses on teaching information literacy skills that are essential to student success in the 21st century and provides students and teachers with a framework for the research and inquiry process.
- The school library is a vital part of the school's overall literacy efforts by providing support for reading instruction and by developing and promoting the love of reading for learning and for pleasure.
- The school library exists beyond its four walls and provides real and virtual access to appropriate, high-quality resources on a 24-hours-per-day/7-days-per-week basis.

• Teacher-librarians are learning leaders and participate actively in curriculum development and delivery through collaboration with other teachers in the design of rich and relevant tasks, and through instructional interventions to help students learn.

• Teacher-librarians are leaders in technology integration and infuse information technology and its appropriate use into their school library programs. This includes the use of various tools of the interactive Web, commonly known as Web 2.0.

• Teacher-librarians are educational leaders who are facilitators for professional learning in their school community.

With this overall philosophy in mind, *Toward a 21st-Century School Library Media Program* is organized into sections on collaboration, curriculum design and assessment, technology integration, 21st-century skills, literacy and reading, partnerships, and issues and management. Each chapter comprises visionary, provocative, and practical articles written by experts in the school library field. It is the our hope that this book is used by practitioners to make the school library essential and central to learning and teaching in the 21st-century school.

Teacher Librarian: The Journal for School Library Professionals, a highly respected publication serving teacher-librarians, has been in publication for more than 30 years. It is published five times per year and contains peer-reviewed feature articles on various aspects of school librarianship, professional book reviews, and regular columns on technology, literacy, authors, best books for various age groups, best web sites, along with a variety of other special elements.

VOYA: The Voice of Youth Advocates is published six times per year and serves librarians, teachers, and others who work with teens. The magazine is well known for its feature articles and reviews rated for both quality and popularity with teens, as well as its annotated booklists in every issue.

PART I

Learning Leadership: Collaboration

①

Building Teaching Partnerships: The Art of Collaboration

Karen Muronaga and Violet Harada

Eleven years ago, *Information Power: Guidelines for School Library Media Programs* (AASL & AECT, 1988) identified three functions of the teacher-librarian: teacher, information specialist and instructional consultant. While the roles of teacher and information specialist remain intact in the recently published *Information Power: Building Partnerships for Learning* (AASL & AECT, 1998), the term *instructional and curriculum partner* replaces that of *instructional consultant* in the new publication. This change signifies a subtle but important shift in thinking about the nature of the collaborative relationship between the teacher-librarian and the classroom teacher.

Consultation generally designates one person, the consultant, as the "expert" (Cramer 1998). It typically denotes an inequality of status between professionals, usually with the implication that the classroom teacher is less qualified than a support services specialist (e.g., teacher-librarian) to provide input and resolve problems (Pugach & Allen-Meares, 1985). Effective collaboration, on the other hand, depends on different-but-equal status between professionals. It assumes joint problem solving and involves mutual efforts by professionals to meet the needs of students (Cohen, Thomas, Sattler, & Morsink, 1997). In short, collaborative interactions enable people with diverse expertise to generate creative solutions to mutually defined problems. As Doiron (1999) states, the dynamics and the nature of such a relationship between teacher and teacher-librarian is the "cornerstone of the school library media program."

Building effective collaborative relationships is a complex and evolving process. Much of the current library literature on teacher and teacher-librarian collaboration focuses on the external or environmental factors affecting such efforts, including flexible scheduling, administrative support, curriculum planning time, and budgets for adequate facilities and resources (Pickard, 1994; van Deusen, 1995; van Deusen & Tallman, 1994). Although these concerns are indeed critical ingredients in building collaborative cultures in schools, equally vital are the internal factors influencing the collaborative relationship itself. These are factors that shape the interpersonal dynamics of how people work effectively with one another. Unfortu-

First published in *Teacher Librarian*, October 1999, Volume 17, Number 1

nately, this aspect of collaboration is not as well documented in library literature.

The experiences at Lincoln Elementary School in Hawaii confirm the need to better understand how such partnerships are developed and sustained. In striving to improve team-building efforts, the school continues to wrestle with the following questions:

- What behaviors and attitudes are critical for collaborative relationships to flourish?
- How are collaborative teams formed, and how do they develop?
- What are the outcomes and benefits of effective teams?

In this chapter, the authors summarize some of the literature on team building and link their understandings to ongoing practices at Lincoln.

BUILDING COLLABORATIVE RELATIONSHIPS

The heart of collaboration resides in developing a climate of trust and mutual respect. This involves identifying and honoring the different perspectives, strengths, and weaknesses of all team partners (Hudson & Glomb, 1997). A sense of parity is critical where each person's contribution to an interaction is equally valued, and each person shares power in making decisions (Friend & Cook, 1996).

To develop trust, partners must develop mutually agreed upon goals and a shared vision for the work (Mattessich & Monsey, 1992). Task completion also depends on shared participation. This does not imply that the individuals involved must divide tasks equally or participate fully in each task required to achieve their goal. However, they must participate equally in the decisions made regarding the appropriateness and possible modifications in the material prepared and in how groups work and how schedules are implemented. Importantly, each individual must have resources to contribute that are valuable for reaching the shared goal. The type of resources depends on roles and the specific activity. Pooling the available, often scarce, resources in schools can lead to tremendously satisfying efforts to the benefit of the students.

An important element in team building is a willingness to collaborate with partners who reflect a range of working styles. Teachers bring diverse classroom and personal experiences, background knowledge, personal abilities and personalities to curriculum discussion sessions (Doiron, 1999). They have preferred methods and favorite activities that they know work for them as effective teaching strategies. Planning sessions need to reflect sensitivity to and respect for their strengths and build on them. This means that teacher-librarians must understand why teachers plan and how they plan. The process should be flexible and must be based on a willingness to examine planning from the "teachers' perspective" (Wolcott, 1994).

In an effective partnership, teacher-librarian and classroom teacher share a crucial underlying assumption that curriculum building is holistic and dynamic. This requires a dramatic shift from envisioning curriculum planning as a linear process with fixed learning goals and implementation strategies to viewing curriculum building as a more fluid process of adjustments and modifications based on a continuing assessment of student performance and needs (Doiron, 1999). It means discarding the notion that curriculum comes in neat, tidy packages that can be repeatedly used with little change.

AN ACTUAL SCHOOL SETTING

In their review of the literature on collaborative practices, the authors found that many of the published observations confirmed their own notions about nurturing curriculum partnerships. They also realized that the journey toward establishing a collaborative culture required a teacher-librarian who was equally willing to lead or to be an active team member depending on the situation and the need. An example of the development of such a collaborative culture is the team-building process at Lincoln Elementary School.

School Context

Lincoln Elementary serves an economically and culturally diverse community in the heart of Honolulu. Hawaiians and part-Hawaiians make up 34% of the K–6 student population of 539; another 12% come from various Asian countries. Over 52% of the children qualify for free or reduced lunches. The teaching staff includes two administrators, 23 classroom teachers, a counselor, a teacher-librarian, a technology coordinator, and eight other support staff positions.

First Task: Building Trust

When teacher-librarian Muronaga first arrived at Lincoln 19 years ago, she knew that teachers needed to perceive her as approachable. Working with all staff, she also realized the importance of keeping confidences and carefully avoiding cliques and factions. Over the years, she has participated in various activities beyond the walls of the library media center. By serving on social and curriculum committees, volunteering for school fairs, and advising the school paper and yearbook, she has developed a highly visible presence in her school community.

She has also involved teachers in promoting the school program through displays at neighborhood malls and through district showcases. In all of these efforts, Muronaga acknowledges teacher contributions through bulletin announcements and handwritten thank you notes. By sharing credit for work well done, she has found that teachers are appreciative and more willing to participate in other activities with the library media center.

Developing Collaborative Relations

During her first year at the school, Muronaga discovered that teachers at Lincoln were not accustomed to planning lessons together with the teacher-librarian. Traditional library skills lessons were taught independently from ongoing classroom instruction. Starting with all willing teachers, Muronaga aimed for a "simple" level of collaboration where she informally linked her lessons to classroom topics. Over time, she developed a network of support for deeper levels of joint planning, delivery and assessment of instruction by linking her efforts with school priorities. For example, the Children as Authors Project emphasized reading, literature, and writing. Through the project, a scope and sequence for writing was developed, the art curriculum was strengthened through classroom demonstrations by a local illustrator, integrated lessons were designed and implemented by the teachers and teacher-librarian, and a poster display of the authoring process and students' books were exhibited at the school's Family Appreciation Night and at a district showcase of best practices.

Today, Muronaga sits with teachers in K–6 grade level meetings to jointly discuss upcoming curriculum priorities. She participates in more "total" collaboration where faculty members discuss how best to weave content area concepts and information literacy skills into integrated learning experiences for students. Given the realities of the busy school year, there are still instances when lessons are linked but not fully integrated; however, 90% of the current instruction involving the library media center reflects more detailed cooperative planning and implementation. Figure 1.1 briefly describes the three categories of curriculum involvement between teacher and teacher-librarian with brief examples.

Creating Leadership Teams

Four years ago, teachers at Lincoln expressed a growing need for technology training and for learning how to integrate technology into the existing curriculum. They realized that establishing new partnerships

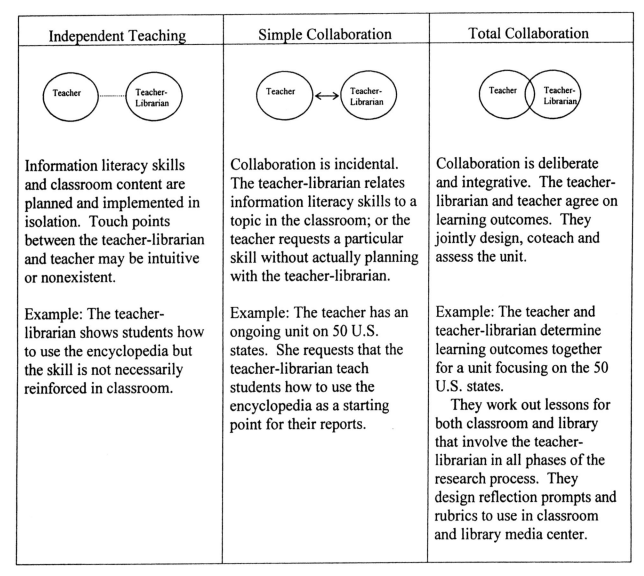

Independent Teaching	Simple Collaboration	Total Collaboration
Information literacy skills and classroom content are planned and implemented in isolation. Touch points between the teacher-librarian and teacher may be intuitive or nonexistent. Example: The teacher-librarian shows students how to use the encyclopedia but the skill is not necessarily reinforced in classroom.	Collaboration is incidental. The teacher-librarian relates information literacy skills to a topic in the classroom; or the teacher requests a particular skill without actually planning with the teacher-librarian. Example: The teacher has an ongoing unit on 50 U.S. states. She requests that the teacher-librarian teach students how to use the encyclopedia as a starting point for their reports.	Collaboration is deliberate and integrative. The teacher-librarian and teacher agree on learning outcomes. They jointly design, coteach and assess the unit. Example: The teacher and teacher-librarian determine learning outcomes together for a unit focusing on the 50 U.S. states. They work out lessons for both classroom and library that involve the teacher-librarian in all phases of the research process. They design reflection prompts and rubrics to use in classroom and library media center.

Figure 1.1. Levels of Curriculum Involvement Between Teacher and Teacher-Librarian

would be vital in meeting these emerging needs. Muronaga volunteered to facilitate the process. She and a team of teachers drafted a proposal for a technology coordinator who would oversee the acquisition and use of computers and appropriate software, and coordinate the use of the technology in effective teaching and learning. The administration and faculty enthusiastically supported the idea. As a result, a new team was born: teachers working with both Muronaga and the new technology coordinator, Lois Ohta.

One of the new team's first major efforts was to secure funding for staff development in computer literacy and in integrating technology into the curriculum. Muronaga and Ohta successfully applied for a Goals 2000 grant that established a networked "student-teacher-parent learning center" equipped with 25 Power Macintosh computers, a laser printer, a scanner, and a direct connection to the Internet. The center provided the school with a new learning environment adjacent to the library media center where Muronaga and Ohta could work together and support teachers in both electronic information access and production of multimedia projects.

Planning Interactive Meetings
Teachers currently meet by grade levels with Muronaga and Ohta at the beginning of each semester to dis-

cuss long-range curriculum plans. These meetings, which last approximately 90 minutes, are crucial for mapping the priorities and areas of emphases for the year. Teachers are asked to bring with them their planning tools including curriculum guides, sample activities, calendars, class lists and lesson-planning forms. The teacher-librarian and technology coordinator also bring copies of the *Information Literacy: Standards for Student Learning*, technology literacy standards and guidelines, and samples of past lessons and units.

The meetings are active conversations in which there are constant checks for perceptions and clarification of meanings. Teachers review curriculum, discuss student assessment strategies, share effective past units and ways to improve upon them. In the fall meetings, they also exchange fresh insights gained from their professional improvement activities during the summer. The spring meetings often center on problem-solving challenges arising from lessons and units being implemented and on reexamining student needs. Muronaga facilitates these sessions. To keep the discussions focused, she uses a simple planning form as an agenda. The defining questions of these sessions are

- What do we want the students to learn?
- How will they learn this best?
- How will we and the students know if they have really learned this?

Note taking is a shared responsibility among team members. Ohta then summarizes the decisions and agreements and distributes them to all team members. These summaries serve as the springboard for more detailed lesson planning among the grade-level teams.

Valuing Strengths

Each member of the team brings skills and knowledge that complement one another. Classroom teachers provide knowledge of student needs, curriculum content, and learning expectations. The technology coordinator offers expertise in software and hardware applications and in designing lessons that use technology for information and communication. The teacher-librarian contributes an information literacy framework, teaching skills, and resources for students and teachers. Occasionally, the roles may change depending on the teacher's knowledge in technology, information literacy, or content skills. All team members, however, learn from each other and pool their knowledge about the instructional process and assessment strategies.

Varying Roles and Responsibilities

Teachers at Lincoln are diverse in their planning behaviors and in their levels of readiness to engage in collaborative work. A few of them are long-term planners who map their curriculum for the entire school year but most teachers tend to do weekly planning. While the veteran teachers are accustomed to working closely with the teacher-librarian and technology coordinator, the newer faculty are often less confident about how to involve the two in curriculum planning. Muronaga and Ohta are sensitive to these differences among teachers and they attempt to share responsibilities in ways that are comfortable for the teachers. Figure 1.2 outlines three examples that reflect a range.

Emphasizing Teamwork

The major goal of the team work is to have students use the resources of the classroom, library media center, and computer lab as one large and seamless learning center. Dependent on the nature of the activity and needs of students, different members of the teaching team guide and support their learning. Typically, a unit is initiated by the teacher in the classroom. As students seek relevant information, the teacher-librarian and technology coordinator assume major roles. Everyone on the teaching team helps students to synthesize their data. The teacher and technology coordinator work together as students design their final presentations. Throughout the process, assessment is done in the classroom, library media center, or computer lab, depending on the task.

Ms. A, Grade 6

Request: Develop a team-taught unit on space exploration with three special areas of study space, stars, interplanetary travel.

Teaming experience: Teacher does long-term planning. She has also worked effectively with the teacher-librarian and technology coordinator in other collaborative projects. Consequently, the team spends less time discussing content and general working relationships and more time on clarifying their specific roles for particular projects.

Teacher's responsibilities:
• takes lead in initiating the unit and maintaining overall co-ordination
• organizes students into three special study groups; sets clear learning expectations
• works specifically with the space study group as they hunt for information, organize and use the information

Teacher-librarian's responsibilities:
• provides print resources for all three study groups
• works specifically with the stars study group
• instructs all three study groups in crediting sources and organizing bibliographies

Technology coordinator's responsibilities:
• provides web resources for all three study groups
• works specifically with the interplanetary travel group
• teaches use of Hyperstudio tools to all three study groups
• takes lead in coordinating student multimedia presentations

Ms. B, Grades 5/6

Request: Assistance with a unit on walls as physical and psychological barriers.

Teaming experience: Teacher has worked closely with the teacher-librarian in past projects but wants more help from the technology coordinator in this unit.

Teacher's responsibilities:
• initiates the unit's theme through literature

• takes lead in all aspects of student work throughout the unit

Teacher-librarian's responsibilities:
• supports the classroom by providing print resources for student investigation

Technology coordinator's responsibilities:
• collaborates with teacher on the unit's theme and learning outcomes
• teaches students web access skills
• assists students with information gathering on the Web
• teams with the teacher on student essay-writing

Mr. C, Grades 2/3

Request: Help with teaching information literacy skills to special education students.

Teaming experience: Teacher is new and eager to team but has no previous experience in collaborating with teacher-librarian or technology coordinator.

Teacher's responsibilities:
• works closely with teacher-librarian and technology coordinator to define area of study and possible sequence of lessons
• prepares students for the library instruction and follows up on it

Teacher-librarian's responsibilities:
• takes lead in helping teacher define area of study and a possible sequence of lessons
• takes lead in introducing various information literacy skills related to the classroom topic of study; may also teach general literacy skills normally taught in the classroom until the teacher gains more experience and confidence in this area
• nurtures teacher's involvement in the planning and implementation process

Technology coordinator's responsibilities:
• takes lead in teaching use of drawing tools for final presentations
• assists teacher with completion of class slide show

Figure 1.2. Team Responsibilities

Viewing Planning as Nonlinear

In working together on units, teams discover that the process of curriculum development is a nonlinear one. As an example, grade 1 teachers wanted to repeat a unit on whales from the previous year. Upon meeting as a team, they decided to shift the emphasis from a topical to a thematic one that explored whales as an endangered species. Early on, the team observed that students were not understanding the simple texts they were reading. They enlisted the Title 1 (learning assistance) teacher who provided additional help in the classroom and suggested the incorporation of comprehension strategies. As the team continued to assess student progress, their data revealed that students needed more time on information-gathering. Accordingly, teachers adjusted their schedules to address this need. Further assessment also indicated that students were excited about using more technology; hence, changes were made to the culminating activity: Students could now create multimedia slide shows instead of posters.

CONCLUSION

Staff involvement in the collaborative process is a dynamic activity as new faculty arrive and curriculum changes occur. The faculty realizes that for collaborative relationships to survive and thrive, all participants must have valued personal and professional resources to contribute. Members need to share resources, decision-making authority, and accountability for the outcomes of their activities. Importantly, the teacher-librarian must advocate and nurture such partnerships (van Deusen, 1995). In this leadership role, teacher-librarians may be called upon to be "harmonizers, encouragers, standard setters, testers, compromisers" (Abelson & Woodman, 1983, p. 131).

What evolves for all participants is refinement of their own professional skills, increased collegial exchange of ideas and strategies, and ultimately, improved and cohesive learning experiences for their students (Thomas, Korea, & Morsink, 1995).

Assuredly, effective partnerships require a realistic and patient view; the nurturing process takes time and a careful scrutiny of an individual's intrapersonal and interpersonal practices. If student learning is the bottom line, however, it makes sound sense to create situations that combine and strengthen faculty knowledge and experience. The Gestalt notion that the whole is greater than the sum of its parts certainly holds true for teaching and learning that builds this sense of community.

ACKNOWLEDGMENTS

The authors thank Lois Ohta and Lois Lum for their editorial assistance with this article. Ohta is Technology Coordinator at Lincoln Elementary School in Honolulu. Lum, a former resource teacher at Lincoln, is now curriculum coordinator at Puohala Elementary School.

REFERENCES

American Association of School Librarians (AASL) & Association for Educational Communications & Technology (AECT). (1988). *Information power: Guidelines for school library media programs.* Chicago: American Library Association.

American Association of School Librarians (AASL) & Association for Educational Communications & Technology (AECT). (1998). *Information power: Building partnerships for learning.* Chicago: American Library Association.

Abelson, M. A., & Woodman, R. W. (1983). Review of research on team effectiveness: Implications for teams in schools. *School Psychology Review, 12*(2), 125–136.

Cohen, S. S., Thomas, C. C., Sattler, R. O., & Morsink, C. V. (1997). Meeting the challenge of consultation and collaboration: Developing interactive teams. *Journal of Learning Disabilities, 30*(4), 427–432.

Cramer, S. F. (1998). *Collaboration: A success strategy for special educators.* Boston: Allyn & Bacon.

Doiron, R. (1999). Curriculum encounters of the third kind: Teachers and teacher-librarians exploring curriculum potential. In K. Haycock (Ed.), *Foundations for effective school library media programs* (pp. 155–166). Englewood, CO: Libraries Unlimited.

Friend, M. & Cook, L. (1996). *Interactions: Collaboration skills for school professionals* (2nd ed.). New York: Longman.

Hudson, P., & Glomb, N. (1997). If it takes two to tango, then why not teach both partners to dance? Collaboration instruction for all educators. *Journal of Learning Disabilities, 30*(4), 442–448.

Mattessich, P. W., & Monsey, B. R. (1992). *Collaboration: What makes it work: A review of research literature on factors influencing successful collaboration.* St. Paul, MN: Amherst H. Wilder Foundation.

Pickard, P. (1994). The instructional consultant role of the library media specialist: A progress report. *School Library Media Activities Monthly, 10*(5), 28–30.

Pugach, M. C., & Allen-Meares, P. (1985). Collaboration at the preservice level: Instructional and evaluation activities. *Teacher Education and Special Education, 8*(1), 3–11.

van Deusen, J. D. (1995). Prerequisites to flexible scheduling. In K. Haycock (Ed.), *Foundations for effective school library media programs* (pp. 223–227). Englewood, CO: Libraries Unlimited.

van Deusen, J. D., & Tallman, J. (1994). The impact of scheduling on curriculum consultation and information skills instruction. *School Library Media Quarterly, 23*(1), 17–26.

Wolcott, L. L. (1994). Understanding how teachers plan: Strategies for successful instructional partnerships. *School Library Media Quarterly, 22*(3), 161–165.

②

America's Most Wanted: Teachers Who Collaborate

Carol Brown

Teacher-librarians are continually seeking opportunities to collaborate with the classroom teacher. Most of us have experienced the professional satisfaction resulting from a successful project, and we've also endured those that were stressful and less productive than anticipated. We have been taught the importance of collaboration in library school and by a society that puts high value on partnership and team endeavors. Indeed, the best schools and the best librarians consistently report that the library must be the heart of the school, and the teacher-librarian must be a proactive team player.

Because of the complexity of collaborative environments, those participating may require an equally flexible and resilient personality. In 1919, Martha Wilson wrote:

> Too much cannot be said about the personality of the school librarian. Her work is of a cooperative nature that requires constant use of all her powers for social adjustment. She needs to understand people and to inspire their confidence in her activities. This is best accomplished by someone possessing steady nerves, an alert mind, a sympathetic and understanding nature, and who is orderly and readily adaptable. In a word, she should be an individual whom both the faculty and the students can respect and admire, a dominant, but not a domineering personality. (cited in Currin, 1939, p. 23)

Althea Currin, a professor of Library Science at Carnegie Library School, revised Wilson's work. Currin's description of the school librarian (1939) could be interpreted as one who is flexible, wise, and a social genius, not unlike expectations for today's teacher-librarian. While her language is more appropriate for the pre–World War II culture, the job description has remained constant—a person with powers for social adjustment who understands people. These same skills and personal attributes are evident in the stories told by librarians and teacher-librarians at conferences, online discussion forums, and in the teachers' lounge.

First published in *Teacher Librarian*, October 2004, Volume 32, Number 1

Many of the personal attributes and dispositions valued in the Carnegie Library School are associated with interpersonal relationships and the ability to work well with one's colleagues. Could a close study of anecdotal stories, personal interviews, and online discussion threads reveal patterns and consistencies in personal attributes, strategies, and environment that lead to successful collaboration? To answer this question, a plan was developed for interviewing teachers, teacher-librarians, public librarians, and other professionals associated with community agencies.

RESEARCH METHOD

Focus groups were interviewed using open-ended questions. Participants responded to me and each other, through dialog and personal reflection. Teacher-librarians from urban elementary and secondary schools were represented in one group. In another, participants of a public school/library partnership funded by a federal grant were interviewed. A third group consisted of K–12 teacher-librarians and instructional specialists attending a professional conference. Each of the three interview sessions was recorded; audiotapes were transcribed and analyzed for recurring themes related to successful collaboration.

Electronic surveys were sent to graduate students enrolled in the Master of Library Science and the Master of Education programs at a large regional university in the eastern United States.

Telephone interviews were conducted with recipients of a federal grant funded through the Library Services and Technology Act (LSTA). Each participant had served on a planning team as the result of a LSTA grant sponsored by the State Library of North Carolina (Brown, 2003, 2004).

To gather information from outside the state, queries were posted to the electronic discussion forum LM_NET. Twenty-four responses came from teacher-librarians located in various regions of the county.

During each of the interviews, surveys, and focus group sessions, participants were asked,

1. Can you tell me about your most successful collaborative project?
2. Why do you think it was successful?
3. What contributed to the success?

Responses were collected and analyzed for recurring key terms and carefully examined for repeated categories or themes within each success story. The analysis of all 66 documents and transcripts yielded several basic attributes for successful collaboration. These were subdivided into environmental factors and social factors (see Table 2.1). Environmental factors can be described as overt and attributed to conditions and policies within the climate of a school. Social factors are not as easily guided by administrative policy. These are covert and are similar to the qualities that lead to social intelligence as described by the early writers involved in training the school librarian.

Environmental Factors	*Social Factors*
Scheduled Planning Meetings	Proactive Team Leader
Impromptu Discussion	Shared Vision
Administrative Support	Self-Confidence in Contribution
Defined Roles	Open Communication
Flexible Scheduling	Trust and Mutual Respect

Table 2.1. Attributes for Successful Collaboration

SCHEDULED PLANNING MEETINGS

According to Twinning (2001), without designated time for joint planning, individuals tend to function separately. Participants for this study would agree. A majority of responses favored regularly scheduled meetings at a specific time and place. Many reported that meetings were the best method for establishing goals, defining objectives, planning activities, and tracking progress.

One teacher-librarian commented,

> Each member needs to attend the group planning sessions for the project to become a success. My least successful collaborative projects were ones that did not provide enough structured planning. I noticed that our collaborative efforts seem to work out better when we have a common time to plan and share ideas.

IMPROMPTU DISCUSSION

Impromptu discussions helped inspire creativity among the team members and sustain motivation to remain committed to the project. Mattessich and Monsey (1992) describe these meetings as cooperative, occurring on an as-needed basis. This teacher-librarian supports this view:

> My best efforts at collaboration come from comments I overhear at lunch or in the hallway. Sometimes I get ideas from children's work displayed in the hall and then suggest a project idea to the teacher. I consistently advertise that I am available for collaboration through newsletters and e-mails.

ADMINISTRATIVE SUPPORT

The support of school administrators was specifically named nine times. References to the power of the principal also appeared numerous times in interview transcripts. As an environmental factor, the support of the building principal is a serious consideration. He or she has the power to induce a value-added climate regarding collaboration, the ability to guide the teachers and staff in planning for flexible or semi-flexible scheduling, and designates funding for the placement of support staff often needed for school-wide or departmental projects.

FLEXIBLE SCHEDULING

Flexible scheduling was reported as a school policy in most of the success stories, but some teacher-librarians experienced success with part-fixed/part-flexible schedules. Those participating in the interviews and focus groups told success stories *because of* flexible or *regardless of* fixed schedules. After surveying teachers, librarians, and administrators from 10 different states, Welch (2000) reported, "Practitioners who value collaboration somehow manage to find time for it, especially if they have routine locations and facilitators to coordinate meetings" (p. 22). A participant for this study commented on fixed scheduling difficulties and the need to pursue collaborative projects:

> I really believe attending teachers' planning meetings to be extremely beneficial. Now, I won't say it is absolutely necessary because we all know that scheduling just may not allow that. We must not give up on trying to collaborate if this happens. We must try to be creative and come up with alternative strategies.

CLEARLY DEFINED ROLES

Many participants emphasized the importance of clearly defined roles for each person involved in a project. Such roles are often based on team members' preferences and areas of expertise:

What I liked about the group was that we did not attempt to "outshine" each other because we saw the successes and failures as a group. We each played an active role in every lesson and we critiqued each other, but we also supported each other. Planning and establishing each person's specific responsibilities helped clarify what our expectations were for each other.

According to Buzzeo (2002), it is important to be aware of the need for varying roles and responsibilities, and the teacher-librarian can be proactive in facilitating the process for role assignments. However, he or she may encounter a variety of responses depending on team members' perception of their own roles as a teacher, information specialist, instructional leader, or a combination of professional roles. Sometimes the teacher-librarian may need to recognize the importance of taking a subordinate role in the project. Serving as support person on the team can be rewarding and provide opportunities to grow professionally. A careful balance between a collegial relationship and support person is needed, as evidenced by these comments from one participant:

We met twice a week in order to plan. As the year progressed, we complemented one another. During our lessons there were three people teaching (a special education teacher, my assistant, and myself). Many [times] the special education teacher was very passionate about her role. I had to learn to accept her as mentor, colleague, and as a learner.

PROACTIVE TEAM LEADER
Proactive team leaders help maintain cohesiveness and accountability for all team members. In one focus group of four teacher-librarians, an experienced teacher-librarian and a recent graduate from a nearby university told contrasting stories about principal support, teachers' perceptions of their roles, and even student response to their respective library programs. The newly minted teacher-librarian described how her collaborative efforts were met with resistance: "I can't get any of the teachers to work with me. They want to drop off their classes and never even come into the library, much less plan a collaborative research project."

The more experienced teacher-librarian countered with this proactive approach:

I've found that if I show an interest in what the classes are doing and offer suggestions for resources, eventually some of the teachers will show an interest. Others will see what we're doing and want to join us or maybe schedule a time to discuss a similar project. . . . Another way I get around [resistance to collaboration] is that I use my media advisory committee as a sounding board. And I meet with them regularly and I try to get the same people to be on the committee the next year by making it fun meetings.

According to De Bono (n.d.), a proactive leader will look around to see how an opportunity can be created. In contrast, a reactive leader focuses on a problem or situation already in existence. To be a proactive team leader, the teacher-librarian will look for opportunities to develop collaboration instead of reacting to strategies or plans already in place.

SHARED VISION
The phrase "shared vision" was often used in the success stories, and has been identified as an important component in collaboration (Muronaga & Harada, 1999; Small, 2002; Welch, 2000). Collaborators must

envision mutual goals and objectives. They must see, with their own professional eyes, a common purpose that also includes shared resources and responsibilities. Each person's contribution is unique and should be considered when planning for the team's common goals. The following story identifies a common goal, purpose, and vision as the basis for a unifying purpose among team members:

> The one reason that one project was more successful than the other was because all parties involved had a common goal . . . being involved, being viewed as part of the team, hearing and seeing firsthand what the teacher or department is trying to accomplish and planning together really builds a foundation for successful collaboration.

OPEN COMMUNICATION

Very often, shared visions were confirmed through open communication. In their research on successful collaboration, Mattessich, Murray-Close, and Monsey (2001) identified five factors that are important for partnerships among schools, agencies, and private industry. Regarding communication, they recommend "open and frequent communication for updating one another, discussing issues openly, and for establishing clearly defined goals" (p. 9). Anecdotal stories and survey responses from teacher-librarians in this study support that conclusion: "Neither project became a total bomb, but communication was a missing link in Project 1." "In particular, time constraints limited the collaboration and created a gap of communication that resulted in poor technique in terms of collaborative efforts." "The successful project contained teamwork, communication, flexibility, and professionalism that the other project lacked. These factors were crucial in the implementation of ideas." "In order for collaboration to work, there needs to be a great deal of trust, lots of communication, and a willingness to share the workload. You could probably write an entire research paper discussing the importance for each of these: teamwork, communication, flexibility, and professionalism."

Based on the following statement, it might be suggested that willing participants are a prerequisite to open communication: "The only way a group project can be truly successful is when all the participants willingly volunteer. Only then can communication be open and create an atmosphere that fosters open and free discussion." Several participants reported similar experiences with teachers who willingly volunteer and reported less favorable outcomes when collaborative projects were mandated through school policy.

MUTUAL TRUST AND RESPECT

For a group of people to share a vision, they must hold each other in respect, and trust one another's professional judgment. The interviews and survey responses contained many comments focused on conditions leading to trust: "There is the trust factor. People must trust and see you as an expert in your field in order for them to invest the valuable time it takes to collaborate and plan with you." "Team members know which individuals have the skills necessary or have support within the organization to build the skills. When someone feels weak they ask for help, building the relationship and the trust." "The unsuccessful project failed to instill trust."

One teacher-librarian responded to resistance and a seeming lack of trust as follows: "Hopefully, we can develop a level of trust among us as a group that will allow us to be creative and supportive of each other so that we can set an example for other teachers in the school system and encourage them to do the same."

SELF-CONFIDENCE IN CONTRIBUTION

Confidence in one's personal ability to contribute to the success of the group was a recurring theme within the stories. There was an assurance that one's skills, whether personal or professional, can be an enabling factor to support the project with unique contributions: "When all members of the group are active participants, the results are very positive, with the majority of the members willing to collaborate together on a regular basis. Each member of the group feels that what they say is important and ideas are shared freely."

IMPLICATIONS FOR SUCCESSFUL COLLABORATION

The 10 attributes described support and further confirm previous research in collaboration. Muronaga and Harada (1999) identified internal factors such as trust, mutual respect, and the importance of shared vision. Others have identified more overt structures, responsibilities and communication (Mattessich & Monsey, 1992) as important to the success or failure for collaborative projects. These same factors were clearly evident within the language of the personal interviews, survey responses, and focus groups throughout the study.

Collaboration is a complex and highly valued endeavor. Most teacher-librarians would agree on certain basic requirements for successful collaboration to occur. Environmental factors include school restructuring, curriculum revision, and strategies for convincing the principal to adopt 100% flexible scheduling (Bishop & Larimer, 1999; Buzzeo, 2002; Oberg, Hay, & Henir, 2000). Social factors, contributing to the complexities of human relationships, appear to supersede the environmental factors. Schedules, time limitations, and administrator support are always serious issues; however, many teacher-librarians remain steadfast in building collaborative partnerships despite environmental roadblocks.

Based on the information gathered from interviews, discussion lists, and surveys, successful collaboration is *directly related* to quality of relationships, goals, and rewards. Without trust and mutual respect within professional relationships, environmental problems can never be resolved. Each person within the group must adopt the attitude, "I have something important to contribute." In addition, each person must admit, "I can't achieve this without the input and expertise of others." Flexibility in both attitude and work ethic is an attribute of the teacher-librarian who is a successful collaborator. This means being able to recognize the possibility of alternative pathways and taking the initiative to pursue a relationship or project idea not yet experienced. Being both proactive and flexible is a winning combination.

Team members should make the effort to schedule meetings. This is important for two reasons:

1. Objectives for the project must be understood and consensus reached.
2. The strengths and talents of each team member should be identified.

Collaboration is more successful when diverse talents and experiences work together to reach clearly defined objectives. This will not happen without opportunity for open communication within some kind of meeting, both scheduled and impromptu.

Rewards should always be directly linked to goals. The teacher-librarian should initiate collaborative projects with those who have an interest in shared resources as well as shared responsibilities. This will lead to opportunities to work with others who see the advantages that come from shared talent and shared responsibility.

Probably the most elusive attribute for successful collaboration is a shared vision by classroom teachers and the teacher-librarian. Even though most would agree that they are "doing it for the children," many will confess that it is difficult to meet on common ground with a shared vision for what is best, educationally and administratively, for students who are the recipients of the project. Understanding the viewpoint of the other can be challenging. One discussion list participant offered the following advice for establishing a shared vision:

> Get to know others. Talk openly and freely about projects, ideas, goals you are excited about. Be positive—like-minded people will respond. Make a plan at informal gatherings and commit to something small. Do it . . . then follow up with larger projects, with bigger goals. When participants feel ownership, that their ideas and efforts are valued, see the purpose and believe the goal they are working toward can happen, they will work very hard to accomplish those goals.

CONCLUSION

In this article five social factors have been identified that affect success in collaboration. By adopting the attributes of proactive (but flexible) leadership, trust, shared vision, open communication, and self-confidence in one's contribution, teacher-librarians may be able to circumvent environmental factors not under their control. Lack of administrative support, time limitations, and rigid schedules may remain as obstacles, but proactive and positive attitudes are more likely to reach that most-wanted group—teachers who will collaborate.

REFERENCES

Bishop, K., & Larimer, N. (1999). Literacy through collaboration. *Teacher Librarian, 27*(1), 15–20.

Brown, C. (2003). Elements of a powerful partnership. *North Carolina Libraries, 61*(2), 52–61. Retrieved May 20, 2004, from **www.nclaonline.org/NCL/ncl/NCL_61_2_Summer2003.pdf**

Brown, C. (2004). Characteristics of successful partnerships between libraries, schools, and community agencies. *Library Philosophy and Practice, 6*(2). Retrieved May 20, 2004, from **http://libr.unl.edu:2000/LPP/cbrown.htm**

Buzzeo, T. (2002). *Collaborating to meet standards: Teacher/Librarian partnerships for K–6.* Worthington, OH: Linworth.

Currin, A. (1939). *School library management* (6th ed.). New York: Wilson.

De Bono, E. (n.d.) Proactive and reactive thinking: Learn the difference between proactive and reactive thinking and increase your creative capabilities. *Thinking Managers.* Retrieved May 20, 2004, from **www.thinkingmanagers.com/management/proactive-reactive-thinking.php**

Mattessich, P., & Monsey, B. (1992). *Collaboration: What makes it work?* St. Paul, MN: Amherst H. Wilder Foundation.

Mattessich, P., Murray-Close, M., & Monsey, B. (2001). *Collaboration: What makes it work* (2nd ed.). St. Paul, MN: Amherst H. Wilder Foundation.

Muronaga, K., & Harada, V. (1999). The art of collaboration. *Teacher Librarian, 27*(1), 9–14.

Oberg, D., Hay, L., & Henri, J. (2000). The role of the principal in an information literate school community: Cross-country comparisons from an international research project. *School Library Media Research, Vol. 3.* Retrieved May 20, 2004, from **www.ala.org/aasl/SLMR/vol3/principal2/principal2.html**

Small, R. (2002). Collaboration: Where does it begin? *Teacher Librarian, 29*(5), 8–11.

Twining, J. (2001). *Collaboration on the information front.* Unpublished dissertation. University of Denver College of Education, Denver, CO.

Welch, M. (2000). Practitioner's perspectives of collaboration: A social validation and factor analysis. *Journal of Educational & Psychological Consultation, 11*(3/4), 357–379.

③

Teacher and Teacher-Librarian Collaboration: Moving Toward Integration

Patricia Montiel-Overall

Preparing students for the 21st century is a challenging and daunting task. It is a responsibility that we have come to realize is best undertaken through the expertise of many individuals working together to enhance student learning.

This is particularly true in light of changing roles, demands on time, and reallocation of resources within educational institutions. Over the past few decades, collaborative relationships among educators have been emphasized as a way of dealing with increased demands and diminished resources that have forced educators to do more with less (Noam, 2001). Collaboration has been promoted in education as a way of preparing students for 21st-century workplace environments where teamwork and problem solvers are in demand (Doiron & Davies, 1998). A considerable body of information from management (Drucker, 1999), nonprofit sectors (Gray, 1989; Gray & Wood, 1991), and education (Pugach & Johnson, 1995) informs us about how to engage in effective collaboration.

The importance of collaboration for educators and teacher-librarians is in its potential to positively affect student learning by working together (Acheson & Gall, 1992). A common understanding across multiple domains, such as technology (Roberts, 2004), special education (Fishbaugh, 1997), and library science (Callison, 1997, 1999; Haycock, 1998, 2003; Loertscher, 1982, 1988, 2000), is that collaboration is a process that improves the way that we develop curriculum and, thus, teaching and learning (AASL & AECT, 1998). This article focuses on face-to-face collaborative efforts involving classroom teachers and teacher-librarians, as a starting point in the discussion of collaboration. It proposes core elements of collaboration that appear to be present across various formats of instruction (face-to-face, computer mediated, and the like), across different domains (education, management, library and infor-

First published in *Teacher Librarian*, December 2006, Volume 34, Number 2

mation science), and among diverse age groups. The core elements may be applicable to teacher–teacher or student–student collaboration.

DEFINING COLLABORATION

The ubiquitous use of the term *collaboration* has led to its multiple interpretations and definitions. Outside of education, collaboration has been defined as thinking together and sharing expertise, resources, and authority (Minnis, John-Steiner, & Weber, 1994, as cited in John-Steiner, 1998). A definition of collaboration provided by Gray (1989) for corporate and nonprofit sectors suggests that collaboration is "a process through which parties who see different aspects of a problem can constructively explore their differences and search for solutions that go beyond their own limited vision of what is possible" (p. 5). In education, collaboration is seen as a way of promoting "the most effective teaching possible for the greatest number of students" (Pugach & Johnson, 1995, p. 178). A similar understanding about collaboration exists in library and information science. Callison (1997) proposed that collaboration for teacher-librarians means "coplanning, coimplementation, and coevaluation" (p. 37). Donham (1999) explained that collaboration involves joint efforts by classroom teachers and teacher-librarians to identify student needs and jointly plan instruction and assessment. More recently, Buzzeo (2002a, 2002b) defined collaboration as equal partners who team design, team teach, and team evaluate. Building on these ideas, I propose a definition of a particular type of collaborative effort for 21st-century classroom teachers and teacher-librarians. This definition of high-end collaboration states that collaboration is a trusting working relationship between two or more equal participants involved in shared thinking, shared planning, and shared creation of something new. Through a shared vision and shared objectives, student learning opportunities are created that integrate subject content and information literacy though jointly planning, implementing, and evaluating student progress throughout the instructional process in order to improve teaching and learning in all areas of the curriculum.

CORE ELEMENTS OF COLLABORATION

At the heart of the definition of classroom teacher and teacher-librarian collaboration are several core elements: interest, innovation, intensity, integration, and implementation (see Montiel-Overall, 2005a). These five elements can be represented on a continuum from low to high. At the high end of the continuum, core ingredients for successful collaboration endeavors are evident and may be the catalyst that results in improved student academic gains. These five elements are further explained as follows.

Interest. High-end collaboration involves a high degree of involvement among participants. The collaborators recognize the joint effort as being mutually beneficial and beneficial to students. Classroom teachers and teacher-librarians realize that time spent collaborating is more interesting than time spent planning alone. They may be more interested in teaching, and they may see greater interest in students during collaboratively planned units.

Innovation. Jointly planned instruction is innovative. The combined ideas from instructors from two backgrounds infuse newness and creativity into the instruction, giving inspiration to those teaching and those learning.

Intensity. Intensity involves commitment by classroom teachers and teacher-librarians to work diligently on jointly planned instruction. In successful teacher and teacher-librarian collaboration, individual ideas develop over time through patience and perseverance to improve instructional units; teacher and teacher-librarian demonstrate a passion for enhancing student learning. Barriers become insignificant in light of the positive student achievement that results from collaborative planning.

Integration. Seamlessly bringing together subject content (math, science, language arts, social studies) with library instruction (reference, research, information literacy) builds a bridge to comprehension. The end product is students' greater understanding of the material being taught.

Implementation. High-end collaboration involves completion of instruction by both collaborators. Joint implementation demonstrates a commitment by the classroom teacher and the teacher-librarian to jointly planned instruction. The transition between content and library curriculum seems effortless, although conscientious planning occurred. Students develop a holistic perspective on subject content and library information when implementation of instruction incorporates the expertise of classroom teacher and teacher-librarian.

RELATED PHENOMENON

Two phenomena associated with collaboration are coordination and cooperation. They are often used interchangeably (Fradd, 1992; Roberts, 2004; Roschelle & Teasley, 1995); however, they do not have the same desired effect as high-level collaboration (Table 3.1). Key elements, such as shared thinking, shared planning, and shared creation of something new from the proposed definition are lacking. For example, coordinated efforts tend to be primarily functional, involving management of time, events, and resources. Cooperation may involve some aspects of high-end collaboration; however, a common practice of cooperation is to divide assigned tasks among participants so that "each person is responsible for a portion of the problem-solving" (Roschelle & Teasley, 1995, p. 70). Participants in cooperative efforts may share responsibilities but do not necessarily share in the creation of something new (Montiel-Overall, 2005b). Program models that were originally identified as cooperative and evolved into more collaborative endeavors or included involvement of the sort described earlier have been renamed as *collaborative* (Haycock, 1995).

LOERTSCHER'S TAXONOMY

Loertscher (1988, 2000) developed two taxonomies as examples of various ways that classroom teachers and teacher-librarians work together: the library media specialist taxonomy, which identifies various types of involvement between teacher-librarian and teacher, and the teacher's taxonomy of resource-based teaching and learning, which describes teachers' involvement with teacher-librarians. These taxonomies have come to be known as Loertscher's taxonomy. Each taxonomy describes distinct levels of involvement between classroom teacher and teacher-librarian. These range from low-level efforts, such as scheduling visits to the library for individuals or small groups of students, to

COLLABORATION				
	Model A: Coordination	Model B: Cooperation	Model C: Integrated Instruction	Model D: Integrated Curriculum
Participant	Designated coordinator to work on project or assignment.	Teacher, Librarian	Teacher(s), Librarian	Teachers, Librarian, (Principal)
Goals and Objectives	Organize, manage, and/or direct events, lessons or activities to ensure efficiency and eliminate overlap of.	Tasks and responsibilities are divided. Individually developed plans are designed to work together for mutual benefit.	Integrate subject content (math, science, language arts, etc.) with library curriculum (collection, references, resources to develop information literacy).	Integrate subject content and library instruction across the curriculum
Impact on Student Academic Achievement	Minimal impact may result. Time is used more efficiently for teaching.	Some impact to improved learning. Students have the perspective of two individuals.	Impact may be significant. A connection between subjects helps students understand content and improves knowledge through multiple sources (references, literature, etc.) Research ability greatly improved and made more meaningful since it is contextualized.	Impact is significant. Students begin to see relationships of all content being studied. Relevance of content areas to real life and to student activities throughout the school day and to the use of library and instruction in library curriculum becomes more apparent to students. Innovation of curriculum increases motivation and interest in learning.
Characteristics Attributes	Shallow trust	Trust/Respect Reciprocity	Deep trust/Respect Reciprocity Propensity to share	Deep trust/Respect Reciprocity Propensity to share

Table 3.1. Models of Collaboration

An example of Model A occurs in a large urban elementary school where one teacher-librarian serves a population of 500 students. The teacher-librarian is on a fixed schedule, and students come into the school library weekly to check out books. There are no computers in the library. The primary role of the teacher-librarian is to help students find literature that is of interest to them and materials for classroom projects. The teacher-librarian is also scheduled for booktalks with primary students once a week. Classroom teachers and teacher-librarian rarely have time to discuss specific curriculum needs.

Text Box 3.1. Model A: Coordination

high-end collaborative efforts involving curriculum development. As an example of high-level collaboration, the teacher-librarian and the classroom teacher both contribute to planning and implementing curriculum. This type of involvement sharply contrasts to activities in which the teacher-librarian solely supports teacher-designed instruction.

MODELS OF COLLABORATION

Collaboration is what Barbara Gray (1989) referred to as an "emergent process" (p. 15) and John-Steiner (1998) described as "shared knowledge of an emergent form" (p. 774). Influenced by these experts on collaboration and using Loertscher's taxonomy, I now describe four different types of collaborative relationships.

At the low end is Model A, coordination, followed by Model B, cooperation. Model C, integrated instruction, and Model D, integrated curriculum, represent high-end collaborative endeavors (Montiel-Overall, 2005a, 2005b). Model A (Text Box 3.1) requires the least amount of involvement between classroom teacher and teacher-librarian. This type of collaboration occurs in many schools where teachers work autonomously and there is little or no contact between teacher and teacher-librarian for instructional purposes (Figure 3.1).[1]

In Model B (Text Box 3.2), classroom teachers and teacher-

Model A: Coordination	Model B: Cooperation	Model C: Integrated Instruction	Model D: Integrated Curriculum
Planning is functional Teachers, teacher-librarians, or principals work together to ensure efficient use of time and space	Planning is carried out by teacher and teacher-librarian independently of each other	Joint planning occurs between the teacher and the teacher-librarian. Teacher and teacher-librarian decide how to incorporate library instruction into the classroom lesson	Joint planning occurs across the school or school district Planning time is provided and supported by the administration
Communication is minimal	Communication is moderate	Communication is essential to good planning and implementation by teacher and teacher-librarian	Excellent communication, foresight, and problem solving occurs between administrators and faculty
Cordial	Collegial	Confidant	Collaborator
Shallow trust	Trust	Deep trust	Deep trust and commitment

Figure 3.1. The Four Models of Teacher and Teacher-Librarian Collaboration
They are Model A: Coordination; Model B: Cooperation; Model C: Integrated Instruction; and Model D: Integrated Curriculum. Each model has certain characteristics that distinguish it from the other models, and sometimes each facet occurs independently of the other models. When all models work together to improve teaching and learning, high-end collaboration occurs. High-end collaboration involves teachers and teacher-librarians planning together to integrate subject content and library instruction. In collaborative educational environments, students benefit from the expertise of two individuals planning lessons that integrate information to make teaching and learning more interesting, holistic, and comprehensible.

When asked if they collaborate, classroom teachers and teacher-librarian at a middle school in the Southwest answer yes. They explain that they are involved in many units, lessons, activities, and events. They share a recent example involving sixth-grade science teachers and the teacher-librarian who worked on a science fair for the district. The teacher-librarian helped students research science topics, format brochures, and create PowerPoint presentations to accompany their projects. Teacher and teacher-librarian met to discuss the types of skills that students would need to complete their projects. They agreed that the teacher-librarian was the most qualified to teach these skills to students.

Text Box 3.2. Model B: Cooperation

Classroom teachers and teacher-librarian schedule four units a year to work on together. After several years of trying different types of meeting arrangements, they have concluded that the best system is to block out the time together at the beginning of the year before school begins. During their designated time together, each teacher meets with the teacher-librarian to talk about the unit and brainstorm ideas about how the teacher-librarian will be able to assist students. One year, the teacher-librarian helped a classroom teacher with a writing project involving the Civil War. She helped teach six traits in the classroom and then worked with small groups of students as they selected their topic on the Civil War, did their research, and completed their report. Outstanding projects were presented in the library at a grade-level poster presentation.

Text Box 3.3. Model C: Integrated Instruction

librarians combine efforts for instruction, but formal planning of lessons is carried out separately. Model C reflects a high level of involvement by classroom teacher and teacher-librarian, who share their expertise to jointly generate new ideas for classroom instruction. This model is an example of high-end collaboration because shared thinking, shared planning, and shared creation of something new occur as classroom teacher and teacher- librarian come together to plan lessons and units of instruction. Model D incorporates the characteristics of Model C; however, it takes place across the curriculum at all grade levels. High-end collaboration involves joint planning as well as evaluation and assessment. In Model C (Text Box 3.3) and Model D (Text Box 3.4), each member's contribution is unique and adds to the process. The combined energy creates something that could not be created individually (Friend & Cook, 2000), and it adds value to the end product.

ATTRIBUTES

The collaborative effort reflected in high-end collaboration (Models C and D) involves certain attributes, such as dedication, respect, and trust. The participants must be good listeners and open to new ideas, which often emerge from discussions generated from diverse perspectives (O'Malley, 1989). Collaboration also involves equal participation and shared responsibilities. In high-end collaboration, there is no leader. Teachers are more receptive and inclined to participate in partnerships where their expertise is valued and where the mission inspires working together. In this type of environment, teaching and learning are enhanced. When teacher-librarians make themselves available to collaborate with classroom teachers as colleagues and equals, they find more partners than they are able to accommodate in the school day.

At a district-level meeting with the curriculum specialist, representatives from several schools discuss completed projects that integrated content and library curriculum. Final evaluation sheets from students indicate a high level of enthusiasm for projects that involve units of instruction created by the classroom teacher and teacher-librarian.

Text Box 3.4. Model D: Integrated Curriculum

INTEGRATION

Integration is the core element of collaboration that may ultimately prove to be a major factor in improved student academic achievement. Although the other core elements (interest, innovation, intensity, and implementation) strengthen collaboration, integration of library instruction—particularly, information literacy across content areas—is key to helping students make connections among different content areas. The holistic view of learning developed by students may result in their cognitive development and enhanced understanding. Seymour Papert (1980) noted 25 years ago that information that was not connected was "dissociated" (p. 65). Through interdisciplinary connections, a deep understanding of information emerges, which may be the most important factor in improved student academic achievement. Collaboration between classroom teachers and teacher-librarians to integrate library curriculum across the curriculum helps students make meaning of a broad range of subjects (math, science, language arts, social studies) while simultaneously developing information literacy and knowledge of other research abilities.

The work by Carol Kuhlthau (1985) has contributed to our understanding of the research process that students engage in when they are confronted with finding information for classroom projects. The process involves cognitive and affective stages that students go through in finding, using, and evaluating information. Through collaboration, students can learn to do library research, not as an end, but as a means to discovering more about subjects they are studying in the classroom. When this process occurs across the curriculum, it becomes a powerful teaching and learning device that taps into students' experiences and schemata (Bruner, 1968; Piaget, 1972) and improves student learning and recall (Howard, 1987).

Finally, integration of content and information literacy through collaboration between classroom teachers and teacher-librarians "is central to the learning process . . . [and] is critical in students' intellectual development" (AASL & AAECT, 1998, p. 15).

Twenty-first century education is a complex endeavor for educators and students alike. Collaboration between classroom teacher and teacher-librarian is one way to improve education, particularly when it involves a high level of interest, innovation, intensity, integration, and joint implementation. An educational environment that is shaped by teacher and teacher-librarian makes teaching and learning more meaningful, and it is an environment where students reach their potential and achieve great success.

REFERENCES

Acheson, K. A., & Gall, M. D. (1992). *Techniques in the clinical supervision of teachers.* New York: Longman.

American Association of School Librarians (AASL) & Association for Educational Communications and Technology (AECT). (1998). *Information power: Building partnerships for learning.* Chicago: American Library Association.

Bruner, J. (1968). *Toward a theory of instruction.* New York: Norton.

Buzzeo, T. (2002a). *Collaborating to meet standards: Teacher/librarian partnerships for K–6.* Worthington, OH: Linworth.

Buzzeo, T. (2002b). *Collaborating to meet standards: Teacher/librarian partnerships for 7–12.* Worthington, OH: Linworth.

Buzzeo, T. (2004). Standards-based education: Library media specialists and teachers meet the challenge collaboratively. *Library Media Connection, 22*(7), 14–16.

Callison, D. (1997). Expanding collaboration for literacy promotion in public and school libraries. *Journal of Youth Services, 11,* 37–48.

Callison, D. (1999). Keywords in instruction: Collaboration. *School Library Media Activities Monthly, 15,* 37–39. (ERIC Documentation Reproduction Service No. EJ608483)

Doiron, R., & Davies, J. (1998). *Partners in learning: Students, teachers, and the school library.* Englewood, CO: Libraries Unlimited.

Donham, J. (1999). Collaboration in the media center: Building partnerships for learning. *NASSP Bulletin, 83*(605), 20–26.

Drucker, P. F. (1999). The new pluralism. *Leader to Leader, 14.* Retrieved March 31, 2004, from **www.pfdf.org/leaderbooks/L2L/fall99/new-pluralism.html**

Fishbaugh, M. S. E. (1997). *Models of collaboration.* Boston: Allyn and Bacon.

Fradd, S. H. (1992). *Collaboration in schools serving students with limited English proficiency and other special needs.* Washington, DC: ERIC Clearinghouse on Languages and Linguistics. (ERIC Documentation Reproduction Service No. ED352847)

Friend, M., & Cook, L. (2000). *Interactions: Collaborative skills for school professionals* (3rd ed.). New York: Longman.

Gray, B. (1989). *Collaborating: Finding common ground for multiparty problems* (1st ed.). San Francisco: Jossey-Bass.

Gray, B., & Wood, D. J. (1991). Collaborative alliances: Moving from practice to theory. *Journal of Applied Behavioral Science, 27*(2), 3–22.

Grover, R. (Ed.). (1996). *Collaboration: Lessons learned series.* Chicago: American Association of School Librarians and American Library Association.

Haycock, K. (1995). Research in teacher-librarianship and the institutionalization of change. *School Library Media Quarterly, 23*(4). Retrieved May 25, 2005, from **www.ala.org/ala/aasl/aaslpubsand journals/slmrb/editorschoiceb/infopower/selecthaycock.htm**

Haycock, K. (1998). Collaborative cultures, team planning, and flexible scheduling. *Emergency Librarian, 25*(5), 28.

Haycock, K. (2003). Collaboration: Because student achievement is the bottom line. *Knowledge Quest, 32*(1), 54.

Howard, R. W. (1987). *Concepts and schemata: An introduction.* Philadelphia: Taylor and Francis.

John-Steiner, V. (1998). The challenge of studying collaboration. *American Educational Research Journal, 35*(4), 773–783.

Kuhlthau, C. C. (1985, Winter). A process approach to library skills. *School Library Media Quarterly, 13*(2), 35–40.

Loertscher, D. V. (1982). *Second revolution: A taxonomy for the 1980s.* Wilson Library Bulletin, *56*, 412–421.

Loertscher, D. V. (1988). *Taxonomies of the school library media program.* Englewood, CO: Libraries Unlimited.

Loertscher, D. V. (2000). *Taxonomies of the school library media program* (2nd ed.). San Jose, CA: Hi Willow Research and Publishing.

Mattessich, P., & Monsey, B. (1992). *Collaboration: What makes it work.* St. Paul, MN: Amherst H. Wilder Foundation.

Montiel-Overall, P. (2005a). A theoretical understanding of teacher and librarian collaboration (TLC). *School Libraries Worldwide, 11*(2), 24–48.

Montiel-Overall, P. (2005b). Toward a theory of collaboration for teachers and librarians. *School Library Media Research, 8.* Retrieved September 22, 2006, from **www.ala.org/ala/aasl/aaslpubs andjournals/slmrb/slmrcontents/volume82005/theory.htm**

Noam, G. G. (2001). *Afterschool time: Toward a theory of collaborations.* Cambridge, MA: Harvard University.

O'Malley, C. (Ed.). (1989). *Computer supported collaborative learning.* New York: Springer-Verlag.

Papert, S. (1980). *Mindstorms: Children, computers, and powerful ideas.* New York: Basic Books.

Piaget, J. (1972). *The child's conception of the world.* Totowa, NJ: Littlefield, Adams.

Pugach, M., & Johnson, L. J. (1995). *Collaborative practitioners collaborative schools* (1st ed.). Denver, CO: Love.

Roberts, T. S. (2004). *Online collaborative learning: Theory and practice.* Hershey, PA: Information Science.

Roschelle, J., & Teasley, S. (1995). The construction of shared knowledge in collaborative problem solving. In C. O'Malley (Ed.), *Computer-supported collaborative learning* (pp. 69–97). New York: Springer-Verlag.

NOTE

1. In previous writing on collaboration, *cooperation* is identified as requiring the least involvement, followed by coordination (Buzzeo, 2004; Grover, 1996; Mattessich & Monsey, 1992). The models proposed reverse this mental model. For further discussion on the reversed order, see Montiel-Overall (2005a).

(4)

From Fixed to Flexible: Making the Journey

Joyce Needham

A class of 25 elementary students rushes into the library resource center for its weekly class. During the 30-minute slot the frazzled teacher-librarian tries to teach "library skills," share literature, provide reader guidance, check out books, monitor behavior, and have the students lined up and ready to leave before the next class arrives at the resource center. Surprises arrive daily as individual students, small groups, or even entire classes arrive unannounced, needing 20 books on Native Americans, biographies of this year's U.S. Olympic team, or information about Christmas traditions on all continents. If you have experienced this, then making the journey from fixed to flexible should be of interest to you.

THE TIME IS RIGHT

Ours is a rapidly changing world. Technology, using improved communication and transportation, has shrunk our world and at the same time is causing an information explosion. Technologies new to one generation (black-and-white television, party phone lines, electric typewriters, eight-track tapes) become obsolete with the next.

These rapid changes affect the needs of our students and our educational system is struggling to meet those needs. Schools are beginning to realize that adding more content to the curriculum has not created the lifelong learning and critical thinking skills required to live successfully in our information-rich world. Sparked by the changing makeup of and emphasis on mandated state and national assessments, there is a realization that information literacy—the ability to find and use information—must be taught in our schools (AASL & AECT, 1998). Information literacy is considered a basic, along with reading, writing, and arithmetic, and one of the skills required of lifelong learners. It is also what the journey from fixed to flexible is all about.

If school libraries are to meet current needs of students, teacher-librarians need "to distinguish be-

First published in *Teacher Librarian*, June 2003, Volume 30, Number 5

tween information and learning, and to promote libraries as instruments of learning, rather than as centers of information" (Hartzell, 2002a, p. 35). The focus must shift from providing information access within the walls of the library to equipping students with a process for finding and using information regardless of its location, a skill they will need all their lives. Students must be encouraged to ask questions, solve problems, think critically, and increasingly accept responsibility for their own learning and in this way become lifelong learners (Ohlrich, 2001). Thus the change to a flexible, integrated, and collaborative information literacy program becomes not just a want of the teacher-librarian but also a need of our students.

How can a flexible, integrated, and collaborative program help teach information literacy? Information literacy is not content (i.e., American history, science, literature) but a three-part process:

- accessing information efficiently and effectively;
- evaluating information critically and competently; and
- using information accurately and creatively.

This process may be actively taught to our students (Todd, 1995). Research by Hardesty and Wright (1982) and Kuhlthau (1989) suggests the following variables appear to be linked to information skills instruction: self-perception, self-esteem, control of learning, mastery of content, focus on task, and reduced confusion and frustration. Within the scope of his study, Todd found integrated information skills instruction had a significant impact on students' mastery of prescribed science content and their ability to use a range of information skills to solve particular information problems. This research supports information skills instruction as a valuable and essential part of the school's educational program. Instruction emphasizing information problem solving and research processes rather than just skills for locating and accessing library resources. Instruction with skills taught within the context of the school's curriculum utilizing innovative instructional methods (Todd, 1995).

PROBLEM-SOLVING MODELS

Many information problem-solving models exist: Kuhlthau (1985), Stripling and Pitts (1988), and Eisenberg and Berkowitz (1990) have all developed models. Because becoming a proficient information problem solver involves a large investment of time, a school may find greater success by selecting one model and implementing it consistently for all students, from grades K–12.

Deciding upon a model to actively teach information literacy is perhaps the first step in building an information literacy program. However, there are three other interrelated components: integration, collaboration, and flexible scheduling.

INTEGRATION

What is integration and why is it important? Integration refers to connecting disciplines, teaching information literacy skills at the point of need in conjunction with other curriculum. Teaching students how to use the encyclopedia after students have been assigned an animal to research and prior to students completing the report using the encyclopedia is an example of integration.

Research on how we learn strongly supports integration as a means of helping students construct knowledge and make connections to prior knowledge, thus increasing the amount of learning that occurs (Fosnot, 1996; Jensen, 1995). The American Association of School Librarians further supports integration as a means of strengthening the teaching/learning process so that students can develop the vital skills necessary to locate, analyze, evaluate, interpret and communicate information and ideas. When the school library program is fully integrated into the instructional program of the school, students, teachers, and teacher-librarians become partners in learning and the library program becomes an extension of the classroom (AASL, 1991).

COLLABORATION

How does collaboration fit within this model? Collaboration between teachers and the teacher-librarian is the key to integration. A study by Tallman and van Deusen (1994) indicates face-to-face communication between teachers and teacher-librarians resulted in increased connections between information skills instruction and classroom instruction. They conclude time teacher-librarians spent meeting with teachers was well spent; however, time for collaboration alone is no guarantee of success. "Successful collaboration is based on common goals, a shared vision and a climate of trust and mutual respect" (Russell, 2002, p. 35). The importance of collaboration is emphasized in *Information Power*: "Effective collaboration with teachers helps to create a vibrant and engaged community of learners, strengthens the whole school program as well as the library media program and develops support for the school library media program throughout the whole school" (AASL & AECT, 1998, p. 5).

FLEXIBLE SCHEDULING

A flexible schedule is necessary to meet the needs of both students and teachers. Flexibility in the library schedule means student needs dictate the schedule. If a class needs to visit the library on three consecutive days to complete a science project, it may do so. In addition, the library resource center is open throughout the day for individuals and small groups who need to access information, select reading material, or simply find a place to read or work in small groups. "Flexible access . . . creates an atmosphere that says, 'Your quest for knowledge is important to us'" (Ohlrich, 2001, p. 7). The flexible schedule also plays an important role in collaboration. Because teachers' schedules in most schools are very inflexible, the flexibility of the library schedule provides the time and opportunity for the teacher and teacher-librarian to plan for integrated instruction. A 1996 study by Miller and Anderson stresses that while a flexible schedule does not ensure the library program will be integrated into the classroom curriculum, if the school library program *is* to be integrated, the schedule *must* be flexible (Miller & Anderson, 1996). Research by Tallman and van Deusen finds the use of flexible scheduling supports consultation between teachers and teacher-librarians. Additionally, as long as teacher-librarians provide planning time for teachers by taking their classes, very little integration of the library program can be expected (Tallman & van Deusen, 1994).

MAKING THE CHANGE

How does a fixed and isolated library program change to a flexible, integrated, and collaborative information literacy program? First an understanding of the nature of change is necessary. Change, because it upsets equilibrium, can be uncomfortable and difficult. Change occurs when someone becomes dissatisfied enough with the status quo to want alternative options. "The change agent needs to be knowledgeable about the change to be made, the people involved, and the school's organization" (Ohlrich, 2001, p. 81). As the change agent in this case, the teacher-librarian must understand that adjusting to a flexible, integrated, and collaborative information literacy program is not accomplished by a few alterations in procedure; rather, "it is a complete change in attitude, resources, and management" (Buchanan, 1991, p. 5). A change of this magnitude will require time and happen slowly.

It is also important to remember the library program belongs to the school—students, teachers, administrators, and teacher-librarian. Any changes to the program will have a direct impact upon all of these people. Thus a successful change must take their needs into consideration and involve them in the creation of the new program.

Students are the reason for schools. Therefore, teaching students to be critical thinkers and lifelong learners must be our focus. As such the retention of facts is secondary to the knowledge of strategies for learning and skill in information retrieval. As the ancient proverb succinctly states, "Tell me, I forget; show me, I remember; involve me, I understand." Children taught that the school library is a place to go when they need information will see the connection in all libraries (Bernstein, 1997). In addition, equipping students with a problem-solving strategy will allow them to enjoy improved performance on mandated assessments.

Any change in instruction obviously affects teachers. The change from fixed to flexible schedule usually means teachers give up needed preparation time and commit additional time to planning with the teacher-librarian. Teachers will commit this additional time only if convinced information literacy is a vital skill for their students. The teacher-librarian can strengthen this commitment by helping teachers understand and experience their roles as guides and coaches. While teachers are accountable for their students meeting district and state standards, they are not responsible for personally teaching each of those standards to their students. By teaming with the teacher-librarian, the teacher is in a position to guide instruction while delegating some of the planning, preparation, and actual teaching to the teacher-librarian. The time saved by such teaming can offset the loss of release time and additional time spent planning with the teacher-librarian. By teaming with the teacher-librarian, the teacher shares some of his or her responsibilities with another professional, making teaching less stressful.

Administrators, as the instructional leaders, are vital to successful change. "Administrators aren't interested in good library media programs because they want good libraries . . . they want students to read better, learn more, and improve achievement" (Hartzell, 2002b, p. 31). To gain administrative support for change to a flexible schedule, teacher-librarians must convince administrators that an information literacy program that teaches students a process and integrates skills into content curriculum can have a positive and direct impact on student learning and achievement. The teacher-librarian can help the administration reach this understanding by diligently communicating information about the library program (projects, weekly schedules, collaboration, etc.) and sharing relevant research. Administrators can be led to an understanding of how collaboration and integration can open classroom doors and build an educational team, not only enhancing student learning but empowering teachers to become guides and coaches, relieving some of the stress that currently exists because of accountability issues (such as mandated testing). It is crucial that the active support of the principal or curriculum director is gained, so these leaders can continually motivate, monitor, model, and provide opportunities for ongoing staff development (Miller & Anderson, 1996).

To build support for the information literacy program, introduce the principal to a process which students can use for solving information problems (in the author's case, Big6© was used). To lead the principal to be an advocate for information literacy, demonstrate how this process can be applied not only to daily classroom information problems (e.g., answering questions in the textbook, solving math word problems), but also to state-mandated assessments and information problems faced by adults in today's society.

Obviously changing to an information literacy program will have a direct impact on the teacher-librarian, and he or she will be crucial to the success of the change. "First and foremost today's school librarian is a teacher, primarily of information literacy. But the school librarian also partners with classroom teachers" (Eisenberg, 2002, p. 47). *Information Power* spells out the role:

> As a teacher, the school librarian collaborates with students and other members of the learning community to analyze learning and information needs, locate and use resources that will meet those needs, and to understand and communicate the information the resources provide. As a partner, the school librarian joins the teachers and others to identify links across student information needs, curricular content, learning outcomes, and a wide variety of print, nonprint, and electronic information resources. (AASL & AECT, 1998, p. 4)

However, research indicates that most students, teachers and administrators do not perceive teacher-librarians and library resource centers as integral to their own success (Hartzell, 2002b). Instead, teacher-librarians are often seen as storytellers and providers of resources rather than teachers who share common goals with classroom teachers (Bishop & Larimer, 1999). The challenge teacher-librarians face, then, is to change this perception. To do so, the teacher-librarian must first ensure that the majority of his or her time is *not* spent telling stories and completing clerical tasks. This may require creativity in delegating clerical duties. Secondly, the teacher-librarian must take an active role in educating staff as to the importance of information literacy and modeling for staff how a flexible, integrated, and collaborative information literacy program fits into the existing curriculum and meets the needs of students.

A PERSONAL JOURNEY

In the author's case, the change from a fixed, release time library program to a flexible, integrated, and collaborative information literacy program was a 10-year journey. The program evolved in two elementary schools (each grades K–5 with approximately 275 students) staffed by one teacher-librarian and one clerical assistant who split time equally between schools, allowing each library to be open every day. The two schools, while located in the same town, had diverse populations. The student body at one was over 90% Caucasian with approximately 13% free and reduced lunch population. The other was 60% Caucasian with approximately 90% free and reduced lunch population.

The process of change was as follows:

1. *Teacher-librarian became knowledgeable about information literacy programs and developed a vision.* Data was gathered through intensive reading of research and literature, discussions about information literacy held with colleagues, administrators and classroom teachers, and visits to schools with information literacy programs.

2. *Program was designed to meet the needs of the school.* Factors such as how many students were served, number of buildings, amount of clerical support, and so on, all shaped the program. Designing a program that met the needs of the school required not only knowledge of information literacy programs but also knowledge of the school. Two tools used to help determine the needs of the school were

• **library advisory committee.** This included the building administrator, teachers, interested parents, and the teacher-librarian. This group shared its vision of the school library program and the role it saw for the teacher-librarian. It was the sounding board, and members became active advocates for the program.
• **needs assessment.** Using information gathered through research and from the advisory committee, staff was surveyed to determine what procedures and policies could be implemented to move toward an information literacy program. As a result of the needs assessment the teacher-librarian was able to:

(a) determine two or three teachers who were open to collaboration and integrated projects and (b) move checkout out of the 30-minute weekly library session to a time when the clerical staffed the resource center. This not only freed the teacher-librarian of many clerical tasks, but also provided a full 30 minutes for instruction.

3. *Foundation was laid.* The teacher-librarian focused on educating (sharing knowledge and experiences) and demonstrating (doing collaborative, integrated projects with interested teachers in addition to the regular fixed schedule) the value of an information literacy program to teachers and administrators. The teacher-librarian also focused on becoming an integral part of the school's staff by taking an active role, serving on school and district curriculum committees and providing staff development on relevant topics. Because teachers began staying with their classes during checkout, they had more contact with the library resource center and began to feel ownership in the facility. The teacher-librarian made connections to classroom content whenever possible during the 30-minute library classes. Students now became conscious of their purpose for coming to the resource center, whether that purpose was to check out a book, locate information, receive instruction, or just relax and read for a few minutes. This consciousness resulted in students accepting more responsibility for their learning.

4. *Flexibility was added to the schedule.* Approximately three years after checkout became a separate activity, the principal, with input from the advisory committee, decided to move grades 3–5 classes to a flexible schedule. In order to allow the teacher-librarian more flexibility, all K–2 classes were blocked into two afternoons. This left five mornings and three afternoons when the teacher-librarian could plan and teach with grades 3–5 classes. At the same time all classroom teachers (grades K–5) began completing a monthly planning form. This provided the teacher-librarian with the content or curriculum connections into which information literacy skills could be integrated. Realizing the value of integration in all areas, these planning forms were also shared with other support staff—the art teacher, music teacher, speech therapist, counselor, resource teachers, and the computer aide. In addition to completing the planning form, grade 3–5 teachers met monthly with the teacher-librarian to collaborate. At the same time, the Big6© information problem-solving process, which had been used by individual teachers, was adopted as the process that would be taught to all students in grades 3–5.

5. *A fully flexible, integrated, and collaborative information literacy program was adopted.* Four years later (10 years after the teacher-librarian initially began the journey), upon the recommendation of the Library Advisory Committee, the principal moved grades K–2 to the flexible schedule. The K–2 teachers began collaborating with the teacher-librarian, continuing to use the monthly planning forms. In addition, annual grade-level planning meetings are held with the teacher-librarian, with further planning sessions as needed. An interim evaluation meeting is held in the second semester to make any necessary adjustments. Thus the journey from fixed to flexible continues in both schools.

CONCLUSION

Why make the journey? Do you believe it is important that our students become information literate— lifelong learners and critical thinkers who can access, process and communicate information? Do you believe in the power of collaboration: educators (classroom teachers, teacher-librarians, and administrators) working as a team toward this common goal? If you share these two beliefs, then the journey from fixed to flexible becomes not only personally rewarding but also critical for the success of our students.

REFERENCES

American Association of School Librarians (AASL). (1991). Position statement on flexible scheduling. Retrieved December 2, 2002, from **http://www.ala.org/aasl/positions**

American Association of School Librarians (AASL) & Association for Educational Communications and Technology (AECT). (1998). *Information power: Building partnerships for learning.* Chicago: Authors.

Bernstein, A. (1997). Flexible schedules: Quality learning time. *Library Talk, 10*(3), 11.

Bishop, K., & Larimer, N. (1999). Literacy through collaboration. *Teacher Librarian, 27*(1), 15–20.

Buchanan, J. (1991). *Flexible access library media programs.* Englewood, CO: Libraries Unlimited.

Eisenberg, M. (2002). This man wants to change your job. *School Library Journal, 48*(9), 46–50.

Eisenberg, M. B., & Berkowitz, R. E. (1990). *Information problem solving: The big six skills approach to library and information skills instruction.* Norwood, NJ: Ablex.

Fosnot, C. (1996). *Constructivism: Theory, perspectives, & practice.* New York: Teachers College Press.

Hardesty, L., & Wright, J. (1982). Student library skills and attitudes and their change: Relationships to other selected variables. *Journal of Academic Librarianship, 8*(5), 216–220.

Hartzell, G. (2002a). Gods of the mind: It's dangerous to confuse information with understanding. *School Library Journal, 48*(8), 35.

Hartzell, G. (2002b). The hole truth: Librarians need to emphasize what they have to offer. *School Library Journal, 48*(7), 31.

Jensen, E. (1995). *Brain-based learning.* DelMar, CA: Turning Point.

Kuhlthau, C. (1985). *Teaching the library research process.* West Nyack, NY: The Center of Applied Research in Education.

Kuhlthau, C. (1989). The information search process: A summary of research and implications for school library media programs. *School Library Media Quarterly, 18*(1), 19–25.

Miller, D., & Anderson J. (1996). *Developing an integrated library program.* Worthington, OH: Linworth.

Ohlrich, K. (2001). *Making flexible access and flexible scheduling work today.* Englewood, CO: Libraries Unlimited.

Russell, S. (2002). Teachers and librarians: Collaborative relationships. *Teacher Librarian, 29*(5), 35–37.

Stripling, B., & Pitts, J. (1988). *Brainstorms & blueprints: Teaching library research as a thinking process.* Englewood, CO: Libraries Unlimited.

Tallman, J., & van Deusen, J. (1994). Collaborative unit planning: Schedule, time and participants. *School Library Media Quarterly, 23*(1), 33–37.

Todd, R. (1995). Integrated information skills instruction: Does it make a difference? *School Library Media Quarterly, 23*(2), 133–138.

⑤

What Works: Gauging the Impact of Teacher and Teacher-Librarian Collaboration

David Loertscher

This feature usually reports a research study and its usefulness in a school library program. No studies were found gauging the impact of individual or group collaborations between teachers and teacher-librarians. Therefore, the *TL* editors have proposed an action research study for your use. We encourage you to carry out a study and report the results for possible publication—e-mail your findings to David Loertscher at *davidlibrarian@gmail.com.*

Background: Administrators and teachers may be interested in the value-added benefits accrued when a classroom teacher and the teacher-librarian collaborate to plan, implement, and evaluate a learning experience taught together. This proposed action research study could be done every time that a collaborative unit happens or just with selected collaborations. The results should be reported by the team to the administrator on a regular basis.

Research Questions: What percentage of learners meet or exceed learning expectations when a classroom teacher and a teacher-librarian team teach a unit of instruction? How does that percentage compare with the normal success rate when classroom teachers teach alone?

METHOD

Step 1: Ask the teacher to judge each student on how well he or she meets or exceeds the expectations of a unit of instruction. Divide the class into three groups: high achievers, average achievers, and challenged students. Compute the percentage for each group.

Step 2: Plan together the objectives of the unit based on what students should know, do, and understand. Be sure that the agenda of both the teacher and the teacher-librarian are included. For example,

---

the teacher-librarian might want the students to do wide reading on the topic, learn an information literacy skill, and use technology to enhance learning.

Step 3: Plan the joint assessment for the unit. Be sure that both partners' objectives are assessed and reflected in the final grade. Regardless of the assessment given, the teacher and the teacher-librarian should be able to judge whether each student met or exceeded unit expectations.

Step 4: Team teach the unit together and assess the students jointly.

Step 5: Determine the number of students in each ability level who met or exceeded expectations.

Step 6: Compare the results with the predictions. This should stimulate a fascinating discussion of the strengths and challenges of the partnership and what might be done the next time to improve the results. Ask such questions as Which students seem to do better when we collaborate? and How could we work more effectively together to maximize the success of every learner?

Step 7: Report the results and make future plans. What happens over time when you collaborate with a single teacher numerous times? What happens when you collaborate with a group of teachers, such as a grade-level team or a department?

Student Name High Ability	Usually Meets Expectations? Y or N	
Total and % Yes		
Student Name Average Ability	Usually Meets Expectations? Y or N	
Total and % Yes		
Student Name Challenged	Usually Meets Expectations? Y or N	
Total and % Yes		
Whole class Total and % Yes		

Prediction Table

Student Name High Ability	Met Expectations? Y or N	
Total and % Yes		
Student Name Average Ability	Met Expectations? Y or N	
Total and % Yes		
Student Name Challenged	Met Expectations? Y or N	
Total and % Yes		
Whole class Total and % Yes		
Comparison With Predicted		
Gain or loss		
What type of student seemed to benefit the most?		
Conclusions and Recommendations		

Analysis and Conclusion Table

⑥

Do Your
Collaboration Homework

Gail Bush

Collaboration favors only the prepared mind. Sound familiar? The 17th-century French chemist Louis Pasteur is quoted to have said that in the fields of observation, "chance favors only the prepared mind." Shamelessly borrowing from this sentiment, we might amend it to read, "collaboration favors only the prepared mind." After all, how can we expect educators to choose to collaborate with us if we ourselves are unprepared for the task? Without collaboration with our fellow educators, we cease to have a purposeful mission in the life of the school. The onus, one could say, is *on us*. So how exactly shall we prepare to position ourselves for effective educator collaboration?

Twenty-first-century educators understand that our students benefit when we weave our programs together; when the school curriculum resembles the world outside of the school. Doing collaboration homework would benefit all members of the school learning community. However, we are directing our attention to the teacher-librarian who is responsible for the school library program. What makes us and our role in the learning community unique?

Having a firm grasp on research and being the resourceful lot that we are, we know that we must do our collaboration homework. We take advantage of the free-ranging role that we have in the school; we are betwixt and between all the teachers and the administrators with our sights set securely on our students. The homework assignments on the following list will help to shape the prepared mind that will serve the valuable collaborative partner well. Add your personal touch, that item that you cannot believe was left off the list, and make the list work for you in your particular school setting. The assignment is due as soon as you want to take the next step toward a fulfilling professional collaborative relationship.

TALK, WALK, AND OWN YOUR MISSION

It is all about the mission. You do have one and you can articulate it in a sentence or two, and we call that

First published in *Teacher Librarian*, October 2003, Volume 31, Number 1

your mission statement. It fits into your school and/or district mission but is unique because it resides in the school library program. What is your interpretation of teacher-librarian best practices as they relate to your unique school situation? Think it through, write it, talk it, walk it, and own it. You are the embodiment of your mission; it is what you and your program are all about. If you cannot articulate it clearly and succinctly and have it permeate your every duty and responsibility, why should anyone else? Use the *Planning Guide for* Information Power: Building Partnerships for Learning (AASL, 1999) for assistance. If you do not feel like you can *own your mission*, go back to the drawing board.

READ *INFORMATION POWER: BUILDING PARTNERSHIPS FOR LEARNING (IP2)*

Read and study *Information Power: Building Partnerships for Learning* (AASL & AECT, 1998) until you are familiar with the concepts of collaboration, leadership, and technology as they impact the roles of teaching and learning, information access and delivery, and program administration. As years go by, another edition of this conceptual foundation will appear. It is your responsibility to stay abreast of the updated standards by which we operate. It is an indicator of your professionalism to stay current in your field, to be able to converse with your colleagues about the roles and areas of concentration as presented in your guiding document.

Let's say you have read *IP2* and you do not feel like you are comfortable using it as your guidebook to an improved school library program. Take that *Planning Guide for* Information Power: Building Partnerships for Learning in hand. It was designed to be that intermediary stepping stone that might be just what you need. If you take the time to work with it, this document will walk you through the steps you need to take to fully appreciate the value of *IP2*.

UNDERSTAND INFORMATION LITERACY

There are honest-to-goodness standards included in *IP2*. Many practitioners bypass these standards and prefer the trademarked, ready-to-wear models. Whether you use packaged models or you choose to create your own research process custom-made for your students, become familiar with the standards presented in *IP2*. Not only do they give us a common language and understanding, they take us a step further than most models. Think about independent learning. Consider how you can promote social responsibility in your students. Information literacy in the way that we normally think about it is only the beginning of student learning. How will you feel comfortable that your students understand information literacy and are independent and socially responsible learners? Simple. Own information literacy standards and use the model of your choice to bring the message home.

FAMILIARIZE YOURSELF WITH YOUR SCHOOL IMPROVEMENT PLAN (SIP)

The term *school improvement plan* refers to a realistic guiding document that leads a school toward desired achievable results. School improvement most often refers to improved student learning and parent involvement. Identifying stakeholders, actions, and processes are standard fare. The responsibility for this blueprint usually sits with the school principal. In some U.S. states, there is legislation that dictates the SIP cycle; in Canada, the Education Improvement Commission sponsors school improvement plan projects. Frequently there are faculty committees mandated to share the ownership of this guiding plan. In every scenario, the impact on student learning is center stage. In no scenario researched (prove me wrong, please) is the school library mentioned. In rare cases, a teacher-librarian may be involved in the school improvement plan committee. Be aware of the status of your SIP. Does your school have one? If so, ask for a copy and study it. Is there a SIP committee? If so, ask to be placed on the committee. If that is not possible, ask to be apprised of their progress so that you can keep your program aligned with their goals.

Interest in your school improvement plan is evidence of your role as an educational leader and it should indicate to your administrator that the school library program requires attention in the development of the plan. The most effective SIPs are long-term (3- to 5-year cycles) and are continuously reviewed. Do not bemoan the plan you read; rather, look for places to involve the library as the plan evolves.

ACQUAINT YOURSELF WITH YOUR ACCREDITING AGENCY

Even if you never think about it, it will not be surprising for you to learn that your school has an independent accrediting agency that provides a framework for accountability. Some agencies are governmental; some are independent. In general, they focus on accountability, monitoring, and reporting. They require educational institutions to conduct self-studies and self-assessments.

The school improvement plan described above is often a component of a school's self-study, which is then reviewed by the accrediting agency. There is usually a school review cycle perpetuated by the accrediting agency. The response of the agency will lead to certain areas of concentration that direct the school's activities during the next part of the cycle. For instance, a school may be directed to increase opportunities for free reading. This focus would naturally be of interest to the teacher-librarian but the language arts department or the reading specialists might not consider including the library program or staff in plans to satisfy the accrediting agency's recommendations.

EXAMINE YOUR CURRICULUM STRUCTURE

Does your school have instructional teams? Is the curriculum delivered through the departments? Are there committees that focus on particular aspects of a curriculum? Does your school have a school curriculum guide? Perhaps your district has a curriculum guide that is not site-specific but covers the curriculum taught by grade level within the district. When your teachers write their lesson plans, do they align the units to learning standards set by the district, subject, state, or a combination? Is there a philosophy or method of curriculum development that they follow? If they are adhering to the *understanding by design* method of determining what they want the students to learn and developing their curriculum in a backward fashion, become familiar with that design. If they follow Curry-Samara and design their curriculum to match Bloom's taxonomy, familiarize yourself with that style of curriculum development. Whichever curriculum gods reign supreme in your school, learn the underlying assumptions, principles, and methods of delivery that distinguish that design.

STUDY INSTRUCTIONAL MATERIALS

When I was the curriculum librarian in a high school library resource center, I read *Catcher in the Rye* every few years. I reread many novels; skimmed biographical sketches of authors; studied historical periods; learned scientific principles; explored trends in the arts; and basically learned as much as I could about every subject that we supported in the library resource center. You might learn about the teacher's focus from previewing the class web site. Do not be afraid or embarrassed to ask for background materials. Teachers love to teach anyone their subject areas; they might feel flattered that you care enough to spend time in the learning process. Perhaps this is a personal bent of mine, but I do not understand how we can attempt to collaborate with a classroom teacher without some understanding of the relevant subject matter.

SUPPORT AND CONDUCT ACTION RESEARCH

Getting back to the curricular structure in your school, your teachers might have a natural structure for conducting action research. If not, it is likely that teams or groups have formed to research specific teaching or management topics relevant to your school. You might do your homework in a few different ways in relation to action research. If your curriculum teams have study questions, support their inquiry by enriching their research capabilities. If this type of research is not currently conducted at your school, consider following up on recommendations by your accrediting agency or by investigating an area of your school improvement plan that would benefit from data-driven research. You will want to discover the best sources for your research needs; which associations and research organizations will you want to explore? Just for a lark, take a minute to visit McREL or AskERIC. Test out an area of inquiry that your teachers are concerned about. Now visit the national association that is related to that inquiry. Resources are in such abundance and isn't that a "good problem to have." Since you have the research skills necessary to conduct effective research, you will need to learn how much you should do for your educators and how much you should refer to them.

As instructional consultants and information professionals, we want to keep our research skills sharp. What better way than to support action research that will ultimately benefit your school by improving student learning? Of course, along the way you will also be supporting improving teacher learning (not to mention your own learning rewards). If your research skills are rusty or not quite up to par, climb onto your learning curve and go for a ride. The teachers and administrators in your building should be able to rely on their in-house research expert for this type of support. It is possible that a new emphasis on developing a professional collection will arise. Another good problem to have.

NETWORK, NETWORK, NETWORK

Certainly some of us come by this networking inclination naturally and you might even wonder at all the fuss made about it. The skills required to network are not second nature to all teacher-librarians. Furthermore, some of us think that this aspect of our work is somehow superfluous to our primary responsibilities. Networking, collaborating with colleagues, visiting other school libraries, connecting with community partners—all serve to improve our practice. Make a special effort to seek out your local public librarians. Participation in district, regional, and state/provincial systems is essential for school library professionals. Additionally, participation in educational networks is important both for us and for our colleagues outside of school librarianship.

We believe that our students benefit when we have a place at the table. There is no point to having a place if we do not actively seek opportunities to have a voice for the school library. You embody the school library program to the greater education community. If we do not take that role seriously we have no business expecting to be taken seriously by other educators.

THINK A STEP AHEAD

If you have done your homework you should be able to get a sense of what is in store for your school and your educators in the future. Use curriculum mapping to help guide your collection development. Write mini-grants focusing on upcoming local, regional, national, and global causes and events.

There are many overlapping cycles of plans, accreditation, grants, and initiatives that impact your school. Stay a step ahead so that you have the statistics you might need for a report. It is not a bad idea to anticipate expenditures that are not part of a line-item budget, so that if you were told that you had X dollars to spend by Friday you would be ready. You might want to have separate wishlists for books, subscriptions, furniture, equipment, hardware, software, and posters-and-such. When the parent organization or a student club or a local club or even a small grant application finds its way into your school library, you want to be ready. No amount is too small because the goodwill it engenders in the donors outweighs the actual purchases made.

EDUCATE THE EDUCATORS

We started this homework assignment by talking, walking, and owning your mission. It is not only possible, it is likely that your mission will change, grow, evolve, as your influence over your school library program deepens. Your knowledge and understanding of the needs of your school learning community will broaden, and become more textured and enriched over time. You will grow as a professional and you will offer more to your colleagues than you ever imagined. In fact, the definition of "your colleagues" might change as well. In our role in the school, we have the possibility to partner with students, support staff, faculty, administrators, parents, and community members. We have a unique position in the school structure. The role that we take in our school library resource centers and how that role is viewed by the school learning community is entirely up to us. Make of it what you will, for better or worse. In either case, you will be educating the educators as to what your library program is, what it can offer, what role you have and can have as a professional educator in the school. Consider this: The next time someone asks a member of your school learning community, "Why do we need a teacher-librarian?" make that seem like the most ridiculous question he or she ever heard. The only way to make this scenario a reality is to educate the educators.

After all is said and done, without collaboration and leadership we simply supply a resource center that is devoid of relevance to any educational mission of the school. Following this bit of logic a step further, if your program is not relevant to your school's mission, how can you be effectively fulfilling your school library program mission? You might even enjoy the expansive nature of collaboration homework so much that you choose to continue your education and become a school principal or district administrator. Whether you choose to do your collaboration homework or not, you are educating the educators and everyone else in your school learning community. Consider what lessons you are teaching them about the school library program and the role that we have in improving student learning. Collaboration favors the prepared mind. On behalf of our fellow teacher-librarians, I beseech you to do your homework.

REFERENCES

American Association of School Librarians (AASL) & the Association for Educational Communications and Technology (AECT). (1998). Information power: Building partnerships for learning. Chicago: American Library Association.

American Association of School Librarians (AASL). (1999). *A planning guide for* Information power: Building partnerships for learning. Chicago: American Library Association.

ERIC Clearinghouse on Information & Technology. AskERIC: Information with the personal touch. **http://www.askeric.org**

Mid-continent Research for Education and Learning. McREL. **http://www.mcrel.org**

Achieve Information Literacy by *Learning for the Future* with *Information Power*!

In addition to *Information Power*, readers will be interested in reviewing and considering the following:
Achieving information literacy: Standards for school library programs in Canada. The Canadian School Library Association and the Association for Teacher-librarianship in Canada. 2003. 90 pp. $20. 0-88802-301-4.
and
Learning for the future: Developing information services in schools (2nd ed.). Australia School Library Association/Australia Library and Information Association. Curriculum Corporation, 2001. 82 pp. $32.95. 1-86366-710-5.

Text Box 6.1. *TL* Extender

(1)

What Works:
Collaborative Program Planning
and Teaching

Ken Haycock

RESEARCH FINDING

Collaborative planning requires a knowledgeable and flexible teacher-librarian, with good interpersonal skills and a commitment to integrated information literacy instruction, and the active support of the principal.

COMMENT

Teacher-librarians recognize the critical importance of their participation in curriculum development; however, their actual involvement in collaboration with classroom teachers does not match the theoretical role and the role they were trained to perform.

Collaborative planning is impacted by the individuals involved, school climate, time for planning, the organization of the school, the facility and collection and training; of these, the characteristics and actions of the people involved is most important.

Collaboration with colleagues and varied student use (individual, small group) is more evident in schools with flexibly scheduled library resource centers. Regardless of whether the schedule is flexible or fixed, classroom teachers tend to accompany their classes—the schedule is thus more a reflection of the school's philosophy and goals.

While elementary teacher-librarians participate more on school curriculum committees than their secondary school colleagues, secondary teacher-librarians plan library-based units with teachers more often and more formally.

First published in *Teacher Librarian*, October 1999, Volume 27, Number 1

Collaboration between teacher and teacher-librarian not only has a positive impact on student achievement but also leads to growth of relationships, growth of the environment and growth of persons.

SOURCES

Cate, G. L. (1998). *A teacher's perceptions of the library media specialist as instructional consultant.* Unpublished doctoral dissertation, Texas Tech University.

Farwell, S. M. (1998). *Profile of planning: A study of a three year project on the implementation of a collaborative library media programs.* Unpublished doctoral dissertation, Florida International University.

Jones, A. C. (1997). *An analysis of the theoretical and actual curriculum development involvement of Georgia school library media specialists.* Unpublished doctoral dissertation, Georgia State University.

Wilson, L. R. D. (1997). *An investigation of the differences between a flexibly scheduled media center and a traditionally scheduled elementary school media center and the effects on administration, faculty, and students.* Unpublished doctoral dissertation, Walden University.

（8）

What Works:
Collaboration Among
School Specialists

Ken Haycock

RESEARCH FINDING

Specialist teachers in related areas (reading, literacy, technology) are encouraged to collaborate with classroom teachers but not with each other.

COMMENT

Effective collaborative partnerships use the expertise of each partner to solve a problem of student learning. It is a process that has demonstrated effective transfer of new learning to classroom pedagogy.

Problems exist in student reading, literacy, and facility with technology, yet the specialist teachers in these areas tend not to collaborate with each other. They work with the same teachers and the same students in the same schools but too often in parallel universes and segregated from each other.

These teachers may have divergent methodologies and theoretical beliefs, for example, about what increases reading motivation, but when they discuss common issues, they find opportunities to learn from each other.

Hindrances to collaboration are time, divergent views (e.g., of literacy acquisition or computer literacy), and district policies. These policies need to include clear definitions of complementary roles such as the technology specialist and the teacher-librarian.

Communication and collaboration would enhance literacy and learning in all its forms for students and teachers alike.

It would be useful to conduct further study on whether there is a correlation between collaboration be-

First published in *Teacher Librarian*, April 2006, Volume 33, Number 4

tween and among related specialists with classroom teachers and student learning and achievement.

SOURCES

Farr, W. J. (2004). *Collaboration among teachers of literacy*. Unpublished doctoral dissertation, University of Connecticut, Storrs.

Gaspar, D. B. (2003). *Stereophonic teaching for literacy: Assessing the parallel approach of library media specialists and reading specialists*. Unpublished doctoral dissertation, Saint Joseph's University, Philadelphia.

Seavers, V. A. B. (2002). *Extent of collaboration between the school library media specialist and the school-level technology specialist within the state of Florida*. Unpublished doctoral dissertation, University of Central Florida, Orlando.

⑨

What Works:
Building Collaborative
Learning Communities

Ken Haycock

RESEARCH FINDING

Principals, teachers, and teacher-librarians collaborate more in professional learning communities.

COMMENT

School reform research reports that schools with high levels of professional community are not only more effective but have school climates wherein teachers' work patterns are cohesive and collaborative.

Principals, teachers, and teacher-librarians indicate that there is more collaboration in professional "communities."

Secondary school principals do not tend to recognize the instructional role of the teacher-librarian. The major role that they indicate is in reference and research services whereas teacher-librarians see their major role in instruction in information literacy. While each group recognizes the importance of staff development as a means of integration of information literacy in the curriculum, principals see the major problem as funding whereas teacher-librarians see the major barrier as negative teacher attitudes.

Positive perceptions and expectations about consultation and collaboration are developed through

role clarification;
modeling;
proactive involvement; and
personal experiences.

First published in *Teacher Librarian*, April 2002, Volume 20, Number 4

SOURCES

Kolenick, P. L. (2001). *Principals and teacher-librarians: Building collaborative partnerships in the learning community.* Unpublished doctoral dissertation, University of Pittsburgh.

Slygh, G. L. (2000). *Shake, rattle and role! The effects of professional community on the collaborative role of the school librarian.* Unpublished doctoral dissertation, University of Wisconsin–Madison.

Straessle, G. A. (2000). *Teachers' and administrators' perceptions and expectations of the instructional consultation role of the library media specialist.* Unpublished master's thesis, Pacific Lutheran University.

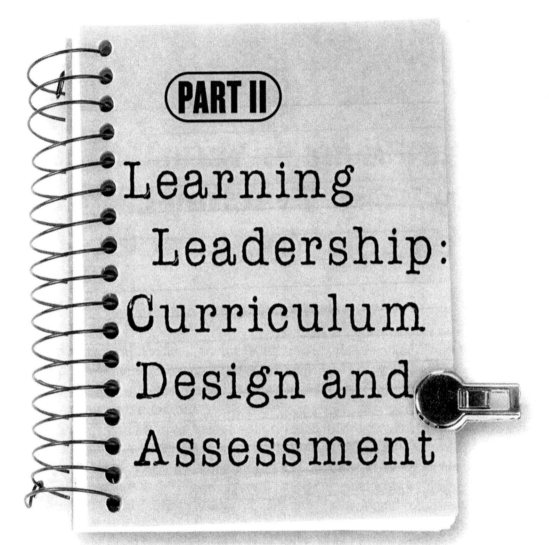

PART II

Learning Leadership: Curriculum Design and Assessment

⑩

What Flavor Is Your School Library? The Teacher-Librarian as Learning Leader

David Loertscher

When results of the Oklahoma study (Miller, 2006) came in, the researchers were in for a surprise. Using Nancy Miller's Time and Task Tracker (2005), under the direction of Ellen Duecker, both professionals and clericals in 14 Oklahoma school libraries documented twice daily for 15 random days what they did with their time. The first finding was gratifying: Professionals and support personnel do quite different things during their day. As in the earlier Alaska study (Lance, Hamilton-Pennell, Rodney, Peterson, & Sitter, 1999), support personnel keep the organization running but do not reach into areas where academic achievement is affected. The professionals all concentrated on professional tasks but were not uniform in their school library program focuses. That is, they emphasized quite different program aspects. Based on this finding, it seems that the Oklahoma professionals exhibited behavior common all across the United States; in other words, there does not seem to be agreement among teacher-librarians about their role in education. Even with the existence of national and state standards for school library programs and that of national standards for teacher-librarian certification, no one unified program focus has emerged over the last 50 years.

FIVE FLAVORS OF LIBRARY PROGRAMS

In the 1960s, the library field fractured into library ladies and audiovisual guys. More recently, the division has been between the teacher-librarian and the technology coordinator. But within these two major categories, there seems to be five major flavors of program focuses, labeled as ice cream flavors in the Figure 10.1.

The particular ice cream flavored program adopted by teacher-librarians seems to depend on one of

First published in *Teacher Librarian*, December 2006, Volume 34, Number 2

Vanilla

organization

Strawberry

reading

Chocolate

information
literacy

Mint Chocolate
Chip

technology

Spumoni

learning

Figure 10.1. Program Focuses

three factors: the professor or mentor originally encountered by the teacher-librarian, the personal philosophy of the teacher-librarian, or the requirements of the school organization in which the teacher-librarian is functioning. In any event, consider the advantages and disadvantages of each of the major flavors.

The vanilla-flavored organization school library consists of a wonderful service facility with a great collection, an array of multimedia and computer equipment, and a super reference staff. "We are here to help you!" they advertise, but you must come into our doors or log onto our networks. Many affluent independent schools often have "academic libraries" on their campuses and are most inviting of patrons who wish to come to use their services. The downside of this vanilla-flavored school library is that many potential patrons never show up. In addition, there seems to be a widespread belief among administrators that the organization or support-supply function of a school library can be handled by a paraprofessional at a much-reduced cost. Thus, there is the trend to replace professional teacher-librarians with support staff, particularly in elementary schools.

The strawberry-flavored reading school library program centers on reading literacy. Here we find the professional who instills the love of reading into every student who will be captivated by book talks, reading initiatives, and a schoolwide reading culture. These professionals fit their programs into whatever reading skills program is being taught in the school, with the objective of helping every child and teen become an avid and capable reader. The positive benefit of a reading focus is its direct impact on achievement, à la Krashen (2004). The downside has been the major expansion of technology and information so that other emphases in school library programs demand attention. Many schools are so focused on the skill of reading that they hire reading specialists or literacy coaches rather than teacher-librarians to boost achievement, and they never mention the love of reading or a lifelong reading habit. The requirements of No Child Left Behind have not helped the strawberry-flavored school library program to expand. In some cases, school library collections suffer as permanent classroom collections are built.

The chocolate-flavored informaton literacy school library program developed in the early 1990s with the issuance of various information literacy models and the national American Association of School Librarians and Association for Educational Communications and Technology's *Information Power: Building Partnerships for Learning* (1998). With the explosion of information and the ubiquitous presence of Google, teacher-librarians adapted and began teaching information literacy as an attempt to help students and teachers cope with the overwhelming crush of data. "Who is saying what to me for what reasons and in what medium?" coupled with a systematic teaching of the research process became the central focus of many school library programs. The upside of this emphasis has been a competition with Google and the realization by many that the Internet, although free, does not contain the best information. The downside of this flavor has been the formulation of courses in information literacy at every grade level, which is disconnected with the curriculum of the school. This downside will be strengthened by the existence of a national information literacy test, with professionals claiming jobs on the basis that they must prepare students for the test.

The mint-chocolate-chip-flavored technology school library program centers on the "if you dazzle them, they will come" idea. Many schools have a veritable graveyard of various tech gizmos dating back to programmed instruction—for example, the single-concept 8-mm loop film and other dazzling devices presumed to cure the ills of education. I am tempted to say, "If you dazzle them, they will come, but will they stay?" Those who have succeeded with this flavor have a reliable technological infrastructure to the point that, when faced with creating a learning experience, teachers and teacher-librarians experience a transparent technological foundation upon which to build. The concentration is on learning rather than on the machine or software itself. The downside of this flavor's emphasis is that networks are often down and equipment is often out of date. The unreliability forces teachers into a low-tech mode.

The final, spumoni-flavored learning school library program focuses on the learner and achievement. Here, the teacher-librarian concentrates on developing collaborative client relationships and transforming tired units of instruction into exciting learning experiences that have lots of reading, information literacy, and transparent technology components. The advantage is that two adults—the teacher and the teacher-librarian—team teach a learning experience, and the percentage of students who achieve the learning unit objectives increases. The downside is that many teacher-librarians have never been able to establish a steady stream of clientele or have not had the necessary training in instructional design.

One might argue, with some success, that every teacher-librarian should build a particular flavored program as a response to the philosophy of the school. In fact, many accrediting bodies require that the various auxiliary programs created in a school fit the school model. In this case, a vanilla-flavored program might be drizzled with toppings of strawberry or chocolate as needed. Others argue that the school organization is so flawed that even a superstar teacher-librarian cannot hope to fix the problem. There are many stories of restructuring, government intervention, state takeovers, and unfunded mandates, and there will be more as schools struggle to meet No Child Left Behind targets.

There is blame enough for teacher-librarians who—for whatever reason—have been unable to burrow their way into the center of whatever flavor program they construct. Everyone can cite schools that brag of reading programs but never mention the school library; virtual schools that have technology but no teacher-librarian; schools where critical thinking is emphasized but information literacy is ignored; and schools claiming great constructivist principles but ignoring the benefits of a strong teacher-librarian. The downside of a divided effort over the years is the result that the role of the school library in education is ignored.

SPEAK THE LANGUAGE

How do teacher-librarians move into the center of the curriculum—the real heart of the school? Dr. Allison Zmuda (2006), the 2005 keynote speaker at the Treasure Mountain Research Retreat No. 12, in Pittsburgh, PA, gave us a challenge. She said that if we wished to push toward the center, we must speak the various languages of our clients rather than expect them to understand our jargonistic eloquence. We should, as a first step, speak the dialects of reading; social studies; science; and the many curricular movements, such as constructivism, understanding by design, and international baccalaureate schools, just to name a few. Our first attack skill, to claim a role on the center stage, is to speak regularly in those dialects. One thing is certain: If the trend of underfunding education continues, there will be few of us around for the push.

Not all is dismal, however. Many ask what states or regions have figured out the best ways to illuminate the benefits of the school library program. Indeed, the research of Keith Curry Lance and Ross Todd keeps adding to the pile of evidence that we are doing something right, even though we might not agree on a central program thrust. Although no state or region seems to have a corner on success, individual teacher-librarians do. In other words, much of our success depends on those who are able to reach up out of the mud puddle of technological breakdown or unshelved books to make a difference. Many of these folks are honored in their state library or technology associations and at the national level.

Returning to the question of how the teacher-librarian can push to the center of the curriculum, I argue that the spumoni-flavored program has the best shot of making the most difference. I have argued this since 1982 (see Loertscher, 1982) when the taxonomy for the school library program first appeared in *Wilson Library Bulletin*. Since that time and across many changes in education, it seems that when we focus on the learner first—rather than on the needs of the organization—other elements of the program come into perspective.

THE LEARNING LEADER CREATES A SPUMONI-FLAVORED LIBRARY

Spumoni is a great ice cream because three distinctive flavors and colors are skillfully blended in such a way that, even though they are separated, the combined taste is absolutely delicious. Likewise, teacher-librarians who successfully implement the spumoni-flavored school library program report stimulating and marvelous careers. Permit me to illustrate how this flavor is created.

The spumoni-flavored school library program is headed by a learning leader known throughout the school as a learning expert in the information- and technology-rich world. Teachers realize that every time they create and teach a collaborative learning unit with a teacher-librarian, a higher percentage of learners succeed. The smart teachers get on the teacher-librarian's calendar. Others . . . well, good luck. Consider the following characteristics of the teacher-librarian as learning leader:

• The learning leader speaks the language of curriculum and its various dialects of reading, social studies, science, or whatever curricular program is popular in the school.

• The learning leader has the ear of the administrator who not only verbalizes support but also eliminates organizational obstacles to a spumoni-flavored school library program.

• The learning leader knows how to collaborate in the best sense, can work with teachers of almost any educational stripe, and can entice a steady clientele for team teaching.

• The learning leader can transform learning experiences in an information- and technology-rich environment so that the result is a "high think" no matter whether the learner is gifted, speaks little English, comes from a different culture, or is a motivated learner (key term: differentiation).

• The learning leader pushes the agenda of wide reading, just-in-time information literacy skills, and wise use of technological applications into each learning experience.

• The teacher and the learning leader halve the teacher–pupil ratio so that each learner receives the appropriate amount of attention—thus, the key to a higher percentage of student success. During the unit, the role of the teacher and the teacher-librarian has become one and the same. Both are helping the learner master content knowledge and information and technology skills.

• The learning leader documents and reports the success of collaborative units, providing data that demonstrate the link to achievement (key terms: data mining, rubrics, authentic assessment).

What does a learning leader's day look like? Perhaps a better question is, What does it not look like? A learning leader does not spend the majority of the day solving organizational snags in the print world or as a tech fix-it whiz kid; those roles are assumed by paraprofessional assistants. Instead, the learning leader concentrates the majority of the day on soliciting clients, planning and transforming units of instruction, team teaching the learning activities, assessing student performance, and assessing the entire program impact.

Let us look at a real example. Janice Gillmore-See has a strange title in her school—information literacy teacher on special assignment. She has no responsibility for the library but spends her days working with grade-level teams on enhancing learning units. She is also a student in the master's degree program at San Jose State University, San Jose, CA, and is taking the instructional design class. As a requirement for the class, Janice decides to work with a team of three first-grade teachers. She has not worked with this team before, because she believed that first graders were not mature enough to understand information literacy.

The unit to be taught in the classroom is about U.S. presidents. The teachers welcome a new face and new ideas to the planning session because they are bored with the previous method of worksheets and brief discussion. The major obstacle is the number of children who are learning English. So, as the learning activities are redesigned, each teacher will have a coteacher, and a group of struggling fifth graders will be recruited as learning coaches.

The first graders use all types of resources in the school library to study various presidents in depth, and the result is a presidential parade that attracts many parents—some to the school for the first time. But does the unit end there? Not if Janice expects a good grade in her graduate class! No, Janice realizes that when each first grader is a mini-expert on a single president, that first grader now has the background knowledge to think. So, the first graders do Venn diagrams comparing presidents, and they write and do analyses of what it takes to be a president and whether they might be president themselves one day. The result? Teachers are surprised that the children can tackle sophisticated learning activities. Perhaps, their expectations of the students have been too low. And Janice learns many new teaching strategies from the experienced teachers. The fifth graders gain a new sense of confidence in their own abilities. All learn that, although not every first grader succeeded, a higher percentage did and that more practice collaborating would fine-tune the process and create a trail of successful experiences over time. Which students gained the most? All students make gains, of course, but fourth-quartile and English learners seem to make the most progress.

Can we afford this expensive model of education? The retort is, in a flat world (Friedman, 2005), can we afford not to provide such a model? Some may have the luxury of spending all day, every day, on collaboration, whereas others learn how to spend a chunk of the day doing it while managing the school library. But what can a professional teacher-librarian do regardless of whether the choice of flavors is spumoni or not? Perhaps persuade every flavor program to at least dabble in spumoni? Can we have a scoop of spumoni on top? Can we all have a trail of evidence that, when we are involved, the percentage of learners who succeed rises? Of course, we can.

BE A LEARNING LEADER IN YOUR SCHOOL

Do we make a difference as a profession? Do you make a difference as a teacher-librarian in your school? Consider the following techniques that are well-known throughout the field:

• Prepare yourself as a learning leader by understanding cognitive psychology, curriculum, instructional design, technology, and how to create high-think learning experiences (see Figure 10.2).
• Establish a learning community in your school and study the best professional practices leading to

What does a person functioning as a learning leader have to know to be effective? Here is a preliminary list.

An effective learning leader knows the best of
- cognitive psychology;
- curriculum;
- instructional design;
- assessment;
- library science;
- technology; and
- a cognate field of choice.

Questions to ponder:
- How should the credentialing of a teacher-librarian be changed to produce more learning leaders?
- Should teachers getting master's degrees get degrees as learning leaders?
- What would happen in a school where heads of departments, grade-level team leaders, or even just a regular classroom teacher had a degree in learning leadership? Suppose there were 10 teacher-librarians/ learning leaders in a single school? How would that work?

Figure 10.2. The Effective Learning Leader

high achievement.

• Link your program to some initiative in the school, but tweak it so that high-think is part of the mix. In other words, cleverly position your program as an essential element in the school agenda.

• Build a repertoire of successful collaborative units where a high percentage of learners succeed. Start with one, then two, and so on.

• Document the success of the collaborations with the teacher partners, jointly presenting to whoever will listen to the results. This is particularly important for those in the profession who are the only professionals in several schools—the most frustrated group we have in the field.

• Write or present your successes in articles, news reports, and conferences that are non-school-library centered with your teacher partner. Ask the principal to be a copresenter or coauthor.

• Nominate supportive administrators for awards, in the library world, the world of curriculum, the local community, and for any other heroic badge you can think of.

• Constantly talk about making a difference for individual learners. Use every trick in the book and then some to push every child to be all he or she can be and then more. This kind of child reads a lot, is a critical thinker in the world of information, and is an efficient learner in the world of technology.

Think spumoni. Dream spumoni. Taste spumoni. You will love it as a teacher-librarian. If you are an administrator, hire a teacher-librarian who loves spumoni. If you are a teacher, hog the time of the teacher-librarian. After all, it is your students who need to achieve.

REFERENCES

American Association of School Librarians & Association of Educational Communications and Technology. (1998). *Information power: Building partnerships for learning.* Chicago: American Library Association.

Friedman, T. L. (2005). *The world is flat: A brief history of the twenty-first century.* New York: Farrar, Straus and Giroux.

Krashen, S. D. (2004). *The power of reading: Insights from the research* (2nd ed.). Portsmouth, NH: Heinemann.

Lance, K. C., Hamilton-Pennell, C., Rodney, M. J., Peterson, L., & Sitter, C. (1999). *Information empowered: The school librarian as an agent of academic achievement in Alaska schools.* Juneau, AK: Alaska State Library. Retrieved July 24, 2006, from **www.library.state.ak.us/dev/infoemp.html**

Loertscher, D. V. (1982). Second revolution: A taxonomy for the 1980s. *Wilson Library Bulletin, 56,* 417–421.

Miller, N. A. S. (2005). *Time and task tracker.* Salt Lake City, UT: Hi Willow Research and Publishing.

Miller, N. A. S. (2006). Oklahoma association of school library media specialists time task study. In D. V. Loertscher (Ed.), *Understanding in the library: Papers of the Treasure Mountain Research Retreat No.*

12, October 5–6, 2005, Gilmary Retreat Center, Pittsburgh, PA (pp. 343–352). Salt Lake City, UT: Hi Willow Research and Publishing.

Zmuda, A. (2006). Designing curriculum for the 21st century classroom. In D. V. Loertscher (Ed.), *Understanding in the library: Papers of the Treasure Mountain Research Retreat No. 12, October 5–6, 2005, Gilmary Retreat Center, Pittsburgh, PA* (pp. 37–48). Salt Lake City, UT: Hi Willow Research and Publishing.

⑪

Assignments Worth the Effort: Questions Are Key

Carol Koechlin and Sandi Zwaan

It is easy for adults to assume that kids can make the connection between the energy and enthusiasm that they feed into a project and the result, but studies have demonstrated that some students are not aware of the fact that the effort that they put into a task has a direct effect on their success relative to the task.

In their book *Classroom Instruction That Works*, Marzano, Pickering, and Pollock (2001) review these studies and assert that educators need to find ways to reinforce effort and help students realize the connection between effort and achievement. The authors offer some practical suggestions for teachers, one of which is sharing with students the stories of super achievers. Teacher-librarians can join the effort campaign by sharing inspirational stories, planning book talks and book displays centered on the theme of personal effort, and introducing students to real superheroes, such as Canada's Terry Fox, who raised an awareness for cancer research in his Marathon of Hope, and Craig Keilburger, who battles for children's rights on the international stage through his Free the Children organization. Although there is no doubt that we need to impress on our students the positive effects of a solid effort, they also need time management skills and task contracts, research portfolios, rubrics, checklists, and other devices to help them stay on task and keep track of their effort and progress.

GUIDING QUESTIONS
Teacher-librarians can help students develop their metacognitive skills by providing them with checklists in the form of guiding questions that they can use throughout the research process. Examples of guiding questions include

- What is the purpose of your research?

First published in *Teacher Librarian*, February 2007, Volume 34, Number 3

- What do you think you will discover?
- How will this assignment be assessed?
- What is important if you are to be successful?
- How do project due dates mesh with your other school and personal commitments?

A simple reflection tool that can be used to build metacognition is a split-page organizer. Have students fold a paper into three columns. Ask them to record in the first column, What was I supposed to do? In the next column, How did I do? In the last column, What can I do better next time? With older students who seem to lack accountability, try giving them practice with a strategy that comes from the business world, called QBQ, or question behind the question. QBQ is based on a great little motivational book with the same title, by John G. Miller (2004). The subtitle of this brilliant text says it all: *What to Really Ask Yourself to Eliminate Blame, Complaining, and Procrastination.* Good QBQ questions to use with students include

- Why didn't the teacher give me more time for this assignment?
- How am I expected to do this if there are no good books in the library?
- Why did I get stuck with this topic, group, or the like?

If you frequently hear these "poor me" or victim-type questions from your students at assignment time, then try teaching them to turn their questions into personal actions by having them ask themselves

- How can I schedule my time better?
- Where can I look for more resources on my topic?
- How can I better understand what my teacher wants me to do?

Having explored some strategies for spurring student effort and personal accountability for that effort, we suggest that there may very well be some legitimate reasons for lack of student effort on research assignments.

LET'S PLAY "WHAT IF?"

- What if the work that was assigned was less than inspiring?
- What if students truly cannot grasp the relevance of the topic that they were assigned?
- What if the only motivation to complete the assignment was the marks?
- What if after the presentations the kids systematically filed their projects in the waste can as they left the classroom?

How would these scenarios be different if the students were personally motivated? Just how do we accomplish this? We know that, regardless of how hard students work, if their actions are not well focused on the outcome, the job will be onerous and unrewarding for them. We are also aware that a task becomes less onerous if students "buy in"—that is, if they are truly interested. So what can we as educators do to help create that interest and fine-tune the focus to ensure that students make the effort required to achieve?

We believe that effective student and teacher questioning can play a huge role toward accomplishing this student buy-in. Motivation is part of our rationale for teaching students to question. We need to revitalize student curiosity, capture their interest, and focus their enthusiasm on the current topic. Curiosity is a critical factor in the learning process, both as a motivator and as a facilitator (Koechlin & Zwaan, 2006). To stimulate curiosity, develop a culture of inquiry in your school by providing an information- and technology-rich environment accessible to all through the school library. Then, design engaging and effective "hands-on, minds-on" learning experiences that enable students to build understanding (Wiggins & McTighe, 1999, p. 21).

In our new book, *Q Tasks: How to Empower Students to Ask Questions and Care About Answers* (2006), we provide an entire chapter to help develop and harness the potential power of curiosity as a catalyst for learning. We revisit some old activities, such as 20 Questions, trivia, and riddles, as relevant kid-friendly starting places for building questioning skills. Of course, it takes more than curiosity about the topic to build an effective learning experience. Students need to learn to turn their curiosity and wonderment into good questions. They also need to be observant as they gather data and watch for patterns as well as conflicts. Questioning also helps with analysis. Because of the volume and complexity of data that are available to students on any given topic or concept, questioning skills must be activated throughout the entire research process.

So, how do questions improve student effort and achievement? When questions belong to the student, he or she is engaged and empowered because now this learning experience is about what the student needs and wants to know. Need, of course, is closely related to effort. Our main objective in teaching students to be effective questioners is the chemistry that takes place between questions and understanding. The number 1 reason that many research projects in classrooms are ho-hum bristol board displays or plagiarized reports is that they are driven by the "all about" syndrome, where students simply hunt and retrieve the data that they discover about a topic and feed it back into the form of a prescribed product with no analysis and with low-level synthesis. It is easy to fix this! If you really want your students to demonstrate their personal growth and understanding through assigned research projects, they must process the data that they have gathered through the lens of a good inquiry question or challenge (Koechlin & Zwaan, 2006).

HOW CAN QUESTIONS AND QUESTIONING ELEVATE THE QUALITY OF RESEARCH PROJECTS?

Questioning

- shifts thinking from product to process,
- moves from simply assigning projects to supporting student-directed learning,
- builds a culture of inquiry,
- is engaging and relevant because the student owns the project, and
- deepens student understanding.

Research based on effective questions

- stimulates curiosity,
- demands rich information sources,
- guides and focuses research,
- provokes deep thought,
- prompts analysis and synthesis,
- enables personal understanding, and
- encourages transfer.

Research without effective questions is fake research and results in

- "all about" regurgitation,
- cut-paste-and-plagiarize,
- fill-in-the-blanks,
- quote-the-experts,
- line-up-the-facts,
- invitational plagiarism (assignments that invite plagiarism by their design), and
- disinterested students.

DESIGNS FOR DEVELOPING UNDERSTANDING WITH QUESTIONS

We offer three ideal designs for developing understanding with questions. When the teacher (T) and the teacher-librarian (TL) collaborate in the design of instruction, we know that student (S) achievement is enhanced (Lance & Loertscher, 2002).

Design 1: Student as Questioner

T and TL provide exploratory activities to build background knowledge.

T and TL instigate activities to spur thinking and help make connections.

S experiments by building questions until S has the "just right" question.

S conducts research with S question as guide.

EXAMPLE

Learning focus. Students identify early European explorers and understand how these explorers affected the development of North America.

Building understanding. Share pictures and video clips of modern-day explorers. Discuss the accomplishments and the challenges of today's explorers, and introduce the European explorers who ventured to North America long ago. In the library, set up discovery stations based on different types of resources, such as books, pictures, videos, Internet sites, and encyclopedias. Provide students with five to six quick-fact trading cards. These cards ask for simple facts that answer the question prompts who, what, when, where, which, how, and why. Have students rotate though the discovery centers to complete as many quick-fact cards as they can in the time available.

Next, have students meet in groups and share and sort their cards into categories. Provide each group with a large question-builder matrix (see Figure 11.1) and instruct them to build questions about European explorers. Have students select questions that they are interested in, and have them experiment with more questioning until they each have the "just right" question. Conference with each student to ensure that he or she has a question that will be a good guide for research.

For more information, see the Background to Question model from *Ban Those Bird Units!* (Loertscher, Koechlin, & Zwaan, 2005, pp. 5–19).

Design 2: Teacher as Questioner

T and TL pose an engaging question.

S builds background knowledge with the question as guide.

T and TL pose a higher-level concept-forming question.

Question Builder Chart

	is	did	can	would	will	might
Who						
What						
When						
Where						
How						
Why						
Which...						
	Your best questions for this project					

Figure 11.1. Question Model

S works with information and ideas to achieve understanding.

EXAMPLE

Learning focus. Students understand the interactions within ecosystems.

Building understanding. Introduce the topic with a good video or picture book that deals with the impact of interference within an ecosystem. Brainstorm for types of ecosystems and build a class web site.

Organize students into ecosystem teams, and pose an engaging investigative question and task to frame their first inquiries—for example, What evidence of life can you find in your ecosystem?

Organize student findings into food chains. Within their ecosystem groups, have students work collaboratively to explore a variety of resources, gather data, and organize data into visual food chains.

Form new groups with students from different ecosystem teams, and pose a new question that allows students to compare their food chains to uncover deeper understanding—for example, What do ecosystems need to remain healthy?

For more information, see the Concept Jigsaw Puzzle model from *Ban Those Bird Units!* (Loertscher et al., 2005, pp. 81–89).

Design 3: Teacher and Students as Question Partners

T and TL design an overarching question to frame the unit.

T and TL provide exploratory activities to build background knowledge.

T and TL instigate activities to spur thinking.

S experiments building questions until S has the "just right" question.

S conducts research with the question as guide.

T and TL bring class back to the unit's overarching question.

EXAMPLE

Learning focus. Students explore the major factors that influence healthy living.

Building understanding. The overarching question is Who is in charge of my body?

Design a web quest where students are investigative reporters who work with partners to research an aspect of healthy living, such as nutrition, substance abuse, dieting, food additives, body image, popular culture, and so forth. The pairs of reporters each write a news column for a teen "zine." During and after sharing the zine, instruct students to record questions about the information shared and its relationship to their personal attitudes and lifestyles. Review levels of questioning and urge students to develop questions that will help them gain deeper understanding.

Provide students with a rubric or criteria checklist for effective inquiry questions—for example, effective questions

- stimulate your curiosity,
- encourage you to dig deep for your information,
- challenge you to think about your discoveries,
- prompt you to analyze your findings,
- guide your research quest,
- keep you on track,
- spark your imagination, and
- help you to make personal meaning.

When students have built good questions, they are ready to start their independent research. Remind them that their presentations should answer the class question, Who is in charge of my body?

WHAT CAN WE DO WHEN THE TOPIC IS ASSIGNED TO STUDENTS OR WHEN STUDENTS SELECT A TOPIC FROM A LIST?

I know we want the kids to ask questions, but how? How, when research is set by the teacher, out of necessity for content standards and time—when kids have the topic and are ready to begin research, how do we get them to ask the question then?

—Participant's comment after a workshop on questioning

What this participant said is often the reality. Students come to the school library with their topics in hand, topics that are to a large extent preprogrammed by the classroom teachers. Of course, content standards drive what we as teacher-librarians do in schools, and our job is to help teachers and students meet their objectives. Even though the student has had little or no choice in the topic, we can use many strategies to generate the spirit of inquiry. Take, for example, the ubiquitous "Know Your Province/State" project or the "Select an Animal, Famous Person, or Ancient Civilization" project. The usual demonstration product for this project is a pamphlet, but it can also be a bristol board display, a slide show, or a written or oral report. The point is that these parameters have already been assigned, and now in the school library you have an opportunity to help students buy in, through injecting questioning techniques at the beginning of the exploration stage and later on throughout the research process.

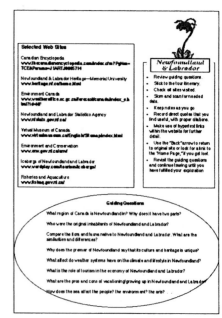

Q Technique 1: Explore With Guiding Questions
HOW CAN TEACHER QUESTIONING HELP STUDENTS BECOME CURIOUS ABOUT A TOPIC?

Take students on an e-tour of their province, state, or city (see Figure 11.2).

Figure 11.2. Guided E-Tour of Newfoundland

Q Technique 2: Question Storming
HOW CAN STUDENT-GENERATED QUESTIONS GET KIDS EXCITED ABOUT A TOPIC?

Question storming is a lively collaborative activity. Teach students how to explore a topic through brainstorming and through webbing lots of questions about it. Model the process by organizing and charting student questions with the students. Use a visual organizer, or have students brainstorm questions on sticky notes and then organize them into a web. Use a software program such as Smart Ideas or Inspiration, and watch the questions and the excitement about the topic grow!

By using this strategy, you will discover that it is much easier for students to narrow a large topic and zero in on a manageable but meaningful inquiry focus. Ask students to highlight the phrases, words, and questions that they are particularly interested in. These subquestions can serve as guideposts or subtopics on which to focus their research. Next, have them develop a list of keywords to help them with online searches.

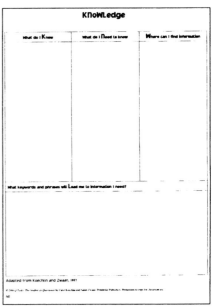

Figure 11.3. KWL Organizer

Q Technique 3: Preparing for Research
HOW CAN QUESTIONING HELP STUDENTS GET ORGANIZED FOR RESEARCH?

Before students embark on a search to find information for their research projects, they need to get their thoughts organized and make some plans. A KWL (know, want, learned) organizer helps students activate prior knowledge, spur questioning, and identify sources and keywords to guide searches. When students complete this organizer, they will be ready to use their searching time efficiently, and they will have time for actually processing the information they find (see Figure 11.3).

Q Technique 4: Evaluating Resources
HOW CAN STUDENT-GENERATED QUESTIONS HELP WITH RESOURCE SELECTION?

You can model effective questioning by providing students with questions that they need to consider when evaluating the reliability and usability of a resource for their projects. Eventually, however, we want the questioning process to become so intuitive that students can assess the quality of a book or web site in their heads—so to speak. Turn over the questioning responsibility to your students and have them generate the questions that they will use to evaluate their resources. You can use an organizer such as question-builder frames to prompt their questions (see Figure 11.4).

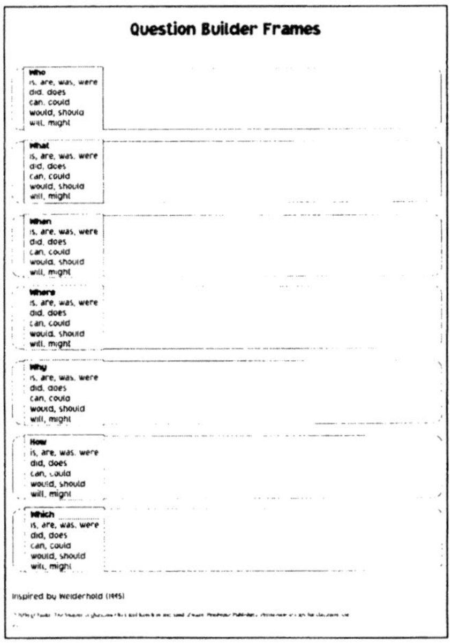

Q Technique 5: Test Ideas
HOW CAN QUESTIONING HELP STUDENTS TO CLARIFY THEIR THINKING AND TEST OUT THEIR IDEAS?

When students have gathered their data information, they need methods of analyzing it before they finalize their thinking, draw con-

Figure 11.4. Question Builder Frames

clusions, and prepare to share their learning. An effective strategy at this stage is to set up peer-to-peer conferences. Instruct the students to prepare the questions that they will ask their partners about the analysis of the data that they have gathered. Model the process first so that students understand how the quality of their questions helps to clarify ideas and uncover new possibilities.

Sample questions include the following:

- What was it about this topic that caught your interest?
- What can you tell me about your discoveries?
- What did you find that surprised you? disturbed you? gave you pause for thought? tickled your funny bone?
- What is really important about your findings? Why? To whom is it important?
- Who or what might this affect? How?
- How did you come to understand . . . (something about the subject)?
- How has your thinking about this changed since you started your research?
- Did you draw any conclusions? find a solution to a problem? make a decision? think of new or different approaches?
- What would you like to see happen now? Who should get involved? How do you fit in?

Q Technique 6: Reflection and Assessment
HOW DO WE CULTIVATE THE ABILITY TO SELF-QUESTION?

After a learning experience, students will benefit from recording their questions as well as their thoughts and feelings. Provide prompts for reflection, and have students start or finish their response journals with questions they are pondering.

You can also give students ownership of the assessment process by asking them to brainstorm the criteria that they believe are key to the success of a presentation, such as an oral report or a multimedia presentation. Agree on the general criteria, and have students work in groups to develop questions for a rating scale or checklist to assess presentations—for example, ask, "Did the presenter communicate effectively with the audience?" Collate the questions and prepare the assessment tool.

OVER TO YOU
We hope that these questioning techniques will inspire many other ideas for elevating what appear to be ho-hum assignments. The teacher-librarian's carefully crafted interventions in the school library should ignite the needed spark to spur student interest and consequently affect student effort. Regardless of whether you are working with classroom teachers in ideal environments (where you work together to design learning for students) or you see students only after the project has been assigned, motivation is key to student effort and success. When research assignments are worthy of effort, kids of all levels and abilities will be motivated to strut their stuff. When students own the questions—they are interested!

Futurists tell us that students will need critical thinking skills and the ability to critically access information in all forms of media. According to Daniel Pink (2005), the future lies with those who possess the aptitude to high concept and high touch. In his book *A Whole New Mind*, Pink tells us that we are moving from the logical, linear, computer-like capabilities of the information age to the inventive, empathetic, big-picture capabilities of the conceptual age, and with that comes a whole new set of skills. Intuitive questioning techniques will become essential in this new era.

We need to keep in mind that learning experiences should provide students with skills and processes that will prepare them for life in the 21st century. Assignments and projects that require students to retrieve only the information and ideas of others belong to the information age, not the conceptual age. We need to think about ways to create relevant real-work tasks that will allow students to engage and grow. If we work on questioning as a major component of assignment design, students will find the experience well worth the effort.

BOTTOM LINE
Questions and questioning will elevate the quality of research projects. Questions are the answer to building knowledge and understanding.

REFERENCES
Koechlin, C., & Zwaan, S. (2006). *Q tasks: How to empower students to ask questions and care about their answers*. Toronto, ON: Pembroke.

Lance, K. C., & Loertscher, D. V. (2002). *Powering achievement: School library programs make a difference: The evidence mounts*. Salt Lake City, UT: Hi Willow Research and Publishing.

Loertscher, D., Koechlin, C., & Zwaan, S. (2005). *Ban those bird units! 15 models for teaching and learning in information-rich and technology-rich environments*. Salt Lake City, UT: Hi Willow Research and Publishing.

Marzano, R. J., Pickering, D. J., & Pollock, J. E. (2001). *Classroom instruction that works: Research-based strategies for increasing student achievement*. Alexandria, VA: Association for Supervision and Curriculum Development.

Miller, J. G. (2004). *QBQ! The question behind the question: What to really ask yourself to eliminate blame, complaining, and procrastination*. New York: Putnam.

Pink, H. D. (2005). *A whole new mind*. New York: Riverhead Books.

Wiggins, G., & McTighe, J. (1999). *Understanding by design*. Alexandria, VA: Association for Supervision and Curriculum Development.

⑫

Beyond the Bird Unit

Jennifer Robins

Lance and Loertscher (2001) warn that it is possible to use high-quality information resources and still create ineffective learning experiences for K–12 students. To illustrate, they discuss the "Bird Unit," the type of research activity where students search for information in order to fill in worksheets that they transform into essays and presentations. By itself, this type of exercise does not go far in promoting information literacy. National standards for information literacy appear in *Information Power: Building Partnerships for Learning* (AASL & AECT, 1998). These standards purport to promote the skills of the lifelong learner as related to information use, self-directed learning, and social responsibility.

This paper contains a brief overview of constructivist teaching strategies followed by a description of this collaborative inquiry where teachers and teacher-librarians pooled their experience and knowledge. This effort resulted in a number of strategies for using information to enrich learning. After presenting the strategies, this paper concludes by suggesting a process for using constructivist methods to enrich any lesson plan. The process integrates information literacy skills with three types of constructivist lessons: problem based, inquiry based, and project based.

CONSTRUCTIVIST STRATEGIES

A traditional view of learning regards knowledge as being outside of the learner. The learner acquires knowledge through the senses. The constructivist view assumes knowledge cannot exist outside the bodies of cognizing beings and that it is created by dynamic interaction with the learning environment (Tobin & Dawson, 1989). Traditional pedagogy values "replicability, reliability, communications, and control," while constructivist pedagogy values "collaboration, personal autonomy, generativity, reflectivity, active engagement, personal relevance, and pluralism" (Lebow, 1992, p. 5). Because constructivist pedagogical strategies are learner centered, they fit well with information literacy skills that are aimed at individual, lifelong learning.

PROBLEM-BASED LEARNING

Problem-based learning (PBL) was introduced in medical schools in the 1960s and is currently used in

First published in *Teacher Librarian*, December 2005, Volume 33, Number 2

many disciplines. The components of PBL are problem formulating, abstracting, applying knowledge, self-directed learning, and reflecting (Koschmann, Kelson, Feltovich, & Barrows, 1996, p. 98). These components fit well with the American Association of School Librarians (AASL) information literacy standards. PBL starts with a real-world problem that might not have a clear solution. The problems are always messy. For example, problems involving case studies work well for PBL. These problems need to be analyzed and reanalyzed by students. The traditional pedagogical approach of carefully sequencing instruction is replaced with more authentic approaches to problem solving and the creation of an environment that has the necessary resources for reaching a conclusion to the problem, if not a solution. Students work in a self-directed manner individually and in groups. They follow their hunches, seeking out information to support or invalidate the leads they generate. Graphic organizers are used by students to analyze the problem and to keep track of knowledge that is acquired during the process. Students determine when the process is complete, either by reaching a solution or a consensus that they have moved as far as they can toward a solution. Teachers and teacher-librarians act as mentors, asking questions that lead students toward deeper reflection, or they provide hints that direct students toward new information sources.

PBL is bounded by the availability of resources and the ability of the mentors to keep students in their zone of proximal development, the area between what a student can do alone and can be done with assistance (Vygotsky, 1978). Mentors assess students' knowledge and skills related to information literacy. They model and promote these skills. At the same time, they must know when to step back and let the student struggle through the problem-solving process (Koschmann et al., 1996). The key to finding suitable problem-based lessons is to find the freedom that comes from letting go of traditional instructional sequences and looking for problems designed for students one or two grade levels ahead and selecting ones that students might manage given a rich information environment, scaffolding, and mentoring.

In PBL the information literacy skills related to information access, evaluation, and use are practiced extensively. To illustrate the process, reading teacher Paula Fagan created a problem-based lesson that has fourth-grade students find and organize information in order to solve the problem, "What type of spider is Charlotte?" The lesson plan is presented in Figure 12.1.

INQUIRY-BASED LEARNING

"The library is the inquiry center in the information age school" (Kulthau, 2001, para. 1). Inquiry-based strategies take advantage of information-rich environments by promoting a student's natural inquisitiveness. The strategies encourage children to make observations and to figure things out. Inquiry-based learning refers to a continuum. On one end is free-ranging inquiry; on the other is highly structured, directed inquiry (Olson & Loucks-Horsley, 2000).

In free inquiry, students generate their own lessons from exploring phenomenon embedded in the world around them. Students are encouraged to explore according to their personal interests. At the farthest point of this end of the continuum, students are not corrected when they make errors as this may discourage inquiry. Instead, they are encouraged by teachers to question their assumptions as they build their knowledge.

At the other end of this spectrum, inquiry is directed toward predefined outcomes. Teachers choose the topics and provide children with hands-on experiences meant to stimulate their curiosity. In between the extremes are many examples where teachers and teacher-librarians create an environment that sparks students' interests. They help students draw the connections between their interests and the learning standards being pursued. In inquiry-based learning students are encouraged to ask questions, but they are also required to find answers to their questions. The inquiry-learning process closely resembles the

Who's Charlotte? Problem-Based Lesson Plan for Grades 4 or 5

by Paula Fagan

The objective of this lesson is for the student to take a description of Charlotte from the book *Charlotte's Web* and through research on the Internet determine what type of spider Charlotte is.

TIME ALLOTTED:

Two 1-hour sessions

SHOW-ME [MISSOURI] STATE STANDARDS:

Communication Arts

Standard 2: Develop and apply skills and strategies to comprehend, analyze, and evaluate fiction, poetry, and drama from a variety of cultures and times

Science

Standard 3: Characteristics and interactions of living organisms

INFORMATION LITERACY STANDARDS:

Standards 1, 2, 3, 7, 8, and 9 from *Information Power* (AASL & AECT 1998)

SUPPLIES NEEDED:

- *Charlotte's Web* by E. B. White
- drawing paper
- crayons, markers, or color pencils
- student worksheet
- one computer per two students with Internet access
- whiteboard, chalkboard, Smartboard, or overhead projector

PRIOR KNOWLEDGE:

The students should either be reading, have read, or be read to the book *Charlotte's Web*. They should also know how to search the Internet.

ANTICIPATORY SET:

Have you ever thought about being a detective such as Sherlock Homes or Cam Jensen? Well, for the next two days you are going to put on your detective caps because you have a mystery to solve. Who is Charlotte?

PROCEDURES:

Day One:
The classroom teacher conducts this part of the lesson.

1. Using a chalkboard, whiteboard, overhead, or Smartboard display the following question: Who is Charlotte?

2. Next, display the following passages from *Charlotte's Web*: "Stretched across the upper part of the doorway was a big spiderweb, and hanging from the top of the web, head down, was a large grey spider. She was the size of a gumdrop." "Yes, but I'm near-sighted" (p. 37). "Next I wrap him up. . . . Now I knock him out. . . . She bit the fly" (p. 38). "You mean you eat flies?" "Certainly, flies, bugs, grasshoppers, choice beetles, moths, butterflies, tasty cockroaches, gnats, midges, daddy longlegs, centipedes, mosquitoes, crickets—anything that is careless enough to get caught in my web . . . I don't really eat them—drink their blood, I love blood. . . . I happen to be a trapper. I just naturally build a web and trap flies and other insects" (p. 39). "However webs get torn everyday . . . a spider must rebuild it. . . . Charlotte liked doing her weaving during the late afternoon" (p. 55). "I'm glad I'm a sedentary spider" (p. 60). "She ripped out a few of the orb lines near the center. She left the radial lines alone" (p. 90).

3. Explain to the class that they are to use the passages to determine what type of spider Charlotte is.

4. Talk about how clues can help us determine what something is. Explain to the students that there are many clues that will help them to determine what type of spider Charlotte is.

5. On the worksheet provided, have the students write down the clues that will help them to solve this mystery. (This can be done individually or as a class.)

6. Next, explain how detectives have sketch artists draw from a description how a person looks. Tell them that it is now their turn to be the sketch artist. They should use the description of Charlotte to sketch a picture of how she looks.

Day Two:
The teacher-librarian conducts this part of the lesson.

1. Redisplay the passage used the previous day.

2. Explain to the students that the next step is to investigate. It could go like this: Yesterday you determined how Charlotte looked by using the clues provided in the passages. Today you will be conducting the investigation to determine what type of spider Charlotte is. There are many different ways that you could conduct this investigation. Who can tell me some of the ways to do this? Generate a list of ideas. For this investigation, you will be conducting your search using the Internet. Remember that like any good detective you will need to make a positive ID. When you think you have found the type of spider Charlotte is, write down the matching characteristics on your worksheet.

3. The students will first need to go to **http://ohioline.osu.edu/hyg-fact/2000/2060.html** and research this site to find out what type of spider Charlotte is.

4. When everyone has determined what type of spider, instruct them to complete this sentence at the bottom of the picture: Charlotte is an orb weaver or garden spider.

5. You can conclude this lesson by collecting worksheets and drawings and display the results on a bulletin board.

CHECK FOR UNDERSTANDING:

To check for understanding you will need to check to see if the students used the given clues to make a positive identification of Charlotte. Conclude this lesson by discussing how the clues in the story helped to determine what type of spider Charlotte is.

EXTENSION TO THIS LESSON:

This lesson can be extended by creating a "Who

(continued)

Am I?" worksheet; descriptions of a variety of spiders can be given, allowing the students to match the description with the spider.

SOME ADDITIONAL WEB SITES ABOUT SPIDERS:

American Museum of Natural History. (1997-1998). *Spiders.* Retrieved on October 28, 2003, from **www.amnh.org/nationalcenter/online_ field_ journal/cp/cpsp/cpspmain.html**
This web site allows students to compare three types of spiders: the funnel web spider, barn spider, and Australian rainbow spider. It also provides online field journals for spiders as well as other creatures. It even provides a section on tips for adult helpers.

Conservation Commission of Missouri. (1995-2002). *Spiders.* Retrieved on October 28, 2003, from **www.conservation.state.mo.us/nathis/ arthopo/mospider/kinds. htm#anchor868086**
At this site, maintained by the Conservation Commission of Missouri, students can learn about the spiders common to the state of Missouri.

Crew, G. (n.d.) *Spiders.* Retrieved on October 24, 2003, from **http://homepage.powerup.com.au/ ~glen/spider.htm**
This site provides a lot of good information on spiders. It provides viewers with many colored pictures of spiders. There are several useful links, including one on lesson plans.

Newton, B. (2002). *The great spider debate.* Retrieved on October 28, 2003, from **www.uky.edu/Agriculture/Entomology/ ythfacts/resourc/tcherpln/spiderdebate.htm**
This site provided by the University of Kentucky, Department of Entomology is a description of a hands-on discovery lab. It can be adapted for students in the primary grades as well as high school.

Oregon Children's Theatre. (n.d.). *The musical Charlotte's web.* Retrieved on October 28, 2003, from **www.octc.org/study%20guides/charlotte _ guide.htm**
Maintained by the Oregon Children's Theatre, this site contains many useful activities that go along with the book *Charlotte's Web.* It also provides seven spider-related lesson plans.

White, E. B. (1952). *Charlotte's web.* New York: Harper & Row.
The inspiration for this lesson came from a suggestion from fellow teacher Kim Marshall.

STUDENT MATERIALS:

Who's Charlotte by E. B. White

DIRECTIONS:

Write the clues under Charlotte that will help you determine what type of web-weaving spider she is. Use the other column to write the findings that match her description.

LESSON GUIDE:

Directions: Write the clues under Charlotte that will help you determine what type of web-weaving spider she is. Use the other column to write the findings that match her description.

Characteristics: Charlotte
Characteristics: Funnel Weaver
Characteristics: Orb Weavers or Garden Spider
Characteristics: House or Cobweb Spider

Answer: Charlotte is a_____spider.

SAMPLE OF A FINISHED STUDENT PROJECT:

Charlotte Characteristics:	Characteristics: Funnel Weaver	Characteristics: Orb Weaver or Garden Spider	Characteristics: House or Cobweb Spider
Builds spiderwebs	Makes large flat sheet like webs	Builds an orb web	Builds irregular webs
Is grey spider	Webs can be built on shrubs	Traps insects	Is gray to brown with dark stripes
Is gumdrop size	Is different colors; can be gray	Has poor vision	Hangs upside down
Hangs head down	Feels the vibrations of the insect	Uses silk to wrap its victims	Eat many types of insects
Is nearsighted	Bites the insects	Bites its prey before eating it	Likes flies
Drinks the blood of flies and other insects	Carries them back to eat	Comes in many colors	Bites them and sucks them dry
Wraps the insect in silk		Hangs head down	
Knocks out the insects with a bite			
Is a trapper			
Rebuilds web daily			
Is sedentary		Answer:	
Web has orb lines and radial lines		Charlotte is a/an <u>orb weaver or garden spider</u>.	

Figure 12.1. Example of a Problem-Based Lesson Plan

information-seeking process. The affective states related to learning are viewed as motivators. "An inquiry approach calls for guiding students in thinking and reflecting in the process of information seeking and use that leads to understanding, learning, and to transferable information literacy" (Kulthau, 2001, para. 17).

Inquiry in the classroom can be bounded by provincial and state learning standards. Left unbounded, it tends to follow youth culture and sports interests, particularly in teens (Nielsen, 2005). However, as students are given the opportunity to develop their historical and cultural imaginations, this problem might be mitigated. The school library is the place for this kind of development to occur.

In inquiry-based learning the information literacy skills related to self-directed learning are practiced extensively. Figure 12.2 presents a lesson created by teacher-librarian Connie King. Connie creates an environment that encourages high school students to explore a number of resources on the U.S. civil rights movement. In the process, students are exposed to multiple aspects of this period in history, motivating them to pursue their own questions.

PROJECT-BASED LEARNING

Project-based learning is the third constructivist strategy explored in this investigation. While problem-based and inquiry-based learning strategies are inherently social, project-based learning is social at its core. Project-based learning has many definitions, but in this discussion project-based learning refers to students working together on a project where the result is the assembling of individual student contributions.

Such projects can vary in scale. They can involve a single classroom or an entire school, city, or country; they can even include international participation. The Internet is great for project-based learning because it enables global cooperation. Agencies like NASA offer such projects continually, and many museums now offer projects. There are scientific studies like the one conducted by RiverWeb (2005) where students around the world monitor rivers and waterways. At the school level themes can be the focal point of projects. For example, a middle school in Portland has ecology as its core emphasis and holds an Earth Day celebration every year. Students work on creating products for performance and display at that cele-

---

What Were the Major Events in the Civil Rights Movement? (Freedom Riders, Desegregation of Birmingham, March on Washington, Lunch Counter Sit-ins, Freedom Summer) Inquiry-Based Lesson Plan for Grades 9–12

by Connie King

DESCRIPTION:

Students will write a newspaper or magazine article about one of the key events in the civil rights movement, written from the perspective of a participant.

MCREL STANDARDS:

United States History, 9–12
Standard 2: Understands the historical perspective
• Benchmark 1: Understands that specific individuals and the values those individuals held had an impact on history

• Benchmark 2: Analyzes the influence specific ideas and beliefs had on a period of history

Standard 29: Understands the struggle for racial and gender equality and for the extension of civil liberties
• Benchmark 1: Understands individual and institutional influences on the civil rights movement (e.g., the origins of the postwar civil rights movement; the role of the National Association for the Advancement of Colored People in the legal assault on segregation; the leadership and ideologies of Martin Luther King, Jr., and Malcolm X; the effects of the constitutional steps taken in the executive, judicial, and legislative

branches of government; the shift from de jure to de facto segregation; important milestones in the civil rights movement between 1954 and 1965; Eisenhower's reasons for dispatching federal troops to Little Rock in 1957)

SHOW-ME [MISSOURI] STATE STANDARDS:

Knowledge:

Goal 1: Acquire the knowledge and skills to gather, analyze, and apply information and ideas
Social Studies:

(continued)

Students will acquire a solid foundation which includes knowledge of

Standard 2: continuity and change in the history of Missouri, the United States, and the world

Standard 6: relationships of the individual and groups to institutions and cultural traditions

Bloom's Level: 4 = Analysis

INFORMATION LITERACY STANDARDS:

Standards 1 and 3 from *Information Power* (AASL & AECT, 1998)

RESOURCES:

Online Reference Databases:
- Grolier's Multimedia Encyclopedia
- World Book Encyclopedia
- Encyclopedia Americana
- EBSCO's History Reference Center
- Gale's History Resource Center U.S.
- Gale's Biography Resource Center
- Corbis Images for Education (to aid in creating a magazine or newspaper article)

I chose the above databases because they are respected, edited, and accurate. The encyclopedias we purchase allow me to differentiate as each set provides a different level of reading. At this time we are encouraging students to carry their Mid-Continent Library number so that students have access to valuable resources that we cannot purchase. I realize this in an equity issue, as some students do not have library cards. However, we have made it extremely easy for students to get a card. We carry Mid-Continent's applications and deliver them to Mid-Continent for the students. The students' library cards are then mailed their home address. We hope that at least 90% of our 10th graders will have Mid-Continent Library cards by the end of the year.

INTERNET SITES:

Internet sites are provided in my instruction folder so that students can simply click on the link to access the information. I chose the Internet sites listed below because they are reputable and provide a wide range of reference possibilities:
- Civil Rights Movement Veterans **www .crmvet.org/**

- Voices of Civil Rights **www.voicesofcivilrights.org/**
- Historical Places of the Civil Rights Movement **www.cr.nps.gov/nr/travel/civilrights/**
- Historical Publications of the United States Commission on Civil Rights

 www.law.umaryland.edu/edocs/usccr/html %20files/usccrhp.asp
- The Martin Luther King, Jr. Papers Project **www.stanford.edu/group/King/**
- Powerful Days: The Civil Rights Photography of Charles Moore **www.kodak.com/US/en/corp/ features/moore/mooreIndex.shtml**

(I encourage teachers to use this site to inspire discussion within their classrooms while studying civil rights. I also encourage students to use photographs in their magazines and newspapers.)

PROCEDURES:

At the high school level we are encouraged to prepare students to be independent when they leave to go on to further education, gain employment, or otherwise move forward in their lives. In our curriculum many search strategies have been taught at the middle school level. However, I still see students struggling as they try to come up with search terms when they go to the Internet. Therefore, I instruct the students in how to perform a search using "advanced" searching techniques. Most search engines come equipped with an advanced option where basic Boolean Logic can be employed. If the teacher and I are truly working as a team, I team teach in that teacher's classroom to formulate search terms before students ever set foot in the library. I try taking the indexes of our general print encyclopedias and the *Reader's Guide to Periodical Literature* to assist in coming up with search terms. I have not done this yet, but my intention is to construct a graphic organizer that students could complete and take to the library for their first day of research. Before students sit down at the computers, I would review the use of the school's purchased databases and Mid-Continent's databases.

I see several barriers that need to be addressed. First, students come to the library having many different reading levels; therefore, some of the students need to locate resources on a much lower level. Doing so requires the teacher's assistance to know who needs this help. Second, teacher-librarians in my district are willing to share resources. Although students should have been instructed in how to use Microsoft Word or Microsoft Publisher, there are students new to the dis-

trict who have not had training on these products. I would conduct some basic introductory classes during study hall or seminar time for students who are not familiar with these products. Third, the teacher and I would have to create a thorough rubric so students would know exactly what was expected of them. As I have not taught this yet, I am certain there will be many pitfalls along the way that I have not considered.

The civil rights movement is usually a high-interest topic, and students have a lot of flexibility as to what they choose to report on. This should encourage buy-in from the students. If a student felt more comfortable doing a traditional report, the newspaper article should appeal to that student. For a student who is more visual, a magazine article might inspire him to research and produce a good product. Advanced placement or gifted students could write an editorial on an event that took place. They could dedicate an entire magazine to an event and the people that were in that event. I have found that a clearly defined rubric greatly aids students in knowing when they have enough information.

ASSESSMENT:

Standard 1: Indicator 4. Identifies a variety of potential sources of information. A ticket-out-the-door strategy could easily assess this on the day that I give them an overview of the resources. They could fill out a graphic organizer showing their top five resource selections. It would be interesting to compare this to their works cited page that I would require even though they are doing a magazine article or newspaper article.

Standard 3: Indicator 1. Organizes information for practical application. I would have the students create a graphic organizer or a formal outline using Inspiration Software that would reflect the organization of their projects.

Standard 3: Indicators 2 and 4. Hopefully the final product would show new information and appropriate format.

Figure 12.2. Example of an Inquiry-Based Lesson Plan

bration (Snow, 2005).

Project-based learning is bounded by the need for articulation work (Schmidt & Bannon, 1992). Articulation work relates to planning and planning to plan. In project-based learning students discuss details and arrangement outside of the content area objectives. For younger children this might be as simple as dividing responsibilities and deciding how they know when a project is finished. Older students might discuss how responsibility will be distributed, how timelines will be planned and implemented, and how the progress of the project will be assessed and managed. At all levels students can learn project oversight through their articulation work as they learn how to work in cooperation with each other.

In project-based learning the information literacy skills related to social responsibility are practiced extensively. In the project-based lesson presented in Figure 12.3, teacher-librarian Karron Ingram worked with a kindergarten class to create an alphabet book. Students looked at examples of alphabet books in the library, and then each took a letter and selected a theme for decorating a page depicting the letter. Together the class created a new alphabet book of their very own.

COMBINING STRATEGIES

Problem-based, inquiry-based, and project-based strategies are not always distinct; moreover, they can be interwoven. Inquiry-based learning can be used to promote social responsibility. Problem-based learning can be self-directed, and project-based learning can involve access, evaluation, and use of information. Teacher-librarian Linda Pierce presents a way to combine strategies by enhancing a fourth-grade lesson on Famous Missourians that is taught to every student. The problem that students faced was to select and

---

Creating an Alphabet Book Project-Based Lesson Plan for Kindergarten

by Karron Ingram

INFORMATION LITERACY STANDARDS (FROM *INFORMATION POWER: BUILDING PARTNERSHIPS FOR LEARNING* (AASL & AECT, 1998)

Standard 3 and 7

RESOURCES:

Students will look at three alphabet books:

Alphabet Adventure and *Alphabet Mystery* by Audrey Wood

Toys ABC: An Alphabet Book by B. A. Hoena

ABC Under the Sea: An Ocean Life Alphabet Book by Barbara Knox

Internet sources are **www.billybear4kids .com/games/online/alphabet/alphabet.htm**, where students can click on the letters of the alphabet to see pictures of things that start with that letter, and **www.primarygames. com/story books/abc/start.htm**, where students can look at

an online animated ABC storybook like the one they will be creating.

Students can come up with the object they want to use to represent their letters and then the teacher-librarian can go to the clip art on the computer and print out an image for the students to either color or one that is already colored and ready for them to cut out and use. However, this can be time consuming for the teacher-librarian and deprives the students of the opportunity to use their own creativity to illustrate their images.

LESSON GUIDE:

1. Assign a letter of the alphabet to each student.

2. Pick a topic. It can be animals, toys, superheroes, plants, and the like.

3. Do research, if need be, to find words for the page.

4. Brainstorm with your classmates for ideas.

5. Create a sentence for the page that starts

with the letter. Example: A stands for _____.

6. Design a page for the class book, putting as many pictures of items beginning with that letter as appropriate plus the sentence.

TEACHER-LIBRARIAN'S NOTE:

Students might have difficulty using the computer to look at the web sites. They might have problems writing their sentences as well. Sticking to a theme may also be confusing or difficult for some students. The easy part should be coming up with words that start with each letter of the alphabet and then illustrating them. Students should be able to actively participate in the discussion process and be able to answer what word each illustration stands for. The teacher-librarian will be able to determine if the students were able to work cooperatively with each other in sharing their resources and in creating the pages for the alphabet book.

Figure 12.3. Example of a Project-Based Lesson Plan

then defend their candidate for Famous Missourian. Creating an inquiry environment, Linda brought in guest speakers and introduced students to a number of perspective candidates. The students' project was to create and populate a timeline with the candidates they selected. This lesson plan is presented in Figure 12.4.

THE COLLABORATIVE INQUIRY

This investigation took place through a course entitled Using Online Resources. This course was a one-semester, seminar-style, distance education graduate-level course in Library and Information Science at Central Missouri State University, Warrensburg, Missouri, I conducted in 2004. The course was a collaborative inquiry designed to uncover processes for using information to enrich any lesson plan in primary and secondary education. The seven students had a variety of teaching experiences: Three were experienced in adult education at the university and corporate level; one was a fourth-year library aid; one was an elementary teacher with 23 years of experience; and the other two students had a combined total of 17 years of experience as teacher-librarians. Each student introduced five lesson plans, one modeled after a traditional approach, three modeled after the constructivist strategies defined herein, and a fifth lesson plan combining strategies.

Each type of lesson plan was discussed online. Before the completion of the fifth lesson, the instructor and the students revisited the 28 plans they had created and produced a written analysis focusing on their strengths and the processes revealed in the plans. The instructor used these discussions, lesson plans, and students' written analyses as data. They were analyzed and coded according to the grounded theory method (Strauss & Corbin, 1998). Collaborative inquiry is recognized as an instruction strategy for adult education, but the new knowledge produced during inquiries often merits distribution (Kasl & Yorks, 2002). Such is the intent of this report on the findings of our investigation.

USING INFORMATION TO ENRICH LESSONS

What is wrong with bird units? Sometimes nothing. There are times when this type of instruction might be exactly right, but the library offers opportunities for richer learning experiences. Bird units are highly scaffolded. A teacher or teacher-librarian has done the work that students might have found interesting and beneficial, and students are not adequately challenged or engaged. On the other hand, a lack of appropriate scaffolding can be frustrating. Work that is too hard can exasperate students. Finding the balance is difficult. Loertscher, Koechlin, and Zwaan's new book *Ban Those Bird Units! 15 Models for Teaching and Learning in Information-Rich and Technology-Rich Environments* (2004) presents models for appropriate scaffolding.

Another problem with bird units is that they rely too much on imposed questions and not enough on student-generated questions. A process that enriches learning through the use of the school library begins with inquiry (Kuhlthau, 2001). The process could be looked at through three facets. The first and most important is the perspective of curriculum standards. These standards reflect the wishes of society for student learning, and because the public funds schools, it is fitting to consider learning standards as paramount (Dewey, 1938). Another lens for viewing the process of using information to enrich lessons is to focus on the collaboration between teachers and teacher-librarians, which ideally drives all library activity. A third focus is the perspective of the learner that is addressed by constructivist teaching strategies. Issues that fall into this category include motivation, social learning, problem solving, establishing credibility, and means for assessment.

The Life of a Famous Missourian: A Lesson Plan Combining an Inquiry, Problem, and Project-Based Approach for Grade 4

by Linda Pierce

This is a great beginning lesson. It or a similar variation is done in most fourth-grade classes throughout the state of Missouri.

The gifted students teacher, Ellen Wright, in the Fort Osage District and I have added to this lesson by adding components of enhanced research of Missouri's history and famous people in order to meet state standards.

SHOW-ME [MISSOURI] STATE STANDARDS:

Social Studies

Standard 2: Knowledge of continuity and change in the history of Missouri, the United States, and the world.

Goal 1: Acquire the knowledge and skills to gather, analyze, and apply information and ideas.

Goal 2: Students will recognize the perspectives of others when planning and making accurate and clear presentations.

Standard 3: Understands the people, events, problems, and ideas that were significant in creating the history of their state
  • Understands how the ideas of significant people affected the history of the state
Language Arts
Standard 4: Gathers and uses information for research purposes

INFORMATION LITERACY STANDARDS:

Standards 1, 2, 3, 4, 5, 6, and 9 from *Information Power* (AASL & AECT, 1998)

RESOURCES:

Worldbookonline database—Missouri resource section has links to famous Missourians, Missouri cities, and Missouri events: **www.worldbook online.com**

Hall of Famous Missourians—State House of Representatives site with descriptions of many famous Missourians: **http://house.state.mo.us/famous/famous.htm**

Thomas Hart Benton—Biography on the famous artist includes photos of his home and carriage house. This web page is hosed by Kansas City Public Library: **www.kclibrary.org/sc/bio/benton.htm**
A Biography of Scott Joplin—An overview of the famous musician's life that explains his ties to Sedalia, Missouri: **http://scottjoplin.org/biography.htm**

The View From Independence—This Missouri Heritage video discusses the leadership of President Harry S. Truman. Click on "The View From Independence" (requires RealPlayer): **www.emints.org/resources/ moheritage**

Timeline of the history of Jackson County, Missouri: **http://jchs.org/175th%20Anniversary_files/Timeline.htm**

Timeline of state history—Missouri: **www.shgresources.com/mo/timeline**

Famous Missourians: **www.fulton.k12.mo.us/bartley/missourian.html**

Famous black Missourians: **www.umsl.edu/~libweb/blackstudies/persons.htm**

Biography.com: **www.biography.com**

Kansas City Missourians: **www.kclibrary.org/sc/bio/default.htm**

PROCEDURES:

Ellen and I collaborated with each other to see what we wanted the students to learn and set up a time frame for the lesson.
  • Week 1: We have access to a great nonfiction historical author, Cheryl Harness, in Independence.

She came to the classroom and explained to the students how she did research for her books. It was a great introduction and provided a lot of ideas for the students, which helped them as we brainstormed what they wanted to do research on. The students decided to create a timeline of Missouri history from 1850 to 1900 (see attached timeline organizer). They wanted a way to share their information with other fourth graders.
  • Week 2: We took a field trip to the Independence branch of the Mid-Continent Library. There in the genealogy department they were able to read old newspaper articles on microfilm and use databases, only available onsite, to look up census records of ancestors and famous Missourians. They also checked out several volumes of the *State History of Missouri* by Parrish to take back to the classroom for research.
  • Week 3: Students will use print and nonprint resources to find the information for the timeline. The students will write a reflection paper about the fieldtrip to Mid-Continent.
  • Week 4: Students will work together to create one huge timeline that will be posted on the bulletin board outside of the library for all students to see.

The students will know when they are done (have enough information) when they have completed the timeline organizer and completed the timeline bulletin board.

One difficult thing has been coordinating my schedule with this class. I am only at that school every other week, so I could not be there for Week 3. Thanks to e-mail, however, Ellen and I can still work out the kinks of the lesson when necessary. What might be difficult for the students is choosing famous Missourians that nobody has chosen. Our plan is to highlight some lesser-known Missourians and what makes them famous. There are 14 students in this class.

Having had Cheryl Harness come and speak to the students has sparked their interest. It has been easy to get the students involved in every aspect of the lesson so far.

(continued)

ASSESSMENT:	LESSON GUIDE:	• State the year.
		• Write two to three sentences explaining the
We will assess the information literacy skill out-	Step 1: 1850–1900 Timeline	person, place, or event.
comes by reading their reflection papers and using	Step 2: Missouri Research	• Cite your resources.
a scoring guide to look for quality and accurate in-	• Investigate 10–15 famous Missourians.	Step 4: Using Word (font 18, Comic Sans MS),
formation on the famous Missourians, places in	• Explore five places in Missouri.	type information and citation page, print, and at-
Missouri, and events that took place in Missouri.	• Examine 10–15 events in Missouri.	tach to timeline bulletin board.
Was the timeline bulletin board factual and com-	Step 3: Record the following information for each	
plete?	finding.	

Figure 12.4. Example of a Combination Lesson Plan

LEARNING STANDARDS

The curriculum standards, not to be confused with the standardized tests, open up the cannon of knowledge that society has deemed to be important enough to pass on to the next generation. Most provinces and states make their curriculum available online, but there is also a compendium of standards available through Mid-continent Research for Education and Learning (McREL). McREL has taken the standards from several countries and compiled them into a single database. Along with this database there is a collection of lesson plans to accompany many of the standards (McREL, 2004). The McREL compendium is not an attempt to build central standards; rather, it is a combining of all the standards currently in use. Other sites that link standards and lesson plans include the e-Themes (eMints National Center, 2005) site, the Ontario-based GrassRoots project (Grassroots Ontario, 2004), and the Gateway to Educational Materials (GEM, 2005).

Curriculum standards can serve as boundary objects, objects that serve as a focal point for discussion between different members of a community, such as teachers, teacher-librarians, and students (Star & Griesemer, 1989). Standards can be used as planning tools that provide agreed-upon lesson objectives. They can provide shortcuts for finding resources in the library and on the Web because mapping is being done between standards and resources in online catalogs and on the Internet. Standards present the essential questions and big ideas that drive learning. This provides cognitive room to think about and discuss how different types of lessons can be used to meet the objectives. At this point the time available for the lesson will be a major factor.

In addition to curriculum standards, information literacy standards can be considered. Information literacy standards often map closely with provincial and state performance standards. They promote skills that are essential to successful learning. Activities that are aimed at achieving curriculum standards are enhanced when activities directed at information literacy standards are added to a lesson plan.

COLLABORATION BETWEEN TEACHERS AND TEACHER-LIBRARIANS

Teachers are the leaders in collaborations with teacher-librarians because it is the teacher's curriculum goals that drive the learning activity. Information literacy goals are folded into curriculum goals. Goals from content standards can be used to create learning objectives and to discuss the essential questions students are to answer. Teacher-librarians locate and discuss opportunities to exercise the information literacy standards related to finding, using, and evaluating information; self-directed learning; and occasions for students to exercise social responsibility.

The teacher-librarian's first step is to consider available information sources that support the lesson and to consider lesson plans being developed by other teachers. Consider where there is a way to combine lessons into a larger project. Next, plan the information seeking process, deciding—in collaboration with the teacher—the scaffolding that is needed to assist individual students with the search process. When possible differentiate the scaffolding for the class in order to meet the diverse needs of the learners. In this part of the collaboration the teacher's knowledge of individual students will drive planning. Constructivist strategies can be introduced by discussing how the learning sequence can be altered and ways to leave time for students to explore and generate their own questions. Are there projects in the community or available through the Internet that might be incorporated into the lesson?

Because everyone in the school community is pressed for time, asynchronous collaboration might help. Instant messenger services, e-mail, and discussion boards can all be used for collaboration. These mediums provide ways to send brief notes during the planning and during the activities. They create a written record of the collaboration that can be useful if the teacher and teacher-librarian wish to showcase their work or provide professional development to others. They also serve as a historical record that can be referred to during future collaborations.

THE PERSPECTIVE OF THE LEARNER

Problem-based, inquiry-based, and project-based strategies all emphasize that knowledge is constructed by the learner. For this process to happen, students must take responsibility for their learning. There is a corollary that proposes that if students have more control over their learning, they are more likely to be engaged. In this investigation there was universal consensus that constructivist methods motivate students to take responsibility for their learning. In an era where teachers are working too hard and students are not working hard enough, constructivist methods are gaining in appeal.

Motivation

Learning is work, and motivating children to work can be a challenge. With younger students it is easier to ignite curiosity and encourage the spirit of inquiry. Dewey noted that the best education occurs when the child's curiosity interacts with organized curriculum (Dewey, 1915). The library is an excellent environment to spark a child's curiosity and love of learning as evidenced by elementary school children's interest in nonfiction books. Book talks are effective in sparking children's interest and work well with both nonfiction and fiction books. Add artifacts and visits from experts, and elementary-age students find intrinsic motivation to apply themselves to learning.

Motivating teenagers to learn can be more difficult. One place that guidance is needed is in both working with and countering the cultural imagination that motivates learning in secondary students. Knowing popular culture is a form of social capital, giving students prestige among their peers. Using the Internet, they gravitate toward sites about sports heroes, cars, beauty and fashion, or rock stars. They demonstrate a well-formed cultural imagination, but they lack a cross-cultural imagination that can only be developed through exposure to other cultures. Teens also often lack a historical imagination.

The library has resources that can be used to explore cultures and history. Every topic in every subject has a history, and all face current issues, many of which are related to multicultural impacts. Adding brief historical and cultural perspectives to learning topics helps students become more engaged and can lead to student-generated questions. Those questions can be transformed into search strategies, and the library is a rich source for answers.

Social Learning

Dewey recognized self-expression as an impulse that could be used as a resource in the classroom (1915).

Students have a desire to "teach about [themselves], as well as to learn and to express [their] ideas, feelings, and values" (Bruce, 1998, para. 3). Because of this desire students are motivated to learn in social environments (Vygotsky, 1978). This social learning is a pedagogical style inherent in problem-based, inquiry-based, and project-based learning. In social learning, students learn both content and process from each other. Today's technology supports social learning through asynchronous communication. Through instant messenger, e-mail, and discussion boards, every student can participate and is encouraged to add thoughts and ideas.

Students not only learn about subject content from each other, but they also see how other students work together to share and build knowledge. They learn how credibility is established among peers by verbally evaluating activities and products. Social learning can activate higher-order thinking as students feel accountable to each other and justify acts and opinions. It also allows students with different intelligences, life and cultural experiences, and values to share their perspectives. The goal of social learning in this context is to demonstrate to students the value of knowledge as social capital in areas other than popular culture and sports.

Problem Solving

The three constructivist strategies explored in this investigation all incorporate a high level of problem-solving skills. Although these skills are not identified as information-literacy skills, many problems require information literacy as part of the problem-solving process, and in a similar way, problem-solving skills are necessary for developing information-literacy skills. Connections between the two include the ability to identify and compare characteristics and properties, the ability to distinguish the parts and the whole of environments and systems, and the ability to identify connections between parts. Problem solving involves the ability to recognize examples of problem types in order to transfer skills developed solving one type of problem to other similar problems. In problem solving, students learn to collect, filter, and examine information, which are all skills that map to information-literacy skills in accessing, using, and evaluating information.

Problem-solving skills are needed in the inquiry cycle that characterizes self-directed learning. Students analyze, categorize, organize, and classify information, making records at appropriate steps. The role of record keeping in information literacy is not addressed directly in the standards but is implicit in learning to use information efficiently. In the traditional bird unit, students record knowledge on worksheets and express knowledge in linear, written form. Constructivist strategies lend themselves to situations where students create their own graphic organizers, a useful skill in lifelong learning. Forms of organizers such as investigation guides, checklists, KWL (Know, Want to Learn, Learn) charts, timelines, and graphs can be used to record information. Mind maps and concept maps can organize information once it is collected. As end products, students can create bulletin boards, posters, murals, games, and job aids in addition to more traditional products. Advanced students can create the graphic organizers to be used by others, thus demonstrating how such skills are arrived at and practiced. Teachers and teacher-librarians can also model the process and invite students to participate.

Establishing Credibility

Establishing credibility is a crucial component of constructivist learning—it is the 21st-century version of critical thinking. It connects to information literacy at two levels. The first relates to the skills necessary to evaluate information sources; the second is the ability to establish one's own credibility. Both of these skills can be taught and developed in the school library. For example, bibliographic instruction in the use of citations serves two purposes. It teaches the correct form for using and creating citations, and it can also include instruction on how citations are used to establish credibility. In a similar way, in teaching the skill of web site evaluation the authority of the site's creator is a factor. Instruction can also include how a reputation is established and how it is ruined.

Rationality is the basis of Western civilization. Rationality is a system for presenting evidence in a logical, empirical way. In order to promote democracy and social responsibility, information-literacy instruction includes teaching students the difference between off-the-cuff opinions and observations and those formed on the basis of evidence. Younger students learn this when they learn to distinguish between fiction and nonfiction books. Older students learn this in dialogue, if given an opportunity to discuss and critique each other's ideas. In planning instruction with teachers, teacher-librarians can take advantage of opportunities to provide activities that reinforce skills related to establishing credibility.

A PROCESS FOR USING INFORMATION TO ENRICH LEARNING

The process of using information to enrich learning starts with the collaboration between the teacher and the teacher-librarian. The teacher takes the lead by deciding which curriculum standards are to be met through the activity. These standards are the focal point of the collaboration. After the big questions are identified, problem-based, inquiry-based, and project-based constructivist strategies are considered. These approaches not only promote information-literacy skills, but they also support learning. The decision on which strategy to use is based on the resources available. The chief constraint is the time available for conducting the lesson.

In deciding on a strategy it is necessary to consider the learning environment available and the nature of the lesson. If the lesson requires students to develop skills in information access, use, and evaluation, problem-based learning is indicated. If there is room for students to question and explore a topic, inquiry-based learning is indicated. If individual products can be combined with those of other students in the classroom, school, community, or online, project-based learning is appropriate.

Regardless of the strategy selected motivation is a factor. Using problem-based learning, scaffolding, and mentoring is a key concern. With inquiry-based learning a stimulating environment is important. In project-based learning it is important for students to create a collective product that is recognizably greater than their individual contributions. In each of these strategies activities are needed that will stimulate motivation. Giving students more responsibility for and control of their learning leads to increased motivation. Social learning is also motivating. Students enjoy teaching each other, and they can model their learning processes while they increase their knowledge. Other factors in the environment relate to the skills and tools needed for problem solving. Problem-solving skills blend well with the skills needed for information literacy. Scaffolding in the form of graphic organizers or mentors can be provided by teachers, teacher-librarians, or other students.

Establishing credibility is interwoven throughout the learning task. It relates to finding reliable sources, engaging in rational discussion, and establishing personal credibility as a holder of knowledge. In the latter case, consider ways to involve students in self-assessment. They can assess their learning process, the extent of learning, and their progress. The assessment can be part of the learning process. Using multiple assessment instruments makes it possible to measure student learning even when it is differentiated.

Finally, after creating and implementing a lesson plan that goes beyond the bird unit, celebrate! Let the school community know what has occurred. Have students exhibit the products of their learning, so they can see how the community values their work. Celebrating information literacy is the best way to promote it.

REFERENCES

American Association of School Librarians (AASL) & Association for Educational Communications and Technology (AECT). (1998). *Information power: Building partnerships for learning.* Chicago: American Library Association. Information literacy standards retrieved July 25, 2005, from **www.ala.org/ala/aasl/aaslproftools/informationpower/InformationLiteracy Standards_final.pdf**

Bruce, B. (1998). Learning through expression. *Journal of Adolescent and Adult Literacy, 42.* Retrieved September 26, 2005, from **www.readingonline.org/electronic/jaal/Dec_Column.html**

Dewey, J. (1915). *The school and society.* Chicago: University of Chicago Press.

Dewey, J. (1938). *Experience & education.* London: Collier Books.

eMints National Center. (2005). *eThemes.* Retrieved May 9, 2005, from **www.emints.org/ethemes**

Gateway to Educational Materials Consortium (GEM). (2005). *Gateway to 21st Century Skills.* Retrieved May 9, 2005, from **http://thegateway.org/**

GrassRoots Ontario. (2004). *The SchoolNet GrassRoots Program.* Retrieved September 26, 2005, from **http://grassroots.enoreo.on.ca/**

Kasl, E., & Yorks, L. (2002). An extended epistemology for transformative learning theory and its application through collaborative inquiry. *Teachers College Record*, ID Number: 10878. Retrieved September 26, 2005, from **www.scu.edu.au/schools/gcm/ar/w/Kasl_and_Yorks.pdf**

Koschmann, T., Kelson, A., Feltovich, P., & Barrows, H. (1996). *CSCL: Theory and practice of an emerging paradigm* (pp. 83–124). Mahwah, NJ: Lawrence Erlbaum.

Kulthau, C. (2001). *Rethinking libraries for the information age school: Vital roles in inquiry learning.* Proceedings of the IASL Conference, Aukland, New Zealand. Retrieved May 9, 2005, from **www.iasl-slo.org/keynote-kuhlthau2001.html**

Lance, K., & Loertscher, D. (2001). *Powering achievement: School library media programs make a difference: The evidence.* Salt Lake City, UT: Hi Willow Research and Publishing.

Lebow, D. (1992). Constructivist values for instructional systems design: Five principles toward a new mindset. *Educational Technology Research and Development, 41*(3), 4–16.

Loertscher, D., Koechlin, C., & Zwaan, S. (2004). *Ban those bird units! 15 models for teaching and learning in information-rich and technology-rich environments.* Salt Lake City, UT: Hi Willow Research and Publishing.

Nielsen, J. (2005). Usability of websites for teenagers. Jakob Nielsen's *Alertbox* (January 31, 2005). Retrieved May 11, 2005, from **http://useit.com/alertbox/20050131.html**

Olson, S., & Loucks-Horsley, S. (2000). *Inquiry and the National Science Education Standards: A guide for teaching and learning.* Washington, DC: National Academies Press.

RiverWeb. (2005). *An introduction to RiverWeb: A digital knowledge network for citizen science.* Retrieved September 26 2005, from **http://archive.ncsa.uiuc.edu/Cyberia/RiverWeb/Intro/intro.html**

Robins, J. (2004). Using online resources. A one-semester, distance education, graduate-level course in Library and Information Science at Central Missouri State University, Warrensburg, MO.

Schmidt, K., & Bannon, L. (1992). Taking CSCW seriously: Supporting articulation work. *Computer Supported Cooperative Work, 1*(1–2), 7–40.

Snow, J. (2005). *StoneSoup: Technology innovation, introduction, and use to support learner-centered education.* Unpublished doctoral dissertation, University of Illinois, Urbana-Champaign.

Star, S., & Griesemer, J. (1989). Institutional ecology, "translations," and coherence: Amateurs and professionals in Berkeley's Museum of Vertebrate Zoology, 1907–1939, *Social Studies of Science, 19*, 387–420.

Strauss, A., & Corbin, J. (1998). *Basics of qualitative research*. Thousand Oaks, CA: Sage.

Tobin, K., & Dawson, G. (1989). Constraints to curriculum reform: Teachers and the myths of schooling. *Educational Technology Research and Development, 40*(1), 81–92.

Vygotsky, L. S. (1978). Internalization of higher psychological functions. In M. Cole, V. John-Steiner, S. Scribner, & E. Souberman (Eds.), *Mind in society* (pp. 52–57). Cambridge, MA: Harvard University Press.

⑬

Focus on Understanding

Carol Koechlin and Sandi Zwaan

Often we have heard teachers say, "This is not what I asked for! These kids just don't get it! Why don't they understand?" We have also heard students express a different point of view, saying, "Why don't teachers understand how we think? How can we make sense of all this stuff? I've got all this information, so what?"

This tension, which exists between teachers and students and students and parents when information tasks are assigned, is very real. There are many causes, but there are also solutions. Students do not need to flail and flounder in a sea of meaningless data waiting for a lightning bolt to strike and sort it out for them. Instead, they need skills and strategies to help them explore and determine their information need, access appropriate data, process the data they have acquired, and communicate their new understanding to others.

This process is not new to teacher-librarians.

WHY THE ANGST?

Students, teachers, and parents all aspire to achieve the current curriculum goals. New curriculum standards have been developed to reflect the growing complexity of global reality. The rapid emergence of information technologies and the glut of information available to students create new challenges. Every grade and subject area has been impacted. Our close investigation of current curriculum identified innumerable expectations that require sophisticated levels of complex information processing. Students are required to form opinions, discover cause, evaluate effect, make relationships, demonstrate understanding, and so on. In practice, however, students are not achieving as well as expected with skills related to the processing of information. This difficulty that students experience when dealing with information is a cross-curricular concern and affects student success in reading and writing as well as content subjects.

Some of the challenges:

• How can we identify the specific problems students are having that contribute to this anxiety?

First published in *Teacher Librarian*, October 2002, Volume 30, Number 1

- How can we help students understand difficult concepts and demonstrate their understanding in meaningful ways?
- How can we help students make connections between their own ideas and those of others so they can create new meaning?
- How can we help students see relevance between the tasks they are asked to perform and real world experiences?
- How can we help teachers to design more effective and engaging information tasks?

Teacher-librarians have the tools and skills set to be of great assistance to teachers in the creation of information tasks. We have knowledge of a wide range of information resources, skills and technologies that are essential for designing effective information-related activities. We know that if information tasks are not carefully crafted, they can lead to plagiarism or a low level regurgitation of facts and data. We understand that if students are not challenged to process the data they gather, they are not likely to do so. We can help teachers carefully structure and scaffold learning experiences to ensure student success. Teacher-librarians can and should have considerable impact on the teaching and learning process. Because we work with all teachers and students, we are in a unique position, with the potential to contribute a great deal to the collective culture of a school. We can impact both teaching and learning.

How can we build the capacity of the school library program to make a difference in student achievement? We offer six key actions for your consideration.

1. Believe that you can make a difference. There is plenty of academic research indicating the strong correlation between student achievement and an exemplary school library program (see Haycock, 1992; Krashen, 1993; Lance, 1999a, 1999b, 2000). As well as sharing this formal research, each of us must work diligently to gather our own personal data and surround our students and ourselves with that evidence. We must

- be confident,
- promote the value of our role in the teaching and learning process,
- share our talents and skills with others, and
- mentor and encourage each other.

2. Treat this problem as a personal professional research project. We need to be proactive about our own learning. We must become active inquirers ourselves. If we are to help students understand, we must investigate the recent research about how students learn and adjust our strategies to take advantage of this knowledge. Find out all we can about brain-based learning, multiple intelligences, learning styles, cooperative learning, facets of understanding, performance tasks, and so on. Experiment with new strategies, reflect on the experience, redesign, consult with others, rework, and try again until we find techniques and strategies that best facilitate student understanding.

3. Find ways to make learning both engaging and effective. Children are innately curious. They come to school in kindergarten hard-wired to ask a lot of questions, particularly those higher-level "why" questions. What happens along the way to short those circuits and dampen their "natural inquiry" approach to life? By the time many students are in middle school, they have difficulty formulating higher-level questions. By high school there is so much pressure to succeed that the only questions students ask are "When is 'it' due?" and "How much is 'it' worth?"

They are so accustomed to doing "it" for the teacher that their focus tends to be on the product rather than the development of personal understanding. All the joy and excitement are gone.

Marks are of ultimate importance to the students. Assessment is undeniably critical to teachers as well. A carefully designed assessment task holds the key to improving student achievement.

The challenge is to design assessment tasks that are effective and engaging (Wiggins & McTighe, 1999), build on students' natural curiosity and capitalize on their desire to mimic adult experiences. Tasks must engage students in authentic real world performances that give them an opportunity to develop personal meaning and utilize their talents as well as their knowledge. If the activities and learning demonstrations are engaging and effective, understanding should improve and even some of the joy and excitement should return.

4. Clarify curriculum goals. We must be very clear about what it is we want understood. For many years teacher-librarians have been witnesses and accomplices to those mega-units of study such as medieval times, whales, famous scientists, and flight. Many were engaging and provided for lots of great learning. But was it the learning we wanted? Did we really know what students achieved? Just what was it we wanted them to learn while they were "doing medieval times" or "flight"?

Today all school districts have clear learning expectations and standards for student learning. It is up to us to select appropriate goals and plan effective teaching and learning experiences. Current pedagogy encourages us to begin planning with targeted learning goals for students (Wiggins & McTighe, 1999):

• What is it that I want my students to know, do and understand?
• How will students demonstrate that understanding? What will be acceptable evidence of their learning?
• How will I construct the learning experience so that students can achieve the desired results?

5. Teach and integrate information literacy skills. We need to think about what students need to know and know how to do before they can build understanding. As well as targeted knowledge and concepts, students need to hone information literacy skills. They also need to know when and where to apply these skills. Students with a solid repertoire of information literacy skills would be better prepared to tackle their schoolwork today and their future world of work and play.

What are the attributes of information literate students? They can

• explore their topic and define their information need;
• use a variety of information-gathering strategies;
• locate and access relevant information from a variety of sources;
• evaluate credibility of sources;
• select only the data they need from all the available sources;
• process and record selected data;
• understand form and format of information;
• analyze and synthesize information;
• share what they have learned through a variety of oral, written, and multimedia presentations;
• engage in literary and media experiences;
• honor the work of others by using appropriate references and citations;
• demonstrate their learning so that others can learn from them;
• apply what they have learned to new and different situations;
• optimize the use of technology to enhance their learning; and

• evaluate their own learning processes and set goals for their improvement (Koechlin & Zwaan, 2001).

6. Commit to focus on student understanding. How can we design information tasks so students can develop real understanding? Just what do we mean by *understanding* anyway? In *Understanding by Design*, Wiggins and McTighe (1999) tell us, "You understand it only if you can teach it, use it, prove it, explain it, or read between the lines."

This definition certainly broadens the scope of an assessment task, doesn't it? It also confirms that authentic performance is the perfect tool for assessment of understanding.

Wiggins and McTighe (1999) offer us an enlightening framework of understanding, which reinforces the importance of analysis, synthesis, and transfer. They have developed in this work a multifaceted view of understanding that they have called the "Six Facets of Understanding." In this model, when students truly understand they can

• explain,
• interpret,
• apply,
• develop perspective,
• empathize, and
• have self-knowledge.

This interpretation challenges us as teacher-librarians and teachers to determine how students will demonstrate the selected goals and understandings, and then design learning experiences that will equip students with the skills and knowledges needed to perform the demonstrations. The demonstration task must measure the desired learning. The learning activities and experiences must prepare the student for this demonstration.

Teacher-librarians need to develop ways to apply this knowledge about understanding to the design of good information tasks. Understanding is student-constructed. Our challenge is to help students reach understanding. In Figure 13.1 we have applied the work of Wiggins and McTighe (1999) to skill building and task design in school library programs.

Commitment to any of these actions, individually, will enhance the school library program. By strategically applying these ideas we can design learning experiences that will help students to construct personal meaning and consequently understanding. When students achieve understanding they will be more successful. When we link all of these initiatives together we are building the capacity of the school library program to enhance student achievement.

Task design considerations for a focus on understanding:

• Blend what is engaging with what is effective. Just because a lesson is engaging does not mean that it is necessarily effective in building understanding for students (Wiggins & McTighe, 1999).
• Do more than just cover desired learning. We must deliberately design to help students uncover difficult concepts and abstract ideas. We need to target complex skills and knowledges and those that are not obvious or could potentially be misunderstood. We must help students become self-directed learners: to probe, discover and inquire (Wiggins & McTighe, 1999).
• Apply the six facets of understanding to the design of student performance tasks (Wiggins &

Facet	Implications for the Design of Tasks for Library Programs	Examples of Tasks for Students
Explanation	Create tasks that require students to give a thoughtful account of how things occur/function and why. Students need to learn how to explore a topic, build a theory/thesis statement, test their ideas, look for relationships, analyze their results, and develop an instructional report/presentation to share with others.	Consider alternatives for using our natural water resources and prepare a press release to report the findings. Assess the use of various disposable products on the environment and synthesize findings to suggest possible solutions.
Interpretation	Create tasks that ask students to make personal meaning and create a demonstration that illustrates their read on the issue/event. Students need to develop communication skills so they can tell their story using a variety of media. Provide prompts to help them build understanding through interpretation, for example, So what? Why is this important? Who is it important to? Why? How does it make a difference to me, my family, or my community?	Represent your understanding of a specific period in history by collaboratively creating a freeze scene. Write a cautionary tale to illustrate your understanding of an environmental issue.
Application	Create tasks that ask students to use knowledge and skills in new and different situations. The problems should be as authentic and real world as possible. Students must have a solid repertoire of critical thinking skills to effectively transfer and apply their understanding to a new problem.	Evaluate web sites to determine their usefulness for specific projects. Create an infomercial that promotes a healthy lifestyle.
Perspective	Create tasks that ask students to identify points of view and examine them critically but dispassionately, to develop understanding. Students need to be able to formulate higher-level questions to be successful in building understanding through perspective.	Analyze a news article to make inferences about the kinds of questions that reporters used to write the news story. Analyze a current controversial issue and identify all the spins on the issue.
Empathy	Create tasks that ask students to walk in someone else's shoes and use their own imaginations and all their senses to explore and project themselves into another person's world. Students will need experiences with drama techniques such as role-playing to help them build understanding in this experiential facet.	Retell a story from the voice of a character in the story. Assume the roles of different citizens expressing their concerns about the effects of urban development in their community.
Self-Knowledge	Create tasks that ask students to probe their own thoughts and actions and reflect on their discoveries to build self-knowledge. Students need a clear understanding of the desired learning outcomes. They need tools and strategies to help them identify their strengths and weaknesses and set goals for improvement.	Use reflective journals or learning logs to record their personal learning journeys. Evaluate how well your group has worked together on a task.

Figure 13.1. Six Facets of Understanding. Based on *Understanding by Design*, Wiggins and McTighe (1999)

McTighe, 1999).

• Help students become skilled information users. They need to develop and strategically apply information literacy skills and information technologies.

• Ensure access to a wide variety of information resources in a variety of formats.

• Scaffold activities to enable students to build understanding and ultimately to construct personal knowledge.

• Overtly teach information processing skills so students can attain understanding and consequently improve their assessment results (Koechlin & Zwaan, 2001).

• Conference with classroom teachers frequently. Keep asking those probing questions: What is working and why? What isn't working and why?

• Rethink, rework, and redesign.

Avoid the angst that results when students "just don't get it." Teach strategically. Use the reflective prompts from the Information Task Design Process (Figure 13.2) to assist you as you design research and inquiry tasks for students. Focus on creating activities that will help students to build knowledge and skills and ultimately reach the targeted understandings. Build into learning tasks the experiences that are crucial to developing understanding. As you are designing tasks, experiment with the Six Facets of Understanding (Figure 13.1) and take care to provide opportunities for students to develop and express their understanding in different ways. Design activities that require your students to process the information they source before they attempt to create a product. Honor the value of all stages of information processing by assessing each component of the process, as well as the product. Marks are powerful. Students believe it is important if it is worth being marked.

Follow this strategy so your students will meet the criteria for success; so they will be able to give you what you ask for.

Finally, collect evidence of their achievements in your library program: display them; share them at staff meetings; tell the world!

REFERENCES

Haycock, K. (1992). *What works: Research about teaching and learning through the school's library resource center.* Vancouver: Rockland Press.

Koechlin, C., & Zwaan, S. (2001). *Info tasks for successful learning: Building skills in reading, writing, and research.* Markham, ON: Pembroke.

Krashen, S. (1993). *The power of reading: Insights from the research.* Englewood, CO: Libraries Unlimited.

Lance, K. (1999a). *Information empowered: The school librarian as an agent of academic achievement in Alaska* [online]. Retrieved from **www.lrs.org/html/about/school_studies.html**

Lance, K. (1999b). *Measuring up to standards: The role of school libraries & information literacy in Pennsylvania schools* [online]. Retrieved July 3, 2002 from **www.lrs.org/documents/lmcstudies/ PA/pabrochure.pdf**

Lance, K. (2000). *How school librarians help kids achieve standards: The second Colorado study* [online]. Retrieved from **www.lrs.org/html/about/school_studies.html**

Lance, K., & Loertscher, D. (2001). *Powering achievement: School library media programs make a difference: The evidence.* San Jose, CA: Hi Willow Research and Publishing.

Ontario School Library Association (OSLA). (1998). *Information studies: Kindergarten to Grade 12.*

Identify desired results.	Just what is it that I want my students to know, understand, and be able to do? How can I cluster and prioritize the learning expectations to peak student interest and ensure student understanding? **Collaborate with the teacher-librarian to identify the information processing expectations required for the task.**
⇩	
Determine acceptable evidence.	How will I know when students have achieved the desired results? What will I accept as evidence of student understanding and proficiency? How will I collect evidence over the course of the information task? How will I provide feedback to students throughout the task? **Design a culminating task that clearly allows students to demonstrate their achievement of the key expectations.** **Establish criteria and achievement levels directly linked to the information and topic/subject expectations. Measure both the process and the performance.**
⇩	
Plan learning experiences and instruction.	**What do I need to consider at each stage of the project process, to ensure that my students are ultimately able to construct knowledge and understanding?** What activities will help students build the needed knowledge and skills? How can I make the stages/steps effectively build on each other? What prerequisite skills need to be in place or reviewed? What will need to be taught or facilitated in light of the desired learning? What resources, materials, and technologies are needed? What student groupings are best for each teaching and learning strategy? What modifications do I need to make for special needs students?

Based on The Backward Design Process, *Understanding by Design*, Wiggins & McTighe (1999); *InfoTasks for Successful Learning*, Koechlin & Zwaan (2001)

Prepare

❑ How will I provide sufficient, informative exploration of the topic so students will have a working knowledge of the topic before they begin their investigation?

❑ What activities will help students define and clarify their information needs?

❑ How will I know when students are ready to proceed?

❑ How can I make sure that students understand the parameters of the task? (e.g., assessment criteria, timelines, presentation format)

Access

❑ Where will students access the necessary data?

❑ What are the best sources for this kind of information? Primary, secondary, or both?

❑ How will they gather the information?

❑ Do students have pre requisite selection and retrieval skills?

❑ How will students keep track of their information sources?

❑ How can I make sure that students have used a variety of resources?

Process

❑ How can I help students evaluate resources for validity and usefulness?

❑ How can I help students analyze their gathered data?

❑ What strategies would help students sort their data and look for trends and relationships?

❑ How can I help students sort out facts and opinions?

❑ What strategies will help students discover cause and effect?

❑ How can I make sure students have explored their issue from multiple perspectives?

❑ How can I help students synthesize the information and make personal meaning?

❑ How can I help students to make judgements, form opinions, and draw conclusions?

❑ What activities would help students to discover the potential consequences or the impact of their discoveries?

Transfer

❑ What strategies would give students opportunities to defend their point of view?

❑ How can I give students authentic opportunities to share their new learning with others?

❑ How can I ensure that students make use of or apply their new learning?

❑ What strategies might help students discover the relevance and importance of their learning?

❑ How can I help students identify their strengths and weaknesses and set goals for personal improvement?

Based on four stages of Inquiry/Research, *Information Studies: Kindergarten to Grade 12*, OSLA (1998) *Info Tasks for Successful Learning*, Koechlin & Zwaan (2001)

Figure 13.2. Information Task Design Process

Toronto: OSLA. Available online at **www.accessola.com/action/positions/info_studies/**

Wiggins, G., & McTighe, J. (1999). *Understanding by Design*. Alexandria VA: Association for Supervision and Curriculum Development.

⑭

Working Smarter: Being Strategic About Assessment and Accountability

Violet Harada

The worth of any school program is based on its contribution to student achievement. How do teacher-librarians contribute to this overall goal? What evidence do we have of the learning that results from our teaching? How do we use the results to inform our school communities and influence improvements? This article provides discussion points related to these issues and scenarios to provoke reflection and action.

No matter which community we live in, we are bound to hear educators deliberating on topics such as quality assurance, data-driven decision making, and curriculum restructuring. Whether these discussions involve parents, teachers, administrators, school board members, or community leaders, two issues consistently emerge: the demand for accountability and the imperative for continuous improvement.

Teachers and administrators' views of the role of assessment have changed dramatically over the past two decades. Spurred on by a national focus on assessment reform, they have come to understand that assessment is both a tool for accountability and a blueprint for instruction (Asp, 1998; Fitzpatrick, 2000). The hard fact is that resources will always be limited in schools, and the programs showing the most "value" are the ones that will receive the funding. Fitzpatrick (2000) defines value as the degree to which the program's impact on the school goals is positive, describable, and visible. That is, decision makers look for and react favorably to information that shows the worth of instructional programs.

We are well aware that student achievement is a critical component in educational improvement and school reform. Administrators are ultimately concerned with what and how well students learn. School personnel who cannot demonstrate a contribution to student learning are marginalized or even eliminated (Neuman, 2000).

First published in *Teacher Librarian*, October 2005, Volume 33, Number 1

The question is whether or not teacher-librarians are active partners in this schoolwide view of assessment. Over 10 years ago, Bob Berkowitz (1993) posed a critical challenge to the profession: What is convincing evidence that our students are competent to enter the information age? What do library programs really do for our students? These questions have taken on a new urgency in the face of continuing cuts in school library budgets and increasing reductions in library staffing across the nation.

David Loertscher and Ross Todd (2003) maintain that school library programs must tell the story of how effective libraries make a difference in the learning outcomes of students. Todd (2003) describes evidence-based practice as "day-to-day professional work that is directed toward demonstrating the tangible impact and outcomes of sound decision making and implementation of organizational goals and objectives" (p. 7).

Following Loertscher's and Todd's train of thinking, my point is this: While we are *working harder* and *teaching harder* than ever, we need to seriously consider ways to *work smarter*. We must show evidence that our dedicated labor produces demonstrated results in student learning. Input is vital; however, documented output is equally critical. In this article, I elaborate on the multipronged nature of assessment and evaluation, delineate a strategic approach to developing a workable assessment plan, and present examples of plans in action.

GOALS OF ASSESSMENT

As teacher-librarians, we focus on what and how well students master information-related skills that are foundational across curriculum areas. Working smarter begins with the understanding that the same evidence can be used for multiple goals and multiple audiences, namely, the following:

- empowering student learning;
- informing instructional effectiveness;
- communicating evidence of learning to parents;
- winning support from administrators.

Empowering Student Learning

By engaging students in assessment, we invite students to reflect on their own progress. Students more clearly understand what is expected. They connect new ideas to prior knowledge and strengthen their ownership over making the learning happen. Assessment also provides them with critical opportunities to give descriptive feedback as they are learning (Davies, 2000).

Informing Instructional Effectiveness

Assessment provides the instructional team—classroom teachers, teacher-librarians, and additional school partners—with crucial information on what students are learning and how teaching might be shaped to help students do even better. Assessment provides a map for planning curriculum and instructional activities (Harada & Yoshina, 2005). The result is more opportunities for peer learning and collaboration, more choices for students in the learning environment, and more integrated and interdisciplinary teaching (Falk, 2000).

Communicating Evidence of Learning to Parents

While parents are interested in their children's scores on norm-referenced, standardized tests, they are also grateful for more personalized information that shows specific examples of what their children are actually learning. If students are creating their own learning portfolios, they include samples of their work; assessments of the samples; and reflections about what they learned, how they learned it, and what future directions they wish to pursue (Harada & Yoshina, 2005).

Winning Support From Administrators

School leaders are besieged with much to do and limited resources and little time with which to do it. When they have to make decisions about allocating funds and staffing positions, they want evidence built on systematically collected data to make their determinations. They also need the evidence in capsulated formats. Providing this type of documentation builds a compelling case for the value of the library program. In short, communicating evidence of what is being learned through library instruction is a vital tool for library advocacy.

ASSESSMENT THAT COUNTS

Teacher-librarians often tell me, "I am already providing a lot of statistical information to everyone. Isn't that sufficient?" The statistics to which they are referring are quantitative reports on collection sizes, new acquisitions, student attendance, lost or damaged book counts, total classes taught, and logs of information requests filled and not filled. While statistics of this nature are helpful in elucidating the resources and input a library provides for learning, these statistics do not measure the extent of the learning.

An analogy might be useful here. Would we determine the success of an operation based on the types of instruments used by the surgeon, or the number of attending personnel in the operating room, or the years of experience of the surgeon? All of these factors might be contributing elements; however, we would surely agree that success should be measured by whether the patient got well as a result of the operation. By the same token, it would not be adequate to measure the *outcomes* of library programs solely by indicators of *input*.

What then might be measures of outcomes? While norm-referenced tests still hold reign in K–12 education, alternative school-level assessment has a legitimate place in the total assessment picture. High-stakes testing figures prominently in No Child Left Behind; however, as Sharon Coatney (2003) points out, this type of large-scale testing is not helpful in determining "individual student needs or informing students about their progress on specific learning goals" (p. 158). To provide a richer and deeper profile of the individual student's learning, achievement of this federal mandate also necessitates that assessment programs include *multiple measures* to appraise students' higher-order thinking skills.

What does this assessment look like? According to Danny Callison (2003), this form of assessment, often referred to as authentic assessment, involves using a range of strategies to examine students' information-seeking efforts and their final products. Anne Davies (2000) categorizes these assessment methods as observations, products, and conversations. The following are examples of tools used with these different methods:

• For observations: checklists of desired behaviors, rubrics that identify criteria for successful performance and describe different levels of performance, and rating scales that place levels of performance along a continuum

• For products: checklists that list criteria for proficiency, rubrics that describe various levels of proficiency, and graphic organizers that organize and synthesize students' work

• For conversations: formal and informal conferences, logs to record thoughts and feelings about the content and process, and notes and letters to self-assess and seek feedback

EMPLOYING A STRATEGIC APPROACH

Working smarter requires that we develop a strategy for action. Figure 14.1 outlines an approach that emphasizes linking library targets to school goals, starting small, and collecting and analyzing data to achieve multiple purposes with different audiences. Assessment must be both *formative* for examining student progress and instructional decisions as well as *summative* in recognizing accomplishments and documenting evidence (Donham, 1998).

The following explanations are given for the strategic approaches listed on Figure 1.

> Step 1: Determine school goals and priorities.
> Step 2: Determine the library's contribution to the goals.
> Step 3: Identify specific learning targets.
> Step 4: Establish criteria to measure student achievement of the learning targets.
> Step 5: Devise assessment tools.
> Step 6: Collect and analyze the data.
> Step 7: Communicate the results to different stakeholder groups.

Figure 14.1. Strategic Approach

1. Determine school goals and priorities. Obviously, the administration will invest most of the school's human and financial resources to meet the targeted priorities. Identifying these goals, then, is a critical first step in strategic planning.

2. Determine the library's contribution to the goals. By carefully identifying the major direction of the school program, we also decide where to channel our time and resources. We need to be visible and articulate regarding our role as partners in improving what and how students learn. By doing this, we emphasize the value-added nature of what we have to offer.

3. Identify specific learning targets. We teach a wide spectrum of skills in our respective information literacy programs. Because we work with entire school populations, it would be impossible for us to formally assess every lesson taught. We need to be selective. Questions that help us make workable decisions include, Which learning targets are most directly related to the school's goals? How do the library's targets match the classroom's learning goals? Which classes or grade levels might be most willing to collaborate with the library? The aim is to narrow our targets and work with a manageable cohort of teachers. We want to establish reasonable boundaries so that we are not overwhelmed with the assessment tasks.

4. Establish criteria to measure student achievement of the learning targets. In assessment-focused instruction, we start with an idea of what the students must be able to do at the end of the learning experience. Grant Wiggins and Jay McTighe (1998) have popularized the term "backward design" (p. 146) to describe this important concept in curriculum planning. The criteria should be stated so that they are understandable not only to the instructors but also to the students.

5. Devise assessment tools. As mentioned earlier, a range of techniques and instruments might be used, including rubrics, rating scales, checklists, and logs. Whichever tool is used, the criteria must be clearly stated so that both students and instructional teams can apply them to determine levels of achievement.

6. Collect and analyze the data. By systematically collecting the data and figuring ways to summarize and analyze the information, we can use the results to drive improvements in learning and teaching. A useful technique is to enter the data on a spreadsheet. This allows us multiple options in terms of formatting, sorting, calculating, and presenting the results.

7. Communicate the results to different stakeholder groups. The same assessment data can be packaged and presented in formats appropriate for different stakeholder groups, including students, teachers, parents, and administrators. With students and parents, the critical focus is the individual student's progress and accomplishments. Instructional partners need the same student-by-student accounting; at the same time, they also require class profiles of this information. Administrators, however, desire broader summaries where the data might be aggregated by grade levels or by courses.

The following two scenarios illustrate how assessment might be used strategically in an elementary school and a secondary school setting. Both are fictional composites of K–12 programs that I have worked with in my state. The scenarios are not intended as recipes to be replicated but rather as examples to provoke critical thinking and conversations about possibilities and options in the reader's school setting.

ELEMENTARY SCHOOL SCENARIO

Step 1: Determine school goals and priorities. Forest Haven Elementary is working to improve reading comprehension scores. In the upper elementary grades, the ability to generalize is one of the critical skills being taught. As a team, the fifth-grade teachers have incorporated this skill into their short research assignments and enlisted the support of their teacher-librarian, Jim.

Step 2: Determine the library's contribution to the goals. The team members decide on recycling, healthy diets, and local history as the three projects that they will implement, respectively, at the beginning, middle, and end of the school year. Jim volunteers to create a graphic organizer that students will use to record their generalizations. He agrees to introduce the skill in the first research project and to review it in the subsequent assignments. In turn, the teachers plan to reinforce the skill through the follow-up tasks in their respective classrooms.

Step 3: Identify specific learning targets. The teachers focus on the language arts content standard that deals with using strategies within the reading processes to construct meaning. This standard requires that students be able to identify a theme, generalization, or big idea from information they have gathered. They must also be able to infer ideas that are not directly stated using information from the text. Jim links this content standard with the information literacy standard that emphasizes the accurate use of information. To achieve this standard, students must be able to integrate new information with prior knowledge. By matching up the language arts and information literacy standards, Jim and the teachers realize that they are working on complementary targets.

Step 4: Establish criteria to measure student achievement of the learning targets. The teaching partners identify the following criteria for this learning outcome: students are able to (1) state generalizations clearly; (2) identify facts that support the generalization; (3) infer ideas from information in the source; and (4) connect new ideas with prior knowledge.

Step 5: Devise assessment tools. Jim creates a graphic organizer that focuses on the criteria established by the team. The components of the organizer are displayed in Figure 14.2.

Step 6: Collect and analyze the data. The team also devises a rating scale to summarize and analyze the students' work on the graphic organizer. Both students and instructors use the same rating scale as in Figure 14.3.

Step 7: Communicate the results to different stakeholder groups. The data are used for several purposes.

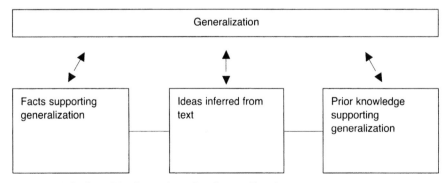

Figure 14.2. Graphic Organizer for Generalizations

Student's name:				
I can . . .	Student Rating		Teacher-Librarian Rating	
	Met	Not yet	Met	Not yet
1. Write a clear generalization.				
2. Give more than one fact that supports this generalization.				
3. Infer something that might not be actually stated but that I can support with facts.				
4. Connect something I already knew to this generalization.				

After conferencing with my instructors, I agree that I am at the following level:
- **EXPERT** because I met 4 of the "I can" statements.
- **PROFICIENT** because I met 3 of the "I can" statements.
- **BASIC** because I met 2 of the "I can" statements.
- **IN PROGRESS** because I met 1 of the "I can" statements.

Figure 14.3. Rating Scale for Generalizations

Mrs. Lee's class

Explanation of code:
1 = Wrote a clear generalization
2 = Provided more than one fact that supported this generalization
3 = Made a supported inference
4 = Connected prior knowledge

Student	Expert	Proficient	Basic	In Progress
Allen			1, 2	
Anglund				1
Barboza				1
Chee				1
Diamond				1
Farias			1, 2	
Fontes				1
Garfield	1, 2, 4			
Lopez			1, 2	
Lindon			1, 2	
Martin				1
Nomura	1, 2, 4			
Patimkin				1
Ross			1, 2	
Samuels				1
Santos				1
Sato			1, 2	
Thompson				1
Viloria				1
Young			1, 2	
TOTAL (20)	0	2	7	11

Figure 14.4. Class Summary on Generalizations

• With students: The students record their work on the graphic organizer and use the rating scale to determine their levels of proficiency. By using these tools to document their learning and assess their progress, the students are able to participate more intelligently in conferences with their instructors. They can thoughtfully and specifically articulate what they are able to do and where they might improve.

• With teachers: Jim knows that the fifth-grade teachers want to see the individual student's proficiency level and the specific criteria that each student has met. Therefore, he provides each teacher with a class summary similar to the one in Figure 14.4.

By analyzing the data, the teachers realize that although students are able to state generalizations, over half of them have problems supporting the generalizations with relevant facts. None of the students are able to make substantiated inferences. As a result of this analysis, Jim and the teachers modify their approach to include more time for conferencing and more work with small groups. The teachers focus on inferences in their modeling and guided practice, while Jim works on helping students support generalizations with facts.

• With parents: Students maintain process folios containing samples of their work for each of the three research assignments. By maintaining the process folios, students deliberately document their learning process. The graphic organizers and the rating sheets are included in the process folios. In three-way conferences that involve the parent, teacher, and student, the pupil assumes the lead in explaining the contents of his or her process folio. In the written introduction to the folios, students identify the teacher-librarian as one of their teachers.

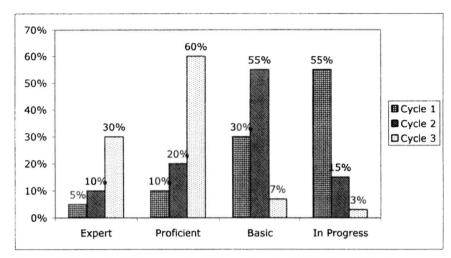

Figure 14.5. Grade 5 Students: Proficiency Levels in Working With Generalizations (N = 60)

• With administrators: Jim knows that his busy administrator needs collective summaries of students' accomplishments. Therefore, he prepares a report from his spreadsheet data that enables the principal to quickly ascertain the students' improvement across the three assignments (Figure 14.5).

By glancing over the summary, the principal is pleased to note that 90% of the students are at the proficient or expert levels by the third assignment, and only 3% of them are at the lowest level.

SECONDARY SCHOOL SCENARIO

Step 1: Determine school goals and priorities. At Beachfront High School, one of the major goals is to integrate technology into teaching and learning. Ninth-grade teachers work in disciplinary core teams comprised of social studies, language arts, science, and mathematics. One of the teams decides on a cross-disciplinary project dealing with the coastal erosion problem confronting the community. Eighty students choose to work in small groups to study the issue from the perspectives of the scientist, environmentalist, and historian. They use various technologies to retrieve, calculate, compile, and analyze their data as well as to communicate their findings. They produce multimedia presentations, displays, brochures, and video casts to raise neighborhood consciousness about the issue and share these products at an environmental awareness fair in their community.

Step 2: Determine the library's contribution to the goals. In this project, students must seek information from government and community agencies through interviews and via the Internet. Sarah, the teacher-librarian, indicates her willingness to help students locate and evaluate web sites for their informational needs. The core team decides that each student must complete at least three web site evaluations.

Step 3: Identify specific learning targets. Sarah and the core team identify the following match between the technology and information literacy standards; these standards form the basis for their learning targets:

• Technology as a research tool: Students must be able to evaluate and select information resources based on their appropriateness for specific tasks.

• Information literacy: Students must be able to evaluate information using such criteria as accuracy, relevance, and credibility of the sources and information in relation to a specific topic or problem.

Name of student: _____		
Name of web site: _____ URL: _____		
CRITERIA	**YES**	**NO**
Criterion 1: Content		
1a. The information relates to my topic and questions.		
EVIDENCE		
1b. The information appears to be accurate.		
EVIDENCE		
1c. The writing is free of bias.		
EVIDENCE		
1d. The information is current.		
EVIDENCE		
Criterion 2: Authority/credibility		
2a. The name of the author or sponsoring organization is stated.		
EVIDENCE		
2b. The author is qualified to speak on the topic.		
EVIDENCE		
Criterion 3: Presentation and ease of use		
3a. Topics, headings, and bullets are used to break up the text.		
EVIDENCE		
3b. Graphics, artwork, and other features enhance the presentation and contribute to understanding.		
EVIDENCE		
3c. Two things that make this site easy to navigate are 1. 2.		
After conferring with my instructors, I agree that I am at the following level: ° Level 4 = I can accurately evaluate the web site on all of the criteria (content, authority, and presentation). ° Level 3 = I can accurately evaluate the web site on 2 of the 3 criteria. Specify the 2 criteria. ° Level 2 = I can accurately evaluate the web site on 1 of the 3 criteria. Specify the criterion. ° Level 1 = I have problems evaluating the web site on all of the criteria.		

Figure 14.6. Web Site Evaluation Tool

Step 4: Establish criteria to measure student achievement of the learning targets. Based on their learning targets, the team works with the ninth graders to identify specific criteria for evaluating the web sites. They agree on indicators for content accuracy and relevance, credibility, and ease of use of the web site.

Step 5: Devise assessment tools. With feedback from the teachers and students, Sarah designs a tool for examining web sites (Figure 14.6). The instructional partners also agree that students must provide evidence supporting their ratings. Students complete this form for each of their three web site evaluations.

Step 6: Collect and analyze the data. Like Jim in the previous scenario, Sarah inputs her data on a spreadsheet. Figure 14.7 is a partial class summary showing how 10 of the students fared on their first web site evaluation. By examining a summary like this one, teachers can see which students are at Levels 1 and 2 and need the most assistance. They can also quickly identify the most problematic criteria for the students.

Step 7: Communicate the results to different stakeholder groups. The compiled data are shared with the following groups.

• With students: The pupils maintain portfolios, which serve as valuable tools to manage and assess learning. With so many instructors involved, the portfolios help the students and teachers to organize assignments and track the students' progress. The web site evaluation sheets are included in the portfolios as work samples. In conferences with the instructors, students use this assessment to identify their areas of strength and the places where they need more assistance.

• With teachers: Summary charts like the one displayed in Figure 14.7 provide information on each student. Teachers can quickly identify the evaluative criteria that the individual student was able to effectively apply, as well as the student's level of proficiency. At the same time,

Explanation of code
0 = Met none of the criteria
1 = Met criterion of content
2 = Met criterion of authority
3 = Met criterion of presentation

Student	Level 1	Level 2	Level 3	Level 4
Ching	0			
Dawson		3		
Furukawa		3		
Hansen			2,3	
Johnson				1, 2,3
Lee			1,2	
Matthews		2		
Olson	0			
Salud		3		
Wilson		3		

Figure 14.7. Partial Class Summary of Web Site Evaluation

the chart provides them with a broader class or group view of competency. Based on their analysis of the data, Sarah and the teachers pinpoint criteria that require more modeling and guided practice.

• With parents: During family conferences that are led by the students, the pupils use their portfolios to articulate their learning goals and accomplishments. In these conferences, students refer to their web site evaluations as evidence of how they are critically analyzing online sources of information. Sarah is invited to participate in the conferences. Families also get to see the students' final products at the environmental awareness fair. Since students must cite sources in their presentations, these citations provide further evidence of the actual use of web-related information.

• With administrators: The team prepares a report that summarizes student use of and proficiency with different technology tools. As part of this report, Sarah includes a summary of students' work on web site evaluations. Having used a spreadsheet, she easily converts the data into a visual presentation (Figure 14.8).

By glancing at the bar graph, the administrators note that the ninth-grade students have made substantial progress in evaluating web sites. While only 10%

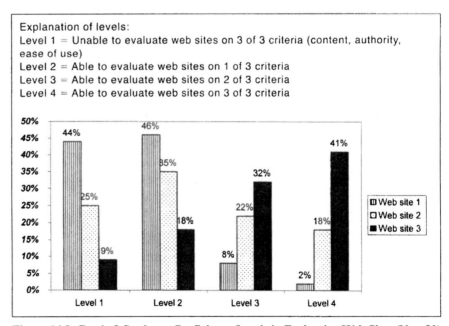

Explanation of levels:
Level 1 = Unable to evaluate web sites on 3 of 3 criteria (content, authority, ease of use)
Level 2 = Able to evaluate web sites on 1 of 3 criteria
Level 3 = Able to evaluate web sites on 2 of 3 criteria
Level 4 = Able to evaluate web sites on 3 of 3 criteria

Figure 14.8. Grade 9 Students: Proficiency Levels in Evaluating Web Sites (N = 80)

of the students were at Levels 3 and 4 in the first evaluation task, over 70% achieved these levels in their third evaluations.

CONCLUSION

Value-added assessment provides critical feedback, stimulates self-assessment, and promotes schoolwide learning. David Loertscher and Ross Todd (2003) maintain,

> At this time in our profession, it is not enough to just say that the library is important. . . . Many school administrators, school boards and parent communities are looking for tangible, documented evidence of the impact of their library on student learning, and use this as a basis for providing more library funding, technology, staffing. (p. 20)

This type of value-added practice involves

- mining the data—collecting and managing pertinent data and information;
- analyzing the data—synthesizing the data to create usable knowledge;
- communicating the results—reporting to support schoolwide learning;
- using the results—implementing improvements (Fitzpatrick, 2000).

Delia Neuman (2000) maintains that the Information Literacy Standards for Student Learning (AASL & AECT, 1998) have given teacher-librarians a voice in the larger school reform movement. She emphasizes that this is a voice we cannot afford to forfeit by remaining outside the discussion regarding assessment. I concur with Neuman that this is a challenge we cannot ignore if we are to be an integral part of the school's teaching and learning community. Assessing for student learning must be a central and strategic part of our mission.

REFERENCES

American Association of School Librarians (AASL) & Association for Educational Communications and Technology (AECT). (1998). *Information power: Building partnerships for learning.* Chicago: American Library Association.

Asp, E. (1998). The relationship between large-scale and classroom assessment: Compatibility or conflict? In R. Brandt (Ed.), *Assessing student learning: New rules, new realities* (pp. 17–46). Arlington, VA: Educational Research Service.

Berkowitz, R. E. (1993). From indicators of quantity to measures of effectiveness: Ensuring *Information power*'s mission. In C. C. Kuhlthau (Ed.), *Assessment and the school library media center* (pp. 33–42). Englewood, CO: Libraries Unlimited.

Callison, D. (2003). *Key words, concepts and methods for information age instruction: A guide to teaching information inquiry.* Baltimore: LMS Associates.

Coatney, S. (2003). Assessment for learning. In B. K. Stripling & S. Hughes-Hassell (Eds.), *Curriculum connections through the library* (pp. 157–168). Westport, CT: Libraries Unlimited.

Davies, A. (2000). *Making classroom assessment work.* Merville, BC: Connections Publishing.

Donham, J. (1998). *Assessment of information processes and products.* McHenry, IL: Follett Software Company.

Falk, B. (2000). *The heart of the matter: Using standards and assessment to learn.* Portsmouth, NH: Heinemann.

Fitzpatrick, K. A. (2000). Seize the data: Maximizing the role of assessment in school improvement planning. In K. Seidel (Ed.), *Assessing student learning: A practical guide* [CD-ROM]. Cincinnati, OH: Alliance for Curriculum Reform.

Harada, V. H., & Yoshina, J. M. (2005). *Assessing learning: Librarians and teachers as partners.* Westport, CT: Libraries Unlimited.

Loertscher, D. V., with Todd, R. J. (2003). *We boost achievement! Evidence-based practice for school library media specialists.* Salt Lake City, UT: Hi Willow Research and Publishing.

Neuman, D. (2000). *Information Power* and assessment: The other side of the standards coin. In R. M. Branch & M. A. Fitzgerald (Eds.), *Educational media and technology yearbook* (Vol. 25, pp. 110–119). Englewood, CO: Libraries Unlimited.

Todd, R. J. (2003). Evidence-based practice: Overview, rationale, and challenges. In D. V. Loertscher (Ed.), *We boost achievement! Evidence-based practice for school library media specialists* (pp. 1–25). Salt Lake City, UT: Hi Willow Research and Publishing.

Wiggins, G., & McTighe, J. (1998). *Understanding by design.* Alexandria, VA: Association for Supervision and Curriculum Development.

(15)

Demystifying the Evaluation Process for Parents: Rubrics for Marking Student Research Projects

Joan Shaw

In school library research programs, a challenge for students doing research emerges when they take their projects home and turn to their parents for assistance. Often parents lack sufficient knowledge of the research process to be able to effectively help their children. Moreover, teachers expect parents to monitor student homework but rarely give parents information about the purpose of the homework or how best to help their children (Fullan, 2001). Many parents are unfamiliar with what is expected of student work, and this inevitably leads to anxiety for both parents and children. Although it is ultimately up to students to create their own successes, research with thousands of parents has shown they want to "motivate, encourage, monitor, keep track of, interact with, and talk about school work at home" (Epstein, 1994, p. 47). In this time of engaged parents (Atlas, 1997), teacher-librarians must see themselves as collaborators with both students and parents if schools are to enhance the lives of students. Coleman suggests that the most important task facing the school in the immediate future is "collaboration with parents in building active communities of learners" (1998, p. 43). Similarly, Connors and Epstein found that "the need for cooperation is forcing a shift in emphasis from changing families to meet the needs of schools to changing schools to meet the needs of children and families" (1995, p. 440). Communicating effectively with families regarding assessment of student assignments can alleviate some of the confusion parents experience in understanding what is expected in their children's assignments. It might also satisfy the public's need for greater accountability in programs being offered in schools.

First published in *Teacher Librarian*, December 2004, Volume 32, Number 2

EVALUATION FROM THE PARENTS' VIEW

Many teachers use the traditional numerical, anecdotal evaluation sheet for marking student research projects, but some find it inadequate for helping parents guide their children. The marking sheet specifies criteria and standards of assessment and gives some details of what is expected. However, it falls short in not including comparisons to other student work that may be stronger or weaker. Often the translation from the isolated numerical mark to the report card letter grade is something of a mystery to parents and their children.

SOLVING THE PUZZLE FOR PARENTS

In 2002, our school staff decided to apply a new assessment technique for marking the collaboratively planned and taught research projects in grades 5, 6, and 7. We began with the performance standards developed by the British Columbia Ministry of Education. They are based on four-level rating scales that describe student performance in reading, writing, numeracy, and social responsibility (British Columbia Ministry of Education, 2002). As there are no specific British Columbia performance standards yet for assessing student research projects, the classroom teachers and I, the teacher-librarian, adapted these rating scales into a rubric assessment design. We completed assessment rubrics for many aspects of the research process: note-taking, draft writing, creative writing, research organization, artistic illustration, and reference list (See Figure 15.1 for one example). The rubric grid allows parents and students to see where the work is lacking and what is expected at the higher levels of the rating scale. (A list of our rubrics, available for your use and adaptation, is provided at the end of this article.)

The four-level rating scale provided by the Ministry of Education consists of (a) exceeds expectations; (b) fully meets expectations; (c) meets expectations (minimal level); and (d) not yet within expectations. We moved to a five-level rating scale, finding the fifth level both critical

Grade 5 Introduction, Conclusion, and Recipe for a Hero
Grade 5 Art and Final Presentation of Hero Project
Grade 6 Note-Taking Process
Grade 6 Introduction, Conclusion, and Reference List
Grade 5 Art and Final Presentation of Report
Grade 6 Fact-Taking and Creative Writing of Japanese Folktale
Grade 7 Note-Taking for Biography of Ancient Egyptian
Grade 7 Creative Writing of Ancient Egypt Story

For copies of any of the above rubrics, contact the author at *shaw8@telus.net*.

Figure 15.1. List of Rubrics

and challenging to create. Our five levels became (a) exceeds expectations; (b) fully meets expectations; (c) meets most expectations; (d) meets some expectations; and (3) meets few expectations.

Our rubrics have gone through multiple revisions and will likely continue to do so as staff, students, programs, and knowledge change. We have only had positive reactions from parents, but we are always open to constructive ideas from parents. On a practical level, lack of time to meet and discuss is a limiting factor for both parents and staff. In some instances we have deliberately sought input from students. Since we intuitively accept that greater student engagement helps deepen understanding of the rubric concept, we will continue to include students when possible. Before physically marking the sheets, a copy of the rubric is given to each student for self-evaluation; this is handed in with the assignment. We then use a yellow highlighter on the teacher copy to mark the phrases applicable to each student and highlight the assigned letter grade at the top. Anecdotal remarks are rarely added.

THE BENEFITS OF CREATING RUBRICS

With a vested interest in their children's education, many parents are eager to help their children succeed in school and in later life. In this light, teacher-librarians are wise to assess student work in a way that aids the many parents who wish to support their children's efforts at research. Our assessment rubrics are helping parents and students understand where the marked work fits on a continuum, why teachers and librarians assign the letter grades they do, and what students must do to achieve a top-level mark. This kind of evaluation is decreasing teacher discussion time with parents and students over the familiar question, "What does the teacher want us to do in this project?" In one parent/teacher interview, the parent of a grade 5 student exclaimed, "This [rubric] is wonderful! It's so clear. I can see where my child is and what he has to work towards."

Teachers who have used both scales overwhelmingly prefer the five-point scale, citing its practicality in matching to the five letter grades and ultimately to the students' report card grades. This more consistent approach in reporting to students and parents is demystifying the evaluation process for many people. With this change to a more transparent assessment technique, teachers are becoming more accountable for their programs.

Our teachers highly recommend this assessment approach for several reasons:

• Parents and their children receive more relevant information about assessment criteria and standards through this five-level rubric. Hence, better designs for library research process evaluation are strengthening the understanding between home and school.

• By using similar language in assessing assignments and preparing report cards, teachers are clarifying their comments, thereby lessening the risk of misinterpretation.

• There is better consistency in assessment design from teacher to teacher and from grade to grade.

• Use of this improved assessment technique is enhancing the well-being and partnership effectiveness among our teachers, parents, and students.

THE TEACHER-LIBRARIAN'S ROLE

Changing from the older, numerical assessment model to a rubric style is easier said than done for some teachers, who find rubrics outside their comfort zone. Fortunately, many classroom teachers are using rubrics successfully in areas other than research projects. It is likely best to start rubric collaboration with teachers who have some rubric experience already, are more willing to take risks, or display a mind-set for making assessment clearer to parents. Success seems to build on success here and the teachers note that some parents have been quite vocal about the rubrics we have created, noting how much more useful they find the information in the rubrics. While parent comments tend to be directed more toward classroom teachers during interview times, several parents have come into the library to tell me the same thing.

Teacher-librarians can guide teachers and students unfamiliar with rubrics by showing them examples such as the one included with this article. They should caution teachers to provide a clear and thorough explanation when introducing this new form of evaluation in the classroom. Students who cannot easily analyze this kind of design need a detailed explanation of the rubric *before* beginning the assignment. Assuming that students automatically comprehend the new system is a mistake. When introduced well, the rubric contains enough detail to satisfy both students and parents. One grade 6 teacher noted that since evaluating assignments with the five-level rubric, students no longer run up to ask why they received the letter grade they did for the assignment. She is very satisfied with this result.

CONCLUSION

In working together, the teacher-librarian and classroom teachers have succeeded in making a difference to their school community. Teachers, parents, and students alike have responded well to the new rubrics.

Although the creation of rubrics is initially time-consuming, the gains far outweigh the time and effort this feat requires. To conclude, one might say that the greatest benefit is both two-pronged and powerful: By communicating more effectively with families, educators also satisfy the current public demand for greater transparency in student evaluation.

REFERENCES

Atlas, J. (1997, April 14). Annals of parenthood: Making the grade. *The New Yorker*, 34–39.

British Columbia Ministry of Education. (2002). *BC performance standards*. Retrieved August 25, 2004, from **www.bced.gov.bc.ca/perf_stands/**

Coleman, P. (1998). *Parent, student, and teacher collaboration: The power of three*. Thousand Oaks, CA: Corwin.

Connors, L., & Epstein, J. (1995). Parent and school partnerships. In M. Bornstein, Ed., *Handbook of parenting, volume 4: Applied and practical parenting* (pp. 437–458). Mahwah, NJ: Lawrence Erlbaum Associates.

Epstein, J. (1994). Theory to practice: School and family partnerships lead to school improvement and student success. In C. Fagnano & B. Werber (Eds.), *School, family and community interaction: A view from the firing lines* (pp. 39–52). Arlington Heights, IL: IRI/SkyLight Training and Publishing.

Fullan, M. (2001). *The new meaning of educational change* (3rd ed.). New York: Teachers College.

PART III

Learning
Leadership:
Technology
Integration

⑯

You Know You're a 21st-Century Teacher-Librarian If . . .

Joyce Valenza

At our state leadership conference this summer, the theme was paradigm shift. The goal was to think outside the box to build a new strategic plan for school libraries in our state. Early in the meeting, a librarian in her twenties asked a question about change. Her honest voice continues to resonate with me. Here is the essence of her question:

> I am recently out of library school, and from what I can see, we're all doing different stuff. The other school librarians I know are not doing what I am doing. Some don't even know about the state databases. Some maintain Web sites and blogs; others do not. Some have seriously retooled; others have not. What should we be planning for? What does a twenty-first-century librarian look like? How do we know what we are really supposed to be doing now?

This young librarian's question got me thinking about how incredibly dramatic the change has been since I first got out of library school in 1976, and then when I had to do that master's over again for my educational credential in 1988. Yet the changes occurring between 1976 and 1988, when the personal computer and automation were becoming ubiquitous in libraries, had nothing on the changes that we have seen in the last two years.

My reflection continued. Within a couple days of our state conference, David Warlick raised the question of library obsolescence in his blog. Colleague Kathy Schrock turned me on to a provocative document, "The Future of Libraries: Beginning the Great Transformation" (**www.davinciinstitute. com/page.php?ID=120**), by Thomas Frey, Executive Director of the DaVinci Institute. He identifies ten key trends that "give clear insight into the rapidly changing technologies and equally fast-changing mindset of library patrons."

First published on e-VOYA, October 2006, www.voya.com. Published in *Teacher Librarian*, October 2007, Volume 35, Number 1. *Teacher Librarian* acknowledges e-VOYA's permission to adapt and reprint this article.

Much of what I am reading these days urges me to consider libraries and change. The public library blogs—Jenny Levine's *Shifted Librarian* (**www.theshiftedlibrarian.com**), Stephen Abrams's *Stephen's Lighthouse* (**stephenslighthouse.sirsi.com**), and Michael Stephens's *Tame the Web* (**http://tametheweb .com**), to name just a few—reflect on the changes now labeled Library 2.0.

My personal vision is very clear. In school libraries, we can do a lot more for learners. We have a unique opportunity to offer customized, 24/7, just-in-time, relevant, and authentic service and instruction—but only if we retool. It is not an option but an urgent need. Teacher-librarians cannot expect to assume a leadership role in information technology and instruction, and we cannot claim any credibility with students, faculty, or administrators, if we do not recognize and thoughtfully exploit the paradigm shift of the past two years.

I began the following list as a blog post and it just kept growing. I welcome your comments and additions.

YOU KNOW YOU'RE A TWENTY-FIRST-CENTURY TEACHER-LIBRARIAN IF . . .

1. you ensure that your learners and teachers can access developmentally appropriate and relevant databases, portals, and web sites. If teacher-librarians don't work toward this goal, we will contribute to the development of an *information underclass*. You are considering federated search solutions for organizing these growing resources.

2. you organize the Web for learners. You create signage and guides for new additions to your "collection." You are investigating the role of informal tagging and folksonomies in helping users to access materials. You have the skills to create a blog or a web site to pull together resources to meet the information needs of your learning community. You consider moving your pathfinders to blogs and wikis, opening them to students and teachers for collaboration and comments.

3. you think outside the box about the concept of "collection." Your collection and your students' best resources might now include e-books, audiobooks, blogs, open-source software, streaming media, wikibooks, and much more! You create guides and search tools for these resources.

4. you are thinking about the interactive services that you might provide online. You are planning to post your materials-suggestion forms, book reviews, and calendar online.

5. you partner with classroom teachers to consider new interactive, collaborative, and engaging communication tools for student projects. You think Web 2.0 for learners. You know the potential that new technologies offer learners as both information consumers and producers. You are exploring the pedagogical uses of digital storytelling, wikis, Podcasts, streaming video, and student-produced learning objects as possibilities beyond paper and PowerPoint. You continually think about the best possible communication tool for a particular project and how you might use the new tools for teaching, practicing, and reflecting on information fluency.

6. you consider just-in-time, just-for-me, blended learning your responsibility and are proud that you own the real estate of one desktop window on your students' home computers, 24/7. You are planning learner-centered, learner-empowered landscapes and are becoming the knowledge-management center of your school. You collect and share the learning tools that your community is most likely to need and you post them in the most effective possible media formats.

7. after reading Tom Friedman's *The World Is Flat: A Brief History of the Twenty-First Century* (2006), the bible for 21st-century change, you wonder what exactly it is you do that might be better done by Google or by Bob or Tiffany in Bangalore. You plan and implement customized services that will *not*, cannot be outsourced to Bangalore.

8. you consider your role as info-technology scout. You look to make "learning sense" of the authen-

tic new information and communication tools used in business and academics. You figure out how to use them thoughtfully and you help classroom teachers use them with their classes. You invite learners to help you in this exploration.

9. you consider ways to bring experts, scholars, authors, and other classrooms into your library and your school using telecommunication tools like Skype and Internet2. You seek partnerships with local universities to help you establish connections.

10. you grapple with issues of equity. You provide open-source software alternatives and Web-based applications to students and teachers who need them. (Here's a starter list: **http://mciu.org/ ~spjvweb/opensource.html**.) You lend flash sticks and laptops and cameras and whatever else it takes to achieve digital equity.

11. you consider new ways to promote reading. You are exploring downloadable audiobooks. You are investigating lending iPods for e-books. You (and your students) are creating digital booktalks. (See examples here: **http://mciu.org/~spjvweb/ movietrailers.html**.) Your literature circles meet with other classrooms around the country or world through telecommunications.

12. you are rethinking the concept of library space. "Library" may become less book space and more creative-production and experience-sharing space. You respond to the increasing need for group creative-production space—iMovie, podcasting, blogging. You recognize "library" as group planning/collaborating space, "library" as performance and presentation space, "library" as event-central for telecommunications and remote author/expert visits, while "library" continues as study/reading/gathering space.

13. you model respect for intellectual property in a world of shift and change. You share examples for documenting new types of media. You insist on appropriate documentation for media in all formats and recognize the growing number of copyright-friendly portals. (Here's a starter list from our web site: **http://mciu.org/~spjvweb/cfimages.html**.) You understand the new, flexible protections and freedoms made possible by Creative Commons (**http://creativecommons.org**) licensing, and use its resources to find copyright-friendly video, audio, images, and more. You point to tools like *Get Creative*, a video describing the White Stripes' approach to sharing their music without intermediaries (**http://mirrors .creativecommons.org/getcreative**), to help explain the new licensing concepts to learners, educators, and content creators.

14. you know that now is only the beginning of social networking. Students will get to their MySpace accounts through proxy servers despite any efforts to block them. You plan educationally meaningful ways to incorporate student excitement (and your own) for social networking.

15. you recognize your iPod as *way more* than a tool for exercising to music or passing time by listening to music. (Contributed by Catherine Nelson, Northside Elementary School of the Arts, Rock Hill, South Carolina.)

16. you read both edtech journals and edtech blogs, not just the print literature of our own profession. Blogs publish professional news and new strategies before they can travel through the traditional publishing process; they are essential strategies for keeping up as a professional.

17. you seek professional development that will help you grow even if you cannot get official credit for that growth. Learning happens between annual conferences. You attend conferences without traveling—by viewing and listening to keynotes online. You use tools like David Warlick's Hitchhikr to visit conferences that you cannot physically attend.

18. you do not take "no" for an answer when a network administrator or technology director refuses to support a pedagogically sound activity. You seek a way to get to "yes" if learners will benefit.

19. you are flexible and recognize that your growth as a professional cannot stop and that you may

learn from unexpected others. You ask your students to help you master additional skills. You engage learners in helping to create learning materials. (Our students began creating learning objects to share with fellow learners this year. See **http://mciu.org/~spjvweb/infoskillsvideo.html**. Much more to come.)

20. even if you are a *digital immigrant*, you learn the language of *digital natives* AND you consider what you want to unpack from the trunk that you carried from the old world. Rigor and information fluency matter, no matter the medium. So do excitement, engagement, and enthusiasm.

The Digital School Library:
A Worldwide Development and a
Fascinating Challenge

David Loertscher

The Internet as an information environment for children and young adults has created a fascinating competitor to libraries of all types. Search engines such as Google are so easy and immediate that many young people, faced with a research assignment, just "google" their way through the Internet rather than struggle through the hoops of a more traditional library environment.

To be sure, the Internet is

- overwhelmingly large;
- mostly irrelevant and largely unreliable for the age group;
- full of advertising, pornography, and other entities designed to lure young people into becoming paying customers or participate in other unwholesome activities;
- getting outdated as many sites age without funding or time for volunteers to update them;
- becoming less and less "free" as corporate entities try to recover costs or make a profit; and
- in some danger of collapsing as its size overwhelms capacity.

Yet in spite of these drawbacks, youth are attracted in such large percentages that library collections, even though superior in content, are ignored. Are we surprised that users gravitate to information systems and technology that suit their needs, whether or not those systems are superior? Teacher-librarians need to realize that to stay relevant, they must embrace the information needs of children and young people on their own terms, not those of well-meaning adults. Many school libraries are rarely accessible at the times when information needs are critical: They are down the hall, filled with classes already, closed in the

First published in *Teacher Librarian*, June 2003, Volume 30, Number 5

evenings, and often their most valuable information resources, the reference collections, are chained to their shelves. Google, on the other hand, is always there as long as the connection is working. And in the age of wireless, it is ubiquitous as well as available 24 hours a day, seven days a week.

What sort of school library information system would young people be attracted to? What system would be so valuable and so convenient that students and their teachers would want to start there first before venturing forth into the information smog of the Internet?

THE LIBRARY AS THE DIGITAL HUB OF THE SCHOOL

In the United States, many school administrators understand that when they give a speech about the library, they should refer to their library as "the hub of the school." In the age of digital information systems, that phrase can be truer than ever before. I would propose that every school library in the world that is able construct a portal/web page that constitutes the central hub of information essential to every student and teacher. This portal would be the home page of every student's and teacher's computing device as it is turned on. The school library would be every student's and teacher's essential information system. To these users, "It all begins at the school library," since it is the gateway to the world. It is *the* place to start: *a safe and nurturing information environment.* In this article, we will explore the academic environment of a total information system for youth. We can imagine a career and personal space in addition, but space does not permit exploration of those worlds. (For more discussion of these concepts, see Loertscher, 2002.)

THE ACADEMIC ENVIRONMENT
A Safe, Nurturing Environment

The first essential element of an information environment that would truly nurture every student and teacher is a closed system with a firewall of protection from the outside world, an *intra*net rather than an Internet. For hundreds of years, librarians have built collections of materials, information, and technology selected for a particular group of users. It never contained everything, but it did contain the highest quality materials targeted at users in a specific community. It was as large as the librarian could influence the community to purchase.

Teacher-librarians have not sought to build libraries containing all that is known. Such collections would not be desirable in any elementary or secondary school. Even in the digital age, teacher-librarians would build a smaller (a relative term) system, yet it would be "enough" to challenge every learner.

The digital information system would also be a safe environment from a number of elements that have become so common on the Internet: advertising, pornography, hackers, and push elements from persons or groups trying to gain access to youth for a variety of nefarious reasons. Just as we protect our homes and school grounds from harmful elements in the community, the digital information system would also be protected from destructive forces. Such a protective environment has nothing to do with the issue of intellectual freedom or with filtering as it is known currently. And this protection extends not just within the library walls, but into the classrooms of the school and into the homes of students and teachers who are accessing this school library intranet.

The intranet envisioned here is no different than many created for professionals in corporate and research environments around the world. Many organizations have intranets protected from the outside world. In such systems, e-mail and instant messaging can take place, but only within the internal environment. Numerous parents understand these intranets because they participate in them at their workplace. Our students might have additional e-mail and instant messaging as a part of independent accounts from home to satisfy their desire to be more independent from the provided intranet from the library resource center. Figure 17.1 shows this protected information environment or the walls of the digital school library.

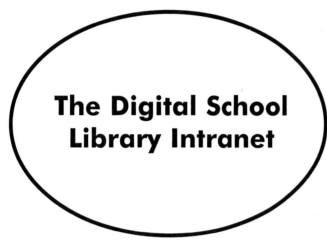

Fig. 17.1. The Digital School Library Intranet

Customization for Every User

Teacher-librarians are accustomed to building "one-size-fits-all" information systems. They build catalogs using search mechanisms and search terminology that all users, adult or child, sophisticated or novice, must use to find materials successfully. A number of libraries targeted at children have subscribed to automation programs that provide simpler and more appealing interfaces. However, even with these specialized catalogs, the interface is still one-size-fits-all at the child level.

A much more optimal interface would allow each user to create and build his own view of the information space within the school library intranet. A child at a certain grade level might wish to view information targeted at her grade level, assignments from only her teachers, e-textbooks for her classes, plus access to information suited to personal interests. This interface could expand or contract within the school library resource center intranet at the discretion of the user under the guidance of the teacher-librarian and the teacher.

Close to the beginning of the school year, students would enter the main school library intranet and, after some exploration of that environment, would design their own home page within that space, gaining access codes/authority at that time which then could be used on whatever electronic device they were using either at home or within the school. For example, students would identify teachers, courses, needed tools, areas of interest, topics for which they want to be notified regularly, languages spoken, cultural and religious preferences, and level of ability; and they would set up e-mail/instant messaging accounts inside the protected information space. At any time during the year, students, perhaps in consultation with teachers and teacher-librarians, could reset their parameters, or they might just choose to see the entire intranet.

The same features could be constructed by teachers who would want to be in contact only with their own students, their classes, their e-textbooks and resources for their classes. If they are collaborating with teachers outside their own discipline, other spaces could be opened up temporarily as needed. Following a common pattern already known in the larger library world, these personalized information spaces might be termed "my school library" as shown in Figure 17.2.

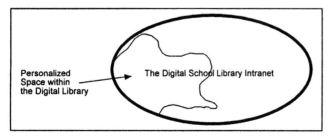

Fig. 17.2. Personalized Space Within the Digital Library

The Digital School Library Ribbon

Another way to think about the digital school library is to think of it as a ribbon down the computer screen of each user. In this system, each user—teacher-librarian, teacher or student—sees the library intranet as a ribbon on the left side of the computer screen and the balance of the screen is devoted to a personal work space. Those familiar with OS10 on Macintosh computers will recognize this concept as a type of library "dock" containing information resources, tools, and communication devices—ever present, handy, and customizable to my needs at any given moment.

BUILDING THE DIGITAL CONTENTS OF THE ACADEMIC INFORMATION SPACE

An Information-Rich Environment

Building a digital information-rich environment for teachers and students draws upon long-known principles of selection: a solid match with the curriculum, appropriate difficulty level, authority and high quality, among others. Publishers and jobbers are still learning how to support the needs of young learners in the digital world and provide affordable resources.

Digital resources for school library collections might contain three levels within the intranet. These are the core collection, the curriculum collection, and the elastic collection.

The Core Collection

Similar to the reference collection of traditional libraries, the core collection contains materials meeting the longstanding Bradford distribution principle that 20% of the collection can usually account for 80% of the inquiries. Thus, encyclopedias, dictionaries, atlases, core databases and captured web sites spanning common curricular topics would be selected. In North America, school districts and even states have licensed many of these core works not only for schools, but for every citizen within their state or province. By doing so, these core works cost much less per capita, and when carefully selected, can provide a rich starter collection available equitably across

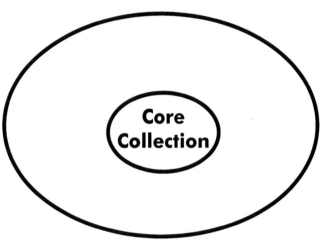

Fig. 17.3. The Core Collection

whole populations. Individual teacher-librarians might create such a core collection, take advantage of core works created by larger entities for use by school students, or add to core collections as needed until the Bradford phenomenon appears to be operational. Figure 17.3 illustrates this concept.

The Curriculum Collection

Using well-known collection development principles, a teacher-librarian would then add resources to the core collection designed to serve a particular curriculum. These might include e-textbooks, collections to support reading initiatives, science and social studies materials, original sources, graphical sources, and curricular information in a variety of languages and difficulty levels. From major projects, such as Access Pennsylvania done in the United States a number of years ago when school library catalogs were joined to form a single online catalog, we learned an important principle about teacher-librarians: The collections they choose to match their curriculums are as different as they are alike across schools.

Some may presume that a school district might build a digital collection that would serve the needs of every elementary school. Not so. With professionals as "chief information officers" at the building level, digital collections would be as diverse and unique as required by the needs of a particular school's

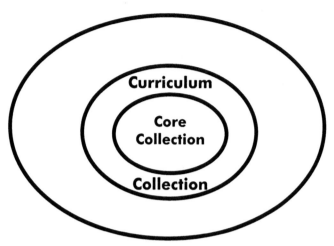

Fig. 17.4. The Curriculum Collection

curriculum and student population, as shown in Figure 17.4.

The Elastic Collection

Information vendors often pitch their information databases to schools and libraries based on a subscription lasting for an entire school year. The idea of the elastic collection would be to open, on the basis of need but on a short-term basis, certain information channels to serve short-term information needs. For example, an advanced high school chemistry class might need access to *Chemical Abstracts* but could never afford to subscribe to such a sophisticated data repository for a year. The teacher-librarian might contract with the company to open that database for 3 hours at an appropriate time when the students and teachers were doing high-level research. Access would then be ended. For some companies, the teacher-librarian might buy a "phone card" in advance that would allow access to a variety of specialized databases based on the minutes used or queries made.

Such access to specialized resources would be termed "elastic" since the school library collection would vary in size from day to day depending on the requirements of teachers and the needs of students at any given moment (see Figure 17.5.) This concept follows the well-known principle that in the digital age, there is a great deal of difference between what a library "owns" as opposed to what it "provides access to."

The elastic concept would work in the world of fiction as easily as in the advanced database arena. For example, as Harry Potter books are released, the teacher-librarian might lease 300 digital copies for two weeks, dropping to 10 copies thereafter. Or, one could imagine that as holidays are observed or popular topics become fads, the digital collection would swell or contract as required by the users. Students and teachers might indeed control the size of the collection at any given moment as they clicked on the Harry Potter book collection. Instead of contracting for a certain number of copies, the users would govern the number of copies required as they clicked their way through the system. A teacher having all students read the same novel would "order" the number of e-copies needed for a short period of time. Thus, within certain parameters, the teacher-librarian, the teacher and the actual users would have control over the contents of the collection at a given moment. It would be interesting to describe the contents of the collection under this system since we would need to have computer reports that could describe these contents at a given time and in a given location. The important notion here would be that the teacher-librarian would be in the driver's seat, setting the parameters within which the users could work and shape the collection. And the chief information officer would often be constrained by the budget available.

The Internet and the Intranet

No matter how large the school library intranet, students and teachers can benefit greatly from ac-

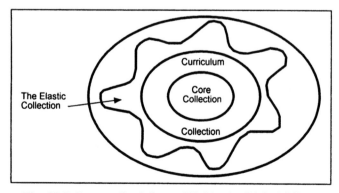

Fig. 17.5. Personalized Space Within the Digital Library

cess to the Internet. In the past, the teacher-librarian or technologist turned on the Internet for everyone with various levels of filtered access. In our view, this responsibility should revert to parents or caregivers who could, for an individual student, allow various size ports to the Internet as pictured in Figure 17.6. This access might vary by levels from a tightly filtered Level 1 access to a full and open Level 3 access, with Level 2 providing some filtered access. If there were no parent or caregiver who would take responsibility, the student would be limited to the school library intranet with no Internet access. Of course, one student might want to borrow from another student's access privilege and that would be a behavior issue to solve.

The Picture of the Whole
Figure 17.6 illustrates the central components of the school library digital collection as a safe, smaller (a relative term), and high-quality information system. It emanates from the school library into every learning space in the school and into homes or other locations where learners are served. It would spread out to homeschoolers and those who could not physically come to school, and would reach out to include distant sites or "sister schools" as partnering occurs locally, nationally, or internationally. Yet it is behind a firewall.

Personalized Features of the Academic Space Within the intranet, every student and teacher should be provided with various other information technologies designed to maximize a learner's opportunities and potential. While others are likely

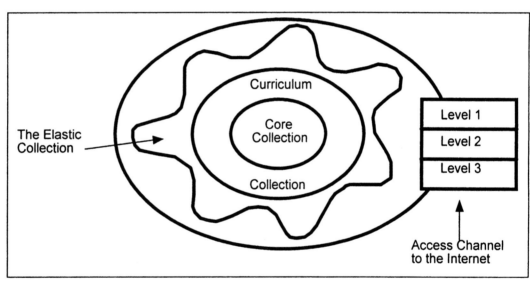

Fig. 17.6. The Digital School Library and the Internet

to develop, the current state of technology allows a description of three important features: tools, push technology and pull technology.

Tools. Young people and their teachers will need the tools to operate within digital space that will boost their potential to learn and provide both sophistication and efficiency in support of the learning process. Current tools that come immediately to mind include

• an office suite (word processor, database, and spreadsheet, including mentoring software such as spelling checks, grammar checks, wizards, or other guidance software to stimulate critical or creative thinking);
• graphics packages (drawing, graphic art software, concept mapping programs, among others);
• web construction editors;
• presentation software (such as PowerPoint or Photoshop);

• communication tools (allowing voice and visual contact with other learners or experts and allowing students and teachers to transmit projects, messages and graphics, or conduct planning);

• translation packages (both language translation and cross-platform translation or conversion);

• assistive technology (for blind, disabled, or other physically challenged users);

• communication tools (certainly within the educational environment and beyond as parents and protective technologies allow);

• course/classroom software (programs such as Web CT or Blackboard where courses are conducted);

• remote sensing devices (allowing collection of data, experimentation or experiencing whether onsite or from afar);

• tutorials for using any of the system tools or their upgrades; and

• management tools for teachers such as grade books and attendance software.

Whether these tools will be resident on the school library server, on the client's device or a combination of both will depend on the sophistication of technology, bandwidth, and a host of other technological issues known now or in the future. Many institutions already license software packages for entire work groups, an entire student body, or small groups with specialized needs. Thus the pattern for this work environment is already in place and will become more and more flexible as schools exhibit the need to equip each individual with the tools required to flourish. These work tools will need to be upgraded on a regular basis as innovation and technology advance. Software operation will need to be seamless across the computing devices in the school, personal technologies, and home-based or mobile technologies.

Push technology. Both learners and teachers can expect software on the intranet that will allow them to become aware of things that will benefit them. Current push technologies might include

• automatic notification software—including calendaring; notification of assignments; alerting messages about new software, new articles on topics of personal interest or research; scholarships and learning opportunities; student activities and service projects; and a whole host of other messages to help the user grow and develop as a responsible member of the learning community. For teachers, this technology would provide notices of new professional articles or research reports of interest, alerts concerning policy changes, or opportunities for professional development, to list just a few.

• messages/news from administrators, teacher-librarians, teachers, parents. For both students and teachers, messages of upcoming events, announcements, reminders, opportunities are designed to help the individual plan and work successfully within the educational environment.

Pull technology. Pull technologies include the various search engines and meta-search engines to allow the user to locate desired information within the information system. Search engines have improved dramatically over the past two decades and there is reason to believe they will become smarter and more adaptable to individual needs. Progress is being made toward a single rather than multiple search engines that will search a wide variety of information databases and sites rather than using multiple engines with a plethora of icons cluttering the computer desktop. A single meta-search engine might allow us to search first within the intranet and then, as the parent allows, outside that environment in the world of the Internet. At the present, the emphasis on building search engines is on *precision*, that is, to provide a selected few sources that meet a need exactly. Dr. David Barr, however, reminds us that learners who are becoming mini-experts in a topic or teachers who want to build comprehensive knowledge, require *recall* as well, where every relevant document is retrieved (Barr, 2002, p. 21–26).

Advantages of the Digital School Library Intranet

Numerous advantages drive the construction of a digital school library, at least one that is ubiquitous, reliable, and available 24/7/365 (24 hours a day, seven days a week, and 365 days a year). The following may not be a complete list:

• The digital school library becomes the *primary information system*—the true hub of the school. Finally, on every digital device, computer screen or instructional space at school or at home, the school library has an essential role as "the place where I begin."

• Digital libraries are available for students who are being *homeschooled* yet who need access to the same information-rich environment that government supporters have provided for those attending public schools.

• If a student for some reason moves to a distant location for a season, the digital school library is *available anywhere and at any time.* It might also provide *distance educational opportunities* for young people with special academic needs not available at the local school.

• By utilizing the personalized space that every user can create, the digital school library can provide many more *cultural and religious* materials that can be accessed or ignored under user control.

• The digital library provides for *individual differences* in ways print libraries could not do very well. Using the personalized space construction tools, the library can serve age ranges, ability levels, personal preferences, languages, and sophistication levels.

• *Equity* issues are served very well by the digital school library and are particularly effective with funding agencies trying to serve every child.

• *Access* to information in the digital world will not depend on access to a single physical location with the traditional organizational restrictions to when, where, and at what time information resources can be used. This concept is discussed further in the section of this article dealing with issues.

• Digital school libraries can be *device-enabled*, making information compatible with a wide range of devices whether they be computers, hand-held devices or other technical devices now being developed.

• The technology is now available to provide an information system for young people including *individualized* customization, using the "my space" concept that is already growing rapidly in many sectors of business and industry.

• Analysis of the digital possibilities allows us to think in terms of a *smaller but high-quality* information environment. Here, searches come up with both reasonable and/or rich results as queries are made.

• The digital school library intranet versus Internet concept *transfers responsibility* of information access to the full Internet to parents/caregivers where it belongs.

• *Safe information environments* are created away from and protected from the rush-hour traffic on the Internet highway. *Predators of all types are locked out.* And the space provides privacy from snooping eyes of internal school workings and operations.

• Digital school libraries still embrace the principles of *intellectual freedom* since all materials within the library are carefully selected under the guidance of selection policies, as has been the case for a century. The tug-of-war of ideas is still alive and well.

• Teacher-librarians will continue to build a *selected collection* utilizing their time-honored expertise. They recognize the needed core materials, materials that will support specific curricular agendas, and they will know which resources belong in the elastic collection for specialized uses.

Issues Related to the Digital School Library

Numerous issues surround the creation of a digital school library. Some have already arisen. Others await more experience, and the development of software and hardware.

Access. The major issue of the digital school library is really identical to the print school library: access. Who can gain access, when, for what periods of time, through what devices, at what speed, and from what locations? Already, the next generation of cell phones is a combination of phone and PDA, and is Internet accessible. It is just a matter of time before a truly portable information device can be furnished to every user at an affordable cost.

The concept of enough. How much information and technology is "enough?" The answer to that question awaits research, but teacher-librarians who use "counters" to analyze behavior of users on their systems and then compare this behavior with learner success, will be able to start discussing this idea intelligently. Right now, we can only speculate.

The redesign of workspace. A number of research organizations and commercial entities are working on workspace design for young people. Because of the "cut and clip" tendency, both individual and group workspaces that track creation of a project through information space, sources used, notes from sources, progress through rubrics, complete with helps, tips, and so on would be extremely useful.

Breaking the googling habit. Well-designed school library portals complete with counters would track student behavior on information systems. When the school library portal is the information avenue of choice for the majority of users, we might be able to declare victory.

Working with the commercial world: Fair use versus copyright. There are a host of issues surrounding intellectual property as the school library collection becomes fluid rather than a collection of physical items. The current uproar in the music industry may result in partial solutions in the tug of war for compensation. Teacher-librarians will need to be fierce advocates of fair use as well as copyright as they purchase various information products for the digital library. No one model has emerged yet that satisfies both demands. It will.

Will books survive? The user will decide. They have already decided in favor of electronic periodicals over print. They will do the same with e-textbooks and other e-books. We need not make the decision for them.

Budgets and the concept of the information utility. Digital libraries cost more. Admit it. Defend it by showing the difference in learning in information-poor versus information-rich environments. We seem to be emerging into an information utility concept. There are costs associated with school buses, heat, lights, and now information. Don't pay the gasoline bill—cancel school. Don't pay the information utility bill—cancel school. Interestingly enough, my calculations show that the cost per child for e-texts and all digital library materials would actually be less per month than the cable or satellite television access bill in the home.

Staffing. Some of the components of the digital school library can be funded and shaped at district, regional, state, and federal levels or their counterparts in various countries of the world. We have some temptation to build one system and serve it out to everyone. While theoretically this could be done, there are a number of important reasons why this will be insufficient. After an extensive review of the research literature on information literacy, Loertscher and Woolls concluded that in the world as we know it, the human interface is a vital component of the information system (Loertscher & Woolls, 2002, p. 21).

Unless computer systems and delivery mechanisms become extremely intelligent, just linking young people in and turning it on will be insufficient. If and when that scenario happens, we will learn what is best. Meanwhile, this generation needs full-time professional, technical and paraprofessional assistance to transform the tools and technologies now known into learning.

CONCLUSION

Not all the features of the digital school library that have been discussed are available at this writing, but every month, new developments seem to enlarge the possibilities. A quick survey of students in any local school asking how many prefer Google or some other search engine to the library databases will give a sense of how urgent the creation of a viable digital library is. It's probably too late already for a segment of our user population. If such is the case in your school, bend over, and here is your *kick*.

P.S. Has there ever been such an exciting time in this field? I think not!

REFERENCES

Barr, D. (2002). The problem of recall in information rich environments: Notes from the field. In David Loertscher and B. Woolls (Eds.), *Information-rich environments: Blessing or curse: Papers of the Treasure Mountain Research Retreat No. 9, Brown County, Indiana, November, 2001* (pp. 21–26). Hi Willow Research and Publishing.

Loertscher, D. (2002). Building knowledge-rich environments for youth: A worldwide challenge for schools and school librarians. *Proceedings of the 2002 Conference of the International Association of School Librarianship*, Petaling Jaya, Malaysia, 4–9 Aug., 1994. Retrieved February 22, 2003, from **www.iasl-slo.org/conference2002-loertscher.html**

Loertscher, D., & Woolls, B. (2002). *Information literacy: A review of the research* (2nd ed.). San Jose, CA: Hi Willow Research and Publishing.

⑱

The Components of Successful Technologies

Steven M. Baule

Books will soon be obsolete in schools. . . . Our school
system will be completely changed in 10 years.

The opening quote sounds like something a modern-day futurist might posit. However, the quote refers not to computer technology but to educational film. The luminary who made the statement was none other than Thomas Edison (as quoted from the New York *Dramatic Mirror*, July 9, 1913; see Saettler, 1990, p. 98). What would it take to truly transform education with technology? Do transformational technologies even exist in education? From the 16th century, futurists have viewed technology as changing education. Of course, in the 16th century, the advent of the printing press was going to make knowledge accessible at everyone's fingertips. Teachers were no longer going to have to be the font of knowledge; rather, they would guide learners to the correct books. Where has that been heard recently?

Computer technologies and the Internet have changed nearly all aspects of society. We bank online and through computerized automatic teller machines. Optical scanning allows us to pass through tollbooths without slowing down to pay tolls. Our cell phones collect our e-mail and allow us to surf the Web while waiting in the parking lot for soccer practice to end. Nearly all universities offer some level of online coursework, and in some cases, one can now obtain a university degree without ever setting foot on campus.

So, why have the same strides not been made in K–12 education? Why have some schools not embraced technology? After all, banks do not seem to think that the ATM is simply a fad, and car dealers have not hesitated to establish web-based show rooms because Internet sales are a transient fad in their business. So why are some educators not embracing effective educational technology? Think of what technology could do for them if they only knew, which leads to the question, what should we be looking for in educational technology?

First published in *Teacher Librarian*, June 2007, Volume 34, Number 5

Early research into what constitutes effective computer technology often focused on three issues: accessibility, professional development, and reliability and support. The canons mentioned the need to provide teachers access to computers in each classroom or workspace. For the most part, that has been done in most schools, and most classrooms in the majority of schools have access to the Internet. Nearly all school libraries have Internet access as one of their primary access points to information. However, technology has not transformed teaching and learning—maybe it cannot. Computer advocates and critics have been arguing about the impact of technology on learning since the invention of the computer. So, what do we know that does allow technology to be both effective and transformational?

USER-FRIENDLY

Transparency, or ease of use, is clearly one of the key components to making technology successful within an educational setting; it may be the most important facet of effective technology. If the technology is not easy for the average teacher to use, it cannot make an impact. As I wander though exhibits at conferences and see various vendor presentations, I often ask or hear, "But will teachers really have time to load this or that data or make this or that connection?" One developer tells his staff, "If your mother cannot figure it out, forget it." As an example, look at Google and the original Dialog (**www.dialog.com**) service. Nearly anyone who can type can use Google to find information. However, Dialog required several steps and often reference to a manual for occasional users. Dialog had few personal home subscriptions. Lots of people are paying $240 or more a year for access to the Internet and, hence, Google. Computer technology has to be as simple as Edison's light bulb. (He did get some things right!) If it is more complicated than a light switch, it will not be as successful.

ENGAGING

Technology must be engaging. Any educational product that is going to be successful must be able to keep learners on task. Studies have shown that the longer the learner remains on task, the more likely he or she is to learn. Technology systems, such as text-based multi-user object-oriented environments and gopher servers, have not withstood the test of time because they were not engaging to the user. However, a fairly simply program such as Oregon Trail (Trinklein & Boettcher, 2003) continues on because students seem enthralled with it. I am unfamiliar with any research showing large test score gains for Oregon Trail users, but it is being used in classrooms around the country.

FILLS A NEED

The next component for technology success is that it must fill a need, curricular or administrative. Nearly every school district has an automated payroll system because the business office staff can be more productive and make fewer errors when using an automated system rather than writing checks by hand. In most cases, the technology tool replaces an existing product or service. A corollary is that it must make sense to replace the existing system with a technology tool. An example of this is the graphing calculator. Nearly every advanced math classroom in the country now includes graphing calculators because they can manage all of the basic operations that a student must complete; plus, they help students visualize advanced mathematical concepts.

FLEXIBLE

Flexibility is another component of successful technologies. Flexibility takes on a number of facets. The flexibility can evidence itself in synchronicity. An example is online courses that allow asynchronous participation. Blogs and wikis are flexible environments that allow for asynchronous collaboration. Wikipedia: The Free Encyclopedia allows an end user to contribute to the site directly, providing a sense of ownership. That was never possible for the masses with the *World Book Encyclopedia*. E-mail is probably my favorite asynchronous technology because I can get quick and sometimes immediate responses without having to play telephone tag. E-mail is so much more flexible than traditional postal mail and telephone service that it appears to be replacing both to some extent.

Flexibility can express itself in differentiation. When properly implemented, adaptive testing may be one of the truly best examples of successful technology. In an adaptive test, the computer will truly find out what level of skill or knowledge the student possesses. If the student gets a wrong answer, adaptive test software can present the next question to address the same learning goal but at a level of skill below the previous question. Other adaptive tests can base their discrimination on which of the distracters (i.e., wrong answers) was chosen. So, one can analyze why the student made the mistake and make the test more of a learning experience for both the student and the teacher. Nearly instant feedback is possible through a computerized test, feedback that would take much longer with paper-and-pencil tests.

At a simpler level, software can adjust its questions and pace to the individual student much easier than a classroom teacher can with 25 students. A student can also work at his or her own pace on a computer, whereas a traditional classroom teacher has to herd 25 learning styles into one uniform direction at a collective pace.

The programmed instruction movement of the late 1960s and early 1970s was a primitive precursor to the best of modern educational software programs. Novel/STARS (Student, Testing, Assessment, and Remediation System; **www.edoptions .com/novel/about.htm**) is an online service that allows students to move through high school courses at their own paces. This software can serve a school by providing a place for late-semester transfers to work on a single course instead of being dropped into a full course load 3 weeks before final exams. Students in need of remediation can work faster and catch up. The ability to catch up to grade-level peers is almost nonexistent in traditional programs, outside of summer school offerings.

Flexibility can also address multiple or nontraditional learning styles. For example, many at-risk learners are labeled as visual learners. A traditional front-of-the-room lecture often provides few visual stimuli for such students. Even simple PowerPoint presentations will often help these students take better notes and stay more engaged. Computer programs that allow students to visualize mathematical concepts, such as Geometer's SketchPad (**www.keypress.com/x5521.xml**) and Maple (**www.maplesoft.com**) are often cited as positive ways to improve math achievement. The student with an interpersonal learning style may do much better in a blog assignment than if asked to write a traditional term paper.

RESULTS ORIENTED

Technology has to be accountable and results oriented. Especially in today's environment of high-stakes testing, other No Child Left Behind measures, and looming financial crises, every dollar spent needs to be able to be supported. To spend money on technology items, the school or district must be able to articulate the positive results. These results must be measurable in a form that the wider public will acknowledge as being valuable. In today's world, that means student achievement scores as measured by tests and other quantitative measures and by reductions in student dropout rates, improved attendance rates, and improved graduation rates. However, the CEO Forum on Education and Technology (2001) articulated five ways in which to measure the results of technology: improved scores on standardized tests; increased application and production of knowledge for the real world; increased ability for students to manage learning; increased ability to promote achievement for special needs students; and improved access to information that increases knowledge, inquiry, and depth of investigation.

How do we measure results in a way that decision makers will value? That is a difficult question to answer. Even since the CEO Forum's report came out in 2001, the landscape has changed. All five measurement criteria are still valid, but some now hold less value in our test-laden world. The simple answer is through standardized achievement testing. Northwest Evaluation Association's Measures of Academic Progress (2004) is an excellent adaptive testing program that is aligned with many states' standards. Such data collection allows a teacher-librarian to work with a group of teachers on a project and then analyze the fruits of their labors by looking for student achievement gains among those involved in the project as opposed to those in classrooms that did not take part. Similarly, the performance of students who did take part in an online learning environment can be measured against those students who completed a traditional module of instruction. Such achievement measurements are strong measures for use in swaying decision makers.

There are other measurements that can be used as well, although potentially not as obvious. In a case where a school has a 1:1 laptop pilot program, attendance rates of those students can be compared to a similar group of students not involved in the pilot. If the laptop program increases the student attendance rate, then there is a positive step forward; in fact, dropout prevention funds might be available to support the project. In an elementary school, are students less likely to miss school on days when they have computer classes? That is another way to measure the impact of technology without having to give students an additional test.

ACTION RESEARCH

One of the most compelling ways to measure achievement is through local action research. If action research projects show a direct impact on achievement at the local school or district level, then that will be viewed as extremely compelling evidence. If a teacher-librarian and a group of teachers demonstrate the achievement impact of a given technology or school library project, then there will be support for that project. In today's educational milieu, dollars will follow projects that demonstrate achievement gains.

Another way to show results is by influencing special learner groups. Many learning style inventories exist that allow a student to determine his or her natural or preferred learning style. One example is the eMINTS learning style assessment site at **www.emints.org/ethemes/resources/S00000718.shtml**. Some also then provide students with tips on how to study to embrace the given style. This process of creating student self-awareness may also assist students in achievement. As a simple experiment, divide your students into two random groups, or collaborate with two classroom teachers. With one group, find a learning style inventory and administer it to each student, and then provide each student with suggestions on how to support his or her learning style. Throughout the next unit or grading period, ensure that students regularly reflect on and actively support their preferred learning styles. Give both groups the same unit test at the end of the period and see if the group that used the learning styles approach does better than the other group or better than expected based on past performance. Action research can be that simple. If the students who took the learning style inventory did better, it might make sense to expand the program and have all students take the inventory.

Similarly, you can make an online discussion group, a blog, or a wiki available to one section of high school literature students and ask them to use it to discuss the unit's reading assignments. With another section of the same class, continue to teach the course without the blogging requirement. At the end of the unit, compare the test results of those students who engaged in blogging and those who did not. If you have a solid and valid unit test, then those achievement results should hold nearly as much weight as standardized test results. If the blogging experiment is successful in improving growth, move to blogging for an entire semester and then measure the semester grades and, potentially, the state exam scores for each group. Post your action research results and share them with your colleagues.

Achievement as measured through real-world production work can be used where teachers have well-defined and agreed-on rubrics. However, within the standardized test climate in which we work, such efforts may not hold as much weight as they did a few years ago. The last item, providing improved access to information that increases student achievement, is difficult to define and provides too many possible variables for causation to be determined, unless the study is working within fairly narrow parameters.

In the end, technology must fill a need, whether academic or administrative. The technology must be easy to use; it must be engaging and flexible; and it must provide results. There is a myriad of further considerations to achieve technology success within a school or district. The systems must be reliable, and the school must provide for proper support and training. The district must also adequately fund the system. However, those are all aspects of the school or district and not the technology products themselves. Good luck and share your action research results widely.

REFERENCES

CEO Forum on Education and Technology. (2001, June). *Key building blocks for student achievement in the 21st century: Assessment, alignment, accountability, access, and analysis.* Retrieved January 15, 2007, from **www.ceoforum.org/ downloads/report4.pdf**

Northwest Evaluation Assocation. (2004). *Measures of Academic Progress (MAP).* Retrieved January 15, 2007, from **www.nwea.org/assessments/map.asp**

Saettler, P. (1990). *The evolution of American educational technology.* Englewood, CO: Libraries Unlimited. (Quoted from the New York *Dramatic Mirror*, July 9, 1913.)

Trinklein, M., & Boettcher, S. (2003). *The Oregon Trail.* Retrieved January 15, 2007, from **www.isu.edu/%7Etrinmich/Oregontrail.html**

⑲

The End of the Teacher-Librarian

James E. Herring

Teacher-librarians around the world face threats to their very existence because of the advance of technology in today's schools. It can be argued that the ubiquitous use of the internet in schools and homes, the development of school intranets, and the increase in use of instructional web sites in schools will make teachers and students retreat from the school library and into their classrooms. As a result, teachers will see themselves as being responsible for student information literacy, further undermining the role of the teacher-librarian. Such a doomsday scenario could cause school managers to take the view that the school library is an unaffordable luxury. While this threat may not be immediate, it is one the teacher-librarian should face and devise ways to counter.

By having a clear purpose for their school library and for their own role, the teacher-librarian can turn potential threats into opportunities. The teacher-librarian's purpose and role in the development of technology in the school must be clear. Otherwise, the "end" of the teacher-librarian (i.e., the demise of the profession) could occur, causing historians to view the teacher-librarian like the lamplighter or the farm servant who walked behind the horse that drew the plow.

INTRODUCTION

In 1983, James Thompson, a university teacher-librarian in the United Kingdom, wrote a book titled *The End of Libraries* in which he examined the potential impact of new technology on various kinds of libraries and the dual use of the word *end*. More than 20 years later, while the "end" (demise) of libraries is not in sight, considerable debate about the "end" (purpose) of libraries and teacher-librarians continues. I seek to challenge teacher-librarians to think ahead and to identify the threats to their own professional role and facility, and to turn these threats into opportunities.

THE INTERNET AS A THREAT

In schools throughout the world, students are being taught to use the Internet—mainly the World Wide Web—at an increasingly early age. When students are taught to use the Web in school as part of a gen-

First published in *Teacher Librarian*, October 2005, Volume 33, Number 1

eral information technology course separated from the main curriculum, they view the technology as no different than software programs such as Microsoft Word or Microsoft Excel. Information technology teachers, also known as technology specialists, focus on teaching students how to use the technology as opposed to how to use the information. The consequences of such instruction, well known to teacher-librarians, are students who

- rarely plan search strategies;
- become overwhelmed by the number of hits they find;
- focus on the first hit(s) they find;
- copy content mindlessly without questioning or analyzing it.

The dangers in this scenario are that students underestimate or ignore the need for information literacy skills and are unlikely to view the teacher-librarian as a possible source of help with their searching. Also, students view the Web as the total research process rather than as part of the research process. Other resources such as books, CD-ROMs, or even the school library's online journal subscriptions are ignored. Students operate on the premise that "everything is on the Web," a fallacy that is reinforced by television and web advertising. For example, broadband Internet subscription advertising emphasizes the educational nature of the Web and its potential for student education. If everything is on the Web and access is available from home or from any wireless classroom or computer lab in the school, then why visit the school library?

A further threat to teacher-librarians is the use of the Internet by teachers. For example, in the United Kingdom, the British Educational Communications and Technology Agency (BECTA, 2002) argues that teachers who exploit the Web for teaching

- "drew on the skills and qualities associated with good teaching in general, such as setting high expectations, intervening purposefully, involving all pupils, and creating a stimulating classroom climate;
- used ICT to genuinely enhance teaching and learning;
- used a range of ICT applications for teaching a range of topics;
- embedded ICT into the schemes of work, using and adapting national frameworks to suit individual needs;
- used ICT to manage teaching, learning, and assessment of the curriculum subject;
- built on and extended the whole-school approach to ICT;
- used ICT to create or adapt highly imaginative resources."

Thus, teachers' use of the Internet appears as a very useful development in education although separated from the teacher-librarian. What if, as many teachers undoubtedly do, teachers search for information from the classroom or from home? What if a teacher prepares for a lesson with a quick check on Google the day before the lesson takes place and then directs her students to the first two (in this case only slightly evaluated) web sites she finds? The point here is that if teachers use the Web on their own and do not recognize any weakness in this approach, why should they take the time to consult with the teacher-librarian?

THE INTERNET AS AN OPPORTUNITY

Of course, some students and some teachers will use the Web effectively; likely they have learned their skills from a variety of sources, including the teacher-librarian. Nonetheless, most teachers and students are not information literate. A schoolwide information literacy program is essential. Enlisting the school's senior management in such an initiative, however, is difficult and sometimes futile. Approaching information literacy at the micro level (i.e., with individual teachers or groups of teachers) is often a less threatening and more effective approach.

Several factors favor this approach. Teachers are under pressure to show that they are incorporating the Web into their teaching, but many teachers have limited training in how to do so. As a resource specialist, the teacher-librarian can identify web sites and web tools that fit a particular teacher's goals or curriculum. Providing students with teacher-selected web sites (a webliography or pathfinder on the school library's web page, for example) will not only focus student learning, but will also avoid the aimless use of search engines about which teachers constantly complain.

Before students use search engines they should be taught the requisite search skills, preferably in front of the subject teacher who will learn them at the same time. The roles or "ends" of the teacher-librarian in relation to the Internet can be seen as

- expert advisor on the use of search engines and subject gateways;
- information gatekeeper and web site mediator;
- information literacy leader and teacher of teachers;
- current-awareness provider on subject-related content in print and online;
- resource coordinator linking web content with print materials, CD-ROMs, and other online material.

By performing these roles in the school, the teacher-librarian ensures that both the library and the teacher-librarian are regarded as key elements in teaching and learning.

THE INTRANET AS A THREAT

Many schools are developing intranets that contain information for staff, students, and even parents. An intranet is accessed using a browser such as Internet Explorer. The main difference between using the intranet and the Internet in school is that a user will have to log on to the intranet via a user name and password. The key areas covered by school intranets are

- learning and teaching materials, such as lesson plans, instructional web sites, and resource guides;
- online access to the school library catalog;
- student information, such as timetables, school events, and school sports;
- staff information, such as timetables, school notices, curriculum syllabi, and school events;
- administrative information only for staff, such as student files, exam results, confidential school reports, and committee minutes.

The potential threat of the school intranet to the teacher-librarian is that school managers, teachers, and students will see the intranet as a "one-stop shop" for all school information. If the school library catalog, web sites, and other learning resources can be accessed through the intranet, what reason do students have to actually visit the school library? If individual teachers develop and post web pages for their classes on the intranet, will they also include links to library materials?

Finally, if the intranet is an outgrowth of the school's technology rather than the school's information system, will it be designed and developed by computer teachers? Will it be influenced by the school managers' emphasis on administrative rather than curricular information? With these questions in mind, one can see how the teacher-librarian could be overlooked as a key player in the development of an intranet.

THE INTRANET AS AN OPPORTUNITY

On the other hand, the development of a school intranet presents the teacher-librarian with a new opportunity to be a key curriculum player. Designing, building, and implementing the school's intranet should be a collaborative effort by school managers, teachers, and the teacher-librarian. As an information professional, the teacher-librarian can advise the team on how to organize the intranet's information structure.

Carter (2002) demonstrates that the teacher-librarian can take on new roles to influence the design and development of an intranet and to ensure that the emphasis remains on information and curriculum, rather than on technology and administrative information. And, as intranet mediator, the teacher-librarian can gather online and print materials to support intranet content on, for example, homework pages. Further, the library section of the intranet should include such resources as information literacy guidelines and tutorials to assist students and teachers with the elements of research. In short, Carter's research in Scottish schools emphasizes that teacher-librarians must take a proactive approach to involvement.

The key roles of the teacher-librarian in the development of a school intranet include

- intranet promoter who demonstrates the advantages of a school intranet;
- intranet team member who contributes to the design of the intranet and, particularly, its information structure;
- intranet content creator who provides links to a wide range of print and electronic resources to support parts of the intranet, such as subject area pages, instructional web sites, links to other schools, and careers information;
- intranet information literacy coordinator who ensures that intranet content for students is linked to information skills guidelines.

In undertaking such roles, the teacher-librarian can ensure that potential threats do not materialize and, rather, that the status of the teacher-librarian in the school is elevated because of these contributions to the intranet development.

INSTRUCTIONAL WEB SITES AS A THREAT

Instructional web sites are becoming increasingly common as students' experience with online learning expands. Many support face-to-face teaching and access to aspects of the curriculum, assessment guidelines, and links to resources. I define instructional web sites as those

- being designed by individuals or groups of school staff;
- relating to the curriculum;
- containing information for student learning;
- engaging students in critical thinking by posing questions;
- containing links to print and electronic resources for students use;
- encouraging students to use information skills;
- including the use of multimedia, such as graphics, photographs, sound, and video (Herring, 2003).

Most instructional web sites are designed by teachers who want to increase or support their students' interest in a curricular topic or subject. The potential threat is that students will assume that using an instructional web site means that they do not have to use the school library and there is no need to consult the teacher-librarian. Poorly designed instructional web pages that do not tie in to the resources of the school library can limit students' intellectual horizons and their learning.

INSTRUCTIONAL WEB SITES AS AN OPPORTUNITY

Well-designed instructional web sites are focused learning instruments. In the United Kingdom, teachers are under pressure to produce them as part of their teaching portfolio. In some schools there is competition among departments to see who can produce the web site with the most multimedia. The teacher-librarian has an opportunity in this instance to help teachers develop web sites that maximize both content and information literacy objectives.

I conducted a case study of a school (Herring, 2003) in which the collaboration between the teacher-librarian and the teachers began with a jointly designed instructional web site with one history teacher, and it resulted in a template for other teachers to use. I looked particularly at the collaborative work between the geography teacher and the teacher-librarian to create an Earth Forces web site. The site contains an outline of the curriculum relating to earthquakes and volcanoes; an outline of the assessment that students complete; links to useful resources, both online and in the school library; and information-skills advice about planning the assignment. The teacher asserts that this site leads to better student understanding, use of a wider range of resources by students, and an improvement in the quality of student work.

This case study identified a range of opportunities for teacher-librarians to exploit. First, the teacher-librarian can develop knowledge of software, such as Dreamweaver or Front Page, and become a source of advice and guidance to teachers. Second, the teacher-librarian can provide teachers with examples of instructional web sites from other schools using such resources as the Blue Web'n gateway. Third, the teacher-librarian can provide teachers with assignment-related links to both print and electronic resources and can ensure that any project outlines given to students make reference to these links. Fourth, the teacher-librarian can ensure that teachers either include information skills guidelines within the specific content area web pages or reference the school library information literacy pages.

Collaboration with teachers ensures that the teacher-librarian's roles or "ends" in relation to instructional web sites include

- instructional web site design tutor and advisor;
- instructional web site content creator and gatherer;
- instructional web site standards coordinator and quality-control evaluator, ensuring that all contain information skills guidelines.

By taking a proactive stance, the teacher-librarian secures a central role in this key area of development.

CONCLUSION

Threats to the role of the teacher-librarian are quite real. Unless the teacher-librarian acts to counteract these threats, both the teacher-librarian and the school library could be seen as peripheral to the school curriculum and considered an expensive luxury that the school cannot afford. Therefore, to remain a key player who is central to the school curriculum as information literacy and resources expert, the teacher-librarian cannot argue that the responsibilities of the current role do not allow time for new ones. Embracing, exploiting, and sharing new technologies is an effective way for the teacher-librarian to promote the position's vast contributions to the school, securing the teacher-librarian a place in the history of education that will be a long and positive one.

REFERENCES

Blue Web'n. Retrieved April 4, 2005, from **www.kn.pacbell.com/wired/bluewebn**

British Educational Communications and Technology Agency (BECTA). (2002). *Designing effective websites*. Retrieved April 4, 2004, from **www.becta.org.uk**

Carter, M. (2002). The connecting school and the intranet librarian. *School Libraries Worldwide, 8*(2), 51–64.

Dreamweaver. Macromedia, Inc. Retrieved April 4, 2004, from **www.macromedia.com/software/ dreamweaver**

FrontPage. Microsoft Corporation. Retrieved April 4, 2004, from **www.microsoft.com/frontpage/**

Herring, J. (2003). *The Internet and information skills: A guide for teachers and school librarians*. London: Facet Publishing.

Thompson, J. (1983). *The end of libraries*. London: Library Association Publishing.

㉒

Something Wiki This Way Comes . . . Are You Ready?

Joyce Valenza

Lately I've been wondering about wikis and their place in student research and their potential as vehicles for student writing. *Wiki* refers to the online collaboration model that allows a community of users to freely create, add, and edit web site content using their browsers. The word derives from the Hawaiian term *wiki wiki*, meaning "quick" or "super-fast." Several web sources note that *wiki* is also an acronym for "what I know is."

Wikipedia (**http://wikipedia.org**) has existed as a free community-based, online encyclopedia since 2001. Not only is it the most popular wiki around, but it is also the fastest growing encyclopedia on the Web, adding articles at a rate of about 3,000 a day. Appearing on the result lists of several major search engines, Wikipedia content is becoming more available to a worldwide audience. Other major projects include Wiktionary, an open-content dictionary, and Wikibooks, an open-content textbook and manual project.

Wikipedia is *not* a traditional encyclopedia. No well-known, reliable publisher solicits experts to write its articles. Maintained in true open-source spirit, Wikipedia is developed, written, and corrected by volunteer editors from around the world—editors who range in experience from casual visitors to hobbyists to scholars. For many of them, contribution is a way of life. They generously spend hours each day creating content and correcting commas. Yet no supervising editorial expert organizes or vets the content of this reference work. Pages change rapidly as volunteer editors negotiate and sometimes argue the content and its accuracy. Hence the accuracy of articles depends on the knowledge and conscientiousness of the particular community of authors who notice (or fail to notice) and correct mistaken entries, and also at what point in the process an entry is viewed. Although anyone can contribute to Wikipedia, the project sets rules for etiquette and dispute resolution, for avoiding bias, and for respecting copyright.

I love the collaborative nature of this and other wiki projects. I love that the project is multilingual. I find

First published on e-VOYA, www.voya.com, October 2005. *Teacher Librarian* acknowledges e-VOYA's permission to adapt and reprint this article.

the chaos and argument behind the editing scenes fascinating. I admire the new ways in which wikis allow communities, businesses, and organizations of all sorts to refine and share information resources. Students who choose to use Wikipedia's free content, however, have many choices. They have online access to excellent databases and traditional subscription encyclopedias—Grolier, Americana, and World Book—brands that we rely on for authority. Should those brands be overlooked? Where does Wikipedia fit in the student research toolkit?

Wikipedia creates interesting challenges for students and teachers. Its founder and director, Jimmy Wales, sees his project as "an excellent teaching opportunity." Wales believes that the site is an extraordinary resource for student use, "as long as they are educated in critical thinking to understand what an encyclopedia is or is not." He feels that "students should only use encyclopedias like Britannica or Wikipedia as a starting point for research—to gain background knowledge—but should turn to more direct sources after that."

I questioned Wales about the quality of Wikipedia's content. "I think that the average quality of entries in Wikipedia is equivalent in many areas to the average quality of entries in Britannica," he said, "but because we are young and because of our open editing process, any given entry might be incomplete or inaccurate at any point in time. Critical analysis is a must!" Wales suggests that students examine an article's edit history. "It's a radical kind of transparency that you don't find in other resources; you can see the discussions."

That's a bit of a problem. Can students really get enough information from an edit history to determine the level of contribution for each collaborator? A large number of contributors prefer to remain anonymous, listed only by IP address, a casual screen name, or links to irrelevant personal information. Evaluating an entry's edit history is a challenge for most adults. It seems a nearly impossible task for the average ninth grader.

"Should a person who is doing research have to look at a long edit list to determine reliability?" asks Tom Paneles, Director of Corporate Communications at Britannica, who expressed serious concerns regarding the value of the open source model in online reference. "Application software is different from knowledge and information. If an application doesn't work, you *must* look for the source of the bad code. Information, on the other hand, can be wrong, and it might sit in an article forever. Having a lot of people who don't know what they are doing edit an encyclopedia is not all that helpful. And is a reference work that simply spreads without limits necessarily good?"

Wales counters, "Encyclopedia articles are essentially a blend of collected knowledge and that is an area in which Wikipedia shines." He also proudly points to the project's multilingual capacity and its extensive network of hyperlinks. He notes the copyright-friendliness of the project. Teachers are free to take articles from Wikipedia and adapt them to meet the needs of their classroom environment. "Everything that we do is placed under a free license," said Wales. Most importantly, "People find Wikipedia useful. In fact, in some areas, the only encyclopedia material that exists is in Wikipedia."

Wikipedia *is* timely; I look to it for Internet- and technology-related articles as well as material relating to popular culture and current events. For some topics, it is indeed the only place where information is seriously being gathered. For more stable areas of knowledge, I generally follow my Wikipedia searches with surveys of reference, journal, and newspaper databases.

Wikipedia does a fine job describing the programming language that I studied in a graduate course last semester, an area about which my subscription encyclopedias were utterly unaware. Although I wouldn't necessarily cite them in my research, I also have examined the particularly up-to-date article on Marburg virus, with its handy links to World Health Organization (WHO) data, as well as the especially comprehensive coverage of the July 7 London bombings, complete with multiple graphics, profiles of the bombers, and a wealth of relevant links. Wikipedia also offers comprehensive information for anyone researching the Twinkie or the phenomena of McMansions.

On the other hand, although the article on Shakespeare appears to be lengthy and impressive, its contributors and sources are not the Shakespearean scholars whom teachers expect students to read. Among many unidentified others, the Singing Badger is a frequent editor, who humbly describes himself as "wise and all knowing" and is renowned for his karaoke rendition of "Don't Go Breaking My Heart." By contrast, Grolier Online's Americana article on Shakespeare is signed by Hallett Smith, a noted scholar of Elizabethan studies who is author and editor of several books on Shakespeare, and it includes a long list of similarly traditional sources. World Book Online's article on Shakespeare is not only authoritative—signed by Frank W. Wadsworth, Professor Emeritus, State University of New York, Purchase—it is also rich in engaging media, impressively organized, and written appropriately for its younger audience.

Bottom line? In my own slightly stodgy wiki prayer, regular and substantial Wikipedia contributors would be listed in edit histories with their real names and credentials, and perhaps a note regarding their potential for bias. It is not likely to happen. It is a fact that Wikipedia is an incredibly popular free source of Web reference, bringing into the classroom wonderful opportunities for discussions involving teachers and librarians and students. Information formats are evolving. In the face of information glut, we are faced with new decisions about the very nature of knowledge and authority. When does it make sense to use Wikipedia, other wiki projects, and blogs as information sources? When might it be best to use other sources? What do your teachers expect in terms of authority in a bibliography? How do the edit histories reflect the quality of the articles?

STUDENT WIKIS?

What about using the wiki model for student projects? Wikis are perhaps best used as a tool for writing, especially when the project involves collaborative authoring. Their major advantage over the paper notebook—or even the blog—is that wikis prepare students to write collaboratively in an authentic networked environment. No one student hogs the disk for the master draft. Everyone gets to contribute and edit. Teachers can easily pop in to comment or to monitor progress and see the various contributions. Wikis allow students to present their work in an authentic way which is increasingly used by business and academia.

Wikis can be used to draft a collaborative document such as a simulated peace treaty or proposed legislation. Students might create an improved and hyperlinked chapter for an American history textbook. They might compile vocabulary words into a wikidictionary or collect general classroom knowledge in a wikitextbook. Wikis are good vehicles for classes engaged in peer-reviewed projects; they function as archived portfolios for classes serious about the writing *process*.

Wikis need not be limited to the enrollment of one class. They can be collaboratively built by classes across the country or the world, or they can be cross-age collaborations across a school district.

Beyond student projects, wikis in schools can support meeting or inservice planning. Professionals can use them for contributing agenda items and linked resources before an event, as notetaking devices during a meeting, and as continuous planning tools following a meeting.

Wiki use has some downsides. Wikis are by nature a bit chaotic and are vulnerable to hacking. They might inspire editing quarrels as groups negotiate content. Yet most wiki users note that the group itself works effectively to keep the content stable.

Democracy is lovely. So is scholarship. Wikis are wonderful tools. They have their place in student research alongside quality online reference products. Students need to know how and when to use and create both. Librarians also must fund and guide students to high-quality online reference sources that offer easy-to-discern authority—and we must make them as easy to get to as a wiki! And finally, we must open new discussions with students and teachers about the nature and authority of knowledge to help students judge when to wiki and when not to wiki.

WIKIS IN EDUCATION—RESOURCES
Projects
Wikipedia (**http://wikipedia.org**).
Wiktionary (**http://en.wiktionary.org**).
Wikibooks (**http://en.wikibooks.org/wiki/Main_Page**). An open-content textbook and manual project.

Wiki Software
Seed Wiki (**www.seedwiki.com**).
List of Wiki Software (**http://en.Wikipedia.org/wiki/List_of_ wiki_software**).

About Wikis in Education
Dodge, Bernie. (2004). *Blogs and wikis as WebQuest tasks*. The WebQuest Page, San Diego State University, June 25. **http://webquest.sdsu.edu/necc2004/blogs-and-wikis.htm**
Lamb, Brian. (2004). *What's a wiki? Tap into the quickest, easiest way to publish on the Web*. e-Strategy Update, The University of British Columbia, January 21. **www.e-strategy.ubc.ca/news/update 0401/040121-wiki.html**
Lamb, Brian. (2004). *Wide open spaces: Wikis, ready or not. Educause Review*, September/October. **www.educause.edu/ir/library/pdf/erm0452.pdf**
My brilliant failure: Wikis in the classroom (A constructivist teacher's cautionary tale). Heather's Blog, Kairosnews, May 21, 2004. **http://kairosnews.org/node/3794**

InfoTech: An Info-Skills Workout: Wikis and Collaborative Writing

Annette Lamb and Larry Johnson

Teacher-librarians are always on the lookout for ways to introduce and reinforce student information skills. Whether evaluating the accuracy of information found at Wikipedia: The Free Encyclopedia, expanding an existing wiki project, or creating original content for a new wiki, collaborative writing projects allow young people the opportunity to exercise their minds and apply essential information skills to authentic activities. To become information fluent, students must be able to use their skills in a variety of situations across disciplines to solve problems and make decisions. Creating and using wikis are a great information skills workout.

WIKI BASICS

Wikis are collaboratively created web sites. They involve young authors in selecting, evaluating, revising, editing, and publishing information and ideas. A wiki uses web-based open-editing tools to provide an easy way for multiple participants to enter, submit, manage, and update web pages. Wiki-based systems are popular because they are simple to install and contributors do not need special software. The word *wiki* comes from the Hawaiian word for "quick" or "fast," meaning that a collaborative team can quickly construct a web site.

Emphasis is placed on authoring content rather than simply viewing existing information. Wiki environments may be text based or can incorporate graphics, audio, video, and animation. Users make changes by selecting from options and filling in forms on a web page. Authorized users can add and delete links, pages, and content. In some cases, a moderator approves changes before they are posted. Most wikis also provide a way to track changes and view earlier versions of pages.

WIKI CHARACTERISTICS

Wikis are a specific type of social technology involving cooperation, interdependence, and synergy. For

First published in *Teacher Librarian*, June 2007, Volume 34, Number 5

instance, individuals, classes, and clubs at different points along an earthquake fault might analyze ground movement and share their findings on a wiki. Or a local historical society might collaborate with the teacher-librarian and high school students to create a city history wiki. They might also invite people who have lived in the area to share their insights and experiences. The resulting wiki contains multiple perspectives likely missed by a single author.

According to Brian Lamb (2004), wikis have five characteristics that separate them from other social or collaborative technologies:

1. *Unique.* Wikis provide an opportunity to share original content in nitch areas that might not be found elsewhere. Rather than duplicate web content, wikis can link to existing information beyond the scope of the project.

2. *Collaborative.* Wikis are designed to be free, open spaces for sharing. Rather than focus on a single author's contribution, wikis concentrate on the synergy that comes from multiple contributers creating a project as a virtual team.

3. *Open editing.* Anyone can add anything to a wiki at anytime. Although many K–12 wiki projects require registration or guest access for outsiders, most allow anyone to join in the fun.

4. *Simple coding.* Even young children can learn to create and edit pages using the web-based forms. In most cases, the tools are similar to a word processor.

5. *Evolving.* Wikis are in a constant state of change. Teacher-librarians can consider ways that young people can build on the work of other students or other classes.

UNDERSTANDING WIKIS

Before jumping into the creation of wikis, students need to understand how they work. Begin by having them explore existing wiki resources. Discuss how these resources are built and the purposes they serve.

Audience. Some wikis are designed for a particular audience, such as an age group, organization, or profession. The Library Success or Teacher Librarian wiki are designed for librarians to share their resources and experiences. The Social Justice Movement wiki was originally created by college students but is now open to the public. Internet Public Library's (IPL's) Teen Poetry Wiki is designed for teens wishing to read and share poetry. This is a wiki that your students may wish to expand.

General. Spend some time exploring Wikipedia. Do a search for your town. Ask students to look for accurate and inaccurate information. Notice that some of the information contains references. The population information may come from the census bureau. Rather than cite Wikipedia as a source, go directly to the primary source and fact-check the information. If you are looking for additional information, use the external links at the bottom of the wiki page. Find a sentence that can be enhanced or expanded. Or look for a piece of information that needs a reference. Demonstrate how the wiki can be edited. Also show the history of the page to see the changes that have been made over time. When citing a Wikipedia page, use the permanent link. For example, a project on Pluto done in the spring of 2006 would be different from one done in the fall of 2007.

Topical. Many individuals and groups have created wikis focusing on particular topics. More Perfect is a wiki focusing on politics and policy. You will find wikis about authors, books, series, and genres that are sponsored by publishers, authors, or fans. For example, Redwall and A Wiki of Unfortunate Events are both based on book series. Check out Wikia for examples of these subject-specific wikis.

WIKIS AND COLLABORATIVE WRITING

Although most educators have used collaborative writing activities in their classroom, these assignments are often more cooperative than collaborative. In other words, teams may work on different aspects of a topic and bring them together to create the final project. Wikis provide an opportunity to synthesize ideas and create a collaborative project that is broader, deeper, and more interconnected than that created in a traditional writing environment.

Wiki setup. Services such as wikispaces are popular with educators because they allow users to set up and build a wiki instantly. Some schools prefer to store wikis on their own web server. Tools such as phpWiki, pmWiki, and TikiWiki are distributed under a general public license.

Wiki basics. Ask each child to create a pseudonym that he or she can use in the project. You may wish to use a generic log-in with younger children. As students gain experiences, allow each student to create a personal username and password. Keep a list of usernames and passwords in case students lose their information. Talk to students about creating and editing pages, linking to pages, and incorporating graphics. Begin with a small project. For instance, small groups can work together to start a page about a book, author, character, or genre. Then, classmates can add their ideas to expand the pages.

Content. Think about designing a project that requires students to generate original works, such as poetry, interviews, and science experiment results. There are many web sites that contain information about the solar system, biomes, and countries of the world. How will your project contribute in some unique way to the body of information already on the Internet? Consider some sample ideas about what wikis can revolve around:

• books, such as analysis and literature circles;
• local and state interests, such as historical buildings, locations, events, noteworthy persons, oral histories, art, and music;
• creative works, such as choose-your-own adventures, invented world, poetry, short stories, artwork, and step-by-step instructions;
• comparisons, such as then-and-now, what-if's, parallel timelines (local, national, and global), pros and cons, issues and perspectives, company profiles; and
•evaluations, such as critical reviews, analysis of a company.

Wikis allow students to incorporate text, graphics, audio, and video. Before posting content, check to be sure that you have permission to use material. Generally, people place their content in wikis under the Creative Commons rule known as "share and share alike." In other words, you can use and link to information found on other wikis as long as it is cited.

Links. Linking is an important aspect of wikis. Students may link within the page. For example, they may create a list of ideas at the top of the page and link to a detailed description further down the page. They may also create links to other pages within the wiki. For instance, if they are creating a wiki based on the book *Crossing the Wire*, by Will Hobbs (2006), they might develop pages on each chapter, character (e.g., Victor, Rico, Julio, Miguel), setting (e.g., Mexico, the border, Arizona), and topic (e.g., smuggling, border patrol, illegal immigration). These pages can then be linked together. Finally, create links to outside resources such as the author's web site and resources related to immigration.

Discussion and editing. One feature that makes wikis so wonderful for collaborative writing is their editing options. Talk to children about the difference between enhancing an article and damaging the work of a peer. Most wikis provide a discussion area where writers can share their ideas for enhancing the page and give an explanation of their reasoning behind additions and changes. This provides a wonderful forum for discussion, as well as a way to track student involvement.

Demonstrate ways that changing the content can make the article better. Discuss the roles and responsibilities of each author. For example, each page may have a main author, contributing authors, and editors. Keep in mind that most wikis do not contain a spell checker, so editing skills are important.

History. One of the strengths of the wiki environment is the history aspect. Students and teachers are able to trace the progress of the project and determine the contribution of each participant. It is also easy to revert back to an earlier version if problems are discovered.

Citations. The power of a wiki is the ability to bring information and ideas together. However, it is important that learners understand how to cite the primary sources that they use in building their wiki. If a student provides a statistic on illegal immigration, he or she should cite the original source, such as the U.S. Citizenship and Immigration Services, and provide a link to the complete set of information.

Wikis provide students an authentic experience applying their information skills. For instance, fact checking is a critical component of wiki development and use. Wiki creators learn to cite their work and provide supporting evidence for their statements, whereas wiki users get practice checking the accuracy of information found in sources such as Wikipedia.

WIKI IN LEARNING

Wikis are useful across grade levels and subject areas. To be effective, young people need to understand the fluid nature of this collaborative format. Consider projects that get students involved in ongoing wiki experiences.

Some possibilities include the following.

Collaborative problem solving. Wikis provide an environment for groups to share their understandings and come to consensus. The wiki can be used to generate lists, narrow topics, outline options, debate issues, make suggestions, and even vote.

Collaborative research. Whether working simultaneously on a project or over multiple semesters, researchers can collate and share their data using a wiki.

Collaborative writing. Wikis are often used for collaborative authorship. In other words, a group of people get together with a final product in mind, such as writing an article or letter; editing a book, guide, manual, glossary; or creating a knowledge base.

Dynamic journal or notebook. Wiki software can be used to organize notes, ideas, and brainstorms. It is a great tool for a book club or study group to organize information. Although generally thought of as a collaborative tool, single-user wikis are a way to collect, organize, and reflect on one person's ideas. The activity is focused on recording ideas and process rather than coming up with a final product.

Electronic portfolio. Some wikis are used for collecting and organizing resources for an electronic portfolio. A wiki is an effective tool for this activity because it allows a learner to constantly select and update materials.

Portal. A portal is designed to be the starting point for a particular topic or subject. Wikipedia refers to main pages on topics or areas. Originally, portals led people to other resources, but they are increasingly being designed as wikis to help people see the big picture of a topic and how it connects to related fields such as arts, biography, geography, history, mathematics, science, society, and technology.

Resource aggregator. Like a bibliography, mediagraphy, or pathfinder, a wiki can be used to organize links to web sites, blogs, and other electronic materials.

Study guide. A wiki is a great tool for creating a collaborative study guide.

Virtual conference. Rather than meet face to face, users can utilize wikis to share resources as part of a virtual conference activity. Because most wikis allow uploading of files, these conference wikis can hold documents, visuals, and audio and video materials.

WIKI USE POLICIES

Examine your school and library collection development and technology use policies as they apply to the wiki environment. Does your acceptable use policy talk about using the discussion option during peer editing in a wiki environment? Does your policy define plagiarism? Are issues such as the use of names and personal photos discussed?

When building wikis, add a short statement and link to your school's policy on your wiki page. Or get students involved in interpreting the policy. They can create their own wiki warranty for their page.

PUT IT ALL TOGETHER

Nancy Bosch, the gifted facilitator at the Nieman Enhanced Learning Center (**http://connections.smsd.org/nieman/el/**), in Shawnee Mission, KS, recently completed her first wiki assignment with students. Her sixth graders were overjoyed to hear that instead of writing an essay, they would be creating a wiki based on the book *The Wright 3*, by Blue Balliett (2006). After setting up the space for her students at Wikispaces, her students jumped into the project, creating chapter summaries, character pages, and topical resources. They also created cross-references within their wiki and linked to outside resources. Their comments told the whole story:

"Boy, I'm glad we didn't have to write!"

"It is so cool to know that somebody might use what I wrote for their research!!"

"I write a lot more carefully knowing the 'world' can read it."

"I liked the fact that we could work together, help each other out, and link to stuff someone else wrote."

"It is so cool to put something ON the Internet, rather than always taking stuff OFF."

REFERENCES

Balliett, B. (2006). *The Wright 3*. New York: Scholastic.

Hobbs, W. (2006). *Crossing the wire*. New York: HarperCollins.

Lamb, B. (2004, September/October). Wide open spaces: Wikis, ready or not. *Educause Review, 39*(5), 36–48.

RESOURCES IN THE COLUMN

IPL's Teen Poetry Wiki: **www4.ipl .org:8080/index.php/Main_Page**

Library Success: A Best Practices Wiki: **www.libsuccess.org/**

More Perfect: **www.moreperfect.org/**

Redwall: **http://redwall.wikia.com/wiki/ Main_Page**

Social Justice: **http://socialjustice.ccnmtl.columbia.edu/index.php/Main_Page**

Teacher Librarian Wiki: **http://teacherlibrarianwiki.pbwiki.com/**

A Wiki of Unforunate Events: **http://snicket.wikia.com/wiki/Main_Page**

Wikia: **www.wikia.com/wiki/Wikicities**

Wikipedia: The Free Encyclopedia: **www.wikipedia.org/**

The Wright 3: **http://thewright3.wiki spaces.com**

Copyright Information

Creative Commons: **http://creativecommons.org/**

Wiki Policies and Safety
Twiki Issues: Keys to a Safe and Positive Wiki: **www.teachersfirst.com/content/wiki/issues.cfm**

Wiki Services
JotSpot: **www.jot.com/**
pbWiki (ads): **http://pbwiki.com/**
Wikispaces (free, no ad spaces for teachers): **www.wikispaces.com/site/for/teachers100K.com/**

Wiki Software
phpWiki: **http://phpwiki.sourceforge.net/**
pmWiki: **www.pmwiki.org/**
TikiWiki: **http://tikiwiki.org/**

㉒

Literacy Links:
Wikis and Student Writing

Keith McPherson

This month's column explores wikis and the possible contributions that they offer teacher-librarians in developing student writing.

THE DEMISE OF THE WRITTEN WORD?

One of the greatest fears that I have about encouraging students to compose in online contexts such as blogs and wikis is that I may well be contributing to the demise of the written word. A quick Google search for and perusal of current Internet student blogs and wikis reveals that modern wiki English contains a great deal more slang and graphics, and a great deal fewer prepositions and capitalizations, than I recall being taught and remember teaching. As a teacher-librarian, I cannot help but ask myself, is this the type of writing that I value and want to promote in my students?

Current articles and research (Allison, 2005; Grant, 2006; Richardson, 2006) exploring the educational use of wikis in the classroom and school library have uncovered many positive possibilities for developing students' writing skills. The first is that wikis provide students with a variety of authentic audiences, ranging from students themselves to anyone in the world with Internet access. Knowing that real people will be reading and possibly responding to their writing is often the impetus to motivate students to write with much more enthusiasm than they would when composing traditional research essays, in which the classroom teacher or teacher-librarian is the only audience.

Another manner in which wikis can positively enhance a student's writing experience and open possibilities for developing writing skills is by providing collaborative writing contexts. By design, wikis allow groups of authors to upload written work—including multimedia—to the Internet and to edit their own and other members' contributions. Such authoring groups typically range from pairs of students to whole classes, but they may also include contributions from anyone on the Internet (such as in the public areas of Wikipedia: The Free Encyclopedia). The size of the authoring group is decided by the teacher-

First published in *Teacher Librarian*, December 2006, Volume 34, Number 2

librarian or classroom teacher, and it includes input from students. These groups then participate in the collaborative and recursive process of adding, deleting, changing, and shaping the group's wiki writing. Examples of wiki writing projects include group poetry, wiki journals, class wikipedias, reader response, and current event discussions.

WRITING AS A SOCIAL PROCESS

When teacher-librarians encourage students to write using wikis, they also encourage students to view and experience writing as a social process (Richardson, 2006). Unlike much of the individualized writing required in school and the real world, writing entries in a wiki demands that students be taught writing skills that emphasize negotiation, cooperation, collaboration, and respect for one another's work and thoughts. Allison (2005) found not only that his secondary students learned advanced collaborative social skills when using a wiki but also that several students learned effective writing strategies and grammar from other students. The result was that his students developed deep understandings and strong social bonds among and between themselves.

Wikis also afford students the opportunity to write using nonlinear text structures. For example, students can use hyperlinks in their wiki writing to create new associations, links, comparisons, and connections within and between their own or other authors' print text or multimedia texts, anywhere on the Internet (Ferris, 2002). Anytime that one clicks on a link in the middle of an online document and is whisked away to new information, that individual has experienced this textual phenomenon (for an example of hypertext writing, visit the Internet Shakespeare site, **http://ise.uvic.ca/index.html**). Such hyperlinking affords the relatively easy creation of connected meaning making previously unknown to student writers and, more important, increases the opportunity for nonlinear thinkers to express themselves using written text.

Another reason that teacher-librarians may choose to use wikis to promote student writing is that they afford students opportunities to express themselves using multiple modalities (Ali Mejias, 2005; Jewitt, 2005; Kress, 2003). For example, students can use wikis to insert music, graphics, video, and photos in their writing and to communicate meanings that were once inaccessible or not fully expressed through the printed word. By encouraging such multimodal compositions, teacher-librarians free those students who struggle to express themselves with written words; as well, they encourage all students to write using a variety of multimodal communicative technologies (visit **www.poemsthatgo .com** for some compelling and spectacular examples of writing that demonstrates multimodal communication).

DRAWBACKS

One of the drawbacks of using online contexts such as wikis to promote student writing is that they may exacerbate students' reading and writing difficulties (RAND Reading Study Group, 2002). Lee (2006) suggested that, in general, online text lacks "recognizable text structures that facilitates the reader's ability to construct meaning found in traditional printed text formats" (p. 10). Thus, wikis that include writing that lacks such text-structure signals will pose additional challenges that greatly reduce a reader's chances of comprehension and learning (Coiro, 2003; Lee, 2006; Literacy Matters, 2006). Literacy teachers and teacher-librarians need to help students realize that wikis can be used to create a variety of writing genres beyond less formal writing; then, they can teach students when and how wikis can be used to compose more formal written works (like the additions to Wikipedia or for their own class-created online encyclopedia). Additionally, Lee (2006) cited Berkowitz (1986) and Taylor (1982) as evidence that teachers and teacher-librarians need to teach students to read and write text structures in the context of online environments such as wikis to "improve students comprehension and memory of text" (p. 11).

A second significant drawback with using wikis to promote and develop writing is that students may be unfamiliar and uncomfortable with collaborative writing. Grant (2006) implemented a 3-week wiki writing segment in her class of 13- to 15-year-olds and found that her students had great difficulties writing in a public space and altering other student's wiki work, because "the social and cultural practices of collaborative working that need to accompany the use of the [wiki] software in order to take advantage of the functional affordances of the tool were not in the students' repertoire of shared practices" (p. 4).

Teacher-librarians must realize that wiki writing requires students to be familiar with how to access and use the wiki, and it requires that they understand, respect, and follow the rules for such a collaborative writing project. The following are some of the issues and questions that teacher-librarians must openly raise and discuss with the students—or have students discuss as a group—to develop clear behavioral statements and student understandings when initiating wiki writing in the classroom:

When and how can we change other people's text (e.g., spelling errors)?
Where and when is written graffiti acceptable? Can graft writers be tracked?
What are appropriate and inappropriate online behaviors?
What is considered appropriate and inappropriate writing?
What are the differences between constructive and destructive feedback, and what are some of the methods for maximizing the former?
How can deleted or modified writing be recovered?
How can hyperlinks and multimedia be used to create dynamic writing?
What technologies and tools can students use online and offline to improve collaborative work?
How can students best solve disputes?
What levels of participation are required and will be assessed (see group participation assessment sheet at **www.readwritethink.org/lesson_images/lesson896/GroupParticipationChart.pdf**)?

Although I am a great believer in as few classroom rules as possible, having these collaborative understandings and rules developed and posted by the group before commencing a wiki will make your students' wiki writing a more positive experience.

DEVELOPING STUDENT-CREATED WIKIS

When attempting to develop student-created wikis as a method to forge literacy links between the school library and classroom, I recommend that you start with easy-to-manage wiki projects. For example, a possible wiki writing/research project for primary-aged children is to create an animal alphabet wiki. Individuals, pairs, or groups of primary students can (a) choose an animal that they wish to add to the class animal alphabet wiki book, then (b) select a picture of their animal from the Internet, and then (c) insert it and the first letter of their animal into their wiki. Depending on the computing skills and writing abilities of you and your students, older students can include information on their animal, such as its full name, habitat, food requirements, size, length, height, how it sounds, art work, clip art, and the like. Young students may require that the teacher or teacher-librarian post their animal information on the class wiki.

Intermediate students can use a wiki to create a story with multiple beginnings and endings (see **www.kidsonthenet.org.uk/porchester/island/index.htm**). Intermediate students can also develop their online and offline map-reading and writing skills by collaboratively adding descriptive text to an online map, such as WikiMapia (**www.wikimapia.org**). Secondary students can use a wiki to create hyperlinks from an existing poem to pages containing their own responses and understandings (see **http://cte.jhu.edu/tech academy/web/2000/baczkowski/hyper.htm**), or they can create their own pair, small group, or class wiki poem.

LITERACY TECHNOLOGY THAT MAKES EFFECTIVE WRITERS

Wikis offer teacher-librarians and students new, dynamic, collaborative, and recursive writing spaces. Teacher-librarians can use these spaces to strengthen social ties among students, as well as to teach students that wikis can go well beyond informal MSN-type writing. By integrating this new writing context into the school library curriculum, we validate the use of wikis in our students' lives, open up opportunities to help students become motivated and powerful writers, encourage students to express themselves using a multitude of communication formats, and expose them to the social dynamics of collaborative writing. Far from being the demise of the written word, which I suggest at the start of this article, wikis may very well be the literacy technology that helps many of our current students learn to be effective writers.

REFERENCES

Ali Mejias, U. (2005). *Social literacies: Some observations about writing and wikis.* Retrieved August 9, 2006, from **http://ideant.typepad.com/ideant/2005/03/social_literaci.html**

Allison, P. (2005). *High school students (and teachers) write collaboratively on a wiki.* Retrieved August 8, 2006, from **www.nycwp.org/paulallison/2005/12/04#a149**

Berkowitz, S. J. (1986). Effects of instruction in text organization on sixth graders' memory for expository reading. *Reading Research Quarterly, 20*(2), 161–178.

Coiro, J. (2003). Reading comprehension on the Internet: Expanding our understanding of reading comprehension to encompass new literacies. *Reading Teacher, 56*(5), 458–464.

Ferris, S. P. (2002). Writing electronically: The effects of computers on traditional writing. *The Journal of Electronic Publishing, 8*(1), n. p.

Grant, L. (2006). *Using wikis in school: A case study.* Retrieved August 3, 2006, from **www.futurelab.org.uk/research/discuss/05discuss01.htm**

Jewitt, C. (2005). Multimodality, "reading," and "writing" for the 21st century. *Discourse: Studies in the Cultural Politics of Education, 26*(3), 315–331.

Kress, G. R. (2003). *Literacy in the new media age.* London: Routledge.

Lee, E. (2006). *New libraries and new literacies for the information generation: Online reading comprehension.* Retrieved August 5, 2006, from **www.lerc.educ.ubc.ca/LERC/outreach/iasl2006/Port06.ppt**

Literacy Matters. (2006). *Text structure.* Retrieved August 7, 2006, from **www.literacy matters.org/content/text/intro.htm**

RAND Reading Study Group. (2002). *Reading for understanding: Toward a R & D program in reading comprehension.* Retrieved June 21, 2006, from **www.rand.org/multi/achievementforall/reading/readreport.html**

Richardson, W. (2006). *Blogs, wikis, Podcasts, and other powerful web tools for classrooms.* Thousand Oaks, CA: Corwin Press.

Taylor, B. M. (1982). Text structure and children's comprehension and memory for expository material. *Journal of Educational Psychology, 74*(3), 323–340.

㉓

Literacy Links:
Wikis and Literacy Development

Keith McPherson

I recently visited a colleague's school library and observed several groups of grade 5 students busily scanning and taking notes from different volumes of print encyclopedias. The teacher-librarian and I struck up a conversation about the students' projects, and I inquired if they would be gathering information from online sources such as Wikipedia: The Free Encyclopedia. Without hesitation, she answered no, explaining that she thought that Wikipedia was too difficult for many of her readers, that some of the information in it was questionable, and that the students did not have access to enough computers that were connected to the Internet. This and the next Literacy Links column reviews my concerns and explores the question, Can wikis be valuable resources for developing strong literacy links between the school library and the classroom?

For those who are new to the term, a *wiki* is a collaborative web space housing a collection of works (textual and multimedia) created and edited by many authors. What makes a wiki unique is that it runs software that permits visitors to add new information and, more important, edit previous authors' submissions. In contrast, a *blog* typically allows visitors to post responses to previous authors' submissions—that is, visitors cannot go back and edit earlier blog submissions. In short, wikis are composed of recursive or editable web pages whereas blogs are composed of salient or uneditable web pages. See Davis (2006) and Dodge (2004) for more information on the differences between blogs and wikis.

TYPES OF WIKIS

There are two major types of wikis of interest to educators: those created in the classroom by teachers and students, which I call *classroom-based wikis*, and those not created by students and teachers, which I call *public wikis*. The best way to become familiar with these two types of wikis is to visit examples of both.

Examples of classroom-based wikis include

First published in *Teacher Librarian*, October 2006, Volume 34, Number 1

• Our Book Wiki—Brandon Middle School, Virginia Beach, VA, book review wiki, **http://books. editme.com/**

• High School Online Collaborative Writing Project—middle school and secondary school online wiki writing project, **http:/schools.wikia.com/wiki/ Main_Page**

• NeighborhoodWiki!—Elementary students' encyclopedia, **www.theneighborhoodschool.org/ wiki/index.php?title=Main_Page**

• Bud the Teacher wiki—student- and teacher-created materials, **www.budtheteacher.com/wiki/index .php?title=Main_Page**

• Best Practices in Mathematics Education—Math teachers' knowledge base, **http://bprime .xwiki.com/xwiki/bin/view/Main/Webhome**

Examples of public wikis:
• Wikipedia—online encyclopedia, **http://en.wikipedia.org/wiki/Main_Page**
• Wikijunior—online information books for children, **http://en.wikibooks.org/wiki/Wikijunior**
• Wiktionary—online editable dictionary, **http://en.wiktionary.org/wiki/Main_Page**
• Canadianwiki—online encyclopedia, **http://canadawiki.org/index.php**

Although there is growing diversity in the types and formats of online public wikis (Richardson, 2006), the most popular wikis with teachers and teacher-librarians seem to be those that resemble online encyclopedias. Wikipedia is an example of this type of wiki. The value of using public wikis to forge literacy links between the school library and the classroom is largely determined by four factors: the wiki's readability, the school's accessibility to the Internet, the objectives of the teacher-librarian and classroom teacher, and the students' ability to evaluate the authenticity and credibility of wiki information.

READING LEVELS

Most public wikis are aimed at capable readers. By *capable*, I mean readers who have been assessed to have at least a grade 7 or higher printed-text reading level. For example, I ran a Flesh Kincaid readability test of 13 randomly generated articles from Wikipedia, and it yielded an average readability level of grade 12. Even wikis created for elementary children scored high readabilities. For example, Wikijunior posted an average readability of grade 8. Thus, my experience—and the experience of many classroom teachers and teacher-librarians—has taught me that most students assessed at a grade 5 or less readability level will likely become bogged down reading Wikijunior and that they will become completely frustrated when trying to read Wikipedia.

If you are considering using public wikis as an online information source with your students, I highly recommend checking the site's readability beforehand. One easy method for testing a wiki's readability is to locate several large chunks of text (totaling 1,000 words or more) that students are likely to read. Copy and paste this text into a word-processing document and run a readability statistics check (for more information on readability tests and running readability tests in KWORD, MS Word, and Corel Wordperfect, visit **http://en.wikipedia .org/wiki/Flesch-Kincaid_ Readability_Test**). Text that is more than two grade levels above a student's recently assessed reading level will likely frustrate the reader. Teacher-librarians should ensure that students approach such text with a great deal of support—for example, through guided reading and by being read to by capable readers.

However, such tests provide only an estimate of a public wiki's readability. For example, a wiki's use of multimedia may provide students with many multimodal (e.g., audio, visual) contextual clues with which to comprehend the text (Jewitt, 2005). Similarly, the student's eagerness to read interactive, hyperlinked online text may be more representative of a constructivist approach to reading, which may in turn help motivate students to stay with it and succeed when reading and comprehending difficult text structures and vocabulary (McNabb, 2006). Students assessed at a grade 3 or grade 4 reading level and who decide to dig their way through the Harry Potter tomes, illustrate the effects of this phenomenon.

Although being motivated to read a wiki might help to lower its readability by one or two grade levels, it has been my experience that, regardless of the multimedia, comprehension of the wiki's content is significantly compromised when students are faced with print ranked two or more grade levels above their own.

INTERNET ACCESS

The school's Internet connectivity is a second factor to consider when using public wikis. Schools with a limited number of Internet-capable computers and schools with limited Internet bandwidth find accessing wiki information a slow endeavor indeed—especially if one wants to have the whole class visit a wiki together. If increasing the school's Internet bandwidth or number of Internet-capable computers is not included in the school's upcoming budget, I suggest applying one or more of the following strategies to increase student access:

• Download the pertinent wiki pages to a local computer and, if possible, share them over a local network.

• Download the pertinent wiki pages to a CD-ROM that can be shared, if possible, over the network or made into copies that the students can use on non-Internet-capable computers.

• Design an information literacy activity that employs a stations approach. In small groups, students rotate through a wiki station comprising 1 to 10 computers. At this station, students learn and practice particular wiki-based information literacy objectives.

Note, though, that these measures are temporary. The lack of access to Internet resources in the classroom or school library is more than just an inconvenience. With research demonstrating that more than 75% of students are accessing the Internet to accomplish their homework (Media Awareness Network, 2005), limited access to the Internet at school not only hinders less economically advantaged children but also exacerbates the growing digital divide between the rich and the poor (Jocewicz, Philbin, Sargent, & Vallejo, 2004). In short, teacher-librarians must continue their advocacy for adequate Internet so that all students can access wikis and have equal opportunity at learning the online information literacy skills that provide them with the opportunity to fully and positively participate in a democratic society.

LEARNING OBJECTIVES

The third major factor influencing the use of wikis as effective literacy teaching and learning technologies involves the goals of classroom teachers and teacher-librarians. Although more and more children are getting their information online, including that from wikis, this format is not the only one that children can access to obtain credible information. Traditional formats such as journals, magazine, encyclopedias, and other peer-reviewed, paper-based materials are still quite valuable sources of information, and they require information literacy skills that are both similar and different to those used with online wikis. For example, locating information in print encyclopedias demands knowledge in using a table of contents and an index to find information, whereas locating information on a public wiki requires knowledge of how to use pull-down menus and hyperlinks.

When developing wiki-based literacy learning objectives, effective teacher-librarians ask themselves questions such as What information literacy skills are unique to this format? Can this literacy be learned faster or more clearly with another technology? and Is this a good use of my precious time on these computers? Answers to such questions help teacher-librarians to develop information literacy skills relevant and specific to the information literacy format (in this case, wikis) while ensuring that students develop an adequate width and breadth of information literacy skills across the variety of information formats.

INFORMATION QUALITY

Finally, one of the greatest challenges to using web resources such as public wikis is in determining the credibility and authenticity of the information. By their nature, wikis encourage input and changes from visitors. For example, a great deal of the information contained in Wikipedia has been entered and refined by many, many contributors. Determining which of Wikipedia's information is correct or has been altered by mischievous hackers lies on the shoulders of the student more than when using peer-reviewed print resources such as encyclopedias. Thus, students must be taught information literacy skills aimed at evaluating the credibility and authenticy of a wiki's information. Examples of library-based activities aimed at helping students determine the credibility and authenticity of web pages and wikis are located at **www.stenhouse.com/pdfs/8196ch09.pdf**.

Interestingly, recent research by *Nature* (Giles, 2005) comparing articles on similar topics from the *Encyclopedia Britannica* and Wikipedia found that both resources had different but similar numbers of errors. As well, the *New York Times* (Hafner, 2006) reported that Wikipedia had protected 82 of its web pages from public editing, and it estimated that 1,000 administrators were working on Wikipeidia's content to ensure that the information was credible.

Public wikis are valuable information sources that teacher-librarians can use to complement and further the width and breadth of literacy objectives developed in the classroom. Although readability and hardware issues create some limitations in using wikis as research and literacy development resources, many of these limitations can be overcome through creative solutions like those mentioned here. Furthermore, students must be taught how to determine the authenticity and credibility of wiki information. In the next issue's column, I explore student-created wikis and the possible contributions that these recursive formats have on developing student writing.

REFERENCES

Davis, V. (2006). *My students compare and contrast wikis and blogs.* Retrieved May 25, 2006, from **http://coolcatteacher.blogspot.com/2006/05/my-students-compare-and-contrast-wikis.html**

Dodge, B. (2004). *Blogs and wikis as WebQuest tasks.* Retrieved June 19, 2006, from **http://webquest.sdsu.edu/necc2004/blogs-and-wikis.htm**

Giles, J. (2005). *Internet encyclopaedias go head to head.* Retrieved June 19, 2006, from **www.nature.com/news/2005/051212/full/438900a.html**

Hafner, K. (2006). *Growing Wikipedia refines its "anyone can edit" policy.* Retrieved June 17, 2006, from **www.nytimes.com/2006/06/17/technology/17wiki.html?ex=1151467200&en=899bc46593b508c6&ei=5070**

Jewitt, C. (2005). Multimodality, "reading," and "writing" for the 21st century. *Studies in the Cultural Politics of Education, 26*(3), 315–331.

Jocewicz, K., Philbin, L., Sargent, E., & Vallejo, V. (2004). *The digital divide and the global south.* Retrieved June 18, 2006, from **http://everyschool.org/u/scu/ddivideworld/**

McNabb, M. (2006). Navigating the maze of hypertext. *Educational Leadership, 63*(4), 76–79.

Media Awareness Network. (2005). *Young Canadians in a wired world—Phase II*. Retrieved June 20, 2006, from **www.media-awareness.ca/english/research/YCWW/phaseII/key_findings.cfm**

Richardson, W. (2006). *Blogs, wikis, podcasts, and other powerful web tools for classrooms.* Thousand Oaks, CA: Corwin Press.

㉔

Beyond Wikipedia

Doug Achterman

The Read/Write Web, also called Web 2.0, offers powerful tools to aid in the collaborative process. Applications such as blogs and wikis allow users to add content to a web page on the fly, generally with little or no knowledge of HTML coding required. And although blogs have gained some popularity and use in schools, the potential of wikis as an educational tool remains largely untapped. The power of a wiki lies in its ability to provide a format for collaborative construction of knowledge. Characteristic features of a wiki include ease of use; ability to create nonlinear document structures through hyperlinks; a built-in mechanism for reflection and metacognition; a means of tracking individual, small group, and whole group progress; and spaces for creating individual, small group, and whole group products. Teacher-librarians and classroom teachers can use these features to design new and improved collaborative learning experiences. This article provides sample assignments and describes free wiki web sites.

BEYOND WIKIPEDIA: USING WIKIS TO CONNECT STUDENTS AND TEACHERS TO THE RESEARCH PROCESS AND TO ONE ANOTHER

It is hard to work in a school library without believing in the power of constructivist learning. Every day teacher-librarians facilitate the process of articulating research questions, locating resources, organizing information from a variety of sources, and synthesizing that information to create new understandings. Some of the most exciting research happens when students collaborate to pool their research and analyze their data, forming a kind of understanding that would be difficult for an individual student to achieve.

The Read/Write Web, also called Web 2.0, offers powerful tools to aid in this kind of collaborative process. Applications such as blogs and wikis allow users to add content to a web page on the fly, generally with little or no knowledge of HTML coding required. And although blogs have gained some popularity and use in schools, the potential for wikis as an educational tool remains largely untapped. While the reasons for this are open to question, it is clear that it is not because students are uncomfortable with these new technologies. In fact, about half of all teens in the United States create some kind of content

First published in *Teacher Librarian*, December 2006, Volume 34, Number 2

for the Internet. These activities include creating web pages, blogs, and wikis, as well as remixing content found online into something new (Lenhart & Madden, 2005).

IN THE IMAGE OF WIKIPEDIA

Many of the suggestions for using wikis are imitations of the general concept of Wikipedia: The Free Encyclopedia, an organic, loosely structured process to produce encyclopedia-type content. Neighborhood-Wiki (**http://theneighborhoodschool.org/wiki/index.php?title= Main_Page**), for example, features elementary students' encyclopedia entries on hundreds of topics, ranging from alligators to *zxcvbnm,./* (the bottom row of the keyboard). Will Richardson (2006) suggested that teachers and students collaborate to create wiki textbooks for individual courses and that each year new classes might add to or edit content. Westwood Schools, in Camilla, GA, maintains a wiki that includes collections of student work, class blogs, student-created study guides, and spaces for students to post pages of interest to other students (Jakes, 2006).

In addition to allowing users to add and edit content, wikis also allow users to weigh in with commentary. Many wiki applications feature a back page, usually labeled "Discussion," which can be used for reflection and feedback. On Wikipedia, users often use this space to post explanations of edits they have made, to evaluate content, or to disagree with other contributors. This feature is being put to good use by teachers who create wikis for their writing courses. Borja (2006) cited Paul Allison's High School Online Collaborative Writing Wiki (**http://schools.wikia.com/wiki/Main_Page**) as an example, on which students used the "Discussion" page to create modern versions of scenes from *Macbeth*, including 20 versions of the opening witch scene.

Many supporters of wikis in education suggest that there is an inherent underlying philosophy that accompanies use of the tool. Richardson (2006) claimed that "early implementations of wikis in educational settings have shown that the more autonomy teachers give to students in terms of negotiating the scope and quality of the content they are creating, the better" (p. 65). Heather James (2004) described her "brilliant wiki failure," in part, the result of assuming too much control. "To really use a wiki," James said, "the participants need to be in control of the content—you have to give it over fully." And Brian Lamb (2004) asserted that wikis are most effective when "students can assert meaningful autonomy over the process. It is not that authority cannot be imposed on a wiki, but doing so undermines the effectiveness of the tool" (p. 45).

WIKIS AND INFORMATION LITERACY

Although it is hard to argue with the goal of independent, self-directed learning, this is often more an ideal to strive toward than it is a reality. In fact, there is evidence that careful structuring and scaffolding of concepts and skills have led to some successful wiki collaborations. Moreover, many of the considerations in effectively setting up a learning wiki are related to the information literacy skills that fall within the teacher-librarian's expertise. For example, in a study of undergraduate engineering students' use of a wiki for a design project, Nicol, Littlejohn, and Grierson (2005) noted that the organization and structure of information and resources affected team sharing and the learning of design principals. In one of two case studies that this team completed, the authors concluded that requiring teams to make their knowledge structures transparent helped teams solidify their ideas about how their ideas were inter-related. The authors also suggested that requiring students to create concept maps of how their resources related to their central design concepts would have deepened students' application of those resources. In debriefing their project, one student stated that it would have been beneficial if they had been required to use the wiki to rank the value of each source that they uploaded to the shared space. Nicol and colleagues (2005) last suggested that some information literacy skills do not come naturally to students and that building in mechanisms to the wiki to assist students through their problem solving is an important role for the instructor.

Phillipson and Hamilton (2004) reflected on a similar issue in relation to their Romantic Audience Project, a class wiki at Bowdoin College, Brunswick, ME, exploring the Romantic poets. In this open-ended project, students analyzed and responded to poetry through annotating the original poems. Words and phrases were linked to pages of explication and reaction; images related to poems were uploaded; poems on similar themes were interlinked; and biographical information was created about influential authors. In spite of students' enthusiasm, there were difficulties. "Wikis lead to dispersion," the authors stated. "It is easy to click around and wander off into paths that feel tangential or idiosyncratic. To a point, such an environment can feel liberating. . . . But disorientation is quickly frustrating, especially in a pedagogical setting."

Phillipson and Hamilton chose a wiki software with navigation features that they thought would help their students. They took an active role in deciding which pages to highlight on the navigation bar, and they barred students from deleting each other's posts. Once again, these instructors intervened in the operation of the wiki in response to their students' information literacy skill levels.

Engstrom and Jewett's middle school wiki project (2005), in which students investigated the long-term consequences of six Missouri River dams, yielded similar conclusions in terms of the need to build in information literacy skills. Teachers realized on reflection that they needed to model and facilitate the exchange of ideas and that students needed some explicit instruction in the inquiry process to help them provide meaningful interactions with each other and the data they were uncovering.

As a matter of pedagogy, Richardson (2006), James (2004), and Lamb (2004) are correct to push for using wikis in the least restrictive environment, giving over control of content and process to students. But providing students with support, structure, and instruction when they lack the skills to assume complete control in no way undermines the effectiveness of the wiki as a tool. Richardson wrote that, in fact, the use of the wiki is as much about collaborative skills as it is about the production of content:

> The collaborative environment that wikis facilitate can teach students much about how to work with others, how to create community, and how to operate in a world where the creation of knowledge and information is increasingly becoming a group effort. (p. 74)

Let us take a closer look at five features of wikis that can make them an effective tool in facilitating such collaborative efforts, including examples from my partnerships with classroom teachers.

Feature 1: *Ease of use.* Contributors simply go to a wiki site and add a new entry or edit an existing one following simple directions. Many wiki sites provide a "what you see is what you get" (WYSIWYG) editing interface with options similar to those seen in a basic word-processing application, such as Microsoft Word. Users click on "Edit," and add or change content, then click on "Save This Page." That is all there is to it. Instant publishing.

Example. At the beginning of the school year, sophomore world studies students come to the library for a minilesson on determining the authority of a web site. Through discussion facilitated by the teacher-librarian and classroom teacher, students generate a set of criteria that they will use to evaluate authority. Working in groups of three, students explore a single site and use the criteria to decide if the site is authoritative. Students record their answers on a wiki page that includes a link to the site. Because students have no difficulty learning to use the wiki after a 1-minute demonstration, they are able to record their answers and share with the whole group right away (Figure 24.1).

Feature 2: *Spaces for students to create products individually, in small groups, and as a whole group.* Any wiki can be designed to contain separate work spaces for individual, small group, and large group products. The digital environment creates an easy means for students to move from one space to the next, taking notes, analyzing, and synthesizing information along the way.

Example. Students in a remedial science class are exploring the similarities and differences between human beings and other primates. Each student locates information on a single species using links off his or her own page provided by the teacher-librarian (Figure 24.2). The student records answers on that page. Then, a group leader copies all group members' work into a matrix. Together, the group members answer the question, "Based on the data here, what does it mean to be human?" (Figure 24.3).

Each group shares its data and answers with the class, comparing and refining answers. In a short period, students are able to collect, organize, and analyze a large amount of data to produce original conclusions and create authentic understanding.

Feature 3: *Ability to create a nonlinear document structure through hyperlinks.* Hyperlinking allows for the creation of assignments whose steps need not be followed in a single order, offering flexibility and choice to students while maintaining clear paths to follow. Again, neither students nor instructors need to know any HTML coding to do this.

Example. Students move easily through all the information and work spaces of the primates wiki mentioned in Feature 2.

Feature 4: *A built-in mechanism for reflection and metacognition.* As mentioned earlier, many wikis offer an option called "Discussion"—some wiki sites call it "Comments"—on which students can engage in conversation about the entry, explaining why they made changes, agreeing or disagreeing with what has been posted, and sharing personal feelings about a topic.

Example. Students work in pairs to explore both sides of a controversial issue before deciding which side to support. On Day 1, one student researches the "pro" arguments while the other researches "con" arguments. The next day, students switch, completing the Day 2 chart by adding concrete details in support of the original arguments or by finding different arguments and support. Students then use the "Discussion" page to communicate with each other (and to the teacher) about which arguments and details are best and why. The teacher may participate in these discussions, too (Figure 24.4).

Feature 5: *A means of tracking individual, small group, and whole group progress through an assignment.* Wikis have a "History" option that allows users to view each change that has been made to an

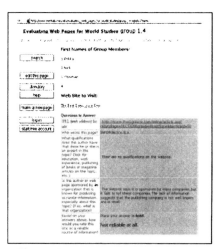

Figure 24.1. Example of Feature 1: Ease of Use

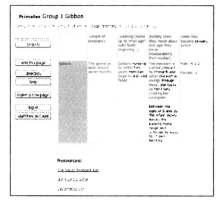

Figure 24.2. Example of Feature 2: Spaces for Students to Create Products

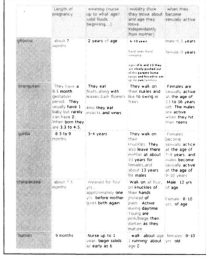

Figure 24.3. Example of Feature 3: Ability to Create a Nonlinear Document

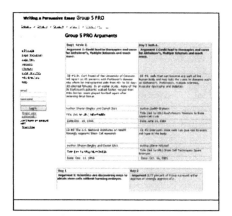

Figure 24.4. Example of Feature 4: A Built-In Mechanism for Reflection and Metacognition

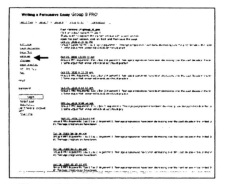

Figure 24.5. Example of Feature 5: A Means of Tracking Progress Through an Assignment

entry since its creation. This makes it possible for the teacher-librarian and classroom teacher to chart progress and identify places in the learning process that require more or less intervention—a useful feedback tool in instructional design.

Example. In the "Writing a Persuasive Essay" assignment, each change to a page automatically creates a link on the "Versions" page—sometimes called the "History" page (Figure 24.5). Some wiki software even allows you to compare new and old versions of a page side by side. This allows both student and teacher to chart progress through an assignment, and it provides opportunities for the teacher to intervene when necessary to keep collaboration on track. It also discourages vandalism because pages can easily be restored to an earlier version.

Each of the examples provides structure and support to meet students' information literacy needs while honing collaboration skills. The collaborative context frequently provides an added dimension to student learning—through multiple perspectives, increased data points, and the heightened demands of clear communication among group members, among other factors. Wikis can help teachers and students negotiate that added dimension.

PRIVACY AND SECURITY

Many educators have concerns about privacy and security in relation to wikis and other Web 2.0 applications. A single response to both is to install wiki software on a school's server and run it inside the firewall. This way, unwanted intruders can neither view nor tamper with students' work. This requires some technical expertise and, perhaps, a relationship with a school district's network administrators—something that is all too rare. There are free wiki sites, however, that can be set up with a password so that only invited guests may visit the site and participate in it. Other sites allow user groups in which only designated registered users gain access to the site.

DELETING ONLINE PREDATORS ACT

Perhaps a greater obstacle is some districts' refusal to allow any social software applications into its schools. In fact, the Deleting Online Predators Act, passed by the House of Representatives (H.R. 5319, 2006) and currently before the U.S. Senate, would deny federal aid to any school library that did not block commercial social networking sites. Although the greatest fears center on MySpace and similar sites, the language of the Deleting Online Predators Act prohibits access to any commercial site that "enables communication among users," a sledge-hammer solution that actually denies students and educators some of the best new learning tools available. It is important that we as information specialists educate our school communities about the far-reaching ramifications of this proposed law.

GETTING STARTED

If you are able to use wikis in your school setting, one final consideration is to choose the best wiki application for your needs. All of the following wiki sites offer free accounts with registration. Each also offers subscription accounts with more powerful options for the account holder.

Seedwiki (**www.seedwiki.com**) and Wikispaces (**www.wikispaces.com**) offer free wikis with WYSI-WYG editors that make them the easiest to use. Seedwiki has a slightly more powerful editing toolbar. Neither site allows a user to password wikis in their free packages, so make certain that students do not include their full names or any personal information on the site.

PeanutButterWiki (**www.pbwiki.com**) and Schtuff (**www.schtuff.com**) are a bit more complicated to use, because they require some simple formatting. PeanutButterWiki allows for passwording of sites, affording teachers and class members some privacy when needed. For this reason, PeanutButterWiki is popular with school staff who are planning and drafting school business. Schtuff incorporates blogs into their spaces and allows changes in permission rights so that different users have different abilities to access or change documents.

REFERENCES

Borja, R. R. (2006). Educators experiment with student-written wikis. *Education Week, 25*(30), 10.

Deleting Online Predators Act of 2006, H.R. 5319, 109th Cong. (2006).

Engstrom, M. E., & Jewett, D. (2005). Collaborative learning the wiki way. *TechTrends, 49*(6), 12–15, 68.

Jakes, D. (2006). Wild about wikis: Tools for taking student and teacher collaboration to the next level. *Technology and Learning, 27*(1), 6.

James, H. (2004). *My brilliant failure: Wikis in classrooms*. Retrieved September 5, 2006, from **http://kairosnews.org/node/view/3794**

Lamb, B. (2004). Wide open spaces: Wikis ready or not. *Educause Review, 39*(5), 37–48.

Lenhart, A., & Madden, M. (2005). *Teen content creators and consumers*. Washington, DC: Pew Internet and American Life Project.

Nicol, D., Littlejohn, A., & Grierson, H. (2005). The importance of structuring information and resources within shared workspaces during collaborative design learning. *Open Learning, 20*(1), 31–49.

Phillipson, M., & Hamilton, D. (2004). *The romantic audience project: A wiki experiment*. Retrieved September 8, 2006, from **www.rc.umd.edu/pedagogies/commons/innovations/rap/toc.htm**

Richardson, W. (2006). *Blogs, wikis, podcasts, and other powerful web tools for classrooms*. Thousand Oaks, CA: Corwin Press.

(25)

Literacy Links:
School Library Blogging

Keith McPherson

A colleague once told me, "Never before in human history has there been more people reading and writing—this is largely due to the Internet." That thought has stuck in my mind. What literacies are happening online?

A review of current Internet usage statistics indicates that 1 billion people now access the Internet (Miniwatts Marketing Group, 2006a). Of this, an estimated 225 million North Americans log into the Internet (Miniwatts Marketing Group, 2006b). A review of the 10 most popular online activities in the United States (see Table 25.1) reveals that surfers must be capable readers and writers of printed text. Although the Internet offers the opportunity for nontextual, multimedia communication, reading and writing are still the cornerstones of online literacy.

Although new online activities appear almost as fast as weeds in my garden, one new Internet pursuit that has captured the attention of many North Americans is the reading and writing of blogs. Indeed, as of 2006, there were close to 30 million unique blogs on the Internet (Sifry, 2006), with this number projected to double every 5 months thereafter. A recent poll (Pew Internet and American Life Project, 2005) indicated that almost 30% of all U.S. citizens have read a blog, 40% of 12- to 18-year-olds have read a blog, and 20% of people have created a blog. At this rate of uptake, blogging may break into the list of top 10 online activities within the next year or two.

A blog is a journal-like web space in which an author raises an issue and the author and fellow bloggers post their responses in reverse chronological order. The content is usually controversial, newsworthy, opinionated, text based (although some blogs include media-like video, audio, animation, pictures, and music), narrative in structure, and does not allow authors to edit previous blog entries. For a clear picture of how blogs are currently being used, listen to the February 28, 2006, American University Radio newscast on blogs at **www.wamu.org/programs/kn/06/02/28.php#**, or visit the list of school-based and Internet-wilds blog examples listed in Table 2 (by *Internet-wilds*, I mean the entirety of Internet sites, es-

First published in *Teacher Librarian*, June 2006, Volume 33, Number 5

pecially sites known and unknown to contain inappropriate content—inappropriate being defined by the school's stakeholders and their local, provincial, state, and federal communities—content such as pornography, racism, sexism, blatant falsehoods, legal infractions, immoral motives, slander, bullying, hate crimes, and the like).

Currently, I am exploring blogs with groups of in-service and preservice educators at the University of British Columbia. One of the first questions that inevitably arises out of our discussions is "How and why should we use blogs with our students?" After visiting the list of school-based blogs cited in Table 25.2, teachers note the educational goal of blogs: to promote reading and writing. Housley (2006) concurs, further suggesting that because blogs provide students authentic and motivating communication contexts and audiences, writers and readers are often committed to writing and reading daily posts. She also notes that school-based blogs can be used to introduce students to new Internet communication technologies while providing opportunities for teachers to help students develop their typing, editing, peer editing, spelling, and reading and writing skills.

	Internet users (%)
Send e-mail	91
Use a search engine to find information	90
Search for a map or driving directions	84
Do an Internet search to answer a specific question	80
Research a product or service before buying it	78
Check the weather	78
Look for information on a hobby or interest	77
Get travel information	73
Get news	72
Buy a product	67

Note: About 72% of American adults use the Internet (approximately 145 million people). Table based on Pew Internet and American Life Project (2005).

Table 25.1. Top 10 Internet Activities in the United States

School-based blogs	Internet-wilds blogs
www.elementary-school.blogspot.com/	**www.boingboing.net/**
www.grandviewlibrary.org/	**http://thinkprogress.org/**
http://stannessecondary.wordpress.com/	**www.engadget.com/**

Table 25.2. Examples of School-Based Blogs and Popular Blogs Found on the Wilds of the Internet

Moreover, teacher-librarians can use blogs to help develop students' online critical-thinking skills. For example, using web site evaluation activities and materials from 2Learn (2Learn.ca Education Society, 2005) and QUICK (Health Development Agency and Center for Health Information Quality, 2006), middle school and secondary school students can visit existing blogs like the Think Progress blog (**http://thinkprogress.org/**) to explore opposing views in current news issues, such as social and economic justice, healthy communities, and global leadership. Similarly, blogs such as Suicide Girls (**http://suicidegirls.com/news/**) can be used to explore the credibility, authenticity, and bias of blog information (both textual and visual), as well as the difference between primary and secondary sources. Most commercial and pop culture blogs can be used to help students become aware of issues around student safety, information privacy, and inappropriate content. Suggested approaches and activities for developing students' safe blogging practices can be found at **www.blogsafety.com/**.

Teacher-librarians can develop students' information literacy skills by having the students evaluate existing blogs. For example, groups of students can be asked to record a list of communication and design criteria representative of effective, safe, and credible blogs. Later, these criteria can be refined across group discussions and then applied by the teacher-librarian or students when developing their own class, school library, or school blog.

Blogs can also be used to develop students' information literacy skills around units of inquiry. For example, students can research and post their own information, insights, and reflections on a particular event, critical question, novel study, author, family history, science experiment, and the like. Blogs can be particularly useful for recording sequential threads of understandings and information, demonstrating change over time. Although an extensive search for examples of such school-based inquiry blogs turned up no examples (possibly because educators choose to keep their school blogs behind firewalls in the deep net), two possibilities include the chronological posting of predictions and observations of a bean seed's growth and the observed cumulative effects of global relief efforts reaching survivors of the 2004 Sumatran tsunami (see **http://tsunamihelp.blogspot.com/** for a non-school-based example of an inquiry-based blog dealing with topics around tsunami relief).

Setting up a school or school library blog is relatively easy. Teacher-librarians or network administrators can download and run blog software such as Wordpress (**http://wordpress.org**) and Movable Type (**http://sixapart.com/movabletype**) on a school or district server. They need to ensure that firewalls and passwords are in place to protect the server from Internet hackers and blog vandals. If networking expertise is not available, teacher-librarians can choose to have their blogs hosted for free on an existing blog service provider, such as **www.blogger.com** or **http://us.blog.com**. Using existing blog services is by far the easiest method of setting up a blog; however, having your blog hosted outside the school or district server brings into question possible access from unauthorized users.

As suggested, the development of school library blogs can offer many opportunities for creating authentic and motivating text-based reading and writing contexts for students. Furthermore, it is within these real-world learning contexts that teacher-librarians can assist their students to develop a foundation of safe, critical, and informed online information literacy skills and practices. Teacher-librarians can also develop students' nontextual information literacies (e.g., visual literacy) through the critical exploration of blogs employing multimedia forms of communication. In essence, blogs are ideal contexts for initiating, connecting, and reinforcing literacies that students develop in the school library and classroom as well as at home.

Students are online and engaging in the blogoshpere. Current research indicates that 75% of our students in grades 6–11 are using the Internet to complete their homework (Media Awareness Network, 2005); 20% of our students have used blogs in general—and this number is likely increasing rapidly (Pew Internet and American Life Project, 2005); and teens are more likely to reveal far more personal data on blogs than in forums and chatrooms (Huffaker & Calvert, 2005). In this context, it is essential that teacher-librarians work with teachers in developing students' reading and writing skills and, more important, ensure that these skills be taught alongside the very information literacy skills, knowledge, and experiences that students require to safely and effectively navigate some of the Internet's most injurious information pitfalls.

REFERENCES

2Learn.ca Education Society. (2005). *Evaluating a web site.* Retrieved March 5, 2006, from **www.2learn.ca/evaluating/evaluating.html**

Health Development Agency and Center for Health Information Quality. (2006). *The QUICK guide to checking information quality.* Retrieved March 5, 2006, from **www.quick.org.uk/**

Housley, S. (2006). *Blogs for kids.* Retrieved March 5, 2006, from Really Simple Syndication's Web server: **www.rss-specifications.com/kids-blogging.htm**

Huffaker, D. A., & Calvert, S. L. (2005). Gender, identity, and language use in teenage blogs. *Journal of Computer-Mediated Communication, 10*(2). Retrieved March 5, 2006, from **http://jcmc.indiana .edu/vol10/issue2/huffaker.html**

Media Awareness Network. (2005). *Young Canadians in a wired world—Phase II: Key findings*. Retrieved March 6, 2006, from the Media Awareness Network server: **www.media-awareness.ca/english/ research/YCWW/phaseII/key_findings.cfm**

Miniwatts Marketing Group. (2006a). *Internet usage statistics: The big picture—World Internet users and population stats*. Retrieved March 4, 2006, from the Internet World Stats web site: **www.internet worldstats.com/stats.htm**

Miniwatts Marketing Group. (2006b). *Internet usage statistics for the Americas*. Retrieved March 4, 2006, from the Internet World Stats web site: **www.internetworldstats.com/stats2.htm#north**

Pew Internet and American Life Project. (2005). *Pew Internet and American Life Project tracking surveys (March 2000–September 2005)*. Retrieved March 4, 2006, from **www.pewinternet.org/trends/ Internet_Activities_12.05.05.htm**

Sifry, D. (2006). *State of the blogosphere, February 2006*. Retrieved March 6, 2006, from the Technorati web server: **www.technorati.com/weblog/**

Literacy Links:
New Online Technologies for
New Literacy Instruction

Keith McPherson

One of the greatest challenges associated with developing students' literacy capabilities is keeping up to date with today's ever-changing Internet communication technologies. For instance, while many of us were busy helping our students to master e-mail and web site construction, diverse telecommunication software like MSN chat (**www.messenger.msn.com**) and Skype (**www.skype.com/**) was being introduced and eagerly embraced by large numbers of students around the globe (Organisation for Economic Cooperation and Development, 2006).

SHOULD WE KEEP STUDENTS CURRENT?

Such change begs the question, Should we try to keep our students up to date with these changes in literacy technologies, and, if so, how? This question has been the focus of a great deal of literacy research, theory, and debate exploring the impact of communication technologies on self and society (e.g., Anstey & Bull, 2006; Forum Barcelona, 2004; Kamil, Intrator, & Kim, 2000; Leu, 2000; New London Group, 1996). Tapscott (1998), Doiron and Asselin (2004), and McPherson (2005) suggest (a) that educators expand their notion of literacy to embrace evolving communication forms that include—but move beyond—just reading and writing and (b) that educators assist their students to develop critical literacy capabilities across a wide set of real-life communication contexts and technologies. They also warn that if we do not, we risk leaving our children at the mercy of less scrupulous players (e.g., advertisers, corporations) using the Internet to communicate their own agenda.

FREE LITERACY WEB SITES

This column introduces five free and relatively new online literacy sites that teacher-librarians can use to

First published in *Teacher Librarian*, February 2007, Volume 34, Number 3

assist teachers to further develop their school's literacy objectives.

Gliffy

Gliffy (**http://gliffy.com**) is a free online drag-and-drop diagram editor that allows K–12 users to quickly and easily create, edit, and share a variety of visuals (see Figure 26.1). I have seen students and teachers using Gliffy to create simple and complex maps, flow charts, tables, timelines, illustrations, graphs, and figures. Five strengths that Gliffy offers literacy educators are that it is intuitive, flexible, collaborative, easily exported, and cost- and time-efficient.

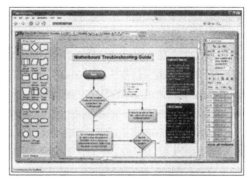

Figure 26.1. Gliffy.com Home Page

Intuitive. The program is so intuitive that my 8-year-old daughter was able to figure out how to use it in less than 5 minutes.

Flexible. K–12 students can graphically represent and communicate simple and complex concepts not easily expressed through words. Gliffy is not tied to any content, so it can be integrated across subjects and is particularly useful for visually representing information associations, sequences, comparisons, and brainstorming.

Collaborative. Teacher-librarians and students can collaboratively create and edit their Gliffy image (or images). This is particularly useful when creating images in which no one user is the information expert and the information is constructed and represented collaboratively. Gliffy also keeps a history of the changes so that authors can go back to resurrect deleted or radically changed segments of their diagram.

Easily exported. Gliffy images can be exported into several common graphics formats recognized by most word-processing and graphics programs. Gliffy also allows users to publish directly to online literacy environments, such as blogs, wikis, and web pages.

Cost- and time-efficient. Like all the online literacy tools being reviewed in this column, Gliffy is free. Similarly, all upgrades are free and instantaneous—no waiting for CD-ROM or Internet upgrades to install. Gliffy also automatically saves your work every 30 seconds, so if your laptop crashes, you still have a copy on the Gliffy server.

Gliffy, however, will by no means replace a graphics editing program, because it does not yet allow for the importing of desktop graphics; it is limited in its editing capabilities (e.g., no eraser or spray can); and its documents can be edited and stored on only the Gliffy web site (raising some concerns over security and privacy). Compared to Gliffy's potential to assist teacher-librarians in fostering students' collaborative and multimodal literacy skills, these limitations become easy to pardon.

Google Docs and Spreadsheets

Initially dubbed Writely and recently bought out by Google, Google Docs and Spreadsheets (**http://docs.google.com**) is a program that, according to its home page, "is a web-based word processing and spreadsheet program that keeps documents current and lets the people you choose update files from their own computers" (see Figure 26.2). The program has been developed and refined over the past 4 years, and educators have recently begun to discover its potential as a literacy technology. Unlike Gliffy, Google Docs is a word-process-

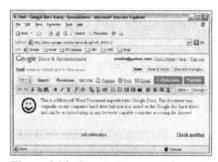

Figure 26.2. Google Docs and Spreadsheets Home Page

ing program that can be accessed and used by grade 3–12 users. The following lists only a few of its many strengths as a literacy learning and teaching technology.

Flexible file formats. You can upload, edit, and download documents in Microsoft Word, pdf, rich text, Open Office, or HTML formats. Being able to access, save, and share your documents in so many formats reduces compatibility issues when moving collaboratively composed word-processed documents between different users and operating systems.

Collaborative writing options. Google Docs offers users the option of allowing other registered Google users to view or edit shared documents. For example, teacher-librarians can use the View option when they want students to view but not alter information (e.g., a set of instructions), whereas the Edit option can be used to allow students to collaboratively compose information (e.g., a news report).

Internet publishing. Google Docs lets teacher-librarians and their students instantly publish documents to the Internet on the Google Docs server or on a class or personal blog. Thus, students do not need to be taught Web-authoring skills before publishing documents to the Internet. This publishing feature also opens up the opportunity of class discussion around the potential benefits and risks of publishing directly to the Internet.

Inserting comments. Teacher-librarians and students can add comments to a document that can be viewed when editing but not displayed when published. Such a feature can be used by teachers and teacher-librarians when editing a student's work or when students are editing each other's work.

Diverse set of writing tools. Google Docs provides authors with a diverse set of the most frequently accessed writing tools found in stand-alone word processors. For example, not only can you do basic word processing, such as cut-and-paste and font formatting, but you can also create levels of headers and insert tables, images, and Internet links.

Google Docs is far more capable a program than presented. I encourage you and your students to explore it when you get a chance. Some limitations, however, that I have encountered when using Google Docs are that the conversion of graphics and tables from a Word document to a Google document is not reliable; some educators find it too easy for students to publish to the Internet; and Google Docs does not run on older browsers and Safari or Opera.

NewsMap, OpenOffice, and del.icio.us

Three other noteworthy online literacy learning and teaching technologies that I recommend exploring and using with your students are NewsMap, OpenOffice, and del.icio.us.

NewsMap (**http://muti.co.za/static/newsmap.html**). This site uses a Google Maps interface for users to quickly locate international, national, regional, or local news. Using the cardinal direction navigation bar in the top lefthand corner of the home page allows one to navigate by zooming out for global news and zooming in for local news. NewsMap is an excellent technology for developing grade 6–12 students' information literacy skills, such as mapping, cardinal directions, current news, critical thinking (Whose news is this?), and media studies.

OpenOffice (**http://openoffice.com**). This bundle of free software contains a word processor, spreadsheet program, and presentation software. All programs are similar to Microsoft products in form and function—so much so that they open and allow you to edit and save files in Microsoft format. MS Office has been and is the staple of many teachers', teacher-librarians', and grade 2–12 students' literacy programs and experiences. Why not try a similar package that is reliable (Rawlinson, 2006) and free?

del.icio.us (**http://del.icio.us**). This is a free social bookmarking system that teacher-librarians can use with secondary students. In essence, del.icio.us is a program that allows groups of people to collect and store bookmarks of their favorite web sites on the site's online storage servers. Such bookmark collections can be created and shared, for example, by a group of students researching global warming and its effect on human diseases. Del.icio.us fosters social construction and expression of knowledge and is excellent groundwork for students participating in research and collaborative literacy projects.

Understandably, all of these online resources require that your school have access to a reliable high-speed Internet connection. If you are thinking of getting a high-speed Interent connection or adding to that which you already have, remember that although the cost for such a connection may at first seem prohibitive (especially if your school is experiencing financial cutbacks), the savings on software costs may help justify the initial outlay of funds.

BUT HAVE A BACKUP PLAN

Note as well that reliable Internet access does not always translate to reliable access to online programs. As with software on a laptop, there is always the possibility that the Gliffy or Google Docs and Spreadsheets software server may crash. In such an instance, instead of having one student experience a laptop problem, the whole class is unable to work. Having a backup plan, such as pencil-and-paper activities, stand-alone word-processing centers, substitute activities, or oral-based research, is a must when using these online literacy programs. Online programs are not recommended for schools with unreliable or intermittent Internet access.

All of these online programs are excellent examples of new online digital technologies that teacher-librarians can use to shape their students' literacy practices in new and powerful ways. Gliffy and Newsmap represent new software that teacher-librarians can use to cultivate visual representation in their school's literacy program, and Google Docs and Spreadsheets and del.icio.us can be used to foster students' social construction and representation of knowledge.

Five years ago, who could have imagined that such technologies would be created and allow our students to access and share their literacy documents anywhere that an active browser-capable computer is located (thus reducing the need for carrying around storage media such as CD-ROMs and flash drives)? And, who could have imagined that the creation of such technologies would develop the current trend toward literacy practices that encourage the social construction and sharing of knowledge (e.g., blogs, wikis, del.icio.us, Gliffy, and the like)?

Ideally, the brief reviews and how-to-use suggestions here will spark in-depth lesson plan ideas of your own. Please e-mail me your ideas for incorporating these new communication technologies into your school library literacy programs, and I will share them with readers in future columns.

THE SCHOOL LIBRARY ALWAYS RELEVANT

It is my belief that these and other online technologies will play a significant role in our students' future literacy practices. Acknowledging these technologies and working with the students toward incorporating them into thoughtful and meaningful literacy learning activities demonstrates to students and the school community that school libraries are as relevant to students' literacy development today as they always have been and always will be.

REFERENCES

Anstey, M., & Bull, G. (2006). *Teaching and learning multiliteracies.* Newark, DE: International Reading Association.
Doiron, R., & Asselin, M. (2004, May). *Gateways to literacies: New libraries for new literacies.* Paper

presented at 49th International Reading Association conference, Reno, NV.

Forum Barcelona. (2004). *New ignorances, new literacies. Learning to live together in a globalizing world*. Retrieved October 24, 2006, from **www.barcelona2004.org/eng/banco_del_conocimiento/ documentos/ficha.cfm?IdDoc=2402**

Kamil, M. L., Intrator, S. M., & Kim, H. S. (2000). The effects of other technologies on literacy and literacy learning. In M. L. Kamil, P. B. Mosenthal, P. D. Pearson, & R. Barr (Eds.), *Handbook of reading research* (Vol. 3, pp. 771–788). Mahwah, NJ: Erlbaum.

Leu, D. J. (2000). Literacy and technology: Deictic consequences for literacy education in an information age. In M. L. Kamil, P. B. Mosenthal, P. D. Pearson, & R. Barr (Eds.), *Handbook of reading research* (Vol. 3, pp. 743–770). Mahwah, NJ: Erlbaum.

McPherson, K. (2005). Of course it's true! I found it on the Internet: Fostering children's online critical literacy. In R. Doiron & M. Asselin (Eds.), *Literacy, libraries and learning: Using books and online resources to promote reading, writing, and research* (pp. 107–118). Markham, ON: Pembroke.

New London Group. (1996). A pedagogy of multiliteracies: Designing social futures. *Harvard Educational Review, 66*(1), 60–92.

Organisation for Economic Cooperation and Development. (2006). *Are students ready for a technology-rich world? What PISA studies tell us.* Retrieved October 24, 2006, from **www.oecd.org/document/ 31/0,2340,en_32252351_32236173_35995743_1_1_1_1,00.html**

Rawlinson, N. (2006, January). OpenOffice 2. *PC Pro: Computing in the Real World, 135.* Retrieved October 24, 2006, from **www.pcpro.co.uk/reviews/80012/openoffice-2.html**

Tapscott, D. (1998). *Growing up digital: The rise of the Net generation.* New York: McGraw-Hill.

InfoTech: Podcasting in the
School Library, Part 1:
Integrating Podcasts and Vodcasts
Into Teaching and Learning

Annette Lamb and Larry Johnson

Listen to Thomas Jefferson's rough draft of the Declaration of Independence.
Learn about Jefferson's passion for music by listening to his favorite works.
Hear how Europeans viewed Americans in the late 18th century.

These are three Podcasts available from the Monticello: Home of Thomas Jefferson web site (see Figure 27.1). A growing number of Internet resources are offering multimedia communications as a way to bring history, literature, science, and other topics alive for visitors. Although some students enjoy reading text as a way to access information, a growing number of young people prefer a multimedia approach. In addition to motivating learners, Podcasts are a way to convey ideas and emotions that are difficult to express in a text format.

DISCOVERING PODCASTS

The word *Podcasting* comes from combining the words *iPod* and *broadcasting*. What distinguishes a Podcast from other multimedia files distributed on the Internet is the addition of a web feed that allows users to subscribe to the audio program. In other words, rather than having to visit a web site to determine whether new content is available, files are automatically accessed and organized by a feed aggregator, such as Bloglines, for immediate enjoyment. Although some people use tools such as iTunes to download

First published in *Teacher Librarian*, February 2007, Volume 34, Number 3

Figure 27.1. Monticello Web Site

media files to their iPod or another portable MP3 player, many users listen to Podcasts on their computer.

With increasing bandwidth, the availability of easy-to-use video-editing tools, and the introduction of the video iPod, many Podcasters are now offering video Podcasts, also known as *vodcasts*.

Because most blog services provide built-in web feeds, many people have chosen this format for their Podcasts, using each posting as an individual episode. These are often called *audioblogs* or *vlogs*.

Although any aggregator can be used to download Podcasts, some people prefer a reader designed specifically for audio feeds. For example, many people use iTunes for their Podcasts because the files are downloaded in the background and are ready whenever the user wants to listen. On the other hand, some people use a Podcast directory and download the files as they use them.

SELECTING QUALITY PODCASTS

Podcasts have become the popular new way to share content on the Internet, so it is easy to become overwhelmed by the thousands of choices. As you begin reviewing these audio programs, use your school library's selection policy as a guide. Although you will be able to find many quality Podcasts, only a few really address the needs of your learners.

Learner Needs

With so many options, it is important to begin with your information need. Look at your selection policy and content area standards. Where are the information needs? Also, think about those information areas that are difficult to express through text communications or learning outcomes where there is a need to differentiate instruction.

As you explore Podcasts, look for the intended audience. For example, the Bobby Bucket web site states that the Podcasts are aimed at kids, parents, and readers of all ages. Listeners will enjoy book reviews, author interviews, reading tips, and other related topics.

Content Quality

Seek out Podcasts that capitalize on the audio feature by providing dynamic dialog, interesting sound effects, and musical elements that engage learners. These Podcasts should hold the attention of listeners and motivate them to ask questions, practice what they have learned, and take action.

Because anyone with a microphone and access to the Web can create a Podcast, it is important to consider the authority of the author. Many interesting programs lack credibility when they fail to distinguish fact from opinion or provide inadequate citations.

The BBC: In Our Time Podcast investigates the history of ideas in areas such as culture, philosophy, and science. One program examines Homer's *Odyssey* in shaping Western ideas. The Podcast is produced by a well-known organization and is presented by experts in this field.

Technical Quality

Given that the focus of Podcasts is audio, look for quality sound elements. Also consider the size of the files and the ease of using the web feeds for downloading. Currently, most Podcasts are produced in the MP3 format and are easy to use. However, the technical quality of the files vary. Some programs are poorly edited, causing concerns regarding sound quality, volume control, and other issues that may interfere with their use.

Design Quality

Consider the usability of the Podcast. Although a program might have good content, it can be difficult to use. For instance, some programs are lengthy, making them difficult to use for only a short segment without editing the work. Look for short single-concept programs that are easy for students and teachers to use, such as programs that are part of a series.

Instructional Quality

Many Podcasts provide scripts, study guides, and other supplemental materials. Look for resources that provide effective guiding questions and engaging, authentic activities for students. The ESL and Archie Comics web site includes an *Archie* comic strip and learning guide with each Podcast.

Check out Kathy Schrock's "Evaluation of Podcasts" checklist (2006) for more ideas on evaluating Podcasts.

EXPLORING PODCASTS

From poetry readings to language learning, there are endless possibilities for audio blogging and Podcasting in learning. Many radio programs translate well to the online environment. For example, National Public Radio's programs, such as *This American Life* and *Living on Earth*, are great examples of quality programming.

Podcasters provide a variety of programming formats and content. Let's explore a few of the options.

Collaborative Projects

Consider Podcasts that have interactive components. Some web sites invite listeners to submit comments or participate in local or global projects. For instance, Podcasting can be used to share audio projects created by reading buddies. These programs provide students with an authentic audience for their work and the opportunity to work as a team toward a joint goal.

The Our City project asks students from around the globe to submit a recording about the city where they live.

Current Events

Most news sources are now producing Podcasts. CNN provides both audio and video Podcasts. Current events for young people can be found on Scholastic Podcasts. Seek out news sources in particular subject areas, such as the Stone Pages archaeological news Podcast.

Government Documents

Many state standards require students to understand well-known documents and interpret primary source materials. Because these works are often difficult for students to understand, audio provides a different format to help students learn from the text.

From the Declaration of Independence to the Federalist Papers, many Podcasting sites, such as Americana Phonic, are sharing audio recordings of primary source documents as well as classic works of fiction.

Interviews

Students enjoy listening to the experiences of experts in content area fields. A Podcast by a NASA scientist can reinforce concepts, provide personal examples, and generate interest in current science events.

The Barnes and Noble web site sponsors a Meet the Writers Podcast. Visitors can download the audio interviews and get updates through an e-mail subscription.

Issues

Some Podcasts focus on advocacy or commentary, providing political statements, persuasive messages, opinions, or specific perspectives. Although these are useful, it is important that students understand the difference between fact and opinion. These web sites are useful in helping students make comparisons among different points of view and develop arguments for debates.

Podcasts can provide unique perspectives or thought-provoking discussions. The Geography for Travelers Podcast discusses the issue of whether people should be allowed to climb Ayers Rock in the outback of Australia. This Podcast can provide a great introduction to issues related to recreation, public lands, and the impact of humans.

Lessons

Podcasts such as language lessons and how-to projects are specifically designed for instruction. These programs often provide support materials in addition to the audio programs.

The Bob and Rob Show provides weekly English lessons including a Podcast and a study guide.

Programs

Many radio and television programs are now available as Podcasts. News programs such as NBC's *Meet the Press* and many of National Public Radio's programming are available in this format. From hurricanes to mummies, *NOVA* is a well-known PBS program that is now producing short audio stories on science topics.

In addition to finding news and nonfiction works, you can find many web sites with prose, poetry, and storytelling programs. Storynory is a source of audio stories for children. Each week, a new story is added to the collection.

Reviews

One of the most popular uses of Podcasts is the critical review of books, television, movies, and games. Many web sites provide reviews of children's books by readers and librarians. Look for the Podcasts produced by publishers such as Penguin Group for author interviews and book excerpts.

Virtual Tours

For decades, audio tours have been a mainstay for museums. This approach is now being translated into the virtual format by museums such as the San Francisco Museum of Modern Art.

The Podcasts from the San Diego Zoo can be used two ways. If you cannot go to the zoo, you can have a virtual experience. Or, if you can go to the zoo with your iPod, it is like having a personal guide walk with you as you visit the exhibits.

LOCATING PODCASTS

With thousands of Podcasts being generated daily and few good search tools, it can be difficult to locate quality programming for young people. A few search tools are designed specifically for locating Podcasts. For example, Podzinger searches for video and audio with RSS (really simple syndication) feeds.

You will quickly become disappointed using traditional search engines to locate Podcasts. However, if you have a specific topic in mind, consider doing a search for your topic and adding the words *Podcast, Podcasting,* or *RSS* into your search. If you know a good web site and wonder if a Podcast is available, do a site search for *Podcast,* and it is likely that you will find a page with Podcast instructions.

An effective way to begin your exploration is to use one of the educational directories to Podcasts, such as Podcast Directory for Educators or the Education Podcast Network. You may also have success searching the education area or content fields in iTunes Directory, Podcast Alley, or Yahoo! Podcasts.

ORGANIZING PODCASTS FOR STUDENT USE

Once you have identified Podcasts that you wish to add to your school library collection, it is time to design an efficient and effective method of storing and accessing these resources. You also need a plan for continually seeking and exploring Podcasts as you mine for new resources.

As you select a Podcast, think about whether you want to monitor the Podcast over time or simply wish to select a particular program of interest. Also think about how students and teachers will be using the resources. This helps determine how you might access the resource.

Podcasting Aggregator

If you plan to come back to the resource over time, it is a good idea to add the web feed to your web aggregator, such as Bloglines. This tool provides a way to organize feeds into folders for easy access, by topic and subject area. Then, you can check the resource regularly for new Podcasts of interest. The advantage of a web-based aggregator is that it can be accessed from any computer with Internet access.

Podcasts for language instruction are particularly popular. For example, the ESL Pod provides audio as well as learning guides. Because new lessons are constantly being posted, it is a good idea to add this Podcast to your web aggregator so that you can get the updates.

Pathfinders and Web Link

In some cases you may identify a Podcast that meets a particular learning standard. In this case, you can simply link to the online resource as part of a web-based pathfinder containing other quality resources on that topic.

DOWNLOADING PODCASTS

An increasing number of school districts are designing intranet systems for storing and sharing multimedia files. You may want to download Podcasts onto your network server and organize them for use by students and teachers. You can also download selected files for use on iPods and other MP3 players that can be checked out from the library. Although some Podcasts have restrictions on use, most allow downloads for educational use. The advantage of downloading files is that you can continue to use the media file even if the web site is no longer available.

The Kedou Kids Pod provides great stories that are divided into short chapters and can be downloaded to an MP3 player for checkout.

INTEGRATING PODCASTS INTO THE CURRICULUM

Before infusing Podcasts into your lessons, focus on the learning outcome. What is the value of the audio medium? How does the Podcast fit with other learning resources? How can it be used to differentiate learning for individual students?

A student who has difficulty reading in the content areas may find Podcasts as a way to access high-quality information. For example, *Earth and Sky* is a radio program with excellent science content.

There are applications of Podcasting across the curriculum. Use the following examples as you start partnering with teachers on potential uses of Podcasts.

Communication Arts

Focus on assignments that ask students to be active listeners and demonstrate their listening skills. The short audio articles at Reader's Digest RD Outload will work well for this type of assignment. Keep in mind that some Podcasts are available in multiple languages, such as Science@NASA, offering both English and Spanish.

Fine Arts

With many museums developing Podcasts, explore opportunities for children to go on virtual field trips and discuss works of art.

Health and Fitness

From sports stories to health information, Podcasts provide easy-to-understand information on popular topics. Family Health Radio provides 2-1/2-minute audio programs on over 500 topics. After listening to a few Podcasts, ask students to generate a list of questions about a topic for further investigation.

Math

The MathGrad Podcast is a series of audio programs that discuss real-world applications of math through topics such as maps, voting, scale, and probability. Ask students to create their own Podcast on a math topic.

Science

Look for Podcasts that discuss practical applications of science. The Jefferson Lab and *New Scientist* magazine both provide news articles and interviews on current issues.

Social Studies

The Colonial Williamsburg web site provides Podcasts on historical topics along with transcripts and web links. Interpreters are used to put students in the time period. For example, students can listen to a reenactment of Thomas Jefferson's reading the Declaration of Independence or to a brickmaker or wigmaker discussing his trade.

CONCLUSION

Like cassettes, audio CDs, and DVDs, Podcasts provide yet another powerful medium to enhance the informational and instructional resources of your school library collection. As you explore the many quality audio and video materials available through the Internet, search for innovative ways to facilitate their use through organization of Podcast web feeds, creation of pathfinders, and the introduction of iPods and other MP3 devices in your library.

To explore the Podcasts discussed in this article, go to our Bloglines at **www.bloglines.com/**

public/eduscapes (see Figure 27.2).

REFERENCES
Schrock, K. (2006). *What makes a good Podcast?* Retrieved November 1, 2006, from **http://school .discovery.com/schrockguide/evalpodcast.html**

PODCAST DIRECTORIES
Education Podcast Network
http://epnweb.org/

iTunes Directory
www.apple.com/itunes/download/

Podcast Alley
www.podcastalley.com/podcast_genres .php?pod_genre_id=7

Podcast Directory for Educators
http://recap.ltd.uk/podcasting/

Podzinger
www.podzinger.com/

Yahoo! Podcasts
http://podcasts.yahoo.com/

RESOURCES IN THIS COLUMN
Americana Phonic
www.americanaphonic.com/

Barnes and Noble Podcast
www.barnesandnoble.com/writers/

BBC: In Our Time
www.bbc.co.uk/radio4/history/inourtime/

Bob and Rob Show
http://englishcaster.com/bobrob/

Bobby Bucket Podcasts
http://bobbybucket.blogspot.com/

CNN Podcast
www.cnn.com/services/podcasting/

Figure 27.2. Bloglines

Colonial Williamsburg
www.history.org/media/podcasts.cfm

Earth and Sky
www.earthsky.org/Kids/

EarthWatch Radio
http://ewradio.org/

ESL and Archie Comics
www.archiecomics.com/podcasts/

ESL Pod
www.eslpod.com/

Family Health Radio
http://fhradio.org/

Geography for Travelers
http://travelgeography.libsyn.com/

Jefferson Lab
www.jlab.org/rss/podcast.html

Kedou Kids Pod
www.jtwgroup.com/podcast.htm

Living on Earth
www.loe.org/

MathGrad
www.mathgrad.com/

Meet the Press from MSNBC
www.msnbc.msn.com/id/3032608/

Monticello Podcasts
www.monticello.org/podcasts/

NASA Pocasting
www.nasa.gov/help/rssnpodcast/

New Scientist
www.newscientist.com/podcast.ns
Our City Podcast
http://learninginhand.com/OurCity/

Popular Mechanics
www.popularmechanics.com/rss/

Reader's Digest
www.rd.com/

San Diego Zoo
www.sandiegozoo.org/podcast/

San Francisco Museum of Modern Art
www.sfmoma.org/education/edu_podcasts.html

Scholastic Podcasts
**http://content.scholastic.com/browse/article.jsp
    ?id=7692**

Science at NASA
http://science.nasa.gov/

Stone Pages
http://www.stonepages.com/news/

Storynory
http://storynory.com/

(28)

InfoTech: Podcasting in the School Library, Part 2: Creating Powerful Podcasts With Your Students

Annette Lamb and Larry Johnson

From children in Nebraska to teens in Australia, young Podcasters are emerging around the globe. Poems, book reviews, radio skits, commentaries, interviews, and news are just a few of their creations.

Because Podcasts are so easy to make, they are a great way to promote technology to reluctant teachers. Dave Fagg (2006), an Australian history teacher, notes that, rather than spend his time confiscating MP3 players from students, he integrates them into learning by involving students in scripting, recording, editing, and sharing Podcasts about Australian history.

Because sound files are simple to produce and deliver, audio sharing is great for teaching and learning. The word *Podcast* comes from combining the words *iPod* with *broadcast*. Although you will find lots of audio on the Internet, Podcasts are different because they are accessible through a web feed and can be downloaded to portable audio players.

PLANNING YOUR PODCAST

Although many schools are producing weekly and even daily Podcasts, you will want to consider starting with a project that does not require a rigorous schedule. For example, you might highlight books nominated for regional awards. Create a Podcast file yourself to kick off the activity; then, post student projects as they are completed.

First published in *Teacher Librarian*, April 2007, Volume 34, Number 4

Choose a Project

Look for activities where audio adds a dimension that would not be available with another medium, such as the intensity of voice found in a commentary or an interview or in storytelling or oral music. Where does voice and sound make a difference? Children at Cefn Fforest Primary School create Podcasts of their book reviews, poems, field trips, artwork, prose, and many other class activities.

Combining text, graphics, and audio into a single project shows the power of this media. Mr. Gates's second-grade class uses audio as an integral part of its blog. On the topic of seeds, each student shared his or her written work, drawing, and an audio recording of this project. This is a great way to maintain a comprehensive record of student literacy.

Identify Your Audience

Podcasts are designed to share with the world, so it is important to think about your audience. Ask yourself whether you really need to share the audio projects or whether you would be better off simply storing the audio files on a CD or on the school's intranet. For instance, electronic portfolios that incorporate audio narration are a wonderful idea but may not need to be posted on the Web. You can also provide password access to a Podcast if you wish parents to visit but want to restrict access by the general public.

Is the project aimed at classmates, parents, community members, or the world? If you are sharing with the world, be sure to identify your school and grade level. However, check your school's student privacy guidelines before identifying individual students by name.

Select a Program Format

If you are planning a series of Podcasts, develop a standard format. For example, most Podcasts contain an introduction (intro), body, and conclusion (sometimes called an *outro*). Think about a title, theme song, and standard structure for your show. Even if the topics vary, consistency makes the production more professional.

Ask students to explore and evaluate Podcasts such as those of the BBC Documentary Archives. Discuss the format used and the elements that were effective and ineffective. The ULiveWhere Podcast interviews people who live in different areas of the world, and it provides maps, satellite images, and photographs about the location, in addition to the audio interview. Ask students to think about visual resources that might accompany the Podcast.

Keep in mind that Podcasts can include many kinds of audio, such as sound effects and music. For instance the Brass Band is a weekly Podcast with brass band music.

Also use existing Podcasts to stimulate ideas. The Every Object Tells a Story Podcast provides a backstory on pieces of artwork. You might ask students to research a work of art and create their own Podcast. Learners could also do a Podcast about their own work of art or about objects that are meaningful in their lives.

Work in Teams

Many projects use collaborative teams for building Podcast programming. An entire class might brainstorm and select topics; then, small groups can write, record, and edit portions of the show. This approach also works well for news programs created by library clubs.

Radio WillowWeb has a formal structure for creating webcasts. It uses planning sheets to help students with planning and organization.

Write a Script

Once you have selected the format, identified content, and assigned work roles, you are ready to write the script. Be sure that students follow the writing process that they use for other classroom activities, providing time for editing and revision. Multiple voices make Podcasts more interesting. Think about ways to incorporate conversations, skits, and interviews.

Try to keep the program short (90 seconds to 3 minutes), or divide it into segments or a series of programs. When students are working on segments independently, assign one person the responsibility of ensuring that the program flows smoothly and uses consistent language throughout.

Check for Copyright Issues

If you or your students use copyrighted materials, you will need to get permission before reproducing these materials on the Web. It is okay to include these cited works in personal projects; however, it is a good idea to create original works so that you do not have to worry about permissions. For example, if you record music played by your school band, audio from a school play, or a work of poetry, check the copyright before Podcasting. Also remember that you need permission to audio record books.

RECORDING YOUR PODCAST: SELECT A LOCATION

Identify a quiet space for recording. It is great if you have a sound-proof video production area; however, a small area such as a meeting room or even a closet will work. A band practice room works well if do not have room in your center. As a last resort, an old-fashioned study carrel will do the job. Be sure that you have a power outlet nearby to plug in your computer. Look for ways to dampen the sound by using rugs or blankets.

Choose a Microphone

Although you can use your internal microphone, it is a good idea to purchase an inexpensive external microphone. Some people like the combined headset with the microphone. You will want an external microphone if your subject is far from the computer or when there is unwanted noise in the area. Although you can purchase inexpensive microphones, you might want to invest in a quality microphone, if you plan to do a lot of recording.

There are three main types of microphones. Unidirectional microphones pick up sound from the direction where they are pointed. These work good for eliminating unwanted background noise. Superdirectional, or *shotgun*, microphones record sounds from far away. Nondirectional microphones work well if you have a small group of people talking at the same time.

Use a Digital Audio Recorder

If you are planning to do interviews or field work, consider using a digital audio recorder or adding a recording unit to your iPod. They are easy to carry and nonthreatening for interviewees. Many of these recorders have a place for an external microphone. These files can then be transferred to your computer and opened in your editing software.

Create Sound Effects

Students love to work with sound effects. Free resources such as the Recordist and the Freesound Project can be used to download MP3 audio files of sounds, such as broken glass, thunder, or rocks sliding. Mr. Jaffe's sixth-grade class incorporated the sound of wind, doors creaking, and an assortment of other effects for their Into the Mummies Tomb Podcast.

Consider setting up a *Foley stage* in your school library. In film production, a Foley artist captures everyday sounds that fit with the dialog of a story. This station includes resources for making interesting sounds, such as blocks of wood, aluminum foil, bells, and other devices. For example, squeezing old audiotape or videotape makes a sound like fall leaves crunching.

Select Software

Of course, you can use purchase software such as Apple's GarageBand, but the most popular software for sound recording is an open-source solution called Audacity, which runs on Windows, Macs, and Linux. There is also software designed specifically for creating Podcasts. For example, Podcaster helps you to create chapter markers and embed images that can be viewed on iPods.

Keep in mind that Podcasts were originally just audio files. However, today's Podcasts can include pictures, video, and animation. For example, Barrett Project Interaction is a blog-based project that incorporates audio, video, and animations.

Rehearse the Performance

You want to practice the Podcast before making your final recording. You may wish to record your rehearsal and talk about the aspects that went well and the areas where the project can be improved. After students become confident with Podcasting, they can go directly to their final recording. Explore some ideas for making your projects professional:

• Talk with students about their speaking voice. Discuss whether the Podcast calls for a formal or informal speaking voice.

• As you evaluate the rehearsal, listen for problems with using the words *like, you know,* and *um.*

• Think about where pauses might be inserted into the script. Although long pauses can be distracting, a few short pauses allow listeners to summarize and reflect on what they are learning.

• Encourage students to use interesting voices. They may even wish to invent characters, or *Podcast personalities,* for themselves. Talk about the use of soft and loud voices, laughter, and sounds to make the project interesting and conversational.

You can record the project dozens of times and never get the perfect performance. Instead, record the program three times and pick your best; then, use the editing process to fix any errors. People do not expect perfection in a Podcast.

Editing Your Podcast

If you have time, edit your work. Editing allows you to add music, cut out errors or unwanted segments, and tighten up the program. As you edit your work, consider the following tips:

• Keep any introductory music short. Rather than start loud, your music should fade in.

• Consider using the same short introduction for each show. For ideas, listen to NPR's radio programs.

• Be sure that you have a clear, concise beginning. Start with questions, problems, and other hooks, to draw in your audience.

• If your program is more than a minute in length, provide an overview to the segments. Each component should have its own short intro and outro.

• Wrap up the program with a concise conclusion.

• Be sure to give credit at the end.

• Carefully listen to the volume of your program as a whole. Balance your audio so that it is all the same volume. Sometimes, one voice can overpower another. However, if you are using background music, be sure that it is quiet enough so that it does not overpower voices.

• Check the recording and playback levels on your computer. You should be able to hear the recording clearly without turning everything to the highest level.

• Save your project as a MP3 file.

Sharing Your Podcast

To share your Podcast, you need a place to store your file on the Web, a web site to create a description and link so that people will be able to find your Podcast, and a web feed such as a RSS file so that people can subscribe to your Podcast. If you are using a blog server, an RSS feed is probably available automatically. If you need to create one, simply use a tool such as ListGarden to create the required file. If you want more extensive feed management resources, try FeedBurner.

PODCAST PROJECT PARTNERSHIPS

You can incorporate Podcasting into school library activities as well as classroom projects in many ways. The key is to develop partnerships with students and teachers. Explore a variety of Podcast projects.

Book Reviews and Booktalks

Book-based projects make great partnership projects. Students at Hopkinton Middle School and High School work with the teacher-librarians to share their Isinglass Teen Read Award Booktalks through Podcasts.

Collaborative Projects

How can you involve students across grade levels or schools? Consider using Podcasts for collaborative projects. In the Sharing Math project between Jamestown Elementary and Hoffman-Boston Elementary, children recorded math story problems for their peers to solve.

Events

From science fair to sporting events, think of ways to capture the excitement of events through your Podcasts. Mabry Podcast Central highlighted the annual science expedition. Think about connecting Podcasts to library promotions such as book fairs, banned book week, and summer reading programs.

Interviews

Local public officials, wildlife experts, and historical reenactors are a few of the many members of the community who would be happy to participate in interview projects. If possible, send the interviewee a set of questions so that he or she can prepare before the recording. In addition to asking prepared questions, ask follow-up questions to provide depth to the discussion. Be sure to pause before asking a new question so that you can easily edit for length.

Students of all ages can produce interviews. In their Reptile Podcast, an honors biology class conducted an interview with Dr. Brady Barr from the National Geographic Channel, whereas the children at Radio Sandaig interviewed a local storyteller.

News Programs
Many schools do a daily or weekly news program. Why not digitize the audio or video and share it on the Web? Planet Sunflower is a daily broadcast of an elementary school in Kansas.

Original Works
From music and poetry to storytelling and persuasive messages, Podcasting is a great tool for sharing original student work. The Cranbrook Composers' Podcasts features student musical compositions. The ilovehistory project involves a collaboration between a teacher and students to produce short history Podcasts. They incorporate historical footage along with original works. Mr. Coley's class shares its favorite literature circle books and activities; *Fortunately, Unfortunately* poems; and field trip experiences (ColeyCast).

Skits, Plays, and Programs
Collaborative teams are a great approach for projects that involve skits, plays, and other radio-type shows. Rather than simply have students read their work aloud, talk with students about engaging listeners and creating ways to make their Podcast voices more dramatic. In an episode of Roadrunner Radio, elementary students incorporate role-playing in discussing the character trait of fairness.

Virtual Tours
Consider projects that can be done in the field, such as field trips to the local museum, park, or zoo. Use digital audio recorders to chronicle the experience, including recording local sounds, recording directions, and documenting the experience.

PODCAST IN THE SCHOOL LIBRARY
Although some teacher-librarians focus on specific projects, such as Podcasts of booktalks, others are working with a variety of classes on many projects. The Dutch Fork Elementary School Library Media Center sponsors the Bookin' It blog as a tool for posting Podcasts of students' work, including interviews, author studies, and student projects. Podcasting can also be used for school library promotions and announcements. At Book Voyages, an elementary school teacher-librarian discusses topics related to children's literature. At the Grandview Elementary Library blog, Podcasts are used to share audio clips from books. The first-grade classes then made their own audiobooks, which were posted on the 1st Grade Huckleberry Room blog.

Use the power of Podcasting to engage students and teachers in exciting audio-rich projects that can be shared both locally and globally.

REFERENCES
Fagg, D. (2006). The iHistory Podcast Project. Retrieved November 1, 2006, from **http://ihistory.word press.com/**

RESOURCES
Podcasts
1st Grade Huckleberry Room
http://huckleberry.edublogs.org/
Barrett Project Interaction
http://barrettpi.blogspot.com/

BBC Documentary Archives
    http://news.bbc.co.uk/2/hi/programmes/
    documentary_archive/
Bookin' It! DFES Podcast!
    http://bookinit.wordpress.com/
Book Voyages
    http://odeo.com/channel/4750/view/
Brass Band
    www.brasscast.com/
Cefn Fforest Primary Podcast
    http://cefnfforest.podomatic.com/
ColeyCast
    http://coleycast.blogspot.com/
Cranbrook Composers' Podcasts
    http://cranbrookcomposers.blogspot.com/
Dream Extreme
    www.dreamextreme.us/Podcast/
Every Object Tells a Story
    www.podcastingnews.com
Grandview Elementary Library
    www.grandviewlibrary.org/
Hoffman-Boston Elementary School
    www.arlington.k12.va.us/schools/hoffman
    boston/students/index.html
ilovehistory
    www.ilovehistory.co.uk/
Isinglass Teen Read Award Booktalks
    www.hopkintonschools.org/hhs/library/
    Podcast.html
Jamestown Elementary
    http://slapcast.com/users/Jamestown/
Mabry Podcast Central
    http://mabryonline.org/Podcasts/index.xml
Mr. Gates' Class
    http://lms.saisd.net/cblog/index.php?blog=6
    &cat=84
Mr. Jaffe's Web Site
    www.cbsd.org/millcreek/jaffe/Podcast/
    index.html
Planet Sunflower
    http://stream.usd385.org/~Sunflower/Site/
    Podcast/Podcast.html
Radio Sandaig
    www.sandaigprimary.co.uk/radio_sandaig/

index.php
Radio WillowWeb
    www.mpsomaha.org/willow/radio/
Reptile Podcast
    http://ghshonorsbio.blogspot.com/2006/05/
    reptile-Podcast.html
Roadrunner Radio
    http://rowland.podomatic.com/
Room5's Podcast
    http://room5.podomatic.com/
ULiveWhere
    www.ulivewhere.com/

RSS Feed Resources
FeedBurner
    www.feedburner.com/
ListGarden
    http://softwaregarden.com/products/list
    garden/

Software
Audacity
    http://audacity.sourceforge.net
GarageBand
    www.apple.com/support/garageband/
Podcaster
    www.kudlian.net/products/Podcaster/

Online Tools
Audioblog
    www.audioblog.com/
ClickCaster
    www.clickcaster.com/
Odeo
    http://odeo.com/
Podmatic
    www.podomatic.com/

Sound Effects Resources
Freesound Project
    http://freesound.iua.upf.edu/
Recordist
    www.therecordist.com/pages/downloads
    .html

㉙

InfoTech: Want to Be My Friend? What You Need to Know About Social Technologies

Annette Lamb and Larry Johnson

Concerned parent—Web sites such as MySpace.com are overflowing with cyberbullies and sexual predators. All social networking web sites should be filtered to protect children and young adults. Enthusiastic teacher—Online learning communities provide wonderful opportunities for students to engage in global discussions, data sharing, and cooperative problem solving.

Like most tools, social technologies have positive and negative applications. Although the news media is filled with scary stories about the harmful consequences of social networking software, little attention is given to the opportunities that this technology provides for children and young adults to share ideas, debate issues, and make global connections.

Over the past several years, people have used the term *Web 2.0* to describe the second generation of web-based services, which allows people to easily socialize, collaborate, and share information online. Children and young adults are attracted to these highly interactive tools. Rather than simply view static web pages, they chat with friends, critique movies, and share digital photographs.

According to Lee Rainie (2006) of the Pew Internet and American Life Project, 87% of all youth between the ages of 12 and 17 use the Internet. Technology plays a special role in the lives of today's teens. As the first generation to grow up with interactive media, they comfortably manipulate, remix, and share content. Rainie notes that 57% of teens contribute to online common areas with creations such as artwork, audio and video, photos, and creative writing.

First published in *Teacher Librarian*, October 2006, Volume 34, Number 1

It is essential that the teacher-librarian work with students, teachers, and parents to understand the harmful and helpful applications of social technologies inside and outside the school setting.

WHAT IS SOCIAL TECHNOLOGY?

Social technology refers to computer-mediated communication environments that connect people for co-operation, collaboration, and information sharing. The result is a dynamic online community.

Weblogs, wikis, forums, instant messaging, and e-mail are all social technologies that facilitate information sharing and online community formation. These communities can be accessed through many types of devices, including laptops and handheld devices such as PDAs (personal digital assistants) and cell phones. Stowe Boyd (2003) identified three characteristics of social software: interaction, feedback, and connections.

Interaction

This software allows conversational interaction between individuals or groups using tools such as instant messaging and collaborative workspaces. For example, teens may get together with friends online rather than meet at the mall. New friends may be invited to join these conversations.

Feedback

Social technology generally provides a mechanism for reacting to others in the form of guest books, comments, or reputation and rating systems. Rainie (2006) notes that, beyond friends whom they know locally, teens expect to have conversations with the creators of web content, and they want to register their critique of others' work.

They also want their voices heard—for example, by voting on issues through online polls and by using rating services to rate reputations, such as those on eBay. Although some people applaud this activism, others are concerned about the potential negative impact of web sites such as RateMyTeachers (**www.ratemyteachers.com/**).

Connections

A third mechanism of social technology is support for the creation of new relationships. For example, MySpace.com (**www.myspace.com/**) uses personal profiles and invitations for friends as a way of establishing new contacts. The core of social software is the ability to identify people with similar interests and needs. A child recovering from cancer may feel isolated; however, a social network such as those sponsored by the American Cancer Society (**http://cancer.org**) can facilitate contacts with others who have similar experiences.

WHY ARE SOCIAL TECHNOLOGIES SO POPULAR WITH YOUNG PEOPLE?

Teens are particularly drawn to social technology because it meets many of their socialization needs. Young people talk about being unique and different from others, but at the same time they seek affirmation from their friends—thus, the ABCs of social networks.

Activism

Young people want to be involved with the world beyond the local community. They want to share. Whether it is voting on *American Idol* or participating in a global warming forum, they want to feel part of what is happening in the world. For some students, their interests lie in participating in online activities related to celebrities and sports figures. However, some young people seek ways to help the environment, become politically active, and build international connections.

Belonging

Relationships are important to tweens and teens. Boyfriends, girlfriends, best friends, and peer-group friends are all nurtured online through the use of rating systems, virtual reputations, and commenting functions. Kids crave a sense of identity and being embraced by a group.

Contact

Students want to be at the center of the action. Because "everyone" is using social networks, students want to be part of the crowd. Young people see social networks as invitations to a party—as a way to meet people and keep up to date on what is happening in their world. They are concerned about missing out on something important, and they use technology to stay in constant contact.

Data Collection

Young people gather information through social networks. They share poems through text postings and ask for feedback; they create polls about school issues; and they ask friends for help with personal problems or homework. Unfortunately, many students are unable to effectively evaluate the information that they gather from these various social contacts.

Freedom

From the mall to the family room, most physical spaces in a young adult's world are supervised. Children seek online environments where they can exert their independence. Although some students experiment with drugs, others use the online environment to test ideas and share fantasies. Although this experimentation can be harmless, it can also be dangerous.

WHAT IS ONLINE SOCIAL NETWORKING?

Social networking is a particular application of social software. Networking web sites facilitate the creation of informal and formal connections among people with similar interests to form online communities. Sometimes called "friend of a friend" sites, they are often associated with places such as MySpace.com. According to the National Center for Missing and Exploited Children (National Center for Missing and Exploited Children, 2006), 61% of 13- to 17-year-olds have a personal profile on a social networking site.

Most social networking sites ask users to enter information about themselves into profiles, and they provide search tools to help participants identify people with similar interests based on criteria from these profiles. Although some social networks are totally open, others require users to be invited to join a group.

Communication can be synchronous (live interaction) or asynchronous (delayed). In addition, it may involve two people or many people.

One-to-One

Some communications are individual-to-individual, such as e-mail, audio and video conferencing, and instant messages.

One-to-Many

Personal profiles, announcements, testimonials, web postings, forum messages, web sites, and blogs are intended for one person to communicate his or her ideas to many people. Many social networks contain digital sharing areas, including reviews, bookmarks, photos, audio, video, or other digital documents.

Flickr (**www.flickr.com/**) is a web site where people share their digital photographs. Delicious (**http://del.icio.us/**) is a social bookmarking web site designed to help people store and share their favorite web sites. MyWeb2.0 from Yahoo! also provides shared bookmarks.

Many-to-Many

Collaborative software such as wikis is used to build projects where many people can share their ideas in creating a joint project, such as Wikipedia: The Free Encyclopedia (**www.wikipedia.org**). Polls, surveys, rating systems, and other data collection tools are also a way for many people to cooperate. Data from remote sites might be used to gain an understanding of a problem or process. For example, students might record and share data about animal migration patterns or river water.

Some people fear that these social networks will replace face-to-face interaction. However, many are finding that, rather than conflict with people's community ties, social networks fit seamlessly with other types of communication. These social networks allow people to maintain contact with family and friends who are geographically dispersed. In addition, social technologies allow people to find support networks for a range of needs.

WHAT ONLINE SOCIAL NETWORKS DO YOUNG PEOPLE USE?

New online social networks are being introduced daily. Most social networking sites, such as MySpace.com, do not allow young people under the age of 14 to join. However, it is common for under-age children to fib about their ages to participate. Because of the notoriety of MySpace.com, many teens are seeking lesser-known web sites with fewer regulations.

Adults

The biggest online social network is MySpace.com. Other social networking web sites include Friendster (**www.friendster.com/**), MSNSpaces (**http://spaces.msn.com/**), Orkut (**www.orkut.com/**), and Yahoo360 (**http://360.yahoo.com/**). Some social networks are designed for photo sharing, such as Flickr (**www.flickr.com/**), Slide (**www.slide.com/**), and Zorpia (**www.zorpia.com/**). There is a growing number of special interest communities, such as BlackPlanet (**www.blackplanet.com/**) and MiGente (**www.migente.com/**). Classmates (**www.classmates.com**), Reunion (**www.reunion.com**), and MyFamily (**www.myfamily.com**) focus on making connections among families and friends.

Media-rich communities such as YouTube (**http://youtube.com**), Multiple (**http://multiple.com**), and Buzznet (**www.buzznet.com/**) emphasize audio, video, and photos, and FriendsOrEnemies (**www.friendsorenemies.com/**) emphasizes music.

High School Students

Although many high school students use adult resources, some web sites are designed specifically for young people. Bebo (**www.bebo.com/**), My Yearbook (**www.myyearbook.com/**), and Facebook (**www.facebook.com/**) were designed for high school and college students. Sconex (**www.sconex.com/**) bills itself as the unofficial web site for "your high school." Study Breakers (**www.studybreakers.com/**) and Tagged (**www.tagged.com/**) are for high school students. Some students prefer to use blog-based tools such as LiveJournal (**www.livejournal.com/**) and Xanga (**www.xanga.com/**) to journal and build communities.

Few social networking sites are designed for younger children. However, two subscription services are being developed for children 8 to 14 years old: Imbee (**www.imbee.com/**) and Thinkronize (**www.thinkronize.com/**), from the producers of NetTrekker (**www.nettrekker.com/**). For a long list of social networks, go to Wikipedia's "List of Social Networking Web Sites" (**http://en.wikipedia .org/wiki/List_of_ social_networking_websites**).

Like any technology, it can be dangerous in the wrong hands. Help young people find and use tools responsibly.

HOW DO SOCIAL NETWORKS AFFECT THE SCHOOL LIBRARY PROGRAM?

Social networks are something that educators cannot ignore. They have become part of the culture of young people. *Information Power: Building Partnerships for Learning* (AASL & AECT, 1998) stresses the importance of preparing students for life beyond the walls of the school. The key is balancing the concerns with the benefits.

Model Positive Applications

Meredith Farkas (2006) is a distance learning librarian at Norwich University in Northfield, VT. In her blog (**http://meredith.wolfwater.com/wordpress/index.php**), she points out that many libraries are using social networks to reach out to their patrons.

Brainstorm ways that you might use the power of social networks in your school. Many schools are developing Intranets that can be used for social technology activities within the school. Show positive applications of social networks through online book clubs; literature circles; and other communication and collaboration-rich activities connected with reading, writing, and information.

If you are still having a hard time relating to the allure of social technologies, try a specialized network. For example, have some fun with LibraryThing (**www.librarything.com/**). This network is designed for people to share the contents of their personal libraries and find out what others are reading. You can review books, find out what others with similar interests are reading, and make social connections. Check out an example at LibraryThing: Educapes (**http://www.librarything.com/   pro- file/eduscapes**).

Discuss Time Management and Multitasking

Although young people are convinced that they can watch music, listen to music, IM (instant message) their friends, and do homework at the same time, they may be overstimulated and less productive than they think. Although they form a generation of multitaskers, they also experience, in the words of Linda Stone (quoted in Levy, 2006), *continuous partial attention.* In other words, they try to accomplish several things at once by scanning through resources looking for the most useful information, which can lead to surface-level perceptions rather than deep understandings. Discuss the importance of study skills and a focus on deep thinking.

Promote Information Skills

Help students make responsible decisions about social networking. Whether it is discussing the threat of cyberbullies or talking about misinformation at social networking web sites, it is important to get students talking about their experiences with social networks. This is a great opportunity to remind students about ethical behavior, the importance of evaluating information, and how to deal with uncomfortable online situations.

SUPERVISE STUDENT ACTIVITY

Focus on supervision rather than restriction, by providing opportunities to participate in meaningful online interactions. In response to concerns about minors who are accessing social networking sites, lawmakers have introduced legislation that would require schools and public libraries to block commercial web sites with features such as blogs, chats, messaging services, and other interactive elements. This enactment would expand the current Children's Internet Protection Act (**www.fcc.gov/cgb/consumer facts/cipa.html**), which requires filtering software. However, filters and blocks will not prevent your students from finding a backdoor into social networks. Make students aware of the dangers, and use the following online resources for added information about online safety:

NetSmartz (**www.netsmartzkids.org/**)
GetNetWise (**http://kids.getnetwise.org/**)
Wired Safety (**www.wiredsafety.org/**)

REFERENCES

American Association of School Librarians (AASL) & Association for Educational Communications and Technology (AECT). (1998). *Information power: Building partnerships for learning*. Chicago: American Library Association.

Boyd, S. (2003, May). Are you ready for social software? *Darwin*. Retrieved May 31, 2006, from **www.darwinmag.com/read/050103/social.html**

Farkas, M. (2006). Libraries in social networking software. *Information Wants to Be Free*. Retrieved May 31, 2006, from **http://meredith.wolfwater.com/wordpress/index.php/2006/05/10/libraries-in -social-networking-software/**

Levy, S. (2006, March 27). (Some) attention must be paid! *Newsweek, 147*(14), 8.

National Center for Missing and Exploited Children. (2006). *Teen Internet safety study*. Retrieved May 31, 2006, from **www.netsmartz.org/safety/statistics.htm**

Rainie, L. (2006, March). *Life online: Teens and technology and the world to come*. Speech to the annual conference of the Public Library Association, Boston. Retrieved May 31, 2006, from **http://www.pewinternet.org/ppt/Teens%20and%20technology.pdf**

㉚

Open the Door and Let 'Em In

Joyce Valenza

Someone's knocking at the door
Somebody's ringing the bell
Someone's knocking at the door
Somebody's ringing the bell
Do me a favor, open the door and let 'em in
—Paul McCartney

After 10 years of maintaining a school library web site of which I was pretty proud, it struck me that it was time to rethink ownership. Here's what I know: Teens who create or collaborate on online spaces are more likely to feel welcome living on them. I see that on my students' MySpace, Facebook, and Flickr accounts.

It makes great sense in a world where learners are used to creating and not merely consuming web content, as documented by the Pew Internet and American Life Project, "Teen Content Creators and Consumers" (**www.pewinternet.org/PPF/r/166/report_display.asp**). Way back in 2005, the report concluded

American teenagers today are utilizing the interactive capabilities of the Internet as they create and share their own media creations. Fully half of all teens and 57 percent of teens who use the Internet could be considered Content Creators. They have created a blog or Webpage, posted original artwork, photography, stories, or videos online or remixed online content into their own new creations.

So what happens when you open the door and let them in?

It's clearly time to open the school library doors. Opportunities are ripe. On the most basic level, librarians can easily create galleries of student art/work or document library activities using tools like Flickr (**www.flickr.com**). I asked several students to collaborate in creating a school clip art gallery

First published on e-VOYA, April 2007, www.voya.com. *Teacher Librarian* acknowledges e-VOYA's permission to adapt and reprint this article.

(**www.flickr.com/photos/ springfieldtownship**). Our curator, Steve, is getting our yearbook photographers to contribute their shots. We have yet to attribute credit and assign labels, but Steve tells me that he's on top of it. Chris, our Art Gallery curator (**www.flickr.com/photos/45367058@N00**), plans to add many more examples of student work, improve the shots I took, and encourage artist reflection as time nears for our spring art show.

You can view a steadily growing archive of videos in our new SpringfieldVideoBlog (**http://spring fieldvideo.edublogs.org**). This work is a collaboration involving the library, classroom teachers, and our video production teacher.

Our students contribute to the learning culture by creating their own learning objects through streamed video or Podcasts. We now have a grammar and an information literacy series. Students are also working with me to create book trailers for our reading list titles. Teachers pull these videos up for just-in-time instruction. I use them regularly. And as I wander, I see students viewing their own videos here in the library. Some pull them up just to show their friends.

Students (mostly Ben) recently wrote and produced our new orientation video (**http://springfield video.edublogs.org/taxonomy/tags/information-skills/orientation**). The library site also now regularly hosts our latest Springfield broadcast news production. Last month's show (**http://springfieldvideo .edublogs.org/taxonomy/tags/springfield-news**) was particularly filled with honesty and humor.

Much more video is coming. The students are working on seven more productions for our grammar series. And I am learning how to convert them to Flash. (They'll open far more quickly once I get that straight.)

Podcasts are coming, too. Martin posted one on Open Source that we need to tighten a bit. He is also helping me to put my own podcasts together for the site.

We are moving our senior seminar projects to blogs to encourage reflection and make peer and faculty interventions more transparent. You can view examples of our curricular blogs and wikis on our on-line lessons page (**http://mciu.org/~spjvweb/jvles.html**). I am beginning to migrate our pathfinders from html to wiki form to encourage student participation. I want to include student discoveries and suggestions for resources.

I am inspired by the discoveries I make as I visit other school library web sites. Northfield Mount Hermon's Reading Room blog (**http://nmhlibrary.typepad.com**) is all about student users and reaches way beyond student research needs to celebrate the whole learner, the whole *teen*. It celebrates and includes its student musicians, its student poets, its workers, its readers, and its lounge lizards.

Pam Allan, associate director of Academic and Library Resources at Northfield Mount Hermon, says of the student involvement, "Some of it was intentional; some of it was discovery. It's a continuing experiment. We knew our library's web site had a different mission and audience from the larger school's Web site."

Northfield's traditional site (**www.nmhschool.org/nmhlibrary/index.php**) is clearly effective but fairly serious and curricular. Allan notes that the library's mission is to serve students and help them with their research. "We spent a lot of time creating a professional Web site that the school could be proud of, but something was missing, something that would reflect the atmosphere of our library. It's a kid-centered library. There's a lot of work going on. There's also a lot of fun going on."

The Reading Room blog (**http://nmhlibrary.typepad.com**) is clearly a student-centered, friendly space. Allan likes its dual purpose. She sees her work, off- and online, as a kind of *guerilla* activity. "Isn't it the nature of librarians to think of learning as fun? Mixing humor and fun with research is what we're all about in the library on the web site."

Allan started with her Lounge Lizards (**http://nmhlibrary.typepad.com/the_reading_room/ lounge_lizard_archives/index.html**), the regulars who show up every day. "The library is their home base. We started taking pictures of them and getting quotes. Then I handed the camera to our student workers, who liked doing it. And they got different kinds of quotes. Now the students do it all. They download the photos; they get the blog entry ready as a draft. I just post it." Allan notes that the Lounge Lizard area has become so popular that kids now just come in and say, "Hey, I've never been Lounge Lizard of the Week!"

Northfield's Acoustic Friday (**http://nmhlibrary.typepad.com/the_reading_room/acoustic_ fridays/index.html**) started a couple years ago. Allan noticed students sitting outside the library with their guitars—"just some low-key musicians playing for their friends." When the weather got cold, she looked for a good time to let them in. "We close at five on Fridays and so we decided to invite them to play during the quiet time between four and five." Allan promoted these events on the web site. The school's webmaster asked about recording them. Now students film and record Acoustic Friday performances and the webmaster posts them as Podcasts.

Posts in Northfield's blog feature student reviews of books, CDs, and DVDs. Sometimes the students read the books. Sometimes Allan just asks students "to go to the new books rack and try to find the book they'd most like to read if they had the time. We advertise these reviews through e-mail. We want the students to say, 'Look at what so-and-so is reading or wants to read.' Students may be more likely to check out what another kid is reading."

Northfield posts photos and profiles of its Library Workjob Crew (**http://nmhlibrary.typepad .com/photos/library_workjob_0506/index.html**). "We ask them to say something they'd like the school to know about them or their work in the library." The site includes student art exhibits as well as winning entries from its yearly poetry contest, a blog-promoted event. Winners of the library's "very silly" Hoggers in Literature Diorama Contest (**http://nmhlibrary.typepad.com/the_reading_room/contest/index .html**) are also featured.

Allan plans to increase student participation. Northfield students are currently involved in helping her to create an online research tutorial. She is planning a student column on the blog and she hopes to post images of an upcoming ALA-inspired contest. Keep an eye on the Reading Room blog for the results of Northfield's Pimp Your Bookcart Contest.

At the Runkle School in Brookline, MA, librarian Teresa Gallo-Toth and educational technology specialist Elizabeth B. Davis collaborate with classroom teachers to post student book review Podcasts (**www.runkle.org/Podcasts/index.html**). Right now, you can listen to book reviews by second, seventh, and eighth graders. But Gallo-Toth and Davis plan to engage the entire K–8 school. Davis says, "The first graders are almost done, and third graders are starting soon. I am hoping that this will become a resource for students looking for a good book. Eventually we want to accept podcasts from other students and teachers—not just at our school—and post them to our site."

In New York state, Greece Athena Media Center's web site (**http://www.greece.k12.ny.us/ath/ library**) features student book reviews and ratings on its supplementary Athena Blogs! (**www.greece .k12.ny.us/ath/library/blogs/index.htm**). At University Laboratory High School (Uni) in Urbana, Illinois, students participate in a long-running Book Discussion Forum (**www.uni.uiuc.edu/bbs/viewforum .php?f=5**). Uni librarian Frances Jacobson Harris fills her own Gargoyles Loose in the Library blog (**www.uni.uiuc.edu/library/blog/index.html**) with images of and stories about her students. Naples High School Media Center in Florida also features images of learners as well as student poems, photos, and art (**www.collier.k12.fl.us/nhs/lmc**). Lawrence High School Library in Kansas has a site **http://library**

.lhs.usd497.org/home.html filled with posters featuring students and photos of student events. The LHS blog (**http://lawrencehighschoollibrary.blogspot.com**) posts student reviews.

So where does all this school library door opening fit in with larger educational trends? Despite moves to prevent student access to social networking tools (the Deleting Online Predators Act or DOPA, for instance), other evidence endorses trends towards engaging learners in interactive online space. SchoolSpan, an organization specializing in school public relations, recently proposed a national rubric for school sites, "Building Blocks to Electronic Communication" (**http://fetc.jssinc.com/release-exh/ SchoolSpanRubricFETC.pdf**). The rubric values contributions from faculty and students, images of students, and the inclusion of student work. The instrument's description of an exemplary site concludes with this statement: "The community-at-large feels empowered as active stakeholders . . . the site reflects that ongoing communication objective."

All this interaction makes great sense in a Web 2.0 world. It puts front and center the kind of learning highlighted in the recently released NETS Refreshed (National Educational Technology Standards) draft (**www.iste.org/Template.cfm?Section=NETS_Refresh_Forum_Meetings&Template=/Content Management/ContentDisplay.cfm&ContentID=16084&MicrositeID=0**). The revised technology standards encourage learning based on Creativity and Innovation; Communication and Collaboration; Research and Information Retrieval; Critical Thinking, Problem Solving, Decision Making; and Digital Citizenship.

Should we lock learners and their creativity out of the very spaces where they spend the largest part of their days? I think it's time to open our doors and let 'em in.

31

InfoTech: Flash: Engaging Learners Through Animation, Interaction, and Multimedia

Annette Lamb and Larry Johnson

I downloaded the new Green Day tunes on my iPod last night.
Do you want to watch last night's episode of Lost *on my cell phone during lunch?*
I saw you online last night. Did you try that new game they were demo-ing?

As students walk through your library, you may catch pieces of their conversations and wonder if they live on another planet. It is not a parallel universe, just the digital world of today's children and young adults. They come to school hoping for a learning environment as multisensory and stimulating as the outside world but are often disappointed by old-fashioned textbooks and low-tech approaches. So how do we balance the need for quality content with the importance of providing varied, engaging resources to meet diverse learning needs?

In his article "Getting Into the Game," Henry Jenkins (2005) notes that students are increasingly bored with school. He suggests that educators apply the power and popularity of gaming when designing classroom activities. Jenkins views electronic simulation games not as something to replace the teacher but as a tool to spark learning and provide a context for experiences.

A DASH OF FLASH

Teacher-librarians are increasingly seeking Flash-based web resources to address this need for engaging, technology-rich learning environments. A few years ago, seeing the Macromedia Flash icon on a web page meant the hassle of downloading plug-ins and the possibility of frequent crashes. However, Flash today often represents the best that the Internet has to offer in terms of free or low-cost, high-quality infor-

First published in *Teacher Librarian*, April 2006, Volume 33, Number 4

mational and instructional materials. Rather than dreading the Flash icon, we now seek out those Flash-based web projects because they are filled with engaging animation, interaction, and multimedia features.

BrainPOP (**http://brainpop.com**) was one of the first web sites to produce animated educational movies for K–12 students, using a fast-paced, multimedia format. Today, more than 25% of school districts subscribe to this service.

Over the past several years, Flash-based projects have become much more sophisticated. For example, Windward (**www.ciconline.org/windward**) from Cable in the Classroom is an elaborate simulation requiring users to "outsmart the weather" with the mission of sailing around the world in record time. Developed in cooperation with Discovery Education, the Weather Channel, and NASA, learners explore concepts in math, science, geography, and history.

FLASH IN A FLASH

Although Flash contains many great features for producing informational, instructional, and persuasive materials, three key elements stand out: animation, interaction, and multimedia (Lamb & Johnson, 2006).

In A Dancer's Journal (**http://artsedge.kennedy-center.org/marthagraham/index.htm**) from the Kennedy Center, readers explore a student's interactive journals as she learns to perform the dances of Martha Graham. In the form of an electronic scrapbook, this virtual experience includes animation, interaction, and multimedia elements.

Animation

Movement is an effective way to communicate concepts, processes, procedures, and other ideas. The animation features of Flash allow developers to create engaging visual presentations. In some cases, the learner has control over the animation. In other words, the child can choose the sequence or speed of the action. Sometimes the animation runs automatically.

The Labs (**www.pbs.org/wgbh/buildingbig/lab/index.html**) at the Building Big web site allows students to control animated sequences while experimenting with forces, materials, loads, and shapes to learn about construction.

Flash is often used to develop short instructional movies that entertain but also have a strong message. The Stop Bullying Now web site (**http://stopbullyingnow.hrsa.gov**), sponsored by the U.S. Department of Health and Human Services, contains 12 short "webisodes" focusing on the message of taking a stand and lending a hand.

As you evaluate Flash-based projects, ask yourself,

- Does the animation contribute to the effectiveness of the project?
- Does the user have control over the animation sequence or speed?
- Does animation attract rather than distract users?
- Is animation used in meaningful ways?

Interaction

The interactive features of Flash allow developers to integrate dynamic functionality through questioning, feedback, branching, and user tools. Seek out Flash projects that immerse students in microworlds where they freely explore ideas, manipulate variables, and experience the consequences of their decisions, rather than merely read, watch, or listen.

Simulations. Inquiry-based approaches help students explore questions, conduct investigations, and solve problems. By providing an environment to analyze information, manipulate variables, examine relationships, and make decisions, users are asked to transfer their skills to new situations.

In Villainy, Inc. (**http://villainyinc.thinkport.org**) students become secret agents and must solve math problems to foil Dr. Wick's goofy evil plan.

In Make a Tide Pool at the Monterey Bay Aquarium (**www.mbayaq.org/lc/kids_place/tidepool/tidepool.asp**) students select the plants and animals that go into a tide pool.

In Making Vaccines (**www.pbs.org/wgbh/nova/meningitis/vaccines.html**) students create six vaccines in a virtual laboratory, applying different techniques for each experiment.

Gaming. Games are based on rules and contain specific goals. Students are intrinsically motivated by the immediate feedback and challenge of solving problems and facing adversity. From conducting experiments on tuberculosis to engaging in international trade, the series of simulations at the Nobel Prize web site (**http://nobelprize.org/search/games-simulations.html**) involve students in the topic related to the award.

The U.S. Department of Agriculture MyPyramid game (**www.mypyramid.gov/kids/kids_game.html**) helps students to explore the food groups and to keep track of their choices as they plan healthy meals.

Tutorials. Tutorials guide students through new information and provide an opportunity to practice. The Edheads web site (**www.edheads.org/**) provides a number of tutorials, including Virtual Knee Surgery, Weather, and Simple Machines.

As you evaluate Flash-based projects, ask yourself,

- Does the interaction contribute to the effectiveness of the project?
- Does the interaction provide levels of access or control to address individual needs?
- Do interactive elements function effectively?
- Do interactive elements contribute to understanding rather than confusion?
- Is the result of interaction clear and effective?

Multimedia

Enriching a Flash project with sounds, speech, music, graphics, scanned images, photographs, and video allows developers to reach varied interests and learning styles.

A More Perfect Union: Japanese Americans and the U.S. Constitution (**http://americanhistory.si.edu/perfectunion/experience/index.html**), from the Smithsonian Institution, offers the option to read or listen.

Many music organizations have interactive Flash web sites that include audio or video elements, including Arts Alive Canada (**www.artsalive.ca/**), Arizona Opera (**www.azopera.com/learn.php**), Dallas Symphony (**www.dsokids.com/**), and San Francisco Symphony (**www.sfskids.org/**).

As you evaluate Flash-based projects, ask yourself,

- Does the multimedia contribute to the effectiveness of the project?
- Are media attributes used effectively without being distracting?
- Do the media elements address alternative learning styles?
- Were media elements clear and easy to understand and interpret?

Putting It All Together

Elements most often incorporated in Flash projects include animation, interaction, and multimedia. These elements can be applied in different ways to create interesting, informative projects. Text, illustrations, maps, slide shows, timelines, and tools are features incorporated into Flash projects.

The Lewis and Clark as Naturalists online exhibit (**www.mnh.si.edu/lewisandclark/**), from the Smithsonian Institution, contains interactive maps, timelines, and illustrations.

Text. Although most often associated with glitzy visuals, Flash is also useful for text-rich projects.

At NOVA's Ancient Refuge in the Holy Land (**www.pbs.org/wgbh/nova/scrolls/babatha.html**), students explore Babatha's Scroll through an interactive translation.

Illustrations. Animated interactive charts and graphics, concept maps, line drawings, scanned documents, and photographs can demonstrate analogies, processes, relationships, cycles, and perspectives.

At the American Museum of Natural History, Ology (**http://ology.amnh.org/**) explores many areas of science and history through Flash animations.

Maps. Animated interactive maps allow users to identify locations, explore changes and make predictions, and examine movement.

The Theban Mapping Project (**www.thebanmappingproject.com/**) allows users to explore archaeological zones of Egypt.

Timelines. Timelines are used across content areas to help users visualize the history of a topic. They can be short term, divided by century or era, or arranged by topic.

The Hip Hop Timeline (**www.emplive.org/explore/hiphop/index.asp**) traces the development of the hip hop musical form from the early 1970s to today.

Tools. Flash can be used to create a variety of utilities, calculators, simulators, and other tools.

At the Artist's Toolkit (**www.artsconnected.org/toolkit/explore.cfm**) users can watch demonstrations, find examples, and create a composition.

INTEGRATING FLASH-BASED ACTIVITIES

It is easy for students to get caught up in the fun of Flash activities. This engagement is important for learning, but it can also distract students from the instructional goal. It is therefore essential that the teacher-librarian and classroom teacher partner to identify specific learning goals matched to curriculum standards, select the best materials to meet these needs, and develop effective minilessons to use these resources efficiently. These learning guides may require students to work with vocabulary lists, concepts maps, or essential questions as they move through the Flash project.

According to Harada and Yoshina (2004), effective partnerships access a range of resources, support varied technologies, and provide opportunities for creative synergy and collegial problem solving.

You probably cannot take students to the National Zoo in Washington, DC, but you can build an exciting learning environment that includes books, videos, manipulatives, and other resources. Through Flash animation, your students can design a panda habitat, go on a habitat adventure, and conduct field research in a virtual forest. Conservation Central (**http://nationalzoo.si.edu/Education/Conservation Central/**), from the National Zoological Park, is an award-winning web site that promotes habitat education. It is also an excellent example of a resource that meets diverse needs. Students who have difficulty reading the words can listen to scientists discussing field research. Students who need concrete experiences can learn new concepts as they build a panda habitat. If they make poor choices, the system provides suggestions and encouragement.

Not all web sites use Flash to achieve their interactive elements. For example, Scholastic's Interactive Skill Builders (**http://teacher.scholastic.com/activities/**) contains a mixture of activities that incorporate Flash as well as other interactive tools.

In the article "Listen to the Natives," Marc Prensky (2005–2006) refers to young people as digital natives. He stresses that technology can have its greatest impact by helping educators adapt to the changing needs of children. Many computer-based environments can adjust to meet the capabilities and skills of individual learners.

However, keep in mind that the multimedia aspects of Flash can cause problems for users who have special needs. For example, Flash is not compatible with all assistive-technology devices and web browsers. As a result, it is important to provide alternative text, descriptive captions, or other devices to ensure accessibility of Flash projects.

FLASH AND THE SCHOOL LIBRARY

Enrich your library pathfinders with links to quality Flash-based learning materials. Using your favorite search engine, add terms such as *Flash, interactive, .swf*, and *animation* to your subject area search, such as *tornado interactive* or *Civil War Flash*.

You will have even better success if you search for projects using popular web sites, such as National Geographic, PBS, Discovery, Scholastic, and NASA. For example, conduct a Google search for *site: nationalgeographic* and add the word *interactive* or *Flash*.

The player software required to use Flash-based projects is free and simple to download and install. Go to the Macromedia Flash Player Support Center (**http://macromedia.com/support/flashplayer/**) for information about the technical aspects of Flash and download requirements.

For many more examples of Flash-based projects across subject areas and grade levels, go to **http://eduscapes.com/flash/explore.htm**.

REFERENCES

Harada, V. H., & Yoshina, J. M. (2004). *Inquiry learning through librarian-teacher partnerships*. Worthington, OH: Linworth.

Jenkins, H. (2005, April). Getting into the game. *Educational Leadership, 62*(7), 48–51.

Lamb, A., & Johnson, L. (2006). *AIM your Flash project: Vision to action*. Available at **http://eduscapes.com/flash**

Prensky, M. (2005, December–2006, January). Listen to the natives. *Educational Leadership, 63*(4), 8–13.

32

Personal Computing: Keeping Up With RSS

Reid Goldsborough

Imagine having delivered to you just the information that you need as soon as it becomes available. That has always been the Holy Grail of the information age. Since the Internet became the Internet, people have tried to come up with better ways to stay informed with the help of the Internet. One of the latest and most successful is a web-based system called RSS, which most people understand today to mean *really simple syndication* (it has meant different things in the past).

For web users, the chief benefit of RSS is convenience. Instead of periodically going to web sites and blogs of interest to find out what is new, you can have that new information automatically delivered to you. This makes it less time-consuming to keep up.

For web site owners, RSS lets you provide people with another means of obtaining your content. If you do not provide RSS feeds, some visitors may opt for similar sites that do. This applies to any business site, news site, personal blog, or other destination with frequently changing information.

You subscribe to RSS feeds through an RSS web service or RSS reader. The most popular RSS web service today is Bloglines (**www.bloglines.com**), a free service that lets you not only subscribe to RSS feeds but also publish your own. The company behind the service was founded by Mark Fletcher, the brains behind ONElist, which eventually became Yahoo! Groups (**http://groups.yahoo.com**), the popular e-mail-based discussion group service.

You can also access RSS feeds from your desktop. RSS is integrated into Mozilla Firefox (**www.mozilla.com/firefox**), the second-most-popular web browser, behind Microsoft Internet Explorer. You can access RSS feeds using Microsoft Internet Explorer with add-on products such as the free Dogpile Search Tool (**www.dogpile.com**). NewsGator (**www.newsgator.com**) is a heavier-duty commercial program that can, among other things, harness RSS to help companies keep track of their competitors.

Other free ways to tap into RSS are Google's Gmail and the latest version of Yahoo! Mail. RSS is built into Tiger, Apple's most recent operating system.

First published in *Teacher Librarian*, February 2007, Volume 34, Number 3

RSS is also used for Podcasting, the delivery of audio and video files of your choice to mobile devices such as Apple's popular iPod.

RSS is bound to become even more mainstream in the future. The upcoming Microsoft Outlook 2007 has RSS integration. According to the beta version, RSS feeds appear as folders in your mailbox. The next version of Microsoft Windows will also have RSS built into it. A competing technology is Atom, with some services and products supporting both RSS and Atom.

RSS, as its name suggests, is fairly simple. On web pages, RSS (or Atom) web feeds are typically indicated with an orange square marked with radio waves, the letters *RSS* or *XML* (RSS is based on the XML page-markup language), or the word *subscribe*. After subscribing, you can click on a headline or summary that is of interest, and the article or post will be delivered to you.

Compared with e-newsletters, which are delivered to your e-mail once a day, RSS lets you keep up with new developments virtually as they happen. More sites provide RSS feeds than newsletters. Some sites provide RSS feeds for discussions, letting you subscribe to a feed not only for the site's articles but also for comments posted in response.

Compared with PointCast, the first popular "push" service that was all the vogue 10 years ago, RSS does not slow down your PC and tie up corporate networks with headlines and ads. You control when you want the information that you request delivered to you, whether every few minutes, hours, or days. RSS works as well on slow dial-up connections as it does on high-speed broadband ones.

There are nearly as many ways to create RSS feeds with your site as there are to subscribe to them, from free on up. As just one example, RSS DreamFeeder (**www.rnsoft.com/products/rssdreamfeeder**) integrates into Adobe Dreamweaver (**www.adobe.com/products/dreamweaver**), the popular high-end web development software.

On the downside, as a clipping service for the Web, RSS can contribute to the problem of information overload. If you sign up for more and more feeds, you may wind up feeling barraged by data. The solution is to "mark all as read" without reading or unsubscribe to feeds that you are consistently not able to get to.

RSS may not be worth checking out if you do not follow any web sites closely. But if you do, it can be an efficient way to track what is new at those sites and receive new information in general about the subjects you are following.

33

InfoTech: Turn Up the Music With Digital Technologies

Annette Lamb and Larry Johnson

A group of young people are picking out music for a poetry slam.
A pair of students are wearing ear buds and playing a keyboard attached to a computer.
A child reads a story into the laptop's microphone as music plays softly in the background.

Turn your school library into a learning laboratory where students can explore all aspects of music as they address standards across the curriculum. Although music plays an important role in the lives of young people, it is often ignored and even censored by educators. Many schools have filtered all MP3 downloads from the Internet and have prohibited music players from school grounds. From the built-in microphone on a laptop to iPods and smart cell phones, the potential for music in learning is enormous. How do we balance concerns about lyrics and "audio cheating" with the benefits associated with the musical medium?

MUSIC IN TEACHING AND LEARNING

The teacher-librarian is in the perfect position to see applications of music across the curriculum. Regardless of whether you have received formal music training or just enjoy listening to songs on the radio, there are many ways to strengthen your school's music collection and support music for learning.

Music is one of the multiple intelligences described by Howard Gardner (1993). Music intelligence is the ability to produce and appreciate rhythm, pitch, and timbre and have an appreciation of the forms of musical expression. Music is for the whole brain and possibly the first of the intelligences to develop. In the decades since Gardner first introduced the theory of multiple intelligences, educators have widely adopted his framework. However, although many schools have structured their school reform around the multiple intelligences, school music programs have been cut or dropped dramatically in favor of funding for testing and basic literacy programs.

First published in *Teacher Librarian*, December 2006, Volume 34, Number 2

Digital technologies provide a range of opportunities for exploring, infusing, and creating music.

EXPLORING DIGITAL MUSIC RESOURCES

Whether seeking information about musicians or looking for music clips, a variety of resources are available on the Internet.

Databases. Many of the popular electronic databases contain a music section, but few provide audio clips. For older students, consider a subscription to Grove Music Online (**www.grovemusic.com/**), where students can find and listen to music, examine musical scores, read biographies, explore world cultures, and learn the parts of instruments.

Seek out web sites that specialize in music files for young people. The National Institute of Environmental Health Sciences maintains a huge collection of sing-along songs (**www.niehs.nih.gov/kids/music.htm**), including musical instrument digital interface (MIDI) audio files and lyrics.

Interactives. From playing in an orchestra to composing music, many web sites provide engaging interactive content and tools for young people. Explore these sites:

Arizona Opera (**www.azopera.com/learn.php**)
Arts Alive (**www.artsalive.ca/**)
Dallas Symphony (**www.dsokids.com/**)
New York Philharmonic Kidzone (**www.nyphilkids.org/**)
San Francisco Symphony (**www.sfskids.org/**)

Music blogs. MP3 blogs, also known as *music blogs* or *audioblogs*, are a type of weblog that makes digital music files available for download. Although some of these Internet DJs post music tracks with granted copyright permissions, others focus on *indie music* (i.e., not connected to the "big four" recording labels) or out-of-print music. In some cases, bloggers post a disclaimer that they are willing to remove any music if the copyright holder objects. Thousands of these blogs exist, with names such as Bubblegum Machine (**www.bubblegum-machine.com/**), Classical Connection (**www.classicalconnection.blogspot.com**), and Destination Out (**http://destination-out.com/**). You can also sample music from several different MP3 blogs at the Hype Machine (**http://hype.non-standard.net/**), an audio blog aggregator. Keep in mind that blogs vary tremendously in content and that some may not be appropriate for school students.

Web radio. People are increasingly listening to live and replayed radio programming through the Internet. Three interfaces are most commonly used for webcasts:

• Apple iTunes (**www.apple.com/itunes/**)
• Real Radio (**http://radio.real.com/**)
• Windows Media (**www.windowsmedia.com/mediaguide/radio/**)

Radio broadcasts are available from around the world, including dozens of languages. Popular webcasts include

• ABC (**www.abc.net.au/streaming/**);
• BBC (**www.bbc.co.uk/radio/d/**);
• CBC (**www.cbc.ca/radio**);
• NPR (**www.npr.org/**).

Popular radio directories include

• Open Directory: Internet Radio (**http://dmoz.org/Arts/Radio/Internet/**);
• Radio-Locator (**www.radio-locator.com/**).

Music video. Some music-video sites are free; others require a membership fee. Keep in mind that many contemporary artists have audio clips and music videos at their personal web sites, such as

• Beck (**www.beck.com/**);
• Jake Shimabukuro (**www.jakeshimabukuro.com/videos.php**).

Music videos can also be found and viewed. They are streamed from varied sites, such as

• AOL Music (**http://music.aol.com/**);
• Yahoo Launch (**http://launch.yahoo.com/musicvideos/**).

Want to know the name of that tune playing on your radio? Visit YES.com (**http://yes .com/index.php**) and enter the station's call letters or key in your zip code. Or just look at the map and see what is starting to play around the country.

Music searching. When attempting to locate a specific title or the work of a musician or group, try using an audio search engine. For example, students can easily find a short segment from the song "War" from the early 1970s (Williams & Edwards, 1970) for use in a project related to antiwar demonstrations. Using Audacity (**http://audacity.sourceforge.net/**), students could create a 10-second clip focusing on the well-known chorus "War, what is it good for? Absolutely nothin'!"

Some popular audio search engines include

• Altavista (**www.altavista.com/audio/default**);
• FindSounds (**www.findsounds.com/**);
• Music Robot (**www.musicrobot.com/**);
• SingingFish from AOL (**http://search.singingfish.com/**);
• Yahoo (**http://audio.search.yahoo.com/**).

Acquiring music. From the earliest Internet days, music has been shared. Today, peer-to-peer (P2P) computer network file-sharing programs, such as Morpheus (**http://morpheus.com/**) and eMule (**www.emule-project.net/**), are used to upload and download music files. Though the technology can be used to acquire accessible copyrighted materials, there are a significant number of copyright hold-ers who have authorized the sharing of their content for noncommercial purposes, often using the Cre-ative Commons (**http://creativecommons.org/**) format license. Remember that most commercially re-leased popular songs are not currently authorized for free redistribution but require separate purchase or licensing.

A huge source for acquiring copyright-free music online is the Audio Archive (**www.archive.org/ details/audio**). Music from the locations on this site can be legally used by students and teachers in their multimedia and web site publications. The music can be remixed and shared.

INFUSING MUSIC ACROSS THE CURRICULUM

Music can set mood, motivate reluctant learners, and address individual differences. However, for music to have a real impact on teaching and learning, it is important to form a collaborative team that includes the teacher-librarian, music educator, and classroom teachers. The resources at ArtsEdge (**http://artsedge.kennedy-center.org/**) are a natural place to begin a discussion of standards-based connections to music. As you explore the possibilities, search Marcopolo (**www.marcopolosearch.org/**) for music connections across the curriculum.

Music and picture books. Over the past several years, music CDs have become popular companions to children's books. Music plays a central role in *The Remarkable Farkle McBride* (2003) and many other picture books by John Lithgow. At his Lithgow Palooza web site (**http://johnlithgow.com/**), you can sample his projects. A series of picture books featuring songs like "Take Me Home Country Roads" (Denver, 2005) have introduced a new generation to John Denver. Recently, original poems by Walter Dean Myers were brought to life through harmonica and guitar riffs, in *Blues Journey* (2003). Poetry and music are a natural combination that can be found in many audio-enhanced picture books.

Music and novels. From historical novels to realistic fiction, seek ways to combine music with literature. Whether reading books from the American Civil War or French Revolution, set the mood with music from the period. For example, *Nory Ryan's Song* (Giff, 2002) is a story set in Ireland during the potato famine and a great opportunity to play Celtic music. In some cases, music may even play a central role. For instance, in *Bud, Not Buddy* (Curtis, 2000), the central character is searching for his jazz musician father. This theme provides a great context for listening to jazz and learning about its origins. Visit NEA Jazz in the Schools (**http://media.jalc.org/nea/**) and PBS Kids: Jazz (**http://pbskids.org/jazz/**) for great lesson materials. Another approach involves students creating their own soundtrack to accompany a novel. Does country, hip-hop, or jazz best fit the story?

Music and mnemonic devices. Whether singing about the functions of conjunctions or the process of passing legislation, teachers have used music in learning for decades. The Emmy Award–winning series *Schoolhouse Rock* is one example that most people remember from their childhoods. Grammar, math, science, and social studies are just a few of the topics covered by the 46 educational music videos, now available on DVD.

The musical approach began long before the days of *Schoolhouse Rock*, though. Listen to science-themed folk songs from the 1950s at Singing Science Records (**www.acme.com/jef/singing_science/**). Today, groups such as AstroCappella (**www.astrocappella.com/**) continue the tradition.

Research has shown that combining simple repeated melodies with accompanying visuals that reinforce the content is effective in learning. So get your students involved in writing their own music.

Music, metaphor, and contemporary issues. Songs such as "The River" by Garth Brooks and Victoria Shaw and "Hazy Shade of Winter" by Paul Simon are rich opportunities to explore metaphor in music and discuss the themes of pop culture. *Stairway to Heaven: Examining Metaphor in Popular Music* (Carmichael, 2006) is the title of one of many lessons at ReadWriteThink (**www.readwritethink.org/**) that uses music in language arts.

Music with a message. Seek out lesser-known musicians with unique perspectives. Consider how the music of someone such as American Indian Jack Gladstone (**www.jackgladstone.com/**) might be used across the curriculum. His songs "Sacagawea" and "When the Land Belonged to God" are biographical; "Tappin' the Earth's Backbone" is environmental; and "Lewis and Clark's Traveling Magical Show" is historical.

Music and culture. Explore the music and culture of a particular area of the world. For example, students might play learn to play the Thumb Piano (**http://pbskids.org/africa/piano/**) as they explore African culture.

Cellist Yo-Yo Ma started the Silk Road Project (**www.silkroadproject.org/**) to encourage the exploration of different cultures and their music. The River of Song web site (**www.pbs.org/riverofsong/**) explores contemporary music along the Mississippi River.

Music and historical recordings. Did you know that there are multiple versions of the "Battle Hymn of the Republic"? You can listen to them and many other patriotic melodies and historical recordings at the Library of Congress Performing Arts Digital Library (**www.loc.gov/rr/perform/ihas/ihashome.html**).

Music and documentary. How does music affect our lives? National Public Radio (**www.npr.org/programs/specials/vote/list100.html**) identified 100 of the most important American musical works of the 20th century. The Experience Music Project (**www.emplive.org/**) explores music in modern culture. Students can listen to music, along with the people and stories behind the music. Ask students to choose a song that represents this millennium and to write their own minidocumentary.

Music and ethics. Issues related to music copyright are an excellent opportunity for student inquiry and debate. ReadWriteThink's *Copyright Infringement or Not? The Debate Over Downloading Music* (Taylor, 2006), at **www.readwritethink.org/lessons/lesson_view.asp?id=855**, explores this topic at the high school level.

All the regulations and restrictions can be daunting for students and teachers who want to use music in the classroom. The portal site Ourmedia (**www.ourmedia.org/**) has become a global community for housing and sharing media, as well as a resource for locating legal music.

CREATING MUSIC

Technology can play a role in all phases of music production, including song writing, recording, editing, mixing, and sharing.

Hardware. A range of peripheral devices can support music applications in the curriculum. First, you need a way to play music. A good set of portable speakers is essential for large group activities. Some schools are now providing ear buds for each student, rather than messing with headsets. If your computers do not have built-in microphones, it is easy to attach an inexpensive microphone.

Many music classrooms use MIDI connections and keyboards (acoustic piano) hooked up to computers to create music. The electronic keyboard can play the sounds of any instrument. Computer technology enables users to arrange the notes and change the timing. Think of it as a musical word processor. Work with your music teacher to develop a music station in your library, where students can explore and create audio resources outside the music classroom.

Software. Before investing in expensive software, explore free, open-source options. For example, Audacity (**http://audacity.sourceforge.net/**) is a popular cross-platform application that allows students to record and edit audio clips for web and multimedia applications. Other examples include

- Band in a Box (**www.band-in-a-box.com/**);
- Bias Peak (Mac only) (**www.bias-inc.com/**);
- GarageBand (Mac only) (**www.apple.com/ilife/garageband/**);
- Sound Forge (**www.sonymediasoftware.com/**).

Mash-ups and remixes. Rather than create original works, some students may to want to produce remixes. Music mash-ups—sometimes called *bootlegs*, *blends*, or *cutups*—are a musical home brew, often of illegal music (derivative works), created by combining elements of two or more songs to form a new piece of music. The ccMixter web site (**http://ccmixter.org/**) is a community music-remixing site that provides users both software and music for cutting up and creating their original mash-up musical work using legal resources.

Music and multimedia projects. Look for music options that are already embedded in other software. For example, PhotoStory for Windows (**www.microsoft.com/windowsxp/using/digitalphotography/photostory/default.mspx**) provides an easy-to-use music generator that can be used with graphics, text, and narration to create high-quality student projects. iPhoto for the Mac (**www.apple.com/dotmac/photocast.html**) also provides a tool for adding audio to slide shows.

Explore examples of student-produced music at Apple Student Gallery (**http://edcommunity.apple.com/gallery/student/**).

MUSIC AND LEARNING

Music can open the mind to learning across the curriculum and pave the way for independent learning. Music embodies the multiple intelligences described by Gardner (1993). Writing lyrics, creating scores, creating complicated patterns, and operating keyboards requires complex critical and creative thinking. Music can be an optimal learning experience, or a *flow experience* (see Csikszentmihalyi, 1990), which completely involves a person. Using an array of digital technologies, today's teacher-librarian can design learning environments that help young people explore, infuse, and create music.

DIGITAL MUSIC PRIMER
Streaming Versus Downloading

Streaming audio means that a remote server sends your computer small amounts of audio data (a *data stream*) that are held in a buffer until there is enough to begin playing. If there is no interruption, the music will play to the end of the stream. As each chunk of the audio is played, the data is discarded.

Downloading music means that the audio files from an Internet location are copied (downloaded) onto a local storage area on your computer. The advantage is that once you have a local copy, you can store it, play as often as you wish, duplicate the file, and distribute it to others based on applicable copyright rules.

A Little About Audio Files

Music, audiobooks, famous speeches, sounds, and sound effects can all be found in a digital audio format. Digital audio is available in a variety of file formats, including RealAudio, WAV (waveform), MIDI, and MP3.

MPEG (Moving Pictures Experts Group) is a set of standards used for coding audiovisual information in a digital compressed format. The MP3 format has become the popular way to store music and other digital audio files. Because MPEG files are highly compressed, they are smaller than other files of the same quality.

REFERENCES

Carmichael, S. (2006). *Stairway to heaven: Examining metaphor in popular music.* Retrieved September 14, 2006, from **www.readwritethink.org/lessons/lesson_view.asp?id=855**

Csikszentmihalyi, M. (1990). *Flow: The psychology of optimal experience.* New York: Harper Perennial.

Curtis, C. P. (2000). *Bud, not Buddy.* New York: Yearling.

Denver, J. (2005). *Take me home, country roads: Score and CD included!* Nevada City, CA: Dawn.

Gardner, H. (1993). *Multiple intelligences: The theory in practice.* New York: Basic Books.

Giff, P. R. (2002). *Nora Ryan's song.* New York: Yearling.

Lithgow, J. (2003). *The remarkable Farkle McBride.* New York: Simon & Schuster.

Myers, W. D. (2003). *Blues journey.* New York: Holiday House.

Taylor, S. (2006). *Copyright infringement or not? The debate over downloading music.* Retrieved September 14, 2006, from **www.readwritethink.org/lessons/lesson_view.asp?id=855**

Williams, P., & Edwards, D. (1970). War [Produced by N. Whitfield]. On *Psychedelic Shack* [album]. Detroit, MI: Gordy.

(34)

InfoTech: Open-Source Software in School Libraries

Annette Lamb and Larry Johnson

I do not see how we can afford to purchase, support, and maintain our technology program. I would like to be optimistic, but look at what is happening to budgets everywhere. We were hoping for an increase in per-student dollars this year, but instead, they have eliminated the software funding entirely. Grants and initiatives have helped our schools get where we are today, but I do not think that we can sustain the program we have built.

Does this scenario sound at all familiar? How much are you spending on computer software? Many schools are examining the fees that they spend yearly to purchase commercial software. Most are finding that they are spending a huge amount of money every year on proprietary software and operating system upgrades. Some are limiting the purchase of specialty software and confining licensing to a core software group. Ever-present budget concerns are leading administrators and decision-makers to look for ways to lessen software costs while at the same time attempting to meet varied classroom and curricular demands.

The purchase of proprietary software provides a license to use but does not allow you to adapt the source code to meet varied needs. The end-user license agreement also narrowly defines how the software is to be used and allows for stiff penalties to be assessed for violations. In addition, you can use the program on only a specific number of computers.

With constantly shrinking budgets and the many restrictions of proprietary software, many teacher-librarians are looking for alternatives, namely, open-source software.

WHAT IS OPEN-SOURCE SOFTWARE?

Open-source software is developed and improved by its own community of programmer users. But in direct contrast to commercial software programmers, these developers are not competing for market share,

First published in *Teacher Librarian*, June 2006, Volume 33, Number 5

nor are they interested in restricting their product's use. They are willing to share the results of their efforts with any interested persons. The source code for these programs is openly shared; no single person or company holds exclusive rights to open-source software programs. Learn more at the Open Source Initiative (**www.opensource.org**), the nonprofit corporation that promotes open-source software.

This free and cooperative approach has evolved into the open-source software movement. With open-source software, a general public license is often used to license the program. There is no worry about software audits, visits from the Business Software Alliance (**www.bsa.org/**), or fines for a misplaced certificate of authenticity (Surran, 2003).

With the general public license of open-source software, users are granted the freedom to

- run the program for any purposes,
- examine the program to see how it works,
- modify the program to improve or fit their needs, and
- release and distribute the program (including their modifications, if they wish; Wikipedia, 2006).

Open-source software is gaining acceptance around the world. According to Goldsborough (2005), there are nearly 100,000 open-source software programs available. Millions of people use the best-known open-source software product, the Linux operating system (**www.linux.org**), an alternative to Microsoft Windows and Mac OSX. According to Netcraft's Web server survey (2006), almost 70% of web sites are now running open-source Apache server software rather than Microsoft, Sun, or others.

WHAT ARE THE ADVANTAGES OF OPEN-SOURCE SOFTWARE?

A primary draw of open-source software is the fact that it is free. Because it costs nothing to download and use, it is immediately available. Although most educators do not change the software's coding, users have full access to source code, allowing them to adapt the program to meet local needs. For example, Moodle is an open-source software course management system that can easily be customized to contain your school's logo and colors.

Open-source software

- is free, allowing money to be used elsewhere;
- can legally be copied and shared with anyone;
- provides alternatives and flexibility to user organizations;
- is constantly being modified and improved;
- has strong technical support;
- is less vulnerable to security threats; and
- has open code so that anyone can examine and see how it works.

WHAT ARE THE CHALLENGES OF OPEN-SOURCE SOFTWARE?

In addition to advantages, challenges are also found with using open-source software. Although most open-source software runs on both Microsoft Windows and Mac OSX, some open-source software runs only on the Linux operating environment. Other issues include the fact that

- programs may not be available to meet specialized needs;
- programs may not be as completely "packaged" as proprietary alternatives;

• open-source software may require more learn time;

• open-source software may require more skill to deploy and maintain;

• open-source software may not be compatible with some preexisting software packages; and

• most open-source developers provide only limited free support and require fees for technical support.

As you might expect, many proprietary software developers are not advocates of open-source software. Critics of open-source products contend that the software is lower quality than that of its commercial counterparts. However, just the opposite may be true. Many open-source packages are equal or superior to their costly competitors. Generally, the programs are more stable than proprietary software because any interested programmer can read, modify, and distribute the source code. There are many more eyes to see program bugs and to provide fixes.

HOW ARE SCHOOLS USING OPEN-SOURCE SOFTWARE?

Open-source software is rapidly emerging as a cost-saving means of providing high-quality technology tools for teachers and students. Schools are introducing and using open-source software in three ways: running the school's servers and furnishing schoolwide network services; providing operating systems for classroom and administrative computers; and supplying applications software in the classroom and for administrative functions (British Educational Communications and Technology Agency, 2005).

The U.K. government's school computing agency, British Educational Communications and Technology Agency (2005), reported on a study conducted in a small number of primary and secondary schools. The study found that when the schools adopted open source operating systems in their office operations, they experienced a potential budget savings of 20% to 50%, with increased reliability and performance and lowered support costs. To successfully migrate and adopt open-source software, the study advocated careful planning and support led by someone who champions the change.

But instead of totally switching to an entirely different operating system, some schools are selectively moving to a few open source programs. This partial open source commitment occurs largely in two patterns: one, through adopting some open-source software programs that run on their existing operating systems; two, through committing a number of their computers to using the Linux systems and software. Many schools are looking at their software service agreements. Instead of switching all computing to open source programs, they are choosing key areas and operations where they can give their budgets some needed wiggle room. Schools that are currently paying significant licensing fees for commercial software stand to gain the most from adopting open source programs.

WHAT OPEN-SOURCE SOFTWARE IS USEFUL IN
TEACHING AND LEARNING?

It is likely that you are already using open-source software. If not, here are a few of the most common applications.

Course Management

If you would like to create online book clubs or promote collaborative writing projects, consider Moodle (**http://moodle.org/**), a popular course management system designed to help educators create effective online learning communities. Like Blackboard, it contains options for threaded discussions, forums, wikis, and many other collaborative tools.

Graphics

Tux Paint (**www.newbreedsoftware.com/tuxpaint/**) is an easy-to-use draw program designed for young children (ages 3 and up). Software such as Blender (**www.blender3d.com/cms/Home.2.0.html**), for modeling and animation; Qcad (**www.ribbonsoft.com/qcad.html**), for computer aided 2-D drafting; the GIMP (**www.gimp.org/**), for image manipulation; and ImageMagick (**www.imagemagick.org/script/index.php**), for creating images from scratch may be able to replace expensive imaging software.

Mind Mapping

For brainstorming to project planning, commercial tools such as Inspiration are often used. However, alternatives are available in the open source community, such as FreeMind (**http://freemind.sourceforge.net/wiki/index.php/Main_Page**) and IHMC Cmap Tools (**http://cmap.ihmc.us/**).

Multimedia

Even free, Audacity (**http://audacity.sourceforge.net/**) is one of the best audio-editing programs available and is widely used by student and teacher developers to record and play sounds, import and export computer files, and more. Consider Dynebolic (**www.dynebolic.org/**) and Jahshaka (**www.jahshaka.org/**) as high-end multimedia tools for sound and video recording, editing, encoding, and streaming.

Productivity Tools

Microsoft Office is something that you will find on most school computers. However, as the cost per computer rises, consider OpenOffice Suite (**www.openoffice.org/**) as an alternative. This multiplatform, multilingual tool includes software for word processing, spreadsheets, graphics, and multimedia presentation.

Reservation System

If you deal with reservations, consider the Online Resource Scheduler (**http://ors.sourceforge.net/**). The software is installed on your web server and can be used throughout the school.

Utilities

Ad-Aware (**www.lavasoftusa.com/software/adaware/**) detects and removes spy/malware, which is placed on a computer to mine data, track usage, and sometimes enact malicious content.

Web Authoring

Although you may currently be using FrontPage or Dreamweaver, open source alternatives are also available, such as Nvu ("new view"; **www.nvu.com/**). In addition, consider JEdit (**www.jedit.org/**) as a text editor and MySQL (**http://dev.mysql.com/**) for database applications. To clean up your HTML, use Tidy (**http://tidy.sourceforge.net/**).

Web Browser

Firefox (**www.mozilla.com/firefox/**) is a relatively fast and intuitive web browser that is an alternative to Internet Explorer, Netscape, and similar programs.

Web Server

Apache web server software (**www.apache.org/**) is a great choice for your school's web server.

Wiki

Wikipedia (**www.wikipedia.org/**) is the public encyclopedia that has been the subject of some controversy and scrutiny but nonetheless continues to gain in use as a handy and relatively reliable desktop reference tool. By its very nature, Wikipedia is self-correcting. That is, when content is identified as being false, correct versions are submitted. In addition, when a topic is controversial or contested, Wikipedia provides direct links to opposing viewpoints and arguments.

Finally, many schools in the United States and other countries (United Kingdom, Canada, Australia) are looking at a total changeover to the Linux operating system and are divorcing themselves from a dependence on proprietary software. Given the choice of having a laptop with open-source software or no laptop at all, which do you think a child would pick?

WHAT IS THE IMPACT ON THE SCHOOL LIBRARY?

Open access to ideas and information is a core philosophy of progressive school library programs. Yet throughout many schools, reliance on proprietary software restricts users to the conditions of an end-user license agreement, so most of the software is closed and locked. As a result, many teacher-librarians have started advocating the use of open-source software as a means to stretch their budgets, as well as to increase access to technology for all.

John McDonald, a teacher-librarian and open source advocate at Connersville Middle School, IN, states that "open-source software functions as an equalizer in many regards because it allows us to focus on effective integration of technology as the need arises instead of worrying about where the funding will come from" (personal e-mail to Larry Johnson, January 29, 2006). He finds that open-source software is an "almost-at-hand resource" for meeting unexpected technology needs. When a student or teacher project has the need for image manipulation, sound editing, or other tasks that cannot be handled with existing packages, they look to open source solutions as a way to try out new ideas without investing in expensive software. For example, say that your poetry club would like to begin a weekly podcast sharing their original poems. At one after-school meeting—and at no cost—students can download and use Audacity to record their poems to an MP3 file that can be uploaded to the school web site.

To plan, facilitate, and implement a successful migration to open-source software in your school, follow these seven steps:

1. Carefully evaluate each piece of software. Explore why and how it will be used, as well as its benefits.
2. Identify the strengths and weaknesses, including the cost benefits connected to existing resources.
3. Select a few software packages, and design tutorials, training materials, and other resources to support the software's use.
4. Begin on a small scale, working with teachers who are likely to embrace change.
5. Help users identify relevant projects where the software can be integrated.
6. Inform decision makers of the software and the benefits that it provided to the trial group.
7. Remember that instruction and support are an ongoing process, not a one-time event.

RESOURCES

For more information and ideas about open-source software, here are resources to explore and learn more:

K–12 Linux Project, Portland, OR (**www.k12linux.org/**)

Making Decisions About Open-Source Software for K–12, from the Northwest Educational Technol-

ogy Consortium and Northwest Regional Educational Laboratory (**www.netc.org/openoptions/**)
Schoolforge (**www.schoolforge.net/**)
Schoolforge News-Journal (**http://opensourceschools.org/**)

REFERENCES

British Educational Communications and Technology Agency. (2005, May). *Open-source software in schools: A study of the spectrum of use and related ICT infrastructure costs.* Retrieved February 14, 2006, from **www.becta.org.uk/corporate/publications/documents/BEC5606_Full_report18.pdf**

Goldsborough, R. (2005, July 4). Open source: Free software at a price. *Community College Week, 17*(24), 18.

Netcraft. (2006, January). *Web server survey.* Retrieved February 14, 2006, from the Netcraft web site, **http://news.netcraft.com/**

Surran, M. (2003, September). Making the switch to open-source software. *The Journal.* Retrieved February 14, 2006, from **www.thejournal.com/articles/16448**

Wikipedia. (2006, February). *Open-source software.* Retrieved February 14, 2006, from **http://en.wikipedia.org/w/index.php?title=Open-source_software&oldid =40664204**

PART IV

Learning Leadership: 21st-Century Skills

(35)

Graduating Students Who Are Not Only "Learned" But Also "Learners"

Jean Donham

In the 19th and early 20th century, a person who had acquired enough knowledge was considered "learned" or "educated." Writing in 1984, Richard Derr quotes from R. S. Peters' 1967 definition of an "educated person":

> According to Peters, we call a person "educated," if (1) he (sic) has some body of knowledge; (2) he has an understanding of principles which provide an organization for facts, (3) the body of knowledge characterizes his way of looking at things, (4) he is committed to the standards on which the body of knowledge rests, and (5) he possess a broad cognitive perspective. (pp. 301–302)

Today's graduates must leave school with knowledge, to be sure. However, the pace of new knowledge generation and change calls for today's graduates to be more than "learned" or "educated." Today's graduates must be learners as well. Learners must possess knowledge, skills, and dispositions that will facilitate continued independent learning past school years.

Consider these facts from *Did You Know?* a video by Karl Fisch, Director of Technology at Arapahoe High School in Colorado; Fisch provides the video and citations for the facts he cites and these can be found at his blog (**http://thefischbowl.blogspot.com/**).

• One in four workers today is working for a company for whom they have been employed for less than one year (United States Department of Labor).

• Today's learner will have 10 to 14 jobs by the time they reach age 38 (United States Department of Labor).

• The top 10 jobs that will be in demand in 2010 did not exist in 2004 (Richard Riley, Former Secretary of Education citing *The Jobs Revolution: Changing How America Works* by Steve Gunderson,

First published in *Teacher Librarian*, October 2007, Volume 35, Number 1

Roberts Jones, and Kathryn Scanland).

• One week's worth of *New York Times* contains as much information as a lifetime's worth of information in the 18th century (Richard Wurman in *Information Anxiety*).

• Over 2.7 million Google searches are performed each month.

• The number of words in the English language is estimated at 240,000—five times the count in Shakespeare's day.

• Technology information doubles yearly. This implies that for a student in a four-year technical program, half of what was learned in the first year could be outdated by the third year!

Fisch's observations bring home the reality that our graduates must leave us as learners in order to survive the dramatic and rapid changes they will encounter in their lives.

We find today a substantial number of initiatives and standards aimed at defining the knowledge and skills graduates should possess. For example, *Results That Matter* is the product of work by a partnership among corporate, education, and government entities to arrive at a vision for 21st-century learning. The vision proposes the following key elements:

• Core subjects: English, reading, or language arts; mathematics; science; foreign languages; civics; government; economics; art; history; and geography

• Emerging content areas: global awareness; financial, economic, business, and entrepreneurial literacy; civic literacy; health and wellness

• Learning and thinking skills: critical thinking and problem solving; communication; creativity and innovation; collaboration; contextual learning

• ICT literacy: ability to use technology to develop knowledge and skills, in the context of core subjects

• Life skills: leadership, ethics, accountability, adaptability, personal productivity, personal responsibility, people skills, self-direction, social responsibility

• Assessments: use of standardized and classroom assessments

Results That Matter is one of many proposals for what students should learn in school. Similarly, each discipline has defined its standards for the knowledge and skills that students must possess, for example, National Council of Teachers of Mathematics, National Council for the Social Studies. Today's pressure for accountability and assessment increase the likelihood of emphasis on knowledge and skills that are readily measured through standardized and/or objective testing.

Knowledge and skills across the disciplines provide an essential foundation for students to face the world of change that they will encounter. However, development of a static knowledge bank will not serve them well in the world they will enter upon graduation, if Fisch's descriptions and predictions are on target. Development of dispositions toward learning and skills to continue to learn will be of utmost importance in their lifetimes. When we say that students must have a disposition toward inquiry, we suggest that they must be curious and ready to pose significant questions. Ron Ritchhart (2001) explores the question of disposition for learning as an alternative view of intelligence. Ritchhart proposes that intelligence may in fact be construed as "a collection of cognitive dispositions that capture one's tendency to engage in certain patterns of thinking" (p. 143). Citing Baron, Ritchhart asserts that dispositions are "learned tendencies or cognitive styles under our control" (para. 2). The notion that dispositions can be learned stands in sharp contrast to the definition of intelligence as a measure of inherent abilities. Upon examination of six researchers' lists of dispositions toward learning and habits of mind, Ritchhart synthesizes them into seven categories.

Costa and Kallick (1999) use the phrase "habits of mind" to describe a similar concept about learners and learning. In their work, they list 16 "habits" not dissimilar from Ritchhart's "dispositions." In their discussion of habits, Costa and Kallick assert that educators are "interested in enhancing the way students produce knowledge rather than reproduce it" (p. 7). They propose that educators want students to inquire and think flexibly.

Similarly, the draft version of the American Association of School Librarians *21st Century Library Learning Standards* (2007) proposes not only skills, but also dispositions. By underscoring the importance of dispositions, this document acknowledges that information work requires a stance characterized by readiness to learn.

The importance of dispositions is evident in initiatives underway to examine college readiness as well. Ritchhart's list of dispositions for learning are generic, that is, cutting across all disciplines. However, there are nuances of dispositions for learning that may be unique to specific disciplines. The Center for Educational Policy Research at the University of Oregon has sought to define what high school graduates need to know and be ready to do in order to succeed in higher education. With funding from the Pew Charitable Trusts and sponsorship from the Association of American Universities, this organization has set out to examine the question of readiness for college. While preparation for higher education is the explicit focus of their work, it is difficult to argue with the appropriateness of their conclusions for graduates who choose other paths after high school as well. Their work is published in three forms: a booklet entitled *Understanding University Success* (Center for Educational Policy Research, 2003), a book entitled *College Knowledge* (Conley, 2005), and a website at **www.s4s.org**. While readers will find here knowledge and skills not unlike those found in other standards and school reform initiatives, the point of emphasis here will be on "dispositions," that is, what attitudes toward learning ought students to have as they leave high school?

In *Understanding University Success*, standards are defined for English, Mathematics, Natural Sciences, Social Sciences, Second Languages, and the Arts. In Table 35.1, descriptions of dispositions for learning from Ritchhart, Costa and Kallick, the American Association of School Librarians (AASL), and *Understanding University Success* are compared. These dispositions are essential for success in an era of rapid and deep change and knowledge growth.

There is remarkable similarity among these portrayals of the disposition of a learner. A challenge for educators is to design experiences that facilitate students developing these dispositions—it is the opportunity to leave school with the dispositions of a learner that should be the entitlement of every American high school graduate.

Library media programs occupy an ideal place for collaboration with teachers from all disciplines to develop in students such dispositions for learning. Library media centers can be the exploratoriums in schools, and teacher-librarians can be the docents, the guides, and the facilitators for students' explorations. If one were seeking a single word to summarize the dispositions Ritchhart and others propose, *inquiry* may be that word. Kuhlthau (2001) describes inquiry in this way:

Inquiry-based learning is an approach to instruction that centers on the research process. . . . Students are guided through inquiry by asking themselves: What do I already know? What questions do I have? How do I find out? And finally, what did I learn? Inquiry takes students out of the predigested format of the textbook and rote memorization into the process of learning from a variety of sources to construct their own understandings. (p. 1)

Ritchhart (2001)	Costa and Kallick (1999)	AASL (2007)	Examples from *Understanding University Success* (Center for Educational Policy Research, 2003)
be open-minded	thinking flexibly taking responsible risks remaining open finding humor listening with empathy creating	maintain openness display resilience demonstrate creativity	"ability to view facts from multiple perspectives"—Second Languages
be curious	persisting responding with awe	display curiosity appreciate literature	"must allow questions to emerge from the text"—English "inquisitiveness and willingness to investigate the steps used to reach a solution"—Mathematics "curiosity and a willingness to explore many layers of meaning"—The Arts
be metacognitive	applying past knowledge to new situations striving for accuracy	demonstrate adaptability demonstrate teamwork	"integrating scientific methods and contextual understanding, critical thinking, and hands-on skills"—Natural Sciences
be investigative	questioning and posing problems	display initiative and engagement	"using experimental thinking"—Mathematics
reason	managing impulsivity thinking independently communicating with clarity	maintain a critical stance	"make connections regularly between public knowledge and personal observations and experiences"—Social Sciences "make connections across disciplines"—Social Sciences
reason	managing impulsivity thinking independently communicating with clarity	maintain a critical stance	"make connections regularly between public knowledge and personal observations and experiences"—Social Sciences "make connections across disciplines"—Social Sciences
use evidence	gathering data with all senses	test against evidence	"make supported inferences and draw conclusions based on textual features"—English

Table 35.1. Dispositions for Learning

Inquiry-based library media programs afford schools the opportunity to provide

- a skill set for learners,
- a context for developing the dispositions necessary to be learners, and
- resources to support learning-to-learn experiences.

Foundation skills are essential for the independent learning that graduates must be prepared for in their adult world of rapid change. These skills can be summarized as the skills necessary to locate, access, evaluate, interpret, and communicate information. While these skills can be readily summarized, they represent a complex set of competencies that depend upon ability to initiate substantive questions, to read and think critically, and to use technology at all stages of the information process. The skill sets are defined more fully in the *21st Century Library Learning Standards* from the AASL (**http://wikis.ala.org/aasllearningstandards/index.php/Main_Page**) and National Educational Technology Standards from the International Society for Technology in Education (**http://cnets.iste.org/students/s_stands.html**).

The challenge for schools to develop the appropriate dispositions for a world of rapid change may be more complex. If we use Ritchhart's (2001) synthesis of the dispositions of learning, we can perhaps consider how the library media program contributes toward developing such dispositions:

• *Be open-minded*. A foundation principle for library collections is the provision of multiple perspectives. By engaging students with a range of resources that bring students into an intellectual exchange, teacher-librarians can create a context that encourages consideration of multiple viewpoints. An environment that fosters acceptance of diverse viewpoints is essential. The library should be the politically and socially neutral environment that avoids pre judgment and encourages exploration. The teacher-librarian can support open-mindedness by offering students a collection that represents a variety of viewpoints and encouraging students to examine topics from various perspectives.

• *Be curious*. By providing an array of resources that can pique interests of students, the school library media center can serve as the stimulus for curiosity. While essential, a collection of current and high-quality resources alone will not be enough to engender curiosity. Teacher-librarians must serve as mediators between students and the collection. In that role, they can model curiosity as they help students consider what questions they could pursue and guide them to resources in that pursuit. Whether they are sharing stories with young children and encouraging questioning and further exploration or they are discussing ideas for a senior research project, teacher-librarians offer unique expertise in the inquiry process.

• *Be metacognitive*. When students engage in any sort of library research, it is important for them to learn to ask and answer the questions "When do I have enough information?" and "Is my information of high enough quality?" and "Am I pursuing a worthwhile question?" and "Have I investigated various perspectives?" A disposition of self-assessment can readily be taught in the context of the library media program. As we consider the world of information change for today's students, such a disposition will be crucial to them as independent learners. Teacher-librarians can encourage self-assessment as students work on research projects by providing frameworks for self-assessment. For example at the web site of the San Benito High School in Hollister, CA,, Achterman and Campbell offer a research guide featuring variety of ways to assist student in their research process. A "checkpoint" strategy encourages students to self assess their research process (**www.sbhsd.k12.ca.us/sbhslib/research/11checkpt1.htm**). Similarly, Abilock's "Noodle Tools Self-Assessment" provides a way for students to reflect on their research process (**www.noodletools.com/debbie/literacies/information/9evaluate/competence.html**)

• *Be strategic*. The library media center provides an excellent laboratory for strategic thinking. To begin, students must have an appropriate mental model of the information search process—they must see it as a process of authentic inquiry, not a process of assembly or transfer of information from a source to their end product. The library media program needs to help students learn to be planful as they pursue interests of their own. If they are engaged in appropriately complex, open-ended assignments so that they generate their own questions and learn to design strategies for information problem solving, they will gain practice at strategic thinking. However, strategic thinking does not necessarily occur without guidance, instruction, and prompting. One way for the teacher-librarian to assist students in developing a strategic approach to research would be adopting an inquiry model. A variety of models are available at **http:// virtualinquiry.com/inquiry/models.htm**. Teacher librarians can select the model most appropriate for the developmental stage of students and acceptable to faculty. Ideally, a model can be adopted school-wide so that students encounter consistent language to describe the inquiry process from class to class, teacher to teacher. Teacher-librarians will need to lead such school-wide adoption in collaboration with teachers. A model will guide students in their understanding of research so that they can approach the inquiry process strategically.

• *Be investigative.* Given appropriate prompts and opportunities, students can use the library media center to explore and to problem solve. Topical queries are too superficial to be truly investigative. Teacher-librarians can help students focus their investigations narrowly enough that they can examine questions in depth and arrive at findings and insights of significance. For example, the Springfield Township High School Virtual Library offers a tool called "Question Brainstormer" at **www.sdst.org/shs/ library/infolitles.html#Information%20Seeking**. Teacher-librarians can use tools like this to help students generate substantive questions that require them to explore and investigate in depth. Too often students are rushed through this early stage of their work out of eagerness to move on to the subsequent stages of their research. Teacher-librarians can play an important role in emphasizing the early stages that result in better focused research queries.

• *Reason.* The library media center offers a reasoning playground. When a teacher-librarian and a classroom teacher plan together, they can create meaningful opportunities for students to develop their abilities to reason. The role for the teacher-librarian is to challenge students' assumptions, question their assertions, point out fallacious reasoning, and insist on adequate evidence and evaluation of sources of information. Engaging students in conversations—whether these are informal or scheduled—is productive and gratifying. One high school librarian actually schedules brief appointments with each student during their class work time in the library so that she can encourage students to challenge themselves in the development of their arguments and their search for viable evidence (Rehmke, personal communication, 2006). A teacher-librarian values persistence in the inquiry process. Teaching students to generate synonyms is another way in which teacher-librarians can give student strategies for being persistent in their information seeking efforts.

• *Use evidence.* By searching for information in the library media center, students can develop an appreciation for the use of evidence to support an argument or to make a decision. Challenging the authority of sources, teaching students to seek verification and to reconcile differences between sources of information are the kinds of critical thinking skills that can be taught when students are working with information from an array of resources—processes not possible in textbook-only instruction.

In order for the library media program to contribute to the development of these dispositions for learning, collaboration between the classroom teacher and the teacher-librarian is essential. Much of what students learn in school is situated in the context of the assignments their teachers design for them. Working with a teacher-librarian, classroom teachers can design assignments that capitalize on the library media program's potential to facilitate students developing dispositions toward learning. A crucial consideration is that these assignments must engage students in work that will challenge them to be curious, to be open-minded, to reason, to be metacognitive, and so on. Gordon (1999) posits that "reporting has masqueraded as researching for so long that the terms are used interchangeably" (para. 1). Indeed, we want students to extend beyond reporting to arriving at insights—at seeking answers to authentic and substantive questions. In the words of Newman, Secada, and Wehlage (1995), they must be assignments that will engage "students in using their minds well" (p. 3). These researchers consider critical criteria for student assignments to be

1. students constructing meaning and producing knowledge;
2. students using disciplined inquiry; and
3. students aiming their work toward production of discourse with value beyond success in school.

To gauge how well assignments meet those criteria, they define four standards of authentic instruction:

1. *Higher order thinking.* Analysis, synthesis, and evaluation are processes residing at the higher order of complexity.
2. *Deep knowledge.* Focusing on central ideas of a topic with enough thoroughness to explore connections and relationships and to produce relatively complex understandings.
3. *Substantive conversation.* Students engage in extended conversational exchanges with the teacher, the teacher-librarian, and/or their peers about subject matter that builds an improved and shared understanding of ideas.
4. *Connection to the world beyond the classroom.* Students make connections between substantive knowledge and personal experience.

Teacher-librarians working in collaboration with classroom teachers can design assignments that meet these criteria. The library media center provides the context where these assignments can be pursued in a setting where the teacher-librarian remains mindful not only of the skills necessary to accomplish information work, but perhaps more importantly of the learning dispositions to be developed. Awareness of dispositions requires that teacher-librarians take proactive and intentional steps to develop and support learning dispositions; these might include

• modeling learning dispositions. Thinking aloud is one strategy for modeling curiosity or open-minded dispositions. For example, a teacher-librarian might be heard saying, "That makes me wonder . . ." Or, "What might be the argument on the opposing side of this question?" Or, "What evidence supports that assertion?" Or "How strong is the evidence on the other side of the argument?"
• posing and encouraging questions that generate authentic inquiry. Teacher-librarians and classroom teachers can use the Newmann, Wehlage, and Secada (1995) four criteria for authentic assignments to design assignments.
• encourage metacognitive behavior. Students may be required to keep a reflective research journal where they record their perceptions about their progress. Or, students might write a reflective self-assessment describing what they might do differently if they were to approach an assignment anew.
• reason and use evidence. Teacher-librarians and classroom teachers together guide students in critically selecting and reading articles to assess evidence and logic.

Intentionality is important. It is not enough to mention or expect that students will develop dispositions of learning as by-products of their school experiences. Developing the disposition of a learner occurs by design. Collaboration between teacher-librarians and classroom teachers can result in assignments and activities that aim intentionally at authentic inquiry and at developing dispositions that will results in graduates who are learners.

Recall the innate curiosity and enthusiasm for learning evident as the kindergarten child arrives at the school house door. It should be the entitlement of every high school graduate to leave the school house with that same curiosity and enthusiasm to learn. It is up to all educators to help not only sustain but enhance those dispositions for learning in order to send off a generation of graduates ready to be learners in a changing world.

REFERENCES

American Association of School Librarians (AASL). (2007). *21st century library learning standards* (draft). Retrieved July 16, 2007, from **http://wikis.ala.org/aasllearningstandards/index.php/ Main_Page**

Center for Educational Policy Research. (2003). *Understanding university success*. Eugene: University of Oregon.

Conley, D. T. (2005). *College knowledge*. San Francisco: Jossey-Bass.

Costa, A. L., & Kallick, B. (1999). *Discovering and exploring habits of mind*. Alexandria, VA: ASCD.

Derr, R. (1984). Education versus developing educated persons. *Curriculum Inquiry, 14*(3), 301–309.

Fisch, K. (2007). Did you know? Shift happens, *The Fischbowl*. Retrieved July 16, 2007, from **http://the fischbowl.blogspot.com/**

Gordon, C. (1999). Students as authentic researchers; A new perspective for the high school research assignment. [Electronic version]. *School Library Media Research Online, 2*. Retrieved March 28, 2007, from **http://www.ala.org/ala/aasl/aaslpubsandjournals/slmrb/slmrcontents/volume21999/ vol2gordon.cfm**

Kuhlthau, C. C. (2001). Inquiry-based learning. In J. Donham, C. C. Kuhlthau, K. Bishop, & D. Oberg (Eds.), *Inquiry-based learning; Lessons from library power* (pp. 1–12). Worthington, OH: Linworth Publishing.

Newmann, F., Secada, W. G., & Wehlage, G. G. (1995). *A Guide to authentic instruction and assessment: Vision, standards, and scoring*. Madison, WI: Wisconsin Center for Education Research.

Partnership for 21st Century skills. (2004). *21st century skills*. Retrieved July 16, 2007, from **www.21stcenturyskills.org**

Ritchhart, R. (2001). A dispositional view of intelligence. *Roeper Review, 23*(3), 143–150.

(36)

Skills for the Knowledge Worker

Doug Johnson

In early 2005, reporter Thomas L. Friedman frightened a great number of Americans with his book *The World Is Flat: A Brief History of the Twenty-First Century* by detailing the impact of globalization on the white-collar workforce in developed countries. Friedman reported that many U.S. jobs once thought to require knowledge economy skills—and, therefore, once thought to be secure—are now being exported to nations such as India and China, which have good telecommunications infrastructures, an overabundance of skilled workers, and (compared to that of the United States) a very low wage scale.

Most Americans, especially those in traditional blue-collar jobs such as manufacturing, have for decades watched nonskilled work being shifted to automated systems (robotics) or cheap foreign labor markets. The conventional wisdom has been that, to be a productive worker in the postindustrial economy, one needs an educated mind rather than a strong back for work that would be done sitting at a desk, not for that done while standing on the factory floor. But Friedman reports that desk jobs in the fields of customer and technical support, computer programming, medical technician diagnostics, tax preparation, and legal research are now migrating abroad. The outsourcing of these kinds of jobs should cause educators to seriously examine what constitutes knowledge worker skills. How might we prepare our graduates to function in jobs that cannot be outsourced and in some way justify the high remuneration that middle-class workers have come to enjoy in developed nations?

This is a problem that is being overstated in the short run but understated in the long run. At the current time, 1 in 10 technical support skills are off-shored; by 2010, it will be 1 in 4 (Morello, 2003). Business analysts predict, "The offshore trend is not a fad, but a mega-trend" (Kalakota & Robinson, 2004, "Conclusion").

Is the educational establishment addressing this trend? (See Figure 36.1.) Levy and Murnane (2004) raise such questions about whether standards-based public education prepares students for mastery of the occupations set to grow in the United States. Using U.S. Bureau of Labor Statistics data, they argue that the greatest job growth will be in well-paying occupations requiring "expert thinking" and "complex hu-

First published in *Teacher Librarian*, October 2006, Volume 34, Number 1

man communication" (p. 80). Schools, the authors claim, need to teach in such a way that these skills become second nature to high school graduates, who can then apply these skills in college or postsecondary training programs, which can lead to success in up-and-coming occupational fields.

But what exactly do we mean when we say "expert thinking" and "complex human communications"? What separates these job skills from "routine cognitive" work? And are there skill sets that students must master before they can be considered complex communicators or expert thinkers?

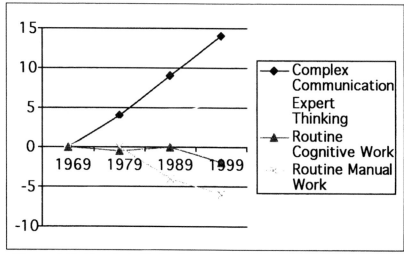

Figure 36.1. Trends in Tasks Done by the U.S. Workforce, 1969–1998 (1969 = 0). Copyright © 2004 by Association for Supervision and Curriculum Development. Reprinted by permission. The Association for Supervision and Curriculum Development is a worldwide community of educators advocating sound policies and sharing best practices to achieve the success of each learner. To learn more, visit ASCD at **www.ascd.org**.

HIERARCHY OF "KNOWLEDGE WORKER SKILLS"

I posit that there is a Maslovian-type hierarchy of knowledge worker skills—skills that need to be mastered before the acquisition and application of higher-order skills (see Figure 36.2). I categorize these as basic skills, discipline- and profession-specific skills, technology skills, information problem-solving and higher-order thinking skills, and conceptual skills.

Level 1: Basic Skills

The ability to read for understanding, interpret visual information, write comprehensibly and persuasively, and solve numeric problems are and will remain the foundations on which all other knowledge work skills rest. To this end, the United States has ambitiously devised systems of testing to help ensure that all students have these literacies. Much of this testing, which varies by state, tests only basic reading comprehension, simple composition, and low-level arithmetic skills.

The danger that many educators perceive in an emphasis on the basics is that, if only the basics are tested and thereby valued, then schools will ignore the affective, creative, and problem-solving sides of education and give students few chances to apply these skills in meaningful

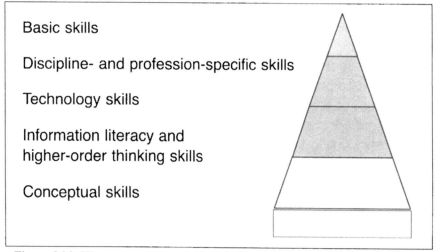

Figure 36.2. Hierarchy of Knowledge Worker Skills

ways. Basic skills, in other words, are an important bar to set for students but an exceedingly low one. Yet, as a primary—if not, the sole—measure of school effectiveness, school leaders are establishing goals and improvement plans addressing student performance on very basic "basic" skills.

Level 2: Discipline- and Profession-Specific Skills

K–12 schools have the obligation to ensure that all students gain some degree of what is often referred to as *cultural literacy*. This is a base of knowledge in history, social science, science, literature, and physical and cultural geography. Cultural literacy cannot be acquired without mastery of the basic skills, and what constitutes as cultural literacy is highly debatable. The memorization of massive numbers of facts without context or application has been rightly criticized as not being a valuable end product of education.

Of course, that postsecondary schools teach the core skill sets and the body of knowledge of science, law, education, architecture, medicine, computer science, engineering, accounting, and other professions will continue to be important. Yet, these occupations are evolving as technology automates routine tasks and creates new procedures and processes that are impossible to do without technology—for example, computer modeling in engineering and CAT scans in medicine.

Level 3: Technology Skills

Because technology has affected nearly every job that might be considered knowledge work, there is an increased recognition that basic technology skills have become a new basic skill. The International Society for Technology in Education attempts to describe what students need to know and need to be able to do, in its National Educational Technology Standards (1998). These standards are divided into six broad categories of application:

1. Basic operations and concepts
Students demonstrate a sound understanding of the nature and operation of technology systems.
Students are proficient in the use of technology.
2. Social, ethical, and human issues
Students understand the ethical, cultural, and societal issues related to technology.
Students practice responsible use of technology systems, information, and software.
Students develop positive attitudes toward technology uses that support lifelong learning, collaboration, personal pursuits, and productivity.
3. Technology productivity tools
Students use technology tools to enhance learning, increase productivity, and promote creativity.
Students use productivity tools to collaborate in constructing technology-enhanced models, prepare publications, and produce other creative works.
4. Technology communications tools
Students use telecommunications to collaborate, publish, and interact with peers, experts, and other audiences.
Students use a variety of media and formats to communicate information and ideas effectively to multiple audiences.
5. Technology research tools
Students use technology to locate, evaluate, and collect information from a variety of sources.
Students use technology tools to process data and report results.

Students evaluate and select new information resources and technological innovations based on the appropriateness for specific tasks.

6. Technology problem-solving and decision-making tools
Students use technology resources for solving problems and making informed decisions.
Students employ technology in the development of strategies for solving problems in the real world.

These clear and well-written standards are focused on the use of the technology itself. And although technology is sufficiently novel, difficult, and mystifying, special standards such as these will be necessary. But technology gurus such as Donald Norman (1998) are beginning to see that the "how to use technology" skills are becoming less important. In his book *The Invisible Computer*, Norman argues that no one really wants to use a computer or even use a word processor. What one really wants to do is write a letter. He predicts that "information appliances" will do a single task simply with minimal technical expertise on the part of the user. Just think how little training is associated with using AlphaSmart (a portable inexpensive word-processing device) compared to that needed to use Microsoft Word. For most beginning writers, AlphaSmart does 90% of the drafting and editing that can be done with Word.

Level 4: Information Problem-Solving Skills and Higher-Order Thinking Skills

While the International Society for Technology in Education standards focus on the technology itself, Information Literacy Standards for Student Learning (American Association of School Librarians & Association for Educational Communications and Technology, 1998) acknowledge technology as one skill from a broader set of skills needed by students to be successful information problem solvers. Released as guidelines in *Information Power: Building Partnerships for Student Learning*, these standards have three major divisions comprising nine standards (pp. 3–9):

1. Information literacy
Standard 1: The student who is information literate accesses information efficiently and effectively.
Standard 2: The student who is information literate evaluates information critically and competently.
Standard 3: The student who is information literate uses information accurately and creatively.

2. Independent learning
Standard 4: The student who is an independent learner is information literate and pursues information related to personal interests.
Standard 5: The student who is an independent learner is information literate and appreciates literature and other creative expressions of information.
Standard 6: The student who is an independent learner is information literate and strives for excellence in information seeking and knowledge generation.

3. Social responsibility
Standard 7: The student who contributes positively to the learning community and to society is information literate and recognizes the importance of information to a democratic society.
Standard 8: The student who contributes positively to the learning community and to society is information literate and practices ethical behavior.
Standard 9: The student who contributes positively to the learning community and to society is information literate and participates effectively in groups to pursue and generate information.

Yet even these standards say little about how information—once found and evaluated—is to be purposefully used.

There is an acknowledgement that students need higher-order thinking skills, of which Benjamin Bloom's taxonomy (1956) is among the most venerated. Bloom identifies six levels within the cognitive domain, with certain verbs often listed in association with each level.

- *Knowledge*: memorize, name, recognize, repeat, recall, define
- *Comprehension*: describe, discuss, explain, restate, translate
- *Application*: apply, demonstrate, illustrate, interpret
- *Analysis*: analyze, categorize, compare, contrast, distinguish
- *Synthesis*: arrange, create, develop, design, formulate
- *Evaluation*: assess, defend, estimate, judge, predict, rate, support

Another interesting look at developing higher-order thinking skills—one that bridges this category of skill and the next, conceptual skills—are 16 habits of mind (Costa & Kallick, 2000), characteristics that good problem solvers demonstrate:

persisting;
thinking and communicating with clarity and precision;
managing impulsivity;
gathering data through all senses;
listening with understanding and empathy;
creating, imagining, innovating;
thinking flexibly;
responding with wonderment and awe;
thinking about thinking (metacognition);
taking responsible risks;
striving for accuracy;
finding humor;
questioning and posing problems;
thinking interdependently;
applying past knowledge to new situations; and
remaining open to continuous learning.

One effort that is attempting to define a holistic approach to technology, information literacy, and higher-order thinking skills is found in North Central Regional Educational Laboratory's *enGauge: 21st Century Skills: Literacy in the Digital Age* (see Figure 36.3). This interesting model is definitely worth a look, but in my opinion, it still may not address all the skills that a postinformation age worker needs.

Level 5: Conceptual Skills

Daniel Pink's book *A Whole New Mind: Moving From the Information Age to the Conceptual Age* (2005) acknowledges Asia (the outsourcing trend described by Friedman) as well as two trends that affect an individual's value in the labor market: abundance (rising affluence, which leads to markets of not just functional but pleasing goods and services) and automation (improvements in mechanized and artificial intelligence labor). He suggests that readers ask themselves three questions about their jobs (p. 51):

Can someone overseas do it cheaper?

Can a computer do it faster?

Am I offering something that satisfies the nonmaterial, transcendent desires of an abundant age? (Are you not just manufacturing toilet brushes, but toilet brushes that satisfy the user's aesthetic sensibilities as well?)

He believes that as a result of these trends, we are shifting from the information age to the conceptual age. Successful players in this new economy will be required to develop and use the right-brain abilities of high concept (seeing the larger picture, synthesizing information) and high touch (being empathetic, creating meaning)—happy news, perhaps, for those of

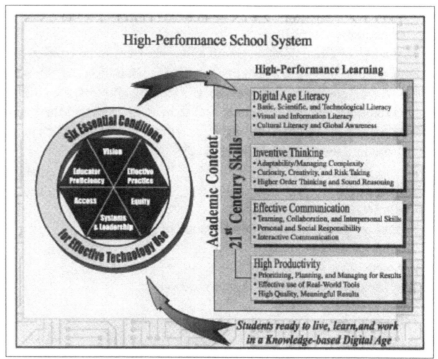

Figure 36.3. enGauge: 21st Century Skills: Literacy in the Digital Age. Copyright © 2003 North Central Regional Educational Laboratory at Learning Point Associates. All rights reserved. Reprinted with permission.

us who never were all that good at the left-brain stuff in the first place. Specifically, he suggests that we work toward developing in ourselves (and I hope, by implication, our students), six right-brain senses to complement our left-brain, analytic skills. He suggests that we need to realize the value of the following (p. 66):

Not just function but also design: "It is no longer sufficient to create a product, a service, an experience, or a lifestyle that is merely functional. Today it is economically crucial and personally rewarding to create something that is also beautiful, whimsical, or emotionally engaging."

Not just argument but also story: "When our lives are brimming with information and data, it is not enough to marshal an effective argument. . . . The essence of persuasion, communication, and self- understanding has become the ability also to fashion a compelling story."

Not just focus but also symphony: "What is in greatest demand today is not analysis but synthesis—seeing the big picture and crossing boundaries—being able to combine disparate pieces into an arresting new whole."

Not just logic but also empathy: "What will distinguish those who thrive will be their ability to understand what makes their fellow woman or man tick, to forge relationships, and to care for others."

Not just seriousness but also play: "Ample evidence points to the enormous health and professional benefits of laughter, lightheartedness, games, and humor."

Not just accumulation but also meaning: Material plenty "has freed hundreds of millions of people from day-to-day struggles and liberated us to pursue more significant desires: purpose, transcendence, and spiritual fulfillment."

I will also be bold enough to add a seventh sense of my own to Pink's list:

Not just knowledge but also learning. Unless a person develops both the ability and the desire to continue to learn new skills, be open to new ideas, and be ready to change practices in the face of new technologies, economic forces, and societal demands, that person will not be able to successfully compete in a global economy.

In the age of educational accountability, we seem to be gearing all our instructional efforts to helping students master left-brain skills, because that is what tests usually measure. But to what extent do we and should we be developing design sense, storytelling abilities, the ability to synthesize information, the ability to empathize, the use of humor, and the ability to detect the importance of the information learned? How do we create lifelong learners? What emphases, using Pink's model, might schools and libraries wish to cultivate in the conceptual age worker?

1. Design

Offer art classes and activities.

Assess not just content but appearance of student work.

Teach visual literacy.

2. Story

Ask for student writing in the narrative voice.

Teach speaking skills.

Use storytelling as a part of teaching.

Give students opportunities to hear and tell stories.

3. Symphony

Design classroom projects that cross disciplines.

Ask for the application of skills and concepts to genuine problems.

Use inductive learning strategies (learning by doing).

4. Empathy

Emphasize reading literature about people from other cultures and socioeconomic groups.

Give students volunteer opportunities or service learning requirements.

Give students the opportunity to take part as an actor in theater productions.

Design group projects.

5. Play

Teach with games.

Offer a variety of athletics and physical education classes.

Offer participatory music classes.

Teach through riddles and jokes, and encourage students to tell them.

6. Meaning

Offer classes in comparative religion, myth, and legend.

Teach ethical behaviors as a part of every project.

Asking for writings to include statements of personal values.

7. Learning

Teach processes, not facts.

Allow students to research areas of personal interest (and tolerate a diversity of interests).

Give students the ability to learn in nontraditional ways (online, early enrollment in college, apprenticeships).

Make available clubs and organizations for students to join in which students learn nonacademic skills.

Provide access to a wide range of information sources.

Sadly, our society and educational system see many of the opportunities listed here that develop conceptual age skills as extras—frills that are often the first to be cut in times of tight budgets. By doing so, we are doing a disservice to our students as future workers and citizens.

CONCLUSION

I admit that I approach the problems of creating knowledge worker skills both from a United States–centric and pragmatic point of view. Yet, conscientious teacher-librarians and educators of every country and professional role should be advocating for attention to be paid to the following questions:

What skills will give individuals value in a global economy?

What skills will allow my students to achieve the greatest level of professional attainment and personal fulfillment?

What projects, activities, and assessments will allow students to practice these skills?

What do schools and library programs look like that help their students and patrons master these skills?

As teacher-librarians, we need to provide access to the resources necessary to support technology, information literacy, and high-order thinking skills. As teachers, we need to model instructional design and delivery practices that build conceptual age skills. And as school leaders, we need to advocate for instructional programs that go beyond the basics, if we are to demonstrate concern for our students' futures.

REFERENCES

American Association of School Librarians & Association for Educational Communications and Technology. (1998). *Information literacy standards for student learning.* Retrieved December 30, 2006, from **www.ala.org/ala/aasl/aaslproftools/informationpower/InformationLiteracyStandards_final.pdf**

Bloom, B. S. (1956). *Taxonomy of educational objectives, handbook I: The cognitive domain.* New York: David McKay. Retrieved December 30, 2006, from **http://eduscapes.com/tap/topic69.htm**

Costa, A. L., & Kallick, B. (2000). *Describing 16 habits of mind.* Retrieved December 30, 2006, from **www.habits-of-mind.net/**

Friedman, T. L. (2005). *The world is flat: A brief history of the twenty-first century.* New York: Farrar, Straus, and Giroux.

International Society for Technology in Education. (1998). *National educational technology standards.* Retrieved December 30, 2006, from **cnets.iste.org/**

Kalakota, R., & Robinson, M. (2004, February 27). *Offshore outsourcing: Will your job disappear in 2004?* Retrieved December 30, 2006, from **www.Informit.com**

Levy, F., & Murnane, R. J. (2004, October). Education and the changing job market. *Educational Leadership, 62*(2), p. 82.

Morello, D. (2003, July 15). *U.S. offshore outsourcing: Structural changes, big impact.* Stamford, CT: Gartner.

Norman, D. A. (1998). *The invisible computer.* Cambridge, MA: MIT Press.

North Central Regional Educational Laboratory. (2003). *enGauge: 21st century skills: Literacy in the digital age.* Retrieved December 30, 2006, from **www.ncrel.org/engauge/skills/skills.htm**

Pink, D. (2005). *A whole new mind: Moving from the information age to the conceptual age.* New York: Riverhead Books.

They Might Be Gurus

Joyce Valenza

The popular media attributes near guru status to young adults in terms of their familiarity and sophistication with technology. In *Growing Up Digital*, Donald Tapscott (1997) describes a generation lap, in which children are authorities lapping adults in all areas involving technology. Mark Prensky (1998) tells us today's student has had "far more experience at processing information more quickly than [his or her] predecessors, and is therefore better at it" (para. 6).

BUT FIRST, ARE THEY GURUS?

Our own literature, the literature of library and information science, documents students' feelings of confusion and frustration and less-than-effective approaches to using information technologies. It reveals troubling data relating to students' searching capabilities, their abilities to navigate the Web to find the resources that they need for school research, the energy that they put into their work, and their understandings of search environments despite common feelings of self-efficacy.

After a couple of years of doctoral study, I am discovering that all of the hunches that I have reached observing young adults and their searching behaviors are documented in nearly 20 years of research. I am now convinced: If we want to graduate information-fluent citizens, we must think beyond our teaching. It is not about teaching alone. Sure, some of the issues relate to what students know and are able to do, but the issues all involve more than just the cognitive aspect. It helps to sort the issues relating to young adult information-seeking behavior into four large *buckets*—cognitive, affective, social, and physical. If we are going to prepare students to be effective adult information seekers and users, then we need comprehensive understandings of how learners connect with information. We need to address the issues in all four buckets.

IN THE COGNITIVE BUCKET

Students do not think like teacher-librarians. Despite their feelings of self-efficacy and the heavily promoted information literacy thrust in our school libraries, young information seekers do not appear to have

First published on e-VOYA, April 2006, www.voya.com. Published in *Teacher Librarian*, October 2006, Volume 34, Number 1. *Teacher Librarian* acknowledges e-VOYA's permission to adapt and reprint this article.

the sophisticated skills or understandings needed to navigate complex information environments and evaluate the information they find. Research points to students' limited understandings of the way that information is organized, the way that results are returned, and the differences in search interfaces. Subject content knowledge, information skills, conceptions of how to determine relevance, and strategies for identifying useful keywords and forming queries are among the significant cognitive variables in student information seeking (Bilal & Kirby, 2002; Chen, 2003; Fidel et al., 1999; Nahl & Harada, 1996; Neuman, 1995).

Students are not planners (Bilal, 2001; Large, Beheshti, & Moukdad, 1999; Shenton & Dixon, 2004; Watson, 1998). Rather than develop queries and identify promising keywords and synonyms in advance, students assume that search engines will understand the sentences and questions that they enter into search boxes—that is, in natural language style. Although this strategy sometimes works effectively in Google, it may not be the optimum approach, and it does not translate well to all interfaces. Researchers (Chen, 2003; Hirsh, 1997; Nahl & Harada, 1996) have observed that students tend to repeat flawed strategies in different search tools, with little or no knowledge of search syntax. Their searches often consist of few words and sometimes use only one word. Neuman's Delphi panel (1995) of expert librarians identified this lack of planning as a significant issue.

Pitts (1994) explored four major learning strands that high school students incorporate during information seeking: content knowledge, information seeking and use, life skills (decision making, problem solving, taking responsibility, planning, and the like), and production. When students encounter difficulties using one strand, they are likely to overcome the problem by using skills from another strand. But without support, weakness of one or more of the strands impedes a student's effectiveness and his or her ability to construct new learning.

Students have trouble naming their information needs (Brown, 1995; Large & Beheshti, 2000; Shenton & Dixon, 2004). Researchers point to the inability of searchers of all ages to use the appropriate terminology in an area of knowledge or predict vocabulary, synonyms, and category patterns used in search interfaces.

Several researchers have commented on students' apparent lack of concern for their ability to discern the quality of their sources; they have noted that students spend much of their time searching and little of their time analyzing and evaluating. Chen (2003) noted that students spend little time evaluating what they have on the screen, apparently not able to distinguish wheat from chaff. Schacter, Chung, and Dorr (1998) find that fifth- and sixth-grade students blindly trust what they find on the Web.

First-year college students favor commercial searches engines over academic databases. According to the Pew Internet and American Life Project study *The Internet Goes to College: How Students Are Living in the Future With Today's Technology* (Jones & Madden, 2002), "Although academic resources are offered online, it may be that students have not been taught, or have not yet figured out, how to locate these resources" (p. 13). The Online Computer Library Center report *Perceptions of Libraries and Information Resources* (2005) notes that 84% of the respondents use search engines to begin information searches, with only 1% beginning searches on library web sites, and that 90% are satisfied with their most recent search using a search engine. Books are seen as the library brand. Libraries are not seen as a starting point for access to electronic resources.

Griffiths and Brophy (2005) observed that college students' use of academic resources was low and that students had little awareness of alternative information-seeking methods beyond their favorite search engine. Students had difficulty locating information, in part, because their use of search engines affected their perceptions and expectations of other electronic resources.

According to Weiler (2005), students are predominantly visual learners. They come to the table at various levels of cognitive development and prefer to learn through discussion and hands-on application more than through lecture. This is a generation concerned about saving time; they are open to instruction only if it helps them save time.

Educational psychologists discuss the role of schema in learning—that is, mental structures or diagrams for understanding. Information science research notes that most students lack the schema necessary for understanding information organization and the types of information available (Agosto, 2002).

IN THE AFFECTIVE BUCKET (ABOUT ATTITUDES AND EMOTIONS)

Carol Kuhlthau's body of work (1985, 1988, 1989, 1991, 1994, 1997) holds that searching is not just an intellectual activity. Students bring their emotions—confusion, uncertainty, optimism, doubt, frustration, and confidence—to the information search process. Kalbach (2003) invokes the work of Kuhlthau in an examination of the affective nature of information seeking on the Web, which he labels "an emotional experience" (p. 1). He observes that feelings of confusion and uncertainty usually trump feelings of enthusiasm and optimism. Kalbach concludes that reducing uncertainty and complexity can improve the information-seeking experience for users. Our understanding of affective concerns is critical when we consider developing web search interfaces.

Students experience the frustration of information overload within both text-heavy individual sites and the Web as a whole. They avoid text-intensive sites in favor of sites with bullets and graphic content. In her theoretical decision-making model, Denise Agosto (2002) refers to this phenomenon as *textual overload* and refers to students' frustration with their overwhelming choice of web sites as *outcome overload*.

Melissa Gross (2001) notes that in the older elementary grades, students trend away from self-generated to imposed queries. Does that affect motivation in information seeking? The trend continues through middle school and high school. Her research indicates that the number of imposed queries continues through middle school and high school and that self-generated library use declines. Bilal (2002) found that students were more successful in self-generated tasks than they were in imposed tasks. Though the seventh graders' behaviors varied by task and by success level, Bilal attributes greater success in the self-generated tasks to student familiarity with and interest in the topic and to the fact that the students involved in these choices had opportunities to modify the task if they could not find relevant information. Bilal, as well as Hirsh (1999), Garland (1995), Pitts (1994), and Small (1999), revealed that students showed greater levels of motivation and challenge when they played a role in selecting the topic and task.

Motivation is related to confidence. Students appear to show greater levels of motivation, challenge, and success when the topic and task are self-generated and when they are familiar with and interested in their inquiries. A number of researchers point to the importance of confidence, although they are quick to note that students tend to overestimate their information problem-solving abilities. Though students tend to overestimate their self-efficacy (Waldman, 2003), confidence contributes to effective performance by sustaining motivation and decreasing anxiety. When students lack confidence, they have trouble recovering from breakdowns or problems encountered when searching.

The Digital Disconnect (Levin, Arafeh, Lenhart, & Rainie, 2002) concludes that even Internet-savvy students experience frustrations, such as finding quality information on the Internet, sorting through the overwhelming number of results returned by general-purpose search engines, attempting to read and understand materials beyond their cognitive levels, ignoring commercial advertisements, and being unable to access trusted sources because they are fee based.

People, teens included, stop their searching at *good enough*. Although teacher-librarians would like to believe otherwise, nonlibrarians—in the face of info-glut—are not always motivated to continue their searching beyond *good enough* to find the best information out there. *Satisficing*, a term coined by Herbert Simon (1955) and frequently used in information science research, is defined as selecting or stopping at results that are good enough to suit a searcher's purposes, though those results are not necessarily optimal—a blend of *sufficing* and *satisfying*. Satisficing resonates with Zipf's frequently cited principle of least effort (1949), the view that, all other things being equal, human behavior tends to follow a path of minimum effort.

Online Computer Library Center's *Environmental Scan: Pattern Recognition* (De Rosa, Dempsey, & Wilson, 2003) points to changes among all types of information consumers. In terms of service, users want to be self-sufficient. In terms of satisfaction, information consumers are largely satisfied with the quality of the information they find, even though information professionals might not deem those choices satisfactory. And users, especially young users, prefer collaborative seamless environments. Their academic, social, creative, and entertainment arenas merge online, in nomadic multitasked landscapes. They do not see the buckets as we do. The concept of leaving a favorite search tool and going to a scholarly database for one task and to a Web portal for another is antithetical to the way that they prefer to work and play.

IN THE SOCIOCULTURAL BUCKET

Constructivist theory views learning as a social activity, and researchers note that information seeking is both a social and an academic event. Studies in young adult information seeking note that students are most successful with the *when needed* intervention of adults, when they can discuss their progress and problems with others who can support gaps in their searching and content knowledge. In the largely independent, often-isolated world of Internet searching, such interventions in the forms of coaching, modeling, and feedback do not always occur.

Kuhlthau (1997), Ryder and Wilson (1996), and others recognize the potential for scaffolding and coaching in virtual libraries. Kuhlthau stresses the importance of online intervention during student periods of uncertainty. Kuhlthau's *zones of intervention* (1994) are times when the user needs help to move ahead and the teacher-librarian participates as collaborator and coach. Researchers also note the importance of peers as collaborators. Team approaches and conversations are critical strategies that allow students to brainstorm, reflect, discuss their ideas, and allow mediators to question and guide. Teacher-librarians and classroom teachers need to design these process interventions into projects to guide students as they construct meaning and seek understanding. Such critical interventions can happen effectively both offline and online.

Among the social barriers that students face as they seek information are the lack of encouragement by others, confusion about their teachers' expectations, and (*sting!*) the perceived unhelpfulness of teacher-librarians. The Pew Internet and American Life Project study *The Digital Disconnect: The Widening Gap Between the Internet-Savvy Students and Their Schools.* (Levin et al., 2002) suggests a kind of slacker culture, where students believe that they know far more about technology than their teachers and are proud to admit that they use the Internet as a way to "complete their schoolwork as quickly and painlessly as possible, with minimal effort and minimal engagement" (p. 9). Many of the students interviewed view their education as an us-versus-them game, with the Web offering strategies for getting by with the least possible work.

IN THE PHYSICAL BUCKET

The Internet removes some physical barriers to information seeking and creates others. Riel (1998) noted the potential for customized just-in-time learning and the growing need for skilled educators to manage online learning environments. The search process no longer has to involve getting up, going to the library, visiting shelves, or physically browsing through indexes or tables of contents. High school students appreciate the speed and physical advantages of the Web over books—all you need do is "type in words and click" (Chen, 2003, p. 29). But teens also note constraints in terms of time and limited resources. Students are frustrated with institutional barriers that prevent them from using resources—school schedules, limited equipment, filters, teacher-librarians, and other users who get in the way.

Discomfort, boredom, and time restraints influence information seeking. Students react negatively to the physical discomfort of excessive Web use—sore bones, headaches, wrist pain, and eyestrain (Agosto, 2002). Though students generally acknowledge the value of the Web as a means of reducing the physical exertion, they describe the time constraints that they face completing school projects, constraints that force them to consider only a few sites before making their selections. Time constraints are self-imposed, as when there is a deadline for a school project, and self-generated, as when the goal is to find, click, and print as quickly as possible.

TWO BUCKETS OF OUR OWN

We have much work to do. In viewing the research in a big-picture approach, it is clear that the work of the 21st-century teacher-librarian must also fall into buckets—two big ones. While we continue to work to make users smarter, we also need to work toward making systems smarter, better able to understand and meet the needs of our students. I am convinced: It is not about teaching alone. Yes, we need to teach both implicitly and explicitly, but we also need to apply our growing understandings to create new and improved learning landscapes—landscapes that are attractive as destinations, landscapes where learners can work and play with intervention and independence.

Making Users Smarter

As an educator and a teacher-librarian, I cannot accept that *good enough* is good enough for the learners whom I teach. I want my learners to know that sometimes *good enough* does work but that some information tasks require greater energy, greater knowledge, greater thought. Our math department does not give up with the teaching of simple functions; it moves students through algebra and trigonometry. It moves many learners on to calculus. Although students may continue to use that mathematical knowledge and training into their adult lives, I suspect that our curriculum has longer legs. Educators and teacher-librarians can work together to change student attitudes about what *good enough* looks like. We can evaluate works-cited lists. We can insist that these lists contain thoughtfully selected, varied, and developmentally appropriate resources. We can teach students to seek quality. We can teach students to produce quality. When it matters, we can move learners beyond satisficing to scholarship.

Despite the major information literacy thrust in our school libraries, we must find better, more scalable strategies to ensure that students become competent information seekers and users before they leave our high schools. We must work to remove both intellectual and physical barriers. We must teach explicitly; we must motivate; we must design projects that challenge learners in meaningful ways; we must change attitudes; we must encourage and support students through their confusion and frustration. Online and offline, we must find ways to intervene in ways that respect young people's existing knowledge.

We must also collaborate to create research challenges that allow students choice, projects that are authentic and that motivate learning. We can use the authentic tools of the Web 2.0 environment. Wikis can support students' group projects. Blogs can support student journaling and reflection; they can be used to create interactive pathfinders. Videoconferencing and webcasting can allow students to interact with authors and experts in powerful new ways. Podcasting can broadcast creativity. Static PowerPoints can make way for digital storytelling.

We must also lead by example, demonstrating solid and forward-looking practice as we guide. We must help teachers and parents understand, deliver, and assess skills for the 21st century. We can hold secondary students accountable for information-process learning as much as we hold them accountable for all content area learning—like algebra and physics.

As for Making Systems Smarter

Eliza Dresang (2005) notes that the meta-analyses of the research on youth information-seeking behavior and use of digital materials tend to focus largely on the deficiencies and need for improvement rather than ferreting out the potential of new and exciting ways of knowing in a digital age. (p. 192)

She suggests that researchers and professionals need more positive perspectives. Dresang urges professionals to examine digital age principles of interactivity, or the similar literacies needed for hypertextual media and handheld text; connectivity, or the importance of collaborative information behavior and online communities; and access, or the breaking of old information barriers.

Jenny Levine (2004), well-known as the Web's Shifted Librarian, describes major differences in our students' approach to information use and the need for teacher-librarians to intervene on their turf and make professional intervention portable. Levine suggests, "Librarians have to start adjusting now. I call that adjustment 'shifting' because I think you have to start meeting these kids' information needs in their world, not yours. The library has to become more portable or 'shifted'" (p. 1).

The urgency to shift, to rethink the information landscape, may be increasing. Though the concept has not yet pervaded the academic literature, library web sites and blogs are abuzz with predictions for a newly interactive Web 2.0 and for our own potential to create Library 2.0 (Crawford, 2006; Miller, 2005). Crawford's compilation of the popular literature concludes that

Library 2.0 encompasses a range of new and not-so-new software methodologies (social software, interactivity, APIs, modular software) that can and will be useful for many libraries in providing new services and making existing services available in new and interesting ways. (p. 32)

Harris (2006), in one of the first articles to discuss the trends as they relate to schools, sees School Library 2.0 as a way that teacher-librarians can adapt to a compelling digital revolution and as an opportunity for school library professionals to remain relevant and effective in the face of technological change.

When we consider library change, as we begin play in new sandboxes, we need first to consider our users. Young information seekers are most successful when they are interacting with systems designed for them, when they have effective system feedbacks and graphic visualizations. As we watch young users interact with interfaces, both those we develop and those we pay others to develop, we need to evaluate their supports. Are those interfaces customized to address the specific learning issues of the groups of teens we serve? Are they engaging? Attractive? Cool? Interactive? Do they offer context-sensitive support and instruction as well as compensations for vocabulary, spelling, and knowledge gaps?

Do these interfaces support teens as they develop schema to make sense of their information options and the information landscape? What can we do to fix them? How can we lobby others to improve them? Can we help make these resources as easy to use as Google? Can we help students to find the best search tools for a task? And once they are there with that perfect tool, can we help them to move the best resources to the top of their result lists? Can we make our own sites—and the databases we invest in—real student destinations?

How can we be there for learners' just-in-time, just-for-me learning experiences? I know that my own online presence scales my guidance and instruction and makes both available to students on weekends and evenings and even when they are sitting 5 feet away. Can we offer independence while we offer as-needed intervention? Can we be available to students beyond our walls and beyond our hours? Our students live online; they need their libraries online. They need their teacher-librarians online.

For today's learners, libraries can be exciting hybrid experiences of face-to-face lessons learned, reinforced with effective online supports.

THEY MAY NOT BE GURUS

Serious examinations of young adults as they seek information appear to be in stark opposition to the assessments of popular media and perhaps to young people's assessments of their own efficacy. Students who are otherwise referred to as savvy are referred to in our literature as naïve, amateur, and incompetent. It is natural for students to face challenges finding information. They confront a trillion-page Web; a Web created primarily for adults; and a Web largely devoid of professional indexing, search standardization, and support.

It is natural for users of any age to be baffled by the multiplicity of choices offered by the free Web, online databases, portals, and the millions of pages that form what we call the *invisible Web*. We can redefine our roles in these new landscapes. We can prove ourselves allies and fellow learners rather than critics. We can prepare young people for efficient and effective experiences on that landscape. We can make the Web and its resources a friendly landscape, even for its natives.

REFERENCES

Agosto, D. E. (2002). Bounded rationality and satisficing in young people's web-based decision making. *Journal of the American Society for Information Science and Technology, 53*(1), 16–27.

Bilal, D. (2001). Children's use of the Yahooligans! web search engine. II. Cognitive and physical behaviors on research tasks. *Journal of the American Society for Information Science and Technology, 52*(2), 118–136.

Bilal, D. (2002). Children's use of the Yahooligans! web search engine. III. Cognitive and physical behaviors on fully self-generated search tasks. *Journal of the American Society for Information Science and Technology, 53*(13), 1170–1183.

Bilal, D., & Kirby, J. (2002). Differences and similarities in information seeking children and adults as web users. *Information Processing and Management, 38*(5), 649–670.

Brown, M. E. (1995). By any other name: Accounting for failure in the naming of subject categories. *Library and Information Science Research, 17*(4), 347–385.

Chen, S.-H. L. (2003). Searching the online catalog and the World Wide Web. *Journal of Educational Media and Library Sciences, 41*(1), 29–43.

Crawford, W. (2006). Library 2.0 and "Library 2.0." *Cites and Insights: Crawford at Large, 6*(2), 1–32. Retrieved April 12, 2006, from **http://cites.boisestate.edu/v6i2a.htm**

De Rosa, C., Dempsey, L., & Wilson, A. (2003). *2003 OCLC environmental scan: Pattern recognition.* Retrieved October 1, 2004, from **www.oclc.org/membership/escan/introduction/default.htm**

Dresang, E. T. (2005). The information-seeking behavior of youth in the digital environment. *Library Trends, 54*(2), 178–196.

Fidel, R., Davies, R. K., Douglass, M. H., Holder, J. K., Hopkins, C. J., Kushner, E. J., et al. (1999). A visit to the information mall: Web searching behavior of high school students. *Journal of the American Society for Information Science, 50*(1), 24–37.

Garland, K. (1995). The information search process: A study of elements associated with meaningful research tasks. *School Libraries Worldwide, 1*(1), 41–53.

Griffiths, J. R., & Brophy, P. (2005). Student searching behavior and the Web: Use of academic resources and Google. *Library Trends, 53*(4), 539–554.

Gross, M. (2001). Imposed information seeking in public libraries and school library media centers: A common behaviour? [Record No. 100]. *Information Research, 6*(2). Retrieved September 20, 2004, from **http://informationr.net/ir/8-2/paper100.html**

Harris, C. (2006, May 1). School Library 2.0. *School Library Journal.* Retrieved May 6, 2006, from **www.schoollibraryjournal.com/index.asp?layout=articlePrint&article id=CA6330755**

Hirsh, S. G. (1997). How do children find information on different types of tasks? Children's use of the Science Library Catalog. *Library Trends, 45*(4), 725–746.

Hirsh, S. G. (1999). Children's relevance criteria and information seeking on electronic resources. *Journal of the American Society for Information Science, 50*(14), 1265–1283.

Jones, S., & Madden, M. (2002). *The Internet goes to college: How students are living in the future with today's technology.* Retrieved September 20, 2004, from the Pew Internet and American Life Project web site: **www.pewinternet.org/report_display.asp?r=71**

Kalbach, J. (2003). "I'm feeling lucky": The role of emotions in seeking information on the Web. Retrieved September 29, 2004, from **http://home.earthlink.net/~searchworkshop/docs/JKalbach_Emotions-InformationSeeking-Web_short21.pdf**

Kuhlthau, C. C. (1985) A process approach to library skills instruction: An investigation into the design of the library research process. *School Library Media Quarterly, 13*, 35–40.

Kuhlthau, C. C. (1988). Perceptions of the information search process in libraries: A study of changes from high school through college. *Information Processing and Management, 24*(4), 419–427.

Kuhlthau, C. C. (1989). The information search process of high-, middle-, and low-achieving high school seniors. *School Library Media Quarterly, 17*, 244–226.

Kuhlthau, C. C. (1991). Inside the search process: Information seeking from the user's perspective. *Journal of the American Society for Information Science, 42*(5), 361–371.

Kuhlthau, C. C. (1994). Students and the information search process: Zones of intervention for librarians. *Advances in Librarianship, 18*, 57–72.

Kuhlthau, C. C. (1997). Learning in digital libraries: An information search process approach. *Library Trends, 45*(4), 708–724.

Large, A., & Beheshti, J. (2000). The Web as a classroom resource: Reactions from users. *Journal of the American Society for Information Science, 51*(12), 1069–1080.

Large, A., Beheshti, J., & Moukdad, H. (1999). Information-seeking on the Web: Navigational skills of grade-six primary school students. In *Proceedings of the 62nd ASIS annual meeting* (pp. 84–97). Medford, NJ: Information Today.

Levin, D., Arafeh, S., Lenhart, A., & Rainie, L. (2002). *The digital disconnect: The widening gap between Internet-savvy students and their schools.* Retrieved September 30, 2004, from the Pew Internet and American Life Project web site: **http://207.21.232.103/ PPF/r/67/report_display.asp**

Levine, J. (2004). *What is a shifted librarian?* Retrieved July 5, 2005, from **www.theshifted librarian.com/stories/ 2002/01/19/whatIsAShiftedLibrarian.html**

Miller, P. (2005). Web 2.0: Building the new library. *Ariadne, 45*. Retrieved April 12, 2006, from **www.ariadne.ac.uk/issue45/miller/intro.html**

Nahl, D., & Harada, V. H. (1996). Composing Boolean search statements: Self-confidence, concept analysis, search logic, and errors. *School Library Media Quarterly, 24*(4), 199–207.

Neuman, D. (1995). High school students' use of databases: Results of a national Delphi study. *Journal of the American Society for Information Science, 46*(4), 284–298.

Online Computer Library Center. (2005). *Perceptions of libraries and information resources.* Dublin, OH: Author.

Pitts, J. M. (1994). Personal understandings and mental models of information: A qualitative study of factors associated with the information seeking and use of adolescents (Doctoral dissertation, Florida State University, Tallahassee, 1994). *Dissertation Abstracts International, 55*, 4.

Prensky, M. (1998). *Twitch speed: Keeping up with young workers.* Retrieved on October 15, 2004, from **www.twitchspeed.com/site/article.html**

Riel, M. (1998, May). *Education in the 21st century: Just-in-time learning or learning communities.* Paper presented at the fourth annual conference of the Emirates Center for Strategic Studies and Research, Abu Dhabi, United Arab Emirates. Retrieved October 15, 2004, from **www.gse.uci.edu/doe home/DeptInfo/Faculty/Riel/jit-learning/**

Ryder, M., & Wilson, B. G. (1996, February). *Affordances and constraints for the Internet for learning and instruction.* Paper presented at the Association for Educational Communications Technology, Indianapolis, IN. Retrieved May 15, 2006, from **http://carbon.cudenver.edu/~mryder/ aect_96.html**

Schacter, J. K. G., Chung, W. K., & Dorr, A. (1998). Children's Internet searching on complex problems: Performance and process analyses. *Journal of the American Society for Information Science, 49*(9), 840–850.

Shenton, A. K., & Dixon, P. (2004). Issues arising from youngsters' information- seeking behavior. *Library and Information Science Research, 26*(3), 177–200.

Simon, H. A. (1955). A behavioral model of rational choice. *Quarterly Journal of Economics, 69*, 99–118.

Small, R. V. (1999). *An exploration of motivational strategies used by library media specialists during library and information skills instruction.* Retrieved September 9, 2004, from **www.ala.org/ala/aasl/ aaslpubsandjournals/slmrb/slmrcontents/volume21999/vol2small.htm**

Tapscott, D. (1997). *Growing up digital: The rise of the net generation.* New York: McGraw-Hill.

Waldman, M. (2003). Freshmen's use of library electronic resources and self-efficacy [Record No. 150]. *Information Research, 8*(2). Retrieved October 4, 2004, from **http://informationr.net/ir/8-2/ paper150.html**

Watson, J. S. (1998). If you don't have it, you can't find it: A close look at students' perceptions of using technology. *Journal of the American Society for Information Science, 49*(11), 1024–1036.

Weiler, A. (2005). Information-seeking behavior in Generation Y students: Motivation, critical thinking, and learning theory. *Journal of Academic Librarianship, 31*(1), 46–53.

Zipf, G. K. (1949). *Human behavior and the principle of least effort.* Cambridge, MA: Addison-Wesley.

(38)

The Generation Z Connection: Teaching Information Literacy to the Newest Net Generation

Caroline Geck

Youths born in or after 1990 are members of the newest net generation, defined in this article as Generation Z. These young people are unique because their birth coincides with the introduction of the graphical Web that resembles the Internet of today. These adolescents are amateur Internet searchers lacking skills in evaluating web content and using resources other than popular Internet search tools such as Google. The Internet can be the perfect medium to introduce and develop information literacy skills because these youngsters will be receptive to any sort of instruction that makes them appear web savvier. Ideas and strategies are offered herein to update both instruction and library service using the Internet as an instructional aid.

According the *Encarta World English Dictionary*, Generation Y is defined as people born in or after 1980. Although Generation Z is not yet defined in the dictionary, the term is sometimes used to describe the already-existing net generation of teenagers born in or after 1990 in technologically advanced countries. Today's Generation Z currently comprises 14-year-olds or those approaching their early teens; these youths were born into a totally different technological world than what their immediate predecessors were, Generation Y. In fact, the Generation Z birth years closely correspond to the conception and birth of the World Wide Web. Tim Berners-Lee created this system of hyperlinks in 1990 and officially introduced this new way of web browsing in 1991. A critical milestone in improved web browsing came in 1993 with the introduction of the Mosaic Web Browser, the first graphical web browser. Mosaic generated huge interest in the Internet because web users could visualize how they were traversing the Web. These initial digital events in the early 1990s triggered an entire technological revolution and are key factors in understanding how this generation's development to adolescence has been affected since birth.

First published in *Teacher Librarian*, February 2006, Volume 34, Number 3

WHY IS THIS GENERATION SPECIAL IN TODAY'S WORLD?

These youths are the first generation to be born into a digital world. What distinguishes these adolescents from those of every other generation is that they are the most electronically connected generation in history. From infancy, these teenagers grew up in an environment surrounded by and using

- graphical web browsers,
- laptops,
- cell phones,
- instant messenger services,
- broadband,
- wireless, and
- video games.

These adolescents have been exposed to many high-tech influences, and today's high-speed digital devices enable them to always be connected to the Internet, their friends, and others. This connectivity permits teens to communicate and collaborate in real-time regardless of physical location; to access a wealth of diverse information, including vast digital collections; and to author or contribute content instantaneously to web sites and weblogs.

These teens will more likely than any previous generation evolve into electronic multitaskers. For example, they will seek information by simultaneously

- searching and using several Internet browser windows at the same computer;
- using several different software applications at the same computer;
- using two computers at the same time, such as computer workstations and laptops;
- instant messenging peers who are not physically located within conversation range;
- using cell phones to contact other peers who are not physically present or are not responding to instant messenging;
- using cell phones for activities other than talking.

These teens also use an arsenal of tools to manage, store, and protect information—including e-mail, peripheral devices such as flash drives and iPods, and file transfer protocol systems. Adolescents have successfully mastered technologies of e-mail to take full advantage of its gathering, organizing, and forwarding capabilities (Levin & Arafeh, 2002, p. iii).

Because these young people know no other reality than their Internet-based world, they are likely to have heightened technical expectations, attitudes, and beliefs. For example, they expect libraries and research resources to be accessible remotely (from home), where they can multitask comfortably and snack and watch television.

ARE THESE TEENAGERS INTERNET EXPERTS OR NOVICES?

Even though these youths have had early experiences with digital technologies, they do not have a deep understanding of the inner workings of the Internet or how commercial search engines rank results. These youngsters are often just familiar with the tip of the Internet iceberg. For example, they are not familiar with information that is part of the invisible Web or deep Web, dynamically generated web pages. Such web databases are often hidden from search engine results and are difficult to find for even those who are considered web savvy. Furthermore, these teens are unfamiliar with electronic resources that are not free on the Internet, such as commercial subscription databases.

Many of these students have never engaged in formal exercises comparing advantages, disadvantages, strengths, and weaknesses of the Web with other informational tools such as books and print journals. Members of other generations are more likely to do this sort of mental comparison automatically, only because they have had more experience with the different types of research tools, especially print indexes and reference books. For example, returning adult college students will often ask, "What electronic index replaced or is similar to the *Reader's Guide to Periodical Literature?*" Younger students have no knowledge of this resource.

Teens will devote large amounts of time out-of-school browsing the Web (Levin & Arafeh, 2002). They tend not to place time constraints on themselves. Their inability to use the Web most effectively causes them to spend exorbitant amounts of time browsing. Evidence suggests that these students will devote large amounts of time engaging in activities personally relevant to them.

These students often started using the Internet before having been given any sort of formal instruction on locating and evaluating web pages. However, they quickly figured out through trial and error that retrieved web results located at the top of a web page are usually more relevant than results found at the bottom of the page. In fact, they do not do any scrolling but will concentrate on results at the top of the screen. This strategy of using only the highest-ranked results on the first page of retrieved results and automatically disregarding the rest implies that these young searchers are not closely evaluating any results and are just viewing all top results as being equal and worthy.

These youngsters believe that the information they need to find a research answer or to complete a homework assignment is freely available on the Internet. According to the Pew Internet and American Life Project, a nonprofit organization that studies digital behavior, statistics concerning the use of the Internet to complete homework assignments among this approximate age group keep spiraling upward (Levin & Arafeh, 2002).

This group's preferred method of Internet searching is to start with a Google search, even if that may not be the most efficient or fastest means to the answer. This generation's overreliance on Google as its first choice to find answers indicates that they may not be aware of other information search strategies and resources, especially print materials that are better suited to answer certain types of questions. These youngsters use Google confidently because they find tens of thousands of results in a few seconds. Their interaction with Google makes them feel self-sufficient, smart, and powerful when retrieving many results. They often do not have the metacognitive skills to know when to stop using Google and other search tools and to try a different information search strategy. Further, these young searchers often use Google carelessly to determine or measure the significance of a topic or individual, thereby leading to faulty conclusions. For example, these students, like many older Google searchers, may type in a person's full name to check how many web pages can be retrieved. If these students do not find any results using Google, they may erroneously assume that the person is neither newsworthy nor historically important.

IS THIS NEW NET GENERATION INFORMATION LITERATE OR ILLITERATE?

According to the American Library Association's "information literacy standards for student learning" (1998), a student is only information literate if he or she "accesses information efficiently and effectively," "evaluates information critically and competently," and "uses information accurately and creatively" (pp. 1–2). The previous discussion suggests that these teens are not information literate.

HOW CAN TEACHER-LIBRARIANS PROMOTE LIBRARY SERVICES AND THEMSELVES AND START HELPING STUDENTS BECOME INFORMATION LITERATE?

Teacher-librarians can begin by

- collaborating with classroom teachers to integrate Internet technologies into the curriculum;
- providing students and classroom teachers with quality information from traditional library sources and from Internet resources;
- showing these students and classroom teachers how to save time when searching;
- supplying students and classroom teachers with web page design technologies to deliver effective presentations;
- creating communities of learners or electronic learning modules by linking classmates' web pages to a central page or starting point.

HOW CAN TEACHER-LIBRARIANS EFFECTIVELY COLLABORATE WITH TEACHERS TO BEGIN INTEGRATING THE INTERNET INTO THE CURRICULUM?

Teacher-librarians will probably have to update their libraries' mission statements to begin integrating Internet technologies in their schools. The new missions may have to be formulated not only to support the curriculum but also to attract foot traffic to the brick-and-mortar library. Teacher-librarians can persuade both classroom teachers and students to visit the library by advertising what is new and exciting. Examples include advertising the addition of new books or technical resources. The library homepage is a crucial element in attracting teachers as well as teens to the actual library. A well-designed web page that is information rich and interactive will capture both groups' attention and encourage them to visit the library. Additional steps include updating policies, signage, broadband connections, and workstations to support multitasking, collaborating abilities and to make visits enjoyable.

Teacher-librarians should take a lead role in establishing and designing online communities of learners. If classroom teachers do not yet see the potential of online learning delivery, teacher-librarians should try alternative approaches, such as creating handouts with visuals that classroom teachers can incorporate into their lesson activities. The handouts can advertise both key print and digital resources, including new web sites and web pages that can be quickly accessed via the school library web site.

Teacher-librarians should clearly identify these handouts as products of their school library and may include brief requests at the bottom of handouts, both in print and e-mail format, to forward copies to colleagues who might be interested. Teacher-librarians should try e-mailing copies to classroom teachers so that they can electronically forward handouts deemed important or useful. The goal is to create a "viral marketing" effort in which key handouts and library advertisements are spread by physical and virtual word of mouth (Diorio, 2002, pp. 72–74).

Another collaborative strategy may be to visit different classrooms. Teacher-librarians can volunteer to do 50-minute sessions on a research topic or information literacy skill of the classroom teacher's choice. The key aim is for teacher-librarians to make themselves indispensable to classroom teachers both virtually and physically.

HOW CAN TEACHER-LIBRARIANS PROVIDE AND PROMOTE PRINT AND DIGITAL RESOURCES?

Because of their early exposure to large amounts of graphic and web content and their comfort level with new digital applications, teens will be receptive to new information incorporated with graphics or introduced using Webquests and other types of Internet-based lessons. Equally important, these youngsters will pay attention and will be motivated to learn material that makes them appear more web savvy or helps them to become more knowledgeable about the Internet.

Using the library homepage, teacher-librarians should offer curriculum-focused web bibliographies or lists of the best quality Internet sites to support the curriculum or grade coursework. Levin and Arafeh (2002) observed that 12- to 17-year-old students prefer to use web sites that are approved and accepted by their schools.

Teacher-librarians can also impress this youthful clientele by becoming the school experts on the invisible Web or even Google. Youths can be offered instructional sessions on how to recognize misinformation and bogus information on the Web, and teacher-librarians can show these students other skills important in evaluating the quality of web resources. To keep these youngsters' attention, teacher-librarians should provide instructional sessions about searching Google effectively, such as using Google Boolean searching and being aware of the Google PageRank system. Other ideas include discussing search engine optimization and how corporations employ webmasters to raise their Google rankings.

HOW DO YOU IMPRESS STUDENTS AND TEACHERS WITH TIME MANAGEMENT SKILLS?

Teacher-librarians can reinforce that Google is not the best or first choice timewise in many situations. By showing students how print resources and electronic subscription databases can be used effectively to find answers, teacher-librarians can make students aware of the enormous amounts of time that may be wasted browsing and sorting through Google results. It is vital to communicate how answers can be found faster than by doing a Google search. Teacher-librarians can also reinforce these efforts by publishing success stories and anecdotes on the school library homepage.

HOW DO YOU IMPRESS STUDENTS AND TEACHERS WITH WEB PRESENTATION SKILLS?

Student research projects, including the presentation component, need to be revamped and reconsidered in the new digital environment. According to the Pew Internet and American Life Project, even though these young people are technologically savvy, only 17% of current 12- to 17-year-olds have created a web page for a school project (Lenhart, Simon, & Graziano, 2001).

Teacher-librarians can serve as experts in web page creation and then help teachers and students gather and organize information for their web pages. If classroom teachers are not initially receptive to having students design web pages as part of a project, teacher-librarians should not give up. Teacher-librarians can demonstrate how to present and use web pages effectively in the learning delivery process.

Many teachers tend to focus on the Internet as a source of content or information, but they need to be encouraged to design assignments that foster the Internet as a communication and teaching tool. In fact, the organization of key concepts themselves as presented on web sites may aid students in the formation or understanding of new knowledge representations—in other words, learning.

Web pages can be used as an important aid in teaching or facilitating the information search process. Instead of having students simply present orally, teachers can have them present using web pages in combination with presentations similar to those using PowerPoint. For example, students' individual web pages can be on their topics of interest, with links to their thesis statements, reports, key informational sites, and graphics. Web pages can serve as starting points for research and can continue as centralized gathering points for information and as a sort of virtual filing cabinet or storage system when students do research over extended periods. In this capacity, the web page can be used as a platform to generate new knowledge and facilitate new learning connections.

Topic-specific web pages will also facilitate students' developing personalized focuses. Central ideas and main links can be located on the main page whereas subtopics and less important information can be accessible from linked pages. Students will constantly need to evaluate and make decisions about what information they will present on their main web pages and what information they will link to other web pages because it is less important. According to Kuhlthau's study (1988) of the cognitive and affective aspects of the library search process, the collection, synthesizing, and organization of key concepts into finished web page products should provide students with increased confidence as well as feelings of satisfaction and achievement derived from completing the web pages before presenting.

HOW CAN TEACHER-LIBRARIANS IMPRESS AND MOTIVATE STUDENTS TO LEARN WITH ELECTRONIC LEARNING (E-LEARNING) MODULES?

It is fairly easy to create a virtual community of learners by linking web pages because the Internet is by definition a hypertext system of links. Linked web pages are a new form of instructional delivery to enhance knowledge acquisition and communicate key ideas. Teacher-librarians can facilitate the creation of these e-learning communities by establishing one centralized main page where students can go and access different class or peer web pages.

Students will enjoy exploring and researching web pages created by their classmates. They will also take pride in having their own personalized web sites and in seeing concrete representations of their research. The students will be part of the e-learning process by sharing this web information with their classmates and by having the opportunity to offer and receive real-time feedback. The other benefits of e-learning delivery systems include convenience, the ability to manage one's learning, and the opportunity to take advantage of learning opportunities any time of day and from any Internet access point.

WHAT WILL IMPLEMENTING THESE STRATEGIES ACCOMPLISH?

Implementing these strategies will not only help teacher-librarians minimize the generation gap between themselves and their students but will also enable them to effectively teach students and to collaborate with classroom teachers. These strategies should also prove beneficial in developing adolescents' technology and information literacy skills and in preparing them to be independent lifelong learners.

REFERENCES

American Library Association. (1998). Information literacy standards for student learning. In *Information power: Building partnerships for learning* (chap. 2). Retrieved November 13, 2005, from **www.ala.org/ala/aasl/aaslproftools/informationpower/informationliteracy.htm**

Diorio, S. G. (2002). *Beyond "e": 12 ways technology is transforming sales and marketing strategy.* New York: McGraw-Hill.

Kuhlthau, C. C. (1988). Developing a model of the library search process: Investigation of cognitive and affective aspects. *Reference Quarterly, 28*(2), 232–242.

Lenhart, A., Simon, M., & Graziano, M. (2001, September 1). *The Internet and education: Findings of the Pew Internet and American Life Project.* Retrieved June 1, 2004, from **www.pewinternet.org/ pdfs/PIP_Schools_Report.pdf**

Levin, D., & Arafeh, S. (2002, August 14). *The digital disconnect: The widening gap between Internet-savvy students and their schools.* Retrieved June 1, 2004, from **www.pewinternet.org/pdfs/PIP_ Schools_Internet_Report.pdf**

RESOURCES

Goodman, L. M. (2003, June 16). E-commerce (a special report). Consumer guide—writing tools: For students researching a paper, online libraries are increasingly the way to go; here's how they stack up. *Wall Street Journal* (Eastern ed.), R11. Retrieved April 12, 2004, from the EBSCOhost Academic Search Premier database.

Jones, S. (2002, September 15). *The Internet goes to college: How students are living in the future with today's technology.* Retrieved June 1, 2004, from **www.pewinternet.org/pdfs/PIP_College_Report .pdf**

Kuhlthau, C. C. (1997). Learning in digital libraries: An information search process approach. *Library Trends, 45*(4), 708–724.

Kuhlthau, C. C. (2003). Rethinking libraries for the information age school: Vital roles in inquiry learning. *School Libraries in Canada, 22*(4), 3–5. Retrieved June 1, 2004, from EBSCOhost MasterFILE database.

Leibovich, L. (2000, August 10). Choosing quick hits over the card catalog: Many students prefer the chaos of the Web to the drudgery of the library. *New York Times.* Retrieved April 12, 2004, from **www .nytimes.com/library/tech/00/08/circuits/ articles/10thin.html**

Lenhart, A., Rainie, L., & Lewis, O. (2001, June 21). *Teenage life online: The rise of the instant-message generation and the Internet's impact on friendships and family relationships.* Retrieved June 1, 2004, from **www.pewinternet.org/pdfs/PIP_Teens_Report.pdf**

Madden, M. (2003, December 22). *America's online pursuits: The changing picture of who's online and what they do.* Retrieved June 1, 2004, from **www.pewinternet.org/pdfs/PIP_Online_Pursuits_ Final.PDF**

Oblinger, D. (2003). Boomers, gen-xers & millennials: Understanding the new students. *Educause Review, 38*(4), 37–47. Retrieved June 1, 2004, from **www.educause.edu/ir/library/pdf/erm0342.pdf**

(39)

Analyzing Student Search Strategies: Making a Case for Integrating Information Literacy Skills Into the Curriculum

Thomas J. Scott and Michael K. O'Sullivan

High school students are not experienced internet researchers. Most students employ the basic search strategy of keyword searching that most search engines use. However, we have observed students get frustrated and end up surfing from one site to another or abandoning their search in frustration. Understanding the nature of information, the structure of the internet, and the ability to efficiently and effectively navigate the hypertext environment of the internet are critical information literacy skills that teachers need to teach and that high school students need master.

Are we as high school educators properly preparing students for the kind of research they will be required to conduct for college classes? Or has the Internet so transformed the structure of human knowledge and learning that, as teachers and teacher-librarians, we need to reassess what skills we teach and how and where we direct students to obtain information? These are the questions we need to ask and analyze as educators.

We know, if given a choice, many high school students will choose to browse or surf the Internet for the information they need for a particular assignment. This approach to research does not require developing sophisticated search strategies or critical thinking skills. Students grow up using Yahoo!, Google, Ask Jeeves, or one of the other search engines where they are instructed to type in a few descriptive words, hit the Enter key, and, viola!—unlimited sources. This search approach is not only seductive, but it is also deceiving.

One can understand the seductive nature of this environment. As one student stated during a survey on Internet use (Scott and O'Sullivan, 2000), distributed to 309 high school students with whom we work:

First published in *Teacher Librarian*, October 2005, Volume 33, Number 1

"One benefit of the Internet is the quantity of information available. When a search is done [on] a topic many thousands of sites come up containing information on that topic, so a person almost has unlimited information." (p. 123).

In searching the Internet for information, the typical high school student simply employs the basic strategy of keyword searching that most—if not all—search engines use. Results of this survey indicated a student infatuation with information; any information is attributed to be good information, and the more of it, the better.

INFORMATION OVERLOAD

Providing access to information is no longer the problem for most school libraries. In fact, students today have access to too much information. The problem is knowing where to find the information you need, efficiently and effectively, among the variety of information sources available. "Choosing which source is best suited to fulfill one's need for information is complex. All kinds of considerations come into play" (de Ruiter, 2002, p. 202). With a vast array of online journal indexes, some subject specific and others multidisciplinary, combined with online public access catalogs and dozens of Internet search engines, one can understand why high school students would opt for the unstructured abundance of information contained in and the simple keyword-search approach of the Internet.

High school students, in spite of their bravura, are not experienced researchers. While seemingly rewarded by the number of hits they receive, students often get frustrated and end up resorting to surfing from one site to another in hopes of discovering that one nugget. Or they abandon their search entirely and claim they could not find anything on their topic. As de Ruiter (2002) claims, surfing alone is not sufficient to unlock the information on the Internet when looking for something specific. "Instruction should be aimed at giving insight into two characteristics of the Internet: the nature of the information it provides and ways to navigate this information" (p. 210).

High school students frequently have difficulty defining exactly what kind of information they need. This inability to define their information needs may account for the frustration voiced by several students on the Internet survey. Many students complained it was "hard to understand where to go" when navigating web sites, and because the Internet "isn't usually organized," conducting research was not an easy or enjoyable task. In spite of this frustration, students persist in pursuing this approach to finding information.

This kind of feedback from the Internet evaluation exercise and continued observation of high school students' tendency to pursue this method of research, even if it is less efficient, caused the authors to speculate on what role the hypertext environment of the Internet plays in a student's infatuation with the medium and in his or her ability to efficiently locate information.

Though many students in our study sample claimed to have accomplished skills in navigating the Internet, in actuality, cyberspace is still a confusing medium for many of them to traverse. Teachers at the high school we work at have also voiced a concern about the students' inability to navigate the Internet. As one teacher noted,

I think the overall structure of the Web is not real organized, nor real useful for a lot of users. It is real easy to get lost, and until that straightens out, it is less than a helpful tool for those kids who do get lost, who tend not think in that manner; you know, who can't pick out a search term.

HYPERTEXT LITERACY

The semiotic nature of the Internet redefines traditional epistemology. Student learning and comprehension has been significantly transformed by this hypertext medium. To account for this transformation, we contend that teachers and teacher-librarians should begin to view the ability to efficiently navigate the Web as another aspect of information literacy. Hypertext literacy plays an important role in a student's ability to formulate knowledge from the information found on the Internet. Synder (1998) asserts that hypertext differs from printed text by offering "readers multiple paths through a body of information: It allows them to make their own connections, incorporate their own links, and produce their own meanings" (p. 127).

The interpretation of the semiotic symbols on the Internet, including graphics, text, sound, icons, images, and video, requires a specific knowledge structure and may pose difficulties for certain types of learners. As an example, de Ruiter (2002, p. 200) cites a friend who could not find what he was looking for at a web site because the buttons to browse the hit list were in an unusual place on the page. Burbules and Callister (2000) claim the structure of the Web may be more understandable for certain people and difficult for others. They state, "The hyperlinked structure of the Web is experienced differently by different users: Some can work through the lateral as well as linear lines of association; others find them confusing or counterintuitive" (p. 26).

As the Internet redefines what we determine to be knowledge, it creates a "cognitive divide" (Scott & O'Sullivan, 2002) between those who can effectively navigate and negotiate the information domains of hypertext and hypermedia (the information rich) and those who cannot (the information poor). Even those individuals described by de Ruiter (2002) as mature researchers "do not bother with the Internet as a source because they know how and where to find what they need efficiently in printed sources. If they do decide to turn to the Internet, they often have great difficulty in finding desired information" (p. 199). One of the obstacles these mature researchers face in using the Internet, like the high school student, is interpreting the navigation information on a screen.

Navarro-Prieto (as cited in Holscher & Strube, 2000) compares web searchers with high and low experience skills and determined that expert searchers plan ahead and develop a search strategy based on their knowledge of the Web. On the other hand, Holscher and Strube (2000) found that novice searchers do not plan at all and seem to be driven by what they see on the screen. This search approach describes the behavior of high school students as they attempt to navigate the hypertext environment of the Internet.

To determine the impact this hypertext environment has on a student's ability to find specific information on the Internet, we developed an action-research study to observe how high school students would proceed in locating answers to specific questions from designated web sites.

NAVIGATING HYPERTEXT

A Hypertext Literacy Exercise was conducted among four ninth-grade social studies classes ($n = 89$), and it was structured to evaluate and observe how high school students would navigate four web sites in order to locate specific information. Data were collected through direct observations of student search behavior as they completed a hypertext evaluation rubric (see Appendix) that we created and through analysis of students' short reflective essays.

The students evaluated four web sites used in the social studies class taught by one of the authors (TJS). The four web sites included the UNESCO home page, the home page of the office of the U.S. Trade Representative, the Institute of Development Studies, and Nike Corporation. The students were asked to locate a specific piece of information from each site and to assess the web site according to its visual design, navigational form, content, and usability.

Comments from the students' reflective essays discussing the search strategies they used, combined with our direct observation of the student search approaches revealed a significant level of frustration and difficulty. In observing the students' difficulties in navigating the web sites to locate the information, their search strategies became apparent, and to some extent, predictable.

STUDENT SEARCH APPROACH

The immediate strategy by many of the students to locate information was to seek out the web site's Search screen, conduct a keyword search, and proceed to go through the list of hits. The students slid into what Holscher and Strube (2000) describe as a "browsing mode" (p. 339) and they continued browsing for several clicks before ultimately returning to the Search screen to alter their query. Many of the students did not change their strategy in spite of continued failure to locate the information requested.

Data from the hypertext evaluation rubric that we developed (see Appendix) suggest that interpreting hypertext presented a variety of frustrations for the students who completed the exercise. A brief sample of student responses regarding their search for information at the UNESCO web page illustrates that graphic design, presentation of links, spatial ordering of text, and the multimedia capabilities of hypertext are all aspects of navigation that cause interpretive difficulties.

The evaluation data from the students regarding the UNESCO web site suggests they had a difficult time locating one of the winners of a Worldwide Poster contest celebrating the UN Year of Tolerance. With respect to the site's visual design, many students found it difficult to navigate. The following responses are illustrative of the students' problems.

- "I couldn't find it; the headings didn't apply; and the search didn't work. I couldn't navigate it."
- "The navigational techniques of this sight were confusing. There were topic headings but no pull down menus or subtopics to aid in the search. The sight had many links to go to, which is sometimes helpful but in this case a bit distracting and could easily get me lost and did get me lost."
- "You could easily get lost because there are so many links off of links."
- "I had to broaden my search field, but then I got too many irrelevant results; it made it too confusing."
- "There was no heading for what I was looking for. I had to do a search, which did not work anyway. It is not easy to get lost, but it was a bit confusing. Information was not easy to find. I tried almost every link and did a couple different searches and still couldn't find anything."

From these responses, it is clear that many students have not developed the cognitive skills to effectively negotiate hypertext. Our observations of the student search strategies verify these difficulties. According to Fidel et al. (1999), many students search in a random manner and appear not to understand the systematic process involved in finding information on the Web. Their search strategies are based on trial and error. The following description is typical of the search approach used by several students in navigating the UNESCO web site:

Student examines the site for the search command.

Finds keyword search, types in "Poster Contest," receives six hits.

Clicks on back button, and changes keyword to "UNESCO Poster Contest." No hits.

Clicks on back button, and changes keyword to "UN Year of Tolerance." No hits.

Clicks on link "UN News Center." Searches screen for "Poster Contest."

Gives up on the UN site and moves onto the next web site where she immediately goes right to the search bar.

The only strategy for many of these students was to make minor changes in their keyword search. These students engaged in what Holscher and Strube (2000, p. 343) describe as "backward-oriented behavior," which is very common behavior for the less-experienced users.

Many of the students adopted a search strategy similar to the approach the AskJeeves search engine encourages. Type in a question or a phrase, and then expect an answer to appear. Rather than initially studying the web site and evaluating it for relevant links, the students would immediately seek the web site's internal search engine. If the answer to the question was not readily available with their initial search, many of the students would compound their problem by pulling additional words from the question and adding these words to their original keyword search, thus creating a lengthy string of words or a phrase.

Some students started out using the keyword search but then abandoned it when the results were not immediately forthcoming. These students went back to the home page of the assigned web site and proceeded to review and analyze how the web site was organized. They reviewed the subject links provided and selected the most appropriate link for the information they sought. These students employed more analytical and critical-thinking skills to locate the answer to the assigned questions.

In their reflective essays, several students admitted to being distracted by what they saw on the screen. For example, one student noted, "Things that seem to get my attention are always flashy. They may be a picture or bright colors or flashing headings. These are sometimes distractions to me when I am trying to find some information in a hurry."

This exercise also revealed several other problems related to navigating hypertext. The inability of students to narrow searches, the inability to discern useful links from nonuseful links, the lack of skill in conducting searches, and the inability to create efficient and effective keyword searches were just a few of the problems encountered by students.

INFORMATION LITERACY IS THE KEY

This action-research study reveals a correlation between a student's search skills and the hypertext environment of the Internet. It also illustrates that hypertext does present distinct challenges to the teaching and learning process. As de Ruiter (2002, p. 208) concludes, it takes experience to navigate the Internet. Recognizing and interpreting navigational pointers on the screen take training and so do surfing and searching the Internet.

The frustrations and difficulties our students encountered emphasize the importance of training and support for students toward learning better and more efficient search strategies for navigating the Web. As Holscher and Strube (2000, p. 340) found in their study, web experts make use of advanced search options like Boolean operators and modifiers much more frequently than the average user. Many high school students do not possess an understanding of how to develop a search strategy or how to refine a search beyond using keywords.

The Internet has impacted education in ways no expert could have foreseen or predicted. The current paradigm for information access, delivery, and retrieval continues to evolve for teachers as well as for students. While the Internet provides students greater decision-making power to accept, reject, modify, and create new forms of information, without the search skills and critical evaluation skills to determine relevancy and reliability, students will not be prepared to undertake the rigorous research requirements of college.

Braun (1997), reflecting on the Internet, states, "The need for teachers to help students develop the ability to discover authentic and relevant knowledge, to distinguish fact from fiction, is greater than ever"

(p. 157). The result of this action-research study highlights the critical need to incorporate exercises and instruction in navigating this hypertext environment. Unless teachers and teacher-librarians show students there are other, more effective ways of finding information, they will continue to pursue this method of information retrieval. Accomplishing this task requires cooperation, collaboration, and support between departments and the library, between teachers and teacher-librarians, and a commitment from the administration to promote this atmosphere.

Teachers at all levels of education, from elementary to higher education, continue to struggle with exactly how to effectively integrate information literacy skills into their curriculum. The key is for teachers to analyze the content of their classes and assignments and then determine which information literacy skills should be applied where and when.

Information literacy skills must be incorporated throughout all areas of a school's curriculum, not just in library orientation classes or in isolated skills presentations. We cannot allow our students to depend solely on the Internet for their information. We need to emphasize and require students to use a variety of sources for their research, and we need to make them aware that the Internet is just another tool they can add to their arsenal of information retrieval sources. As Dupuis (1997) observes, "Unless [both teachers and] librarians educate users about finding information, users will continue to underutilize and misuse information" (p. 98).

It is apparent that the Internet will continue to influence the school curriculum. Given

Gender: Male ___ Female ___	**URL:** www.un.org **Web Site:** United Nations

Question: Find an example of a winning poster from the "Worldwide Poster Contest" organized by UNESCO, for the UN Year of Tolerance. Write the title and name of the author of one of the winning posters.

Visual Design
In what ways did the design of this web site help or hinder you in locating the information?
Items to consider when answering this question:
- Is the site text-based or graphic-based?
- Are the major elements of the site easily identified (e.g., a photograph, a logo, graphic art, headline, major subject headings)?
- Are the colors used for the text and background distracting or hard to read?
- Is advertising used, and if so, did it distract you from finding your information?

Navigational Form
What navigational technique does this web site use, and did it help or hinder you in locating the information?
Items to consider when answering this question:
- Are Topic or Subject Heading lists provided? Drop down Menus? Keyword Search of the site?
- Does the site prevent you from getting lost?
- Is navigation consistent throughout the site? How easy was it to retrieve your information?

Web Site Content
Was the content (subjects covered) at this web site easy to follow and determine?
Items to consider when answering this question:
- Was a list of the major content areas provided?
- How was the content organized (e.g., by subject area, general categories)?
- What was the main message or purpose of the site?

Usability
Overall, was this web site easy or difficult to use?
Items to consider when answering this question:
- Was the download time reasonable or too slow?
- Were the special effects distracting?
- Did the hyperlinks function properly and were they still active?
- Was the text easy to read (e.g., font size, style, color, grammatical and spelling errors)?
- Does the site require additional plug-ins to function (i.e., RealPlayer, Adobe Acrobat, QuickTime)?

Appendix: Hypertext Evaluation Criteria

this reality, students need to master the information literacy skills if they are to harness the potential of this "new age of information." By working together, we can prepare students with the necessary analytical and information literacy skills for college and life to ensure that this new millennium is not remembered as the "age of misinformation."

REFERENCES

Braun, J., Jr. (1997). Past, possibilities, and potholes on the information superhighway. *Social Education, 61*(3), 149–153.

Burbules, N., & Callister, T., Jr. (2000). *Watch it: The risks and promises of information technologies for education*. Boulder, CO: Westview Press.

de Ruiter, J. (2002). Aspects of dealing with digital information: Mature novices on the Internet. *Library-Trends, 51*(2), 199–209.

Dupuis, E. (1997). The information literacy challenge: Addressing the changing needs of our students through our programs. In L. E. M. Martin (Ed.), *The challenge of Internet literacy: The instruction-web convergence* (p. 93–112). New York: Haworth Press.

Fidel, R., Davies, R., Douglass, M., Holder, J., Hopkins, C., Kushner, E., et al. (1999). A visit to the information mall: Web searching behavior of high school students. *Journal of the American Society for Information Science, 50*(1), 24–37.

Holscher, C., & Strube, G. (2000). Web search behavior of Internet experts and newbies. *Computer Networks, 33*, 337–346.

Scott, T., & O'Sullivan, M. (2000, May–June). The Internet and information literacy: Taking the first step toward technology education in the social studies. *Social Studies, 91*(3), 121–125.

Scott, T., & O'Sullivan, M. (2002, October 14). *The epistemology of Internet use: Implications for teaching and learning*. Presented at the Association of Internet Researchers, Maastricht, The Netherlands.

Synder, I. (1998). Beyond the hype: Reassessing hypertext. In I. Synder (Ed.), *Page to screen: Taking literacy into the electronic era* (p. 127). London: Routledge.

㊵

Critical Literacy: A Building Block Toward the Information Literate School Community

Linda Langford

In my paper entitled *Information Literacy: Seeking clarification* (Langford, 1999), I grapple with semantics. This came as a result of my frustration over a concept that was being bandied around, written into schools' mission and vision statements and being toted as the teacher-librarian's core business. It was frustrating because one's understanding of the concept, depended on what end of the elephant you had in your grasp.

I was able to tease out a number of literacies that were being generated as fast as I could read the literature on literacy or digest what research was available. Critical literacy was one aspect that I had included in my map of information literacy (Langford, 1999, 49). It was grouped with ethical, moral, and information problem-solving literacies.

Today, I question what critical literacy is about and how we develop this literacy. In a global society endeavouring to make sense of the information surrounding us, critical literacy has proved to be a difficult concept. Misson and Christie (1998) posit the definition that critical literacy is both process and practice and that it centers on making clear new ideologies and the consequent ideological working of texts. Certainly the struggle between the existing model of industrial age schools with the demands of a communication age society begs that we come to some pedagogical grip with a literacy that finds its challenge in emerging communication technologies.

If we are serious about the new teaching and learning paradigm that is emerging as a consequence of the '*Net Education System* so aptly coined by Mal Lee (1999), then critical literacy must lie in a learning culture that is informed by a conceptual understanding of information literacy. As a society, we are evermore conscious of the need to be continuously learning, to keep developing as information literate human

First published in *Teacher Librarian*, June 2001, Volume 28, Number 5

beings. The development of the skills and practices of critical literacy are more vital than ever to school curricula. How will schools take on this challenge? Can they emerge as information literate school communities?

I believe that Industrial Age schooling must crumble and give rise to a more student-centred, goal-oriented, caring environment, which fosters active involvement and risk taking, and ongoing personal mastery. This paper supports the thesis that critical literacy, as a subset of information literacy, relies on the development of critical and creative thinking within the information process: the scaffold for continuous learning.

CRITICAL LITERACY: POSSIBLE UNDERSTANDINGS

Critical literacy has as many points of view as information literacy. It is my thesis that critical literacy is but one literacy that combines with other literacies to develop a continually inquiring human mind. One never becomes critically literate because one never becomes information literate (Langford, 1999; Henri, 1999). The continuum is dynamic and centers on our continuous learning if we are to be effective and creative beings, able to relate and reassess the ideological workings in a text . . . from an advertising flyer to an economic/political initiative like GST.

As a concept, it can be manifested in an aspect of the information process, that is, the development of thinking. The information environment, tied to emerging technologies, forces us to adopt a manner of continuous learning in order to function well in society at whatever point in time, using whatever skills we have developed, to make sense of an ever changing information climate (Buckland, 1991). Critical literacy is but one building block toward this societal imperative to make sense of all that seeks to inform.

Critical literacy could be defined as "taking the learner beyond thoughtful reflection to analysis and a determined course of action" (Jones, 1996). Within a conceptual view of information literacy; a view that perceives learning as a series of multiple arrivals along a continuous journey, critical literacy's foci rests on the developing skills of thinking.

To develop critical literacy, that is our ability to recast our thinking through metacognitive processes (McGregor, 1999; Paul, 1993), we may need to experience, adopt, and apply a degree of skills and attitudes that free us to recast our thinking. These skills and attitudes would enable us to shift our mental models of *what is* to *what can be* as we hone the skills necessary to differentiate between fact and opinion, examining extrinsic and intrinsic assumptions, remaining focussed on the big picture while examining the specifics. Awareness of fallacious arguments, ambiguity, and manipulative reasoning (Jones, 1996) coupled with flexibility and open-mindedness would contribute to a state of deep critical thinking.

CRITICAL AND CREATIVE THINKING: SUSTAINING CRITICAL LITERACY

Analyzing the work of academics like Jones, McGregor, Paul, Todd, and Meyer provides a good base for developing identifiers of critical and creative thinkers. These identifiers have significantly extended the concept of critical literacy, as understood by those who coined the term, as the "use of language in all of its forms, as in thinking, solving problems, or communicating" (Venezky, 1982). These identifiers support the notion of critical literacy as a set of processes centering on the development of thinking.

The following set of features (Jones, 1996; **www.library.ucsb.edu/untangle/jones.html#savery**) serve to identify some of the characteristics that may define a critically literate community:

- can approach something new in a logical manner;
- can look at how others have approached the same question or problem, but know when they need

more information;
* can use creative and diverse ways to generate a hypothesis, approach a problem or answer a question;
* can take their critical thinking skills and apply them to everyday life;
* can clarify assumptions and recognize that they have causes and consequences;
* can support their opinions with evidence, data, logical reasoning, and statistical measures;
* can look at a problem from multiple angles;
* can not only fit the problem within a larger context, but decide if and where it fits in the larger context;
* are comfortable with ambiguity.

Further to this list, the CTILAC Advisory Board (1998–1999) **http://ir.bcc.ctc.edu/library/ilac/ critdef.htm** adds that critical and creative thinking implies that there is purpose to the thinking, that is, that there is an information problem to be solved. Therefore this would call upon the skills inherent in analysis, synthesis, and evaluation. They add weight to Jones's summation by pointing out that critical and creative thinkers recognize

* patterns and provide a way to use those patterns to solve a problem or answer a question;
* errors in logic, reasoning, or the thought process;
* what is irrelevant or extraneous information;
* preconceptions, bias, values, and the way that these affect our thinking;
* that these preconceptions and values mean that any inferences are within a certain context;
* ambiguity—that there may be more than one solution or more than one way to solve a problem.

Does critical literacy therefore have a relational role to critical and creative thinking? Can critical literacy be the platform for a whole school curriculum? And if so, can this whole school approach translate to an information literate school community: a learning community that is in the business of "continually creating its future" (Senge, 1992)?

CRITICAL LITERACY: BEYOND RHETORIC IN EDUCATION

Perhaps a more useable perspective for schools might be in viewing critical literacy as interpreting the intellectual and social value of information (Buckland, 1991; Langford, 1999, p. 49). This then would call up the higher order thinking skills that lead to decision-making, creating, and synthesizing the outcomes of the myriad forms of literacy.

If critical literacy can develop from a metacognitive approach to recognising the need to think critically and creatively, then the *skills* involved can be developed. It is especially pertinent that educators appreciate that critical literacy, which has as its twin skill sets critical and creative thinking, is not a set of sectoralised skills reserved for say, the English classroom, but is a shared set of skills across all disciplines. As Meyers (1995) so clearly delineates,

* critical thinking is a learnable skill with teachers and peers serving as resources;
* problems, questions, and issues serve as the source of motivation for the learner;
* courses are assignment centred rather than text or lecture oriented;
* goals, methods, and evaluation emphasise using content rather than simply acquiring it;

• students need to formulate and justify their ideas in writing;
• students collaborate to learn and enhance their thinking.

If we agree that critical literacy emphasizes mental attitudes or dispositions and the concomitant application of reasoning to everyday situations, then we might argue that the building blocks of analysis, synthesis and evaluation are the building blocks that develop critical literacy. How we apply those building blocks will determine the extent of our critical and creative thinking (McGregor, 1999). No matter how we view the building blocks, we must be conscious that literate practice is always morally and politically loaded; and that our world view stems from our ability to "render explicit the belief systems inscribed in the text, and so negate their power" (Misson & Christie, 1998, p. 11). We must also be conscious that critical literacy be a shared understanding if it is, as it should be, a foundation to sound education.

CRITICALLY LITERATE: THE LEARNING COMMUNITY

However we view critical literacy, it must center on thought and our belief that, through developing the processes of thinking, our attitudes will be shaped. Our values and beliefs, coupled with the ability to solve problems, are partners in developing and shaping our worldview. And this sharpening and developing of our worldview critically asks us to appraise our information environment . . . to assess the *ching-dou* (Handy, 1997) as we seek meaning.

A highly critically literate learning community acts through an *unconscious consciousness*, aware only that the determined course of action takes the group onward toward successful outcomes, toward functioning well in society. The processes and practices that inform critical literacy, that is the *tools of truth making*, are well honed. The capacity to think about their thinking, analyze and apply thought, create knowledge and act will reflect the quality of that learning community; the quality of that information literate school community.

BACK TO SCHOOL

Information literacy, as seen from an holistic platform, is perceived within a journey of multiple arrivals, connecting to the continuous honing of our mental capacities: our critical literacy, our technological literacy, our cultural literacy, our functional literacy. Let us not argue about the nature of information literacy anymore. Let us accept that we must move beyond the jargon of learning how to learn and critically examine and synthesize the connecting aspects of the information literacy map (Langford, 1999) as teachers and as teacher-librarians. Let us reconstruct our understanding of an information literate school community. Let us acknowledge a paradigm shift from information skills thinking to lifelong learning thinking, complete with the metacognitive skills of critical literacy: critical and creative thinking. Let us truly set our young people onward toward the goal of functioning well in society.

My belief is that this is a far more regenerative concept for educators to be a part of then some narrowly defined information literacy concept.

The truth is out there!

REFERENCES

Buckland, M. (1991). Information as thing. *Journal of the American Society for Information Science, 42*(5), 351–360.
CTILAC Advisory Board, Bellevue Community College. (1998–1999). Critical thinking definition [online]. **http://ir.bcc.ctc.edu/library/ilac/critdef.htm**

Handy, C. (1997). *The hungry spirit.* London: Hutchinson

Henri, J. (1999). The information literate school community: Not just a pretty face. In J. Henri & K. Bonanno (Eds.), *The information literate school community* (p. 4). Wagga Wagga: Centre for Information Studies

Jones, D. (1996). Critical thinking in an online world [online]. **www.library.ucsb.edu/untangle/ jones.html#savery**

Langford, L. (1999). Information literacy: Seeking clarification. In J. Henri & K. Bonanno (Eds.), *The information literate school community.* Charles Sturt University, Wagga Wagga: Centre for Information Studies.

Lee, M. (1999). A new global education system. *Access, 13*(2), 15–16

McGregor, J. (1999). Critical literacy and the Internet. From seminar May 26, 1999, at Charles Sturt University, Wagga Wagga, Australia.

Meyers, C. (1985). *Teaching students to think critically.* San Francisco: Jossey Bass.

Misson, R., & Christie, F. (1998). *Literacy and schooling.* London: Routledge.

Paul, R. (1993). *Critical thinking: How to prepare students for a rapidly changing world.* J. Willsen & A. J. A. Binker (Eds.). Santa Rosa, CA: Foundation for Critical Thinking.

Senge P. (1992). *The fifth discipline: The art and practise of the learning organization.* New York: Random House.

Venezky, R. (1982). Linguistics and/or reading or is applied linguistics a caveat emptor technology? In W. Frawley (Ed.), *Linguistics and literacy* (pp. 269–283). New York: Plenum Press.

Literacy Links: Supporting Comprehensive Literacy Instruction in Your School: Guiding the Inclusion of Information Literacy

Marlene Asselin

A major recommendation from the 2000 Program for International Student Assessment (PISA) calls for increased attention to instruction and assessment of information literacy processes. Results of the PISA showed significant differences in processes and student capabilities among different types of reading, specifically between reflective and informational reading. The report states: "In the future, demands on individual literacy abilities are likely to include more fluent information retrieval and processing along with reflection and evaluation, so literacy that is balanced in these regards is desirable" (Topping et al., 2003, p. 12). Teacher-librarians are well prepared to spearhead professional development in this new area of literacy in their schools. This column reviews evidence of the growing importance of the place of information literacy in educational reform, outlines challenges to including it as part of regular literacy instruction, and suggests ways that teacher-librarians can advance professional development in this area in their schools.

INFORMATION LITERACY: A CENTRAL FOCUS OF EDUCATIONAL REFORM

Teacher-librarians should be well informed about the broader political and educational rationale for information literacy instruction. Current educational reform movements are shaped by political agendas aimed at competing in a global knowledge-based economy. Key themes of these movements are lifelong learning, a learning society, and knowledge generation (Darling-Hammond, 1997). Like many countries, the Canadian government has established a national agenda for competing in the new global economy and developed descriptions of workforce skills to enable this vision, at the heart of which is information lit-

First published in *Teacher Librarian*, April 2004, Volume 31, Number 4

eracy—for example, "manage information: locate, gather, and organize information using appropriate technology and information systems" (Ministry of Education, Government of British Columbia, 2000). In accordance with these political directions, Canada views education as "a lifelong learning process where educators strive to create a learning society in which the acquisition, renewal, and use of knowledge is cherished" (Canadian Council of Ministers of Education, 1999).

As a starting point for professional development on information literacy, teacher-librarians need to know the relevant learning outcomes already embedded in classroom core curriculum. In the United States, 3 of the 12 national literacy standards encompass information literacy—for example, "use a variety of technological and informational resources to gather and synthesize information to create and communicate knowledge" (National Council of Teachers of English & the International Reading Association, 1996). Examples from Canadian provincial language arts curricula are "collect specific information from a variety of sources, including print, oral discussions, electronic media, and computer technology" and "identify viewpoints, opinions, stereotypes, and propaganda in literary, informational, and mass media communications" (British Columbia Ministry of Education, 1996). In one province, a new curriculum document contains a comprehensive breakdown of information literacy skills and strategies organized within four major components of the inquiry or research process (Alberta Learning, 2003).

WHY ISN'T INFORMATION LITERACY INSTRUCTION ALREADY HAPPENING?

Teachers are not prepared to teach this aspect of literacy either at the preservice or inservice level. A study of Canadian teacher education programs found minimal inclusion of information literacy (Asselin & Doiron, 2003). While literacy is a major focus of professional development for inservice teachers across North America, programs do *not* address information literacy. In turn, teachers' lack of understanding about information literacy explains low levels of teacher-librarian and teacher collaboration for information literacy instruction (Whelan, 2003).

Classroom instruction that is happening is limited. It follows from teachers' lack of preparation in information literacy that instruction, where it does exist, is neither systematic nor explicit. As with other aspects of literacy, teachers need to learn a progressive, developmental curriculum of information literacy skills and how to use explicit instructional strategies with students (modeling, demonstrating, explaining). Too often students are left to carry out information tasks without sufficient instructional support.

Literacy assessments do not include information literacy. If assessment drives instruction, then what is assessed should give us insight into what is being taught. Preliminary findings from a study of standardized literacy tests across all 50 states comprehension and evaluation of information on the Internet is not included in more than three-fourths of state tests (Leu, 2002).

LEADING PROFESSIONAL DEVELOPMENT IN INFORMATION LITERACY

1. Using mind maps in paper or electronic form, guide teachers (and administrators) to explore their current concepts of information literacy and instructional methods. Prepare an overhead or handout of information literacy outcomes from each grade and curricular area as an anchor point for these explorations. Guide teachers to discuss how these outcomes are being taught and their students' abilities and needs in these areas.

2. Design an interactive small group learning activity, such as a web quest, that helps teachers deepen their understanding of the concept of information literacy, provides instructional exemplars (video ideally), shows examples of collaborative units in which information literacy instruction is embedded in content area learning, and illustrates how to develop valid assessment measures of information literacy. Introduce one or

two models of information processes and an example of an information literacy curriculum (or scope and sequence) by grade so teachers can refer to them for their own information literacy instruction.

3. Provide a variety of relevant readings selected according to questions and concerns of your particular group of colleagues. You may have your own favorite readings but also check out collected resources that can be found on various web sites such as the International Association of School Librarianship (**www.ials-slo.org**), Jamie McKenzie's Libraries and the Information Literate School Community (**http://newlibrary.org/**), Kathy Schrock's Guide for Educators (**http://school.discovery.com/schrock guide/**) and ERIC (**http://eric.ed.gov/**).

4. Help teachers develop a plan for teaching one aspect of information literacy to their class. The plan should include these elements of effective instruction: setting purpose, building background knowledge, direct instruction of new skill, guided practice, closure, and assessment.

5. After teachers have implemented their plan, share and reflect in small groups. Use this opportunity to illustrate how student competency in information literacy improves their learning and to emphasize the instructional support that teacher-librarians offer through resources and discipline expertise.

REFERENCES

Alberta Learning. (2003). *Focus on inquiry: A teacher's guide to implementing inquiry-based learning.* Edmonton, AB: Learning and Teaching Resources Branch.

Asselin, M., & Doiron, R. (2003). An analysis of the inclusion of school library programs and services in the preparation of preservice teachers in Canadian universities. *Behavioral and Social Sciences Librarian, 22* (1), 19–32.

British Columbia Ministry of Education. (1996). *Language arts instructional resource package.* Victoria, BC: BC Ministry of Education. Retrieved November 19, 2003, from **www.bced.gov.bc.ca/irp**

Canadian Council of Ministers of Education, Canada (1999). *Shared priorities in education at the dawn of the 21st century: Future directions for The Council of Ministers of Education, Canada.* Retrieved January 27, 2003, from **www.cmec.ca/reports/victoria99.en.stm**

Darling-Hammond, L. (1997). *The right to learn: A blueprint for creating schools that work.* San Francisco: Jossey-Boss.

Leu, D. (2002). Assessment practices in reading and writing with new technologies. Paper presented at the 52nd National Reading Conference, December 2002, Miami, FL.

Ministry of Education, Government of British Columbia. (2000). *The critical skills required of the Canadian workforce.* Retrieved February 28, 2003, from **www.bced.gov.bc.ca/careers/planning/ work/critskll.htm**

National Council of Teachers of English & the International Reading Association. (1996). *Standards for the English language arts.* Retrieved November 17, 2003, from **www.ncte.org/standards/standards .shtml**

Topping, K., et al. (2003). *Policy and practice implications of the Program for International Student Assessment (PISA) 2000: Report of the International Reading Association PISA Task Force.* Retrieved December 3, 2003, from **www.reading.org/advocacy/pisa.pdf**

Whelan, D. (2003). Why isn't information literacy catching on? *School Library Journal, 49*(9), 50–53. Retrieved January 19, 2004 from **http://slj.reviewsnews.com/index.asp?layout=article& articleid=CA318993&publication=slj**

42

Literacy Links:
Online Information Literacy:
Moving from the Familiar to the New

Keith McPherson

Many of the Internet sites visited by our students exhibit text structures that parallel those of information books. A teacher-librarian coworker summed up this observation while searching for plagiarism web sites to use with her grade 10 students. She stated, "Surfing the Internet is more challenging than finding information about needles in a set of Dorling Kindersley's Eyewitness Guides [or Eyewitness series]!" Having scanned many Dorling Kindersley's Eyewitness Guides for a variety of information (other than needles), I completely related to this parallelism. I thus chuckled a reply to her, "If only the Internet came with as good a table of contents or index!"

Although the feasibility of an Internet index can be debated, most web page designers will not argue the necessity for clearly organizing web site content. Consequently, most Internet web sites incorporate information text structures similar to those found in books. For example, tables of contents and indexes are the organizing "backbones" of most successful medium to large web sites like the Smithsonian Institute (**www.si.edu/**), the Louvre (**www.louvre.fr**), and Encyclopædia Britannica Online (**www.britannica .com/**). Similarly, popular student recreational web sites, like gaming sites (**www.runescape.com**), student-created sites (**http://agirlsworld.com/**), blogs (**https://teenblogs.studentcenter.org**), and "hangouts" (**www.gurl.com/**) are crafted around some very complex, inventive—and yet intuitive—index and table of contents structures.

Understandably, table of contents and indexes are not the only information text structures our students will interact with when surfing the Internet. For example, other familiar print-based-information text characteristics found online are keywords, graphs, headers and titles, timelines, glossaries, photographs, family trees, classification graphics, and so forth. New information text structures found with the Inter-

First published in *Teacher Librarian*, October 2005, Volume 33, Number 1

Figure 42.1. June 26, 2005 Homepages of Encyclopædia Britannica (© 2005, Encyclopædia Britannica, Inc.) and gURL (© iVillage Inc., 1995–2005. All rights reserved).

net's multimedia environment include, but are not limited to, fly-out menus, pull-down menus, textual and pictorial hyperlinks, audio and video demonstrations, search engines, chat-with-an-expert option, and the like. As highlighted in the screen shots of the Encyclopædia Britannica Online and gURL home pages (see Figure 42.1), many sites contain wide combinations and permutations of both familiar and new information structures.

These screenshots highlight just the tip of the massive information-rich online-iceberg with which our students will be interacting. Combined with data from related research studies (Ipsos, 2003; Kaiser Family Foundation, 2003) that finds 88–96% of all North American secondary students regularly using the Internet for pleasure or school work, it is no surprise that the job of honing our students' online information literacy skills falls to information literacy experts like us—teacher-librarians.

Where does one begin? If you are just beginning to develop curriculum aimed at expanding your students' online information literacy skills, I highly recommend contacting your local, state, provincial, or national teacher-librarian organizations to determine if there are current school library information-learning objectives already in place. Many of these organizations have strands of learning outcomes that focus on developing online information literacy skills. If not, or if you wish to expand your students' existing skill sets, then I suggest that you visit the following four exemplar links that contain a wide variety of curricular tools for developing your grade K–12 students' online (and offline) information literacy skills:

• American Association of School Libraries, Information Literacy: **www.ala.org/ala/aasl/aaslissues/aaslinfolit/informationliteracy1.htm**
• Information Literacy Learning Outcomes (K–12), British Columbia: **www.lerc.educ.ubc.ca/LERC/courses/461/infolit/infolit.htm**
• Missouri Department of Elementary and Secondary Education, K–12 Curriculum and Integrated Information and Technology Literacy Skills: **www.dese.state.mo.us/divimprove/curriculum/literacy/document.pdf**
• Building Information Literacy (K–12), Prince Edward Island: **www.edu.pe.ca/bil/**

When developing online information literacy lessons and units, I try to remind myself that many skills required on the Internet are identical or very similar to those required to successfully interact with and comprehend information in books. In other words, an online index has a very similar structure and function to those in books. Therefore, before jumping into learning how to teach children to use complex online information literacy structures (e.g., how to download and troubleshoot browser plug-ins for interactive online searching and multimedia playbacks), try helping children to use more familiar information literacy tools, like identifying headers and keywords or skimming and scanning. Such skills may have been originally developed in books, but they are essential when searching and reading dense or multiple web sites. Once comfortable using these familiar tools in this new environment, you can move on to tackle fly-out or fly-down menus, which are just fancy interactive subtables of contents and indexes.

Sometimes, though, we may resist teaching online information literacy skills because we are unfamiliar with the technology or Internet environment or because our students are unable to stay on task while browsing. A suggestion here is to develop these online skills away from the computer. I have established the foundations of grade 6 students' advanced Google searches without ever turning on a computer. How? First, I stand eight students in front of the class, telling them that they represent the total pool of Internet web sites containing information on cats and dogs. I tell three students that they are web sites containing information on *cats*, the next three represent web sites on *dogs*, and the last two contain information on both *cats and dogs*. Then, after a quick explanation of what basic Boolean operators *and* and *or* are supposed to do, I use the operators to have specific sets of "student web sites" step forward from the pool.

For example, when I search for *cat* web sites, five student web sites should step forward—all but the three *dog* web sites. A search for *cats* and *dogs* will bring the two web sites on *cats and dogs* forward (thus narrowing the search), whereas a search for *cats* or *dogs* will bring all eight student web sites forward (thus expanding the search). I then explain that double quotes around the words *hairless cats* will bring forward only those sites with that exact phrase. After repeating this activity several times, I then encourage students to write out Boolean expressions using keywords from their current research projects. The intention is to visually and experientially develop students' abilities to use Boolean operators to focus their online searches without being distracted by the computer. Combined with keywords (also generated offline), many students are delighted with the speed and accuracy at which they can identify Internet information using their computers.

As I have pointed out in this and earlier columns, forging literacy links between the classroom and school library goes well beyond just the teaching of reading and writing. I believe if we are serious at developing and maintaining dynamic and relevant school libraries supportive of our students' real-world literacies, then we must provide opportunities for students to learn in a variety of real contexts where a variety of literacies are valued, taught, modeled, and expressed. Since students are online already, and the Internet is largely built on information text structures, it seems prudent to help our students become more adept (and critical) of these new online structures and literacies. Making bridges between familiar print-based materials and these new online environments is one way to start. Such approaches to teaching literacy will, I believe, develop powerful online literacy skills in students and continue to demonstrate to the school community that the school library is relevant, progressive, and sensitive to changing times and students' multiple real-world literacies.

REFERENCES

Encyclopædia Britannica Online. (2005). Home page. Retrieved June 26, 2005, from **www.britannica.com/**

gURL. (2005). Home page. Retrieved June 26, 2005, from **www.gurl.com/**

Ipsos News Center. (2003). The Internet is changing the way Canadians socialize. Retrieved June 27, 2005, from **www.ipsos-na.com/news/pressrelease.cfm?id=2008**

Kaiser Family Foundation. (2003). Growing up wired: Survey on youth and the Internet in the Silicon Valley. Retrieved June 27, 2005, from **www.kff.org/entmedia/20030518a-index.cfm**

(PART V)

Learning Leadership: Literacy and Reading

㊸

Teacher-Librarian as
Literacy Leader

Michael Cart

According to proverbial wisdom, all politics is local, and so, I would argue, is all literacy leadership. Okay, I am exaggerating here for dramatic effect, but nevertheless, I do believe that to be effective, literacy leadership must begin at home and, further, that home base for literacy leadership must be the school library.

BE A LITERACY LEADER

Joel Shoemaker, past president of the Young Adult Library Services Association and a teacher-librarian at South East Junior High School in Iowa City, IA, recently wrote to me, "I want my library to be an integral part of the entire school environment that keeps students constantly awash in a sea of books, authors, and ideas" (personal communication, November 5, 2006). To Joel, being a literacy leader means keeping his focus on creating, sustaining, and promoting a community of readers. Of course, such communities always begin with individuals—individual readers and leaders.

David Loertscher wrote in the December 2006 issue of *Teacher Librarian*,

> While no state or region seems to have a corner on success, *individual* [emphasis added] teacher-librarians
> do. In other words, much of our success depends on the individual who is able to reach up out of the mud
> puddle of technological breakdown or unshelved books to make a difference. (p. 10)

I could not agree more, and though Loertscher was writing about teacher-librarians as learning leaders, so much of what he wrote is so directly relevant to their companion role as literacy leaders that I make frequent references to his article throughout what follows.

For starters, I believe, like Loertscher, that the ability to make a difference is one hallmark of successful leadership. But *how* do we make that essential difference? Well, it begins, again, with individuals.

First published in *Teacher Librarian*, February 2007, Volume 34, Number 3

You—as individual teacher-librarians—must focus on individual students. As some of you know, I do many, many presentations all across the country about young adult literature, and whenever I do, I always stress the same thing to the teacher-librarians in my audiences: When it comes to deciding which of the many books I am discussing are the right books for the right students at the right time, it is you teacher-librarians—not me—who are the experts. Because it is you who know—or should know—your kids as individuals, as living, breathing, wonderfully idiosyncratic human beings with equally individual needs, skills, abilities, and interests.

As teacher-librarians, you know how different individual students are. And you know what a tremendous disservice society has done to young people, especially to teens, to regard them as a homogeneous whole. There is nothing homogenous about them. Indeed, they are a study in heterogeneity, and nobody is more aware of, or anxious about, their individual differences than the young people themselves. That is why I believe that it is imperative for all children and teens to see their faces reflected in the pages of good books—because that opportunity offers the reassuring, sometimes even lifesaving knowledge that they are not alone, that they are not the only one of their kind, and, accordingly, that they are not the total freaks that they thought they were (yes, I was a teen once myself, and I have a vivid emotional memory of those awful days).

The trouble, of course, is that most young people do not have a clue that books can offer such healthy reassurance, such life-affirming comfort. And that is where the teacher-librarian comes in: the teacher-librarian who can lead the young person to the right book.

MODEL READING BEHAVIOR

Of course, you can lead a horse to water but you can't . . . well, you know the rest of it. How do you get the horse—excuse me, the kid—to open a book and discover the amazing experience of reading that waits inside?

Well, I was a public library director for 25 years before I took an early retirement to focus on what I believed was my true reason for being: to inhabit the world of books on a full-time basis—to write them; to edit them; to read them; and to talk, talk, talk about them. During those years as a director, I always believed that I could lead by example. I could model the behavior that I expected of my staff. This strategy worked often enough to reaffirm my faith in it, and now that I am a reading and youth advocate, I always have a book with me because I believe that I can model reading behavior for anyone who happens to see me. And I think that teacher-librarians can—no, *must*—model such reading behavior, too, if they are to be literacy leaders. But it does not always have to be a book that is being read. It can be a magazine, a newspaper, a comic, or if that is too radical, how about a graphic novel that combines captivating words with captivating pictures?

It is not enough, however, just to be seen reading; you must be seen enjoying reading, and you must share what you have read, enthusiastically, even passionately. The act of sharing your reading is tremendously important. In a 2005 survey of teenagers conducted by **www.SmartGirl.org** in association with the Young Adult Library Services Association's annual Teen Read Week, 63% of respondents said that they would read more "if they knew about more good books to read." Who better to tell them than literacy leaders? But—and this is a big *but*—literacy leaders can do that only if they are thoroughly grounded in literature—all kinds of literature but especially in literature that the young people themselves like to read. When the SmartGirl survey asked its respondents, "What kinds of books do you like to read?" the answers were gratifyingly diverse, but the eight categories most often identified were, in descending order, fiction, adventure, teenlit, humor, fantasy, true stories, horror, and romance.

This knowledge can help you focus your own reading. But how do you determine what are the best books in these categories? Well, speaking for myself, I am forever looking for authoritative books about the history of children's and young adult literature to give me necessary context for the countless reviews that I read of new books in all the professional journals (e.g., *Booklist, School Library Journal, VOYA, The Horn Book*, and the rest). But I do not stop there: I also read reviews in the mass media; in newspapers; in magazines; in online publications such as *Slate, Salon*, and Teenreads.com; and many, many more. I am also an inveterate browser among the new titles in bookstores. This gives me a sense of what new books are being noticed and what new titles are being talked about. I also subscribe to YALSA-BK, the Young Adult Library Services Association's electronic discussion list devoted to young adult literature and reading. In my opinion, it is hands-down the best such forum for keeping abreast of trends, developments, new titles, and stimulating discussions of middle school and young adult literature. (You do not have to be an association member to participate. To subscribe, simply go to **http://lists.ala.org/wws/info/yalsa-bk**, select "Subscribe" on the lefthand side of the screen, enter your e-mail address, hit the gray button, and you are in!)

TALK ABOUT BOOKS

Of course, there is more to literacy than knowledge of children's and young adult literature. Julie A. Walker, executive director of the American Association of School Librarians, acknowledged this in a recent e-mail to me in which she said,

> School library media specialists must also understand those skills that students need to read and, most importantly, to read for understanding. The school library media specialist has the special expertise necessary to bridge the technical skills of reading with the experiential side of reading. (personal communication, November 7, 2006)

One way to help students understand what they are reading is to talk with them about it. This seems like a good place to mention that I have always loved to talk, in person and online, about the books that I am reading. But it was not until I started lecturing about books and reading that I discovered that, apparently, I bring a lot of passion to the process. Audience members began thanking me for sharing that passion and then telling me they could not wait to get back to their school libraries to read the books that I had been talking about.

The lesson here is obvious: You need to bring the same kind of passion not only to your conversation about books with other teacher-librarians but also to your conversation with the kids in your personal and professional lives.

Loertscher (2006) quotes Allison Zmuda (2006) as saying, "We must speak the various languages of our clients rather than expecting them to understand our jargonistic eloquence" (p. 10). This means that we need to speak plain English to our students. Does it also mean that we should try to sprinkle our book talk with the latest teenage argot? God forbid! There is nothing more pathetic or wince inducing than someone my age trying to sound hip. It does, however, mean that we need to respect the abilities of kids by bringing a kind of collegiality to our conversation with them. It also suggests, I think, that sometimes we need to shut up and simply let the kids do the talking, let them talk in unstructured ways about their reading, and let them tell us what they are feeling about their reading as well as what they are thinking about it. Reading is a visceral as well as an intellectual experience. In fact, the lion's share of the kids who responded to the Smartgirl.org survey said that they read about things they are passionate about. Though I have been avidly reading for more than 55 years, I know that my own first reaction to reading a new title is still to think, "Oh, I *love* this book" or "Oh, I *hate* this book."

The key is to establish a welcoming, nonthreatening forum for informal, honest, and heartfelt conversation. Shoemaker says,

> I want my students to know they can come to the library and talk to us about books they have read, books they want to read, and books they liked or disliked. I want them to know that their reading can be seen as a conversation between themselves and the author, and that they can continue that conversation with others. (personal communication, November 5, 2006)

To help students continue that conversation, you might consider a structured environment, such as a book discussion group. You might even consider asking your students to help you conduct a sort of Smart-Girl.org survey of your own because—again—all literacy is local. What turns on your kids and their friends might repel teens in other localities, and vice versa. The professional literature is replete with sample surveys so that you do not necessarily have to create a unique one for yourself (who has the time?). A good sample survey is Denice Hildebrandt's Reading Interest Survey (2001), which is available at the Young Adult Library Services Association's Teen Read Week web site or at Smartgirl.org.

OFFER MORE AND THEY WILL READ MORE

Once you know what kinds of reading materials engage your local students, you need to tailor your collections to those specifications. Then you need to be sure that your community knows what is available. Joel Shoemaker says,

> I work hard to make my collection current, attractive, and constantly "out there," promoting it by displays, signs, bulletin boards, announcements, booktalks (in classrooms, in the community, and on various cable broadcasts). I am also heading toward using more online resources—including my library web site—to promote this literate environment. (personal communication, November 5, 2006)

Remember that the more you can offer, the more they will read. The October 20, 2006, issue of *PEN Weekly NewsBlast* (Public Education Newtork) included an article that is instructive in this connection. It was headlined "The Rise and Fall of Reading School Library Books." "New books really do make a difference," it noted in its report of the results of the Indiana School Library Printed Materials Grant (**http://mgrn.evansville.edu/library%20report%202006.pdf**). From 1997 to 2001, when the General Assembly provided matching funding for the purchase of new books, the average circulation among Hoosier students rose from 33.8 per student to 43.1. When the funding was terminated, circulation fell precipitously to 32.7 in 2006.

KNOW YOUR COMMUNITY OF READERS

Of course, the parameters of literacy keep expanding beyond books. Shoemaker writes,

> Besides the traditional literacies involved in reading/writing, we work to provide support and instruction in literacies that are auditory/visual, kinesthetic, multicultural, informational, historical, political, mathematical, scientific . . . you get the idea. Once you get started, there's no stopping! (personal communication, November 5, 2006)

So, yes, to be a literacy leader you need to know your community of readers and their evolving needs, but you also need to know your larger community. The more intimately you know your global community—local, state, national, and even international—the more chances you can find to assume leadership opportunities and make important connections. Networking is still a nonpareil of leadership development. One way to get to know your community is to get out of the library and into the larger world. A literacy leader is involved in the community, not only for the sake of knowing that community, but also for the sake of being known by that community. The same applies for the community that is your school.

Loertscher (2006) writes about what he calls the *organization school library* that trumpets "We are here to help you" but then adds "But you must come into our doors or log onto our networks." The downside, he notes dryly, is that "many potential patrons never show up" (pp. 8–9). This is further substantiated by the SmartGirl.org survey (2005) that shows that the most common response to the question "How often do you visit your school library?" was a disheartening "Never." Also disconcerting was the fact that 14% of respondents said that they did not even know if their school had a librarian or a library media specialist.

The point of all this is that a leader needs to be visible. One way to enhance that visibility is to establish a network of allies, supporters, and partners. One of the most important of those partners should be your local public librarian (do I betray my origins?). Leadership is a responsibility, but it is also an opportunity that is made for sharing and for working cooperatively. "The learning leader," Loertscher (2006) writes, "knows how to collaborate in the best sense [and] can work with teachers of almost any educational stripe" (p. 11)—and, I would add, with other librarians.

Speaking as a former public librarian and consultant, I found it difficult to establish any kind of meaningful cooperation with local schools, which often seemed to be more interested in building barriers than bridges. To ensure that this is not the case in your community, do not wait for others to approach you. Take the first step to cooperation yourself.

It may sound corny to say, "Reach out and touch someone," but I think that literacy leadership begins that way. And it must be rooted in passion, the passion called love, the love for reading, and, yes, the love for the young people whom you hope to inspire to share the bliss of reading. Could there be a more powerful incentive to become a literacy leader than to guide kids to books that they will love to read?

Well, perhaps there is one: In today's world of No Test—oops—No Child Left Behind, it is worth noting that wide reading improves test scores, but don't take my word for it. The respected reading authority Stephen Krashen has already made a passionate case for that. As David Loertscher (2005) notes in a recent review of the second edition of Krashen's *The Power of Reading: Insights From the Research* (2004), "To Krashen, the more a child or teen reads, the higher he scores on achievement tests, and students who have plentiful resources read more, which in turn affects their scores" (p. 47).

This brings us back to the following point: To ensure success as a learning and literacy leader, it is important to be able to speak other "languages." Loertscher (2006) cogently points out that "the learning leader speaks the language of curriculum and its various dialects of reading, social studies, science, or whatever curricular program is popular in the school" (p. 11). So does the literacy leader, who must also be fluent in what I call *administratese*, being able to speak—to power—the truth of the fundamental importance of the school library to both literacy and learning.

At heart, though, literacy leadership must be rooted in an absolutely fundamental belief in the beneficial power of reading. I often tell about the time, some years ago, when I interviewed the British literary critic Brian Alderson in 1980 and asked him why he thought books were so important. His answer is still resonant today. "Well," he said thoughtfully, "I suppose books are only important if reading is important. And I suppose reading is only important if civilization is important."

Loertscher (2006) argues persuasively in his recent *Teacher Librarian* article, "There does not seem to be agreement among teacher-librarians about their role in education" (p. 8). True, but I argue, in conclusion, that there must be agreement about at least one thing: the imperative need for every teacher-librarian to become a literacy leader. For, after all, civilization depends on it.

REFERENCES

Hildebrandt, D. (2001). *Reading interest survey*. Retrieved November 7, 2006, from **www.ala.org/ala/yalsa/teenreading/tipsenc/reading_interest_survey.pdf**

Krashen, S. D. (2004). *The power of reading: Insights from the research* (2nd ed.). Portsmouth, NH: Heinemann.

Loertscher, D. (2005). Enhancing teaching and learning. *Teacher Librarian, 32*(4), 47.

Loertscher, D. (2006). What flavor is your school library: The teacher-librarian as learning leader. *Teacher Librarian, 34*(2), 8–12.

Public Education Network. (2006, October 20). The rise and fall of reading school library books. *The PEN Weekly NewsBlast*. Retrieved November 7, 2006, from **www.publiceducation.org/news blast/October06/October20.htm**

SmartGirl. (2005). *Report on teen read week 2005*. Retrieved November 7, 2006, from **www.smart girl.org/reports/5100284.html**

Zmuda, A. (2006). Designing curriculum for the 21st century classroom. In D. V. Loertscher (Ed.), *Understanding in the library: Papers of the Treasure Mountain Research Retreat No. 12, October 5–6, 2005, Gilmary Retreat Center, Pittsburgh, PA* (pp. 37–48). Salt Lake City, UT: Hi Willow Research and Publishing.

Literacy Links: Harry Potter and the Goblet of Motivation

Keith McPherson

Late one evening last year, I was walking past my 7-year-old daughter's bedroom when I noticed that she had left a flashlight on under her bed. Getting down on my hands and knees, I saw that the light was not coming from a flashlight. Light was filtering down from the covers above. Standing up, I said, "Sweetheart, please turn off the flashlight, put the book away, and go to sleep. It is 11 o'clock, and tomorrow your teacher would appreciate you being awake in class."

From under the covers came a muffled and surprised, "How did you know?" I explained that I, too, had spent my fair share of late nights conducting my own underground reading. She then pulled back her covers and revealed her partner in crime, *Harry Potter and the Chamber of Secrets* (Rowling, 1998).

Reflecting on this incident, I realized that I was not surprised at my daughter's late-night reading habit (she is, after all, a night owl like her father). I was surprised, though, at the tenacity with which she was reading the Harry Potter series, especially when considering that the books registered an average readability of at least three grade levels above her own. Moreover, I wondered how we as teacher-librarians could foster such reading motivation in our own students. This column surveys some of the key research on reading motivation and suggests instructional approaches aimed at fostering strong reading motivation in students.

RESEARCH ON READING MOTIVATION

Current research into reading motivation finds strong relationships between engaged reading and achievement. For example, children who read frequently and actively exhibit higher comprehension rates (Cipielewski & Stanovich, 1992; Wang & Guthrie, 2004) and attain higher achievement scores than children who do not read as such (Perie, Moran, & Lutkus, 2005). Similarly, children who read more make more rapid gains in their reading abilities than do children who read less (Stanovich, 1986). Furthermore, as reading competencies increase, so does the motivation to read, creating an upward spiral of achievement

First published in *Teacher Librarian*, April 2007, Volume 34, Number 4

(Guthrie, Wigfield, Metsala, & Cox, 1999).

Current research also suggests that motivated readers hold positive beliefs about themselves as learners (Guthrie & Wigfield, 1997; Valentine, DuBois, & Cooper, 2004). Schunk and Zimmerman (1997) found that children who doubt their ability to learn (in this case, learning to read) give up quickly when faced with challenges. Such students often assume that they are responsible for their learning inabilities, instead of recognizing that it may be due to a faulty or unknown learning strategy or approach. In a research review of reading motivation, Cunningham and Cunningham (2002) suggest that students must view reading as a pleasurable activity because "children who dislike something may avoid it or give only partial attention to learning it, although they have the self-confidence to learn lessons and attempt assigned tasks" (p. 90).

FOSTERING READING MOTIVATION

The most probable obstacle facing many unmotivated readers is a lack of self-confidence. Whether told by others that they are not as good a reader as their older siblings or whether they have developed the attitude from peers that reading is not cool, many young readers have come to believe that they are poor readers or cannot read altogether. Although reading specialists suggest a variety of approaches aimed at reversing these attitudes (Guthrie & Wigfield, 2000), one of the most powerful is to tell students again and again, individually and as a group, that they are capable of reading and that they will learn to read.

Wlodkowski (1985) suggests that such praise must be sincere, specific, and based on the teacher's or teacher-librarian's genuine conviction in his or her students' learning abilities and potentials. Otherwise, students will ignore the praise and interpret it as being manipulative. However, genuine praise may be one of only a few voices (the teacher-librarian's and the classroom teacher's) combating years of negative reinforcement underlying students' poor reading self-confidence. It may also be one the most important seeds from which future positive reading attitudes may germinate.

Another effective method for increasing a learner's self-confidence toward reading is to ensure that students know that most reading struggles are not due to a deficiency in personal ability but rather a lack of knowing the appropriate reading skills, strategies, and approaches and knowing when to use them. Research by Schunk and Zimmerman (1997) and Powell, McIntyre, and Rightmyer (2006) suggests that the intentional teaching of reading strategies and skills (e.g., reading recovery, guided reading) increases students' abilities on task behavior and self-efficacy. Thus, teacher-librarians and teachers can foster students' reading motivation by identifying reading strategies that each student lacks, overtly modeling and teaching these strategies, and giving students time to practice them.

Teacher-librarians can also help increase students' reading motivation by making concerted efforts to provide students with access to interesting texts. In this case, *interesting texts* means a variety of reading materials that captivate students' attention and that are written at students' independent reading levels. Thus, noncanonical reading materials such as *Archie Comics*, graphic novels, Nancy Drew stories, computer game instructions, 'zines, Internet blogs and wikis, and Manga should be offered to students through the school library, along with more traditional materials such as literature circle novels, magazines, chapter books, novels, print encyclopedias, textbooks, and print dictionaries. Furthermore, teacher-librarians should make every effort to identify students' reading levels and match them with books at the same levels. Research of reading motivation supports the matching of readers with interesting books because such efforts encourage students to read more (Guthrie, 2001; McLoyd, 1979) and because students learn more content (Schiefele, 1996).

Because there is great variance in students' experiences and sociocultural backgrounds, the resources that students find interesting are diverse. Thus, the school community and teacher-librarian must develop a school library collection with great breadth and depth. Considering the current budget restraints facing most schools, it is not surprising that this type of resource development lacks adequate administrative support and is rarely afforded adequate funding (Allington & Guice, 1997; American Library Association, 2006). Therefore, when advocating for increased funding as a method for promoting motivated readers, teacher-librarians are well advised to draw on research by Elley (1992) and Lance (2006) that found that large, well-stocked school libraries (guided, of course, by a full-time teacher-librarian) correlates with a general increase across the school in students' reading achievement and overall academic achievement.

Reading-related research finds that reading motivation increases when students are actively engaged with real-world reading materials in real-world interactions (Brophy, 1998; Csikszentmihalyi, 1991; Yair, 2000). Furthermore, Anderson (1998, cited in Guthrie & Wigfield, 2000) found that students who are actively engaged with real-world learning activities are motivated to read with intensity and thus comprehend more of the content. Teacher-librarians can encourage this type of deep motivated reading by developing hands-on learning activities in the school library that reinforce and parallel concepts being read in print. For example, for a research project on insects, teacher-librarians can have students bring into the library their favorite insects (in a sealed jar, of course). The students can then observe and record their insects' physical characteristics and habits before and while researching and reading about these creatures.

Students' choice of reading materials is another factor that affects their reading motivation. Grolnick and Ryan (1987) found that when teachers give students choices in their reading materials, students' reading motivation and comprehension increase. Furthermore, Skinner and Belmont (1993) found that the more that teachers taught students to be responsible for their own learning and allowed them more choice and control over the design of learning activities, the more that students gained self-confidence and the more that they were intrinsically motivated to take control of their learning.

Teacher-librarians know full well the power of allowing children to select their own pleasure reading materials. Nonetheless, the research into children's choice of reading materials suggests that when the teacher or teacher-librarian encourages students to choose their reading material and have input and control into their learning activities, students are often intrinsically motivated to deeply engage with the text. Unfortunately, current research (Yair, 2000) indicates that most students are rarely given choices in designing their learning experiences; thus, "the structures of instruction that disaffect students are overwhelmingly represented in students' daily school life; those that spark their hearts are not frequent enough to motivate students" (p. 191).

However, not all students are familiar and comfortable with intrinsically motivated reading and learning environments. Many students have little experience with learning contexts that de-emphasize extrinsic rewards but emphasize social responsibility, setting personal and group goals, taking ownership for actions, and developing individually and group motivated critical thinking and reasoning skills. Thus, teacher-librarians must be sure to identify such students and provide strategies for helping them become self-directed learners and readers (Lehtinen, Vaurus, Salonen, Olkinuora, & Kinnunen, 1995).

Another instructional approach geared toward fostering reading motivation is to recognize the importance of social support structures. Wentzel (1996, 1997) and Oldfather and Dahl (1994) found that when students sensed that they were accepted by their peers as part of the learning community and when the teacher actively developed prosocial behaviors between students (e.g., students help each other, encourage risk taking in the community, and take responsibility for each other's learning), students were more likely to be motivated toward reading. Accordingly, teacher-librarians can foster reading motivation by allowing students to explore, discuss, and develop a set of prosocial behaviors and learning strategies at the beginning of the year, which the teacher-librarian and students can reinforce during their activities in the library and the classroom.

CONCLUSION

This very brief discussion of key research regarding reading motivation and instructional strategies over-simplifies the growing body of research and underrepresents the instructional complexities integral to the process of motivating readers. Ideally, though, it has sparked your interest toward further exploring the positive effects of reading motivation. Additional information on this subject can be found at **www.literacy trust.org.uk/Research/readmotivabstracts.html**; see also, the work by Guthrie and Wigfield (2000), Robb (2000), and Guthrie and Knowles (2001).

Teacher-librarians are entrusted to unique positions in schools. They have the opportunity to motivate many different readers through a variety of classes and across multiple grades. Furthermore, they can take a leadership role in the school by modeling to other educators instructional approaches that promote student reading motivation, to which these educators can take these approaches back to their own classrooms.

The impact that we have as teacher-librarians on students' reading motivation cannot be underestimated. This very point was driven home two nights ago when my now-8-year-old daughter commented excitedly, "Dad! Dad! Guess what! GUESS WHAT! I can read *Harry Potter* all over again. My teacher-librarian gave me *Harry Potter and the Philosopher's Stone* in French!" (Rowling, 2000).

REFERENCES

Allington, R. L., & Guice, S. (1997). Literature curriculum: Issues of definition and control. In J. Flood, D. Lapp, & S. B. Heath (Eds.), *Handbook of research on teaching literacy through the communicative and visual arts* (pp. 727–734). New York: Macmillan.

American Library Association (2006). *School library funding: Funding problems for school library media centers nationwide causing cutbacks in library media specialists, resources, and hours.* Retrieved December 14, 2006, from the American Library Association's web server: **www.ala.org/ala/news/ libraryfunding/schoollibraryfunding.htm**

Anderson, E. (1998). *Motivational and cognitive influences on conceptual knowledge acquisition: The combination of science observation and interesting texts.* Unpublished doctoral dissertation, University of Maryland, College Park.

Brophy, J. (1998). *Motivating students to learn.* Boston: McGraw-Hill.

Cipielewski, J., & Stanovich, K. E. (1992). Predicting growth in reading ability from children's exposure to print. *Journal of Experimental Child Psychology, 54,* 74–89.

Csikszentmihalyi, M. (1991). Literacy and intrinsic motivation. In S. Graubard (Ed.), *Literacy: An overview by fourteen experts* (pp. 115–40). New York: Noonday Press.

Cunningham, P. M., & Cunningham, J. W. (2002). What we know about how to teach phonics. In S. E. Farstrup & S. J. Samuels (Eds.), *What research has to say about reading instruction* (pp. 87–109). Newark, DE: International Reading Association.

Elley, W. B. (1992). *How in the world do students read?* Hamburg, Germany: International Reading Association.

Grolnick, W. S., & Ryan, R. M. (1987). Autonomy in children's learning: An experimental and individual difference investigation. *Journal of Personality and Social Psychology, 52,* 890–898.

Guthrie, J. T. (2001, March). Contexts for engagement and motivation in reading. *Reading Online, 4*(8).

Retrieved December 12, 2006, from **www.readingonline.org/articles/art_index.asp?HREF=/ articles/handbook/guthrie/index.html**

Guthrie, J. T., & Knowles, K. T. (2001). Promoting reading motivation. In L. Verhoeven & C. E. Snow (Eds.), *Literacy and motivation: Reading engagement in individuals and groups* (pp. 159–176). Mahwah, NJ: Erlbaum.

Guthrie, J. T., & Wigfield, A. (1997). Reading engagement: A rationale for theory and teaching. In J. T. Guthrie & A. Wigfield (Eds.), *Reading engagement: Motivating readers through integrated instruction* (pp. 1–14). Newark, DE: International Reading Association.

Guthrie, J. T., & Wigfield, A. (2000). Engagement and motivation in reading. In M. L. Kamil, P. B. Mosenthal, P. D. Pearson, & R. Barr (Eds.), *Handbook of reading research* (Vol. 3, pp. 403–422). New York: Erlbaum.

Guthrie, J. T., Wigfield, A., Metsala, J. L., & Cox, K. E. (1999). Motivational and cognitive predictors of text comprehension and reading amount. *Scientific Studies of Reading, 3*, 231–257.

Lance, K. C. (2006). *School library impact studies.* Retrieved December 14, 2006, from the Library Research Services web server: **www.lrs.org/impact.asp**

Lehtinen, E., Vauras, M., Salonen, P., Olkinuora, E., & Kinnunen, R. (1995). Long-term development of learning activity: Motivational, cognitive and social interaction. *Educational Psychologist, 30*(1), 21–35.

McLoyd, V. (1979). The effects on extrinsic rewards of differential value on high and low intrinsic interest. *Child Development, 50*, 1010–1019.

Oldfather, P., & Dahl, K. (1994). Toward a social constructivist reconceptualization of intrinsic motivation for literacy learning. *Journal of Reading Behavior, 26*, 139–153.

Perie, M., Moran, R., & Lutkus, A. D. (2005). *NAEP 2004 trends in academic progress: Three decades of student performance in reading and mathematics* (NCES Publication No. 2005-464). Washington, DC: Government Printing Office.

Powell, R., McIntyre, E., & Rightmyer, E. (2006). Johnny won't read, and Susie won't either: Reading instruction and student resistance. *Journal of Early Childhood Literacy, 6*, 5–31.

Robb, L. (2000). *Teaching reading in middle school: A strategic approach to teaching reading that improves comprehension and thinking.* New York: Scholastic.

Rowling, J. K. (1998). *Harry Potter and the chamber of secrets.* London: Bloomsbury.

Rowling, J. K. (2000). *Harry Potter à l'école des sorciers* [Harry Potter and the philosopher's stone]. Paris: Gallimard Jeunesse.

Schiefele, U. (1996). Topic interest, text representation, and quality of experience. *Contemporary Educational Psychology, 21*, 3–18.

Schunk, D. H., & Zimmerman, B. J. (1997). Social origins of self-regulatory competence. *Educational Psychologist, 32*, 195–208.

Skinner, E. A., & Belmont, M. J. (1993). Motivation in the classroom: Reciprocal effects of teacher behavior and student engagement across the school year. *Journal of Educational Psychology, 85*, 571–581.

Stanovich, K. E. (1986). Matthew effects in reading: Some consequences of individual differences in the acquisition of literacy. *Reading Research Quarterly, 21*, 360–407.

Valentine, J. C., DuBois, D. L., & Cooper, H. (2004). The relation between self-beliefs and academic achievement: A meta-analytic review. *Educational Psychologist, 39*, 111–134.

Wang, J. H. Y., & Guthrie, J. T. (2004). Modeling the effects of intrinsic motivation, extrinsic motivation, amount of reading and past reading achievement on text comprehension between U.S. and Chinese students. *Reading Research Quarterly, 39,* 162–186.

Wentzel, K. R. (1996). Social and academic motivation in middle school: Concurrent and long-term relations to academic effort. *Journal of Early Adolescence, 16,* 390–406.

Wentzel, K, R. (1997). Student motivation in middle school: The role of perceived pedagogical caring. *Journal of Educational Psychology, 89,* 411–419.

Wlodkowski, R. (1985). *Enhancing adult motivation to learn.* San Francisco: Jossey-Bass.

Yair, G. (2000). Reforming motivation: How the structure of instruction affects students' learning experiences. *British Educational Research Journal, 26,* 191–210.

NOTE

Reading motivation research and associated strategies discussed in this month's column do not include studies involving students with severe learning disabilities. Furthermore, the term *reading* is defined as that including decoding and comprehending the traditional alphanumeric print-on-page text, with acknowledgment to other supporting texts, such as photos, pictures, video, and so on.

45

Mrs. Travis's Traveling Library: A Teacher-Librarian's Attempt to Gather Data About Reading Aloud to Students

Leslie Travis

Reading out loud to students improves their test scores.
Teacher-librarians do not do enough to document the effect that their programs
have on the academic achievement of the students.

Hearing these two statements on the same day at teacher-librarian workshops in Chicago persuaded me to set up what I hope will be a 6-year longitudinal study to document the effect of reading out loud to students in the primary grades.

The program itself is quite simple. I give kindergarten students a bag of seven different children's books to take home each Monday of the school year. In the bag is a request that an adult in the student's house read one book each day to the student. Students get a different set of books each week of the school year.

I will continue this program for at least 3 years, giving these same students seven books a week while they are in kindergarten, first grade, and second grade. During these years, I will collect data from parent and teacher surveys and students' test scores. I will analyze the data to determine if there are statistically valid qualitative or quantitative differences between this group of students and a control group. For the purposes of this study, I am using this year's first graders—who did not receive the books—as my control group. I will conduct the study at several different schools so that the data I collect will give statistically valid results.

First published in *Teacher Librarian*, June 2006, Volume 33, Number 5

Why am I doing this study? First, because I think that getting the books and hearing them read aloud will be good for my students. I predict that there will be long-term, measurable improvements in their academic achievement as a result of hearing more than 600 books—both fiction and nonfiction—read aloud to them at home during their first 3 years of school. My principal suggested that I begin with kindergarten students with the hope that the program will jump-start their first-grade experience as they enter first grade with larger vocabularies, better listening skills, and established patterns of reading and discussing books with family members.

Second, I think that it will be good for teacher-librarians. We need to publicize and document the positive effect that reading has on our students. Teacher-librarians work with all students in a school and are uniquely situated to do schoolwide longitudinal studies with students and their families.

Third, I am the only adult in a library that serves over 700 students, and I have observed that the number of books that I can allow students to circulate is limited not by their desire to obtain books but by my ability to reshelve them. This program is a way for me to keep hundreds books in active circulation without having to reshelve or recard items. Fourth, it allows me to use donations of books quickly because I do not need to wait until I have had time to get each book shelf-ready.

What materials did I need to begin this project? Bags, books, labels, a storage box, a record book, a file drawer, and access to a copy machine. The bags that I am using this year are heavy-weight clear plastic and have handles that snap shut. I ordered them from a library supplier's catalog. I have written a number in permanent marker on the inside and outside of the handle of each bag so that I can keep track of which bag a student has been given. I made at least 12 extra sets of books for each classroom, so a class of 28 students has about 40 bags of books. In that way, fewer than 300 books are enough to enable an entire class of students to read a different book each day for an entire school year. Each book is labeled with a computer-generated label affixed to the upper right-hand corner of the cover, which says, "This book is from Mrs. Travis's Traveling Library."

Each classroom that is participating in the program needs a box to hold the extra sets of books. The only time that the entire set of books needs to be stored in a classroom is the day before the books are passed out to students and the day after they are collected for the final time, at the end of the year. I use a grade book to record the number of the bag that a student receives, ensuring that students get different bags of books each week.

Each bag contains a letter to parents that explains the program. At the beginning, middle, and end of each school year, a one-page survey is sent home for parents of kindergarten and first-grade students to complete. Kindergarten, first-grade, and second-grade teachers are asked to fill out a survey at the beginning, middle, and end of each school year. Next year, I will survey parents of kindergarten, first-grade, and second-grade students. This year, I am working with three different schools, and I have color-coded each survey so that every piece of paper from a particular school is the same color. I will simplify the record keeping, enabling me to analyze the data more efficiently years from now. I keep every document that I collect in the same file drawer.

Where do these materials come from? The bags for the project were paid for by a small grant from the Chicago Foundation for Education, which funds collaborative projects that cost under $400. For this grant, I am collaborating with the three kindergarten teachers at my school. The books for the project come from an annual Book Trade that I host at my school in the spring. For the month leading up to the Book Trade, I "buy" used children's books from the students, using Book Bucks. For every three books that a student brings in, he or she receives two Book Bucks. On the day of the Book Trade, all the books that students have brought in are "for sale." Each book at the Book Trade costs one Book Buck. I set up this system to allow students choice as they trade; students bring in books that they have outgrown, and they choose books that they are now ready to read. Many books that are left from the Book Trade are the right interest level and length for the Traveling Library program. Additional books have come from donations of used books to the school and thrift stores, which sometimes sell books at 10 cents apiece.

How much time is this program taking this year? To begin the program, I first consulted my principal. Then, I had to contact the kindergarten teachers at my school and then find principals with kindergarten teachers or teacher-librarians at other schools who were willing to work with me. All three kindergarten teachers at my school were enthusiastic about the idea. Finding people at other schools was labor intensive, but I did find a teacher-librarian at one school and a kindergarten teacher at another school who were willing to try the program. The principals at both of those schools were supportive of the idea.

Over the summer, I weeded through the books that I had amassed as a result of the Book Trade. I decided that I needed to make enough sets of books for seven kindergarten classrooms—three at my school and two at each of the other schools. This meant that I needed 280 sets of books. After the bags that I ordered arrived, I numbered them. It took an entire day to arrange my books into 280 sets of seven, label them, and put them into the bags. I tried to make sure that each bag contained nonfiction, but I was definitely working with a random assortment of literature. I divided the bags into seven classroom sets. I wrote parent surveys, instructions to the people who would be running the program, an insert letter for the bags, and letters to parents introducing the program (see Appendixes A, B, C, and D for copies of these documents). Another day was required to deliver the boxes of books, surveys, and instructions to the two other schools.

In the first week of the school year, I asked the three kindergarten teachers at my school if they would like to handle the book-bag exchange and record keeping each week or if they would like me to do it. One of the teachers said that she would do it on her own. The other two teachers asked me to handle the exchange of bags and the record keeping. It takes me about 40 minutes every Monday morning to do the exchanges in the two kindergarten rooms. In one of the rooms, I take care of the exchange while the students are at lunch. In that room, the teacher collects all of the Traveling Library bags in a box, and I change the name tags on the bags without seeing the students. In the other room, I exchange bags with the students directly with the assistance of an older student.

What has been the teachers' reaction to the program? In general, the teachers seem to like the program. They have been very willing to include the oral reading into their weekly homework assignments. The teacher whose room I go into has been supportive in giving me and her students time to talk about what they have read; she does not view it as an interruption of her work time. The teacher who handles the book transfer personally is using the book bags to hold the students' weekly homework—and she is the teacher with the highest weekly return rate for Traveling Library bags. The third teacher is always quite willing to send students to the library if they have forgotten to put their book bags into the box of bags to be exchanged.

The teachers have all reported positive parent feedback about the program. They have also reported that the program is a relief for their classroom libraries. Because students have access to books that they borrow from the school library as well as the seven books a week from the Traveling Library program, they do not need to take classroom library books home. The teachers have also been willing to distribute and collect the parent surveys, and they report that they hear from both students and parents that many of the books are being read to students at home.

What has been the students' reaction to the program? Students have told me that they like to get their books in the bag. The Traveling Library program gives students a daily opportunity to talk about books with adults as they read one each day. It gives students another opportunity to talk to me about a particular book that they enjoyed and a chance to recommend a book to another student. They enjoy all of these activities. Students and their parents even come to the library to get a new bag of books for the week if they were absent on the day the exchange took place.

What results have I already seen from this program? I have developed close relationships with students, parents, and teachers. I have increased contact with the kindergarten students, especially in the classroom where I do the exchange directly. Obviously, I see those students twice a week instead of only once a week, but the direct exchange gives me an opportunity to speak personally with each student about a book that she or he has just enjoyed hearing. As a student returns a bag, I ask that student if there is a particular book that he or she wants to recommend to the next student who will receive the bag, and I listen to that student share his or her thoughts with me and the other student.

I have additional contact with the kindergarten teachers because the program requires that I be in their rooms with them at least once a week. That time is an informal opportunity for us to share observations about books, individual students, curriculum plans, and suggestions on how to improve this program.

I also use the book distribution time to work with a student who has reading difficulties and attends a self-contained special education class; this student assists me with the distribution of books in the class where I exchange the books directly with students. She helps me by lining the students up, counting to be sure there are seven books in the bag (although I also have to count), and makes certain that students remember to put their bags in their backpacks. I have observed that she is fascinated with the books. She often tells a particular student that a book is good, and she often asks to borrow a particular book for herself.

What has parent reaction been to the program? I now have more contact than ever with parents. I have contact with parents through the classroom homework assignments because the library reading program is now a part of the regular homework routine. Thus, the parents see the teacher-librarian collaborating with the homeroom teacher. Several parents who have older children in the school and realize that this program is new have thanked me for starting it and have encouraged me to continue it next year for their children. Parents say that even if they have lots of books at home, their children enjoy getting different things to read—and so do they. Parents often come to the library to get a new bag of books if their child is absent on the exchange day; they say that reading the books is a favorite routine.

Parents have discussed the program at Parent–Teacher Association meetings and local school council meetings and have voiced their approval of it. The program has given me more opportunities to speak directly to parents about their children. For example, with the parent of one child who can read but who forgets his book bags, I discussed how to set up a regular place at home to keep the books so that they would not get lost. Several other parents have asked me to put specific books into their children's bags for the week, and several families have offered to donate books to the program.

What observations do I have about how the program is working at my school? At my school, all three kindergarten classes are getting their books, and the speech therapist for the hearing-challenged preK class has asked if these students can join the program. It is interesting for me to note that there seems to be a higher rate of return for the books in a bag than for the individual books that the kindergarten students circulate from the library. I guess the reason is that the teachers, the parents, and I are all involved in helping the students remember the book bags, especially in the room where the bags also function as homework folders. Students tell me that their parents do read the books in the bag aloud to them but that they do not read the library books to them as often. Students have told me that they like the books, and parents have reported that students think that I chose the books that they get specifically for them, even though they see me take a bag from another child and hand it directly to them.

When I started this program, I thought that hardcover books are desirable because they are prettier and bigger. I now realize that paperbacks are actually better because seven hardcover picture books are too heavy for a kindergarten student to easily carry in a backpack. I do not give a student a new bag until that student returns the one that he or she has, but I find that most students return their bags regularly. To accommodate those students who lose a bag, I do give them another bag after a couple of weeks. In many cases, that second bag has been a reminder, and the student has returned both bags the next week.

During the winter vacation break, I switch the sets of books between homerooms to ensure that students receive different books every week. The school weeks that do not have a Monday are harder for me to handle because of scheduling conflicts; the book exchange on those weeks has to occur during my lunch break. I have learned that I must count the number of books in each bag before I circulate it again—both to be certain that there are still seven books in it and to be sure that a regular library book has not made its way into the Traveling Library bag.

I also need to have the individual child's name inside the bag of books that she or he has for the week, so that if it gets misplaced in the classroom, the other students and teachers have a way of knowing to whom it belongs on a particular week. For that reason, the next time I order a new set of bags, I would like to order bags that have card pockets inside. This year, I have started putting a Post-it note with the child's name written on it inside the bag.

How is the program working at the other schools? Both of the other schools experienced complete reorganizations of their kindergarten programs after the school year started. At one of the schools, only half of the kindergarten students are receiving books from the Traveling Library program. The teacher-librarian at that school says that the students who do get the Traveling Library books enjoy them.

I will continue to distribute books for the Traveling Library project next year, attempting to get books to kindergarten and first-grade students at my school and the other participating schools. I plan to supply these students and their families with books to read aloud through the end of second grade. In the fall, I will be able to do the first data-driven comparison of students, when I can look at the reading habits of families of beginning first graders whose parents read to them regularly as kindergarteners and compare them to the reading habits of families the year before, who did not participate in the program. If you are interested in trying the program at your school and are willing to collect data to add to the study, please contact me at *ljtravis@sbcglobal.net*. Even if you decide not to collect the data, I think you will find that the Traveling Library program is rewarding.

APPENDIX A: INSERT LETTER FOR THE BAGS

Please keep this note in the bag of books. Thank you.

This bag contains books for you to read to your child at home. Please do not expect your child to be able to read them by himself. Every Monday, your child will be given a new bag of books to keep until the following Monday. The purpose of this activity is to expose your child to a variety of children's literature as well as build your child's reading comprehension and vocabulary. As you read to your child, be sure to engage her by asking questions, such as, "Why do you thing the character did that?" or "What do you think will happen next?" In addition, have your child ask you questions about the story and let him read sight words that he already knows. It may be helpful to set up a specific time when you read together daily, such as after dinner or before bedtime.

Make a special place in your home for the books. In the event that a book should be misplaced, please replace it with a picture book of your own so that the bag is returned to school with the same number of books it had when your child brought the bag home. This way, we can be sure we will have enough quality books to share with all kindergarten families. Thank you, and *ENJOY!*

APPENDIX B: LETTER TO PARENTS INTRODUCING THE PROGRAM

Date _____

Dear Parents,

Reading out loud is one of the most important things that you, as a parent, can do for your kindergarten student. Many things happen when you read to your child. Your child begins to learn about books, develops a larger vocabulary, increases his general knowledge, has an opportunity to talk about what is being read, and his comprehension improves. Your child sees you reading with him and realizes that you think reading is important—so important that you sill spend time reading with him. In addition to our school's regular library program, we will be participating in a new program that will make it possible for you to read a different book to your child each day. The program is called Mrs. Travis's Traveling Library.

Each Monday, your child will receive a bag of seven books. Please read a different book a day to your child, and return the bag of books the following Monday. If your child would like to substitute a book of his choice for one of the books in the bag, feel free to do so. The purpose of the program is to guarantee that each kindergarten student hears a different book read each day. If a book gets lost, please replace it with one from your home library so that the bag contains seven books when it is returned. During the course of the year, you will be asked to fill out three short surveys. The first survey is attached to this letter. Please fill it out and return it to your child's teacher.

If you have questions, contact Mrs. Travis at ljtravis@sbcglobal.net, or talk to your child's homeroom teacher.

Sincerely,
Leslie Travis
Ray School

APPENDIX C: PARENT READING SURVEY

Date _____

Student's Name_____ Grade_____
Room Number_____

Please circle your answer:

What kinds of materials are regularly read at home? Circle all items that apply.
Magazines   Books   Newspapers   Online materials

How much time do adults in your home spend reading each week?
None   1–2 hours
3–4 hours   More

How much time do adults in your home spend watching television and playing video games each week?
None   1–2 hours
3–4 hours   More

Do adults in your home read aloud to your child? Yes   No

What kinds of materials are regularly read to your child?
None   Magazines   Books   Newspapers   Online materials

How many books do adults read to your child each week?
None   1–2   3–4   6–10   More

How much time is spent reading to your child each day?
None   15–30 minutes   30–60 minutes   More

How much time does your child spend watching television and playing video games each day?
None   15–30 minutes   30–60 minutes   More

Is there a regular time of day when someone reads to your child? Yes   No
Can your child read?   Yes   No

Does your child look at books when no one is reading aloud to him or her? Yes   No

Does anyone in your home have a public library card?   Yes   No

APPENDIX D: INSTRUCTIONS TO THE PEOPLE RUNNING THE PROGRAM
Dear Coordinator:

Thank you for volunteering to coordinate the distribution of books and surveys for the Traveling Library project. I would like you to do these jobs:
Week 1:
• Distribute parent letters and surveys to all kindergarten students for their parents to fill out.
• Distribute only the surveys to first-grade students for their parents to fill out.
• When they have been completed, please return them to:
Leslie Travis, Library, Ray School, Mail Run 41
• Decide who at your school will be responsible for rotating the sets of books among the kindergarten students and where the book distribution will take place.
• If you wish to apply for a Small Grant Award that covers the cost of bags and a cart for storage, I have included a sample.
Weeks 2–39:
• Collect the returned bags of books, and give each kindergarten student a different one.
Week 39:
• Collect the bags of books for the last time.
• Distribute the end-of-year survey to kindergarten and first-grade students for their families to fill out.
• Return the surveys to Leslie Travis.
If you have any questions, e-mail me at ljtravis@sbcglobal.net.

Thank you very much,
Leslie Travis

(46)

Challenging the Gender Divide: Improving Literacy for All

Les Parsons

Teacher-librarians are rushing to the front lines to help battle the latest crisis in education. A gender gap exists in reading proficiency: Boys do not read as well as girls. Even worse, that gap has been growing over the past decade.

The challenge of enticing boys into reading has led teacher-librarians into a variety of inventive and proactive experiments. They have started "boys only" reading clubs, for example, and when necessary have enlisted male staff members to help run the clubs and serve as role models. They have purchased materials specifically for their appeal to boys and organized "gender specific" book displays in their libraries. As some schools move toward reorganizing reading classes on the basis of gender, some teacher-librarians have even considered the unthinkable: Should the library collection be reorganized in the same manner?

Before we move any further into pedagogy based on segregation and exclusion, however, we need to examine more closely the source and nature of this current "crisis" in reading and only then decide how best to serve our students' needs. History offers some clues.

THE MORE THINGS CHANGE . . .

Thirty-odd years ago, teachers did not talk about a "fourth-grade slump" in reading or an "eighth-grade cliff." We talked instead about students' self-esteem "falling off the tabletop" after grade 3, and we worried about the number of boys dropping out after grade 8 or 9. We knew then that a gap between the most and least proficient readers existed from the time students entered the school system; we also knew that gap widened as students moved through the grades.

The solution to the reading gap problem seemed obvious. Schools began to reorganize their reading classes across grade lines on the basis of ability. Known as the Joplin Plan (Molnar, 2002), this approach offered teachers a group of students at the same reading ability level. At a prearranged time, all students

First published in *Teacher Librarian*, December 2004, Volume 32, Number 2

within a three-grade limit went to a class with students of their own reading ability regardless of age. No one, of course, was too surprised to see how gender marked these classes. Older boys reluctantly moved to younger classes and younger girls nervously entered older classes. A partial de facto gender divide was inevitably created.

The Joplin Plan faded in popularity partly because of the self-esteem and social problems that accrued, but more directly because it failed to address the source of the difficulties students were having with reading (Molnar, 2002; Smith, 1986). The real crisis in reading today, in fact, is the same crisis that plagued schools more than three decades ago. The issue is not how you organize your readers but rather what you do *with* your readers, regardless of how you organize them.

LOOKING FOR THE CAUSE

If a stream stops flowing, where do you look for a solution to the problem? Before inventing a variety of rainmaking machines, you are likely to first check upstream to see if anything is blocking the water. Something is certainly blocking the reading flow, and boys are not the only ones affected.

Reading is a complex and multifaceted activity. Students grow into reading in individual and idiosyncratic ways. If gender is such a pivotal issue, why do we see so many exceptions in the way students approach reading? We should be as curious about the boys who read well, for instance, as we are about boys who do not: Did they stumble at an early age into books on hockey and auto mechanics? We should be as curious about girls who do not read well as we are about the girls who do: Were they immune to the universal attraction of Nancy Drew and Sweet Valley High? Clearly, essential factors other than this simplistic and stereotypical reaction to the problem of boys and reading need to be addressed (Allington & Cunningham, 1997; Flurkey, 2003; Graves, 1990).

When gender is a factor, we need to explore why it is and make certain the "cure" is not worse than the "disease." Where do so many boys pick up the idea that reading is for "sissies"? Why do we expect girls to relate to both male and female characters, but assume that boys really only relate to male problems? If we start making decisions about "gender-appropriate" materials, are we in danger of reinforcing negative connotations about what is and is not suitable to read? What will happen to those unfortunate few who dare to read a book from the "wrong" side? What will the teacher do when the homophobic slurs descend on the boy reading *Anne of Green Gables*?

Teacher-librarians, of course, cannot remodel the world. Many of the factors that influence reading exist outside their schools and outside their control. Gender acculturation, socioeconomic factors or the introduction of standardized reading tests (Parsons, 2001; Smith, 1986), for example, have much to do with attitudes toward and facility with reading, but there is little teacher-librarians can do about these. Where they can make a difference, however, is where students spend most of their time and where they learn what reading in school is all about: the classroom. When teacher-librarians organize "boys only" clubs and create "boys only" book displays, they should be wondering why it takes such a drastic step to put materials into boys' hands that match their interests and their abilities. What exactly is going on in classroom reading programs?

READING IN THE CLASSROOM

If students were to define reading by what they do in classrooms, many would say it is reading a story and answering questions (Allington & Cunningham, 1997; Smith, 1986). Usually they are all reading the same story and answering the same questions.

Beginning in the elementary grades, students are introduced to the routine of answering main idea, supporting details and vocabulary questions. Somewhere around grade 4, they are introduced to terms such as theme, plot, setting, climax, and character study, and are asked more questions. By that time, to augment the reading anthology, the entire class is given the same novel to read, chapter by chapter, answering questions, of course, as they go along. The students' comprehension is largely measured by rating their written answers to teacher-made tests that stress plot recall, application of literary terms, vocabulary, and written fluency.

When they reach middle school, students are usually treated as blank slates, reintroduced to the same, tried and true English catechism, and cranked through an arbitrarily chosen selection of short stories and novels, one by one. Teachers may call it English literature, but students recognize it as the same old game.

The wonder is not that we lose so many potential readers with this nonsense but rather that we don't lose more. The purpose for reading becomes so devalued that function is lost to form. We ask questions to generate answers rather than thought; students answer questions to obtain marks not to demonstrate understanding. If you do not read much or well before you get on this question-answering, reading merry-go-round, you may end up just going around in circles.

Instead of jumping on a "boys only" bandwagon, perhaps it is time to take a closer look at reading practices in classrooms. Are students learning that reading is an open-ended opportunity to find out more about themselves and the world around them or are they concluding that it is a series of hurdles to overcome and marks and grades to acquire? Do they see their teachers, especially male teachers, avidly reading during the Language Arts/English period or do they notice them marking papers, filling out their daybooks or chatting with the teacher next door? Are they listening to their teacher animating the characters from Roald Dahl's *The Witches* in a stirring read-aloud or waiting for their turn to stumble through a passage in the daily, oral, round robin read-along?

What is a good reading program for boys? To paraphrase Gertrude Stein, a good reading program is a good reading program is a good reading program.

WHAT TEACHER-LIBRARIANS CAN DO

This is where teacher-librarians can make a crucial difference. Specific reading practices have been demonstrated over time to be highly effective for *all* students. As school literacy leaders, teacher-librarians can make teachers aware of these practices and help them develop the kinds of reading programs that produce good readers, boys included.

The following questions highlight effective reading practices. As you reflect on the reading programs in your school, consider how many of these questions you can answer in the affirmative. For those questions you cannot answer in the affirmative, a few implementation suggestions are included.

• *Do the programs feature frequent and regular read-alouds of both fiction and nonfiction by the teacher? (And is the teacher reading them well?)*

• Successful oral reading is a combination of an acquired skill and the choice of appropriate materials. Classroom teachers often need help with both. You can demonstrate how to make books come alive either in a short inservice or during an outreach program in the classrooms. Set up displays of sure-fire read-alouds for each grade level in the staff room and encourage teachers to choose books that appeal to them personally as readers. Be certain that they and you are including nonfiction in read-alouds.

• *Do teachers model independent reading during class time?*

• Suggest an "everybody reads" time for your school and collaboratively set up some ground rules. Even 15 or 20 minutes a day can make a crucial difference. Stress the fact that students learn to value independent reading when they see that their teachers value independent reading for themselves.

• *Are there enough materials in the school library to match individual student interests and abilities? Are students encouraged to venture outside their usual or expected reading patterns?*

• Reading cannot be forced. While we certainly would like all students to experience award-winning literature, we also have to be sensitive to the variety of reading needs in our schools. When purchasing, remember that high-interest materials are essential to every collection and that a range of reading levels need to be addressed with nonfiction materials. Reading aloud some of these high-interest materials will ensure their circulation.

• *Do the students have frequent opportunities to select their own materials and not just from a range picked by the teacher? Do teachers readily assist students who have trouble finding "a good book"?*

• When teachers come to you for "a good group novel," be prepared to suggest how they might implement and evaluate an independent novel study as a replacement and indicate to them all the advantages of such an approach. Encourage teachers to send you those students who cannot seem to settle on a book and work your magic on them.

• *Are students provided with regular and significant amounts of in-class time to read as opposed to answering questions based on their reading? Are they then punished by having to take the questions home for homework?*

• Work with your administration team to establish priorities for the improvement of reading in your school. With their backing, explain to your teachers what the research says about on-task reading and settle on some basic guidelines that everyone can follow. Again, a relatively few minutes a day of "just reading" can work wonders.

• *Do students have frequent opportunities to respond to materials in a personally significant manner, not just in ways dictated by the teacher or in response to questions asked by the teacher? Are they given guidance and direction in how to do this?*

• Journal writing is one of the most misunderstood and abused techniques in a reading teacher's arsenal (Parsons, 2001). You would benefit your teachers enormously if you would do some research on the "do's" and "don'ts" of personal response and assist your teachers in developing a more satisfying and effective approach to this vital technique.

• *Do students have many opportunities to discuss with someone else what they are reading?*

• When students come to you in the library, try instructing them in various reading circle, personal response and small-group discussion strategies. Follow up with the classroom teachers and ask them to reinforce your teaching with some in-class practice. You will find that teachers who were not familiar with these strategies often continue with them after this kind of introduction.

• *Do students seek out and value peer opinions and advice?*

• The real experts on "what's good" and "what's not" in reading are the students themselves. They know each other, the elements in their environment that shape their interests and their struggles and triumphs as they come to terms with books in your collection. Seek out their counsel. When they see that you value their opinions and advice, they will begin to value each other's expertise. When a student is considering a particular book, refer to someone in his or her class who has already read and enjoyed it.

• *Do the programs include the flexibility to allow students to employ a variety of strategies to comprehend material (e.g., retelling, predicting, relating to personal experience, reflecting, discussing, dramatizing, expanding on the text, comparing, hypothesizing, making inferences and judgments)?*

• Teachers often have little knowledge of, experience with, or confidence in such techniques as readers theater, dramatic reenactment, open-ended questioning, or personal response. You might choose one strategy a month and briefly highlight it at a staff meeting. Encourage teachers to come to you or others on staff who use that strategy for more guidance.

• *Is the reading program an integral part of an integrated language arts/English program?*

• This is the most difficult of all the components of an effective reading program since it requires teachers, including the teacher-librarian, to define for themselves what literacy entails. The word *integrated* is used so often in discussing English and language arts programs that the term needs clarification. The term is usually used in three ways. An integrated program is one that is (1) a blend of all the aspects of English: reading, writing, speaking, viewing, and valuing; (2) individualized to the personal growth, skills and cultural needs of the individual student; or (3) coordinated with other aspects of a student's program, such as art, music, science, or computer studies. Conversely, the other aspects of a student's program should be integrated with the English program (Parsons, 2001). With these three aspects in mind, who else on a staff is better qualified to understand and speak to an integrated program than the teacher-librarian?

READING AS A LIFE SKILL

Teacher-librarians obviously have their work cut out for them. In the current teach/test hysteria gripping the profession, many of these proven practices have fallen into disuse. If teacher-librarians can convince their teachers to include these components in their programs, however, students will begin to understand that reading is an essential life skill. Through reading, they can discover how others cope with disappointment, confusion, and frustration. They can recognize that they are not alone in feeling inadequate about their bodies, their abilities, or their social graces. They can learn how discrimination and bullying, such as racism, sexism, and homophobia, emerge and what to do about them.

But your school cannot operate on a double standard; the values that students observe in the school library resource center have to be the same values taught and modeled in their classrooms. If a teacher-librarian tries to sell students on the true value of reading and the students go back to the classroom to answer the same old set of questions on the same old novel, nothing is going to change. Teacher-librarians and classroom teachers have to be on the same page. If teacher-librarians can break down some of the barriers to effective reading practices in classrooms, on the other hand, students will come to understand what reading is truly all about.

Reading is a purposeful activity. Anything that limits the scope and potential of reading, from filling in the blanks for marks to pandering to gender stereotyping, undermines that purpose. When students, regardless of gender, are finally convinced that reading can help them cope with and make sense of their world and their lives, inevitably, the reading will flow.

REFERENCES

Allington, R., & Cunningham, P. (1997). *Schools that work: Where all children read and write.* Boston, MA: Addison Wesley.

Flurkey, A. (Ed.). (2003). *On the revolution of reading: The selected writings of Kenneth S. Goodman.* Portsmouth, NH: Heinemann.

Graves, D. (1990). *Discover your own literacy.* Portsmouth, NH: Heinemann.

Molnar, A. (2002). *School reform proposals: The research evidence.* Greenwich, CT: Information Age.

Parsons, L. (2001). *Response journals revisited.* Markham, ON: Pembroke.

Smith, F. (1986). *Insult to intelligence: The bureaucratic invasion of our classrooms.* New York: Arbor House.

Overcoming the Obstacle Course: A Look at Teenage Boys and Reading

Patrick Jones and Dawn Cartwright Fiorelli

Almost any school or public librarian who has visited a secondary school classroom to booktalk could tell the tale about the student, always a male, who will defiantly and proudly announce to the librarian that he doesn't read. Chances are much of that is for show, to mark turf and to challenge. Chances are that boy does read. But not the stack of novels the booktalking librarian no doubt has in front of her; instead, that male is probably reading newspapers (especially comics, sports and entertainment), magazines (same list of subjects, but throw in video game magazines for younger teens) and maybe even heavily illustrated nonfiction.

After years of neglect, there is now a growing body of research to explain the reading and non-reading habits of boys. In the first chapter of Michael Smith's indispensable book *"Reading Don't Fix No Chevys"* (2002) is a quick review of a dozen major findings of that research related to boys (not just teens) and reading:

- Boys don't comprehend narrative (fiction) as well as girls.
- Boys have much less interest in leisure reading than girls.
- Boys are more inclined to read informational texts.
- Boys are more inclined to read magazine and newspaper articles.
- Boys are more inclined to read comic books and graphic novels than girls.
- Boys like to read about hobbies, sports, and things they do or want to do.
- Boys tend to enjoy escapism and humor.
- Some groups of boys are passionate about science fiction or fantasy.

First published in *Teacher Librarian*, February 2003, Volume 30, Number 3

• The appearance of a book and cover is important to boys.
• Few boys entering school call themselves "nonreaders" but by high school, over half do.
• Boys tend to think they are bad readers.
• If reading is perceived as feminized, then boys will go to great lengths to avoid it.

Thus, the boy at the booktalking session saying he doesn't read might simply be saying that he doesn't read what libraries offer.

Most young adult (YA) sections in public libraries are filled with fiction; there is little recreational nonfiction. If there is recreational nonfiction, it is more than likely to be self-help, health-related, about teen issues or pop star biographies. There might be magazines, but the chances are they are aimed more at girls than boys. Comic books are more than likely not to be there, and graphic novels, if collected, are not featured. There probably isn't a newspaper lying around. Boys who venture into the YA area will find shelves so jammed that they won't have a catchy cover catch their interest and it is doubtful if anything but new books (which again, no doubt are all fiction) will be on display. Given these choices, the teen boy, especially a younger one, will opt for something safe like a series (boys like brands) only to get the message from a teacher, parent, or maybe even a librarian that the book is okay because "at least they are reading something." Secondary school libraries, which rarely and mystifyingly don't even have YA areas to highlight materials to be read outside of the curriculum, offer boys just as few options. Thus, for most boys finding something to read in a library is like running an obstacle course.

WHAT BOYS SEE AS OBSTACLES
A national survey conducted as part of YALSA's (Young Adult Library Services Association) 2001 Teen Read Week celebration netted more evidence about what boys see as obstacles to reading. One question on the survey (see full results at **www.smartgirl.org/speakout/archives/trw/trw2001.html**) asked, "If you don't read much or don't like reading, why?" The chart illustrates the responses of teenage boys; the average age of the survey respondent was 14:

Boring/not fun	39.3%
No time/too busy	29.8%
Like other activities better	11.1%
Can't get into the stories	7.7%
I'm not good at it	4.3%
Makes me tired/causes headaches	2.5%
Video games/TV more interesting	2.3%
Too much school work	1.4%
Books are too long	0.09%
Friends make fun of me	0.01%

What is interesting is that virtually no teen boys responded that negative peer pressure served as a major obstacle. The rest of the obstacles can be overcome, but not by doing more of the same, which is building YA areas filled with teen problem novel fiction; that is not what most boys want to read.

But more than research, the library world is filled with case studies (also known as anecdotal evidence). As a teacher-librarian in a middle school in New York, co-author Dawn Fiorelli learned to be creative and theatrical in her approach to booktalking, putting on quite a show to prompt boys to want to pick up a book, check it out of the library, and then actually read it. One of her favorite experiences was with Shawn, a "very cool" seventh grader. Dawn was booktalking *Harris and Me* by Gary Paulsen and told the class that it was the funniest book she had ever read. Shawn said, "Books can't be funny," to which Dawn replied, "Oh yeah? I bet if you read this book you'll laugh out loud." He shrugged his shoulders, took the book, and read it! Satisfied to simply get a book in his hands, she was ecstatic when he returned it and said, "Yeah, pretty funny."

Dawn then moved on to her current position as a YA librarian in a public library in an affluent town in Connecticut where she spends lots of time showing moms books that their sons may enjoy. Parents have ideas about what appeals to their children, and she always wonders about the conversation that goes on at home after they leave the library. She recalls a recent encounter involving a parent telling her that her son, in grade 8 and a skateboarder, "would not be interested in the Tony Hawk biography because it was too long." After she left, Dawn realized that if the customer had simply had a list for her to take home, her library experience would have been more productive in many ways. She could have taken it home to her son, he could read over the list and choose for himself, and maybe some of those books would get into his hands. That experience prompted Dawn to ask fellow YA librarians across the country what their "sure thing" titles for boys were. The list (appended at the end of the article) is rich in its variety and provides one more opportunity to connect our boys with books. Creating such a list for both boys and parents of boys is one simple thing every library could do to help males jump the hurdle of finding a good book.

WHAT THE TEACHER-LIBRARIAN CAN DO

Here are 10 other things which teacher-librarians can do *this week* to increase reading behaviors and improve attitudes toward reading among teenage boys. Few of these items involve additional resources; almost all involve rearranging priorities.

• Link from the library web site to the guysread.com website which contains list after list of books recommended by guys for guys.

• Plan at least one program aimed just at boys, which may or may not be directly related to reading. For example, have a martial arts demonstration and workshop, but make sure on every chair in the meeting room is a book or magazine about the subject. Take a look at Kirsten Edwards' *Teen Library Events* (2002) and RoseMary Honnold's *101+ Teen Programs That Work* (2003) to learn more about planning exciting teen programs.

• Get into the classroom and booktalk, including lots of nonfiction. Don't just hold up the covers; use PowerPoint to show the covers and illustrations. Boys want to see stuff, not just hear about them. See Jennifer Bromann's *Booktalking That Works* (2001) to learn the tricks of the booktalking trade.

• Buy every ALA Read poster featuring a male. Given that within their school the majority of English teachers and librarians are likely female, any example of a male reading is worth something.

• Engage the coaches of the boys' sports teams in a Guys Read project. From read-alouds on the bus to away games to having athletes read to younger children, get coaches (of whom most are teachers; few are librarians) involved.

• Buy a few less novels and put that money into periodicals: magazines, comic books, and newspapers, particularly *USA Today* and at least one tabloid such as the *Weekly World News*. See *Do It Right* (Jones & Shoemaker, 2001) for information on teen magazines.

• Actively recruit teenage boys to volunteer and work in your library. Related, make sure that the teenager, often male, who is volunteering at your library because of community service gets to do more than stamp date due cards; give them a chance to have an experience with reading, from reviewing web sites to reading book reviews to whatever you can imagine. Recruit first for volunteers in the short term; recruit for the profession in the long term.

• Ask teen boys about their reading. Find out any book they have ever read and learn what they liked about it. Do this not by asking, "What did you like about it?"; rather, ask them to tell you the story of the book. Seek suggestions, do surveys, but talk one-on-one with boys whenever you can about reading and leave the "at least you are reading something" back in the 20th century where it belongs.

• Teen boys do use libraries: they use computers, copiers and study tables, but the books are on the shelves. Put the books where the boys are. Move next to the computers the books about subjects which boys are looking at online: sex, sports, and animation.

• Buy books that boys want to read.

BUILDING A GUY-FRIENDLY COLLECTION

So what are those books? Lists abound in print and on the Internet. In the forthcoming *Creating a Core Collection for Young Adults* (co written with Patricia Taylor and Kirsten Edwards; to be published by Neal-Schuman), there are lots of fiction and nonfiction for guys ages 12 to 18. YALSA's annual "Quick Picks" list (among the lists featured at **www.ala.org/yalsa/**) is put together by a committee which seeks books that teens will pick up on their own and read for pleasure. The list is geared to the teenager who, for whatever reason, does not like to read. Teen input is a vital aspect in the final decision of the committee. The visual appearance of a book and the standard considerations in the quality of content is equally important when selecting books for reluctant young readers. While the list is not "books for boys" per se, the majority of the titles on the list *do* have high guy appeal, especially for those boys who struggle with reading. No one wants to do anything they associate with failure, so libraries need books that allow boys to succeed at reading. The "for more information" list at the end of this article contains numerous books and articles, most of which provide suggested titles, such as Kathleen Odean's *Great Books for Boys: More Than 600 Books for Boys 2 to 14* (1998).

The tools and titles are there; the research is there, and the need is there staring us right in the face. One more statistic: In the United States, one in 32 people is in or has been in the criminal justice system. One in 32 people in the United States according to the Justice Department is currently in jail, in prison, on probation, on parole, or has been one of these things. The majority of these people are male. The majority of the male prison population has limited education; many are high school dropouts. The limits of education are almost always related to reading problems. If we want young men to have their hands clutching a graduation diploma rather than the bars of cell, then it is time to start overcoming the obstacles course we've set up in school and public libraries in order to ensure that guys read.

TWENTY GREAT FICTION BOOKS FOR GRADE 7 BOYS

We've listed only one title for each author, but most have several titles with high boy-appeal.

1. *Downriver*. Will Hobbs. Atheneum, 1991. 0689316909
2. *Enders game*. Orson Scott Card. T. Doherty, 1985. 0312932081
3. *Harris and me*. Gary Paulsen. Harcourt Brace, 1993. 0152928774
4. *Heart of a champion*. Carl Deuker. Joy Street, 1993. 0316181668
5. His Dark Materials trilogy. Phillip Pullman. Knopf. *Golden compass*, 1996, 0679879242; *Subtle knife*, 1997, 0679879250; *Amber spyglass*, 2000, 0679879269

6. *Hitchhiker's guide to the galaxy.* Douglas Adams. Harmony Books, 1989 (anniversary edition). 0517542099

7. *Last mission.* Harry Mazer. Delacorte, 1979. 0440057744

8. *Maniac Magee.* Jerry Spinelli. Little Brown, 1990. 0316807222

9. *Monster.* Walter Dean Myers. HarperCollins, 1999. 0060280786

10. Net Force series. Tom Clancy.

11. *No more dead dogs.* Gordon Korman. Hyperion, 2000. 078682462X

12. *Oddballs.* William Sleator. Dutton, 1993. 0525450572

13. *One fat summer.* Robert Lypstye. Harper & Row, 1977. 006023895X

14. *Raven of the waves.* Michael Cadnum. Orchard, 2001. 0531303349

15. *Silent to the bone.* E. L. Konigsburg. Atheneum, 2000. 0689836015

16. *Slot machine.* Chris Lynch. HarperCollins, 1995. 0060235853

17. *Soldier's heart.* Gary Paulsen. Delacorte, 1998. 0385324987

18. *Stormbreaker.* Anthony Horowitz. Philomel, 2001. 0399236201

19. *Tangerine.* Edward Bloor. Harcourt Brace, 1997. 015201246X

20. *Touching spirit bear.* Ben Mikealsen. HarperCollins, 2001. 0060291494

NONFICTION AREAS OF INTEREST TO GUYS, IN DEWEY ORDER

000/100/200s: World records / Computers / Bigfoot / UFOs / Unexplained / Monsters / Parapsychology / Mythology

300s: Scary stories / Urban legends/ True crime / Forensics / Military / Study guides

500s: Dinosaurs / Snakes / Sharks / Wolves / Outer space / Reptiles / Natural disasters / Math riddles

600s: Anything with wheels (bikes, cars, trucks, etc.) / Sex / Electronics

700s: Almost any sport, both professional and participatory / Gameboy codes / Magic / Drawing / Comics / Optical illusions / Hip hop / Rock music / Cartoons / Star Wars / Special effects / Puns

800s: Jokes / Poetry / Story collections / How to write poetry / Riddles

900s: Wars / Biographies of athletes, musicians, actors, and explorers

RESOURCES

Aronson, M. (2001). *Exploding the myths: The truth about teenagers and reading.* Landham, MD: Scarecrow Press.

Baxter, K. (1999). *Gotcha! Nonfiction booktalks to get kids excited about reading.* Englewood, CO: Libraries Unlimited.

Barrs, M. (2000). Gendered literacy. *Language Arts, 77,* 287–293.

Bromann, J. (2001). *Booktalking that works.* New York: Neal-Schuman.

Brooks, B., O'Dell, K., & Jones, P. (2000). Will boys be boys? Are you sure? *Voice of Youth Advocates, 23,* 88–92.

Brozo, W. (2002). *To be a boy, to be a reader: Engaging teen and preteen boys in active literacy.* Newark, DE: International Reading Association.

Brozo, W., & Schmelzer, R. (1997). Wildmen, warriors, and lovers: Reaching boys through archetypal literature. *Journal of Adolescent & Adult Literacy, 41,* 4-11.

Cart, M. (2000). What about boys? YA novels with male protagonists. *Booklist, 96,* 892.

Crowe, C. (2002). An antidote for testosterone poisoning: YA books girls—and boys—should read. *Eng-

lish Journal, 91 (3), 135-138.

Cox, R. (2001). Lost boys. *Voice of Youth Advocates, 24*, 172–173.

Edwards, K. (2002). *Teen library events: A month-by-month guide.* Westport, CT: Greenwood Press.

Flynn, J. & Rahbar, M. (1994). Prevalence of reading failure in boys compared with girls. *Psychology in the Schools, 31*, 66–71.

Gorman, M. (2002). What teens want: Graphic novels. *School Library Journal, 48*(8), 42–44, 47.

Gurian, M. (2000). *What stories does my son need? A guide to books and movies that build character in boys.* New York: Jeremy P. Tarcher/Putnam.

Honnold, R. (2003). *101+ teen programs that work.* New York: Neal-Schuman.

Jacobson, L. (2002). Longitudinal study finds gender and race gaps among 1st graders. *Education Week, 21*(27), 7.

Jones, P. (2001). Teen nonfiction: The real stuff. *School Library Journal, 47*(4), 44–45.

Jones, P., & Shoemaker, J. (2001). *Do it right! Best practices for serving young adults in school and public libraries.* New York: Neal-Schuman.

Langerman, D. (1990). Books & boys: Gender preferences and book selection. *School Library Journal, 36* (3), 132–136.

Lodge, S. (1999). Get ready for "boy power." *Publishers Weekly, 246*(32), 212–213.

McGillian, J. (2002). Get boys crazy about books! *Creative Classroom, 16*(6), 30–32.

Maynard, T. (2002). *Boys and literacy: Exploring the issues.* New York: RoutledgeFalmer.

Murphy, J. (2001). Boys will be boys. *School Library Journal, 47*(1), 31.

Nilsen, A. (2001). It's deja vu all over again! *School Library Journal, 47*(3), 49–50.

Nicolle, R. (1989). Boys and the five-year void. *School Library Journal, 35*(3), 130.

Nodelman, P. (2002). Who the boys are: Thinking about masculinity in children's fiction. *New Advocate, 15*(1), 9–18.

Odean K. (1998). *Great books for boys: More than 600 books for boys 2 to 14.* New York: Ballantine.

Orellana, M. (1995). Literacy as a gendered social practice: tasks, texts, talk, and take-up. *Reading Research Quarterly 30*, 674–708.

Robb, D. (2001). *Crossing the water: Eighteen months on an island working with troubled boys—a teacher's memoir.* New York: Simon & Schuster.

Simpson, A. (1996). Fictions and facts: An investigation of the reading practices of girls and boys. *English Education, 28*, 268–279.

Smith, M. (2002). *"Reading don't fix no Chevys": Literacy in the lives of young men.* Portsmouth, NH: Boynton/Cook.

Wilhelm, J. (2001). It's a guy thing. *Voices from the Middle, 9*(2), 60.

Young, J. (2001). Displaying practices of masculinity: Critical literacy and social contexts. *Journal of Adolescent & Adult Literacy, 45*, 4–14.

Young, J. (2001). Boys will be boys, or will they? Literacy and masculinities. *Reading Research Quarterly, 36*, 316–325.

48

Where the Boys Are

Allison Haupt

As much as I enjoyed reading, in the world in which I was living it had to be a secret vice. When I brought books home from the library, I would sometimes run into older kids who would tease me about my reading. It was, they made it clear, not what boys did. And though by now I was fighting older boys and didn't mind that one bit, for some reason I didn't want to fight about books. Books were special and said something about me that I didn't want to reveal.
—from *Bad Boy: A Memoir*, by Walter Dean Myers

Where *are* the boys? Well, they're not breaking down the doors to the public library. Are they haunting the school libraries? And while we're pondering that question, what has happened to "boyhood"? Has it vanished into some sort of virtual war game? Why has it become impossible to imagine a teenage boy curling up with a good book? Are our boys all so eager to become men, or more importantly, have they all adopted the position that "real mean don't read," to the extent that reading has become an anathema to them by the time they hit grade 7?

Literacy scores from different continents are consistent in showing that boys are not performing as well as girls, and these scores have precipitated a new wave of concern regarding boys' reading habits (or lack thereof). Some have blamed the lack of appropriate literature or role models. Others blame television, the media, or computer games. Others blame pedagogical models.

Is there a problem or isn't there? Has it become impossible for boys to find the time to lose themselves in a good book these days? In blaming "the boys" for declining literacy scores are we dooming them to an endless vortex of standardized testing? Do too many questions diminish or destroy the sheer pleasure and power of reading? Are issues of masculinity actively preventing young men from becoming readers?

A 1996 joint publication from the Equal Opportunities Commission and the Office for Standards in Education, *The Gender Divide,*

First published in *Teacher Librarian*, February 2003, Volume 30, Number 3

confirms the fact that in England girls are more successful than boys at every level in examinations at age 16. In the three core subjects of English, mathematics and science, English is notable in that girls outperform boys at each of the assessment stages (ages 7, 11, 14 and 16). A report entitled *Boys and English* points out that boys' attitudes towards reading and writing tend to be more negative than girls'. (Hall & Coles, 1997, para. 1)

The same authors also write that boys "often have narrower experiences of fiction, write more predictably and have difficulty with the affective aspects of English" (para. 1). This assessment echoes a 1996 Australian literacy survey, which indicated that literacy levels had not improved in the past decade, and that for boys, scores had in fact declined (Bantick, 1996). And Canada's *Toronto Sun* newspaper reported that 80% of girls passed the provincial grade 10 literacy test required for graduation, while only 70% of boys did (Fenlon, 2002). I think we can all admit that there is a problem, and since it is international rather than regional or cultural in scope, it obviously has something to do with the structure of the brain and developmental differences.

Recently I've read several books that have totally changed my "nonsexist" approach to reading and library promotion. I used to assume that a good book was simply a good book, regardless of the sex of the protagonist or the narrative style. When I went out to schools to do booktalks, I always tried to be fair and introduce books that I felt had equal male/female appeal. I always included nonfiction, following the adage that boys are often more interested in fact than fiction. But now, I've decided to be overtly and blatantly sexist in everything from the way I approach storytelling to the books I promote. It's not that I don't think that boys and girls, or men and women, can't read and enjoy the same books. Not at all. But several research papers and studies have convinced me that our ability to promote reading can be greatly enhanced by recognizing biological and developmental differences between the guys and the gals.

My interest in this topic began when I started getting repeated requests for more booklists for boys; more suggestions for boys' book clubs. The request that always made me cringe was the demand for books for reluctant readers, more "hi-lo" titles—a request based erroneously on the assumption that if boys didn't want to read, all you had to do was find them something dead simple to read. Curiosity led me to Michael Gurian's *Boys and Girls Learn Differently: A Guide for Teachers and Parents* (2001). I'd like to add librarians to the list of individuals who must read this book. Whether or not you ultimately agree with Gurian, he proposes some interesting and challenging notions about how male and female brains differ and therefore how developmental, hormonal and societal influences affect learning. Gurian quotes researcher Camilla Benbow as stating, "After fifteen years of looking for an environmental explanation and getting zero results, I gave up" (p. 17). The differences, she discovered, were in the brain, with culture playing an important part but not the defining role that many people have wished to believe.

Gurian (2001) touches on many issues including technology and gender, communication styles, mentoring and learning and behavioral disabilities. Toward the end of the book he states,

As brain-based research assumes power in educational culture, and as brain-based gender research increases its usefulness, we generally notice what so many reading specialists already know: the vast majority of reading-traumatized and reading-deficient high school students are young men. (p. 297)

Gurian identifies and then suggests very practical and significant ways that we can adapt teaching styles to recognize and utilize the research he has introduced. From deductive versus inductive reasoning, from the abstract to the concrete, from language acquisition to motivating readers, Gurian brings together biological, linguistic, and pedagogical research in a practical and revealing way.

Gurian pointed me to what he called the "best primary text we know of for getting a whole picture (on a worldwide scale) of brain-based gender differences"—*Brain Sex* (1989) by Anne Moir and David Jessel. Despite its slightly lurid cover, I found the book to be as lucid, provocative, and controversial as it claimed to be. The authors begin with the premise that a "baby's brain is born sexually biased" and never look back. Gender-neutral language and equality may be one thing, but Moir and Jessel claim that "it makes infinitely more sense to reform our educational system in a way that acknowledges, and adapts to, our basic sex differences" (p. 184). The researchers look at everything from the print bias that exists for teaching and testing in schools to their belief that the discipline of school is deeply unnatural to boys. "His is a world of action, exploration and things. But school tells him to sit quiet, listen, not fidget, and pay attention to ideas; everything, in fact, that his brain and body are telling him not to do" (p. 64). *Brain Sex* examines the biological differences in brain development and function and has massive implications for everyone seeking a basic understanding of male/female differences in education, including reading acquisition and communication.

A massive amount of reading and research is required, but obviously once gender differences are identified and recognized, it's possible to address the research and adapt our philosophies and practices to fit. There are many subtle ways that we can change our approach to reading acquisition in light of this new research. For me, it has resulted in a reborn belief in the power of oral storytelling, and a renewed and passionate plea for parents, librarians, and teachers to read aloud to children of all ages as often as possible and a more liberal attitude toward expression, movement, and participation.

Through participation in storytimes at the public library, and through an active family involvement with books, parents can set the stage for success for a preschool child's acquisition of language. As boys grow older and enter school, the acquisition of reading skills becomes critical. Even though they may struggle with that acquisition, in the same way that girls may struggle with mathematical/spatial comprehension, boys can gain the language and reading skills they need unless a true reading disability is involved. It's like every other skill, from playing soccer to the piano. You need access to the materials, you need supportive parents, you need encouragement, and you need time to play.

As boys move up into grades 4 and 5, the learning differences seem to become much more pronounced. It seems to me that this is the critical point in a boy's reading education. If he's not a reader by now, he's not apt to become one without massive encouragement or change. Reading mentors that the boy admires are important. Book clubs, Young Readers' Choice Awards, and social acceptability might change the social perception of "readers." At this age children diverge, becoming even better, more passionate, more devoted readers or those who only read what is required.

From the developmental stages outlined by Gurion (2001), this would appear to be the critical moment when hormones are building, aggression is increasing, and boys become even more focused on action and exploration. As they enter high school, the emphasis on strength, masculinity, social acceptance, sports, aggression, hierarchies, and power increases even more. If reading isn't perceived as important, if students don't have an academic or professional goal, or if reading is identified as being "soft" or feminine, then reading would diminish rather than develop their fragile sense of self and growing masculinity. If boys have no male role models or strong women to introduce them to relevant and exciting books, they may not pick up another novel other than those required for high school English.

Who are the culprits? Everything has been blamed, from the curriculum to television. According to Brozo (2002),

Recent reports suggest that the average 5–7 hours per day that children spend in front of television and computer screens regardless of content, results in less intellectually stimulated and more emotionally disconnected adolescents and adults (Greenspan and Lewis, 2000). Boys who are mired in this video malaise take fewer and increasingly limited flight of imagination. (p. 27)

The Australia literacy survey (Bantick, 1996) blames the "crowded curriculum" for the lack of reading time and therefore the declining literacy scores. It's a sentiment I hear repeated regularly from busy teacher-librarians who no longer have time to booktalk great new titles and from middle school teachers who don't have time to read aloud. And pointing to another cause, Hashway and Austin (1997) state,

Quantitative literacy would increase if more leisure time was spent on thought-provoking activities and less on television viewing. This places a burden upon the family to prepare their children by spending quality time and provide experiences by which the children will evolve as humans prepared to live in and contribute to a quantitatively demanding society. (p. 3)

Despite the number of parents who come up to my desk towing a miserable-looking 12-year-old and loudly announce, "My son won't read;" despite the near panic in the voices of adults who proclaim there aren't *any* books for boys; despite headlines that announce that "boys don't read"—I soundly disagree. Boys *do* read. I am surrounded by boys who love to read: little boys who are barely five and who love books, boys in kindergarten and grade 1 who roll around on the floor, laughing at a funny story, boys in grades 4 and 5 who currently outnumber the girls in our book club. I am surrounded by men who read: friends, brothers, fathers, colleagues. And these men aren't teachers or librarians; they are engineers, insurance salesmen, bus drivers, computer specialists, managers, scientists, longshoremen. In fact it seems that almost every male within spitting distance is an avid reader, and I'm not talking about the evening paper. Was their childhood so radically different from the childhood of today's youth? If you ask most people who are readers, you typically hear one of two major conditions: They had a parent or teacher or librarian who read aloud to them, or books were available around the home and collections were augmented by frequent, lengthy visits to a library.

As a result of reading Gurian (2001) and Moir and Jessel (1989), I have changed the way I talk to boys about books. Small, subtle shifts in the way we look at behavior and what encourages rather than discourages reading behavior are incredible important. Book club meetings are a lot noisier now—I let the kids do most of the talking. Another example which rang alarms in my head was Gurian's discussion of the "reader interview." I have often asked, "What have you read before that you've liked?" Gurian points out two massive assumptions inherent in that question that automatically put the young male on the defensive: (1) He has read something before, and (2) he *liked* something he read. Neither may be true.

We should become knowledgeable about and accept the "real" boy, the loud and sometimes aggressive being that he is. We can find male mentors or be strong role models and introduce the "all boys book clubs" where boys control the selection, the action and the discussion about books. We can participate in initiatives like the Young Readers' Choice Awards that run in many states and provinces and that attract male readers with their competitive and structural edge.

I will be eternally thankful to J. K. Rowling for proving three things:

• Boys will read a book, no matter how difficult or foreign, if they're motivated.
• Boys' books don't have to be simplified play-by-play sports dramas, novels full of potty humor, or

"plots in hyper-drive."
  • Children, even boys, *will* read hardcover fiction.

The Potter phenomenon has created a window of opportunity, not only for publishers who have re-sponded with a myriad of new and rereleased fantasy titles, but for parents, teachers, and librarians. It's an opportunity to offer other titles that will interest, challenge, and fascinate boys. If the commercial wheels can make hay out of the Harry Potter phenomena, why can't we capture the moment and lead these young men on to the fantasy titles of Diana Wynne Jones, Ken Oppel, Jane Yolen, Susan Cooper, and Lloyd Alexander? As readers get older we can introduce them to Philip Pullman, Terry Pratchett, David Eddings, Garth Nix, and Robert Jordan. Boys will broaden their reading tastes and discover their own fa-vorite authors—if they have the time and motivation to read and access to great books.

SO WHAT *DO* BOYS READ?

In "Gendered Readings," the authors point out that although book reading declined for 14-year-old boys, the reading of magazines and newspapers increased.

> Boys' underachievement in school relates to a complex of factors of which reading patterns might well be one, but attempting to develop boys' reading habits through a careful look at what boys do choose to read as they get older, and an analysis of the successes in improving reading amongst younger boys, seems to us more profitable than a deficit model which focuses on what boys do not do. . . . A greater percentage of boys' reading diet is science fiction and fantasy, sports-related books and war and spy stories. More boys than girls read comic and joke books, annuals and humorous fiction. Interestingly, crime and detective works are equally popular as a proportion of the reading diet of both sexes. (Hall & Coles, 1997, Children's Reading Choices section, para. 14)

Another finding of the study is that

> boys' book reading is primarily narrative. This is counter to the prevalent conception in England that boys are interested primarily in non-fiction books . . . . Invented stories from "facts" are an increasing element in our culture evidenced, for instance, by popular television programmes like *999* and *Police, Camera, Ac-tion* (which use police film footage from surveillance cameras to create stories), and "faction" and "fic-tionographies." (Developing Critical Readers section, para. 4)

The final book which rounded out my recent exploration of the literary landscape of the young male psyche was William Brozo's *To Be a Boy, to Be a Reader: Engaging Teens and Preteen Boys in Active Lit-eracy* (2002). I liked the emphasis on "active" literacy. Brozo's dedication in the front of the book speaks volumes: "I dedicate this book to the first man I saw reading—my father." He then sets out to examine the psychological needs of the male reader, and to discuss how male archetypes in literature can satisfy those deep intellectual, emotional and psychological needs of boys. "I explore in-depth the origins and modern applications of ten positive male archetypes: Pilgrim, Patriarch, King, Warrior, Magician, Wild-man, Healer, Prophet, Trickster and Lover" (p. 4). Brozo then introduces each of these archetypes with a discussion of their relevance to a boy's development and gives examples of novels and informational books that fulfil that need.

Contrary to the British research, Brozo cites a study that found boys were "reading fewer magazines and newspapers on a daily basis than females. The survey also revealed that students, particularly boys, would rather watch television" He does concur, however, with the British report on the subject of nonfiction and adds,

> For most boys, however, reading nonfiction in school consists almost exclusively of reading textbooks, which has been found to be a principal culprit in creating disaffection with reading for both boys and girls. . . . These observations reinforce how rarely young adults are exposed to nonfiction books written specifically for them. (Brozo, 2002, p. 17)

SO WHAT CAN WE DO?

Brozo (2002) says boys need choice and control:

> Typical remedial reading schemes tend to strengthen a boy's self perception as an incompetent reader because they leave little or no room for choice and control. . . . I saw how boys need personally meaningful reading material to genuinely improve their literacy abilities. (p. 21)

Returning to his main premise he states, "Archetypal literature that resonates in the male psyche has the power to reveal the delight and necessity of reading." He recommends biographies such as *Simon Wiesenthal: Tracking Down Nazi Criminals*, *Rocket Boys: A Memoir*, *Never Cry Wolf*, and such novels as Robert Lipsyte's *The Chemo Kid*, Will Hobbs' *The Bearstone*, and Paul Fleishman's *Whirligig* to name just a few.

I asked another friend, an artist who struggled with reading when young, what made the difference for him. His reply: "Graphics. Design. Illustration." True. The guys in my libraries are definitely attracted to the graphic novel as an alternative narrative. Just as film plays a prominent role in the lives of young people, the combination of heroic quest story and fantasy and the graphic visual elements of comic books appeal to the young male reader. As do the bodacious babes.

"We need to be seen laughing over books, being unable to put books down . . . gasping over horror stories. . . . If children don't know we love to read, how will they realize what an absorbing rewarding activity reading is?" says Mem Fox (1993, p. 21).

What books do I believe guys will laugh over, find heroes in, be drawn away from the television by? I have prepared a lengthy booklist called *Guy Time: Novels for Young Men from Grades 4–9*. It is available on the National Book Service web site at **www.nbs.com**. If I had to narrow it down to just a few, these would be on my current Top 10 titles for boys aged 10 to 15:

- *Devil and his boy*. Anthony Horowitz. Philomel, 2000. 0399234322
- *Ender's game*. Orson Scott Card. Tor (rerelease), 1994. 0812550706
- *Holes*. Louis Sachar. Farrar, Straus and Giroux, 1998. 0374332657
- *Jack on the tracks*. Jack Gantos. Farrar, Straus and Giroux, 1999. 0374336652
- *Joey Pigza swallowed the key*. Jack Gantos. Farrar, Straus and Giroux, 1998. 0374336644
- *Lord of the nutcracker men*. Iain Lawrence. Delacorte, 2001. 0385729243. (Also his High Seas trilogy.)
- *Maniac Magee*. Jery Spinelli. Little, Brown, 1990. 0316807222
- *Shade's children*. Garth Nix. HarperCollins, 1997. 0060273240
- *The subtle knife*. Philip Pullman. Knopf, 1997. 0679879250
- *Woodsong*. Gary Paulsen. Simon & Schuster, 1990. 0027702219

And what are my new current favorites? *Amazing Maurice and His Educated Rodents*, by Terry Pratchett (HarperCollins, 2001, 0060012331); *Boy in the Burning House*, by Tim Wynne-Jones (Farrar, Straus and Giroux, 2001, 0374309302); *Kit's Wilderness*, by David Almond (Delacorte, 2000, 0385326653); and *Summerland*, by Michael Chabon (Miramax, 2002, 0786808772).

In his introduction to *Boys' Own: An Anthology of Canadian Fiction for Young Readers*, Tim Wynne-Jones (2001) asks,

What is a boy's story? Well, it kind of depends on what you think a boy is. Based on personal experience and observation, I would have to say that a boy is, typically, brave and scared, full of strutting self-confidence one moment and as wobbly as a first bike-ride the next. Boys are thoughtful and reckless, amiable and gross, noisy and withdrawn, smart and sometimes, thick as a brick! So a boy's story, I guess, who have to reflect some of that. (p. vii)

So what are your favorite books for boys, and what are you going to do with them?

REFERENCES

Bantick, C. (1996). Literacy survey. *Youth Studies, 15*(4), 5–6.

Brozo, W. (2002). *To be a boy, to be a reader: Engaging teen and preteen boys in active literacy*. Newark, DE: International Reading Association.

Fenlon, B. (2002, January 10). Test results tickle Tories: Grade 10 literacy scores up 7% this year. *Toronto Sun*, p. 17.

Fox, M. (1993). *Radical reflections: Passionate opinions on teaching, learning, and living*. San Diego: Harcourt.

Gurian, M. (2001). *Boys and girls learn differently: A guide for teachers and parents*. San Francisco: Jossey-Bass.

Hall, C., & Coles, M. (1997). Gendered readings: Helping boys develop as critical readers. *Gender and Education, 9*(1), 61–68. Retrieved December 6, 2002, from Academic Search Premier database.

Hashway, R., & Austin, D. (1997, June). Education as the key to adult quantitative literacy. *Education, 117*(4), 592–598.

Moir, A., & Jessel, D. (1989). *Brain sex*. New York: Laurel.

Wynne-Jones, T. (2001). *Boys' own: An anthology of Canadian fiction for young readers*. Toronto: Viking.

⑭

Boy Books, Girl Books: Should We Reorganize Our School Library Collections?

Ray Doiron

Many of us with years of teaching experience in a school library or in a classroom have seen the reactions children have to different books. Some look at the cover with a beautiful horse riding across an open field and immediately gush and goo about what a great book this would be. Others pick it up and say, "Oh, that's a girl book."

As a class of grade 3 or grade 4 children tumble into the school library for book exchange, we can hear the cries for joke books, hockey books, and dinosaur books. We've seen children walking with their arms folded around a book hugging it close to their body as if it was a newly discovered treasure. We've seen other children immediately open up a new book and start talking animatedly with a friend or laughing and giggling about a gross scene or a "naked picture."

We've seen some children jockey for position with their friends to take out the same book the friend just had, as if their social status will somehow rise if they are seen with that same book choice. We have seen children scrunch up their faces, almost in disgust, as we hold up the latest Caldecott or Newbery winner and tell them this is a great book to read.

We've seen many trends come and go as The Baby-Sitters' Club, The Boxcar Children, Goosebumps, Animorphs, Sweet Valley High, and the current Harry Potter series wash over the school like a tidal wave of reading interest that can't be stopped or even redirected. We've seen many children get stuck in the same genre or category of book and refuse to take anything but a sports book or a horse book or a paperback novel. What is problematic I think, as teacher-librarians and classroom teachers, is the feeling that we are somehow failing if we *don't* redirect children to what we feel are the "best" books, when in fact, children are exercising their freedom of choice when they pick books and they are showing us what they

First published in *Teacher Librarian*, February 2003, Volume 30, Number 3

are really interested in and what they like to read.

RESEARCHING GENDER READING PREFERENCES

These experiences formed the foundation of my research over the past few years on elementary children's reading preferences. While working as a teacher-librarian and as a classroom teacher, there seemed to be "trends" in boys' and girls' reading choices which were at once very evident and impossible to change. For instance, boys generally chose books about sports, space, science, jokes, and vehicles; girls picked picture storybooks and books about horses, cats, and crafts as well as novels, particularly ones about friends. Both boys and girls chose books about seasonal holidays and humorous stories; both chose animal books, although with animals, boys really liked sharks, snakes, and dinosaurs, while girls liked pets and animals like deer, bears, and raccoons.

These observations gave rise to a series of questions: Were these generalizations from my experience true or simply examples of an inherent stereotype? Could the whole issue be reduced to the simple fact that boys prefer information books and girls prefer fiction? How do children's preferences develop and what can we do as adults to affect them? Do boys and girls come wired this way or are we as a culture teaching them to identify themselves in these choices? These questions propelled me into a major research project where I examined the content of elementary classroom libraries across a large school district in my home province. It was evident in that study (Doiron, 1995) that children were presented predominately with fiction paperbacks as reading choices from their classroom libraries. Over 85% of the books counted in those classrooms were paperback novels purchased by classroom teachers from book clubs and book fairs. My "informal" study while working as a teacher-librarian in a large elementary school library, plus my discussions with fellow teacher-librarians, suggested many students preferred information books when they came to the school library. Counts from my school library automated circulation indicated that students were choosing twice as many information books as novels.

In addition, a second study I completed of school libraries across my province (Doiron & Davies, 1996) indicated that elementary school library collections broke down into 60% fiction (combined novels and easy fiction books) and 40% information books (trade books only). This was just the opposite of what our provincial guidelines suggested as a normal balance in an elementary school library. Either the guidelines established by our Department of Education (and evident in other national jurisdictions) were wrong or we were adding more fiction books than recommended. When the findings from the two studies were combined, the indications were that elementary students were given primarily fiction books to choose from for their reading. In order to identify what book types boys and girls were choosing for their independent reading when they came to the school library, I completed a third study in three large elementary schools. If these children preferred to take information books and, as educators we were presenting them with more fiction books from which to choose, it would have implications for instruction and for future book selection.

In this 3-year study, I asked teacher-librarians to track all books signed out by students in grades 1–6. This was done through an informal data gathering sheet on which a research assistant recorded the sex of each student, grade level, the number of fiction and number of information books signed out, the subject area of the information book choices, and whether the books were for independent reading or school work. Only books identified as chosen for students' personal or independent reading were included in the data. Other choices were assumed to be part of classroom projects or required reading set by the teacher and thus were not free book choices. More than 10,000 transactions were analyzed by grade level, gender, and book type. There are some general things I can report to you so far.

• First of all, the students signed out more fiction than information books. The split was about 60% fiction to 40% nonfiction.

• Broken down by gender, the data indicates girls are taking more books out than boys, but not in significantly different numbers.

• Broken down by book type (fiction and information), boys signed out 1.029 fiction books and 0.753 information books per transaction. Girls signed out 1.405 fiction books and 0.449 information books per transaction.

• Boys took out over two-thirds of all information books signed out, with less than one-third taken out by girls.

DISCUSSION AND IMPLICATIONS

It's obvious from these three studies that elementary children are telling us something in the book choices they are making. Both boys and girls enjoy reading stories including novels and easy fiction books with boys choosing 1.029 fiction books each and girls choosing 1.405 fiction books each. As educators, it appears we are doing a good job of presenting and promoting the reading of fiction. In fact, the studies indicated that we are presenting elementary children with many fiction choices both in our classroom libraries and in our school libraries from which to develop their reading interests. However, the third study indicated that when it comes to information books, there is a serious gender difference in the number of information books chosen by students for independent reading, with boys choosing 0.753 books each and girls 0.449 information books each. Girls were three times as likely to choose a fiction book as an information book (1.405 fiction to 0.449 information books), while boys were only 1.3 times more likely to choose fiction over information books (1.029 fiction to 0.753 information books). This strikes me as a serious imbalance in the reading choices girls are making. Boys clearly choose fiction and information books in a more equitable way, so we seem to be doing a good job of encouraging them to balance their reading choices. Girls however, were less likely to choose an information book, while they were in fact shown to be choosing slightly more books overall than boys. Girls seem to need more encouragement to balance their reading choices.

IMPLICATIONS FOR TEACHER-LIBRARIANS

As educators, this suggests several things. We need to reexamine the way we use fiction and information books in all aspects of our literacy programs. Clearly we need to encourage boys to do more reading just as a matter of good literacy promotion, while we need to encourage girls to be more balanced in their reading choices and to add information books to the book choices they make. This may be particularly important at grades 3 and 4 where there seems to be a great deal of interest in information books. We should be promoting information books in a big way at this age and we should be using them to directly teach many literacy skills. If children have a strong preference for information at this time in their elementary programs, we need to capitalize on it and use it to promote reading and the use of their school libraries. We should model the reading of information books and promote their inclusion in classroom libraries and on visits to the school library. Let's do booktalks, read-alouds, author studies, book displays, and the many other things we do to promote reading; only let's use information books.

There are groups of educators who suggest we should be using a more balanced approach for the use of fiction and information books in our literacy programs. Reese and Harris (1997) see there is a "power and beauty" in using information books with young readers. Others suggest we need to encourage teachers to read aloud information books to balance their reliance on fiction (Doiron, 1994; Oyler & Barry, 1996). The use of information texts as part of writing programs is also seen as crucial in developing young writers who can create writing for a wide variety of purposes (Stead, 2002).

It is also important for teachers to get excited about information books themselves, because children will mirror that enthusiasm (Roser & Firth, 1983). The teacher-librarian may have a particularly important role to play here by encouraging teachers to become more familiar with information books and to show them how these books can be used effectively in programs that encourage reading. Many classroom teachers are not comfortable with information books and the teacher-librarian can show leadership here as well, by including information books as part of curriculum planning sessions, reading-aloud programs, and other literacy activities aimed at supporting classroom literacy programs.

So to return to my original title and the questions that gave rise to my research projects, I guess I would have to say, yes, there are "boy books" and "girl books." There are books targeted especially for stereotypical views of boys and girls. But I don't believe the differences break down completely along the fiction/information book divide. As educators, we are definitely working with some stereotypical views ourselves and we need to examine how we are using fiction and information materials in our programs. Do we see reading for pleasure as predominately reading stories and novels? Can we not get pleasure from reading good quality information books? Do we see information books solely as resources we go to when we do research or have an information problem?

I think the children in these studies have taught me that we need to watch them carefully and they will quickly show us that they like information books a great deal and they want to read them. We need to re-examine what it means to read so that browsing through a book, stopping at things that catch our attention, reading captions, looking at pictures and visual materials are all ways of reading. If this type of reading was not pleasurable we would have no such thing as "coffee table" books or the successful Eyewitness series or biographies, magazines and cleverly engineered books. Reading is reading and when we motivate people to read we need to be sure that we are helping them find materials they are interested in reading and that we are not telling them that fiction is "better" to read than information books. Remember, there is no accounting for people's taste and as teacher-librarians we must provide our students with the best quality examples of all types of texts and then celebrate everything they ever read.

REFERENCES

Doiron, R. (1994). Using nonfiction in a read-aloud program: Letting the facts speak for themselves. *The Reading Teacher, 47*(8), 616–624.

Doiron, R. (1995). *The relationship between elementary classroom collections and the school library resource centre program.* Unpublished doctoral dissertation, University of British Columbia, Vancouver, BC.

Doiron, R., & Davies, J. (1996). *Reflection and renewal in Prince Edward Island school libraries.* Provincial research study prepared for the Department of Education, Charlottetown, PEI.

Oyler, C., & Barry, A. (1996). Intertextual connections in read-alouds of information books. *Language Arts, 73,* 324–329.

Reese, D. A., & Harris, V. J. (1997). "Look at this nest!" The beauty and power of using informational books with young children. *Early Child Development and Care, 127,* 217–231.

Stead, T. (2002). *Is that a fact? Teaching non-fiction writing.* Markham, ON: Pembroke Publishers.

(50)

Going Beyond the Debate: Using Technology and Instruction for a Balanced Reading Program

Valerie Grenawalt

As the debate over the value of computerized reading management programs continues, teacher-librarians should consider how they may be used together with a reading skills program to help schools implement a balanced literacy program. Such a program would promote collaboration and help teachers to implement differentiated instruction.

Reading management programs such as Accelerated Reader and Reading Counts! offer students the opportunity to select books at their own reading levels, to read independently, and to verify their work by taking a computerized test upon completion of the book. Interested teacher-librarians can help teachers individualize language arts instruction by using reading management programs combined with reading skill instruction as an alternative to the traditional classroom novel approach. In content area classes, teacher-librarians can help teachers promote reading and differentiate instruction by requiring supplemental enrichment reading that reinforces reading skills. Both these uses of reading management programs will increase the teacher-librarian's opportunities for collaboration.

THE CLASSROOM NOVEL

Not so long ago it was considered standard practice for language arts teachers to assign a class novel that every student was expected to read. For a month or two the class would study one piece of fiction on which class lessons were based. More than likely, students were assigned a specific number of pages to read each weeknight, then faced quizzes on certain chapters and a major "unit" test at the end of the book. In some more creative classrooms, students might be encouraged to dress up as characters or cook food to learn more about the period in which the novel was set. In the less creative classrooms, study guides

First published in *Teacher Librarian*, December 2004, Volume 32, Number 2

would be assigned. Students would be required to answer basic plot questions for each assigned chapter.

Under this "class novel" model, the school library existed quite separately from classroom instruction. Most students would visit the school library with a teacher only if reference resources were needed for other, nonfiction assignments. A few teachers asked students to read fiction independently and have their parents sign something verifying their children spent certain amounts of time reading. But since most teachers felt this assignment was only as valuable as the supervising parent required it to be, it was not heavily emphasized in grades or class time. Consequently, if students wanted fiction from the school library, they usually went on their own time.

There were several advantages to this class novel approach:

• Teachers and school districts selected "quality" materials that were "appropriate and educational" for students. Every book selected for students had been approved, usually by at least three professionals, and was on an "approved list." Such lists provide safety nets for teachers and school districts.

• Reading a book together as a class allowed students to participate in a teacher-led discussion of specific elements of the piece of literature. Teachers could point out important themes or other literary elements of literature.

• Teacher-led discussions also allowed students to experience and/or process difficult issues as a group with an adult leader.

• Spelling and vocabulary lists and history lessons could be related to the class novel, providing an integrated learning experience.

There are also several disadvantages to this approach:

• Many students were "turned off" reading by having no choice about what they were assigned to read.

• The reading level of the assigned piece was too easy for good readers and too difficult for struggling readers, further alienating some students.

• The assigned reading pace was too fast for some, and too slow for others.

• Typically, a few students who liked and understood the book would carry class discussions while other students slumped down in their chairs, avoiding participation.

• There was no accountability for outside student reading. Parents could sign off indicating students had read 30 minutes per night, but no one knew for sure.

READING MANAGEMENT PROGRAMS

New technology, however, has drastically changed the way fiction can be taught. Programs such as Accelerated Reader and Reading Counts! are commercial reading management programs. Schools that purchase such programs buy software that includes computer-based tests for books. Books are assigned point values based on length and level of difficulty and students earn points by reading books and taking the tests. In some schools, students are graded or earn prizes based on their points, though the prize aspect of the program has met with much criticism (Biggers, 2001; Carter, 1996) and may just as easily be avoided altogether. Teachers can easily print reports showing what students have read and the points they've earned.

Do reading programs work? While some students come to school loving to read, and others may learn to love to read by being introduced to outstanding literature, it has been my experience that requiring students to read, as my school's use of Accelerated Reader did, resulted in more students discovering that they liked to read than had I not had this tool. Simply put, some students did not know they like to read until they were required to do so. Once required, they discovered favorite authors and genres. In my opinion, our school could not have required students to read without using a reading management program for accountability purposes. Such is the nature of our educational climate.

THE ACCELERATED READER DEBATE

A review of current research related to reading management programs reveals a plethora of what I judge are inconclusive studies, most of which have been discredited by researchers with opposing viewpoints. Some studies have found that similar students who participated in reading management programs showed significant improvement in reading comprehension and attitudes toward reading, and even showed better attendance (Paul, VanderZee, Rue, & Swanson, 1996; Topping & Paul, 1999; Vollands, Topping, & Evans, 1999). Another study determined a sample of grade 7 students showed no significant gains with Accelerated Reader compared with those who do not use it (Pavonetti, Brimmer, & Cipielweski, 2002). Paul's studies have lost credibility with some because of his relationship with Renaissance Learning, Accelerated Reader's parent company. He and his wife were its cofounders in the mid-1980s (Chenoweth, 2001). The research by Pavonetti et al. is criticized because of an unscientific research design and because "their experimental and control groups were not matched for socioeconomic and other factors" (cited in Krashen, 2004, p. 444), while others argue the schools in the Pavonetti study did not follow the best practice guidelines set forth by Renaissance Learning in implementing Accelerated Reader (Kerns, 2003; Tardrew, 2003). Yet those same critics have also been discredited because they too are associated with Renaissance Learning (Krashen, 2004). Adding fuel to both sides, there are ample practitioners offering criticisms of different aspects of the Accelerated Reader program (Biggers, 2001; Carter, 1996; Chenoweth, 2001; Prince & Barron, 1998), and a few enthusiasts purporting to have seen success (Anderson, 2001; Greer, 2003; Guastello, 2002). So goes the research to date, without conclusive significant findings on either side of the debate.

At this point, only one researcher, William Sanders of the University of Tennessee, who seems to be accepted by both critics and proponents, provides an explanation for this phenomenon. He concludes, "Basically what the company [Renaissance Learning] offers is a good tool. If teachers use the tool as feedback on the progress of kids, that is very useful. It is not a stand-alone reading program" (cited in Chenowith, 2001, p. 50).

A BALANCED, INDIVIDUALIZED LITERACY PROGRAM

The effect that reading management programs can have on middle school language arts instruction varies by teacher, but can be quite dramatic. For some, these programs have offered a solution to some of the major problems with the traditional "class novel" approach to teaching. For instance, rather than assigning everyone the same novel, with tests and quizzes to check for understanding, teachers can assign students to earn a certain number of points during a grading period. Under this system, each student chooses his or her own book, based on reading ability and interest. Students also read at their own pace and take the computerized test when they finish their book(s).

Instead of spending class time trying to force a discussion over assigned chapters and quizzing students over plot details, teachers can spend time teaching and practicing real reading skills such as those outlined by Stephanie Harvey and Anne Goudvis in *Strategies That Work: Teaching Comprehension to Enhance Understanding* (2000). This important work shows teachers how to ensure that they are actually *teaching* higher-level reading skills such as making connections, making inferences, synthesizing information, and determining importance (Harvey & Goudvis, 2000; Zimmerman & Keene, 1997). The pairing of reading skills instruction with reading management programs that require students to spend time reading and practicing these skills is at the heart of a balanced literacy program. Thus reading management technology may be used as a tool for teachers to keep up with the ever increasing demand for teachers to "individualize and differentiate" instruction for each student.

Incorporating higher-level thinking skills into classroom discussions also serves as a counterbalance to the recall-based comprehension tests used in reading management programs. Students can use the books they choose for independent reading to practice these skills. Class discussions change from "What happened in Chapter 14?" to sharing enthusiasm for books and examples of inferences or other reading skills. In this system all students are accountable for reading. In addition, students cannot rely on others to carry them during class discussions or to provide answers on a study guide.

And ultimately, in classrooms where reading management programs are used well in combination with reading skill instruction, teachers and teacher-librarians work together to help students get to know themselves as readers, in much the same way adults do. Students learn genres of fiction and discover their personal preferences for action/adventure, mystery, fantasy, and so forth. Thus language arts teachers and teacher-librarians may work together as readers' advisors, sharing the joys of reading and selection with students.

READING MANAGEMENT PROGRAMS AND CONTENT AREA CLASSES

Content area teachers are under increasing pressure to reinforce literacy skills and provide opportunities for reading across the curriculum. This is problematic for some, as they feel that their expertise is in their content area and not literacy. They may also feel pressured to cover a vast amount of content, as set forth in their curriculum guide. This is where a teacher-librarian utilizing a reading management program can help content teachers meet their curricular objectives while addressing demands for literacy, reading and differentiated instruction. By simply providing teachers and/or students with lists of titles related to the content area, teacher-librarians can help teachers use reading management programs to meet all these goals.

As in language arts, the content area teacher can require students to earn a specified number of points using a title list, related to units of study, created by the teacher-librarian. While many districts encourage literacy skills to be reinforced across the curriculum, it is likely the language arts teacher will provide the bulk of literacy skills instruction. Thus incorporating a reading management program and requiring students to use reading skills allow the content teacher to meet the schoolwide goal of encouraging literacy skills while maintaining the primary focus on content and achieving curricular objectives.

Following are some best practices for using reading management programs schoolwide. Many of these suggestions and more are also included in the best practice recommendations by Renaissance Learning.

• Reading practice time should be a part of a balanced literacy program where reading skills such as those espoused by Harvey and Goudvis (2000) are taught separately from reading practice time.
  • Students need significant amounts of practice reading time at school.
  • Students must be engaged during this time, and accountable for it.
  • Student goals must be differentiated, so that all feel successful.
  • Teachers must vigilantly monitor, diagnose, intervene, and support their students.
  • Students must be allowed to use alternative assessments at times.
  • Students must be allowed to read outside their reading range at times.

CONCLUSION

Amidst all the research and rhetoric, is it really all that surprising that, as is the case with most instructional practices, they are only as effective as the teacher who implements them? In the end, reading management programs are mere tools, to be used well or poorly. But if they *can* be used well, to create enthusiastic readers, to help students know themselves, including their abilities and preferences as readers, and to provide teachers with a way of holding students accountable for practicing reading skills in a differentiated manner, should they not be embraced, or at the very least recognized as valuable tools in some cases? It is time for outspoken opponents of reading management programs to confine their comments to specific situations where poor implementation is not helping students or teachers. Similarly, opponents need to realize that some practitioners—and I include myself among them—have experienced the joy of watching middle school students learn to love reading as a result of being required to read. With the proper conditions for implementation, reading management programs can be powerful tools that no willing teacher, teacher-librarian, or school should be discouraged from using.

REFERENCES

Anderson, J. (2001). Using Accelerated Reader. *Teacher Librarian, 47*(7), 31.

Biggers, D. (2001). The argument against Accelerated Reader. *Journal of Adolescent & Adult Literacy, 45*(1), 72–76.

Chenoweth, K. (2001). Keeping score. *School Library Journal, 47*(9), 48–51.

Carter, B. (1996). Hold the applause! Do Accelerated Reader and Electronic Bookshelf send the right message? *School Library Journal, 42*(10), 22–25.

Greer, J. (2003). A positive experience with Accelerated Reader. *Teacher Librarian, 30*(4), 32.

Guastello, F. (2002). Accelerated Reader. *Knowledge Quest, 30*(4), 53–55.

Harvey, S., & Goudvis, A. (2000). *Strategies that work: Teaching comprehension to enhance understanding.* Portland, ME: Stenhouse.

Kerns, G. (2003). Accelerated Reader: Lasting effects. *Journal of Adolescent & Adult Literacy, 47*(1), 4.

Krashen, S. (2004). A comment on the Accelerated Reader debate: The pot calls the kettle black. *Journal of Adolescent & Adult Literacy, 47*, 444–445.

Paul, T., VanderZee, D., Rue, T., & Swanson, S. (1996). Impact of the Accelerated Reader technology-based literacy program on overall academic achievement and school attendance. *Reading and Writing Quarterly, 15*, 197–211.

Pavonetti, L., Brimmer K., & Cipielweski, J. (2002). Accelerated Reader: What are the lasting effects on the reading habits of middle school students exposed to Accelerated Reader in elementary grades? *Journal of Adolescent & Adult Literacy, 46*(4), 300–312.

Prince, R., & Barron, D. (1998). Technology and reading, part II: Computer-based reading programs and rewards: Some misleading intentions. *School Library Media Activities Monthly, 114*(8), 48–50.

Tardrew, S. (2003). Accelerated reader: Lasting effects. *Journal of Adolescent & Adult Literacy, 47*(1), 4.

Topping, K., & Paul, T. (1999). Computer-assisted assessment of practice at reading: A large scale survey using Accelerated Reader data. *Reading and Writing Quarterly, 15*, 219–232.

Vollands, S., Topping, K., & Evans, R. (1999). Computerized self-assessment of reading comprehension with the Accelerated Reader: Action research. *Reading and Writing Quarterly, 15*, 197–211.

Zimmerman, S., & Keene, E. (1997). *Mosaic of thought: Teaching comprehension in a reader's workshop.* Portsmouth, NH: Heinemann.

Technology Meets Literature: Meeting Authors Through Their Blogs

Teri Lesesne

Nearly 2 years ago, I made a resolution to begin writing my own blog (**www.livejournal .com/users/professornana**) as one way to let people know about the books that I was reading and what I thought about them. A web log, or blog, seemed to be something relatively simple that would permit me to readily reach a wide audience.

I thought that some former colleagues and students would visit the blog from time to time, but basically I was creating one for my own use and benefit. To my surprise, I connected with a whole new community through this simple blog. I discovered a whole new world of friends and colleagues—others who kept blogs for a variety of reasons. As it turns out, many of these new friends were writers of children's and young adult literature. There they were, writing about books and related issues for all the world to see. What a terrific asset to anyone who lives and breathes books.

Technology has now made it possible for all readers to connect to authors in new and incredibly intimate ways. So, in this column, let us take a journey into the land of bloggers and meet some of the authors whose blogs can make their more traditional writing more meaningful. Here are a handful of sites featuring talented writers for children and young adults. Most sites are blogs of individual writers, but also included are a few association sites that provide links to many authors' blogs.

YA (young adult) author Gail Giles (*Shattering Glass, Dead Girls Don't Write Letters*) maintains a blog at **http://notjazz.livejournal.com/**. Giles writes about her writing process, as well as about her life outside of the novel, offering readers an incredible insight into the person behind the books. Giles is witty, opinionated, and heartfelt in her postings, ranging from the work of her fellow writers to the loss of her beloved pet. Note, too, that authors frequently talk about works still in progress on their blogs so that vis-

First published in *Teacher Librarian*, June 2006, Volume 33, Number 5

itors know what to expect down the road.

Mary Pearson, author of *A Room on Lorelie Street*, maintains her blog at **http://mary-ohhh.live journal.com/**. Like Gail, Mary is quick to offer kudos to her fellow authors for the awards and honors that their books receive. Quotes that touched her, photos from her travels, and other odds and ends fill her entries, giving readers an inside look at this talented YA author.

Want to see inside the brain of a writer? Visit Brent's Brain (**http://brentsbrain.livejournal.com/**), the blog spot for Brent Hartinger, author of *Geography Club, Order of the Poison Oak,* and *The Last Chance Texaco*. Hartinger's site literally pulses with color; the firing neurons in the background of this author's blog might just reflect the new way of thinking and connecting to books and other media that you will encounter here.

If you have ever wondered what reaction an author has upon learning the news that he or she has won a prestigious award, wonder no more. Printz-winning author of *Looking for Alaska*, John Green, can be seen at his web site's blog (**www.sparksflyup.com/weblog.php**) receiving the phone call from Michael Cart and the 2006 Printz Committee informing him of his award. How much fun is this? Of course, there is more in the blog than just this life-changing moment, and readers will enjoy learning more about this gifted young author.

Cynthia Leitich Smith maintains her blog at **http://cynthialeitichsmith.blogspot.com/**, and it is loaded with tons of great information about this talented author and her interviews with leading figures in the field, including Newbery author Cynthia Kadohata, and newcomers Scott Westerfeld and Tanya Lee Stone (who maintains a blog of her own at **http://tanyaleestone.livejournal.com/**). Be sure to take some time to explore Leitich Smith's web site as well; at **www.cynthialeitichsmith.com/**, you will find a veritable cornucopia of information about children's and YA literature.

E. Lockhart, author of *The Boyfriend List* and *Fly on the Wall*, connects readers to a wide variety of links and topics at her blog site, **www.theboyfriendlist.com/e_lockhart_blog/**. Read about the books that she loved madly at age 14, important events in the lives of her friends and fellow authors, and lots of other subjects. While exploring this blog, make sure to read "Twenty-One Things You Don't Know About Me." One aspect common to many of these author blogs is that they contain lots of news about new books and book events, as well as personal remarks about writing. Lockhart is quick to acknowledge reviews of other authors' books and to comment on her own reading.

Neil Gaiman (**www.neilgaiman.com/journal/**) keeps a journal at his web site, where readers can see what books are forthcoming from this talented author of many, wide-ranging books. Graphic novels, picture books for older readers, sci-fi, and fantasy are all products of Gaiman, whose novel *Coraline* is still a huge hit with middle school kids whom I talk to in Texas.

Another interesting addition to blogs and online journals is the chance to see photos of the various authors. Gaiman's site has several professional and candid shots of himself. Some other blog sites use clip art in lieu of photos. Kids might be interested in seeing which icons various authors utilize—Laurie Halse Anderson has a red Converse sneaker, for instance.

Children's author Anastasia Suen's web site, **www.asuen.com/blog.central.html**, contains links to dozens of blogs maintained by children's authors and illustrators, including Erik Brooks, **http://erik brooks.blogspot.com/**, and Holli Conger, **www.agirlwhocreates.com/**. This is a great place to begin exploring the entire world of juvenile literature, as Suen provides links to editors and others in the field. Reading pieces from the blog of editor Arthur Levine (his is the imprint for the Harry Potter books, among others; **www.arthuralevinebooks.com/blog.asp**) can also provide interesting tidbits about trends and issues in the field of juvenile literature.

Instead of a single-author blog spot, a community of YA authors at **http://community .livejournal.com/yawriterblogs/** draws together an assortment of writers whose blogs serve as an introduction to YA literature. Postings about events and opportunities are also part of this community blog site.

Another community of interest is AS IF! (Authors Support Intellectual Freedom) at **http://asifnews.blogspot.com/**. The creation of this blogging community was spurred by the decision of a private school in Austin, TX, to refuse a sizable donation and to not remove the story *Brokeback Mountain* from its library. Several authors, including Brent Hartinger, Jordan Sonneblick, and Mark Williams, formed this community, which reports on various challenges to books. For some of the latest news on the challenges to books for young readers, visit this blog spot regularly. Postings here are from authors and others fighting against censorship of books.

The Children's Literature Web Guide, **www.ucalgary.ca/~dkbrown/authors.html**, provides links to dozens of children's literature and YA authors' web sites. Other links included at this site can take you to pages with information about various genre in the field, such as series books, folktales, and much more. Discussion boards and other resources are only a click away.

Monthly chats (sometimes more often) and much more are available at YA Authors Chat, **http://mysite.verizon.net/selimsa 803/default.html**. Anyone can join in the chats—even kids. The home page lists the upcoming chats with times (always on Tuesdays) and dates. There are, of course, links to other sites of interest.

And finally, the Society of Children's Book Writers and Illustrators has a rather comprehensive list of its members' web sites, **www.scbwi.org/links/mem_links.htm**. Check out Paul Zelinsky's newest project, or find out who the subject of Sue Macy's newest nonfiction book is. Browse the portfolio of illustrator Chuck Galey. There are more than a hundred links here to the fine folks who bring us the best on books.

BOOKS MENTIONED

Gaiman, N. *Coraline.* HarperTrophy, 2003. 0-380-80734-3.
Giles, G. *Dead girls don't write letters.* Roaring Brook Press, 2003. 0-7613-1727-9.
Giles, G. *Shattering glass.* Simon & Schuster, 2003. 0-689-85800-0.
Green, J. *Looking for Alaska.* Dutton, 2005. 0-525-47506-0.
Hartinger, B. *Geography club.* HarperTempest, 2003. 0-06-001221-8.
Hartinger, B. *The last chance Texaco.* HarperTempest, 2005. 0-06-050914-7.
Hartinger, B. *Order of the Poison Oak.* HarperTempest, 2005. 0-06-056730-9.
Lockhart, E. *The boyfriend list: 15 Guys, 11 shrink appointments, 4 ceramic frogs, and me, Ruby Oliver.* Random House, 2005. 0-385-73206-6.
Lockhart, E. *Fly on the wall: How one girl saw everything.* Random House, 2006. 0-385-73281-3.
Pearson, M. *A room on Lorelie Street.* Henry Holt, 2005. 0-8050-7667-0.

(52)

Literacy Links: New Literacies: Toward a Renewed Role of School Libraries

Marlene Asselin

The notion of "new literacies" is appearing increasingly in the news; in literacy research, journals and books; and in preservice and inservice teacher education. What does *new literacies* mean? How do new literacies relate to school libraries? What does new literacies teaching and learning look like? How can teacher-librarians take a leadership role in including new literacies in the school literacy curriculum?

WHAT ARE THE NEW LITERACIES?

What was counted as literacy a generation ago (let alone 500 or 1,000 years ago) has changed dramatically. To function effectively in society now requires more than basic reading and writing with "old technologies" or print materials. Today, in the workplace, in our communities, and in our private lives, we use a variety of print and electronic technologies to communicate and learn. In recent decades, literacy researchers began to examine the many different ways of reading and writing in cultures and groups other than those of white Western upper-middle class. This work forms the foundation of the concept of "multiliteracies." Literacy is now conceived as being both more expansive and more complex than ever before.

New literacies refers to the unique ways of reading and writing with the new technologies of information, communication, and multimedia. While many adults are learning how to be comfortable with new technologies, today's youth have been "bathed in bits since birth" (Tapscott, 1998) and regard technology as an inherent and integral means of creating themselves and the world. As Alvermann notes, "Digital culture locates adolescents in new ways—ways that necessarily challenge earlier views on what counts as literacy, for whom, and when" (2002, p. ix). Many students are well practiced in technical skills such as

First published in *Teacher Librarian*, June 2004, Volume 31, Number 5

word processing and managing software; however, researchers have identified intellectual skills where they need help: searching and locating information on the Internet, comprehending hypermediated text and critically evaluating online information (Kinzer, 2003; Leu, 2002; Todd, 2004).

As well as technical and intellectual competencies, new literacies include social abilities necessary for living in today's diverse and multicultural world. Thus, critical literacy perspectives should also shape new literacies education (Street, 2003). Critical literacy theorists emphasize that students should be taught not only to learn with and through information but, most importantly, to learn about the political, economic, and cultural production and use of information. Thus, students should investigate such questions as "Who posed this information problem? Why was it adapted and others precluded? How was the resultant information solution arrived at? What role did the resources I used play in the investigation and construction of the solution?" (Kaptize, 2003, p. 52).

HOW DO NEW LITERACIES RELATE TO SCHOOL LIBRARIES?

New literacy skills should certainly sound familiar to teacher-librarians as key aspects of information literacy. In our school systems, new literacies are being incorporated into mandated curriculum in both the language arts and ICT (information and communications technology) domains. School library programs already include relevant learning outcomes (but are limited in the critical literacy competencies); however, their curriculum is not mandated. As is the situation in some other areas of literacy education, the school library field and the literacy research community are working apart from each other. I recently presented a paper at a major literacy research conference outlining the extensive research on information literacy in the school library literature. Attendees at my session were both surprised at its existence, and, at the same time, recognized the obvious reason why intellectual aspects of new literacies would be such a strong area in the library field.

WHAT DOES NEW LITERACY TEACHING AND LEARNING LOOK LIKE?

Although researchers know it when they see it, they are just beginning to articulate the particular components that comprise new literacy learning environments. Consider the elements in the following list (Kist, 2001):

- ongoing, continuous use of multiple forms of representation;
- explicit discussion of symbol usage, past and present;
- students in ongoing meta-dialogues in an atmosphere of cognitive pluralism;
- a balance of individual and collaborative activities;
- evidence of student engagement;
- a balance of choice and collaborative activities;
- work centered around projects; and
- evidence of a breakdown of traditional teacher and student roles.

HOW CAN TEACHER LIBRARIANS TAKE A LEADERSHIP ROLE IN INCLUDING NEW LITERACIES IN THE SCHOOL LITERACY CURRICULUM?

Implications from the new literacies perspective extend those described in my last column on information literacy. In your school's literacy study groups, begin with teachers' current understandings and gradually develop shared knowledge of practical instructional strategies.

1. Guide teachers to represent their current understandings of and attitudes towards new literacies. Based on other professional development projects focused on the integration of new literacies into literacy programs, I suggest framing initial discussions around these points: (a) the relationship between traditional and new literacies; (b) which curriculum area(s) new literacies belong in; (c) what pedagogy of new literacies looks like.

2. Develop or find lessons that are relevant to the students and curriculum in your school that illustrate each of the four major competency areas of new literacies (locating, comprehending and evaluating online information, and critical analysis of information). Lessons should be at different learning levels—primary, middle, secondary—depending on your teachers' needs. You can find a multitude of ideas online that can be adapted to your particular context. Explore the CyberSmart School Program (2004), ideas in the New Literacies section of the International Reading Association's (2004) *Reading Online*, and other sites listed at the International Association of School Librarianship's (2003) web site section, Links to Educational Resources. Lessons can be adapted to different degrees of collaboration between the teacher and teacher-librarian.

3. Build a professional resource base for teaching and learning new literacies. Construct it as an online resource on your school library web site and include resources for both teachers and students.

4. Model and debrief collaborative planning, instruction, and evaluation of new literacies education. With the study group, reflect on the strengths and weaknesses of these pilot collaborations, and refine and revise the teaching process as appropriate. Showcase success to all stakeholders. Begin teaching new literacies with one teacher and add as teachers' interest and confidence increases.

REFERENCES

Alvermann, D. (Ed.). (2002). *Adolescents and literacies in a digital world*. New York: Peter Lang.

CyberSmart School Program. (2004). Retrieved January 5, 2004, from **www.cybersmartcurriculum.org/home/**

International Association of School Librarianship. (2003). Links to educational resources. Retrieved December 15, 2004, from **www.iasl-slo.org/edresources.html**

International Reading Association. (2004). New literacies. *Reading online*. Retrieved February 16, 2004, from **www.readingonline.org/newliteracies/lit_index.asp**

Kapitze, C. (2003). Information literacy: A positivist epistemology and a politics of outformation. *Educational Theory, 53*(1), 37–53.

Kinzer, C. (2003). The importance of recognizing the expanding boundaries of literacy. *Reading Online, 6*(10). Retrieved February 3, 2004, from **www.readingonline.org/electronic/elec_index .asp?HREF=/electronic/kinzer/index.html**

Kist, W. (2001). Searching for new literacy classrooms: An invitation. *Reading Online, 5*(1). Retrieved November 20, 2004, from **www.readingonline.org/newliteracies/lit_index.asp?HREF=/new literacies/kist/index.html**

Leu, D. (2002). The new literacies: Research on reading instruction with the Internet and other digital technologies. In S. J. Samuels and A. E. Farstrup (Eds.), *What research has to say about reading instruction* (pp. 310–336). Newark, DE: International Reading Association. Retrieved January 31, 2004, from **www.sp.uconn.edu/~djleu/newlit.html**

Street, B. (2003). What's "new" in New Literacy studies? Critical approaches to literacy theory and practice. *Current Issues in Comparative Education, 5*(2). Retrieved January 11, 2004, from **www.tc .columbia.edu/cice/articles/bs152.pdf**

Tapscott, D. (1998). *Growing up digital: The rise of the net generation*. New York: McGraw Hill.

Todd, R. (2004). Adolescent information behaviours. In M. Manning and S. La Marca, (Eds), *Reality bytes: Information literacy for independent learning*. Carlton, Vic.: School Library Association of Victoria [in press].

⑤③

Literacy Links: Dramatic School Library Literacy Programs

Keith McPherson

Last month, I quietly entered a colleague's elementary school library resource center and stood transfixed upon seeing a blur of activity and hearing a cacophony of "cawing." It seems I had stepped into a murder of crows desperately trying to get a "frozen" duck and a "frozen" goose to either blink or move! The interesting part was that the intensity of the crows' actions was so riveting that neither the birds, nor their teacher, nor their teacher-librarian had noticed my entrance.

By now the title of this article and the activity I've just described has alerted you to this month's literacy links topic, drama in the school library resource center. The above activity involved a grade four class' dramatic interpretation of the teacher-librarian's reading of the picture book, *Don't Fidget a Feather*, by Erica Silverman (1994). In the story, two best friends, a duck and a goose, use a freeze-in-place game to determine who is "the best" no matter how much the woodland animals pester them (when I came in, the crows were having their turn), even if one of the animals involved a hungry fox! The point of this "dramatic illustration" is to make you think about how drama and literacy are connected, and how this relates to the school library resource center.

WHY DRAMA IN THE SCHOOL LIBRARY'S LITERACY PROGRAM?

Many grade K–12 teachers and teacher-librarians know through first hand experience that drama provides students with very powerful, often nontextual, context in which to build new meanings and avenues for representing and communicating understandings (Worthman, 2002). Similarly, most school districts' language and literacy standards and curriculum reaffirm these experiences and encourage the use of drama as another powerful form of communicative expression (New Jersey Department of Education, 2005; British Columbia Ministry of Education, 1996; Ontario Ministry of Education, 2005; Texas Education Agency, 1998). Current examples of language and literacy research and projects indicate that drama is effective for: (a) stimulating imagination and shaping powerful writing contexts (Schneider & Jackson,

First published in *Teacher Librarian*, April 2005, Volume 32, Number 4

2000); (b) promoting social and emotional development of students through oral communication (Evans, 2004); (c) engaging children in critical interpretive readings of text (Hertzberg, 2003); (d) promoting reading comprehension (Rose, Parks, Androes, & McMahon, 2001); (e) engaging students who struggle with reading traditional print-based narrative structures (Morado & Rosalie, 1999); and (f) enhancing students' social skills and overall academic learning and achievement (Arts Education Partnership, 2002).

Furthermore, a growing number of literacy experts (Armstrong, 1994; Eisner, 1997; Greene, 1997; Leland & Harste, 1994) argue that by increasing children's opportunities to learn and communicate using *less* textual and "verbocentric" modalities (e.g., drama, music, painting, etc.), we also increase their opportunities to build knowledge and increase "marginalized" and "at-risk" language learners' chances of successfully acquiring, communicating, and representing knowledge. Similarly, by developing a school library literacy program that embraces multiple modalities for knowing and communicating—in this case drama—the school library also becomes a model of literacy instruction that values the expansion of the communication potential of all learners.

WHAT ABOUT DRAMATIC DRAWBACKS LIKE NOISE?

Noise, space, and resources are the biggest concerns teacher-librarians face when integrating drama into their school libraries. I have had many neighboring teachers and school staff close their doors in an effort to shut out particularly noisy library drama sessions. Teacher-librarians should always be alert to noise and activity levels in their resource center and ensure that students are well within appreciable decibel levels. As well, I highly recommend alerting neighboring teachers and staff to potential "noisy drama days," or try developing activities in your school library that are much quieter. The following are some suggested ideas for reducing noise:

- Pantomime dramatic interpretations.
- Use vignettes or freeze frames to capture interpretations of books or experiences.
- Move the noisy drama activity to a gym, music, or band room.
- Have students assist you in alerting the class to increasing sound.

Space is always an issue in most school library resource centers. In many cases the arrangement of fixed furniture combined with inadequate floor space eliminates the possibility of conducting any drama that requires a large "stage" or any sort of gross body movements like wide arm and leg gestures. Again, temporary relocation to another room is one recommendation. I made the following five changes to my current resource center that has opened significant amounts of floor space, allowing me to accommodate drama sessions: (1) installing locking castors on tables; (2) acquiring lightweight stackable chairs; (3) installing industrial wheels on low-level shelves; (4) replacing computer stations with laptops; and (5) mounting the library's presentation equipment from the ceiling (e.g., computer projector and TV).

Fortunately, the most required resource for integrating drama into your school library literacy program is your students' imagination. There is still the demand for superbly illustrated traditional fiction and nonfiction resources (e.g., books, videos, posters, newspapers, etc.) with which to stimulate their imagination and to activate background knowledge, but, by and large, such resources are used only as prompts. Incidentally, being an elementary school educator, I firmly believe that a variety of puppets are a staple when infusing dramatic experiences into the school library literacy program.

BIG BOOK DRAMA

My copious use of references in this article does not indicate drama expertise on my part. On the contrary, it is because I have little experience "doing drama" that I draw heavily on the authority of such experts. But as many educational drama colleagues teach us (e.g., Tchudi & Mitchell, 1999), drama expertise and experience is usually not essential for a great deal of classroom drama. Much of the required expertise can be acquired by attending drama workshops, reading literature on infusing drama throughout the curriculum, starting with low-risk drama activities, and, most importantly, spending our energy in creating safe classroom and school library resource center environments that value imagination.

The following is an example of an engaging low-risk drama activity recently introduced to me—"The big pop-up book": Read the class a picture book containing a variety of characters like Silverman's (1994) *Don't Fidget a Feather* (elementary) or Wiesner's (2001) *Three Pigs* (middle school and secondary). Next, draw an imaginary outline of a VERY big book on the floor (maybe 10 feet by 10 feet). Indicate to the class that this big book is also a pop-up book and that they are going to be the pop-up characters as you read. Assign students to be the characters for certain pages. Ask the students to think about what pop-up shapes they'll be when you turn to their page. Now, ask the students who have the characters on the next page to lie down inside the book outline. Read the text for the next page, and using your imagination, pretend to turn the page in the book upon which the characters pop up and take their shape. Ask the class to comment on the positive manners in which the pop-ups have captured and expressed their segment of the story. Now, have the next set of characters for the next page lie down and repeat the process until the end of the story. The goal of this activity is to encourage children to use their imagination to physically represent actions, feelings, and characters in the story while you assist the rest of the class to develop their visual acuity in identifying effective methods of using the human body to express and communicate story elements.

THE IMPORTANCE OF DRAMA IN THE SCHOOL LIBRARY LITERACY PROGRAM

Whether using puppets to read a picture book or interpreting Shakespeare on stage, effective teaching practice and educational research indicates that drama strengthens students' literacy development. The inclusion of drama in the school library literacy program, then, actively demonstrates this understanding while sending a clear message to the school that an effective and progressive language arts program must be supportive of a variety of communication styles and meaning-making approaches. As I noted the day I walked into that dramatic flurry of grade four crows, drama in the school library resource center is an engaging, motivating, and creative meaning-making activity that further reinforces the school library as a place valuing all voices and multiple ways of being literate.

REFERENCES

Arts Education Partnership. (2002). *Critical links: Learning in the arts and student academic and social development*. Retrieved February 25, 2005, from the Arts Education partnership web site: **http://aep-arts.org/CLhome.html**

Armstrong, T. (1994) *Multiple intelligence in the classroom*. Alexandria, VA: The Association of Supervision and Curriculum Development.

British Columbia Ministry of Education (1996). *Language arts integrated resource package: Grade 7–communicate ideas and information (presenting and valuing)*. Retrieved on March 11, 2005, from the Province of British Columbia, Ministry of Education's web site: **www.bced.gov.bc.ca/irp/**

elak7/7compre.htm

Eisner, E. (1997). Cognition and representation: A way to pursue the American Dream? *Phi Delta Kappan, 78*(5), 349–353.

Evans, A. (2004). Communication through performance. *Literacy Today, 39*, 8.

Greene, M. (1997). Metaphors and multiples: Representation, the arts, and history. *Phi Delta Kappan, 78*(5), 387–394.

Hertzberg, M. (2003). Engaging critical reader response to literature through process drama. Reading Online, Retrieved February 24, 2005, from **www.readingonline.org/international/inter_index .asp?HREF=hertzberg/index.html**

Leland, C., & Harste, J. (1994). Multiple ways of knowing: Curriculum in a new key. *Language Arts, 71*(3), 337–345.

Morado, C., & Koenig, R. (1999). Miniperformances, many stars! Playing with stories. *Reading Teacher, 53*(2), 116–124.

New Jersey Department of Education. (2005). *New Jersey Core Curriculum Content Standards for Language Arts Literacy.* Retrieved March 11, 2005, from the New Jersey Department of Education's web site: **www.state.nj.us/njded/cccs/s3_lal.htm**

Ontario Ministry of Education. (2005). *English: The Ontario curriculum, grades 9 and 10.* Retrieved March 11, 2005, from the Ontario Ministry of Training, Colleges and Education's web site: **www.edu.gov.on.ca/eng/document/curricul/secondary/english/englful.html#ENG1D**

Rogers, T., & O'Neill, C. (1993). Creating multiple worlds: Drama, language, and literary response. In G. E. Newell & R. R. Durst (Eds.), *Exploring texts* (pp. 69–89). Norwood, MA: Christopher-Gordon.

Rose, D. S., Parks, M., Androes, K., & McMahon, S. D. (2001). Imagery-based learning: Improving elementary students' reading comprehension with drama techniques. *Journal of Educational Research, 94*(1), 55–63.

Schneider, J. J., & Jackson, S. A. (2000). Process drama: A special space and place for writing. *Reading Teacher, 54*(1), 38–52.

Silverman, E. (1994). *Don't fidget a feather.* New York: Simon & Schuster.

Tchudi, S., & Mitchell, D. (1999). Classroom talk, drama, and performance. In *Exploring and Teaching the English Language Arts* (4th ed., pp. 314–337). New York, NY: Longman.

Texas Education Agency. (1998). *Texas essential knowledge and skills for English language arts and reading,* and *Texas essential knowledge and skills for Spanish language arts and English as a second language: Subchapter C, high school.* Retrieved March 11, 2005, from the Texas Education Agency's web site: **www.tea.state.tx.us/rules/tac/ch110_128c.html**

Wiesner, D. (2001). *The three pigs.* New York: Clarion Books.

Worthman, C. (2002). *"Just playing the part": Engaging adolescents in drama and literacy.* New York: Teacher's College Press.

Literacy Links: Visual Literacy and School Libraries

Keith McPherson

Recently I watched the third Harry Potter movie, *Harry Potter and the Prisoner of Azkaban*, and was disappointed with the cinematic interpretation of the book. The filmmakers completely eliminated one of my favorite scenes, the quidditch championship match, and one of my favorite characters, Nearly Headless Nick. Unlike the first two Harry Potter movies, for which I thought the producers captured the books' essential imagery, the third Harry Potter movie was so vastly different to my own visualizations that I concluded the producers had not read the book!

The point of this anecdote is not to debate the validity behind movies bringing fresh visual interpretations to books, but to illustrate the innate ability humans have for bringing texts (defined here as any symbol system used to convey meaning, including traditional alphabetic print and script, images, body gestures, drama, music, etc.) alive in their "mind's eye" through mental pictures. Whether "reading" page-bound printed text or visual texts (e.g., film, photographs, paintings, drawings, charts, graphic arts, maps, graphs), people make sense of various texts by creating their own unique set of mental images. Often these images expand the reader's understandings as they coalesce with, build upon, and recreate images from previously read texts (Keene & Zimmerman, 1997). For some students, these mental pictures prompt responses that are best expressed in drawings, paintings and other graphic art forms aside from page-bound text (Millard & Marsh, 2001). This ability to see, to comprehend and to think, re-create, and communicate graphically is termed *visual literacy*.

The creation of mental images during and following the "reading" of texts has become a hot topic in educational literature on reading comprehension. Research by Beers (1998) found that reluctant readers were unable to create mental pictures from printed text and became frustrated with their inability to bring texts alive in their "mind's eye." Similarly, Keene and Zimmerman concluded, "The propensity to create vivid images during reading correlates highly with overall comprehension" (1997, p. 129). Unfortunately, they also noted that "too often in school [students have] been conditioned to pay attention only to the lit-

First published in *Teacher Librarian*, December 2004, Volume 32, Number 2

eral interpretation of text" (p. 140). Millard and Marsh (2001) further argued that by privileging the written word above all other forms of communication in the literacy curriculum, educators ignore the complex social and cultural contexts of language, limit students' (and especially visual learners') opportunities to communicate using multiple communication forms, and hinder students' ability to critically engage with the images that predominate their world (e.g., Internet, television, computers).

VISUAL LITERACY IN THE SCHOOL LIBRARY

Not convinced that teachers and teacher-librarians were actively suppressing their students' visual literacy, I decided to conduct informal interviews with four local teacher-librarians (three elementary and one secondary) attending classes at the university where I instruct. All four indicated that though their libraries were rich sources of key visuals ranging from laminated posters to historical films, many of these visual resources were either untouched or used by teachers to stimulate student writing. Rarely were school library visuals used to stimulate students' talk about the images that they formed in their minds, or to encourage students to graphically represent their understandings. One teacher-librarian stated that this was because "our school's mission is to get our kids reading and writing."

INTEGRATING VISUAL LITERACY INTO THE SCHOOL LIBRARY

Knowing that the development of students' visual literacy skills has a positive effect on reading comprehension and provides students with a choice of modes in which to make sense of their social and cultural contexts, the question arises: How can teacher-librarians improve their own and their students' visual literacy skills? Following is a brief list of practical suggestions taken from Begoray (2003), Keene and Zimmerman (1997), and Millard and Marsh (2001) aimed at improving teachers' and students' visual literacy skills:

• Begin by developing your own visual literacy skills through careful observations and visual records (e.g., travel photo journals).

• Attend conferences and workshops on improving your and your students' visual literacy.

• Initiate and maintain conversations on visual literacy with other knowledgeable adults.

• Model risk taking to your students by demonstrating your own developing visual skills.

• Bring examples of your community's authentic use of visual literacy (e.g., computer graphic designers, draftpersons, billboard advertisers, local artisans) into the school library.

• Develop a deeper understanding of your students' learning preferences by scheduling sufficient time to talk to them (and their parents) about these preferences.

• Use a reader's workshop approach to evoke mental images.

• Start by using interesting but relatively unchallenging short passages of fiction to model for your students how the creation of mental images from text "helps the reader to understand the text deeply" (Keene & Zimmerman, 1997, p. 142).

• Encourage students to participate in whole-group discussions to develop a reflective awareness of their own and each other's mental images and how these images help them "see" or comprehend the text.

• Gradually move to conferences and then small groups where students are encouraged to think aloud and share the mental images they created while reading.

• Provide students with opportunities for constructing meaning using a variety of response options (e.g., sculpture, drama, drawings, painting, speech) rather than always insisting their writing be "front and center" and completed first.

• Provide students with "more time to think about the processes involved in finding ideas, composing and expressing meaning, rather than being hustled from one skills-based target to the next" (Miller & Marsh, 2001, p 61).

• Call upon university and college experts to conduct professional development sessions on visual literacy.

One of the keys to being successful at developing your and your student's visual literacy abilities is to "remember that you are not alone in seeking more understanding about how to integrate viewing and representing into your content area lessons" (Begoray, 2003, p. 194). Many colleagues like yourself are just beginning to integrate visual literacy into their school library programs and would be glad to share their experiences and ideas with you. It is through this sharing and incorporation of best literacy practices that the school library resource centre will continue to be "literally" visualized as the heart of the school.

REFERENCES

Beers, K. (1998). Choosing not to read: Understanding why some middle schoolers just say no. In K. Beers & B. Samuels (Eds.), *Into focus: Understanding and creating middle school readers* (pp. 37–63). New York: Christopher Gordon.

Begoray, D. (2003). Integrating the literacies of viewing and visually representing with content reading. In J. Richards & M. McKenna (Eds.), *Integrating multiple literacies in K–8 classrooms: Cases, commentaries, and practical applications* (pp. 190–209). Mahwah, NJ: L. Erlbaum Associates.

Keene, E., & Zimmerman, S. (1997). A mosaic in the mind: Using sensory images to enhance comprehension. In *Mosaic of thought: Teaching comprehension in a reader's workshop* (pp. 123–143). Portsmouth, NH: Heinemann.

Millard, E., & Marsh, J. (2001). Words with pictures: The role of visual literacy in writing and its implication for schooling. *Reading, 35*(2), 54–61.

PART VI

Learning Leadership: Partnerships

Why Should Principals Support School Libraries?

Gary Hartzell

Principals should support school libraries because it is in both their students' and their own best interests to do so. Quality library programs can enhance student achievement, and informed, committed teacher-librarians can help principals enhance their own administrative practice.

STUDENT ACHIEVEMENT

Improving student achievement is a vital principal interest, but many principals overlook libraries and teacher-librarians as potentially powerful instruments in that work because they have not been educated to the library's value, and school library research rarely appears in administrator publications (Wilson & Blake, 1993). Consequently, principals often leave library potential untapped despite 50 years of research evidence that effective library programs—when led by active, involved teacher-librarians—can have a discernible positive impact on student achievement *regardless of student, school, and community demographics.*

The evidence is drawn from elementary, middle, and high school studies reaching back to the 1950s. While the volume of evidence alone is cumulatively persuasive, the most recent research is especially powerful because its authors statistically controlled for demographic differences among the schools they studied—a feature missing in the pre-1990 research. This is important because the evidence is largely derived from statistical correlation studies, which cannot unequivocally prove causation. Correlation research can, however, identify relationships and degrees of association among variables. Cause-and-effect probability is strengthened if similar correlations appear in multiple settings over time, which is what occurs here.

Most effectively illustrated in recent work by Lance and his associates in Colorado (Lance, 2001; Lance & Loertscher, 2001) and by Smith (2001) in Texas, the research identifies statistically significant positive correlations between (a) student achievement levels on various types of standardized measures

First published in *Teacher Librarian*, December 2003, Volume 31, Number 2

and (b) library services and school librarians displaying these 11 characteristics:

Library program characteristics
- large, varied, and up-to-date collections;
- one or more full-time qualified librarians;
- library support staff large enough and skilled enough to free certificated librarians from routine clerical duties and to allow them time to teach, to collaborate with teachers, and to engage in leadership activities outside of the library;
- free student and teacher access to the library during and beyond school hours;
- networked computers providing student and faculty access to catalogs, licensed databases, and the Internet;
- budget adequate to support the previous five items;
- staff commitment to teaching;
- individual student library use well beyond scheduled class visitations; and
- information literacy instruction integrated into the curriculum.

Teacher-librarian characteristics
- extensively collaborates with teachers; and
- extensively involved in curricular, organizational and operational school leadership activities outside of the library.

Of particular interest is the recent evidence (Lance & Loertscher, 2001) that the positive effects of library programs increase when the teacher-librarian's traditional role is expanded to include involvement well beyond the library. One great barrier to full library utilization is a lack of faculty awareness of what the library and teacher-librarian have to offer. Exposure to and experience working with effective teacher-librarians is a first step in correcting that deficiency.

ADMINISTRATOR SUPPORT
Role expansion allows teacher-librarians to deliver additional important services, such as research support for administrators. Freed from clerical duties and aware of developing challenges and opportunities through their extra-library involvement, teacher-librarians can draw on the Internet and subscription databases to supply principals with up-to-the-minute information on any given topic in planning sessions and prior to any board, faculty, parent, or business partner meeting. Consistent access to such information can only result in improved administrative decision-making.

Teacher-librarians also can support targeted faculty and student groups, including counselors (White & Wilson, 1997); beginning teachers (Barron, 1998); and at-risk (Bluemel & Taylor, 1991), latchkey (Feldman, 1990), and special needs youngsters (Wesson & Keefe, 1995).

HOW CAN PRINCIPALS SUPPORT LIBRARIES?
Principals determine school library program quality as much as teacher-librarians do (Haycock, 1999; Oberg, 1995; Oberg, Hay, & Henri, 2000) because they influence or control each of the 11 factors listed above. Collection size, currency, service hours, staff size, and the employment of full-time qualified teacher-librarians and adequate support staff all are tied to the principal's budgeting decisions.

As important as money is, however, it's not the only measure of support. Equally important is the principal's role in creating a school environment where student library use and faculty/librarian interaction are valued and promoted (Campbell & Cordiero, 1996; Wilson & Lyders, 2001). For example, the teacher-librarian's opportunity to collaborate with teachers depends on the school schedule, which the principal controls (McGregor, 2002; van Dusen & Tallman, 1994) and on how effectively principals encourage collaboration among faculty members. Teachers collaborate more with other teachers and with teacher-librarians when principals openly encourage the practice in word and deed (Haycock, 1999; Oberg, 1997; Pounder, 1998; Tallman & van Dusen, 1994a; Tallman & van Dusen, 1994b). How often students use the library similarly follows how well principals encourage faculty/librarian collaboration and their willingness to financially support services beyond regular school hours. As instructional and curriculum leaders, principals also powerfully affect the extent to which information literacy instruction is embedded in the body of the school's curriculum and how the school addresses meeting state standards in varying disciplines.

Perhaps nowhere is a principal's power to affect library programs more apparent than in the extent to which the teacher-librarian has the opportunity to serve in a leadership capacity outside the library itself. Principals structure and populate the committees, teams and task forces that recommend and implement school policy and practice changes. Principals decide who will have the opportunity to take part in boundary-spanning activities to interact with district-level committees, parent groups, business partners, and community organizations (Hoy & Miskel, 2001; Morris, Crowson, Porter-Gehie, & Hurwitz, 1984). An active and committed teacher-librarian may be eager to engage in these activities, but will not have the chance unless the principal wills it. This is a particularly important point because many principals do not perceive teacher-librarians as potential faculty leaders (Schon, Helmstadter, & Robinson, 1991).

The school library elements that foster increased student achievement are interactive and their effects are cumulative. Even under optimum conditions, none is sufficient in itself. External leadership opportunities won't increase faculty interaction opportunities if the library is impoverished. The most extensive collection will not produce maximal achievement results unless qualified teacher-librarians and support staff are available to help students and teachers use it. Enrichment services to targeted groups and administrative research support cannot be delivered if teacher-librarians are saddled with clerical duties. Principal support must be broad based and multidimensional.

Albert Einstein is reputed to have said that problems cannot be solved using the same thinking that created them. How then can principals best support their libraries?

- educate themselves to library and teacher-librarian potential;
- reconfigure the teacher-librarian's job to maximize realization of that potential;
- hire high-quality, forward-looking, energetic, innovative librarians;
- provide budget resources adequate to new roles and demands; and
- effectively and accurately evaluate both the program and the teacher-librarian on jointly developed criteria recognizing school library work as simultaneously integral to instructional quality but distinct from classroom teaching itself.

FINDING ASSISTANCE

Principals interested in developing their libraries as instruments of school improvement can ask their teacher-librarians to assemble a research collection to share with board members, district administration and faculty. Ireland's (2001) regularly updated annotated bibliography of school library and academic achievement research is a useful starting point. Several ERIC digests (Lance, 2001; Lowe, 2000; Russell,

2000, for example) also point to original sources. A number of useful books (such as Lance & Loertscher, 2001; McQuillan, 1998; Wilson & Lyders, 2001) similarly identify and summarize research findings.

REFERENCES

Barron, D. (1998). In the beginning: Resources for school library media specialists helping new teachers. *School Library Media Activities Monthly, 15*(2), 46–50. (ERIC Document Reproduction Service No. EJ 577 807)

Bluemel, S., & Taylor, R. (1991). *Current status of Texas library media specialists' intervention with at-risk students.* Paper presented at the annual conference of the Texas Library Association. (ERIC Document Reproduction Service No. ED 335 046)

Campbell, B., & Cordiero, P. (1996). *High school principal roles and implementation themes for mainstreaming information literacy instruction.* Paper presented at the annual meeting of the American Educational Research Association, New York City. (ERIC Document Reproduction Service No. ED 399 667)

Feldman, S. (1990). *The library and the latchkey.* ERIC Digest. (ERIC Document Reproduction Service No. ED 331 512)

Haycock, K. (1999). Fostering collaboration, leadership, and information literacy: Common behaviors of uncommon principals and faculties. *NASSP Bulletin, 83*(605), 82–87. (ERIC Document Reproduction Service No. EJ 585 580)

Hoy, W. K., & Miskel, C. G. (2001). *Educational administration: Theory, research, and practice* (6th ed.). New York: McGraw-Hill.

Ireland, L. H. (2001). *The impact of school library services on student academic achievement: An annotated bibliography* (5th ed.). (ERIC Document Reproduction Service No. ED 450 807)

Lance, K. (2001). *Proof of the power: Recent research on the impact of school library media programs on the academic achievement of U.S. public school students.* ERIC Digest. (ERIC Document Reproduction Service No. ED 456 861). Available online: **http://ericit.org/digests/EDO-IR-2001-05.pdf**

Lance, K., & Loertscher, D. (2001). *Powering achievement: School library media programs make a difference—the evidence.* San Jose, CA: Hi Willow Research and Publishing.

Lowe, C. (2000). *The role of the school library media specialist in the 21st century.* ERIC Digest. (ERIC Document Reproduction Service No. ED 446 769). Available online: **http://ericit.org/digests/EDO-IR-2000-08.shtml**

McGregor, J. (2002). Flexible scheduling: How does a principal facilitate implementation? *School Libraries Worldwide, 8*(1), 71–84.

McQuillan, J. (1998). *The literacy crisis.* Portsmouth, NH: Heinemann.

Morris, V., Crowson, C., Porter-Gehrie, C., & Hurwitz, E., Jr. (1984). *Principals in action: The reality of managing schools.* Columbus, OH: Charles E. Merrill.

Oberg, D. (1995). Principal support: What does it mean to teacher-librarians? In *Sustaining the vision: Selected papers from the annual conference of the International Association of School Librarianship*, Worcester, England (pp. 17–25). Kalamazoo, MI: International Association of School Librarianship. (ERIC Document Reproduction Service No. ED 400 834). Available online: **www.slis.ualberta.ca/oberg_support.htm**

Oberg, D. (1997). The principal's role in empowering collaboration between teacher-librarians and teachers: Research findings. *Scan, 16*(3), 6–8.

Oberg, D., Hay, L., & Henri, J. (2000). The role of the principal in an information literate school community: Cross-country comparisons from an international research project. *School Library Media Research, 3.* (ERIC Document Reproduction Service No. EJ 618 497). Available online at: **www.ala.org/Content/NavigationMenu/AASL/Publications_and_Journals/School_Library_Media_Research/Contents1/Volume_3_(2000)/Volume_3_(2000).htm**

Pounder, D. (Ed.) (1998). *Restructuring schools for collaboration: Promises and pitfalls.* Albany, NY: SUNY Press.

Russell, S. (2000). *Teachers and librarians: Collaborative relationships.* ERIC Digest. (ERIC Reproduction Service No. ED 444 605). Available online: **http://ericit.org/digests/EDO-IR-2000-06.shtml**

Schon, I., Helmstadter, G., & Robinson, D. (1991). The role of school library media specialists. *School Library Media Quarterly, 19*(4), 228–233. (ERIC Document Reproduction Service No. EJ 433 168)

Smith, E. (2001). *Texas school libraries: Standards, resources, services, and students' performance.* Austin: Texas State Library and Archives Commission. (ERIC Document Reproduction Service No. ED 455 850). Available online: **www.tsl.state.tx.us/ld/pubs/schlibsurvey/index.html**

Tallman, J., & van Dusen, J. (1994a). Collaborative unit planning—schedule, time and participants. *School Library Media Quarterly, 23*(1), 33–37. (ERIC Document Reproduction Service EJ 493 343)

Tallman, J., & van Dusen, J. (1994b). External conditions as they relate to curriculum consultation and information skills instruction by school library media specialists. *School Library Media Quarterly, 23* (1), 27–31. (ERIC Document Reproduction Service No. EJ 493 342)

van Dusen, J., & Tallman, J. (1994). The impact of scheduling on curriculum consultation and information skills instruction. *School Library Media Quarterly, 23*(1), 17–25. (ERIC Document Reproduction Service No. EJ 493 341)

Wesson, C., & Keefe, M. (Eds.) (1995). *Serving special needs students in the school library media center.* Westport, CT: Greenwood. (ERIC Document Reproduction Service No. ED 385 999)

White, M., & Wilson, P. (1997). School counselors and teacher-librarians: A necessary partnership for effective schools. *Emergency Librarian, 25*(1), 8–13. (ERIC Document Reproduction Service No. EJ 552 633)

Wilson, P. J., & Blake, M. (1993). The missing piece: A school library media center component in principal-preparation programs. *Record in Educational Leadership, 12*(2), 65–68.

Wilson, P. P., & Lyders, J. A. (2001). *Leadership for today's school library: A handbook for the library media specialist and the school principal.* Westport, CT: Greenwood Press.

Moving the Fence: Engaging Your Principal in Your School Library Program

Diane Gallagher-Hayashi

During a battle in Belgium in the midst of the Second World War, a particular soldier was killed. In the aftermath of the battle, his friends approached the local priest and asked if this soldier could be buried in the town's churchyard. The priest was torn; he could understand the desires of the friends of the soldier, but the soldier had not been a Catholic and it was forbidden to bury a non-Catholic in the consecrated churchyard. After some consideration, the priest decided to bury the soldier just outside the fence of the churchyard. Although this was not what the friends had hoped for, they had to be satisfied, as the priest assured them it was the best he could do. The war continued, then ended, and the soldier's friends moved on with their unit, and then their lives. Several years later, one of the friends returned to that small town in Belgium to seek out the grave of the soldier that had so bravely died. The friend searched and searched around the outside of the fence in vain. The soldier's grave seemed to have disappeared. Upset, the friend entered the church and was met by the very same priest he had spoken to on the day of the soldier's death. "Father, I've searched all around the outside of the fence. Where is my friend's grave?" "My son," the priest replied, "I thought long and hard about your friend, and finally, I decided to move the fence." (Vrooman, 2000)

Getting the support that teacher-librarians need for our school library programs is not always as easy or as straightforward as might be hoped. In many instances, it is a case of "moving the fence," as it is easier to build the program around the administrators than it is to expect them to move into "the churchyard."

First published in *Teacher Librarian*, June 2001, Volume 28, Number 5

THE PROGRAM

What makes a strong school library program? The Library Power Initiative, a 10-year, $45-million school improvement program, lists the following seven characteristics of a "more fully adapted school library media program" (Hopkins and Zweizig, 1999):

- leadership from the school administration (both principals and vice-principals)
- shared vision
- professional development programs
- ample planning opportunities
- adequate support staff
- complementary school reforms
- community and district advocacy

It is my contention that characteristics two to seven cannot exist without characteristic one: leadership from the school administration.

Shared vision. A shared vision of the school library program should fall in line with the shared vision of the school as a whole. As a result, the vision needs to be reached through professional in-service supported by the principal in collaboration with the teacher-librarian, classroom teachers, and other members of the administration.

Professional development programs. In order for workshops and in-service to occur during the school year, the principal must provide time and opportunity, thus encouraging and/or requiring staff members to take part in school library program-based professional development. In addition, teacher-librarians need time to be able to attend conferences, visit other school libraries with successful programs, and meet with other teacher-librarians and district staff.

Ample planning opportunities. Time for regular planning sessions between the teacher-librarian and classroom teachers is essential and must be supported by the administration in order to integrate the school library program into the curriculum. In addition, collaborative planning at the community level (e.g., local Parent Advisory Councils, the public library) is much more meaningful with the presence of the principal.

Adequate support staff. By hiring sufficient technical staff, the principal allows the teacher-librarian to focus on student learning and classroom instruction, rather than clerical duties. In addition, a strong and integrated system of volunteers must include recognition for their valuable contributions. The administration can provide some funding to support this recognition, as well as to show awareness of the assistance provided.

Complementary school reforms. Principals can choose to support school reforms that complement the school library program such as resource-based learning, critical thinking, and cooperative teaching. By providing in-service, and by modelling the target reforms, the administration can encourage the teaching staff to reform and improve their instructional practices.

Community and district advocacy. As the first line of communication between school district staff and the school, the principal is in an ideal position to foster advocacy at the district level. In addition, as the most visible member of a school staff, the community looks to the principal as the representative of the school, offering the principal a unique opportunity to develop advocacy at the community level.

THE UNINFORMED ADMINISTRATOR

It is clear, then, that the administration of a school plays a critical role in the development and mainte-nance of strong library programs. Yet, in spite of this information, and the recent research in Colorado, Alaska, and Pennsylvania which shows a strong correlation between such library programs and academic success, many principals still do not support their libraries and teacher-librarians. It is this apparent con-tradiction that prompted Hartzell to ask the following question in his 1997 article:

> Why don't teachers and administrators rally to support libraries? Even worse, why are they often the ones who, in fact, get behind library cuts? The answers to these questions are also simple.
>
> Many, perhaps most, of them do not understand the value and educational potential of libraries and li-brarians. It isn't that they don't like them, and they certainly aren't out to "get 'em." Mostly, it's just a mat-ter of indifference—and people regard as expendable those things about which they are indifferent.

The source of this indifference can be found in the syllabi of the principal training programs. Sadly, information regarding school libraries seems to be strictly in terms of law. Therefore, school libraries are viewed, consciously or unconsciously, as a source of potential trouble, rather than a support for academic achievement and a critical factor in the development of lifelong learning.

In a 1996 study by Wilson and MacNeil, 250 university administrator training programs were sur-veyed regarding the inclusion of school library programs in course work. Only 18% actually integrated school library information into their programs. In interviews with professors of these programs, most in-dicated that it was a good idea to include information on school libraries; however many felt that their course topics were already too packed with material to cover. Thus, after their training is complete, it does not occur to many administrators that they should be engaged in a meaningful way in their school's li-brary program.

"Once through their training, these educators get caught up in the imperatives of their own worlds and it becomes very difficult for them to expand the conceptual horizons established at the beginning of their careers" (Hartzell, 1997).

THE RETICENT TEACHER-LIBRARIAN

As a collective, teacher-librarians are a hardworking lot. While we may have been working hard, however, we have not been working "smart." If we are to indeed "move the fence" to include school administration in our library programs, and more specifically, in educational reforms such as resource-based learning, teacher-librarians need to examine our professional practices as colleagues in a larger system.

Teacher-librarians are often less visible in their schools than their co-workers in other departments and often isolated, in most cases there is only one teacher-librarian in most schools. In addition, teacher-librarians may take their lunch and breaks at different times than other staff in order to be available for students, thereby losing opportunities to "systematically build visibility, relationships, and influence with teachers and administrators" (Hartzell, 1997).

Another area in which many teacher-librarians are lacking is advocacy. We have not, in our training, learned how to be advocates for our programs. Therefore, traditional school library culture does not en-courage us to "toot our own horns," so to speak. Instead, we quietly go about our work, hoping to attract others, rather than promoting our own programs.

Many people prefer to believe that merit inevitably bestows recognition on the meritorious. We all are attracted to the notion that something of quality will enjoy support just because it is so obviously right. But research and experience show that while this idea is wonderfully attractive, it's also fundamentally flawed. (Hartzell, 1997)

The one exception to this shortcoming lies in teacher-librarians' ability to present information to each other. Many teacher-librarians regularly take part in conferences, write for professional journals and meet together to discuss what we are doing in our programs. On the surface, it may seem that we are reaching out to promote school library programs. The problem is that we are preaching to the converted. It is not other teacher-librarians who must be convinced; it is the administrators and classroom teachers. So our responsibilities are two-fold: to educate students in lifelong learning and information literacy skills such as resource-based learning, and to educate principals and classroom teachers in the importance of school library programs.

MOVING THE FENCE

Before a teacher-librarian begins to "move the fence," she must set goals. Possible goals might include

- to have the teacher-librarian's work viewed, by stakeholders, as critical to the success of the school;
- to build influence in the school and school district;
- to increase understanding of the role and job of the teacher-librarian;
- to include information on school libraries in training programs for administrators;
- to become more proactive in the cause of school libraries and reforms such as resource-based instruction and critical thinking at several levels.

Once the teacher-librarian has set some goals, several strategies can be adopted to achieve them.

RAISING EXPECTATIONS

Teacher-librarians generally have low expectations of their principals (Oberg, 1995). Teachers know that students will typically achieve or perform only to the level of expectation. Why should this not be the case with principals? Teacher-librarians must raise the expectations they hold for their administrators. This can be done in a number of concrete ways:

- Approach the principal with a positive attitude. Encourage her to demonstrate personal commitment to the school library program and resource-based learning with the attitude "Of course you want to support this—here's how we can do it."
- Approach the principal with solutions, not just problems. Try to show how he can support a budget for materials and technical staff. Introduce him to research supporting educational reforms such as resource-based learning, information literacy, and critical thinking.
- Make the principal aware of the depth and breadth of training for teacher-librarians and why continued training is so important. Invite her to join you at an in-service on educational reforms, or to sit in on coplanning meetings.
- Encourage the principal to use his role as school leader to enable the school library program. Make requests for support directly and in specific terms.
- Encourage the principal to hire classroom teachers already familiar with and supportive of resource-based learning and cooperative teaching. Volunteer to provide sample interview questions and appropriate answers.

• Encourage the principal to find solutions for classroom teacher preparation time other than assigning the teacher-librarian to the class. Suggest alternatives. List the strengths of the teacher-librarian. Outline the reasons why preparation time replacement is not the best use of these strengths and show how they could be used if not already engaged in "prep coverage."

• Encourage the principal to support flexible scheduling. Introduce him to research supporting the importance of reforms such as resource-based learning and teaching information literacy skills. Offer to organize parent volunteers.

MEET REGULARLY

Meeting regularly with the principal can help to build a positive and influential relationship between administration and the teacher-librarian. Such meetings can change the principal's perceptions of the school library program and help create support for professional growth and advocacy (Hartzell, 1997). Possible topics of discussion can include

• provincial/state standards;
• how the school library program fits into the overall program;
• the education required to be a teacher-librarian;
• what the teacher-librarian can provide beyond cataloging and checking out books, for example, curriculum planning;
• joint visits to a school library with an outstanding program to broaden the principal's understanding of what may be possible;
• setting joint goals for the school library (Wilson & MacNeil, 1998).

In addition to regular meetings with the principal, the teacher-librarian can initiate a task force with the purpose of evaluating the school library program and establishing a library policy. This committee should be composed of at least one of each of the following stakeholders:

• teacher-librarian;
• administration;
• classroom teachers;
• parents;
• students;
• district staff members;
• community members, such as public librarians.

The committee can address the program and policy through the following questions (Hopkins & Zweizig, 1999).

Common vision

1. To what degree is there a common vision of the role of the school library program in promoting student learning amongst the teacher-librarian, the administrators, teachers, parents, and community leaders?

2. How can district and school planning focus on promoting the use of the school library in ways that best support learning?

Professional development

3. What professional development activities relating to the school library program are available to the teacher-librarian, administrator, and classroom teachers?

4. How does district level professional development planning promote a common school vision of school library support for the curriculum?

Planning opportunities

5. How can collaboration between the teacher-librarian and classroom teachers be made a natural approach to instruction?

Leadership of administration

6. What leadership or support is offered for the school library program?

Support staff

7. To what degree does school library staffing support multiple activities for individual, small group and class use?

8. To what degree can the teacher-librarian be engaged in professional rather than clerical responsibilities?

School reforms

9. Do the educational initiatives promoted in the district and in the school emphasize areas that are compatible with the desired school library program such as resource-based learning?

Community and district advocacy

10. What community groups are currently or are likely to be interested in the school library program's role in promoting student learning (e.g., Parent Advisory Council, public library, universities, civic groups), and how can their interest be activated?

11. How can district level leadership for the school library program be encouraged and/or maintained?

BECOMING ACTIVE

We must become more proactive in our quest for support for educational reforms, such as, resource-based learning. It is important to do more than merely join a professional organization; teacher-librarians must have an active voice. We must call for more workshops on advocacy, and we must push our associations to put pressure on universities to make changes in training programs for teachers and principals (Hartzell, 1997).

At the district level, teacher-librarians can meet in local professional associations to brainstorm strategies for gaining support for programs. We must take part in and develop a strong and active network committed to ongoing professional development, mentoring, advocacy, and policy development (Oberg, 1995).

Individually, teacher-librarians can volunteer to lecture for principal training and teacher training classes, and we can offer our library as a site for a visit for such classes (Wilson & MacNeil, 1998). In addition, teacher-librarians can write articles and make presentations for educators other than librarians. We must put the ideas of reforms such as resource-based learning, information literacy, and critical thinking in front of principals and classroom teachers in nonthreatening way; we must show that these reforms are successful and available (Hartzell, 1997).

CONCLUSION
Teacher-librarians, through our programs, are the gatekeepers of reforms such as resource-based learning. Although the task may seem daunting, it is our responsibility to do as the priest in the small town in Belgium; we must move the fence to ensure that all stakeholders are included in supporting school library programs.

RESOURCES
Hamilton-Pennell, C., Curry, K. L., Rodney, M. & Hainer, E. (2000). Dick and Jane go to the head of the class. *School Library Journal Online.* Available at **www.slj.com/articles/articles/20000401_7475.asp**

Hartzell, G. (1997). The invisible school librarian: Why other educators are blind to your value. *School Library Journal Online.* Available at **http://206.236.152.83/articals/articals/19971101_5664.asp** and **http://206.236.152.83/articles/articles/19971101_5693.asp**

Haycock, K. (2000). School Libraries make a difference. *Teacher Librarian, 28*(1), 39.

Hopkins, D., & Zweizig, D. (1999). Power to the media center (And to the people, too). *School Library Journal Online.* Available at **http://206.236.152.83/articles/articles/19990501_6433.asp**

Lance, K. C. (2000). *How school librarians help kids achieve standards: The second Colorado study* [online]. Available at **www.lrs.org/pdf/lmc/execsumm.pdf**

LaRocque, L., & Oberg, D. (1991). The principal's role in a successful library program. *The Canadian School Executive, 11*(4), 17–21.

Manzo, K. K. (2000). *Study shows rise in test scores tied to school library resources* [online]. Available at **www.edweek.org/ew/ewstory.cfm?slug=28libe.h19**

Oberg, D. (1995). Principal support: What does it mean to teacher-librarians? *Sustaining the vision: A selection of conference papers, 24th International Association of School Librarianship Conference.* Worcester College of Higher Education, Worcester, UK, 17–25. Available at **www.ualberta .ca/~doberg/prcsuplhtm**

Vrooman, G. (2000). Stories, quotes and anecdotes. *AHA! 10*(1), 8.

Wilson, P., & MacNeil, A. (1998). In the dark: What's keeping principals from understanding libraries. *School Library Journal Online.* Available at **http://206.236.152.83/articles/articles/19980901_6372.asp**

(57)

Administrator's Perspective: Helping Leaders to Learn: Teaching Principals About School Libraries

Marla W. McGhee

Administrators matter when it comes to making important decisions about school libraries and their place, purpose, and function in the learning life of a school. Yet, most campus administrators do not learn much, if anything, about teacher-librarians or libraries during their preservice training.

In a 1996 survey of 250 graduate preparation programs, researchers discovered that most future principals are unlikely to learn about the library or the role of the teacher-librarian in their training programs (Wilson & MacNeil, 1998). When asked whether they spent any substantive time on the topic of school libraries, more than three-quarters of the program representatives said *no*. Only 18% of those surveyed integrated information about school libraries into the curriculum. What we can make of this then, is that *most* future principals, assistant principals, and superintendents are not learning about library programs prior to becoming campus or district leaders.

So, if most educational leaders don't learn about the power of the school libraries in their preparation programs, how can they become more aware of library standards and practices? Well, that's the good news. There are other opportunities for learning.

Consider, for example, my experience as a campus administrator. Several years after opening a school in a growing suburban district, our teacher-librarian, Barbara Jansen, handed me a copy of *Information Power: Building Partnerships for Learning* (AASL & AECT, 1998). The book was tabbed and dog-eared in several places where she especially wanted me to read and pay attention. And I did. I read about the importance of the library program and the role of the teacher-librarian as a teacher,

First published in *Teacher Librarian*, June 2005, Volume 32, Number 5

collaborator, and leader, and I learned how the principal must be knowledgeable about and supportive of the library program.

I watched and listened as Barbara began to use the information search process with students across the campus. She worked successfully with special-needs students and gifted learners, and she meaningfully and authentically implemented technology across the campus. I witnessed, first hand, model collaboration and cooperation between the library program and teachers at every grade level.

Luckily I went on to serve as principal in two other schools where I had the privilege and joy of learning from outstanding teacher-librarians—Carlin Gray skillfully rebuilt an ailing middle school library program, and Jill Stimson provided incredible professional development for teachers about the power of classroom-library collaborations.

So, my learning did not come from the university classroom; it came, instead, from the talented individuals I worked alongside. Now, as a professor working with preservice educational leaders, I have the opportunity to help our graduate students initiate their learning about libraries before they enter the leadership field. In our unit of study, students read the Texas standards for school libraries and then examine a program through observation and interviews. When we meet together in a seminar format in a local school library, we share our findings as well as explore several other broad concepts. We also interact with a practicing teacher-librarian and a district library media director who offer information and answer questions from the group. The other "big ideas" we promote and discuss are listed below.

• A teacher-librarian is a powerful teacher, not someone who simply checks out books or manages resources. The teacher-librarian can *and should* collaborate with classroom teachers to meaningfully infuse information and technology skills into and across the curriculum.

• The library program can have a profound impact on student learning *if* the teacher-librarian is available to plan and teach alongside teachers to integrate skills and promote literacy throughout the school.

• How campus leaders organize the school and manage organizational mechanisms can either promote *or impede* student learning and professional effectiveness.

• Look at the teacher-librarian's priorities in job responsibilities—if the duty helps students to master the curriculum and instills in them a lifelong love of learning and reading, then the responsibility is worthwhile. If not, then reconsider it.

Dr. Carl Glickman, one of our finest contemporary authors on issues of educational leadership, school improvement, and democracy in education, in his foreword in *The Principal's Guide to a Powerful Library Media Program* (McGhee & Jansen, 2005) reminds us of the importance of leader knowledge and support for school library programs.

Perhaps many school leaders think as I did as a school principal that the library is an important place but best left alone in the hands of competent professionals. I now understand that the result of such benign neglect is terrible underutilization . . . the culprits are not the librarians or teachers, as in most schools they respect each other. But they simply don't have the time to make the library media center central to teaching and learning. It takes steadfast and knowledgeable leaders to change this detachment to powerful collaboration.

May we all dedicate ourselves to becoming those steadfast and knowledgeable leaders who will help to promote active and effective libraries for all.

REFERENCES

American Association of School Librarians (AASL) & Association for Educational Communications and Technology (AECT). (1998). *Information power: Building partnerships for learning.* Chicago: American Library Association.

McGhee, M., & Jansen, B. (2005). *The principal's guide to a powerful library media program.* Worthington, OH: Linworth.

Wilson, P., & MacNeil, A. (1998). In the dark. *School Library Journal, 44*(9), 114.

Developing the Respect and Support of School Administrators

Diane Oberg

Gaining the respect and support of school administrators is the number one challenge facing school library professionals in the 21st century (Ishizuka, Minkel, & St. Lifer, 2002). The school library literature from its earliest years contains discussions of the role of the principal in school library programs, often centering on the notion of principal support. "The principal's support of the library as a vital part of the educational system is extremely important," Winifred B. Linderman wrote in an article entitled "What Should the School Librarian Expect of the School Principal?" in the December 1944 issue of *The School Review* (p. 614). This quote, from 60 years ago, could easily have come from a much more recent source.

WHY PRINCIPAL SUPPORT MIGHT BE LACKING

Principals have a critical role in the implementation of change in schools. The educational change research (see, e.g., Fullan, 1991, 1993) and the effective schools research (see, e.g., Rosenholtz, 1985, 1989) have helped us to understand the contributions of the principal in terms of vision building, evolutionary planning, empowering others, resource mobilization, and problem coping and monitoring. Effective principals are collaborative leaders who use these strategies to facilitate the transformation of school culture. Research in the school library field has shown that although teacher-librarians generally view principal support as being critical to the success of the library program (Haycock, 1995), they often have low expectations of principal support (J. M. Campbell, 1991) and rarely engage in the kind of activities that would increase their principals' understanding and support (Edwards, 1989).

A growing body of research from around the world centers on what principal respect and support involve (see Table 58.1). However, not surprisingly, not all principals respect and support the school library programs or teacher-librarians. In the worst-case scenario, the principal believes that libraries are basically warehouses, that teacher-librarians are fussy introverts whose most important role is selecting and

---

First published in *Teacher Librarian*, February 2006, Volume 33, Number 3

- Principal support was critical to school library program development (Baldwin, 1996; Charter, 1982; Gehlken, 1995).
- Principal attitude was positively correlated to school library program implementation (Corr, 1979; Turner, 1980).
- Principal support involved encouraging the school library program's use by teachers and students, integrating it into curricular work, and providing flexible scheduling (Farwell, 1999; Hellene, 1974; Yetter, 1994).
- Principals needed to serve as advocates for collaborative planning and information literacy instruction, especially if high school students were to become information literate (B. S. Campbell, 1995; Farwell, 1999).
- Principals rarely recognized the instructional role of the school librarian (Dorrell & Lawson, 1995; Hauck & Schieman, 1985; Kolencik, 2001).
- Many principals were hampered in their support for school libraries by lack of knowledge about the management and function of school libraries (Wilson, Blake, & Lyders, 1993).

Table 58.1. Principals and School Libraries: Research Findings

circulating materials, and that teacher-librarians are not leaders or proactive educators but service providers who merely respond to teacher or student requests.

Hartzell (2002) suggests some of the reasons that may underly the worst-case scenario. He points out that when information is limited, people tend to rely on stereotypes to make judgments. Teacher-librarians suffer from occupational invisibility, and the occupational socialization of principals rarely focuses on libraries or teacher-librarians. Teacher-librarians tend to be invisible because the nature of their work involves empowering others, and building relationships with other educators—including the principal—is limited by their physical isolation in the library and by scheduling.

Teacher-librarians also tend to be invisible because of their low profile in the educational literature. Principals often had limited exposure to the role of the teacher-librarians when they were students in school and when they were classroom teachers. Few had opportunity to learn about the role of the teacher-librarian in their education as teachers or as administrators. Additionally, media images rarely add positively to their perceptions of teacher-librarians or librarians in general.

Teacher-librarians' occupational invisibility is exacerbated by the low levels of librarianship education within the profession. When some members of a professional group lack appropriate professional education, their potential clientele are unsure about what to expect in expertise and quality of service, and the image and status of the whole group suffer from this uncertainty.

However, many teacher-librarians are visible leaders in their schools, and many principals are supportive of the work of their teacher-librarians; we can learn a great deal from those principals and their teacher-librarians. My own understanding of what is involved in gaining the respect and support of principals comes from over a decade of work as a teacher-librarian in three schools as well as from the research done by myself and others. Since the 1980s, I have been analyzing the professional literature and research literature dealing with the concept of principal support (see, e.g., Oberg, 1995).

With a colleague from the field of educational administration, I have conducted research, through interviewing principals, teacher-librarians, and district leaders in a district with exemplary school library programs, on how school culture facilitates school library programs (LaRocque & Oberg, 1991). Our case study of two teacher-librarians' establishing library programs in schools where the programs were new to them as well as teachers and principals expanded my understanding of the role of the principal in supporting the school library program and that of the teacher-librarian in gaining the respect and support of the principal (Oberg & LaRocque, 1992). Most recently, I was part of an international survey on the role of principals in supporting school library programs (Henri, Hay, & Oberg, 2002). Drawing on this research, I explore three questions:

- How does the principal support the school library?

• What do principals believe about the teacher-librarian and the school library program?
• How can teacher-librarians develop principal respect and support?

HOW DOES THE PRINCIPAL SUPPORT THE SCHOOL LIBRARY?

The research involving principals who support the school library program and the teacher-librarian indicates that principal support occurs through four key roles of the principal: that as a supervisor working directly with teachers, that as a model demonstrating personal commitment, that as a manager enabling the program, and that as a mentor providing visibility and importance. The first three roles focus on the principal's support for the school library program and the fourth, on the principal's support for the teacher-librarian.

As supervisors working directly with teachers, supportive principals outlined expectations for library use and provided professional development for teachers. These principals made it clear that teachers were expected to be involved in the school library program on an ongoing basis. For example, principals required that evidence of collaboratively planned projects be provided as part of the teachers' annual performance reviews (LaRocque & Oberg, 1991). Principals encouraged teachers' professional development in relation to the school library program by providing in-service education and by providing time for discussions related to the program in staff meetings.

As models demonstrating personal commitment, supportive principals explicitly expressed their understanding of the value of the school library program, and they were visible in the library. These principals conveyed the importance of the library program to teachers (Mandrusiak, 1993). They also interpreted the role of the school library program to students and parents and to district-level personnel and other principals (LaRocque & Oberg, 1991). They demonstrated an understanding of the value of information literacy and encouraged teachers to embrace it (Hay & Henri, 1995). Principals who also taught in the classroom modeled their commitment by using the program in their teaching.

As managers enabling the program, supportive principals created the school context and structures within which the principal, the teachers, and the teacher-librarian could work collaboratively (Nasedkin, 1989). These principals ensured the provision of adequate budgets for materials and information technology. They arranged for the flexible scheduling that allowed collaborative work between teachers and teacher-librarians (Hay & Henri, 1995). In addition to providing flexible schedules for the teacher-librarians, principals built into school schedules common planning times for teachers at the same grade or level. Some principals used their administrative time to release teachers from their classrooms for planning, and others used discretionary funds to hire substitute teachers or provide additional clerical support in the library (Oberg, 1997). Principals ensured that the school library program was integrated into the planning and evaluating structures of the school.

As mentors providing visibility and importance for the teacher-librarians, supportive principals spoke highly of the teacher-librarians in their schools and gave clear evidence that they trusted the teacher-librarians' knowledge and expertise. They made time for meetings with the teacher-librarians and encouraged their personal and professional development. Principals also provided resources to teacher-   librarians to allow release from teaching to undertake professional development (Hay & Henri, 1995; Oberg, 1997).

In both the professional and the research literature, the role of the principal in supporting the school library program is often referred to as simply "principal support." An analysis of the complex relationships between principals and school librarians has demonstrated that principal support involves at least four kinds of principal actions or role categories. Only one of these roles involves what is often seen as the core of principal support, which is that of ensuring collaborative planning time and providing funding for program resources.

WHAT DO PRINCIPALS BELIEVE ABOUT THE TEACHER-LIBRARIAN AND THE SCHOOL LIBRARY PROGRAM?

The research involving principals who support the school library program and the teacher-librarian indicates that these principals have positive perceptions about the contributions of the program and those of the teacher-librarian to teaching and learning in their schools. For example, principals in Alberta, Canada, who had teacher-librarians working half-time or more in their schools stated that teacher-librarians improved the quality of teaching and learning through in-servicing staff, cooperative planning and teaching, and collection development. The principals believed that teacher-librarians had valuable expertise and should inform their principals about issues affecting the potential of the library. The principals also believed that teacher-librarians should be key players in the school's information literacy programs and that an important part of the teacher-librarian's role in the school was providing appropriate in-servicing to the teaching staff. The strengths of their libraries, according to these Alberta principals, were the qualified and cooperative staff, the resources and equipment, and the focus on learning and curriculum.

These findings are consistent with those of studies in other parts of the world. Principals interviewed in an Australian study (Hay & Henri, 1995) expected their teacher-librarians to have a vision of the future development of the library's program and services and to have or develop the skills needed to be leaders in the school. They were prepared to support teacher-librarians as senior members of staff as long as the teacher-librarians met those expectations. Principals in a U.S. study (J. M. Campbell, 1991) reported that their major source of information about library programs was that of their teacher-librarians; that is, teacher-librarians provided professional development for principals as part of routine communications with principals.

HOW CAN TEACHER-LIBRARIANS GAIN PRINCIPAL RESPECT AND SUPPORT?

Teacher-librarians gain the respect and support of their principals in three key ways: by building their professional credibility, by communicating effectively with principals, and by working to advance school goals.

Teacher-librarians must build their credibility as experts in the field of teacher-librarianship as school leaders and as agents or catalysts of change. According to Alberta principals (Hay, Henri, & Oberg, 1998), being experts in teacher-librarianship means having qualifications in both education and librarianship. Teacher-librarians should have the same level of education as the other leaders in their schools; in most schools and school districts, school leaders are expected to have master's degrees. Expertise in librarianship brings to teaching and learning the core values of librarianship (including freedom of information and the right to privacy) as well as the practical knowledge required to deal with issues such as censorship, cultural diversity, and Internet filtering.

By contributing as school leaders to schoolwide initiatives and concerns, teacher-librarians build their credibility as educators and increase the willingness of others to work with them (Lance, 2001). When asked to list the tasks that the teacher-librarian does that are critical to the quality of teaching and learning, both principals and teacher-librarians identified those of in-servicing staff (Oberg, 1997), cooperative planning and teaching, and collection development. The teacher-librarians put the strongest emphasis on the cooperative planning and teaching role, whereas the principals put the strongest emphasis on the in-servicing role.

Time and money alone are not sufficient for meaningful change. Principals and teacher-librarians need to have a shared view of the potential of the school library program as one that reaches beyond the library and into the teaching and learning of the whole school. Together principals and teacher-librarians need to develop a deep and rich understanding of resource-based and inquiry-based learning that will allow them to link these changes to restructuring efforts focused on improving opportunities for student learning. This may mean discussing the implication of research, such as studies showing that integrated resource-based instruction is the most effective means of acquiring information skills (Hara, 1997) and that it leads to improved levels of content knowledge (Todd, 1995).

Teacher-librarians must communicate effectively with their principals. Teacher-librarians need to begin by enhancing their principals' knowledge of the school library program and the role of the teacher-librarian. This includes clearly explaining the goals of the school library program and the teacher-librarian. Some studies have found that principals seemed uncertain about how to evaluate the success of library and information literacy programs (Hay & Henri, 1995; Wilson, Blake, & Lyders, 1993). However, where district, state, or provincial guidelines were made available to them, principals reported feeling confident in evaluating their teacher-librarian and the library program (Dekker, 1989; Wilson, Blake, & Lyders, 1993). Teacher-librarians also need to clearly explain their professional needs, in terms of both mentoring and professional development.

Teacher-librarians must work to advance school goals. Teacher-librarians should begin by knowing and promoting with others their principal's views of school goals. The principal needs to be able to see the teacher-librarian as an ally, not as someone with an endless list of demands and complaints. The teacher-librarian needs to be able to share the principal's worldview (or find another, more compatible assignment). Teacher-librarians should help their principals see the strong connection between library program goals and school goals, that a close alignment between the principal's vision and the teacher-librarian's vision is of benefit to both of them (Oberg, 2000). Principals have valuable resources to share with teacher-librarians; teacher-librarians need to be clear that they have valuable resources to share with principals. Together, the teacher-librarian and the principal can form a strong team.

Finally, teacher-librarians need to be patient and understanding of the evolution of the school library program. Gaining principal support can be a difficult task and may take several years of effort based on a planned approach and taking advantage of the opportunities that occur. With each new school assignment, teacher-librarians have to begin anew the work of communicating with the principal about their role and the school library program. Hartzell (2002) put it this way: "The only way to change principal perceptions is to assault them directly, repeatedly, and from a multiplicity of directions. Reshaping perceptions takes time and effort and commitment" (p. 106).

WORKING TOGETHER AS A TEAM

Research has shown that the principal is the key factor in the development of the collaborative school culture that is needed for a strong school library program. The principal gives support for the program and for those working to build the program. The principal provides opportunities for teachers to work and learn together. A foundation activity for any school is working together to decide on a vision for the school, a vision that clearly describes what it is that students are to learn and how they are to show what they have learned. This requires active leadership from the principal.

The expertise of teacher-librarians in information literacy, collaboration, and program design and implementation can provide a valuable contribution to teaching and learning. For example, teacher-librarians often begin their work in a school by analyzing the changes that will be needed in the ways that educators have traditionally organized and thought about teaching and learning. Teacher-librarians understand that teachers work from different philosophical bases or platforms, something that complicates the task of collaboration. They often initiate an explicit sharing and examination of these differing platforms. They are experienced in working with teachers to develop learning activities for students, and they are accustomed to working with others to develop schoolwide approaches—this requires active leadership from the teacher-librarian.

The active leadership of the principal and teacher-librarian team is facilitated by district support for collaboration. The support provided by school district administrators, school trustees, and district policy and administrative structures has been shown to be important in enabling principals and teacher-librarians to work together. This teamwork also appears to be much less difficult where teacher-librarians have access to a strong and active teacher-librarian network that is committed to ongoing professional education and mentoring as well as advocacy and policy development. Teacher-librarians need to be aware of and utilize professional networks throughout their professional lives; certainly, most principals are aware of and utilize their own professional networks. As has been pointed out (see, e.g., Haycock, 1992; Strachan, 1995), principals and teacher-librarians have a lot in common and a great deal to gain by working together.

REFERENCES

Baldwin, M. K. (1996). Enhancing learning through library and information services in K–12 education: A future search conference (Doctoral dissertation, Seattle University, 1995). *Dissertation Abstracts International, 56*(08), 2918A.

Campbell, B. S. (1995). High school principal roles and implementation themes for mainstreaming information literacy instruction (Doctoral dissertation, University of Connecticut, 1994). *Dissertation Abstracts International, 56*(03), 770A.

Campbell, J. M. (1991). Principal school library media relations as perceived by selected North Carolina elementary principals and school library media specialists (Doctoral dissertation, University of North Carolina, 1991). *Dissertation Abstracts International, 52*, 2336A.

Charter, J. B. (1982). Case study profiles of six exemplary public high school library media programs (Doctoral dissertation, Florida State University, 1982). *Dissertation Abstracts International, 43*, 293A–294A.

Corr, G. P. (1979). Factors that affect the school library media specialist's involvement in curriculum planning and implementation in small high schools in Oregon (Doctoral dissertation, University of Oregon, 1979). *Dissertation Abstracts International, 40*, 2955A.

Dekker, B. (1989). Principals and teacher-librarians—Their roles and attitudes regarding school libraries: Results of a survey of elementary schools in Ontario. *School Libraries in Canada, 10*(2), 32–37.

Dorrell, L. D., & Lawson, L. (1995). What are the school principals' perceptions of the school library media specialists? *NASSP Bulletin, 79*(573), 72–80.

Edwards, K. K. (1989). Principals' perceptions of librarians: A survey. *School Library Journal, 34*(5), 28–31.

Farwell, S. M. (1999). Profile of planning: A study of a three-year project on the implementation of collaborative library media programs (Doctoral dissertation, Florida International University, 1998). *Dissertation Abstracts International, 59*(11), 4042A.

Fullan, M. (1991). *The new meaning of educational change.* Toronto: OISE Press.

Fullan, M. (1993). *Change forces! Probing the depths of educational reform.* London: Falmer Press.

Gehlken, V. S. (1995). The role of the high school library media program in three nationally recognized South Carolina Blue Ribbon secondary schools (Doctoral dissertation, University of South Carolina, 1994). *Dissertation Abstracts International, 55*(11), 3338A.

Hara, K. (1997). A study of information skills instruction in elementary school: Effectiveness and teachers' attitudes (Doctoral dissertation, University of Toronto, 1996). *Dissertation Abstracts International, 57,* 3376A.

Hartzell, G. (2002). The principal's perceptions of school libraries and teacher-librarians. *School Libraries Worldwide, 8*(1), 92–110.

Hauck, P., & Schieman, E. (1985). *The role of the teacher-librarian in Alberta schools.* Calgary, AB: University of Calgary. (ERIC Documentation Reproduction Service No. ED262788)

Hay, L., & Henri, J. (1995). *Leadership for collaboration: Making vision work.* Paper presented at 61st International Federation of Library Associations Conference, Istanbul, Turkey. Retrieved August 11, 2003, from **www.ifla.org/IV/ifla61/61-hayl.htm**

Hay, L., Henri, J., & Oberg, D. (1998). The principal's role in developing information literacy: Findings from Australia and Canada. In S. Shoham & M. Yitzhaki (Eds.), *Education for all: Culture, reading and information—Selected papers of the 27th International Conference of the International Association of School Librarianship* (pp. 36–80). Seattle, WA: International Association of School Librarianship.

Haycock, K. (1992). Career alternatives: The teacher-librarian as school principal—A natural progression. *Emergency Librarian, 19*(5), 21–22.

Haycock, K. (1995). Research in teacher-librarianship and the institutionalization of change. *School Library Media Quarterly, 23,* 227–233.

Hellene, D. L. I. (1974). The relationships of the behaviors of principals in the state of Washington to the development of school library/media programs (Doctoral dissertation, University of Washington, 1973). *Dissertation Abstracts International, 34,* 3835A.

Henri, J., Hay, L., & Oberg, D. (2002). An international study on principal influence and information services in schools: Synergy in themes and methods. *School Libraries Worldwide, 8*(1), 49–70.

Ishizuka, K., Minkel, W., & St. Lifer, E. (2002). Biggest challenges for 2002. *School Library Journal, 48*(1), 50–53.

Kolencik, P. L. (2001). Principals and teacher-librarians: Building collaborative partnerships in the learning community (Doctoral dissertation, University of Pittsburgh, 2001). *Dissertation Abstracts International, 62*(05), 1784A.

Lance, K. C. (2001). Proof of the power: Quality library media programs affect academic achievement. *Multimedia Schools, 8*(4), 14–20.

LaRocque, L., & Oberg, D. (1991). The principal's role in a successful library program. *Canadian School Executive, 11*(4), 27–30.

Linderman, W. B. (1944). What should the school librarian expect of the school principal? *School Review,* 611–617.

Mandrusiak, S. J. (1993). *The role of the teacher-librarian as an informal instructional leader in addressing program continuity.* Unpublished master's project, University of Alberta, Edmonton, Canada.

Nasedkin, S. (1989). *The teacher-librarian/principal partnership in operating an effective school library program.* Unpublished master's thesis, University of Alberta, Edmonton, Canada.

Oberg, D. (1995). Principal support—What does it mean to teacher-librarians? In *Sustaining the vision:*

A selection of conference papers from the 24th Annual Conference of the International Association of School Librarianship (pp. 17–25). Kalamazoo, MI: International Association of School Librarianship.

Oberg, D. (1997). The principal's role in empowering collaboration between teacher-librarians and teachers: Research findings. *Scan, 16*(3), 6–8.

Oberg, D. (2000). Educating your principal: Lessons from research. *Teacher-Librarian Today, 6*(2), 24–28.

Oberg, D., & LaRocque, L. (1992). Learning to be a teacher-librarian: A play without a script. *Alberta Learning Resources Journal, 11*(1), 17–21.

Rosenholtz, S. (1985). Effective schools: Interpreting the evidence. *American Journal of Education, 53*(3), 352–359.

Rosenholtz, S. (1989). *Teachers' workplace: The social organization of schools.* New York: Longman.

Strachan, B. D. (1995). Crossing the hall: Teacher-librarianship as a route to school administration. *School Libraries in Canada, 15*(1), 10–15.

Todd, R. J. (1995). Integrated information skills instruction: Does it make a difference? *School Library Media Quarterly, 23*(2), 133–138.

Turner, P. M. (1980). The relationship between the principal's attitude and the amount and type of instructional development performed by the media professional. *International Journal of Instructional Media, 7*(2), 127–138.

Wilson, P. J., Blake, M., & Lyders, J. A. (1993). Principals and teacher-librarians: A study and a plan for partnership. *Emergency Librarian, 21*(1), 18–24.

Yetter, C. L. (1994). Resource-based learning in the information age school: The intersection of roles and relationships of the school library media specialist, teachers, and principal (Doctoral dissertation, Seattle University, 1994). *Dissertation Abstracts International, 55,* 1130A.

ACKNOWLEDGMENTS

This article grew out of presentations given in 2003 at the Alberta Library Conference in Jasper, Alberta, and at the American Library Association/Canadian Library Association Conference in Toronto. I acknowledge with thanks the contributions of the participants whose questions and comments helped to shape my thinking about this topic.

Beyond the Frontline:
Activating New Partnerships
in Support of School Libraries

Ray Doiron

I n the daily efforts of developing school library programs, there is no one better able to bring about change than a teacher-librarian working in partnership with administrators, classroom teachers, and students. The frontline is where the goals of school library policies and programs are realized. At the same time, there are other players "beyond the frontline," who have key roles to play in facilitating that change, in supporting school-based efforts and in championing the integrated school library program. My colleague, Judy Davies, and I spent over 20 years on the frontline as teacher-librarians in two successful elementary school library resource centers in Prince Edward Island. During the past few years, we have left those frontline positions and accepted new positions—Judy, as a consultant with the Department of Education and me, as a teacher educator at the University of Prince Edward Island. Throughout the transition from "being" a teacher-librarian to facilitating the role of teacher-librarians, I have been struck by the similarities in the work we do now and what we did as teacher-librarians and by how that frontline experience informs and influences our new work. This article outlines some of the similarities in the roles of the teacher-librarian, curriculum consultant, teacher educator, and administrators in general, and then describes new partnerships that can be nurtured when frontline teacher-librarians move into other educational roles.

SIMILAR ROLES IN DIFFERENT CONTEXTS

Teacher-librarians have four major components to the roles they play in the development of a school library program. They act as instructional leaders; they work in partnership with classroom teachers to develop curriculum; they champion the cause of school libraries through various advocacy programs; and they manage a budget, a support staff, and a set of learning resources. Curriculum consultants, teacher

First published in *Teacher Librarian*, February 1999, Volume 26, Number 3

educators, and administrators can be seen as playing much the same role, but at different levels of the system and within different contexts. A few examples will help to clarify the point.

INSTRUCTIONAL LEADERSHIP

1. Teacher-librarians work with a team of teachers in the school to actively create resource-based learning activities. They use a variety of teaching methods that integrate school library program goals; they lead the development of the school library program that includes a plan for information skills development and a school library mission statement.

2. Consultants work with a team of colleagues to lead the development of new teaching strategies, one of which includes resource-based learning. They work with district or provincial/state committees to make connections in curriculum development that include the goals of an integrated school library program. They run pilot projects that demonstrate how resource-based learning works; and they work to develop new programs and policies at the board or department level.

3. Teacher educators work with a team of colleagues to teach preservice teachers new teaching strategies that incorporate resource-based learning and the role of the school library. They lead the development of a faculty-wide view of information literacy; they teach courses using resource-based learning strategies and teaching methods common to school library programs; and they provide advice and input in new policy and program development by the Department of Education.

CURRICULUM DEVELOPMENT

1. Teacher-librarians work in collaboration with a school staff to design, implement, and evaluate a plan for teaching information skills and strategies within the overall school curriculum. They use cooperative planning and teaching to develop the curriculum; they sit on school committees in the areas of technology and new programs; and they collaborate in research projects.

2. Consultants work in collaboration with department colleagues to integrate school library program goals across the curriculum. They develop resource-based learning projects that demonstrate how it works and what it "looks" like; they work on curriculum committees to develop new programs and initiatives; and they collaborate in research projects.

3. Teacher educators work in collaboration with faculty colleagues to integrate school library goals into the teacher education program. They work with their colleagues to refine the teacher education curriculum to include a more visible role for school libraries and resource-based learning. They become involved in Department of Education curriculum committees deciding on new programs and new curriculum initiatives; and they collaborate with teachers, teacher-librarians, and consultants in research projects.

ADVOCACY

1. Teacher-librarians communicate news about the school library program through library newsletters, websites, Home and School notices, and parent memos. They keep principals and teachers up-to-date on school library issues; they promote various school library activities and special projects; they mount displays of work students have completed; they hold author visits, Library Week activities, and other promotional activities; and they lead professional development activities with staff and fellow teacher-librarians.

2. Consultants communicate across the school system through newsletters, teacher networks, listservs,

and other electronic routes. They keep the message front and center for administrators in schools and in the Department of Education. They share with other consultants examples of "best practice"; they promote school library issues by sharing articles and current information on resource-based learning; they lead professional development activities; and they make presentations at local and national conferences.

3. Teacher educators also communicate through local newsletters, electronic networks, and national and international journals. They advocate across the faculty for the role of the school library in teacher education; they incorporate resource-based learning projects/assignments into course work and share those with other faculty members and students. They make presentations at conferences and professional organization meetings and they disseminate research results.

MANAGEMENT

1. Teacher-librarians manage collection development, circulation, maintenance, and inventory of a wide range of print, nonprint, and electronic learning resources. They manage the school library facility on a daily basis; they manage the human resources that support the school library program; and they manage a budget for resources and the operation of the program.

2. Consultants maintain a district or province-wide perspective on learning resources and examine where and how they are accessed. They identify ways that resources can be shared; they identify what resources will be needed to support newly implemented programs; they make suggestions to other consultants for professional development and new resources; and they gather information on the state of collections and resources across the school system.

3. Teacher educators manage in-service course offerings for teachers that reflect their professional needs and interests. They examine resource issues through their research projects; they identify what resources will be needed to mount and maintain course offerings; they select resources for teacher education programs; and they develop awareness among preservice teachers that all teachers need resources and that the school library and a teacher-librarian are crucial to the success of their classroom programs.

When looking at these four areas, it is obvious there are similarities in what teacher-librarians do and in what consultants and teacher educators do. In fact, the management, organizational, and pedagogical skills honed as teacher-librarians working on the frontline provide an excellent base from which to work in other areas of the system. These skills transfer easily to many other instructional and administrative positions in the system. In fact, leadership, knowledge of curriculum, a commitment to advocate for change, and sound management skills are essential for all successful roles in the school system.

UNIQUE OPPORTUNITIES TO SUPPORT THE FRONTLINE

As well as sharing many similar characteristics in the nature of their work and the skills needed to do that work well, consultants and teacher educators who have been on the frontline of school librarianship have many unique opportunities to support and facilitate the integration of school library programs across the system. Their new work puts them in a unique position to affect change across the school system in a variety of ways.

HOLISTIC PERSPECTIVE

One of the first things you notice when moving from a teacher-librarian or classroom position into a consultant or teacher educator position is that your focus changes. Instead of being primarily concerned with the needs of your single school library, you take a more holistic view of the entire district or provincial/state system. You step back from the frontline and see the whole system and the set of issues facing all administrators, teacher-librarians, and classroom teachers. You see that, while some of your problems were unique, they are very similar to what others are facing. You are able to bring the firsthand experience of handling your own school library program to the wide-angled view provided from this shift in work. Your experience on the frontline gives you great credibility among your new colleagues and allows you to go back to the schools and speak with the authority of someone who has "been there" and knows what it is like slugging it out on the frontline. Consultants visit schools across the system and work with administrators and classroom teachers, while teacher educators work with preservice and in-service teachers from all aspects of the system. In both positions, you are able to see how problems may be unique to one type of situation, such as small schools trying to bring about the goals of an integrated school library program, and you learn that all educators are struggling with many of the same issues like how we bring about the change needed to fully realize our goals.

RESEARCH

As a teacher-librarian, you work many hours with teachers and students as they research topics of interest chosen from the curriculum. In some cases, teacher-librarians even conduct action research projects in their own school library related to the use of resources or the development of information skills. When you become a consultant or teacher educator, the opportunities for professional research really open up and become essential to your new work. In our former positions, we have developed a sound understanding of the research process by teaching others how to activate it and fully use it to solve information problems. In our new positions, this helps us understand more clearly the issues and problems that face teacher-librarians. You start to develop a research agenda that involves teacher-librarians in the process and that provides them with research findings that enhance and support what they do on a daily basis.

Doiron and Davies (1996) recently completed a province-wide study of the impact of the Prince Edward Island School Library Policy on school library programs in the province. All teacher-librarians and administrators were involved in the research process which included an extensive survey, 48 research interviews, and 2 days of professional development where the research findings and recommendations were presented and discussed. The findings of the study became the focus of professional development activities, as well as a solid foundation on which to advocate for improvements in programs and services at the Department of Education and the Faculty of Education. This study involved teacher-librarians in a very real way in determining what issues needed to be addressed and how best we could accomplish our goals. It helped clarify for consultants what needs to be done and facilitated a process in which all levels of the education system can come to terms with issues in school librarianship in our province.

TEACHER EDUCATION

Teacher-librarians are involved in many ways with "teacher education." They lead professional development activities at their schools and provide leadership in bringing about some of the major curriculum changes underway. However, most of their teaching time is spent with students who are looking for reading materials or who are actively involved with the information problem-solving process as part of their learning. Consultants and teacher educators at universities, on the other hand, work mostly with teachers and administrators. Since you come from the frontline of school librarianship, you have a unique opportunity to develop in all educators a clearer understanding of information literacy, resource-based learning, the role of the teacher-librarian, and how crucial school libraries are to achieving the learning outcomes set for all students.

As a consultant or university-based teacher educator, you become involved in setting short and long-term in-service goals for teachers and administrators. You design professional development workshops, as well as credit and noncredit courses, summer institutes and distance learning activities. While all of these undertakings may not center on school libraries, they provide useful opportunities to include the role of the teacher-librarian and the school library program in any course outline or in-service workshop. Consultants and teacher educators work with teachers and administrators in understanding new theory and acquiring new pedagogy, and they use their previous classroom or school library experience to lend credibility and authority to what they do. The same holds in work with preservice teachers who are often seen as the hope for the future or the new energy source needed to bring about change in the system. Having had frontline experience in the classroom or the school library, you are able to make connections for new teachers and show them how the goals of an integrated school library program will help them develop richer and more effective programs for their students. The benefits are not immediate but long-term change will definitely happen if we spend time teaching new teachers the importance of resource-based learning and school library programs.

INCLUSION

While working on the frontline, teacher-librarians are often frustrated by the way they are excluded from decision making that directly affects their daily jobs. New curriculum is brought in without any thought for the resources needed to support its full implementation; teacher-librarian positions are cut in a time when information literacy and the use of information technologies are paramount; and vast sets of learning outcomes are developed for schools with little evidence of the many information skills that learners will need for their future. Once you move to a consultant or teacher educator position, you find you suddenly have many opportunities to have the role of school libraries and teacher-librarians included at the level where decisions are made.

Consultants can lobby to have a teacher-librarian included on any curriculum committee; they can see that information literacy is included as a broad strand in any curriculum development; and they can find many subtle ways to have the role of the school library resource center included in all levels of their work. Teacher educators can see that resource-based learning, integrated school library programs, and the role of teacher-librarians are included in any courses they teach, and they can lobby to make these educational concepts pervasive across the Faculty of Education in which they work.

These efforts to include school libraries at the decision-making level are really attempts to infiltrate the system and change concepts many people have of the school library. Instead of being conceptualized as having only a peripheral role to play in education, former teacher-librarians can help educators understand the school library as part of our curriculum and as essential to achieving the ambitious sets of learning outcomes expected by the education system.

Teacher-librarians on the frontline will have to continue their individual efforts to lobby for change in their schools, but with more former teacher-librarians moving into administrative, consultant, or teacher educator positions, we should be able to have the school library included more fully so that we make sound educational decisions that will ensure that students develop the lifelong learning skills said to be crucial to their full literacy development.

NEW AND EMERGING PARTNERSHIPS

A reflection on these examples of the similarities between the work of teacher-librarians on the frontline of school librarianship and those who have moved beyond the frontline to take consultant or teacher educator positions, as well as the examination of the unique opportunities offered by these positions to further the goals of school librarianship suggest that we need to recognize and celebrate several new and emerging partnerships that hold the potential of forging real change across the system. These new partnerships reflect a growing awareness by administrators, trustees, parents, and governments that we have to find new solutions to the problems inhibiting the realization of the fullest potential for our education system.

CURRICULUM PARTNERSHIP AROUND INFORMATION LITERACY

The concept of information literacy is one that is quickly becoming a rallying point for many different groups. Information literacy is defined as "the ability to acquire, critically evaluate, select, use, create and communicate information in ways that lead to knowledge and wisdom. It encompasses all other forms of literacy." (Ontario Ministry of Education, 1995). Core curriculum documents developed in several regions of the country give information literacy a central role in the curriculum programs of the future. Technology innovators are recognizing that this concept needs to be integrated into their goals of having learners use technology in more meaningful ways. Teacher-librarians are very comfortable with the concept of information literacy and recognize it as a natural progression in our understanding of resource-based learning, research, and information skills. As consultants or teacher educators, we are gravitating to this concept as well, since it embraces several areas such as curriculum development, technology, lifelong learning, and the development of skills related to learning "how to learn." This seems to suggest that information literacy may be a unifying concept that can bring us all together to form a curriculum partnership in which consultants, administrators, teacher educators, teacher-librarians, and classroom teachers can work together for a common set of learning outcomes. In this way, one part of the system is not in competition with the other for value and support; all partners have a role and a place in the overall plan.

DEPARTMENT OF EDUCATION/FACULTY OF EDUCATION PARTNERSHIPS

For too long these two components of the education system have operated at arm's-length from each other. However, the experiences we have shared suggest that there is much that consultants at the Department or Ministry of Education and teacher educators in universities can do to work together and forge improvements in the programs and services available for students and teachers. Research partnerships are one of the more obvious connections. The school system is often criticized for making decisions that are not rooted in sound or relevant research, while university researchers are criticized for conducting studies that fail to consider the reality or context of classrooms and school libraries. Clearly it is a win-win situation when consultants and university personnel work together to develop research agendas that further our understanding of learning and pedagogy. In fact when we stop to consider the idea, there are many opportunities for all educators to come together and develop research that truly informs our work.

In addition to research, more communication is needed among faculties of education and departments of education, school districts and teacher organizations to develop better professional development programs for all educators. Whether the delivery is handled through credit or noncredit courses, workshops, or distance learning, all players need input into designing and presenting the program. Faculty can also partner with consultants and frontline teacher-librarians to make presentations and to develop various professional development activities.

NEW PARTNERSHIPS AROUND LEARNING RESOURCES

There is plenty of evidence that all players in education are forced to do more with less. It has become increasingly difficult to find the resources we need to deliver all the programs and services we have established. New solutions to the problems of resource provision need to be found. When you work in a school library, you see the immediate benefits to building a central resource collection that can be shared and used to the maximum by all students and teachers. This point is driven home even more emphatically when you move beyond that frontline. In the past, curriculum initiatives were often started without any evidence for what existing resources would be available or useful to support the program. As well, programs were implemented with a core set of materials, but without a clear plan for providing additional resources or maintaining any losses or destruction of materials. It seems duplication, inefficiency, and inconsistency abound, and when you have worked in a school library you become very frustrated when no collection development plans seem to exist at the district or provincial/state level to ensure that selection of resources is well done or that an efficient system is in place for acquiring resources and placing them in schools.

It is obvious there is need for improvement in this whole area. New programs today are more likely to include a greater variety of learning resources in several formats. Publishers promote these as "resource based," but this type of programming leads to several questions that still need to be addressed. Does every classroom require all available resources? Is it possible to centralize some of these in school or district collections? Is it possible to order some resources centrally and house them in school libraries? The point is that when curriculum is in the developmental stage, the use of teacher-librarians is essential. Consultants who have worked in school libraries can take a leadership role here and show how centralized selection, ordering, and delivery of resources makes sound economic and pedagogical sense. Luckily, there are ways technology can bring people together to streamline the whole resource management system. There are also several examples of integrated library systems where resources in public, school, academic, and specialized libraries are accessible to everyone through union catalogues and electronic networks. It makes all kinds of sense for people to work together to remove the duplication of effort and the waste of limited funding so that we get the most "bang-per-buck" and learn to share resources in new ways that are more effective and efficient.

NEW PARTNERSHIPS AROUND THE INTEGRATION OF TECHNOLOGY

Technology innovators are aggressive in their desire to make technology a priority across the school system. Business interests also want to see more attention and time given to teaching students how to use all types of instructional technologies. Educators at all levels of the system are spending great efforts to learn about new technologies and to find ways to integrate them into their teaching. School libraries are taking a leadership role here by recognizing the value of information technologies and by embracing their use in many management and instructional activities. This interest by so many players in using new technologies presents us with the unique chance to come together and combine our efforts and make real change happen.

Everyone needs to be talking about technology as an integrated part of curriculum. We need to keep the curriculum message loud and clear so that we link our use of technology with our expected learning outcomes. We want to be sure that educators use technology as part of the instructional program and not as something to learn for its own sake. We want to place technology within a holistic view of our system. This will mean bringing the players together and creating a partnership around technology where we work together and achieve common goals.

CONCLUSION

It could be said, "Once a teacher-librarian, always a teacher-librarian." It seems that no matter what position you take in our education system, once you have worked as a teacher-librarian to develop an integrated school library program, you learn valuable lessons about collaboration, resource management, instructional leadership, resource-based learning, integrating technology, and lifelong learning. These experiences form the foundation for your future work. Moving beyond the frontline is not abandoning the cause of school librarianship or cutting your connections with your teacher-librarian colleagues. It means you can bring to administrators, consultants, and teacher educators all of the positive energy you used to develop your school library program and you can take a new leadership role transferring the concepts inherent in the vision of an integrated school library program to a wider context and to all educators, which will help those ideas become pervasive throughout the entire education system.

REFERENCES

Doiron, R., & Davies, J. (1996). *Reflection and renewal in PEI school library programs*. A research report prepared for the Prince Edward Island Department of Education.

Ontario Ministry of Education and Training. (1995). *Information literacy and equitable access: A framework for change*. A draft document for discussion and response. Toronto: Ontario Ministry of Education and Training.

(60)

Strategy: Working With Your School Board Members

Carol-Anne Hutchinson

A unanimous vote? How can that be? I wrote my school board member a letter, and she should have supported me! A group referred to as the "school board" or the "school trustees" governs most school districts. These individuals are normally elected at the municipal level; however, there may be political appointments among them. They are not usually teachers, teacher-librarians, or school district employees. Rather, they are individuals who reside in the school district and have an interest in school district and policies. Many hold down full-time jobs in addition to the time they spend as board members. Most school board members are well-meaning. Often a personal situation has launched them into the world of school politics—perhaps a child with special needs, distaste for the educational direction of the district, or a calling to serve. These individuals are important, regardless what you think of their motives, education level, or their personalities. They are the governance of your school district, and they have the power to close schools, cut budgets, hire and fire senior administrators, and lobby provincial or state governments. Many of these individuals become quite familiar with politicians and bureaucrats at the municipal and state/provincial level. Never underestimate your school board member's influence or potential influence.

Get to know the school board member responsible for the school in which you work. In fact, at election time, do your homework! Contact candidates by phone or drop in for a personal visit and ask them questions about school libraries. When people are seeking office they are very willing to talk to you—they need you and the support you can bring. It has been my sad experience that most people seeking election to a school board know little about school libraries and the current situation in their district. This is an ideal time for you, the teacher-librarian, to educate and find an ally. Ask about funding: Is there designated funding? Is it global? How much? Put your suggestions forward. Ask about staffing: Does this potential board member know how school libraries are staffed? Have the discussion. Make sure that she or he knows. Give the recent history of the district and the province/state. By meeting this person in advance of the election, you

First published in *Teacher Librarian*, April 2002, Volume 29, Number 4

can provide a platform, accurate information, and a new healthy attitude of respect for school libraries. It also allows you to determine for whom to vote and for whom to encourage others to vote.

Don't limit your contact to one-on-one. Make sure that your school library association has members contacting every person running for election. Then the association, which is not normally connected to the school district, can take a political stand and recommend certain individuals, based on their school library views. Upon election, every single board member will have talked and met with one or more teacher-librarians, and together the board knows the names and faces of many teacher-librarians. This will be helpful down the road.

Don't approach your board members only when there is a problem. They have been elected to serve. They are interested in your schools and the life of these schools, and school libraries are a part of that. When you have an author visit, invite a board member. Invite a board member to read to students as part of a guest reading program. Invite your board members to special school library functions such as public speaking competitions and Remembrance Day/Veteran's Day ceremonies. You may be pleasantly surprised at the times they will accept and participate. Always have someone meet them at the door and make sure you introduce her or him formally. A follow-up thank you note is also a good idea.

Don't limit your invitations to special events. Have the school board member, or a small group of interested board members, take part in a resource-based learning activity. It is critical that they see and come to understand the kind of information literacy work that teacher-librarians do. Send them copies of projects and photos of projects of which you and the teachers with whom you have worked are proud. Do not hesitate to send interesting e-mails and articles to your board members about school library and literacy issues. This keeps them up-to-date, and keeps you in the communication loop with them.

We often complain that there are too many school committees. I cannot stress strongly enough that school board members be invited to serve on committees. No committee is too small! It can be your own school's library committee. If you don't have one, then form one and have the school board member serve as a standing member. If they don't have time to be a regular committee member, invite school board members to attend committee meetings when you know an important library issue will come forward. This level of participation helps the school board member to know and understand the educational, financial and political agendas that impact school libraries. And most importantly it provides you, the teacher-librarian, with support at a level higher than the school.

Remember to include your school principal in your plans. Under no circumstances should you lobby or reach out to a school board member "behind the back" of your administration. What could merely be a logistical oversight may be perceived as duplicity, so always seek the approval of your supervisors. It can be lonely out there in school library land, so don't do anything to further the isolation.

Attend your school district's school board meetings. Most school districts hold open, monthly meetings. Only at these meetings can you discover how the board members and administrative school district staff interact. Simply reading the agenda or the minutes of these meeting does not give you the perspective and feeling for the individuals' political alliances and the set of their political compass. It is also good for school library public relations for you to be interested in the governance of the school district. Then, when the time comes to make a presentation to the board or ask questions, you will be handled with courtesy and enjoy personal confidence as these are the same people who have been in your school library and served with you on committees.

Contact, connect, and communicate. Be visible and allow your board member visibility. Enjoy the process. Forge alliances and relationships, which will endure your whole career.

Catch Them (Preservice Teachers) While You Can!

Audrey Church

Research shows that preservice and practicing classroom teachers are typically unaware of the role of the teacher-librarian as a collaborative instructional partner and that university teacher preparation programs do little to address this issue. This article addresses one university school library instructor's approach to remedy this deficit by working through the Education Department using a multilayered approach—that is, meeting with preservice teachers early in their sequence of coursework, again during their junior year, and finally just before their going out for student teaching. The article concludes with a challenge to catch them—preservice teachers—while we can.

This year I began my 25th year in the school library profession. After 20 years as a building-level teacher-librarian in K–12 public schools, I am in my 5th year as a faculty member in the Department of Education of a 4-year public university. My experience tells me that the majority of classroom teachers do not have a clue as to what teacher-librarians can do to help them with instruction and their students with learning. My experience also tells me that the majority of preservice teachers are not learning in their teacher preparation programs about the benefits of collaborative partnerships with teacher-librarians. Neither practicing teachers nor preservice teachers see teacher-librarians as teachers and instructional partners, and this issue needs to be addressed.

Sadly, my personal experience is confirmed by the literature. In a study conducted at the University of Pittsburgh, School of Education (Getz, 1991), there was no difference in the attitudes of preservice education students and practicing teachers toward working cooperatively with the teacher-librarian in the instructional process: Although both groups viewed teacher-librarians positively, neither engaged in cooperative activities. Wolcott, Lawless, and Hobbs (1999) examined preservice teachers' beliefs about the role of the teacher-librarian, looking at whether teacher education programs are preparing tomorrow's teachers to expect and accept teacher-librarians' taking an active role in teaching. The researchers found that preservice teachers look to teacher-librarians more for information access and delivery than they do

First published in *Teacher Librarian*, June 2006, Volume 33, Number 5

for teaching and learning.

In a recent issue of *Knowledge Quest*, Chesky and Meyer (2004) report on a grant they received from the Institute for Library Information and Literacy Education, Kent State University, OH. Noting that "teacher education programs in our area do not portray the school library media center as a curriculum resource or the school librarian as a collaborative partner" (p. 20), Chesky and Meyer are targeting new teachers to make them aware of the collaborative instructional role of the teacher-librarian and the benefits that they and their students can gain from such collaboration.

Hartzell (2002) notes that "aspiring teachers are not provided with any model or expectation that school librarians should be regarded as partners in curriculum and instruction" (p. 2). Unless we tell them, they will not know. In fact, Getz (1991) recommends that "schools of education and schools of library science provide their students with instruction in school librarianship and offer opportunities to practice cooperative attitudes" (p. v). At Longwood University, we are attempting to do just that.

HIGHER EDUCATION

My first challenge as a faculty member in the Department of Education is to make fellow faculty members aware of the collaborative instructional role of the teacher-librarian in today's schools. Hartzell (2003) describes college and university professors as "a target that librarians have long neglected . . . the people who prepare new teachers and administrators, shaping their initial professional values in the process" (p. 41). No opportunity for advocacy with my colleagues therefore passes me by! From decorative reading and library theme pins worn daily, to bulletin boards outside my office promoting reading, libraries, and collaboration, to sound bites at department faculty meetings, I constantly "talk" libraries, teacher-librarians, and our role in today's schools. Once faculty members' awareness is raised, my next step is to volunteer to speak to their classes. I have a three-pronged approach to catch preservice teachers while I can: first, when our students are taking introductory education courses; second, when our partnership students are working out in the schools during their junior year; and third, when our student teachers are in their final semester before program completion.

INTRODUCTION TO THE TEACHING PROFESSION

All students in our education program are required to take an Introduction to the Teaching Profession course, typically during their sophomore year. This course provides

> an overview of teaching and schooling that addresses the foundations of education and the professional aspects of teaching. Emphasis on the history and philosophy of education; school organization; governance; legal and financial issues; teacher preparation; professional development; practicum preparation; and lesson planning. (Longwood University, 2004, Education Course Descriptions section, 3)

Each semester I volunteer to speak to the Introduction to the Teaching Profession classes.

My primary objective in visiting these classes is to raise awareness of what today's teacher-librarian can do to assist in instruction—laying the groundwork for library use early in their teacher preparation training—to broaden the perspective of these early preservice teachers. When I visit the Introduction to Teaching classes, I discuss the information specialist role of the teacher-librarian, pointing out that the teacher-librarian will be the one to provide them with professional, informational, and instructional resources. As an example, I share with them information that I think will be helpful to them as they move through teacher preparation coursework—information about copyright, databases that will be useful in their research, and web sites for lesson plans—and I emphasize that, once they are in schools, their teacher-librarians will be their sources for similar pertinent information.

However, as I talk with these teaching students, my primary focus is the teacher and instructional partner roles of the teacher-librarian. Many of the students have said to me, "Wow! I did not know that librarians did that," or "I did not know that the librarian would teach with me or would reinforce in the library what I might be teaching in the classroom." I give examples of areas that the teacher-librarian might teach, such as evaluation of potential sources for a project, and examples of areas that lend themselves well to partnerships between the teacher-librarian and the classroom teacher, such as author studies or research projects. We also discuss the importance of communication between the classroom teacher and the teacher-librarian. In this introductory course, I try to plant the seeds for an understanding of the active role of the teacher-librarian in today's schools.

PARTNERSHIP SCHOOLS

During their junior year, our students in elementary school and middle school teacher preparation participate in the partnership semester: This semester provides the second opportunity for me to talk with them about the importance of working and collaborating with their teacher-librarians. For the partnership experience, our students spend 4 days a week for the entire semester in an area school. Half of each day is spent in university methods coursework taught by a university professor onsite in the public school; the other half of the day is spent in the classroom with the teacher and class to which they are assigned. During their partnership semester, because they are actually working on a daily basis in the classrooms, our students are ready for concrete examples of how the teacher-librarian can assist them in curriculum and instruction. At the request of the university partnership professor, I spend about 2 hours talking with the partnership students.

Again, my approach is how the teacher-librarian can assist the classroom teacher as an information specialist and as a teacher and instructional partner. In small groups, students analyze content area standards and brainstorm ways in which the classroom teacher and the teacher-librarian could collaborate to address these standards. Going beyond reading and language arts, in the context of the various content areas, we discuss databases appropriate for the K–12 environment, such as SIRS Knowledge Source and the Gale Infotrac products, and information literacy skills that the teacher-librarian can teach students, such as information access and retrieval skills, note taking and paraphrasing skills, and methods for citing sources. These partnership students—preservice teachers—admit to thinking of the teacher-librarian in a different light following our discussions.

For our students in secondary school teacher preparation, there is no semester partnership experience, so I must work through various content areas to reach these future teachers. Again, advocacy and outreach are required to make the connection with colleagues in the College of Arts and Sciences—the professor "in charge" of science teacher education, English teacher education, math teacher education, and so forth. Given the opportunity to speak to these classes, I title my presentation "Powerful Partnerships @ [name of library]," "Every Student Succeeds @ [name of library]," or "10 Thoughts on How the TL and the Science Teacher [for example] Can Partner to Help Students Learn!" For each presentation, I have 10 discussion points—namely, to

1. provide quality resources,
2. tape public television instructional programs,
3. create connections to "good" teacher web sites,

4. create connections to professional journals,

5. assist students with the research process,

6. assist students with searching for resources effectively,

7. assist students with locating and evaluating resources for research,

8. teach students how to evaluate web sites and how to cite sources,

9. prepare pathfinders for students to help focus their research, and

10. encourage and promote ethical use of information.

For each point, I give specific content examples of how the teacher-librarian can partner with the secondary classroom teacher to affect instruction.

STUDENT TEACHERS

My third opportunity to speak to our preservice teachers to reinforce the concept of today's teacher-librarian as a collaborative teaching partner comes at the beginning of their student teaching semester. Here I use a modified CPR model, reminding them that teacher-librarians provide resources and promote reading but that they also assist with research process instruction and reinforce classroom learning (R); that teacher-librarians are all about collaboration, that communication is critical, that teacher-librarians have tremendous curriculum knowledge and provide connections to the world, and that we are colleagues in teaching (C); and that partnerships promote learning (P). I even give the student teachers a homework assignment: In their first days in their assigned school, they are to make it a point to meet with the teacher-librarian.

Concurrently, I post a message to our state school library association listserv, alerting teacher-librarians to fact that the student teachers will soon be in their schools. I remind them that a library convert early in the career may be a library user and supporter for life. Successful experience with a teacher-librarian during student teaching goes a long way to develop a library user for the remainder of an educational career. Teacher-librarians across the state respond, as evidenced by this reply to my posting:

> Thank you so much for doing this. If we get one of your students, I will be on the look out and go for him/her if they do not come to me. I will pass this on to my friend who is a 5th-grade teacher at another school; she is getting a Longwood Student. I once mentioned this idea to [the division contact for student teachers]. It really pleases me to see it coming from the college. (J. Koch, personal communication, January 18, 2004)

SPECIAL REQUESTS

Of course, there is always room for special requests, and I believe in capitalizing on every opportunity. One of our education professors invites me to address her junior level assessment classes each semester. She requests that I share with her students all the resources available on the Web for our state Standards of Learning—the SOL themselves, curriculum framework and scope and sequence guides, test blueprints, and sample test items from previous years' tests. As I demonstrate how to access these resources, I emphasize that my field is school library media, that I can share this information with them because I am an information specialist, and that teacher-librarians in their schools are just as in tune with the standards and curriculum as I am. I point out that teacher-librarians are concerned with student achievement and that they work to connect information literacy instruction to standards that are tested.

Last year, one of the partnership professors requested a special twist on my presentation for her elementary preservice teachers. In addition to asking me to talk about the teacher-librarian as an instructional partner, she asked me to focus on literature connections to curriculum standards, particularly in the areas of math and science. Elementary teacher-librarians from across the state shared almost 150 titles of books that connect with and reinforce concepts in various Standards of Learning. When I met with the partnership students, for math connections, for example, we discussed *Millions to Measure* (Schwartz, 2003; calculating measurement using the metric system) and *Mathematickles* (Franco, 2003; poems written in the form of mathematical problems, in seasonal themes). For science we discussed *Pumpkin Circle* (Levenson, 2000; life cycles of plants) and *All You Need for a Snowman* (Schertle, 2002; snow and winter weather). The preservice teachers left the session with useful information (books correlated to state curriculum standards) and with new ideas about ways to connect with their teacher-librarians.

Another special request sometimes comes from our special education program faculty. Of course, collaboration is integral to special education, but our professors ask me to specifically address the role of the teacher-librarian in collaboration with the special education teacher. We discuss how partnerships promote learning, how the teacher-librarian can serve as a resource person and information provider, and how the teacher-librarian can team-teach with the special education teacher.

MODEL COLLABORATIVE PARTNERSHIPS

To provide a model for collaboration and partnerships between teacher-librarians and classroom teachers, one project that we have instituted at Longwood is our Longwood Literature Page. Several publishing companies donate new children's books. Students in our school library program write book reviews; then preservice teachers in various methods courses write matching lesson plans. Students enrolled in the special education and communications disorders programs write adaptations for the lesson plans. Through cooperative ventures such as these, we work to promote the concept of collaboration and teamwork at the onset of these educators' careers.

CHALLENGES

Hartzell (2002) asserts that "once into positions as teachers . . . they [teachers] get caught up in the imperatives of their own environments, and it becomes very difficult for them to expand their conceptual horizons. Teaching is demanding" (p. 3). Our strategy should therefore be to catch them while we can. With repeated exposure to the concept of teacher-librarians as collaborative instructional partners while they are preservice teachers, we can affect these educators during the formative stages of their educational philosophy and thought processes. Hartzell notes that "few teacher-training programs contain any systematic instruction in how librarians might improve instruction, serve in staff development projects, assist with special student populations, or provide administrative support" (p. 2). Our challenge then, for those of us in college and university settings, is to connect, inform, and advocate. For those in libraries who are working as teacher-librarians, volunteer to speak with preservice teachers at colleges and universities; approach and convert preservice, student, and new teachers. We must use every opportunity to catch them while we can.

REFERENCES

Chesky, P., & Meyer, M. E. (2004). Creating partnerships: A grant-funded collaborative information literacy project. *Knowledge Quest, 35*(1), 20–21.

Franco, B. (2003). *Mathematickles*. New York: Margaret K. McElderry.

Getz, I. (1991). Inservice and preservice teachers' attitudes towards working cooperatively with school librarians (Doctoral dissertation, University of Pittsburgh, 1991). *Dissertation Abstracts International, 53*(03A).

Hartzell, G. (2002, June). *White House conference on school libraries: What's it take?* Retrieved August 22, 2004, from **www.imls.gov/pubs/whitehouse0602/garyhartzell.htm**

Hartzell, G. (2003). Ready . . . aim . . . aim again. *School Library Journal, 49*(2), 41.

Levenson, G. (2000). *Pumpkin circle.* Berkeley, CA: Tricycle Press.

Longwood University. (2004). Education 260: Introduction to the teaching profession. In *Longwood 2004–2005 undergraduate catalog.* Retrieved September 8, 2004, from **www.longwood.edu/catalog/ 2004/Educ.htm**

Schertle, A. (2002). *All you need for a snowman.* New York: Silver Whistle.

Schwartz, D. M. (2003). *Millions to measure.* New York: HarperCollins.

Wolcott, L. L., Lawless, K. A., & Hobbs, D. (1999). *Assessing pre-service teachers' beliefs about the role of the library media specialist.* (ERIC Document Reproduction Service No. ED437065)

PART VII

Learning
Leadership:
Issues and
Management

62

The Seven Most Critical Challenges That Face Our Profession

Doug Johnson

It certainly seems like our profession is in a state of crisis! Various places in different parts of the country are

- reducing school library programs and cutting professional and clerical staff;
- providing minimal budgets for library materials;
- supplanting "library programs" with "technology initiatives";
- closing university library programs; and
- establishing "teach to the test" curricula.

And you can probably add to the list.

However my sense is that most professions are facing one sort of crisis or another much of the time and similarly, school library programs in general have always been in a crisis situation. But at the same time, my sense is that there are as many vital, successful library programs in schools today as there have ever been.

Let's just face it, good school library resource programs may *never* be seen as a permanent part of the educational landscape. Gifted and talented programs, art programs, academic and athletic extracurricular programs, and even school counseling programs—anything in a school that goes beyond one teacher, 30 students, and a textbook—can and will be seen as nonessential by some decision makers.

I am not sure that this is a bad thing. Our very vulnerability demands that we as a profession need to continually find ways to strengthen our programs and roles. I would suggest we take a hard look at the

First published in *Teacher Librarian*, June 2002, Volume 29, Number 5

challenges we currently face and see how we can rise to meet them. Below I suggest seven areas where every teacher-librarian can and should take action.

1. Tying our library program goals to the larger goals of our educational system. Too many teacher-librarians create lovely programs that have very little to do with what transpires in the rest of the school. While I'm sure their library skills and activities do wonderful things for students, teachers and administrators are too often unaware of them and see little impact on the school's overall learning goals. Classroom instruction is and will remain the primary focus of education, and unless we have an impact on it, we will be seen as superfluous. Our library program goals must be directly aligned to the instructional goals of the district, building, and classroom. Sometimes I sense that we work very, very hard to climb one mountain only to find the rest of the school on a completely different peak.

While it is probably the most daunting part of our jobs, we must continually enhance our collaborative efforts with teachers. This is the only way that what we do in the library will tie directly to what is happening in the classroom. We need to work with *every* teacher on staff (not just the living, as we like to joke). That will only happen with initiative and persistence. Make it your goal to work one-on-one with four additional teachers *every* year. Hone those interpersonal skills, identify and articulate the areas where you can be seen as someone who can be helpful, and keep at it. Also, our best teacher-librarians are ones who serve on site-based councils, technology committees, and curriculum teams, and in other decision-making positions. The credibility established by serving as a "leader" often goes a long way in gaining acceptance by teachers in collaborative efforts.

2. Demonstrating and publicizing our effectiveness through accountability. While we certainly have responsibilities that go beyond direct student instruction, our role as a teacher of critical skills is the one that is the most important in an educational setting. In order to be seen as true teachers it is imperative we

• establish an integrated information/technology curriculum with clearly defined and measurable skill benchmarks by grade level;

• collaborate with teachers in designing and teaching units in which students learn, practice, and demonstrate those skills within a content area;

• collaborate with teachers in designing and administering the student performance assessment that accompanies those units; and

• report attainment of skills to students, parents, and community though progress reports, conferences, and public reports.

Perhaps the most challenging task we have ahead is helping our administrators and public understand how our information literacy curricula complement and support school accountability efforts that use standardized testing as a critical measurement. A publicity effort that informs those outside our profession about the findings of studies like those of Keith Curry Lance's Colorado studies needs to be undertaken by every district.

3. Remaining experts in helping others make meaning out of technology. Schools have made a rapid technological transformation. They have gone from institutions devoid of technology to institutions full of under-used, rapidly aging technology. Teachers need training, not just in basic productivity tools such as word processors and web page design, but in learning how to construct instructional units that help students master technology skills, content concepts, and higher-level thinking skills.

Thoughtful information literacy units can also teach most, if not all, technology competencies needed by students. Technology used to locate, assess, synthesize, and communicate information in order to answer questions and solve problems is technology used in its most powerful and meaningful way. Teacher-librarians must be seen as the experts in this use. We also need to make sure teachers and students are truly technologically literate: They know when technology is *not* the best solution to a problem as well.

New and changing technologies create a need for exceptional staff development opportunities for teacher-librarians. But if we demonstrate to our administrators that we will teach to our staff members what we have learned though workshops, conferences, and other training opportunities, we can justify receiving those extra staff development dollars.

We can also do some of the technology tasks in our buildings that are rapidly becoming very important. These tasks include web mastering, network management, and technician supervision. Remember that there is rarely a position that is indispensable, but there are specific tasks that *must* be done. Personally, I like to stay valuable by doing jobs no one else is willing or able to do.

4. Retaining our professional teaching status. The most distressing talk I hear revolves around decertifying the position of teacher-librarian. Not requiring a teaching license and certification in library science and educational media is too often seen as a quick fix for finding folks who can staff our school libraries. Along with the rest of the teaching profession, good teacher-librarians are in short supply in many areas of the country. An aging teaching profession, low retention rate of beginning educators, opportunities in the business world, and stress-related burnout are all contributing to this problem.

Yet our professional skills in constructivist teaching, authentic assessment, program management, material selection and organization, and information and technology ethics are growing, rather than diminishing, in importance. We must work with our boards of teaching and other certifying agencies to educate them in what we do, why our skills are vital to schools, and why total reliance on clerks and technicians will short-change students.

5. Attracting the best to our field. Each teacher-librarian's work reflects on all other teacher-librarians. Unfortunately many teachers, principals, and parents have never had the opportunity to work with an excellent teacher-librarian. But once they have, they understand and support the position. It's imperative that our profession actively recruits the best and brightest of teachers to our field. Each of us needs to encourage teachers we feel would make good teacher-librarians to consider this career path. And we need to encourage our postsecondary institutions to adopt a rigorous selection procedure for admittance into the school library certification program.

I am perhaps even more worried about the status of postsecondary library media education than anything else. Universities are closing or reducing library schools. Library schools seem to be having a difficult time hiring and retaining those dynamic professors who not only teach the next generation of teacher-librarians but also guide and lead those now practicing. Poor or nonexistent library schools *will* doom the profession.

6. Keeping our core values. Michael Gorman's important book *Our Enduring Values: Librarianship in the 21st Century* (2000) speaks eloquently to how public librarians must adapt to, but not be co-opted by, technologies and societal change. The tools we use may change, but not our mission to provide our patrons information and the skills to use it.

As teacher-librarians we also need to continually remind ourselves of some our core values when faced with institutions that may seem to be forcing us into the roles of babysitter, technician, or clerk. While I certainly advocate that we must master the new tools of information technology, we must also continue to

• use technology only as an empowering device that extends students' and teachers' talents;

• make higher-level thinking skills taught through information literacy projects a part of *every* child's education;

• make the ethical use of information and technology a part of every curriculum, paying special attention to safety, intellectual property, and appropriate use issues;

• demonstrate that all forms of media, including print, are and will remain critical sources of information, and that school library programs must continue to play a role in developing both the ability to read, as well as the desire to read, in all students;

• advocate intellectual freedoms for children that extend to both the print and digital worlds by fighting all forms of censorship;

• celebrate those uniquely human attributes of teaching—personal guidance, empathy, judgment, encouragement, wisdom, and caring—that cannot be duplicated by programmed instruction or teacher-proof curricula or measured on standardized tests;

• celebrate cultural and human diversity through the range of materials our collections offer, the stories and booktalks we give, and the topics studied through our information literacy units; and

• continue to advocate for children by providing programs and facilities that meet individual needs and by creating low-stress environments.

7. Staying connected. My friend and fellow teacher-librarian, Tom Ross of Aitken, MN, reminded me of a final challenge after reading an earlier version of this paper. He says it well:

> I am struck by our need to meet with each other to willfully engage in a battle for an optimistic vision for what we do. While the struggle for improving our media programs is often political and social, it is also a battle of the *mind.* If we remain alone in our understanding of the gifts we share with our students, we fail to feed ourselves the vital truths that will empower us to go once more "into the breach." We spend so much time flailing against the wind that we forget to rejuvenate, and that tiredness too can undermine our goals, our programs, and our best intentions for our students.
>
> How do we rebuild our vigor? By supporting each other, by taking classes where we sharpen our skills, by sharing our woes, by calling on each other, and by meeting together at conferences. We must celebrate the moments of magic we have experienced and strategies we developed to obtain those moments. In short, we must be colleagues to one another. Because we usually don't have another media specialist next door, we must break out of our buildings and our districts and go and seek these experiences. If we don't, we will mentally wither and die, educational dinosaurs.

Despite the challenges that face our profession, I remain wildly optimistic about its future. We are by far the most caring, smartest (and probably best-looking) group of educators now working in schools. Savvy communities are realizing that their best natural resource is a well-educated work force, and in today's economy well-educated means being not just literate, but information literate. A powerful teacher-librarian is indispensable to schools who are dedicated to graduating citizens who can use information in meaningful ways and know how to keep on learning.

A person recently commented to me that one must be mad to go into school librarianship. He's right, of course, on a number of levels. You have to mad (passionate) for stories, computers, and especially work with kids. You have to be mad (angry) about how poorly our schools under-serve too many vulnerable children. And finally, you have to be mad (crazy) enough to believe that you as one little individual have the power to change your institution, your political systems and especially the lives of your students and teachers. Hopefully, everyone who reads this will get just a little bit madder.

REFERENCE

Gorman, M. (2000). *Our enduring values: Librarianship in the 21st century*. Chicago: American Library Association.

Using Data in the School Library

Mary Jo Langhorne

Teacher-librarians are awash in data. Studies on the impact of school library programs on student achievement have now been replicated in 12 states (more are in the works) with amazingly consistent results. These are added to studies dating from the early 1960s that support the importance of school library programs to student achievement and the importance of libraries and librarians in developing readers. Even the much-discussed No Child Left Behind legislation passed by the U.S. Congress in 2001 has taken note of this research by including a section in the bill whose purpose is stated as follows: "To improve literacy skills and academic achievement of students by providing them with access to up-to-date school library materials; technologically advanced school library media centers; and professionally certified school library media specialists" (NCLB, 2001).

In our own schools, we maintain sophisticated electronic library circulation and catalog systems that provide us with a wealth of data on collections and circulation. We have purchased online tools with built-in statistical recording features. Teacher-librarians maintain records of classes and individuals using our libraries and assessments of student progress in our teaching and learning programs.

So, we have all of this data . . . what are we to do with it? I suggest three responsibilities for teacher-librarians in regard to data about library programs.

KNOW IT!

Teacher-librarians need to clearly understand the data that is available to them from national as well as local sources. If your state has done a school library impact study, be sure that you have read it and understood its major findings. If your state has not done a study, use the Library Research Services web site (**www.lrs.org/impact.asp**) to identify a nearby state or a state whose demographics are similar to your own and secure a copy of that state's study, or read some of the many articles that have been published summarizing the results of the studies (see bibliography accompanying this article). Sometimes the statistical portions of the studies can be complex; be sure you understand the limitations of the studies as well as the strengths so that you are able to deal with questions from administrators and others who may

First published in *Teacher Librarian*, December 2004, Volume 32, Number 2

be skeptical of the results.

Utilize in-house record-keeping systems to generate local data on circulation, strengths, and weaknesses in collections (e.g., numbers of books in current areas of curriculum emphasis, age of collections, materials added). Keep records on the use of your library and its resources—not just raw numbers but what students are doing and what you are doing while they are there. Are your online databases being used? How does the "hit" rate compare to numbers of articles printer or e-mailed? How many classes did you teach this week, and what was the content? Record unmet needs in the library as they occur: Did a teacher ask to bring classes at a time you could not accommodate them? Did a student need materials on a particular subject that you did not have in the library? Were there not enough computers for students who came to the library to do research on a given day?

Record-keeping systems need not require a huge time commitment—once you develop simple recording documents, data can be kept easily and quickly. Support staff can do much of the record keeping for you, counting numbers of students using the library, transcribing information from your schedule book to a weekly or monthly recording form. Figure 63.1, a table generated in a high school at the end of each month from the library's schedule book, is a simple record-keeping device for summarizing use by classes and correlating that with information process model instruction and local standards. Putting data into a spreadsheet or database allows for tracking over time and provides a way to easily generate charts and graphs to present your data to others.

Key to level of instructional support:	**Key to areas of information literacy curriculum:**
1. Gathering information in response to a teacher request	1. Define the information need
2. Working with students on a small-group or individual basis during a teacher-planned activity	2. Locate information
3. Teaching classes in support of a teacher-planned activity	3. Process the information
4. Sharing equal responsibility with the teacher for planning and delivering instruction.	4. Create and communicate results
	5. Assess process and product

Date	Teacher	Periods	Level	Activities	Info. Skills
February 4,5	Rinken	1,8	3	China/Japan Booktalks	1,2
February 11–14	Beckhold	1,2,6,7	3,4	English 10 research papers	1,2,3
February 13,14	Brocksmith	3,4	3,4	Science issues research projects preparation - HyperStudio	3,4,5
February 15	Talbot	1,2,4,7	3	Word processing letters and envelopes for book of myself thank you letters	4
February 13–15	Koenick	5	2	Honors biology research	1,2
February 11,12,13,14,18	Witson	2	2	World War II issues research	1,2,3
February 18,20,21	Black	1,2,5,7	4	Begin English 9 I-Search project: search strategy lesson, sources of information	1,2
February 19,20	Sabrose	6,8	3	Health issues research: Magazine indexes, SIRS	2
February 19,20,21	Putnum	3	2	Legal issues research; government class	2,3
February 20,22,23	Philton	2,4,5,6,8	2,3	Research on authors; poetry unit	2,3
February 19,20,25,26	Beckhold	1,2,6,7	3,4	English 10 research papers: Bibliography preparation, begin word processing	3,4,5
February 28	Rinken	1,8	3	Begin "forces of change" research	1,2

Figure 63.1. City High School Library Resource Center

SHARE IT!

Clearly, all of this data is of little use to us unless we share it with our teachers, administrators, parents, school board members, and other stakeholders. In 2002, the State Library of Iowa instituted an annual survey to collect data on school libraries in our state. We believe that Iowa is the only state currently requiring such data collection on school libraries. Over time, this survey will provide invaluable information to our teacher-librarians and administrators on the status of programs. One striking finding in the first year of the survey is the small number of teacher-librarians who engage in sharing data with administrators and others as illustrated by the following statistics:

• only 41% of teacher-librarians in our state submit an annual (or more frequent) report to their principal;
   • 30% submit an annual budget request;
   • 13% have a library advisory committee (State Library of Iowa, 2003).

All three of these are areas where valuable data supporting school library programs can and should be shared.

Annual—or better yet monthly or semi-annual—reports to the principal allow you to document and share the variety of things occurring in your library. A sample form for reporting statistical information is shown in Figure 63.2. We must be sure not to report just "inputs" (how many books circulated, how many classes scheduled), but "outputs" as well (what specific language arts units impacted circulation, what were classes doing when they used the library, what specific teacher requests were filled during the month). Combining a statistical report with an instructional report such as that shown in Figure 63.1 gives the administrator or parent group a better all-around picture of what is going on in the school library.

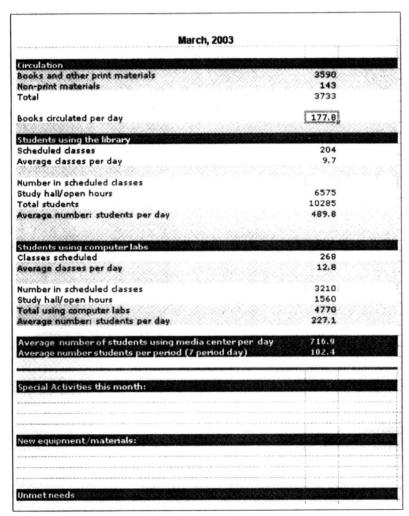

Figure 63.2. Sample Monthly/Quarterly/Annual Reporting Form

Similarly, annual budget requests need to be connected to curriculum goals. In an Indiana study, Daniel Callison (1994) documented a direct, positive correlation between how frequently the teacher-librarian communicates with the administrator about the budget and the library's budget allocation—in other words, submitting an annual budget request and following it up with monthly contacts with the principal about budget needs result in a larger budget! Care must be taken that communication about budget is also connected to curriculum goals (e.g., we need to spend $500 on earth science books because the newly adopted curriculum has units on weather, geology, and astronomy; we need to purchase a complete set of Newbery books because the language arts teachers are requiring students to read two during the year).

Library advisory groups, composed of parents, teachers, interested community members, and often students, are also a natural place to share data about the school library program. There are three excellent reasons to initiate such a group in your library:

1. You can directly model the collaboration that we speak of so frequently in the school library world.

2. Such a group affords the opportunity to consider input on decisions that may allow you to see things more clearly or differently because of others' perspectives (two—or more—heads really are better than one!).

3. You will be creating a built-in group of advocates for your program. If you have a group of people who are already informed about program, collections, and curriculum, you will not be alone in making the case for increased budgets or in lobbying for resources when times are tough.

Data should also be shared with the larger community. Our public library colleagues are skilled at publicizing data in support of their programs—usage and circulations statistics, special programming, and so forth. We should do the same. This is another area where the advisory committee can be of help.

USE IT!

The terms *data-driven leadership* and *data-driven decision making* are everywhere in the education literature today. We all understand that in times of diminishing resources, care must be taken to assure that those resources are used in support of programs that have proven impact on student learning. Our challenge is to learn to present our needs and requests in terms that are supported by data.

In our area, school administrators are being taught a model called QIC-Decide, wherein they use a four-step process (develop question, decide what information is needed, collect and analyze information, make the decision) to facilitate decision making in the school setting. Teacher-librarians have been teaching others a similar process for arriving at decisions by assembling and synthesizing data for many years. Information problem-solving models such as those developed by Eisenberg and Berkowitz (1996) and others have value for us as we use data to bring about improvements in our libraries.

We begin by identifying the question or "defining the information need." What is it we wish to change? The questions we seek support for may vary along a continuum from things that are relatively easy and that we can make happen with little need for data or involving others (e.g., rearranging the furniture in the library, deciding to purchase another set of popular paperbacks) to the more complex and expensive (e.g., I want to add a staff person, we need more space in the library). The complexity and cost of the issue being addressed will impact who needs to be involved in the problem-solving process. We do not operate in a vacuum; to bring about substantive changes will require the participation and support of others.

The second step is to decide what information is needed. Again this will depend upon the improvement you are hoping to make. For example, if you are making a case for expanding your facility, records of classes using the library as well as activities you have not been able to schedule will be needed. Comparative data on other libraries in schools of your size will be useful. Articles in national publications provide useful data on staffing, collections, budgets, and facilities in other school libraries. Local data can be collected through focus groups, interviews, and surveys with impacted populations, in addition to the sort of statistics mentioned earlier. The most important data you can gather and present is that which shows the impact on student achievement. Data from the Library Research Services studies (2004) cited above, as well as the work by Lance (2002) and Lance and Loertscher (2002), will be useful here.

Next, you must organize and analyze the data you have gathered. We know that information presented visually is more accessible to most people than pages and pages of narrative. Most teacher-librarians have access to Excel or other programs that can easily generate charts and graphs from data. Presenting information in this way is professional and convincing. (Isn't this what we tell students?)

Obviously, some goals are going to be more difficult to achieve than others. Requests for additional staffing are especially difficult because they represent ongoing expenditures. However, once the case is made and the information communicated clearly, the likelihood of the change occurring is dramatically increased. On the other hand, if you do not make the effort and use data to make your case, the likelihood that positive change will occur is very low. Figure 63.3 will serve as a guide as you identify areas for improvement and the data that can be used in support of your proposals.

CONCLUSION

Gary Hartzell, in a speech at the 2002 White House Conference on School Libraries, stated that school administrators are accustomed to thinking of the library program as a *cost*. "Our challenge is to get administrators to think of our library programs as an *investment* that pays rich dividends in student achievement" (Hartzell, 2002, emphasis added).

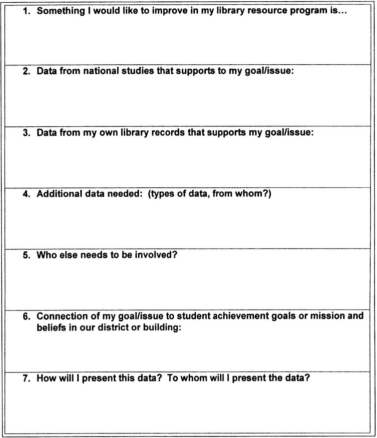

Figure 63.3. **Using Data to Improve School Library Resource Programs**

1. Something I would like to improve in my library resource program is...
2. Data from national studies that supports to my goal/issue:
3. Data from my own library records that supports my goal/issue:
4. Additional data needed: (types of data, from whom?)
5. Who else needs to be involved?
6. Connection of my goal/issue to student achievement goals or mission and beliefs in our district or building:
7. How will I present this data? To whom will I present the data?

This requires some adjustment in our thinking: We can no longer express program needs in terms of "mores"—more books, more staff, more space. Instead, we must learn to express program needs in terms of their potential to improve teaching and increase student achievement. We have much of the data that we need in hand. We need to begin to use it skillfully to influence decision makers.

REFERENCES

Callison, D. (1994). The AIME statewide survey of school library media centers: Relationships and associations from the data. *Indiana Media Journal, 17,* 103–162.

Eisenberg, M., & Berkowitz, R. (1996). Information problem-solving: The Big Six Skills approach to library & information skills instruction. Norwood, NJ: Ablex.

Elementary & Secondary Education Act, Subpart 4 — Improving literacy through school libraries. (2001). Department of Education. Washington, DC. Retrieved August 17, 2004, from **www.ed.gov/policy/elsec/leg/esea02/pg7.html**

Hartzell, G. (2002). What's it take? White House Conference on School Libraries. Retrieved August 17, 2004, from **www.imls.gov/pubs/whitehouse0602/garyhartzell.htm**

Lance, K. C. (2002). Impact of school library media programs on academic achievement. *Teacher Librar-*

ian, 29(3), 29.

Lance, K. C., & Loertscher, D. (2002). *Powering achievement: School library media programs make a difference.* San Jose, CA: Hi Willow Research and Publishing.

Library Research Service. (2004). School library impact studies. Retrieved August 17, 2004, from **www.lrs.org/impact.asp**

State Library of Iowa. (2003). School library survey. Retrieved March 3, 2003, from **www.silo.lib.ia.us/for-ia-libraries/statistics/schools/index.htm**

SUGGESTED RESOURCES FOR DATA

Association for Supervision and Curriculum Development. (2003, September 2). School libraries and their impact on student performance. Retrieved August 17, 2004, from **www.ascd.org/publications/ researchbrief/volume1/v1n18.html**

Haycock, K. (2004). Effective roles for student achievement. *Teacher Librarian, 31*(5), 34.

Krashen, S. (1993). *The power of reading: Insights from the research.* Englewood, CO: Libraries Unlimited.

Whelan, D. (2004). 13,000 kids can't be wrong. *School Library Journal, 50*(2), 46.

Using Focus Group Interviews to Improve Library Services for Youth

Sandra Hughes-Hassell and Kay Bishop

Imagine a small group of teenagers sitting around a table in your school library discussing the programs and services you offer. If they knew you valued their ideas and opinions, what would they say? What ideas would they have and how could you use their ideas to better meet their needs? Experienced librarians understand the importance of involving their patrons in the development and evaluation of the programs and services they offer. Finding out about the needs and expectations of patrons, especially children and young adults, however, is often viewed as too time-consuming, expensive, and staff intensive to perform on a regular basis, thus causing many librarians to continue to develop programs for children and young adults "largely embedded in librarian wisdom, based on the notion that what has worked, will work, and on the belief that as long as children come and their parents seem satisfied, the program is working" (Holt, Dresang, & Gross, 2000, p. 6). Developing library services based on past experiences, good intentions and little information is not, as Veldof points out, "the ticket to delighting, or even satisfying, one's customers" (1999, p. 33). Instead, librarians need to find practical and cost effective ways to determine what their patrons want. In this article we will discuss the focus group interview, a data collection tool that teacher-librarians can use to discover the perceptions, feelings, and beliefs of their patrons (Everhart, 2002; Glitz, 1998; Simon, 1999; Veldof, 1999). In our discussion we will define the focus group interview, outline the benefits and challenges associated with this data collection technique, and suggest steps for conducting an interview. We will end the article with examples of how focus groups have been used in schools to improve programming and services for youth.

WHAT IS A FOCUS GROUP INTERVIEW?

A focus group is "an interview with a small group of people on a specific topic" (Patton, 1990, p. 335). Participants are usually a group of 6 to 10 people who share a common experience or set of characteristics. For example, they may be grade 3 students who use the library on a regular basis or principals who

First published in *Teacher Librarian*, October 2004, Volume 32, Number 1

are responsible for hiring and supervising teacher-librarians in a specific school district. For 1/2 to 2 hours, participants in a focus group interview are asked to reflect on a carefully prepared set of open-ended questions asked by an interviewer. The goal of the interview is not for the group to solve a problem or reach consensus, but to consider their own views about the topic under discussion in the context of the views of others. As participants hear each other's responses, they are encouraged to express their ideas and opinions, provide alternative viewpoints, and supply details that will lead to a broader understanding of the topic under discussion. The data collected from a focus group interview is analyzed and used in planning; making decisions; evaluating programs, products, or services; enriching findings from other research methods; and constructing questionnaires or surveys for further data gathering.

When to Use a Focus Group Interview

Focus group interviews can be used by librarians in all types of settings and with all ages of patrons, including children and young adults, to measure the effectiveness and efficiency of their services, as well as to better understand the needs of their patrons (Glitz, 1998). They are especially useful when librarians want to learn about patron perceptions of current resources, programming, and services; generate lists of problems, unmet needs, or ideas for new services or programs; test and refine new products, services, and programs; improve written documentation such as help screens and pathfinders; or construct questionnaires or surveys (Drabenstott, 1992). Table 64.1 provides a list of issues teacher-librarians might explore using a focus group approach.

* exploring student attitudes and perceptions of the collection;
* understanding how teachers use the collection to support the curriculum;
* determining the need for expanded reference services;
* investigating the role of the school library resource program in the school's instructional program;
* designing a library web site or portal;
* studying student use of computers and the Internet;
* evaluating after-school outreach programs;
* designing a new facility;
* evaluating the library's instructional program;
* determining continuing education needs of the library staff or school faculty;
* discovering parent perceptions of the library program;
* developing programs and services for parents.

Table 64.1. Possible Issues for Focus Group Interviews in School Libraries

Benefits of Focus Group Interviews

Focus group interviews offer several benefits to time-strapped teacher-librarians. In one hour a teacher-librarian can gather the ideas, views or opinions of six to eight people instead of only one person. The social interaction involved in the interview typically helps participants focus on the most important aspects of a topic or issue, thus getting to the core of an issue in less time. Plus, the format allows the interviewer to probe for clarification or solicit greater detail throughout the interview, thus enhancing the completeness of the data collected.

Focus group interviews also tend to encourage "more openness and candor in the participants' responses than other techniques" (Glitz, 1998, p. 33). By hearing other people speak about similar experiences and feelings, members of the group are able to overcome their own anxieties or hesitations about offering their views, opinions, or thoughts about a topic. This is especially important when dealing with populations whose views have often been overlooked or dismissed, like children and young adults.

Challenges of Focus Group Interviews

Like any method of data collection, there are challenges associated with focus group interviews. The primary challenge involves managing the group so that the interview is not dominated by one or two people, and so that those participants who tend to be reticent are able to share their views (Glitz, 1998; Patton, 1990). This is made easier when the group is kept small, thus allowing real participation and discussion by all. Although there is no exact number for membership, the typical number of focus group participants is 6 to 10.

The success of a focus group interview also depends on the interviewer's ability to transform the "various individuals into a collective whole" (Glitz, 1998, p. 10). Each member of the group must feel included as a vital member and want to contribute. The interviewer can facilitate this transformation through self-introductions, going quickly around the room and giving each person a chance to speak. Another method is to start with a simple question and ask each person in turn to answer. Both of these methods make it clear to all members of the group that each person is "expected to contribute, and demonstrates that all opinions and ideas will be heard" (Glitz, 1998, p. 11).

Another challenge involves accurately capturing the discussion. Most interviewers overcome this challenge by recording the interview—with the permission of the participants—and transcribing the discussion at a later time. Often, a pair of interviewers will work together, with one asking the questions and the other taking notes. Interviewers may also share the transcription of the interview with the participants to check that their ideas and views have been represented correctly.

Lastly, it is important to remember "no single focus group is likely to reflect the range of opinions, interests and involvements of the full patron population of a library" (Glitz, 1998, p. 38). Before decisions are made, the data collected from a focus group interview needs to be validated by additional focus group interviews or data collected using other techniques such as surveys.

HOW TO CONDUCT A FOCUS GROUP INTERVIEW

Conducting a focus group interview involves a series of steps outlined below. As with any project, a basic plan of action should be developed to guide the implementation of the focus group interviews. Teacher-librarians need to develop a timeline, determine the number of interviews to be conducted and how participants will be contacted, choose a site for the interviews, and make a list of the equipment and supplies needed. Table 64.2, adapted from *Recipe for Focus Groups* (Bishop, 2000), provides some lessons we have learned about conducting focus group interviews.

Step 1: Identify the Goals and Objectives of the Interview

The first task in conducting a focus group interview is to determine the purpose of the interview. Ask yourself,

Why are you holding a focus group?

What do you hope to learn from the interview?

What type of information do you need to gather?

How do you plan to use the data collected?

* Limit the size of the group to 6 to 10 people.
* Don't allow people to join the group after it begins.
* Be sure everyone in the group is aware of the purpose of the interview and what kind of information is being sought.
* Limit the number of questions to 5 to 10.
* Share questions with the participants prior to the interview in order to give them time to reflect on their ideas, views, and opinions.
* Don't be so structured with questions that there is not allowance for spontaneity.
* Use a protocol, or set of procedures, that creates a structure that ensures that each person gets to speak and be heard.
* Ask people to lean toward the tape recorder when speaking.
* Have a backup in case the tape recorder doesn't work—involve an additional interviewer as a note-taker or use two tape recorders.
* Be prepared with techniques for handling diversions or conflicts.

Table 64.2. Tips for Successful Focus Group Interviews

Step 2: Choose an Interviewer

Choosing a trained interviewer is critical to the success of a focus group interview. An effective modera-tor is people oriented, interested in the topic, well organized, a skilled communicator and interviewer, and has a good short-term memory (Glitz, 1998). Because of the importance of the role, you may choose to hire a professional interviewer rather than conducting the interview yourself. This has several advantages. Since they do not work for the library or school district, professional interviewers tend to be more objec-tive in their conduct of the focus group and are less likely to bias the comments of the participants. Their extensive training also enables them to effectively manage the group interview process (Glitz, 1998).

Step 3: Determine Who Should Be Interviewed

The goal in selecting focus group participants is to bring together a group of individuals who have opin-ions and ideas that will provide meaningful input to the discussion (Drabenstott, 1992). Consider draw-ing from formal groups that already exist in your school, such as the young adult advisory council, parent-teacher organization or site-based decision-making team. Select individuals who are willing to par-ticipate and who have knowledge of and/or experience with the topic to be discussed, as well as the abil-ity to reflect on the topic in a group (Glitz, 1998). To ensure a wide range of viewpoints and opinions, pay careful attention to characteristics such as race or ethnicity, gender, socioeconomic status and age. Make sure to include library users and nonusers—students, teachers, administrators, and parents who do not use your library services can often provide valuable insight.

Step 4: Recruit Participants

Once a pool of potential participants has been selected, the recruitment process can begin. It is important to identify more participants than you need since not everyone you contact will be able to attend. During the recruitment process, be sure to let participants know how they will be remunerated. Will they be paid a nominal fee, served lunch, or a given a small gift such as a paperback book? Will they be reimbursed for the cost of transportation?

Step 5: Formulate Questions

This is the most important—and difficult—task associated with focus group interviews (Glitz, 1998). The questions should flow naturally from the goals of the project, enable the interviewer to gather the data needed to meet the project goals, and stimulate but not bias the discussion. Effective questions are clear and con-crete, open-ended to encourage maximum participation, free of jargon, and precise. No more than 5 to 10 questions should be asked per session and the questions should be asked from general to specific.

Step 6: Run the Session(s) and Record the Discussion

Before the actual interview begins, it is important to explain the purpose and scope of the discussion, ex-plain the protocol or structure that will be used to guide the next 1 or 2 hours, and invite the participants, including the interviewer, to introduce themselves. The goal is to set a relaxed tone that makes it clear to the participants that their ideas are valued, that they should feel free to ask for clarification at any point during the discussion, and that they should enjoy themselves (Drabenstott, 1992; Glitz, 1998). If the dis-cussion is being recorded, participants should be reminded of this and assured that the information they provide will be reported as "group data" and that no individuals will be identified by name or position.

Once everyone is aware of the procedures that will guide the discussion, the interviewer asks the pre-pared questions, being sure to allow each person to respond. The interviewer's task throughout the interview is to pay close attention to what is being said, keep the discussion focused and on the topic, and prompt for greater detail when necessary.

Once the listed questions have been asked, the interviewer brings closure to the discussion. This can be done in a number of ways. The simplest approach is for the interviewer to review the purpose of the interview and ask for final comments. Another useful strategy is for the interviewer to invite each participant to sum up their feelings about the topic and add anything they may have forgotten earlier. Finally, the interviewer can summarize the discussion, asking the participants to verify their impressions or conclusions (Glitz, 1998).

Step 7: Analyze the Data

Data analysis involves reviewing the transcripts to determine what the group said about each issue discussed and to draw conclusions. After transcribing the interviews, organize the group's comments into categories. Usually the interview questions and the goals of the interview provide the framework for doing this. For example, if the goal of the interview is to understand how teens use the library's electronic resources, the categories might include the Internet, CD-ROMs, electronic databases, and electronic journals. Each participant's comments are then placed into the appropriate category. Remember that relevant comments about a topic may be located anywhere in the text, not just in response to a specific question about that topic. For example, in response to a question about the use of electronic journals, a teen might talk about an e-zine that he reads on a regular basis because it publishes teen poetry. This comment would be categorized under Internet. After the data is categorized, review it again to identify patterns, relationships, and trends among the various comments.

Step 8: Report the Results

In order for the data to be used it must be synthesized and presented in a useful format. The presentation format will depend on the original purpose of the project and the intended audience. The simplest format involves organizing the data by participants under each topic. This method, while providing all the data needed for decision making, can be overwhelming to the reader especially if a number of focus groups have been conducted. A more succinct way to report the data entails providing summary statements that emphasize patterns and trends. A summary statement should be written for each topic and should include direct quotations from the participants that illustrate typical responses, key observations, and the range of ideas expressed. The summary statements should be as comprehensive, balanced, and objective as possible. Any conclusions reached in the summary statements must be supported by the data.

Step 10: Use the Results

The final step in the process is to use the results. What you ultimately do with the knowledge gained from the interviews will depend on the purpose of the project and on the findings themselves. They may lead to actions like adding new services, revising or dropping old services, making changes to the collection, increasing the library budget, or hiring new personnel. In some cases, they may result in no visible action, but may increase your understanding of a particular issue, thus improving how you go about your daily work.

FOCUS GROUP INTERVIEWS IN ACTION: MIDDLE SCHOOL STUDENTS AND THE SCHOOL LIBRARY

Kay Bishop, one of the authors of this article, currently director of the School Library Media Program at the State University of New York at Buffalo, was a case study evaluator for the National Library Power initiative. Her charge as an evaluator was to determine how the Library Power initiative affected student learning at a middle school (grades 7–9) in Lincoln, NE. The following questions guided her research:

- Are students having different learning experiences as a result of Library Power?
- Are students engaging in more independent research?
- Are students approaching topics/subjects in new ways?
- Are students conducting high-quality independent research?
- Are students acquiring a broad in-depth understanding of topics?
- Are students performing new tasks that can be associated with constructivist learning?

As part of her research, Bishop wanted to understand what impact projects that were collaboratively developed between teacher-librarians and teachers had on student learning. She used approximately 20 focus groups of four to six students each as one of the methods of answering that question. She asked the students in the groups to bring some of the study projects produced in the interdisciplinary units made possible through Library Power funding. These products included posters, booklets, research papers, models, games, drawings, and various other items. The interviews were focused on questions relating to whether the learning extended beyond getting a grade for an assignment. Among the initial questions Bishop asked were the following:

- What, if anything, did you learn from this unit or project?
- Do you remember much about this project?
- How did you use what you learned?
- How was this project different from what you did previously in your classes?
- Do you like being involved in interdisciplinary projects that are worked on in more than one of your classes?

Although Bishop initially utilized a list of general questions, other more specific questions evolved from the student responses. She found the students eager to share their thoughts about the units and the products they had created. Students were unanimously enthusiastic about the interdisciplinary units and commented on the transference of learning from one subject to another, as well as to their lives in general.

COLLECTION DEVELOPMENT AND FOCUS GROUPS

Successfully meeting the resource needs of the learning community requires teacher-librarians to understand the learner and the teaching/learning context. The most effective way to do this is by working collaboratively with teachers, students, parents, and other members of the learning community. When she was developing the library collection for a new elementary school, Sandra Hughes-Hassell (coauthor of this article) used focus group interviews to gather data from teachers about their students, the curriculum, and the methods of instruction used in their classrooms. Hughes-Hassell first sent a survey to all the teachers who would be employed at the new school asking them to identify key curricular areas, specific literature and authors studied at each grade level, and their students' favorite books. After analyzing this data, she conducted a focus group with the lead teachers from each grade level to gather additional data and to discuss overlaps in curricular areas. For example, in reviewing the survey data, Hughes-Hassell noticed that biomes were studied in grades 3 and 4. In the interview, she asked the teachers to provide details about what students in each grade would be expected "to know and be able to do" about biomes and to describe how the grade 4 curriculum built upon what students learned in grade 3. By actively engaging teachers in the collection development process, she was able to not only create a library collection that better met the requirements of the learning community, but to involve teachers in a preliminary discussion of the curriculum.

CONCLUSION

Focus groups are cost effective techniques for gathering qualitative information that can be used for decision making. The interviews can provide teacher-librarians with valuable insight into many issues. They can be used to identify interests or needs, gather information for planning, determine problems encountered, suggest possible solutions or strategies, and evaluate existing services. Most importantly, focus group interviews allow teacher-librarians to hear directly from those whom they serve and to involve them in the planning, implementation and evaluation of programs and services.

REFERENCES

Bishop, K. (2002). *Recipe for focus groups.* Retrieved January 14, 2003, from **www.ala.org/aasl/ kqweb/kqweb_30_3.html**

Drabenstott, K. (1992). Focused group interviews. In J. D. Glazier & R. R. Powell (Eds.), *Qualitative research in information management* (pp. 85–104). Englewood, CO: Libraries Unlimited.

Everhart, N. (2002). Focus groups in school library settings. *Knowledge Quest, 30* (3), 36.

Glitz, B. (1998). *Focus groups for libraries and librarians.* New York: Forbes.

Holt, L., Dresang, E., & Gross, M. (2000). *Reducing the digital divide: An outcome-based model for evaluating school-aged children's use of technology in an urban public library (Project CATE).* Unpublished research proposal. Retrieved October 20, 2002, from **www.imls.gov/grants/library/ pdf/nlg01nrd.pdf**

Patton, M. (1990). *Qualitative evaluation and research methods* (2nd ed.). New York: Sage Publications.

Simon, J. (1999). *The Wilder nonprofit field guide to conducting successful focus groups.* Saint Paul, MN: Amherst H. Wilder Foundation.

Veldof, J. (1999). Data driven decisions: Using data to inform process changes in libraries. *Library & Information Science Research, 21*(1), 31–46.

Marketing Reflections:
Advocacy in Action

Gail Bush and Merrilee Andersen Kwielford

Teacher-librarians are often their own worst enemies in the marketing department. When we think of marketing, our service-oriented hackles are raised as we consider ourselves to be above the marketing mindset. We do good work, we know that it has lasting value, that it benefits our schools, and we do not see the need to make a nuisance of ourselves getting the point across. Talk about self-serving—the last thing our teachers and administrators want to hear is the library staff promoting itself and the library resource center.

While we admire library programs that excel in public relations, we understand the viewpoint described above because we shared it ourselves. It wasn't until we were asked to make a presentation about marketing (Marketing? Us? We don't do it—how will we talk about it?) that we realized that our style of marketing is subtle but it is definitely there. And furthermore, since we discovered that we do in fact market our program in various ways, we came to realize that our brand of marketing enhances our opportunities to expand and deepen our program. The focus could be described as "less talk and more action." We hope that some of the levels of marketing that are described in this article will find resonance with your program and you will see your way to enhance your advocacy in your school. Perhaps this approach can be viewed as a preliminary step to a bona fide public relations plan.

The primary difference between our concept of marketing and the traditional viewpoint is that we promote our actual programs and projects; we do not have separate strategies or marketing ideas that are used for the explicit purpose of promoting our school library. The promotion that our library receives from this type of marketing is a natural consequence of making our programs more visible. The various members of our school learning community are our audience; perhaps we should call the marketing of our program "learning community relations."

Our philosophy for the library media program is one that defines our mission as a means but not an end within the school. We do not consider marketing our library resource program to be worthy just for

First published in *Teacher Librarian*, June 2001, Volume 28, Number 5

the sake of bolstering our self-esteem or our position in the building or district. Advocating for our program is generative. It is illustrative and therefore it motivates teachers and administrators to see the library media program with fresh eyes. That new slant is what we seek to enhance and broaden our program, all the while knowing that a strong library resource program will benefit our students academically and every which way. As each "level" appreciates the marketing we do for the level above, the generative nature of this advocacy is realized. We often find ourselves in the position of starting an initiative that we then pass on to others to more fully develop. Enjoying the creative phase of project development necessitates giving up some of our "babies." And that brings us back to the library media program as a means and not an end in and of itself.

The following discussion illustrates each of the six levels of marketing as shown in the inset. We invite you to engage in your own marketing reflections and consider how you think about advocacy at each level. Perhaps, like us, your marketing is more of an attitude than an explicit plan.

BASIC ASSUMPTIONS: SETTING THE FOUNDATION

Do your homework. There are some basic elements that must be paid attention to before all else. These basic assumptions fall into two categories, the physical and the professional:

• The physical concerns include books and computers, paper and toner, tables and chairs. First things first.

• Professional concerns include adequate (or working toward that goal) staffing and a shared vision (if there is more than one of you!).

As professionals we are familiar with *Information Power: Building Partnerships for Learning* (AASL & AECT, 1998) and the information literacy standards described therein. As members of our school learning community we refer to our school's curriculum standards and our state learning standards. A comprehensive program evaluation can be found in *Program Evaluation: Library Media Services*, published by the National Study of School Evaluation (Fitzpatrick, 1998). We "walk our

6. **STATE AND NATIONAL**
Practitioner as visionary

5. **COMMUNITY**
Awareness

4. **ADMINISTRATION**
Program Support

3. **SCHOOL**
Collaborative Environment

2. **LIBRARY RESOURCE PROGRAM**
Attitude for Success

1. **BASIC ASSUMPTIONS**
Setting the Foundation

Figure 65.1. Levels of Marketing

talk" by writing and following a mission statement that clearly states our role as it relates to all our learners. Before you proceed any further, understand that taking care of business at this level is necessary to set your foundation firmly and to proceed to the next levels of engagement.

Beyond the basics, read the books published by Greenwood, Libraries Unlimited, ALA, Linworth, Hi-Willow, and the other school library publishers (there are too many worthy titles to list here). You will find them to be helpful and encouraging. Keep current by reading the school library journals and join a school library electronic discussion list. Take advantage of those generous souls in our profession who have gone before us and have experiences, good and bad, to share.

LIBRARY RESOURCE PROGRAM: ATTITUDE FOR SUCCESS

It takes an attitude. Some of us come by this naturally. We put ourselves into every library research project and add twists and tweaks at every opportunity. If this does not describe you or your program, here are a few simple pointers to liven things up:

• We believe very strongly in our mission of curricular support. However, our definition of "curricular" is rather broad. When our students are studying China for their social science class, we play Chinese folk music on the CD player as an accompaniment to the students' research. We have music for most cultures and most decades covered by our classes. Our favorite musical enhancement was during our freshman orientation. The physical education classes came into the library to research the Olympics. As the students and teachers entered the library they were welcomed with John Williams' "Olympic Fanfare." Our goal is not to "promote our program" but to empower the teacher by providing a dynamic learning environment for his or her students.

• Weeding is a practice that sometimes creates ruffled feathers. The teacher that uses the one resource one day annually is the one who will come looking for it two months after you weed it out of the collection. To prevent these occurrences and to share the ownership of the weeding of audiovisual materials, we created "Tropical Friday," when we invite our faculty to review all materials in the "to-be-weeded" stage. Tropical Friday began on a cold Friday in the dead of winter; we strung up suns, wore Hawaiian shirts, played Jimmy Buffet music, and served tropical juices and treats in our workroom. It sounds silly and it was a little bit, but it was also fun and memorable.

• As a good neighbor in the school, we invite various groups and committees to meet in the library. We serve as the school art gallery when we display art on modular walls every spring. We hang panels of the AIDS quilt and provide room and time for classes to view and discuss the quilt project.

These examples illustrate the attitude we have about our role in the school learning community. If you were in our school you would get the message that our program is an integral part of our school. Everything that we do reinforces that attitude. We are fortunate to have three professional teacher-librarians on our staff. As we started working together as a team, we learned about each other's strengths. We felt that our program would benefit if we could all function primarily in an area that suited our strengths. Certainly, all of us can function in any capacity as needed. It is in the discretionary areas that we go with our strengths and bring interested faculty and staff along for the ride. Fortunately, we all agree that not every idea works. We are always prepared to flop. We generate many ideas and sometimes the best idea may be a weak idea improved by input from another staff member.

SCHOOL: COLLABORATIVE ENVIRONMENT

Think holistically. We strive to develop innovative programs that impact the entire school and bring it together as a single learning community. Ideally, the role of the library staff is one of facilitation and collaboration with other faculty and staff. We seek to share in the ownership of programs that cast a wide net and unexpectedly lure an unusual mixing of members of our school community. Some of these programs are now run by faculty in other departments, some were one-shot deals, and others we enjoy as annual fetes.

The Open Mike Café (OMC), now presented twice annually, started as an idea in the school library resource center. It is a poetry reading cafe held during lunch periods in the faculty cafeteria. The entire school community is invited. Since its inception, OMC has had standing room only. Students, teachers, staff (including support and custodial staff), and administrators participate. Like the other events described at this level of marketing, this event breaks down the walls within the school and makes us enjoy learning together. In order to organize the first OMC, we partnered with the two English teachers who sponsor our school's literary magazine. Their magazine editorial staff provided the student labor that we needed. The day following the first OMC, we received glowing comments in equal parts from students, support staff, and faculty. The OMCs are now organized by the literary magazine sponsors.

Spaceday 1999 started with an innovation grant from our library system. We learned about the NASA-sponsored celebration of space in 1998 from one of our special education teachers. Spaceday is celebrated in May. We wrote and received a grant that allowed us to purchase t-shirts, mugs, decorations, and prizes. Two science teachers were interested in participating prior to the event. We planned to view the webcast on a projection system, host a trivia contest and other guessing games, participate in a distance learning lecture from the Adler Planetarium, and have a Star Wars film festival running all day in our Little Theater. Our CyberWest (tech club) members wore Spaceday t-shirts and helped with the games and technology. We invited the junior high school tech club students and sponsor, community members, school board members, and science classes. More than 600 people attended our events and our school was listed in the Congressional Record.

Random Acts of Poetry is a project that continues annually. During National Poetry Month every April, we randomly stuff mailboxes in our school with poetry throughout the month. Teachers and staff post, read aloud, and share the poetry we distribute. Contributions come from faculty and staff—this year, an art teacher and a secretary made the first contributions. After writing about this project a number of years ago we now have samples from other schools' library staff who are also participating in Random Acts of Poetry.

And just for fun, we were the back-up singers (no, we can't sing but that didn't stop us) in the faculty band act for the school Variety Show. The band was composed of teachers (some of whom are now administrators) from the English, physical education, and foreign language departments. We had television broadcasting students produce a music video of our "gig"; if you must know, the song was "Twist and Shout" (Bush, 1997).

ADMINISTRATION: PROGRAM SUPPORT

"They don't know what we do." It is a lament common to many of us. Our administrators do not have a clear picture of our mission, our daily work, or our place in the school learning community. Understand that it is our responsibility to relay to our administrators in the most effective manner feasible how we define our program. Administrators are busy people. It is not our aim to inundate them with trivial matters that illustrate our labor-intensive daily chores. We prefer to include our administrators as members of our learning community so that they will comprehend the integral role we have as a learning center in the school. Administrators are invited to every event and in-service. We share our involvement in the community and in our profession with them. As the role of technology filters through our program we strive to clarify the place that it has to enhance, but not replace, other valuable resources. Our proactive stance increases our visibility without creating a management-by-crisis atmosphere. We do not adhere to the "no news is good news" mantra of many departments with regard to their administrators. We prefer to share our program with our administrators so that in those (inevitable) times of crisis we do not feel like we are crying wolf.

Standards, recertification, and the professional growth program in our state and district are now including areas that relate directly to the school library program. Information literacy, technology, differentiated instruction, and other markers of education in the 21st century reside comfortably within our domain. We empower our administrators by sharing our knowledge and our role as educational leaders in these areas. And, in return, we receive the program support that is essential to continue to provide the type of program that can impact our mutual bottom line, student achievement.

COMMUNITY: AWARENESS

Awareness is a two-way street. We feel that we have a responsibility to be a part of the local community. Maine West is the only public high school in our community. There are many ways that we like to make contact with local institutions. Sometimes we enrich standing programs, and other times we may create a new project (Spaceday, for example) that includes community members.

One of the simplest ways that we include the community in our program is to invite public library staff to our library to register students and staff for library cards. During our National Library Week Open House, we invite library staff and set up a registration table for them. This is a great way for the students to make the connection between the libraries. The Des Plaines Public Library had a poster project where a photographer was taking photos of various library users for display as posters in the public library. Each of the teacher-librarians went to the public library to be photographed, so as public library users entered their library, they saw photographs of us on the poster, creating a bridge between the public and school libraries. We also made an opportunity for the public library staff who work with teenagers to shadow us for a day. Again, this is a small step but it helped the public library staff get a greater understanding of how we work with our students.

We visited the Kiwanis during a lunch meeting. When we were writing a grant that included a broadcasting component, one of the teacher-librarians attended the cable commission meetings at the civic center. We attended training in the Great Books program (even though there is not a program in the high school) along with the middle school and elementary teacher-librarians and parent volunteers.

In our school library community, we network both informally and formally with the feeder school teacher-librarians and our fellow high school teacher-librarians in neighboring school districts. We attend meetings and will just call up a colleague as needed. We feel very strongly that networking strengthens all of our programs; none of us operates in isolation and we all learn from each other.

STATE AND NATIONAL: PRACTITIONER AS VISIONARY

We walk our talk. We also have a responsibility, as professionals, to participate in the grand discussion that is reserved for practitioners. In the years since we started building our program, members of our school library's professional staff have (collectively) earned an educational administration certificate, an educational administration master's degree, and a doctorate in educational psychology. We take what we learn in the classroom and through research and we apply it to practical situations. We take that mix and consult with our teachers and administrators with a broad scope of understanding regarding their work. To take our program to this level and not to participate in ongoing discussions amongst teacher-librarians would be to fall short of our positions as professionals.

Our program and our individual work have been recognized in various ways. In each instance, we sought out the recognition. We apply for awards, we seek out and write grant applications, and we contribute to school library and education journals. We do not always get funded but we are guaranteed to *not* receive funding for those grants for which we do not apply. Yes, it's true, in the school library biz: no guts, no glory. The important message here is that the "glory" is generative and the visibility garnered filters through each level of relationships noted in this article. A stamp of approval from an outside source carries great weight with school districts. Each group identified in our school learning community has its own peer group. As we share ownership of our program with them, they then share in our recognition.

There are many ways to participate in our profession at the state and national levels. Some teacher-librarians are organizationally oriented and enjoy committee work. Some may like to write for journals, while others may prefer to present in-services and workshops. Go with your strength and you will find wonderful colleagues who are willing to share and learn in every corner of our profession. Start by reading the journals, attending the conferences, and participating in local workshops. Avail yourself of all we have to offer and before you know it you will be a contributing member in the school library conversation.

CONCLUSION

If you noticed that the levels of marketing reflect the learning community as described in *Information Power: Building Partnerships for Learning* (AASL & AECT, 1998), we would agree with you. These levels are not revolutionary by any means. We have distinguished among these six levels based on the focus of our program as we relate to each group. We do feel that there is a hierarchical arrangement. "Basic Assumptions" is a foundation that must be built before developing any other part of the school library program. Then, taking care of business within the library resource center at a fundamental level comes next, before looking to build school and administrative support. Going outside the school to the community and to the professional school library community follows as a natural progression of the program.

We are not so coy as to deny the marketing benefits of involvement at each of the levels described. However, it is the quality of the programming that carries the day in our scenario.

Ralph Waldo Emerson could be describing our program when he commented, "What you do speaks so loudly, I can't hear what you say."

REFERENCES

American Association of School Librarians (AASL) & the Association for Educational Communications and Technology (AECT). (1998). *Information power: Building partnerships for learning.* Chicago: American Library Association.

Bush, G. (1997). Twist & shout: It starts with an attitude. *Emergency Librarian, 25*(2), 20–21.

Fitzpatrick, K. A. (1998). *Program evaluation: Library media services—A comprehensive guide for standards-based program evaluation committed to continuous improvement.* Schaumburg, IL: National Study of School Evaluation.

⑥⑥

Are Libraries (and Librarians) Heading Toward Extinction?

Doug Johnson

As a profession, librarians have gone on the defensive, justifying in increasingly worried and frantic tones, just why they and their institutions are ever so much better than the Internet. Mark Herring's article "10 Reasons Why the Internet Is No Substitute for a Library" (Herring, 2001) and even a column of mine, "Why Do We Need Libraries When We Have the Internet?" (Johnson, 1998) are examples of this concern about our physical resources, space, and even profession being replaced by Google and its virtual ilk.

I am beginning to wonder how helpful such articles and arguments really are for the health of our profession. Neither article suggests ways to keep our patrons from having their information needs increasingly met independently of print, libraries, and librarians, other than to shout ever more loudly, "But we are so much better!" to each other.

Okay, true confession time. I don't blame Jane and Joe Blow for increasingly using the Internet rather than libraries. I'm doing it myself, despite the fact I am a big fan of libraries and my livelihood depends in large part on their continued existence. For example, I recently saved a very short walk from my office to our lovely high school resource center for a copy of an R. L. Stevenson short story by finding it in about three minutes on the Web and printing it out. And my 17-year-old son deems anything not on the Internet is not worth knowing and is nearly a stranger to both his school and public library. According to the Pew study, *The Digital Disconnect* (Pew Internet Project, 2002), he is typical of his generation. People of all ages are simply finding it is really, really handy to have information needs met right at their desks or in their homes.

Yet, I have no doubt that many libraries and librarians will evolve and survive despite the increasing use of the Internet to fulfill needs those libraries and librarians previously met.

The libraries that will continue to thrive will be those which meet *real* needs that *cannot* be met by the Internet (or bookstores or classrooms). Our profession should be defining, discovering, and empha-

First published in *Teacher Librarian*, December 2003, Volume 31, Number 2

sizing those needs in the current budgetary and political climate rather than simply complaining and justifying our existence to each other through professional publications.

There are a great number of physical businesses and institutions that might have felt just as threatened by the public's increased use of the Internet: bookstores, travel agents, public libraries, and banks, just to name a few. Even virtual schools are now taking the place of brick and mortar buildings for many students. Just how are the savvier among these institutions escaping being replaced by the Internet?

• By providing a physical comfort that the Internet does not. I still buy books and spend time at our local Barnes & Noble bookstore because I like having coffee there, sitting in the comfy chairs, and handling physical books. I still buy more books there than I do online.

• By providing expertise an Internet user may not have. My travel agent knows more about vacation destinations than I do—or am willing to take the time to research and read about on the Internet. She can find better fares under some circumstances than I am able to. And she has the time to the time to look for "deals" that I don't have.

• By providing "high-touch" experiences to offset the "high-tech" environments. John Naisbitt, in his book *Megatrends*, predicted that the more people use isolating technologies, the greater their needs will be for face-to-face human interaction and socialization (Naisbitt, 1982). This is why I still like going to the public library to read the paper sometimes instead of reading it online—I see and meet people there. Internet usage is lonely—even for the chronic chatters, I'm guessing.

• By recognizing and using the Internet to complement one's mission. I still value my bank down on Hickory Street even though I check my miserable account balances online, have my paltry paycheck direct deposited, visit impersonal instant tellers to get cash, and pay my horrendous bills electronically. I don't go in the physical building much anymore, but I use their banking services more than ever. I don't see the Internet displacing Wells Fargo anytime soon.

Let's take just these four ways in which our physical existence may be superior to or can be enhanced by the virtual experience and think about how we in school libraries can capitalize on these qualities rather than try to compete head-to-head with the Internet. (Darwin called this adaptation and recognized successful species were good at it.)

PHYSICAL COMFORT AND WELCOMING ENVIRONMENT

This means creating a library where kids and teachers *really* like to be. Comfy chairs, friendly atmosphere, low-stress, safe, and forgiving. If my library is not a wonderful place to be, everyone will stay on the Internet or in the classroom. Period.

A frightful quote was given in the Pew study by a middle school student: "The Internet is like a librarian without the bad attitude or breath" (Pew Internet Project, 2002, p. 15). *Ouch!* What does this say about how welcoming my staff and I need to be to our kids and staff? In practice:

I'm lucky enough to have been able to design our own new library and I think one of the choices that I made that has pleased the students the most are the chairs. The soft seating area chairs are soft and comfortable, "comfy." And the tables all have three-position chairs which I call "teenager chairs." I don't have to tell them to stop leaning back in their chairs and I don't miss that. Perhaps most importantly, so much of creating a welcoming atmosphere is being a nonjudgmental, supportive person who can help students and faculty find out the answers to the serious and the silly. (Sara Kelly Johns, Lake Placid Schools, Lake Placid, NY)

Instead of worrying about making the library welcoming, perhaps our efforts would be better spent making the students welcome. Think about that for a moment. It's not just a turn of phrase. Kids will hang out together on a street corner, in the parking lot of 7-Eleven or wherever they feel comfortable. I think it has less to do with the physical comfort than acceptance of each individual. Your library furnishings can be hopelessly dated, your chairs uncomfortable, and you may not have an espresso machine; but if kids know you're happy to have them there, and if they can sense that you value them, they'll come. It all comes down to being child-centered. (Herb Wilburn, Ashby Lee Elementary School, Quicksburg, VA)

EXPERTISE

Classroom teachers should send kids to the library because the librarian is better at helping them find information or complete a task (especially in technology) than the teacher. We need to have responsibility for a curriculum and important, identified skills that no one but us *can* teach. We must be better at selecting books and other print materials, organizing them, and especially getting them into the kids' hands than the reading or English teacher. Teachers and administrators must come to *us* for help with problems only we can solve. In practice:

Show students and teachers how to use information for learning on an ongoing basis. Support teacher efforts by organizing higher-order mini-research projects around essential topics and then working with students to build the critical thinking skills that should be the basis of Information Literacy. Most teachers don't know how to do this because they teach from textbooks and give multiple-choice tests. Librarians know how to do this and that makes them important in an era of state testing that integrates critical thinking processes more and more. (Carl Janetka, ProQuest-Bigchalk)

[In my] inner-city school we had few proficient readers in the lower grades and a new "school reform/reading" program that had taken all the fairy tales, nursery rhymes, and holidays out of the K–1 curriculum, which gave me a ready curriculum. (Dorothy Tissair, Old Saybrook, CT)

Do whatever you can to make teachers' lives easier even if it's something that makes yours a little harder. If you can get the teachers to feel like you really care about them, they will also send in their students more often and ask you for your help. (Lorraine Smith, Lake Pointe Elementary School, Austin, TX)

SOCIAL EXPERIENCES

Are our libraries places for kids to interact with each other in positive ways? Instead of the library being the tomb and the study hall/computer lab being socialization central, maybe we should reverse those atmospheres. In practice:

I keep the library open for an hour after school Monday through Thursday. It is a very popular gathering place. We call it "Hang Time." Students may use the computers for homework or recreational use (I am there to supervise), play board games, sit and visit, or do jigsaw puzzles. We currently have Mancala and Pente tournaments underway. I keep music playing and we usually have some sort of snack provided by the school lunch program. I am looking to offer a few more activities to pull in some of kids who don't always know how to mix with others. I plan to make an Origami Table and a Create a Bookmark Table. I would like to find some "brainy toys" for the kids. (Robie Martin, Parsons Middle School, Parsons, KS)

If you took everything out of my library, you would have a large barn, so what I have done is partition it into "rooms" using the shelves (no lines of stacks here) and so immediately it is more inviting. This year about a third of it is for seniors (grades 5/6) only at lunch time, and they have a lounge suite, coffee tables, computers, work spaces, their senior fiction collection AND a loud CD player which is on all the time during lunch break. Never have I seen so many in there at lunch, and the most unlikely kids! Chess is popular, some do their homework (and there is research evidence to suggest that this age group cannot work in silence), others just chat or read. But they are there—they are exposed to what we offer and are forming habits and attitudes about libraries. (Barbara Braxton, Palmerston District Primary School, Palmerston, Australia)

COMPLEMENTARY USE

This means not buying (or buying less of) the sorts of things kids are now getting online—paper magazines, current events sources, print indices, and so forth. It means buying more online resources, since that is the format kids find most useable and convenient. It means having a very useable library web page tailored specifically to meet the needs of the school curriculum that is accessible from the classroom, computer lab, and home. It may mean providing online reference services. In practice:

Show off. Use the web to get what they're looking for as they watch. Point out those databases that nobody uses. Teach classes for your staff. (Maggi Rohde, Allen Elementary School, Ann Arbor, MI)

I have relied upon the online databases to supply much of what we formerly got from magazine subscriptions. Now that I don't have to order as many for research I find that I can order things like *Car & Driver*, *Motor Trend*, and the like. These types of magazines really attract the kids that I have noticed are reluctant researchers. Those that didn't "hang" in the library are now here before and after school reading the magazines and using the computers. They seem to be more relaxed in the library and unafraid to talk to us when they have questions. I think that has been the greatest payoff I have seen from the investment in the online databases. (Pati Daisy, Southern Cal Schools, IA)

We also may need to remind administrators that a primary reason libraries exist is to share commonly used instructional support materials. While book collections, magazines, and videotapes would be nice to have in every classroom, having a central pool of resources that all users can draw from makes more sense economically. Materials that are cataloged, inventoried, and circulated tend not to be materials that walk out the door when a teacher leaves the building. Didn't libraries start because not everyone could afford a copy of every book?

I am deeply troubled by reading about cut after cut after cut in school library programs throughout the nation and deeply sympathize with those whose jobs are gone and feel their work has not been appreciated. We can and should mourn with and for them. As my dad used to say, "There but for the grace of God go I."

But as professionals, we simply cannot let our reactions end with only being sorrowful. We need to figure out how our services should change in order to meet the needs of teachers and students who *do* use the Internet, to remain absolutely vital to schools that *are* strapped for funds, and to be seen as important by decision makers who *do* allocate funds in a zero-sum game.

We all keep thinking about things we can do that the Internet can't.

Oh yeah. And do them.

REFERENCES

Herring, M. (2001). 10 reasons why the Internet is no substitute for a library. *American Libraries, 32*(3), 76–78. Retrieved September 16, 2003, from **www.ala.org/Content/NavigationMenu/Products_ and_Publications/Periodicals/American_Libraries/Selected_articles/10_Reasons_Why_the_ Internet_Is_No_Substitute_for_a_Library.htm**

Johnson, D. (1998). Why do we need libraries when we have the Internet? *Knowledge Quest,* 27(1). Retrieved September 16, 2003 from **www.doug-johnson.com/dougwri/internet.html**.

Naisbitt, J. (1982). *Megatrends: Ten new directions transforming our lives.* New York: Warner.

Pew Internet Project. (2002). *The digital disconnect: The widening gap between Internet-savvy students and their schools.* Retrieved September 16, 2003, from **www.pewinternet.org/reports/toc.asp? Report=67**

How One Child Learns:
The Teacher-Librarian as
Evidence-Based Practitioner

Gail Dickinson

Evidence-based practice is a process used in the helping professions to systematically improve results by focusing on one child, patient, or client. Although not widely used in the school library profession, evidence-based practice could be used to provide a strong foundation for the teacher-librarian's role in student achievement. The process of evidence-based practitioners develop an answerable question, search for known evidence in the literature, apply possible solutions, evaluate the results, and share their findings with others in the profession.

BEST PRACTICES AND ACCOUNTABILITY

How do we know that best practices really are best? Can a "one size fits all" approach work in our library—with our students? What about what we as professionals know and can do? Where does the professional judgment of the teacher-librarian enter the process of implementing best practices in our school library programs?

One important way to prove to our colleagues that school libraries make a difference in the educational achievement of students is to concentrate our efforts not on justifying our existence but on investigating how we can improve student learning. That effort to use achievement tests and other school-wide measures has been ongoing since the late 1950s. Mary Virginia Gaver's study on the effect of school libraries on elementary reading scores was one of the very first and is often cited as the pioneer research study (Gaver, 1963). The current research conducted in Ohio by Ross Todd and Carol Kuhlthau, commissioned by the Ohio Educational Library Media Association (OELMA, 2004), and the work of Keith Curry Lance (Lance, 2004), are just a few of the recent studies. This article focuses on a more direct approach:

First published in *Teacher Librarian*, October 2005, Volume 33, Number 1

how one child learns.

Accountability is standard operating procedure in education. In some ways, the school library field has always collected data as a measure of program evaluation, such as circulation or attendance statistics. A more recent approach to improving practice in the health and social service fields can also be used as an accountability measure in school libraries. The evidence that we are looking for may exist not only in the analysis of the schoolwide standardized testing results but also through analysis of what is happening in front of our eyes each day. The research methods of evidence-based practice suggest that the path to accountability in educational best practices starts with attention to how one child learns.

EVIDENCE-BASED PRACTICE IN THE LIBRARY DEFINED

Evidence-based practice is a systematic approach to increasing results by focusing on the effect of best practices on an individual patient, client, or student. Writings on evidence-based practices are slim in the educational and library literature but are extensive in the literature of other helping professions. Nursing and social work in particular have a number of articles and books devoted to this topic. In those professions, results mean that a patient gets well or a client's particular situation improves. In education, it means that one child learns. This does not detract from the current emphasis on analysis of large-scale testing but rather gives it a rational foundation. The more that we know about how one child learns in the school library, the closer we are to recognition by our peers of our role in the education of all students.

Evidence-based practice uses action research techniques to formulate a question, research the literature, implement a solution, and analyze those results. Gibbs's (2003) handbook of evidence-based practice for the helping professions gives the following operational definition:

> Placing the client's benefits first, evidence-based practitioners adopt a process of lifelong learning that involves continually posing specific questions of direct practical importance to clients, searching objectively and efficiently for the current best evidence relative to each question, and taking appropriate action guided by evidence. (p. 6)

An interpretation of Gibbs's definition for school library programs is the following:

• *Placing the client's benefit first:* Notice that *client* is singular. The helping professions tend to the needs of hundreds of clients throughout the course of the daily and weekly grind. The sheer number of clients, all with pressing needs, can blur the edges of accountability conducted on a large scale, just as the number of students in a large high school may do in school library accountability measures. Evidence-based practice means focusing on one student. In the description used by Norlander-Case, Reagan, and Case in their work on the teacher as reflective practitioner, the focus is on "how one child learns" (1999, p. 23). The unit of study is the child in evidence-based practice, not the school library program, not the class, and not the school. Evidence-based practice means focusing on what school library services can bring to this one child, using the class and the school as minimal context.

• *Reflecting and acting on evidence-based observations:* Conceptual frameworks in schools of education abound with the term *reflective practitioner*, which refers to a teacher who uses skills of inquiry and self-analysis to embark on a journey of lifelong learning and growth as a professional educator. Becoming an evidence-based practitioner takes that definition a step deeper, past reflection into action. Becoming evidence-based means that practitioners must learn new skills, most importantly, the skills needed to produce evidence that will improve practice. The teacher-librarian sees the child through a different lens than the classroom teacher. The skills that a child exhibits in reading, in using technology, and in using information skills may provide opportunities for reflection that are in different arenas than for the classroom teacher.

• *Adopting a process of lifelong learning:* Although lifelong learning has long been our catchword, we may be more comfortable applying it to others than to ourselves. Phrased in this way, lifelong learning becomes a lifestyle, a way of behaving that we model for others. It also hints at lifelong learning being a conscious effort, something that we reach for and work at making our own. The process of lifelong learning becomes a series of steps to improve practice. It is a way for us to model the inquiry learning that we teach.

• *Continually posing specific questions of direct practical importance to clients:* The questions that evidence-based practitioners are researching are very specific. Patterson, Santa, Short, and Smith, in their earlier work on action research, give the direction "not car, but Cadillac" to help with forming an action research question (1993, p. 8). For our purposes, questions for evidence-based teacher-librarians may not be how the school library program encourages reading, but, instead, may track how booktalks on different genres over the course of the semester affect the voluntary reading of one student in one class. Until we know the answer to that specific question, we will fumble in giving specific answers to the larger questions. "Direct practical importance" also has to mean that the questions are important to the client, not just to the school library program or to the teachers. The questions of direct practical importance to our selected student in information skills inquiry usually involve finding the answer to a question in the most efficient way possible.

• *Searching objectively and efficiently for the current best evidence relative to each question:* This phrase is a way to model the "direct practical importance" mentioned previously, which requires that questions be important to the client. It is hoped that in keeping with the client's benefits first, this will also mean that the question has the potential to create change in the school library program. Finding the best evidence—the best ways to encourage reading, to teach information skills, or to integrate technology—is part of the training for teacher-librarians. Gibbs's practical guide (2003) devotes an entire section to ways to search in the literature for the best evidence. Teacher-librarians know how to do that and know how to teach others to do it. Evidence-based practice is one way that we can model not only how to search efficiently for the best evidence, but it can also demonstrate why being able to search efficiently is such an important skill.

• *Taking appropriate action guided by the evidence:* If through the literature we find that students learn information skills best when they have a specific need to know those skills, then it is against that evidence to continue to teach just-in-case library skills. Collaborating with classroom teachers to integrate information skills with subject content is teaching just-in-time skills. Students will learn by doing, rather than going through the motions of skills to be put to use weeks or months later. If we know that book displays promote reading, then the requisite action would be to place displays and carefully watch to see which type and which books seem to have the greatest impact on students. In addition, the phrase *guided by evidence* means to me that we are not alone, even in our isolated profession. We are guided by the evidence provided by others who came before us. A virtual hand-holding results when the school library becomes a true learning community.

Gibbs's definition places the teacher-librarian profession in a self-study course that requires adopting action-research questions that we have constructed through observations of practical situations in school library programs, searching the literature for research behind best practices, and then applying those practices in the library program.

AN EVIDENCE-BASED APPROACH TO BEST PRACTICES

What are the best practices used in school library programs today? Throughout this issue, best practices are highlighted as teacher-librarians illustrate ways that they have implemented areas such as collaboration, flexible access, advocacy, and other practices.

BRIEF REVIEW OF BEST PRACTICES

Collaboration teaching of information skills integrated into classroom content is a direct order in *Information Power* (AASL & AECT, 1998) and is confirmed by Zweizig and Hopkins's report of Library Power (1999). Working with classroom teachers has always been a school library best practice. In 1958, Berner wrote,

> The degree to which the library succeeds in helping teachers to become familiar with the uses of the library, to develop proficiency in library skills, and to grow in confidence in their ability to teach their students how to utilize the resources of the library—to that degree the librarian will be providing the adolescent with the keys to the rich storehouse of knowledge called the library. (p. iii)

The importance of working with teachers, seen here in the very early history of the school library, is key to the current best practice. There is no moat filled with alligators as described in Berner's account of the library program at the fictional Plainview Junior High. We know that the teacher-librarian is a teacher of information skills. This practice is evident in the writings of Wilson (1928), Douglas (1949), and many others.

Flexible access is an important precursor to success in school library programs, as shown in the research conducted by noted researchers such as Donna Shannon (1996) and Jean Donham van Deusen (1999). Flexible access has also long been a best practice, but it is still far from being universal. Currin (1939) cautions in her school library management text against tying the teacher-librarian to a fixed schedule and noted that over half of each day should be available for flexible activities (p. 25). Flex access can best be defined by its opposite. A teacher-librarian operating under the crushing weight of back-to-back classes in the library has no time to plan with teachers, assist small groups, or work with individual students. Excellence cannot be achieved under such circumstances. It would be valuable to have evidence to show exactly how and why a flexible schedule is the best learning environment. Evidence-based practitioners may be able to provide such evidence.

Steven Krashen (1993) is the oft-cited resource for the power of reading in our schools. We know from Trelease (1989) and others that a rich and diverse collection of resources best tempts students to read. We know the importance of reading, and we know how best to encourage students to read. Despite the heated debate in the field over computerized reading programs such as Accelerated Reader, we have little solid evidence from practitioners to fuel either side of the debate. Casual observations and general impressions are important, but they will not aid in proving the point to the extent that carefully planned action research will.

The above brief list of best practices barely skims the surface. We have the literature representing the found knowledge of the field passing under our eyes in a daily stream. What remains is to apply that literature to a question of library practice.

APPLYING THE LITERATURE IN LIBRARY PRACTICE

Formulating the question. The field of the school library is incredibly broad and has within it a tremendous range of areas crying out for further study. There is no universal best question, nor is there an area in the field that is imperative to the areas focused on by evidence-based practitioners. Remember that the questions should be student-focused and place the student's benefit at the highest level. Use Figure 67.1 to help scale down broad issues to answerable questions.

The first step is to select a broad issue around which to build a question. Make a list of issues of interest to you, enough that the energy the question gives you will last for at least a semester. A good think-starter is the mission and vision of *Information Power* (AASL & AECT, 1998). Read through it and think of the issues that students have in your school library. From the list, circle two or three that are of particular interest.

In the library literature or ERIC database, do quick searches for the topics you have chosen. Scan the list of citations to help narrow your choices. Choose one area of particular interest. You are ready for a more thorough search once you have selected a specific topic. Pick out and scan through several articles of interest. At this point, you are not determining the answer; rather, you are determining how to form the question. Sample questions that can be focused on one student appear below.

• Your school is adopting Schools Attuned (**www.allkindsofminds.org**). What is the effect of this program on information skills instruction?

> Step 1: "Should" questions
> Which activities should make students read more?
>
> Step 2: Literature search
> What are some good ways proven to have encouraged reading?
>
> Step 3: If/Then questions
> If I had a book display of both fiction and nonfiction books on current topics, then which ones would be checked out by avid readers and which ones by reluctant readers?
>
> Step 4: Methodology questions
> How many book displays can I set up weekly, monthly?
>
> Step 5: Evaluation questions
> How can I tell whether this is working?
>
> Step 6: Results questions
> Who would be interested in my results?

Figure 67.1. Formulating a Research Question

• What is the difference in reading behavior for strong readers within the Accelerated Reader program and those that opt out of the program?

• We assume that students are all comfortable with technology. Are there some that are not? What are the needs of those students?

Searching efficiently. This step is aimed at the skills of the teacher-librarian. Searching efficiently means to use the best resources. We need to be able to locate information in both the library literature and that from the education professions. In some cases, when dealing with student motivation or behavioral issues, consulting the social science literature might be best. Using the best resources is a crucial step in evidence-based practice, and that includes using interlibrary loan resources at our public or university library if they are not available in the school.

The best literature may not be that which is readily available or covered in a current issue of our favorite journal. We need to read deeply, but we also need to begin noting articles that may be a lead for a further question.

Appraising the evidence. Many of the questions we will pose may be controversial. For example, we may decide to investigate if flex access versus fixed access is the best way to encourage second graders to read. While realizing that flex access is the accepted best practice, we also know that there are those who believe that keeping the primary grade students on a fixed schedule works best for them. It would be nice if this topic were debated, with pro and con research conducted and reported, but this is not the case.

As with many such issues in the field, disagreements exist but rarely find their way into print.

The key is not to search for the answers you think you already have, but to search for the answers that others have found, regardless of whether you like those answers. An objective view of the literature should give a broad view of the topic.

Implementing a solution and analyzing results. Choose a course of action. Action plans were all the rage several years ago. The statement "I will" still remains an extremely powerful choice. The sheer size of the school library universe can be overwhelming. In a high school with 1,000 students, tracking increased reading or differences in inquiry learning can be overwhelming. In evidence-based practice, however, the tracking is student-centered. We test "Does this work?" by looking at individual students.

Teaching others by example and illustration. The final step in the scientific method is to publish the results of the experiment. The caveat to publish is the concluding step in any research, and so it is with evidence-based practice. Conference presentations are important but can only reach the immediate audience. Transforming those presentations into publishable articles is crucial to sharing results. Retrieving information in a literature search is a transaction that must be two-way. For every article that you find helpful, you owe an article to give help to someone else.

CONCLUSION

Professionalism is a continuum of improving skills. Although referring to classroom teachers, Norlander-Case et al. (1999) note that,

> to be a profession, there has to be a group of [SLMS] who . . . have knowledge and skills, understand the values and beliefs underlying the profession and be willing to take risks to implement those values and beliefs; inquire and reflect; respect diversity, and be altruistic towards their profession. (p. 1)

Teacher-librarians are supremely situated to perform this professional obligation, improve practice, and through that, improve our profession.

Evidence-based practice is one way that teacher-librarians can improve the school library program and their own performance, while at the same time making a difference in the lives of students. The best times as teachers come when we feel we have made a difference with one child. It is unlikely that a teacher-librarian will say that it was a good day because the 150 students in the fifth grade enjoyed a booktalk. More likely, it was the one student in the back row who came alive with one particular book and even asked to check it out. Evidence-based practice is a way for the teacher-librarian to take the euphoric moment of reaching a child and to translate it into an analysis of why that one book reached that one child at that moment. Why didn't the other books have the same effect? Would other books on the same topic have the same effect?

Evidence-based practice is a way to take the "I wonder" moments and to provide a structured way to track changes within the school library program. The changes that improve learning for this one child will change both teacher and learner and provide a sound foundation for the place of the school library program in schoolwide instruction.

REFERENCES

American Association of School Librarians (AASL) & Association for Educational Communications and Technology (AECT). (1998). *Information power: Building partnerships for learning.* Chicago: American Library Association.

Berner, E. (1958). *Integrating library instruction with classroom teaching at Plainview Junior High School*. Chicago: American Library Association.

Currin, A. M. (1939). *School library management* (6th ed.). New York: H. W. Wilson.

Donham van Deusen, J. (1999). Prequisites to flexible scheduling. In K. Haycock (Ed.), *Foundations for effective school library media programs* (pp. 223–227). Englewood, CO: Libraries Unlimited.

Douglas, M. P. (1949). *The teacher-librarian's handbook* (2nd ed.). Chicago: American Library Association.

Gaver, M. V. (1963). *Effectiveness of centralized library service in elementary schools*. New Brunswick, NJ: Rutgers University Press.

Gibbs, L. E. (2003). *Evidence-based practice for the helping professions: A practical guide with multimedia*. Pacific Grove, CA: Brooks/Cole.

Krashen, S. D. (1993). *The power of reading: Insights from the research*. Englewood, CO: Libraries Unlimited.

Lance, K. C. Retrieved February 27, 2004, from **www.lrs.org**. (Most of Keith Curry Lance's research can be found on this site.)

Norlander-Case, K., Reagan, T. G., & Case, C. W. (1999). *The professional teacher: The preparation and nurturance of the reflective practitioner*. San Francisco: Jossey-Bass.

Ohio Educational Library Media Association (OELMA). (2004). *Student learning through Ohio school libraries*. Retrieved February 27, 2004, from **www.oelma.org/studentlearning.htm**

Patterson, L., Santa, C. M., Short, K., & Smith, K. (1993). *Teachers are researchers: Reflection and action*. Newark, DE: International Reading Association.

Shannon, D. (1996). Tracking the transition to a flexible access library program in two Library Power elementary schools. *School Library Media Quarterly, 24*(3), 155–163.

Trelease, J. (1989). *The new read-aloud handbook* (2nd rev. ed.). New York: Penguin.

Wilson, M. (1928). Score card for school libraries. In *School library yearbook* (pp. 32–64). Chicago: American Library Association.

Zweizig, D. L., & Hopkins, D. M. (1999). *Lessons from Library Power: Enriching, teaching, and learning*. Westport, CT: Libraries Unlimited.

(**68**)

Bringing Vision to Practice: Planning and Provisioning the New Library Resource Center

Lisa Wilson

For school librarians, envisioning the ideal library resource center and placing into practice the best ideas gleaned from visiting dozens of libraries, reading hundreds of articles, attending professional conferences, coursework, collegial conversation, and personal experience presents a tantalizing professional challenge. By the time the doors open to welcome the first students, the teacher-librarian will have negotiated a gauntlet of selection decisions and purchasing compromises. Pitfalls abound and mistakes can be costly and difficult or even impossible to correct. In a perfect world, every time a new school library is commissioned, the teacher-librarian would be selected at the same time as the architect. The two professionals would work cooperatively to bring the ideal library resource center to reality. In practice, however, such forward-thinking collaboration is seldom the situation, and the teacher-librarian is almost always hired long after all major architectural decisions have been made and well into the construction process. Many fine books and professional articles are available regarding the design of library buildings (see Erikson & Markuson, 2001; Klasing, 1991; Woodward, 2000), but I found nothing satisfactory in my search for the practical and political realities of provisioning a new school library resource center with a comprehensive collection, appropriate technologies, furniture, equipment, and operational supplies.

The opening of Angelo Rodriguez High School in 2001 was the realization of a dream for the communities of Fairfield and Suisun, CA, which despite burgeoning population growth had not seen the opening of a new high school for 36 years. It was also the realization of a personal dream when I was appointed as Rodriguez's first teacher-librarian. Thus began an exhausting yet exhilarating year of incredibly steep learning curves that continually required that I step out beyond my role as teacher-librarian; become an

First published in *Teacher Librarian*, October 2004, Volume 32, Number 1

administrator of a million-dollar operation; and step into the unfamiliar territories of facilities planner, designer, technology consultant, and budget authority. What I learned can serve to guide others who find themselves with the exciting, overwhelming, and rewarding task of setting up a new school library and help you succeed in bringing your vision to practice.

BEGIN WITH A VISION

As simplistic as that sounds, and as eager as you may be to jump in and get started, it is critical to spend time reflecting on and developing a vision of the mission, culture, and atmosphere of the new library. A clearly developed vision will, and should, drive all purchasing decisions. To this end, tour other libraries—both school and public—to develop a critical eye for spotting exemplary layouts and avoiding functional errors. Review the school district's vision and mission statements to ensure that the library seamlessly supports the school's efforts. Visit popular bookstores for insight into design elements such as unique shelving, tables, and slat walls that make for effective book promotion and display. Interview teacher-librarians and ask what works in their libraries, what they wish they could change, and investigate what they see as emerging needs, trends and problems. The collective experience of other library professionals can guide you in fine-tuning your vision and avoiding costly errors.

FINANCES

Creating a quality library resource center is an expensive enterprise and undoubtedly the library's large budget will come under close scrutiny. Obtain solid financial commitments from the school district with separate budgets for the collection, technology, furniture and equipment, and supplies. It is impossible to establish purchasing priorities when budget figures are not set. At Rodriguez, the collection budget was well established, but the balance of library funding was always nebulous. When the district finally closed the coffers, I had authorized the purchase of a few luxuries such as mobile book display pedestals, but had not yet purchased necessities such as book carts.

Research costs and prepare realistic estimates of all expenditures. Build in contingency funds for cost overruns or unforeseen expenditures. Create a comprehensive budget document that can be presented to board members to establish legitimacy to funding requests. Attend all budgetary meetings and be prepared to defend library expenditures. Establish staffing requirements for clerical and information technology positions. Examine the quality of library services provided by other new schools and determine their costs. Comparing an underfunded, mediocre library program to a concretely described vision of an outstanding library resource center can make a powerful funding argument.

Inevitably there will be items that were overlooked or holes in the collection that won't become apparent until the books are on the shelves and patron service begins. Can unspent start-up funds be carried over, or will second-year funding provide for these additional items? Obtain written commitments for future funding that includes dollar amounts and a timeline.

THE BUILDING

Obtain blueprints of the library building, and make sure you understand every symbol and measurement. During construction, meet with the architect and construction manager to review all concerns and questions and arrange for a guided walk through. Provide them with written specifications for the security and circulation systems. Communicate needs for electrical outlets and data ports.

Ask for copies of all change orders that occurred after the initial design drawings were completed. The original plans for the Rodriguez library depicted alternating rows of tall and short shelves. Imagine my surprise in arriving on scene to find the shelves completely installed, all at a height of 42 inches. The shelving change was documented in a change order written months prior to my appointment—an order I never knew existed that cut a third of our shelving.

Don't assume anything and document everything. At Rodriguez, a false floor hides a 6-inch deep well that contains all the data lines for the 30 computers located in the center of the library. Wrongly, I assumed that electricity would be installed along with the data lines. The plans did not indicate installation of power to the floor. It took nearly 6 weeks of negotiation to get electricity to the computers resulting in a 1-month delay of the opening of the library. Ensure that adequate electricity is provided to the building. In the media production room of our new library, no electrical outlets were placed above the entire length of the work counter.

Finally, expect that some construction delays, alterations, and mistakes will occur. Document all items that need repair or adjustment. Be present at the final "walk-through" inspection, share your remaining concerns, and keep your own notes of the meeting. If you have taken the time to develop an excellent working relationship with the construction managers, resolutions to these problems will be much easier to come by. Small courtesies such as calling ahead to arrange for a site visit will lessen construction disruption and will foster a spirit of respect, trust, and cooperation.

COLLECTION DEVELOPMENT

Because our nearest public library is approximately 5 miles away via a busy interstate freeway, my vision for the school library included breadth and depth of coverage for all curricular areas with a large, noncirculating reference collection; duplicate copies of many in-demand nonfiction titles; quality, electronic subscription databases with remote access; and strong support for student recreational reading.

Every book vendor I spoke with offered prepackaged, opening-day collections, but as the late humorist Erma Bombeck once said, "One size fits all, fits nobody." This pithy observation of life applies to library collections as well. Each school has an individual identity and needs particular to that identity. At Rodriguez, the social science department is deeply committed to project-based, constructivist learning. Numerous and wide-ranging resources, including primary source materials, are required to support these assignments. Becoming familiar with state and local standards, objectives, and outcomes and taking the time to appreciate the individual preferences of your teachers will allow you to build a collection that successfully supports both mandated curricular areas and specific projects.

Beginning a full year in advance of opening and starting with the basics, I used *Senior High School Library Catalog* (Yaakow, 1997) to develop a professionally sound foundation print collection. Even this highly regarded collection development tool, however, suggested titles that I omitted as I knew they would sit unused—for example, a recommended biography of Adolf Hitler more than 1,000 pages long.

Most major book vendors provide free access to online collection development tools. Experiment with a few of them to see which you prefer. The best of these tools allow you to search by any combination of title, author, publisher, subject, or Dewey classification; permit the use of limiters such as copyright date, grade, or interest level; let you create lists based on specific review sources; provide flexible printing options; and very importantly, permit you to save your lists for future revision. For example, when searching for science and mathematics books, I specified Dewey numbers 500–699, young adult/adult interest level, and copyright dates of 1998 and newer, and required at least three reviews including *Senior High School Library Catalog*. By printing an annotated list, I could easily go through the titles one by one.

After developing a core collection, I reviewed the book orders for the past 2 years at my previous high school and added those titles. A search of the catalogs of preferred publishers and book series generated many additional titles. Circulation reports provided valuable input about books that were actually being checked out. Examining the reference collections of other school libraries proved very fruitful.

Every provider of electronic information resources offers free trials, usually for a 30-day period. Though it can be time-consuming, meeting with salespeople for demonstrations of their products will give you a much better idea of the depth and capabilities of these programs than plodding through them on your own. Online subscriptions with current biography, country, health, and science information, magazine and newspaper articles are essential for providing teachers and students with up-to-date information and must be considered an integral part of collection development.

Even if it costs a little more, order your collection from reliable, tried-and-true vendors. Remember that construction schedules are hopeful at best and bald-faced lies at worst. The completion of Rodriguez fell more than 100 days behind. Remaining flexible will allow you to keep some hold on your sanity. Therefore, when you need to reschedule the delivery for the third time an accommodating vendor will cheerfully handle your request.

Customer service is a major consideration in selecting a book vendor. When the collection was being delivered at Rodriguez, a careless truck driver allowed two pallets of books to fall from the deck of his truck, spilling dozens of boxes onto the concrete, breaking book spines and denting the covers of our beautiful new books. My sales representative arrived early the next morning and arranged for the replacement books to be shipped immediately. What seemed like a catastrophe at the time was resolved with a single phone call because I was dealing with a vendor willing and able to make things right.

Neither is this the time for processing surprises. Time will become very precious in the last few weeks before opening, and the last thing you want to do is fix poor cataloging records or type new spine labels.

At the time of ordering, insist that your price include delivery into the library—*not* the nearest building. Boxes of books are incredibly heavy and finding volunteers willing to risk lower back injury is difficult.

FURNITURE AND EQUIPMENT

When hiring personnel, government agencies remind us to "describe the job and not the person." This adage holds true for furniture and equipment as well. Your furniture and equipment needs will very likely be put out to bid. The more complete your description, the better the chances are of getting exactly what you want. An excellent reference for writing furniture and equipment specifications is *Designing a School Library Media Center for the Future* (Erikson & Markuson, 2001.) Obtaining to-scale drawings of the floor plan and furniture enabled us to visualize furniture placement and determine correct quantities. An empty library building can appear cavernous, but as the shelving is installed and furniture delivered, the space will fill quickly.

It is unlikely that you will be able to order your circulation desk, worktables, computer stations, library tables, and chairs all from the same vendor. If your furniture has laminate tops, specify the brand name, and color of the laminate you have chosen. These are standard throughout the furniture industry and will assure that your pieces will match exactly. Keep wood finish samples and fabric swatches of all furniture under consideration.

Purchase furniture that allows for flexibility in arrangement. Round tables encourage conversation and participation in group work but aren't practical for combining to create larger workspaces. Consider the comfort of your patrons. Soft seating sofas and chairs create a welcome reading retreat. A huge hit with the students at Rodriguez are the two-position wooden rocking library chairs. The selection of glass-topped computer tables with recessed monitors creates a sleek, uncluttered look but more importantly, provides tabletop space for student books and binders. Computer chairs with pneumatic height adjustment are essential for accommodating the wide range of sizes of high school students.

Request bids from equipment suppliers. Competitive bidding resulted in price reductions of 25–30% from nearly every supplier. Insist that all bids include delivery, assembly, installation, and setup, and demand that all packaging material be hauled away from the site by the vendor. If you have your heart set on a particular manufacturer or supplier, contact the company and advise them when your contract has gone to bid. After a year-long search for furniture, the manufacturer I was most excited about never even put in a bid.

None of your purchasing decisions exists in a vacuum; the collection, building layout, furniture, and equipment should all enhance your vision of quality library service. However, in the modern school library resource center, technology may well be the tie that binds all of the other aspects together into a seamless information portal. One of the goals at Rodriguez is that students will be proficient users of information technologies. In support of that goal, the library purchased quality electronic databases, powerful computers with T-1 Internet connectivity, and state-of-the-art production software; created a media production center within the library with dedicated computers, television, VCR, digital cameras, scanners, and CD recorders; and linked all library resources, including the catalog, on the library web page.

Visit schools with commendable reputations for employing technology to advance student learning and access to information. Ask specifically what their future technology plans include. Begin your technology plan a year in advance of opening, but hold off writing your equipment specifications until the last possible moment as advancements and enhancements appear almost daily. The digital cameras first specified for Rodriguez were ultimately replaced by models that offered higher resolution, were more compact and easier to download, and cost nearly $400 less each.

SUPPLIES

Order enough of everything to last through the first year. Once the facility is operating, you may find that once-open purse-strings are drawn tightly shut, as other district needs become more pressing. Obtain a commitment to fund those items that were overlooked in the original order.

Keep and continually update lists of required supplies. The final supply list for Rodriguez consisted of a 20-page spreadsheet. Consider all the functions of and services to be provided by the library: book repair, photocopying, printing, project binding, laminating, and sales of student supplies such as posterboards and diskettes. Open every drawer and cabinet in your existing library and write down every item. Ask clerical staff to make lists of necessary supplies and have them keep notes of everything they use over the course of a typical week. Walk through your library, inspecting from floor to ceiling, and note the number of bulletin boards, trashcans, tape dispensers, and staplers. List book display materials, signage, literature holders, printer cartridges, copier paper, and toner. Don't forget bookends—I nearly did. If you don't currently work in a library, ask a colleague in a busy library to allow you to make detailed observations and interview the clerical staff.

MOVING IN

During the year of planning and provisioning, I interviewed four teacher-librarians who had recently opened new library resource centers. While all of them offered invaluable guidance and individual insight, each of them cautioned me to take time—lots of time—to think about the layout of the collection on the shelves, to consider how students will enter and exit the library, to envision classroom visits and busy lunchtimes, to plan for active learner groups and quiet study areas, and to anticipate a logical and pragmatic flow to the library.

Our opening-day print collection arrived in 300 extraordinarily heavy boxes that the vendors had clearly labeled with the Dewey range of the enclosed books. We recruited students from phys ed classes to place the boxes in Dewey order next to their assigned shelves. Filling the shelves only half full and leaving the bottom shelf of each row empty has allowed for future expansion without needing to shift the entire collection. Placing the books on the shelves in their exact order before processing made for a quick inventory and cut down on the number of times the books had to be handled.

Recruit a minimum of 10 reliable volunteers from local churches, service organizations, seniors groups, or neighborhoods to help with inventory and processing. Order at least a dozen of each of your book stamps. While you will never need this many stamps again, it will allow many volunteers to speedily stamp large numbers of books. At Rodriguez, I ordered only three sets of stamps and this shortsighted cost-saving measure likely delayed the library's opening by 10 full days.

Provide your district Information Technology department or computer installers with approximate dates for installation, a sketch showing where all equipment is to be placed, and a list of all programs and databases to be provided. Confirm that computer furniture will be delivered, assembled, and in place prior to installation. Finally, test your circulation software and security system and ensure that all computer programs and databases are fully functional.

CONCLUSION

Opening a new high school library proved to be a challenging yet rewarding episode in my professional life. The most critical factor in creating a successful school library is the development of a clear vision of the mission and functionality of this integral learning space. However, the process of bringing a vision to realization involves harsh realities and sensible planning. The budget will determine many purchasing decisions and therefore it is essential to have solid funding figures. You should be prepared to defend the financial investment in your library to the school board and the community. Develop a collection integrating print and electronic media that support curriculum, standards, and student literacy, while being attentive to the individual teaching styles of your staff and the recreational reading needs of your students. Furniture and equipment selections should enhance instruction and student learning. Invest in supplies that will free you from clerical tasks to enable more time to be spent on your most important role as teacher-librarian.

Ultimately, a year of planning, preparation, and hard work and an incredible amount of money resulted in the opening of the Angelo Rodriguez High School Library Media Center. The adventure of bringing the vision of an active, student-centered library that serves as the academic hub of the school to practice is an accomplishment to celebrate.

REFERENCES

Erikson, R., & Markuson, C. (2001). *Designing a school library media center for the future*. Chicago: American Library Association.

Klasing, J. P. (1991). *Designing and renovating school library media centers*. Chicago: American Library Association.

Woodward, J. A. (2000). *Countdown to a new library: Managing the building project*. Chicago: American Library Association.

Yaakow, J. (Ed.). (1997). *Senior high school library catalog*. New York: H.W. Wilson.

School Library Accessibility: The Role of Assistive Technology

Janet Hopkins

While doing research into the topic of assistive technology in libraries, I found many examples of libraries providing assistive technology and special services for clients with disabilities. However, most of those examples are in postsecondary and public libraries. It was difficult to identify K–12 school libraries that are providing access to assistive technology for students with disabilities. This is understandable for a couple of reasons. Assistive technology is a relatively new and rapidly developing field of educational technology specialization. Additionally, many special educators remain unaware of the range of enabling technology options for special needs students. Teacher-librarians can help students with disabilities make the most of media-rich school library resources by implementing accessible technology options.

Most people visualize a school library as a room with many shelves filled with a variety of reference, fiction, and nonfiction books. These traditional resources certainly have the potential to influence students' knowledge of themselves and the world they inhabit. Teacher-librarians have further expanded these collections with the multimedia resources and information technology now available in school libraries. It is easy to take for granted the ability to gain knowledge through print and electronic resources —unless one lives with a disability that makes this difficult or impossible.

Inclusive education presents many challenges for schools and educators. Diverse student groupings in K–12 classrooms have prompted education leaders to explore new ways of meeting the needs of all learners. Most schools now address accessibility issues in the architectural design of buildings and classrooms (see National Clearinghouse for Educational Facilities, 2003). Wheelchair lifts and ramps are part of the modern school structure. But how do we move beyond structural accessibility issues and make K–12 learning materials more accessible as well? How can library resources be of greater use to students and staff with special needs?

Fortunately, more students with physical, perceptual, communication, cognitive, and learning disabil-

First published in *Teacher Librarian*, February 2004, Volume 31, Number 3

ities are now benefiting from the wide range of assistive technologies being developed to facilitate educational participation and access to learning.

DEFINING ASSISTIVE TECHNOLOGY

What is assistive technology and how is it being used? Assistive technology (AT) refers to a broad range of enabling strategies, technologies, and devices that allow individuals with special needs to work around their areas of challenge. Appropriately selected AT helps people with disabilities to provide or access information or perform a task more independently and efficiently. In an educational setting, AT can assist a student with a disability to participate in an activity or complete a task that he would have found difficult or impossible to do on his own.

AT differs from reference and instructional technology such as encyclopedia and learn-to-read CD-ROMs. These products may include accessibility features such as enabling hyperlink, multimedia, and text-to-speech options built into the software, but their primary purpose is to provide selective instruction and information.

This definition of assistive technology comes from the Individuals with Disabilities Education Act (IDEA), which is federal law in the United States:

> As used in this part, **assistive technology device** means any item, piece of equipment, or product system, whether acquired commercially off the shelf, modified, or customized, that is used to increase, maintain, or improve the functional capabilities of a child with a disability." (Individuals with Disabilities Education Act, 1999, §300.5, from IDEA Practices, 2003)

AT applications are used by many professionals in the fields of health, rehabilitation and education. Low-tech strategies and tools that are frequently used in libraries include large-print books, color-coding techniques and the use of symbols as visual cues. Audio books and videotapes are other popular resources used by disabled and nondisabled persons. A diverse collection of materials helps to create an inclusive library. However, other more sophisticated high-tech options are also available.

RATIONALE FOR USING ASSISTIVE TECHNOLOGY

AT services in the school library provide new opportunities for students with disabilities and the people who interact with them. K–12 teacher-librarians have a new and important role to play in helping youngsters with disabilities develop skills with AT that will allow them to enjoy literature, research, and learning throughout their lives.

AT products can help students living with a disability to function more productively in a variety of circumstances. The functional value of an AT product is one obvious benefit and usually the primary reason for institutions, individuals, and families to acquire these products. This important functional role of AT often has a positive psychological influence on users and those who interact with them (Community Research for Assistive Technology, n.d.).

AT can be applied to address a variety of personal needs. For example, students with visual difficulties can make use of portable magnification devices, specialized software with screen reading and magnification capabilities, CCTVs (Closed Circuit Televisions or video magnifiers), audio products (talking books), and Braille computer technologies (Braille translation software, refreshable Braille displays and Braille printers), as well as large-print resources.

Students with hearing challenges benefit from various assistive listening devices, captioning features, and text telephone (TTY) or telecommunication devices for the deaf (TDD).

Students who are unable to communicate verbally make use of portable augmentative and alternative communication (AAC) devices to speak for them. These devices allow customized programming to facilitate communication in multiple environments. A variety of specialized AAC hardware and software is available. Some AAC users have a dedicated device to speak for them, which functions exclusively for communication. Other AAC users prefer to install AAC software on a multifunctional laptop or handheld computer. (For information on AT devices, see the online journal *Assistive Technology Journal*, **www .atnet.org/news/**.)

Students with limited movement can take advantage of environmental control units, mobility devices such as wheelchairs and alternative computer access technologies such as head mouse tracking systems or switch controls with scanning software (Phillips, 2003).

These are just some examples of the assistive technologies available to support students with special needs. Consult an online searchable database such as ABLEDATA **www.abledata.com/** or assistivetech .net **www.assistivetech.net/** to learn more about the range of products available.

WHY USE AT IN THE SCHOOL LIBRARY?

• *Access to information*: Barrier-free information access facilitates student self-determination and the ability to make good decisions. If information is difficult to access because of a reading, sensory, or mobility impairment, a student becomes reliant on the assistance and advice of others. AT can improve access to information, allowing students with disabilities to independently seek out solutions and meet more of their own needs.

• *Skill development and progress*: All students need to feel capable of setting and achieving their own goals. Achievable goals will, of course, vary from student to student. Learning to use an AT device to produce desired outcomes encourages relevant goal-setting for a student with a disability. Recognizing that there are ways to function more productively through well-matched AT and observing other students who have developed AT skills can provide strong motivation. As a student enhances his own abilities through AT, there is bound to be a realization that new goals could be accomplished. Success in AT task accomplishment provides encouragement. Positive results achieved through the use of AT can create incentive for students to set the bar a little higher next time.

• *Competency and efficiency*: A student who has mastered basic skills in AT use can proceed to more complex levels of skill acquisition and efficiency. Anyone who has attempted to maneuver a wheelchair for the first time will quickly appreciate the skill and performance competency of wheelchair athletes who participate in basketball, volleyball, and other athletic events. AT skill development can provide challenge and motivation for people who strive for greater independence and enhanced performance.

• *Specialization*: Beyond AT competency and efficiency lies the ability to inspire and mentor students who want to learn about AT. Students and staff who develop a high level of knowledge and skill in specific areas of AT will be valued resource people for others wishing to learn. Sharing AT expertise is rewarding for staff and students who have developed knowledge and skills. The ability to assist others through specialist skills and knowledge brings with it the power to influence attitudes. With the ability to influence lies the potential for expanding the school community's knowledge and support of AT and inclusive library services.

• *Self-esteem and self-reliance*: The education system must strive to nurture the self-esteem of all students. AT helps to alleviate frustration for students with disabilities having to rely on others to assist with tasks they would rather perform for themselves. Progress toward greater independence provides a sense of achievement and relief for students with disabilities, their families, and their caregivers.

• *Peace of mind*: AT products function as problem-solvers for students with disabilities. There are still challenges to face on a day-to-day basis even with well-selected AT, but it helps make life more manageable for students and their families. AT provides opportunities for success and optimism, while allowing educators to better serve students with disabilities. AT helps to create bonds through problem solving and teamwork while reducing feelings of dependence.

• *Peer acceptance*: Technology that promotes increased interaction with others helps to prevent social isolation. AT that allows a student to access information, communicate, or participate in school promotes acceptance. Universal design initiatives in architecture and technology help to bring students with disabilities into contact with their nondisabled peers. When the school community is able to observe the achievements and contributions of students with disabilities, it leads to increased awareness. School libraries that provide accommodations for students with disabilities can help to create a welcoming environment.

• *Lifelong learning tools*: AT is evolving to meet the needs of a range of students with disabilities with products available to address many learning needs. Teacher-librarians can play an important role in familiarizing students with the AT options available to help during their school years thus promoting lifelong learning skills.

WHAT TEACHER-LIBRARIANS CAN DO

Here are 10 ideas for addressing library accessibility issues for students with disabilities:

1. Consult with special educators at your school to learn about your students with disabilities and their challenges. Do these students use the library? Why or why not?

2. Seek out colleagues or members of the school community with AT expertise. Find out which resources and services already exist in your school or district.

3. Tour your own library to identify barriers to learning and assess the variety of technology and resource formats available for students with diverse needs.

4. Allocate professional development time for learning about library accessibility and AT. Visit other libraries, schools, and suppliers; meet with district specialists; or attend conferences where you can learn more.

5. Consider forming a focus group including colleagues who share an interest in library accessibility issues.

6. Become familiar with the built-in accessibility features already available on your computer operating systems. (See resource list below for links.)

7. Assess your need for funding and identify budget and grant options.

8. Talk to administrators about the library accessibility issues that you consider most urgent.

9. Ask vendors to provide trial products before purchasing products. Most AT software companies provide time-limited downloads through their web sites. Use the trial to consider hardware and software compatibility issues.

10. Publicize your accessibility initiatives and new technology acquisitions. Inform the school community of your progress in newsletters, staff meetings, and other announcements. Share your experiences with your colleagues.

CONCLUSION

AT is making a difference in the lives of many students with disabilities. Teacher-librarians, in partnership with special educators and other members of the school community, can assist in expanding the educational opportunities available to all students by promoting and developing accessible school libraries.

REFERENCES

Community Research for Assistive Technology. (n.d.). Success story: Assistive technology and function. Retrieved October 20, 2003 from **http://www.atnet.org/CR4AT/PositionPapers/Function.html**

IDEA Practices. (2003). *IDEA '97 law & regs*. Retrieved October 17, 2003 from **http://www.ideapractices .org/law/regulations/index.php**

National Clearinghouse for Educational Facilities. (2003). *NCEF resource list: Accessibility in schools*. Retrieved October 20, 2003 from **http://www.edfacilities.org/rl/accessibility.cfm**

Phillips, B. (2003). Headpointing technology: A comparative project. *Proceedings of the Technology and Persons with Disabilities Conference 2003*. Retrieved October 20, 2003 from **http://www.csun .edu/cod/conf/2003/proceedings/209.htm**

ONLINE RESOURCES

http://trace.wisc.edu/world/computer_access/

The "Designing More Usable Computers and Software" page on this site from Trace Research and Development Center includes links to major technology company accessibility resources.

www.rit.edu/~easi/lib.htm

The Equal Access to Software and Information (EASI) site has a page devoted to library accessibility issues, including a collection of useful links.

http://bpm.nlb-online.org/contents.html

Library Services for Visually Impaired People: A Manual of Best Practice was produced by the United Kingdom's National Library for the Blind.

http://sussex.njstatelib.org/njlib/disabilities/dsequtoc.htm

Created by the New Jersey State Library, the publication *Equal Access to Information: Libraries Serving People with Disabilities* is available online, and includes links to print and online services.

www.washington.edu/doit/UA/

This page from the DO-IT link on the University of Washington web site includes helpful resources on technology and universal design.

⑦⓪

Corey's Story

Barbara Braxton

Once upon a time, there was a little boy with curly red hair, big brown eyes, a smattering of freckles on his nose, and a smile as big as the whole outdoors. His name is Corey and this is his story. Corey had seen a lot in the 5 years he had been on this planet—more than most little boys should see in a lifetime. When he was very little, he lived with his mummy and daddy just like lots of little boys do. But his daddy did not want Corey to see his mummy shoot poison into her veins, so he took Corey to live in another town far, far away. Corey's mummy was so stoned that she did not even notice they were gone, and, to this day, Corey has not seen or spoken to his mummy again.

The months went by, and life was good for Corey—as good as it could be for a little boy with a daddy who worked all day while he played with the other kids in the childcare center. But every night, his daddy was there to tuck him into bed, read him a story, and give him a kiss. Corey loved stories. He loved to let his mind wander to the lands of make-believe where children had mummies who loved them and looked after them. Sometimes he even dreamed that he was in a family like that, but each morning he woke up, and he knew it was just that—a dream.

Then one day his daddy found him a new mummy—one that came with a brother and sister too! Corey was happy for a while. But it was so hard to understand why his new mummy did not love him as much as she loved his brother and sister, and no matter how hard he tried, she always yelled at him and sometimes even hit him, even when he had been especially good. But the hardest part for Corey to understand was why his daddy did not read him stories anymore or tuck him into bed, and why, sometimes, he hit Corey too.

Corey needed to escape, but being such a little boy, he did not have anywhere to escape to—except inside his books. Even though he was only four, he would find a quiet spot, curl up with his favorite stories, and tell them to himself over and over again. It was not long before Corey realized that he could read! Although he did not have many books to read, when he read those he had, he got the same pleasure over and over again. Lots of times he read them to his teddy Scruffy because Scruffy seemed to enjoy the stories as much as he did.

First published in *Teacher Librarian*, October 2005, Volume 33, Number 1

Where Corey lives, children can go to school when they are five, and that day was soon coming for Corey. He could hardly wait because he knew that at the school there was a library full of books that could take him on magical adventures to faraway places, and that while he was there, he could forget about the yelling and the smacking and the bruises that made his back and his bottom so sore.

That day came and off Corey went to school with his shiny new school bag, his shiny new lunchbox, and his shiny new library bag. Oh, how he hoped he would be able to go to the library on that very first day. Even if he couldn't borrow a book, what fun it would be just to look and choose what he would borrow just as soon as he could.

To his delight, his teacher took him to the library on that first day, and he was allowed to choose a book. The library lady had worked very hard to get all the new students' names on the computer just so they could borrow books.

The library was a wonderful place, and there were books and things everywhere just waiting for him to choose them. The library lady showed all of the children where their favorite characters were, like Winnie the Pooh and the Rainbow Fish. It was so hard to decide. Finally, he selected a little book that looked like fun and very proudly took it to the counter, so that it could be scanned before he popped it into that shiny new library bag. The library lady had introduced them to a teddy called Dr. Booklove and told them how Dr. Booklove liked to read rather than repair books, so he liked the books to go home in library bags so they did not get damaged.

Dr. Booklove had also said that it was important to keep your library books in a special place at home away from your little brothers and sisters and pets, and Corey knew exactly where he was going to keep his book. That night after he had read the book to himself—because no one else read to him anymore—he put it in his special place.

And that was the last Corey ever saw of his very first library book.

Just as he was going to sleep, a lady came to the house, and before Corey knew what was happening, all his clothes and Scruffy were shoved into his shiny new schoolbag, and he was being put in a car with the lady. He didn't even have time to tell her about the library book in its special place.

That night, he and Scruffy slept in a new bed, one "where you will be safe" the lady said.

Corey did not go back to school for a few days, but when he did he was too scared to tell the nice library lady what had happened. He really did not understand it himself. So when it was time for him to go to the library again, and she asked him where his book was, he just said it was at his dad's house.

Because lots of children at that school spend one week with their mummies and the next with their daddies, the library lady assumed he would bring it the next week. "When you bring it back, you can borrow another one," she said. Corey's heart broke. How could he tell her that the book was at his dad's house, but he was not?

Four weeks went by, and each time, the library lady said the same thing, "When you bring it back, you can borrow another one." She even gave him little reminder notes and said she would phone his dad to get him to put it in his bag for him. She was used to lots of little children not being able to remember.

Then one day the library lady was talking to Corey's teacher, and she mentioned that he had not returned his book and she was going to call his dad. That's when she discovered what happened to Corey on that night all those weeks ago. No wonder that big smile he had on that first day had disappeared, and he looked so forlorn each time he could not borrow a book.

As soon as lunchtime was over, the library lady went to Corey's class and asked his teacher if he could come to the library for a few minutes. When they got there, the library lady said that under special circumstances she could break the rules, and even though Corey had not returned his library book, he could choose another one anyway. The smile was back! In a flash, he was off to the shelves to choose the story he had wanted all those weeks.

Meanwhile, the library lady found a very smart library bag with a special message on it, and she gave it to Corey. The smile nearly split his face as he went back to class.

The next morning Corey was back at the library before school to see if it was all right to get another book because he had already read that one to Scruffy. "No worries," said the library lady, "you can come every day if you want. We are always open before school and at lunchtime and even after school. You do not have to wait until your library day."

As Corey went out the door, he punched the air and shouted, "YES!"

Every day since, Corey comes to the library before school and changes his book, always placing it in the library bag with the special message. His smile is still as wide as the outdoors, and whenever he sees the library lady in the playground, he comes up and slips his hand in hers and says, "Hello library lady."

The library lady smiles too and, inside, blesses the day she broke the rules.

As for the special message on Corey's library bag, it says, "To teach is to touch lives forever."

⑦⑪

The School Library as Sanctuary

Lynn Evarts

Two weeks after the Columbine High School shootings, where 15 people died at the hands of Dylan Klebold and Eric Harris, Dan Savage wrote in his Seattle newspaper column, "The tenth or eleventh time DanCBS/PeterABC/TomNBC told me the massacre in Littleton, Colorado, was especially horrific because it happened in a high school, 'somewhere children feel safe,' I started screaming at the television. What high school were they talking about?" ("Savage Love: Fear the Geek," *The Stranger*, May 6, 1999, **www.thestranger.com/seattle/Content?oid=915**).

Klebold and Harris did not feel safe in their school community, and thus they set out to take away any feelings of safety that anyone ever felt in a school. To a large extent, they were successful. School librarians will never forget that the school library was the site of some of the shootings. Resonating with all of us is the panicked voice of the library aide who dialed 911 that day and screamed for students to "Get down" as shots were heard. Unfortunately that culture of isolation and feeling of not being safe continues to pervade high schools almost 8 years later. Fortunately there is a way that school librarians can wield more power than people with guns. We can combat that isolation in students who feel disenfranchised and unprotected.

Why the library and the library media professional? We are the keepers of the books and the supporters of the curriculum. What can we do to help marginalized students who feel that their high schools offer absolutely no safe place?

Have you ever looked around your library and noticed the boy in the back, sitting alone and reading the world's biggest fantasy novel? I'm sure you've seen the petite girl in the long army coat, huddled behind a bookcase, writing in her journal. We are well acquainted with the isolated students in our schools; I advocate that library media professionals become proactive in helping these students find a safe place in their schools—their school libraries. Librarians have a head start because isolated teens are already hanging out in the library. All we need to do is reach out to them. Occasionally educators and librarians bemoan the fact that we are powerless in so many ways. But when it comes to helping isolated students,

First published in *VOYA: The Voice of Youth Advocates*, December 2006. *Teacher Librarian* acknowledges *VOYA*'s permission to adapt and reprint this article.

we have amazing power—if we use it effectively.

Supporting isolated students costs little in time or money, but the benefits that both the school library and the students reap are enormous. In these times of budget and personnel cuts, school libraries should rely not only on how well we support the curriculum but also on how we support the students—particularly the isolated students. As schools purchase programs and line up speakers to explain how to reach and help all students, almost none of them mention the power of the library.

TWO TYPES OF ISOLATION

Young people can be isolated in one of two ways: self-isolated or actively isolated by their peers. Self-isolated teens might be insecure, shy, or unsure of their sexual identity. They might be hiding tense family situations, eating disorders, or drug use, often going to great lengths to stay away from others. They might feel that they aren't good enough for a friend or even good enough for anyone to notice them. They are frequently the invisible students in the school. Ask many members of your school community and you will find very few people, teachers included, who recognize the self-isolated student.

The second type, peer-isolated students, are more easily identified because they are harassed and ostracized by their peers. Among the numerous reasons that they are harassed might be the way they are dressed, their race or ethnicity or sexual identity, their problem acne, or their lack of social skills. Adults notice the peer-isolated student because of bullying training and the frequent need to intervene on the harassed student's behalf.

The library and the librarian are ideally poised to help these young people because the library is not a structured classroom environment; there are no grades or assessments, and the librarian does not carry the stigma that a counselor sometimes holds for students. The library can simply provide a safe space and resources for those students who are self-isolated. Because the librarian can be very proactive about harassment, peer-isolated students can feel safe as well.

Some students who need a safe environment will automatically find the library. Look around your library and you will see them right now. But there are other students who desperately need a haven in the school environment and don't know how to find you. As you move around the school during the day, keep an eye out for students who seem to sequester themselves. Lunch is one of the most stressful times for isolated students, so wander down to the cafeteria and look for teens sitting alone. Make sure that the teachers in your school know that you're actively searching for students who would benefit from a safe space. A student whom you know is struggling with self-mutilation might learn that she is not so alone if she "finds" *Cut*, by Patricia McCormick (2000) or *The Luckiest Girl in the World*, by Steven Levenkron (1997). When she discovers that she's not the only one in the world, she might see the library as a safe space.

Another subtle way to draw in these (and all) students is to work at remembering what individual students like to read. Most librarians do it anyway, but it's important to do it consciously. Students are flattered if you simply ask them how they liked a book that they're returning. You draw them in just by asking about the plot of a book that you haven't read yet.

This technique works with nonfiction books that support the curriculum, but it works even better with fiction. Take one school year's budget and focus on fiction. Ask students for suggestions. Buy paperbacks to double the number of books you can purchase. When you bulk up your fiction collection, they will come, isolated students among the others. Read the books yourself or at least read reviews and keep notes on cards. Start a set of cards headed with the names of students, listing titles that you think they might like. Keep the cards nearby when you're reading review journals so you can jot down titles as you come across them. If a book arrives that you know a particular student will like, set it aside and make sure that she sees it when she comes to the library. Better yet, find out what class she's in and do a delivery.

Such personal consideration helps you create more of a connection with students and costs nothing. You are the matchmaker; when you find just the right book for a student, you will be rewarded when he returns to tell you that he has never read a book before—but do you have another one just like this one? It's even more rewarding when he is one of your isolated students.

LUNCH IN THE LIBRARY

One controversial idea that truly creates a safe space and a sense of community in your library is to allow students to eat lunch there. Many schools have strict no-food policies in the library; you must do what works in your particular space. In my experience, lunch in the library has been a stunning success for the past 6 years. During one lunchtime early in the school year, I counted 42 students with hot lunch, bag lunch, salad bar, or no lunch—just a book. They were in groups all over the library. Some students were studying, some were reading quietly, some were doing the Sudoku together in the newspaper. There is a garbage can available for their use; the problems that I used to have with lollipops stuck in books and Twinkies shoved behind shelves have disappeared since students began eating lunch in the library.

Library lunches are one of the most effective ways to draw in isolated students because the scariest place in any school is the cafeteria at lunchtime. You get your tray and you turn around to face a sea of potential harassment incidents. Where do you sit? What if you don't have any friends—or any friends in your lunch period? I have discovered that interesting combinations of students develop in the library during lunch. I look up to see two football stars sharing a table with one of our cognitively disabled students. I cruise by to see if the players are sitting there just to harass him, but I find that they're all talking about the upcoming football game. School staff and community members who mentor at our library often comment on the unusual combinations created during lunch.

STARTING SLOWLY

Making some of these changes may indeed cause controversy in your school. Ultimately you need to know your own community limits and environment. On the other hand, you can't live in fear that you might upset the apple cart. These students desperately need your support. If you're initially hesitant, go slowly. Often isolated students who are most in need of help have fallen through the cracks. Perhaps a student was evaluated for special education, but she didn't meet the requirements. Or maybe comments from someone's former teachers lead you to believe that a certain student has slowly walled herself off. If you notice her looking in one particular area for books, place books that might interest her there.

I once had a student who was suffering from anorexia but refused help. She frequented one display rack in the library, so I made sure to load it with titles about eating disorders and body image. I was thrilled when I noticed that she was looking them over. (She rarely checked anything out.) If you develop the philosophy that you'll change the world one teen at a time, this method is perfect.

GATHERING SUPPORT

Administrative support for what you do in this arena is important because often you are dealing with sensitive issues. With so much media attention on disenfranchised youth, now is the time to garner such backup. Show your administrators how important you are to your school community by demonstrating that you can support the curriculum and reach out to at-risk students at the same time. Collect facts and statistics from the media to reinforce your cause.

Another ally within your school building is your counseling department. School counselors might be able to give you back-ground information about a particular student (without breach of confidentiality) or help the student with a specific issue. Because isolated students are often hesitant to reach out to strangers, it might be helpful for you to make the initial contact or accompany the student to the counselor's office. Just having a friendly face nearby might help a young person open up to someone else who can get the professional assistance needed.

School employees are required, by law, to report any instances of child abuse (sexual, emotional, and physical) to the authorities. It is often helpful, if you notice a conversation with a teen headed in that direction, to remind her that you're bound by law to report any instance in which she is being hurt, is hurting herself, or might harm others. I often use this yardstick when deciding when to take our conversation to someone else. Cultivating relationships with other staff members will give you an outlet for your own feelings about what you're hearing; often they can help you judge what to report and what not to report.

Occasionally you can affect a student's life by reaching beyond school walls. Network within your community to find creative ways to help these students. Get to know your local counselors and therapists so that perhaps you can help a student and/or his family to get low-cost counseling. (Make sure that you're aware of what permission you need to involve the student in counseling outside of school.)

Match members of your community with students who are searching for employment. One girl whom I knew well was unsuccessfully looking for a job because she was painfully shy. For weeks, we talked about jobs she could do that didn't involve contact with a lot of people. When one of my friends had a stroke, she needed a cleaning person. Success! I introduced the two of them, and the girl is still working for my friend, 6 years later. The cleaning job became more of a personal assistant job, giving the student a chance to spread her wings in a safe environment. She is now cleaning several places, offering a needed service to some of the older people in our community.

Not all librarians are comfortable with such a role. Some readers of this article might scoff at adding one more hat on their already full heads. Yet all it really takes to offer this important service is genuine interest in the community you serve. Teenagers are fun—when you notice a student looking at a book, you can brighten your day a great deal by simply having a conversation about the book.

Also remember to take care of yourself. Set boundaries with which you will be comfortable and see what happens from there. Don't try to change the world in one fell swoop; just change it one teenager at a time. It will all be worthwhile when you get a thank-you note that says, "You've had a very positive influence in my life and I'll never forget my crazy high school library lady."

Books are our stock in trade, but the teens are really why we're here. When we remember that, we'll do our best to create those safe spaces that all teens so desperately need.

REFERENCES

Levenkron, S. (1997). *The luckiest girl in the world*. New York: Scribner.

McCormick, P. (2001). *Cut*. Asheville, NC: Front Street.

Savage, D. (1999, May 6). Savage love: Fear the geek. *The Stranger*. **www.thestranger.com/seattle/ Content?oid=915**

Safe Haven: Libraries as Safe Havens for Teens

Gail Bush

*Aquamarine. The color of water. "I bought them so I could paint the island," Carrie
said matter-of-factly, as if she had known it all along. And then she flopped, stomach-down,
on her bed and wondered for the millionth time why it was the island she wanted to paint.*
From *The Language of Goldfish*, by Zibby Oneal (1980)

We are here for the children. All educators believe that we can help our students live good and meaningful lives that are both personally rewarding and socially responsible. That *is* the long and the short of it. Has this vision changed along with so much else in our fragile world? What does it mean now? And where does it leave us, holding that wonderful, sappy old poster that reads, "It's a beautiful world in the library"?

No one will dispute that 2001 was a tough year in every school in America, for every grade level, and in every region of the country. But at our suburban public high school, the heartache began a week earlier than most. That was when we suffered the first of two student suicides in our school community. We were hoping to begin to heal when the world collapsed in Manhattan.

Ann* was a girl, a senior, a loner, a sullen child.

Tragically, tragically, three months later, we were shaken to our core once again.

Mike* was a boy, a freshman, a team player, a friendly child.

Writing these words, knowing these students, I struggle for something to hold onto. As humans, we seek to create order out of chaos. We are impelled to look for patterns so that we might say, "Oh, well, that might give us a clue to a mystery that even the experts cannot unravel." Perhaps if we find another clue and another, we will feel as if we have learned something significant, something that will help us to

First published in *VOYA: The Voice of Youth Advocates*, February 2003. *Teacher Librarian* acknowledges *VOYA*'s permission to adapt and reprint this article.

cope, to avert tragedy in the future. Every person, every child and adult in our school community was looking for an answer.

Everyone was hurting. When one of the social workers stopped me in the hall in mid-January, naturally I asked her how she was coping. She talked about Ann and about Mike and about their blatant differences. She said, "I just cannot see any connection, any pattern in their behavior. We have looked and looked."

"Oh, I know one," I replied sadly. I proceeded to share my recollections of Ann and Mike.

Ann had come to the library during her free periods every single day of her four-year high school career. Mike was just a freshman but he had quickly become a library "regular." Both students headed for their same spots every day. Ann would never make eye contact with us (try as we might) as she walked to a study carrel in the rear of the library; she sat alone and somber, gazing out the window. Mike sauntered in, friendly as can be, and sat right up front eyeing everyone who walked through the library.

My colleague stood dumbstruck, staring at me, seeing in my expression what we as librarians know in our hearts. Our libraries *are* safe havens. Done properly, we provide a sanctuary not only for language and mutual respect, but constancy and openness and acceptance and tolerance. Our "zone" is a safety zone; our purpose goes far deeper than information literacy and technology planning. Our collection has all the best books about teen suicide, depression, adolescence and its pitfalls. That is not what these reflections are about. The collection, facility, budget, personnel, planning—all may be well in place. This piece also is not about the belabored fact that the rest of our colleagues are blind to the unwritten role we perform. Rarely are we in the student services loop in the schools. But let's talk about us, about that part of the library program that eludes standards and guidelines. All the pieces are in the right places; now let us consider our true mission.

I have come to believe that there are certain elements that help foster a safe haven in any school library:

• *The environment:* A soft chair here and there—some visible and some tucked away; a rug from home; a window with a view; the privacy of a study carrel; natural lighting; lots of plants; a quiet hum of human activity. (Depending on where you are in our library, it is either a quiet or loud whisper.)

• *A place:* We talk about the library as a place. For colleagues, it is sometimes a conference space, sometimes a salon with ideas being tossed around. For some students, it is home base in a daily game of tag. (Our only other nonclassroom space for students is the cafeteria which is, for some, the social equivalent of being thrown to the lions.)

• *Judgments:* None allowed. You don't get a grade in library. Assessments fall neatly off our shoulders. Although we do teach, we are usually behind-the-scenes assessors.

• *Familiarity:* On two counts. Students like depending on seeing the same faces as they walk in the door. Maybe this familiarity will make them inclined to seek out the public library. Maybe they can find a home base at the public library when the school is closed.

• *An oasis:* Sure, we encourage homework before *Teen People*, but there are more avenues for leisure here than anywhere else in the school. It is all leisure brought to you by the written word, whether it is between the covers of a magazine or on the Web site on a computer screen.

• *Everyone is welcome:* Every grade, ability level, gender, sexual orientation, hair dye, tattoo, piercing. You name it, we've either seen it or read it on their T-shirts.

• *A constant:* Yep, we are here all through high school and before and after school every day—while the rest of the experience is fresh every 45 minutes when a new opportunity for adolescent angst is born. The place, the people, the air, the familiarity—students can bank on it.

• *Relationships:* Now this element interests me the most. Let's talk about relationships, the heart of it all. All education of significance comes hand in hand with a relationship that has been established between student and teacher, coach, counselor, librarian. Think back to your own memorable learning experiences in formal education. What was at the heart of the matter for you?

Relationships. The funny thing about being an institution within an institution is that we have some very unnatural bonding with some of these kids. Those whom I have tossed out, debated with, written up—they come back year after year after they graduate, just to check in. Here are just a few for the books:

When Steve was a senior, he felt as if he was not a reader. Not that he did not know how. But he felt that it did not matter when he read. He could not connect with anything in books. He was unmotivated. Yet Steve was an ambitious boy. He had a lawn-mowing business after school, which was where his interests dwelled. So I made literacy competitive for him. When he had to read a sizeable novel during senior year, I said that I would read it, too. We would see who would finish first. It was a true challenge for me because I had started the book previously and never engaged with it. When I told that to Steve, we were on. I think we put one dollar on it. I said that if I won, I would give my dollar to charity. Steve came into the library every day and read right in front of me, winning the dollar handily. I have seen Steve many times since he graduated from high school. He has a lawn maintenance company and a family now. He tells me that he is going to be sure that his children become readers.

It was mid-afternoon in the dead of a Midwestern midwinter day. George had engaged me in conversation. We stood talking and leaning over the reference shelves for 10 minutes or so. There was a pause as we watched students enter and leave the library. George said, "Don't you have anything *important* to do? Don't you have to work?"

"You," I said to George, "are my work, and you are important."

George smirked and replied by indicating that my life was "pitiful," that I was "stuck in this high school." It was not so bad for him but for me, well, this was my "real life being wasted at this school. Too bad you don't have a real job."

Five or 6 years later, George saw me at the airport and literally chased me down. He just wanted to say hello, wanted me to know that he works there as a translator. He wanted to thank me for always seeming to have time to talk to him. It made him realize that he liked to "be in conversation" with others.

Last spring, the oddest thing happened. We were all still bruised from the wounds of the year. In walked Robert, a graduate from a few years back. He looked very familiar, but I could not place him without the aid of our trusty yearbook collection. Even then, he was one of so many over the years who I had held to a standard, sat on, showed that I cared in a steady and routine way. He walked over to me in his white shirt, suit, and tie. He asked if he could give me a hug. "You know what you said to me?" he asked.

"No," I said, "What?"

"You said, 'Do a little more. You can do better. I believe in you, Robert, even if you can't see it yourself right now.'"

Robert said, "Do you believe that? I acted so jerky when I was here. You told me you believed in me and it always seemed so weird because you didn't have to. I figured my teachers wanted me to do better in their classes so it would make them feel better, but you didn't have anything riding on it. It always seemed so 'out there.' So I came here today because I wanted you to see that I did a little more, I did better, and now I believe in myself. I have a company. People work for me. I tell my employees that they can do better. And I came to give you a big hug so that you would know what you did for me."

I was touched, to be sure. But I remember thinking that I told Robert the same thing that I told hundreds of students—because that is just what I say to students. And now that is what I want to say to you. Do a little more. Do better. Believe in us.

We all create a space in our schools. What is in your space? New books? Instructional technology? Displays? All important and all good. But do not undersell the gift that we give our young friends who are struggling through adolescence. On any given day, we all have moments when we want to "paint the island." On those days in particular, take the time to peel back the layers of the adolescent shell. See inside where the truth, beauty, and goodness resides deep within. Be the adult in that teen's day who takes the time to stop and listen for that which he or she simply cannot express to the outside world. Create a safe haven. Ensure that it is a safety zone for everyone who crosses your threshold. Do a little more. Do better. Believe.

* *All names have been changed.*

Index

Note: Italic page numbers refer to figures.

About the Editors
and Contributors

Doug Achterman is the teacher-librarian at San Benito High School, Hollister, CA, and is a doctoral student in the interdisciplinary studies library and information science program at the University of North Texas. He can be reached at *dachterman@sbhsd.k12.ca.us*.

Marlene Asselin is an assistant professor in the Department of Language and Literacy Education at the University of British Columbia, Canada. She teaches graduate and teacher education courses in reading, language arts, and literature instruction. She also coordinates the teacher-librarian education program. Her research interests are teacher knowledge, collaboration, literature response, and school library programs. She can be reached at *marlene.asselin@ubc.ca*.

Steven M. Baule is the superintendent of schools for Community Unit School District 201 in Westmont, IL. He has served as an assistant superintendent, high school principal, technology director, teacher-librarian, and classroom teacher. He can be reached at *sbaule@cusd201.org*.

Kay Bishop is director of the School Library Media Specialist Program in the School of Informatics at the State University of New York at Buffalo. She can be reached *atkgbishop@buffalo.edu*.

Barbara Braxton is the teacher-librarian at Palmerston District Primary School in Palmerston, Australian Capital Territory. She can be reached at *barbara@iimetro.com.au*.

Carol A. Brown is associate professor and program coordinator in the Department of Librarianship, Educational Technology, and Distance Instruction at East Carolina University. Her research interests include strategies for successful collaboration between technology and library professionals in K–12 schools. She can be reached at *browncar@mail.ecu.edu*.

Gail Bush is professor and director, Center for Teaching Through Children's Books, National-Louis University, Skokie, IL, and author of *The School Buddy System: The Practice of Collaboration* (2003). She can be reached at *gail.bush@nl.edu*.

Michael Cart, a recipient of the Grolier Foundation Award for distinguished contributions to young people and literature, is a *Booklist* columnist and reviewer. The former director of the Beverly Hills (CA) Public Library, he teaches young adult literature at the University of California, Los Angeles. He can be reached at *mrmcart@sbcglobal.net*.

Audrey Church is coordinator of the School Library Media Program at Longwood University in Farmville, VA. Prior to this position, she was a public school teacher-librarian for 20 years. She is author of *Leverage Your Library Program to Help Raise Test Scores: A Guide for Library Media Specialists, Principals, Teachers, and Parents* (2003). She can be reached at *churchap@longwood.edu*.

Gail Dickinson is assistant professor of school librarianship in the Darden College of Education at Old Dominion University, Norfolk, VA. She is the author of the *Achieving National Board Certification for School Library Media Specialists* (2005). Her other work on evidence-based practice appears in the papers of the Treasure Mountain No.11 Research Forum. She can be reached at *gdickins@odu.edu*.

Ray Doiron has been a primary school teacher, administrator, and teacher-librarian. Dr. Doiron is assistant professor in the Faculty of Education at the University of Prince Edward Island, where he teaches courses in the postbaccalaureate Diploma in School Librarianship, as well as courses for preservice teachers in general methods, literacy in the primary grades, and instructional communications. He can be reached at *raydoiron@upei.ca*.

Jean Donham is the college librarian at Cornell College in Mt. Vernon, IA. She was associate professor in School of Library and Information Sciences at the University of Iowa before moving to Cornell. Her courses have included Research Methods, Resources for Children, Information Literacy, and Strategic Management. She can be reached at *jdonham@cornellcollege.edu*.

Lynn Evarts is a school library media specialist at Sauk Prairie High School in Prairie du Sac, WI. As a recovering isolated student, she realized early the power of a brief acknowledgment from someone and has gone on to empower young adult and school librarians to make a difference in the lives of their patrons. She can be reached at *levarts@aol.com*.

Dawn Cartwright Fiorelli is a young adult librarian with Scranton Library in Madison, CT. She can be reached at *fiorellid@madisonct.org*.

Diane Gallagher-Hayashi is a teacher-librarian at Stelly's School in the Saanich School District in British Columbia. In addition to being a teacher-librarian, she also teaches Japanese. She can be reached at *Diane_Hayashi@sd63.bc.ca*.

Caroline Geck is a bibliographic instruction librarian at Kean University Library and is interested in young people and how they seek information. Her ongoing research project is developing subject web bibliographies for faculty and student use at the library. She can be reached at *cgeck@kean.edu*.

Reid Goldsborough is author of *Straight Talk About the Information Superhighway*. His column has been in syndication since 1997.

Valerie Grenawalt taught middle school language arts for 9 years in Littleton, CO. She holds an MA in education from the University of Denver, where she also recently earned her MLIS. She can be reached at *grenawalts@alumni.tufts.edu.*

Violet H. Harada is a professor at the University of Hawaii and coordinates the School Library Media specialization. She is a frequent presenter at state, national, and international conferences. She has coauthored two books with Joan Yoshina: *Learning Through Inquiry: Librarians and Teachers as Partners* (2004) and *Assessing Learning: Librarians and Teachers as Partners* (2005). She can be reached at *vharada@hawaii.edu.*

Gary Hartzell is a former high school principal and professor of educational administration and supervision at University of Nebraska, Omaha. A keynote speaker at the White House Conference on School Libraries in June 2002 and a member of the advisory board for the Laura Bush Foundation for America's Libraries, Professor Hartzell works to bring the school library to administrator's attention through conference presentations, articles, and books.

Allison Haupt is coordinator of Children's and Young Adults' Services with North Vancouver District Public Library in North Vancouver, BC; has taught contemporary children's literature in the School of Library, Archival, and Information Studies at the University of British Columbia; and is a collections consultant for National Book Service. She can be reached at *allison.haupt@telus.net.*

Ken Haycock is professor and director of the School of Library and Information Science at San Jose State University, San Jose, CA. He has been president of several national and international professional associations and is a member of the council of the American Library Association and past president of the Association for Library and Information Science Education. He was editor-in-chief and publisher of *Teacher Librarian* until January 2005.

James E. Herring is lecturer in the Center for Studies in Teacher Librarianship at the School of Information Studies, Charles Sturt University, Wagga Wagga, Australia. He is author of *The Internet and Information Skills: A Guide for Teachers and School Librarians* (2003). He can be reached at *jherring@csu.edu.au.*

Janet Hopkins, a British Columbia certified teacher and certified assistive technology practitioner, is the author of the forthcoming book *Assistive Technology: An Introductory Guide for K–12 Library Media Specialists*. She is also moderator of the Assistive Technology Canada discussion list (**http://ca.groups.yahoo.com/group/ATCanada/**) and can be reached at *AT_Consulting@canada.com* or through her web site **http://ca.geocities.com/janethopkinsbc/**.

Sandra Hughes-Hassel is associate professor in the School of Information and Library Science at the University of North Carolina at Chapel Hill. She can be reached at *smhughes@email.unc.edu.*

Carol-Anne Hutchinson is technical services/school library advisor for the Halifax Regional School Board in Dartmouth, Nova Scotia, and a doctoral student studying issues related to school libraries and educational leadership. She can be reached at *cahutch@staff.ednet.ns.ca.*

Doug Johnson has been the director of media and technology for the Mankato Public Schools since 1991 and has served as an adjunct faculty member of Minnesota State University, Mankato, since 1990. His regular columns appear in *Library Media Connection*, *Leading and Learning*, and the *Education World* web site. Visit his web site at **www.doug-johnson.com** and read his Blue Skunk Blog at **http://doug-johnson.squarespace.com/**.

Larry Johnson teaches in the School of Library and Information Science at Indiana University, Indianapolis, as part of the Teacher of School Library Media Leadership Online Blue Ribbon Certification program, available to educators around the world (**http://eduscapes.com/blueribbon/**).

Patrick Jones is author of several books on library service to young adults, including the forthcoming *Creating a Core Collection for Young Adults*. He can be reached at *patrict@connectingya.com*.

Carol Koechlin is an educational consultant for school library programs and resources. She is an award-winning author whose work has been recognized both nationally and internationally. A popular conference presenter and staff development leader, she is on an ongoing quest for techniques that assist teacher-librarians in developing programs and strategies to make information tasks more meaningful and successful for students. She can be reached at *koechlin@sympatico.ca*.

Merrilee Andersen Kwielford is the lead librarian at Maine East High School in Des Plaines, IL. She can be reached at *mandersen@maine207.org*.

Annette Lamb teaches in the School of Library and Information Science at Indiana University, Indianapolis, as part of the Teacher of School Library Media Leadership Online Blue Ribbon Certification program, available to educators around the world (**http://eduscapes.com/blueribbon/**). Visit **http://annettelamb.com/** for more exciting teaching ideas.

Linda Langford is teacher-librarian at Mary Immaculate Primary School in Sydney, Australia. She is the editor of Australian School Library Association's professional journal *Access*. She can be reached at *llangford@csu.edu.au*.

Mary Jo Langhorne has 26 years of experience as a teacher-librarian, including 8 years as media and technology coordinator for the Iowa City Community School District, which won the National School Library Media Program of the Year Award. Langhorne is an adjunct professor in the School of Library and Information Science at the University of Iowa and does consulting and training on school library issues. She can be reached at *mjlanghorne@mchsi.com*.

David Loertscher is a professor at the School of Library and Information Science at San Jose State University, San Jose, CA, and coeditor of *Teacher Librarian*. A past president of the American Association of School Librarians, Loertscher is a respected expert in library and information science. He can be reached at *dloertscher@teacherlibrarian.com*.

Teri Lesesne is a professor at Sam Houston State University, Huntsville, TX, where she teaches graduate and undergraduate classes in young adult and children's literature in the Department of Library Science. She can be reached at *lis_tsl@shsu.edu*.

Marla W. McGhee teaches in the master's and doctoral programs in educational leadership at Texas State University, San Marcos, where she is also the codirector of the National Center for School Improvement. She is the coauthor of *The Principal's Guide to a Powerful Library Media Program* (2005). She can be reached at *mmcghee@txstate.edu.*

Keith McPherson is lecturer and coordinator in the Language and Literacy Education Research Centre of the University of British Columbia, Vancouver, Canada. He can be reached at *keith.mcpherson@ubc.ca.*

Patricia Montiel-Overall is assistant professor at the University of Arizona, College of Social and Behavioral Science, School of Information Resources and Library Science, Tucson. She can be reached at *overall@email.arizona.edu.*

Karen N. Muronaga is library media specialist at Lincoln Elementary School in Honolulu, HI. She can be reached at *kmuronag@k12.hi.us.*

Joyce Needham is the teacher-librarian at Sequiota and Weller Elementary Schools in Springfield, MO. She can be reached at *jneedham@spsmail.org.*

Dianne Oberg is a professor in teacher-librarianship in the Faculty of Education at the University of Alberta in Canada. Oberg is the editor of an international journal, *School Libraries Worldwide*. She can be reached at *dianne.oberg@ualberta.ca.*

Michael K. O'Sullivan is the instructional media coordinator at Rosemount High School, Rosemount, MN, and a reference librarian at Hamline University in St. Paul. He can be reached at *michael.osullivan@district196.org.*

Les Parsons, a former teacher and teacher-librarian, is the author of numerous professional books, including *Grammarama*. He can be reached at *les.parsons@tel.tdsb.on.ca.*

Jennifer Robins is an assistant professor in the Library Science and Information Services program at Central Missouri State University, Warrensburg, MO. She can be reached at *jrobins@cmsu1.cmsu.edu.*

Esther Rosenfeld is the former districtwide coordinator of Library and Learning Resources for the Toronto District School Board and past president of the Ontario School Library Association. After years of overseeing program support for Toronto's 570 elementary and secondary school libraries, as well as a professional library, media library, and technical services, Rosenfeld is now an educational and school library consultant and coeditor of *Teacher Librarian*.

Thomas J. Scott is a social studies teacher at Rosemount High School, Rosemount, MN, and an adjunct professor at St. Mary's University, Minneapolis, MN, and at Metropolitan State University in St. Paul, MN. He can be contacted at *thomas.scott@district196.org.*

Joan Shaw is a teacher-librarian at Upper Lynn Elementary School in North Vancouver, BC, and a veteran teacher with more than 30 years' experience. She is a doctoral student in educational studies at the University of Western Ontario and can be reached at *shaw8@telus.net.*

Leslie Travis has been teaching for 26 years, 14 of which have been as a teacher-librarian for the Chicago Board of Education. She can be reached at *ljtravis@sbcglobal.net*.

Joyce Kasman Valenza is a library information specialist at Springfield Township High School, Erdenheim, PA. She is a frequent speaker on issues relating to libraries, technology, and education, and she writes the techlife@school column for the *Philadelphia Inquirer*. Visit her web site at **http://mciu.org/%7Espjvweb/jvweb.html** and e-mail her at *joyce_valenza@sdst.org*.

Lisa Wilson is the teacher-librarian at Angelo Rodriguez High School in Fairfield, CA. She can be reached at *lisaw@fsusd.k12.ca.us*.

Sandi Zwaan is an educational consultant for school library programs and resources. She is an award-winning authors whose work has been recognized both nationally and internationally. A popular conference presenter and staff development leader, she is on an ongoing quest for techniques that assist teacher-librarians in developing programs and strategies to make information tasks more meaningful and successful for students. She can be reached at *hzwaan@sympatico.ca*.

LaVergne, TN USA
15 February 2011
216570LV00001B/9/P